THE CENTURY PSYCHOLOGY SERIES
Richard M. Elliott, *Editor*
Kenneth MacCorquodale, *Assistant Editor*

PERSONS and PERSONALITY

Persons and Personality
AN INTRODUCTION TO PSYCHOLOGY

by

SISTER ANNETTE WALTERS

in collaboration with

SISTER KEVIN O'HARA

Both of the College of St. Catherine
St. Paul, Minnesota

New York

APPLETON-CENTURY-CROFTS, INC.

COPYRIGHT, 1953, BY
APPLETON-CENTURY-CROFTS, INC.

All rights reserved. This book, or parts thereof, must not be reproduced in any form without permission of the publisher.

559-6

Library of Congress Card Number: 52-13695

PRINTED IN THE UNITED STATES OF AMERICA

Dedicated to
OUR LADY,
SEAT OF WISDOM

Nihil Obstat

Louis J. McCarthy, Ph.D.
Censor Deputatus

Imprimatur

✠ Joannes Gregorius Murray
*Archiepiscopus Sancti Pauli
de Minnesota*

Preface

This book is frankly partisan in its approach to psychology. It has two major objectives: (1) to present the data of scientific psychology in such a way that the *person* rather than isolated mental functions is the center of interest, and (2) to relate scientific psychology wherever feasible to relevant theological and philosophical considerations.

In keeping with the first of the above objectives, the subject matter of this book is the whole human being—man as a biological organism, man as a social animal, and man as a person. Psychology, as treated in this book, grows out of several distinct but related disciplines—natural science, social science, the humanities, and theology. Studied in this way, psychology encourages the student to integrate his knowledge, since it transcends the usual boundaries of curricular divisions.

In keeping with the second of the above objectives, this book attempts to put at the student's disposal the means for beginning a synthesis of our scientific, philosophical, and theological knowledge of man. These means are rudimentary, to be sure; they are adapted to the intellectual level of the college sophomore. The Christian student in his study of psychology raises many questions which do not occur to the non-Christian student. He wants to know, for example, if it is true that miraculous cures are nothing more than suggestive psychotherapy. He is often disturbed by the seeming disharmony between psychological science and Christian principles. He finds it difficult to reconcile the amoral point of view adopted by psychologists with the moral view inculcated by his religion. He is confused by the implicit philosophy of popular books that tell him how to win friends and develop his personality. If he has studied philosophy, he is confused by the different meanings that philosophy and psychology sometimes give to the same term, and he wants to know which is "right." The present textbook attempts to answer or to help the student find the answers to these and to similar questions.

The book is intended primarily as a basic text for the first course in psychology at the college level. It should also prove useful as a reference book for courses in applied psychology, developmental psychology, theoretical psychology, child study, and child guidance. The intelligent layman, as well as the college student, will find this book a helpful introduction to the vast literature of contemporary psychology.

We wish to acknowledge our debt of gratitude to the many students, fellow psychologists, publishers, librarians, and friends who have helped us in the preparation of this volume. Hundreds of students have commented on the preliminary edition of the book and have assisted us in writing the present edition. Students and colleagues have helped most generously in typing the manuscript, in reading proof, and in doing numerous other tasks involved in preparing a textbook. We wish to thank the following people especially:

His Excellency, the Most Reverend John Gregory Murray, S.T.D., Archbishop of St. Paul, for reading the entire manuscript.

Sister Helen Margaret and Sister Mary William of the English department of the College of St. Catherine for reading the manuscript and for making many helpful suggestions and criticisms.

The Reverend Louis J. McCarthy, rector of Nazareth Hall, for reading the entire manuscript and for making invaluable suggestions both as to content and style.

The Reverend William C. Bier, S.J., of the psychology department of Fordham University, for reading the entire manuscript and for assistance with both the psychological and the philosophical content of the book.

The Reverend William B. Murphy, O.P., of the philosophy department of the College of St. Catherine, for helping us with a number of philosophical and theological problems.

Mr. Peter Lupori and Sister Judith of the art department of the College of St. Catherine. Mr. Lupori contributed the many beautiful original drawings that appear throughout the book. Sister Judith did the lettering.

Our superiors, Mother Antonius and Mother Antonine, for encouraging us to write the book and for making the administrative adjustments necessary to bring it to completion.

The many individuals and publishers who gave us permission to reproduce copyrighted materials. Specific acknowledgment of each of these contributions is made on the page at which it appears.

Dr. Richard M. Elliott, our editor, for suggesting that the book be written, for his constant intellectual stimulation, for his unfailing patience and optimism, and for his splendid editorial help. Any clarity of style that the book may have achieved is largely the result of his efforts.

Miss Eileen Gavin, for valuable assistance in reading and correcting proof.

The administrative officers and faculty of the College of St. Catherine for their inspiration and example. Daily association with these dedicated people has, more than anything else, impelled us to make our own small contribution to the Christian apostolate of higher education.

THE AUTHORS

Suggestions for Outside Reading

The six basic references listed below contain selections to accompany nearly all of the chapters of this textbook.

L. W. Crafts, T. C. Schneirla, E. E. Robinson, and R. W. Gilbert, *Recent Experiments in Psychology* (New York, McGraw-Hill Book Company, Inc., 1950).
W. Dennis (ed.), *Readings in General Psychology* (New York, Prentice-Hall, Inc., 1949).
H. E. Garrett, *Great Experiments in Psychology*, Third Edition (New York, Appleton-Century-Crofts, Inc., 1951).
E. L. Hartley, H. G. Birch, and R. E. Hartley (eds.), *Outside Readings in Psychology* (New York, Thomas Y. Crowell Company, 1950).
R. G. Kuhlen and G. G. Thompson, *Psychological Studies of Human Development* (New York, Appleton-Century-Crofts, Inc., 1952).
W. L. Valentine and D. D. Wickens, *Experimental Foundations of General Psychology*, Third Edition (New York, Rinehart and Company, Inc., 1949).

In preparing outside readings to accompany the chapters of this book, we have been guided by three criteria: (1) Is the material suitable for college sophomores? (2) Will it help the student to get a more intensive or extensive knowledge of the subject matter treated in the chapter? (3) Can the book be easily secured in sufficient quantities by the undergraduate library?

In keeping with these guiding principles, we recommend that the books listed above be provided in sufficiently large quantities so that every student will have access to one or more of them at the appropriate time. It is not essential, however, that all of these books be available.

In addition to the six basic references, we have included other suggestions at the end of some of the chapters whenever it seemed desirable to do so.

SUGGESTIONS FOR OUTSIDE READING

The correlation of the basic references with the present textbook is as follows: [1]

Ch. I: Hartley, 1–4
 II: Crafts, 1; Hartley, 16; Kuhlen and Thompson, Ch. 1; Valentine, 1–3
 III: Dennis, 11
 IV: Crafts, 2; Kuhlen and Thompson, 2, 3, 15; Valentine, 5, 6
 V: Hartley, 8; Kuhlen and Thompson, 1, 8, 15, 19, 36, 51, 53–57
 VI: Crafts, 8, 9; Dennis, 1, 2; Hartley, 25, 26, 29
 VII: Crafts, 10–12; Hartley, 13–15
 VIII: Crafts, 6, 7; Dennis, 4; Garrett, 8; Hartley, 50–61; Kuhlen and Thompson, 1; Valentine, 10–14
 IX: Dennis, 5
 X: Crafts, 21, 22; Dennis, 3; Garrett, 14; Hartley, 17–24; 30–32; Kuhlen and Thompson, 4, 35; Valentine, 15
 XI: Crafts, 5, 10, 15–19; Dennis, 6; Garrett, 1–6; Hartley, 34–49; Kuhlen and Thompson, 14, 16; Valentine, 16–18, 20
 XII: Crafts, 14; Dennis, 8; Garrett, 11–13; Hartley, 10–12, 63, 64, 66, 68; Kuhlen and Thompson, 20, 21, 24, 25, 29, 33; Valentine, 7, 8
 XIII: Crafts, 23, 24; Dennis, 7; Hartley, 33, 69–75; Valentine, 19
 XIV: Crafts, 20; Hartley, 62, 76, 86–92
 XV: Crafts, 9; Hartley, 65, 67; Kuhlen and Thompson, 26–28
 XVI: Garrett, 7; Hartley, 5–7, 9; Kuhlen and Thompson, 11, 32, 34, 46, 47, 68, 69
 XVII: Kuhlen and Thompson, 12, 30, 40, 43, 58, 60
 XVIII: Kuhlen and Thompson, 5–7, 37, 48, 59, 62, 63; Valentine, 4
 XIX: Crafts, 25; Dennis, 10; Garrett, 9; Valentine, 21
 XX: Crafts, 4, 26; Dennis, 9; Garrett, 10; Hartley, 77–85; Kuhlen and Thompson, 41, 42, 44, 45, 49, 67
 XXI: Crafts, 13; Hartley, 93–97; Kuhlen and Thompson, 10, 13, 38, 39, 52, 64–66; Valentine, 9
 XXII: Kuhlen and Thompson, 8, 17, 22, 23, 31, 50, 71
 XXIII: Garrett, 15, 16; Hartley, 98

[1] The references to Hartley and to Kuhlen and Thompson are to numbered readings unless otherwise indicated. References to the remaining four books are to chapters.

Contents

PREFACE vii

SUGGESTIONS FOR OUTSIDE READING xi

PART I. NATURE, SCOPE, AND METHODS OF PSYCHOLOGY

Chapter I. THE NATURE AND SCOPE OF PSYCHOLOGY . . 3
The Study of Psychology. Meaning of Terms. Study of People Not Limited to Psychology. Psychology and the Physical Sciences, Mathematics, and Statistics. Application of Psychology to the Professions. Psychology and Ethics. Subdivisions of Psychology. Our Point of Departure.

Chapter II. METHODS OF PSYCHOLOGY 20
Scientific Observation. Scientific Method. The Scientific Experiment in Psychology. Field Studies in Psychology. Life History Methods. Clinical or Case Study Method. Validity of Generalizations Based Upon Clinical Observations. Paper and Pencil Devices. Statistical Analysis. Objective and Subjective Observation.

PART II. CONSTITUTIONAL, ENVIRONMENTAL, AND PERSONAL FACTORS THAT INFLUENCE PSYCHOLOGICAL DEVELOPMENT

Chapter III. THE DEVELOPMENTAL APPROACH TO PSYCHOLOGY: INTRODUCTION 45
What Is Involved in a Developmental Study? What Is the Psychology of Development? Reasons for Studying the Psychology of Development. Cross-Sectional and Longitudinal Methods of Studying Development. Psychology of Development and Social Class. Psychology of Development and Culture. Heredity, Environment, and Free Choice.

Chapter IV. ROLE OF HEREDITY, ENVIRONMENT, AND HUMAN FREEDOM IN PSYCHOLOGICAL DEVELOPMENT 59

Interaction of Heredity, Environment, and Human Freedom. The Biological Basis of Heredity. Interference with the Normal Environment of the Embryo and Young Animal. Is There Inheritance of Acquired Characteristics? Studies of the Relative Effects of Heredity and Environment on Specific Traits. Maturation and Learning. Human Freedom.

Chapter V. THE ROLE OF THE FAMILY, SCHOOL, COMMUNITY, AND CULTURAL MILIEU IN PERSONALITY DEVELOPMENT 95

Introduction. General Principles of Social Learning. The Marginal Person. Influence of the Family. The Role of the School in Personality Development. Informal Learning. Environment and the Human Organism.

PART III. *THE HUMAN ORGANISM*

Chapter VI. RECEPTORS, SENSORY EXPERIENCE, AND EFFECTORS 127

Receptors and Sensory Experience in General. Vision. Hearing. The Skin Senses. The Gustatory Sense. The Olfactory Sense. The Kinesthetic Sense. The Sense of Equilibrium (Static Sense). The Organic Senses. The Senses: Their Treatment in Contemporary Psychology and in the Traditional Philosophy. The Effectors.

Chapter VII. THE HUMAN ORGANISM: THE NERVOUS SYSTEM 159

Nervous Tissue. Nerves. The Nerve Impulse. The Synapse. Overview of the Nervous System. The Central Somatic Nervous System. The Peripheral Somatic Nervous System. The Autonomic Nervous System. Prefrontal Lobotomy. Development of the Nervous System and Behavior.

PART IV. *DYNAMICS OF HUMAN ADJUSTMENT*

Chapter VIII. EMOTIONS, MOTIVATION, AND PATTERNS OF ADJUSTMENT 183

Affective Experiences. Emotion. Cycles of Mood. Motivation in Human Life. Patterns of Human Adjustment.

Chapter IX. THE PROBLEM OF HUMAN ADJUSTMENT . . . 213

The Meaning of Adjustment. Criteria of Adjustment. Natural Levels of Adjustment. Supernatural Level of

Adjustment. The Whole Person Adjusts. The Role of Habit in Adjustment. Psychology of Adjustment and the Christian Vocation.

PART V. HUMAN ACTIVITY AND ADJUSTMENT

Chapter X. How People Perceive the World 239
Some Basic Facts About Attention. Visual Perception. Sound Perception. General Facts About Perception. Inaccurate and Abnormal Perception. Eidetic Imagery. The Perception of Time. Extra-Sensory Perception. Perception in Relation to Other Psychological Phenomena.

Chapter XI. How People Learn and Remember . . . 272
The Problem of Learning. The Learning Curve. Kinds of Learning Problems. Transfer of Learning. Theories of Learning. Human Learning. Learning and Memory. The Methods of Studying Memory. Forgetting. Efficiency in Learning and Remembering. Learning and Memory in Relation to the Whole Personality.

Chapter XII. Intelligent Behavior 308
The Human Intellect. Intelligence. Achievement and the IQ. Educational and Occupational Level in Relation to the IQ. The Distribution of Intelligence in the Population. Interpretation of IQ.'s. Racial, National, and Cultural Differences in Intelligence. Rural and Urban Differences. Theories about the Nature of Intelligence. Attributes of Intelligence. Intelligence and Personality. A Clarification of Some Statistical Terms Commonly Used in the Measurement of Psychological Characteristics. Individual Differences and the Study of the Individual.

Chapter XIII. Thinking and Creative Imagination . . 342
The Role of Thinking in Human Life. The Meaning of Thinking. The Scientific and Clinical Study of Thinking. Creative Thought. Thinking and the Vocation of Man.

Chapter XIV. Disorders of Personality 361
The Problem of Mental Disorder. Mental Hygiene. Types of Personality Disorder. Double or Multiple Personality. Mental Disease in Childhood. Causes of Personality Problems.

Chapter XV. Adjustment of the Atypical Person . . 393
Blindness. Deafness and Hearing Defects. Orthopedic Defects. Illness and Accident. Feeblemindedness. The Slow Learner. Left-Handedness. Speech Defects. What Constitutes a Handicap?

CONTENTS

PART VI. STAGES OF GROWTH AND DEVELOPMENT

Chapter XVI. THE PSYCHOLOGY OF DEVELOPMENT: INFANCY AND EARLY CHILDHOOD 415

Period of Infancy. Sex Differences. Training and Personality Development. Fundamental Needs of the Young Child. The Preschool Period of Development. Emotional and Social Development of the Preschool Child. Sex Awareness and Instruction. Common Behavior Problems of the Preschool Period of Development. Linguistic Development. Intellectual Development of the Preschool Child. Perception. Social Class and Caste Differences. Geographical and Cultural Differences. Religious Education.

Chapter XVII. THE PSYCHOLOGY OF DEVELOPMENT: CHILDHOOD AND PREADOLESCENCE 448

The Period of "Middle" Childhood. Developmental Tasks of "Middle" Childhood. Studies of Character and Moral Development. The Developing Concept of Self. Special Gifts or Talents. The Preadolescent.

Chapter XVIII. THE PSYCHOLOGY OF DEVELOPMENT: PUBERTY AND ADOLESCENCE 469

What Is Adolescence? The Body in Adolescence. Developmental Tasks of Adolescence. The Underprivileged Adolescent. Differential Educational Opportunities of Adolescents. Characteristics of College Students. Adjustment Problems of the College Student.

PART VII. PERSONALITY AND SOCIAL PSYCHOLOGY

Chapter XIX. HUMAN PERSONALITY 507

The Individual "Whole Personality" in Psychology. The Ego or Self. Methods of Studying Personality. Depth of Understanding. The Glands and Personality. Family Resemblances in Personality. Personality Types.

Chapter XX. THE PERSON IN SOCIETY 548

Man and Society. Culture and Personality. Group Dynamics. Prejudice as a Barrier to Human Understanding. Discrimination and Scapegoating. Antisocial Behavior. Social Psychology and Christian Principles.

PART VIII. MATURITY AND OLD AGE

Chapter XXI. ADULTHOOD IN OUR CULTURE 575

Early Maturity in Relation to the Whole Life Span. Sex Differences. The Adult Woman in Our Culture. Marital and Familial Adjustments. Work and Job Satisfaction. Other Factors Associated with Adult Adjustment and Happiness. What Is Maturity?

Chapter XXII. LATER MATURITY AND OLD AGE . . . 600
The Culture Pattern in Relation to Aging. Changes in Ability with Age. Age and Productivity. What Is Old Age? Longevity. Adjustment Problems of the Aged. Mental Disease in Later Life. The Mental Hygiene of Old Age. Viewpoints in Psychology.

PART IX. *THEORETICAL FRAMEWORK OF PSYCHOLOGY*

Chapter XXIII. TRENDS AND VIEWPOINTS IN PSYCHOLOGY TODAY 623
Psychology as a Science and as a Profession. Historical Roots of Contemporary Psychology. Schools of Psychology. Evaluation of Psychological Schools. Psychology and the Future.

Chapter XXIV. SCIENCE, PHILOSOPHY, AND THEOLOGY IN THE STUDY OF MAN 643
Psychology and Common Sense. Psychology and Science. Apparent Conflict of Truth. Psychology and Life.

INDEX 659

PART I

Nature, Scope, and Methods of Psychology

The psychologist's peculiar contribution to the study of people is his objective and scientific approach.

I

The Nature and Scope of Psychology

The notion of the person is at the centre of all our human problems.—JEAN MOUROUX [1]

1. THE STUDY OF PSYCHOLOGY

Psychology is the systematic, scientific study of human beings. It is a body of facts and principles that can make it easier for you to understand people in your everyday contacts with them. Psychology develops this understanding by giving you insight into the factors that influence the development of human personality and character throughout life. This understanding is valuable because it leads to greater appreciation and tolerance of yourself and others. Understanding helps provide a suitable environment in which the best potentialities of human beings can find fulfillment. Understanding enables you to predict what people are likely to do in given circumstances of life and to get some notion as to *why* they act as they do. And lastly, understanding can show you what to seek and what to avoid in trying to become the kind of person you want to be.

A good way to begin your study of psychology is to observe the people about you—in your home, at school, at social gatherings, and in public places. Ask yourself *why* these people behave as they do, feel as they do, and think as they do. You will be astonished to find out how little you really know about the motivation of these people. You will be especially surprised, no doubt, to discover how little you know of the reasons behind the behavior of people with whom you rub elbows every day. You can easily observe *what* people do; you cannot observe *why* they do it.

You may think, because you can predict what a certain person

[1] From *The Meaning of Man*, by Jean Mouroux. Copyright, 1948, Sheed and Ward Inc., New York.

will do in a given situation, that you understand him, but this is not necessarily true. You may be very sure, let us say, that the boy in the front row will always give the right answer to any question addressed to him. You may be equally sure that the girl across the aisle will ask the instructor to repeat the question addressed to her before she answers it. You can predict how these people will act, not with absolute certainty, but with such a high degree of probability that for all practical purposes it is the same as certainty. You can predict what a person will do in the future because you have observed how he has behaved in the past. At any moment, of course, a person may surprise you and adopt a new course of action. But ordinarily you can depend upon people to do what they habitually do. If any great change in their behavior takes place, it is usually so gradual that you can adjust your predictions accordingly. The boy who always gives the right answers habitually studies; the girl who always asks the instructor to repeat his question habitually daydreams.

Because you can predict what a person will do in a given set of circumstances, you can indirectly control some of his responses by appropriately manipulating his environment. This does not mean, however, that you understand him. You understand the well-informed student only when you know *why* he studies; you understand the daydreamer only when you know *why* she daydreams. In short, you understand a person only when you know what makes him act as he does, feel as he does, and think as he does. The *why* behind human behavior is a major problem of psychology.

In studying psychology you will learn the general principles that govern the behavior of people in general. Yet an inescapable fact of everyday experience is that all people differ. No two people, not even identical twins, are exactly alike. How are you going to use psychology to help you understand *individuals?* Psychology, like other sciences, is comprised of a body of facts and principles which apply to the general class rather than to the individual case. Nevertheless, psychology will enable you to understand individual people by providing you with the principles which explain how individuality arises.

Psychology today is vitally concerned with all aspects of human life and human interaction. The most recent science to be differentiated from philosophy, it is undergoing a rapid expansion of both subject matter and method. Without a knowledge of what psychologists do, what they have accomplished, and what they hope to accomplish, it is impossible to understand the nature and scope of contemporary psychology. A definition of psychology can be given at the beginning of this book. Your understanding of what the definition implies must keep on growing right up to the end of the book.

II. MEANING OF TERMS

Since this is a book on *psychology* that deals with *persons* and *personality*, and since we are using these and other common terms in a special sense in this book, we shall explain here what we mean by them. This explanation will not be a complete definition; it would take a whole book to define them properly. But later we shall have occasion to point out that man differs *essentially* from the other animals; that during a man's lifetime *accidental* changes take place in him; and that the human being has a certain *nature*. To give you a working idea of what we mean by these terms, we offer a brief explanation of them here.

A. Psychology

The word *psychology* comes from two Greek words, *psyche* (soul) and *logos* (word); therefore, it was used to mean the *study of the soul*. For Aristotle psychology meant just that, as is indicated by the title of his famous outline of psychology, *Treatise on the Soul*. Aristotle's treatise dealt not only with the human soul, but with the soul in general, as the principle of life, whether vegetative, sensitive, or intellectual.

In the thirteenth century St. Thomas Aquinas, recognizing the perennial nature of Aristotle's philosophical psychology, used Aristotle's works as the basis for some of his own systematic writings. For St. Thomas, however, *man,* the composite of body and soul, rather than *soul* was the proper subject matter of psychology. It is the Thomistic notion of psychology as the study of man that will, we hope, permeate this book.

Historically, psychology was first defined as the study of the soul. Later, to eliminate the theological implications of *soul*, the term *mind* was substituted. Later still, psychology was defined as the study of consciousness. Today most psychologists define psychology as the science of behavior. One commentator dryly summarizes these trends as follows: psychology first lost its soul, then it lost its mind, then it lost consciousness, but it still has behavior!

B. Person, Personality, and Character

In studying the human being, we must distinguish three commonly used terms: *person, personality,* and *character.* By *person* we mean the very substance of man, the subject of his actions, that is, what is unchangeable in him. Everyone, by reason of his spiritual soul, is a person from the moment of conception. Being a person does not change or grow; it is immutable. We do not mean to be taken literally when we say of someone that "he is a changed person."

Personality, on the other hand, primarily refers not to the substance, but to the "accidents" of man, and it can therefore be changed. Personality develops as an individual's potentialities are gradually made actual. An individual personality is at any moment the sum total of all potentialities which have become actual.

Character has more of an ethical connotation than the word *personality.* *Character* is personality evaluated; it is an ethical and social concept. Character is the aggregate of traits, mental and moral, comprising the personality as evaluated by a particular set of standards.

C. Substance and Accident

In defining person and personality we used the words *substance* and *accidents.* These words are used in the special philosophical sense. *Substance* is being which exists in itself and not in any other being.[2] An *accident* is that which cannot exist except in another being.[3] Everything in the world either exists through itself or inheres in something else. For instance, the black in a black table exists in the table, and not apart from it. The table does not belong to anything else in the way in which the black belongs to the table. Smallness exists in the acorn; the acorn itself is complete for its own existence. You can find many exam-

---

[2] St. Thomas Aquinas, *Summa Contra Gentiles,* Book I, Chapter 25.
[3] This definition is satisfactory for the present book on psychology. It is not, however, comprehensive enough to include theological concepts.

NATURE AND SCOPE OF PSYCHOLOGY

ples of substance and accident. Anything which you can experience with your senses is an accident; for instance, the hardness and height of a table. Substance, on the contrary, can be known only by the intellect.

D. Nature and Activity

Substance can be considered from another point of view besides that of existence. Substance considered as the source of a thing's activity is called *nature*. Everything in the world has some activity. Even a stone will roll down a hill if you do not stop it. All the various activities of things are accidents. They must belong to some substance. They must be *acts of something*. The *accidents* of a thing reveal something about its substance. The *activities* of a thing reveal its nature. Once you have seen a thing in operation, you begin to understand something of its nature. Thus, stones and men have some activities in common: a man as well as a stone has mass and consequently weight. Stones and men have some activities which are not common: a stone does not learn statistics nor eat meals. A man eats a meal and studies statistics. From man's activities we can deduce that his substance must support the accidents of (1) assimilating food and (2) thinking. We may say that man is both animal and rational in nature.

E. Essence

Through the accidents we know *that* a substance *exists*. *What* the substance *is* that exists, is called the *essence*. Between a man and a tree there is an essential difference—each one has a different essence, each is a different kind of being.

III. STUDY OF PEOPLE NOT LIMITED TO PSYCHOLOGY

Psychology is not the only field of study which has human nature and behavior as its subject matter. *Anthropology*, for example, is by very definition the study of man. Yet historically it has approached its subject in a very different way from that of psychology. Anthropology is a branch of knowledge distinct from psychology, but one which is enriched by the contributions of psychologists and which in its turn enriches psychology through its own research. *Cultural anthropology*, the study of human life in different cultural milieus, is of particular value to the psychologist. In recent years many psychological generalizations based upon studies of individuals drawn from one culture group only (middle class, western European and American) have had to be revised in the light of anthropological studies.

Sociology is the study of man in society and should be a prerequisite or companion course for all students of psychology. Personality does not develop in a social vacuum. It develops in a particular family and community setting. Sociologists have contributed much to our knowledge of social factors which help to develop an individual's personality. Of special interest to the student of psychology are sociological studies such as the following: environmental factors conducive to delinquency, crime, and disease; problems of ethnic groups; social class and caste in relation to personality.

Psychiatry is the branch of medicine which deals with the diagnosis, causation, and treatment of mental disease. Like anthropology and sociology, it contributes to and borrows from the field of psychology.

Biological sciences—biology, anatomy, physiology, nutrition and the like—deal, for the most part, with more restricted aspects of human development than does psychology. Since man is a biological organism, a familiarity with the basic facts and concepts of these sciences is a prerequisite for the understanding of the total personality and therefore helpful to the student of psychology.

The Humanities by definition deal with subject matter which is essentially human. They include philosophy, literature, and the fine arts. Until rather recently, psychology was called upon to give knowledge to rather than to receive it from the humanistic studies. Creative art and literature, for example, have been profoundly influenced by psychological concepts—particularly by those of the psychoanalytical school. Psychological principles have for many years played an important part in literary and artistic criticism. More recently, however, psychologists have discovered that the humanities provide rich source materials for psychological research, and it is clear today that psychological research and the humanistic studies play complementary roles in the study of man.

IV. PSYCHOLOGY AND THE PHYSICAL SCIENCES, MATHEMATICS, AND STATISTICS

In 1796 Kinnebrook, a young assistant in the Greenwich astronomical laboratory, was discharged for making what appeared to be an error in recording the transit of a star. Many years later it became evident that Kinnebrook had not been in error, nor had the observers with whom his records had been compared. The truth is that no two observers ever give exactly the same measurements. These differences in measurement came to be known as the "personal equation," and techniques for correcting the resulting "errors" of observation were soon developed. The Kinnebrook incident highlights the relationship between psychology and the physical sciences. Observations in the natural sciences depend for their accuracy upon the perception and reporting of sense data. A knowledge of psychology, and particularly of the conditions necessary for securing adequate data and interpreting them correctly, is a prerequisite for scientific experimentation.

On the other hand, the physical sciences contribute to psychology in a number of important ways. Physical studies of sound and light, for example, have yielded important information about the stimuli that arouse human activity. Apparatus developed through the application of physical principles has made possible the exact measurement of physiological conditions and changes in the human organism—conditions and changes which are significantly related to psychological states. The psychogalvanometer which measures directly changes in the galvanic skin reflex (and indirectly changes in emotional states), the sphygmomanometer which registers changes in blood pressure, and the electroencephalograph which records brain waves, are examples in point.

Lastly, in certain of the more highly developed aspects of scientific psychology, as in other sciences, mathematics is used as an instrument of discovery and as a language in which to express the relationships and truths discovered. In this sense, psychology is part of that "Book of Nature" which Galileo declared "is written in mathematical language." The use of statistical techniques which are tools for the analysis of data is widespread in psychology today.

V. APPLICATION OF PSYCHOLOGY TO THE PROFESSIONS

Psychology can be applied in all areas of life: in person-to-person or person-to-group relations within the family, in the school, or within the community; in group-to-group relations such as those of political parties, labor unions, or international relations; and in the understanding and improvement of oneself. There are certain occupations, however, in which psychology has particular applications. A few of these will be discussed briefly.

A. Law

It is obvious that the lawyer needs to know psychology in order to understand his clients, to interpret them to others, and to plead in their defense. Other applications of psychology to the legal profession, however, are equally important but not so generally known. In this category are psychological studies such as those concerned with (1) lie detection, (2) the adequacy and validity of legal testimony, (3) factors which contribute to delinquency and crime, and (4) the value of different methods of handling offenders.

B. Medicine

Doctors, of course, need an understanding of modern psychology. It is not enough for a doctor to have a proper bedside manner, and to assume that he knows "how to handle" people; his understanding of people must be based upon a sound comprehension of psychological facts and principles. Every organic disease affects and is, in turn, affected by the whole personality. In the past, doctors have often treated with drugs, or even with surgery, patients whose symptoms were chiefly the result of unresolved personality conflicts. Modern doctors trained in psychology can avoid such mistakes and make applications of psychological principles in the treatment of patients a valuable therapeutic aid.

C. Nursing

Psychology is also applied in all types of modern nursing: in bedside nursing, in the pediatric ward, in the nursery, in the school health service, in public health nursing, and in the nursing of mental and nervous cases in conjunction with occupational therapy.

NATURE AND SCOPE OF PSYCHOLOGY

The nurse who knows when and how to apply psychological principles has acquired a skill of great importance in the art of healing.

D. Social Work

Modern social work, especially social case work, is closely related to clinical psychology on the one hand and to psychiatry on the other. The social worker is professionally concerned with helping people out of their troubles; a deep knowledge of psychology is basic to such work.

E. Teaching

Knowledge does not transfer automatically from the mind of the teacher to that of the pupil simply by his being exposed to it. The pupil must want to learn and must usually identify himself with the teacher if he is to improve. While it is probably true that the personality of the teacher is the most important factor involved in teaching, still a knowledge of psychology added to a knowledge of whatever subject is being taught is extremely important. Of particular concern to teachers are such topics as the psychology of motivation, personality adjustment, learning, intelligence, maturation, and characteristics of the different developmental stages.

F. Business and Industry

Psychology has numerous applications in present-day business and industry. Its techniques are used in consumer research, in advertising, in the study of efficiency and morale, and in the selection and placement of employees.

G. Military Science

World War II witnessed a tremendous increase in the application of psychological facts and principles to military procedures. Psychologists worked with military specialists on such varied problems as the selection and placement of recruits, testing of skills such as those of gunners and airplane pilots, teaching, screening out the mentally unfit, promoting the morale of soldiers and civilians, maintaining efficiency under various conditions encountered in war, and psychological warfare. Military psychology is now a required subject in all schools which train officers for the armed services.

VI. PSYCHOLOGY AND ETHICS

In considering the different areas in which psychology can be applied we must not overlook the dangers which can and do result from applying psychology for unethical or inhuman ends. Psychology, like other sciences, deals with *means,* not ends. It can never, as science, tell us what *ought* to be; it can merely tell us what *is* or what *will be* under given conditions. It can, for example, and does, study the values of individuals and groups. It can give us statistical data on the percentage of people holding given values and reporting that they live according to their scale of values. Such studies are important to the applied scientist, the clinical and social psychologist, and the social planner. They supply data which serve as a guide in many practical situations. But to assume that statistical studies of the values people hold or what they do should serve as guides to standards of morality is going beyond science into the realm of religion and philosophy. The scientist, as scientist, has no techniques for setting up ethical values.

This does not mean, of course, that the psychologist is not morally responsible for the ways in which he applies his knowledge. On the contrary, his responsibility as a person with specialized knowledge and with great potentialities for good or evil is exceedingly great. Most American psychologists today fortunately recognize this fact. Until a short time ago, however, most scientists, including psychologists, tended to think of ethical ends as something quite distinct from their professional purposes. Then came the atomic and hydrogen bombs. The scientists whose research made the production of these devastating weapons possible made clear in many public utterances that they could not be indifferent to their social consequences nor could they comfortably dodge the question of their own moral responsibility.

The scientist, as scientist, it is true, is not equipped to solve questions of values. But the scientist is more than a scientist; he is also a human being, living in close association with other human beings. As a human being he has certain rights which other men are bound to respect, and other men have rights which he

NATURE AND SCOPE OF PSYCHOLOGY

is bound to respect. The occupation which he chooses and the way in which he carries on his work are not indifferent matters. The scientist, like the business man, statesman, butcher or baker, is not outside of the moral law in the conduct of his profession. The scientist, whether a Christian or not, is bound to obey the natural law. The fact that his field of research is ethically neutral does not exonerate him from personal responsibility.

Glaring examples of the misuse of psychological and medical knowledge are the legal farces periodically enacted in the so-called "peoples' courts" of Soviet-controlled countries. Over and over again in these courts men who have been subjected to Soviet psychological treatment have "confessed" to crimes which, in the nature of their cases, was manifestly absurd. Many of these men were known to be moral giants who had previously defied every attempt, physical or moral, to intimidate them. Furthermore, they had nothing to gain by making these confessions. The information we have about these Soviet trials forces us to recognize that psychological knowledge can be used not only to advance human progress and welfare but also to destroy human personality and drag men down to barbarism.

VII. SUBDIVISIONS OF PSYCHOLOGY

Psychology as a whole is comprised of a number of highly specialized but mutually related subdivisions. The major subdivisions and some typical problems with which each is concerned are as follows:

General psychology is the scientific study of the normal individual's activities in adjusting to his environment. It is called "general" because it deals with what is characteristic of individuals in general rather than with what is true of one individual or class of individuals. Studies in general psychology, for instance, show us the laws governing perception, memory, and learning.

Experimental psychology overlaps general psychology and parts of other subdivisions of psychology as well. Historically, its scope was limited to the "generalized human, normal, adult mind" as revealed by laboratory experiments. The experimental psychologist, for instance, has determined experimentally how it is that blind persons avoid obstacles in their paths. Before conducting his experiments the psychologist had a number of "hunches" as to what sense cues the blind person might be using. He did not know, however, whether any one or several senses working in combination were essential for avoiding obstacles. By bringing blind subjects into his laboratory and by blindfolding normal people, he systematically eliminated the stimulation of all sense organs but one at a time. In this way, he found that the only essential cues for avoiding obstacles were auditory stimuli.

Developmental or *genetic psychology* is the study of psychological changes throughout life, from conception or birth until death. A variety of methods are used in making these studies. Experiments are sometimes made to ascertain what factors influence the growth of an animal or of a human being. One investigator, for instance, wanted to find out what effect the prevention of activity would have upon the development of swimming behavior in the tadpole. He designed his experiment in such a way that one group of tadpoles was prevented from swimming until after the time at which swimming movements normally took place. The tadpoles in another group used for a comparison were allowed to engage in swimming movements as soon as they were ready. The first group of tadpoles was raised in an anesthetizing chloretone solution which successfully prevented them not only from swimming but from making all other visible bodily movements. They went through the same sequence of developmental changes, however, as the second group that was raised in tap water. Within a half hour after they were placed in the fresh-water environment, the previously drugged tadpoles were swimming almost as well as the non-drugged animals. Apparently, the mechanisms necessary for swimming developed independently of exercise.

Besides experimentation, as just illustrated, developmental psychologists employ a number of other methods, among which are the study of diaries, biographies, and autobiographies with a view to understanding the factors that influence development throughout the life history.

Child psychology is similar to developmental psychology but is limited to the early years of life and deals for the most part with the preschool child. Studies of grade school children, apart from the already well-advanced work on intellectual development, are now beginning to get more attention. Child psychology

NATURE AND SCOPE OF PSYCHOLOGY

deals only with human beings, whereas developmental psychology is often concerned with animals as well.

Comparative psychology is usually considered synonymous with the study of animal behavior. It is concerned with investigating and comparing the behavior of different species. Comparative psychologists have been most ingenious in devising methods of studying the most complex as well as the simplest types of behavior in various species of animals, from the amœba to the great apes. They have, for instance, worked out methods for determining how well animals can discriminate colors, what they do instinctively and how well they can learn, and what factors motivate their behavior.

Differential psychology deals with the nature and extent of human differences. The differences it investigates may be between individuals, races, sexes, or age groups. It also studies differences in the same individuals at different times. Elaborate studies have been made, for instance, of the measured intelligence of various national and racial groups in the United States, and of people from different geographical localities and age groups. Other studies include the relative incidence of specific kinds of mental disease in different groups of the population and differences in attitudes and social behavior.

Social psychology studies the influence of society upon the individual and of the individual upon society. It is concerned with such questions as the social determinants of personality and with the nature and origin of prejudice, the factors operating in leadership, the spreading of rumors, the building of morale, and other human problems which grow out of and which find expression in the interaction of individuals and of groups in our own and in other societies.

Abnormal psychology has traditionally dealt with people and groups that differ markedly from the average, irrespective of whether these deviations are desirable or not. Its proper subject matter, however, is the kind of deviation that results in social maladjustment, as, for instance, mental retardation, neurotic personality, and mental disease.

Clinical psychology is concerned with understanding and diagnosing individuals and helping them to change their behavior and attitudes. Clinical psychology is not only a subdivision of the total field of modern psychology; it is a highly developed field of professional specialization as well. The clinical psychologist finds employment in many different kinds of situations—schools for exceptional children, hospitals (general and psychiatric), prisons and reformatories, child guidance clinics, social welfare agencies, business and industry, and private practice.

Physiological psychology contributes knowledge of the sense organs, ductless glands, and nervous system as they affect behavior. Such knowledge is basic to the understanding of man as a biological organism. Physiological psychology differs from physiology in that it is chiefly concerned with the psychological significance of physiological functioning. It is not, for instance, interested primarily in the ductless glands as such, but in the role of these glands in initiating emotions and moods and in influencing personality structure. It studies the sense organs and muscles, not as ends in themselves, but as means for understanding how man gets to know his world and how he reacts to it.

Theoretical psychology deals with the basic assumptions underlying psychological study of all kinds. It is closely connected with a subdivision of the field of knowledge known as the "Philosophy of Science." It goes beyond the immediate observational data of psychology to the problems of how they are ordered to form a consistent whole and to the formulation of the most general psychological laws which enable the psychologist to interpret his data.

Applied psychology is directed to the solution of practical problems. As we have already shown, it has a place in many diversified fields and a value in many human endeavors. Among the fields of application are education, vocational guidance, advertising, selling, industry, medicine, law, military strategy, public opinion research, and social planning.

VIII. OUR POINT OF DEPARTURE

The subject matter of this book is the development of human personality throughout the entire life history. We are trying to present a systematic picture of all of the factors which in the course of an individual life influence this development. In doing so, we have dipped into the various subdivisions of psychology whenever we have found it instructive to do so. We have also

NATURE AND SCOPE OF PSYCHOLOGY

tried to integrate psychological research to some extent with the humanities and with data from the other sciences which deal with man, notably: (1) biology, (2) sociology, (3) anthropology, (4) education, and (5) medicine. In addition, we have tried to tease out the personal, sociological, and educational implications of the factors which influence personality growth at each of its several stages. The fact that supernatural grace as well as the natural factors studied by psychologists also affects human personality, we explicitly recognize. The place of revelation and philosophy as well as of science in the study of human beings is presented specifically in Part IX, and their relation to particular psychological problems is pointed out in various chapters throughout the book.

The present textbook is primarily scientific in nature. Like other textbooks in the field, it stresses particularly those aspects of psychology about which there is adequate scientific evidence to warrant generalizations. It aims, among other things, to inculcate respect for careful scientific research. It stresses the need for a critical attitude and for suspending judgment on a problem until all of the facts are assembled. In addition it stresses the truth that philosophy and revelation (as well as science) give us valuable insights into human nature and behavior.

Compared with the works of artists and novelists, spiritual writers, theologians, and philosophers, the writings of experimental psychologists have been thought to be singularly sterile in throwing light upon people as people. Yet the findings of scientific psychology, when placed in their proper setting, are tremendously important for the understanding of human beings. Among the many source materials from which one can derive valid generalizations concerning the growth of human personality are several which are not often used by authors of psychology textbooks but which we have felt should be used. Some of these resources are experimental; some have been derived from psychological and psychiatric clinics; some are found in the researches of anthropologists and sociologists. Still others are found in the creative work of artists, musicians, and novelists; the speculative researches of theologians and philosophers; and the diaries, letters, and autobiographies which people have written throughout the ages. If you wish to obtain a deep knowledge of human nature, you must despise none of these sources. You must avoid the "provincialism" of mind which comes from wedding yourself too early to one "school" of psychology, to one method of study, or to the "most recent findings of psychology."

This book aims to give you a deep and sympathetic understanding of the *individual human being* rather than a knowledge of the *generalized human mind*. To accomplish this objective it takes its subject matter from any legitimate source of knowledge that is relevant, whether such knowledge be obtained through revelation, reason, or scientific experimentation.

This book aims to provide you with the facts and principles basic to understanding *why* people behave as they do and *how* they become what they *are*. As we pointed out in the beginning of this chapter, human motivation is a central problem of modern psychology. Psychology is interested not only in *how* people behave and *why* they behave, but also in *what* people *are*. In the last analysis, the most important thing to know about a person is not what he *does* but what he *is*. Our study of psychology will be sterile if it does not give us insights into how people can become wholesome, mature, and well-integrated personalities.

We have tried to emphasize in our discussion of each of the several stages of life the whole personality rather than isolated mental functions. For this reason we have avoided as much as possible the discussion of any specific aspect of development, such as "social development," "motor development," and "sensory development" apart from the discussion of its role in the entire economy of the human personality at any particular stage of its development. In other words, we have tried to center attention at every moment upon the human being himself rather than upon any one of his mental or physical functions. Necessarily, we have had to deal with sensation, perception, intelligence, and other components of human personality in separate chapters for the sake of clarity. But you must remember that these are only aspects of the whole personality. Unfortunately, you can learn a great deal about such human mental functions in isolation without, however, gaining much genuine insight into human personality.

We have seen in this chapter what is the basic problem of psychology—the understanding of persons. We have also pointed out in what ways psychology is related to other fields of knowledge. We have indicated some of the more important applications of psychological knowledge. In the following chapter we shall complete our introduction to psychology by discussing methods of learning about people.

SUGGESTED READING

BERRIEN, F. K., *Practical Psychology* (New York, The Macmillan Company, 1944).

BORING, E. G. (ed.), *Psychology for the Armed Services* (Washington, The Infantry Journal, 1945), Chapter I.

MÜNSTERBERG, HUGO, *On the Witness Stand* (New York, Clark Boardman Company, Ltd., 1923).

II

Methods of Psychology

Every object of our investigation belongs to a whole in which it acts and is acted upon, in which it is subject to conditions and imposes its own; one cannot study it apart. What we call specializing or analysis may indeed be a method, it must not be a spirit. Shall the worker be the dupe of his own device?—A. D. SERTILLANGES [1]

I. SCIENTIFIC OBSERVATION

Writers of biography, fiction, and poetry are as much concerned with human behavior as psychologists. But they treat their subject matter in a very different way. The psychologist's peculiar contribution to the study of people is his objective and scientific approach. He tries to eliminate from his scientific pronouncements his personal preferences and intuitive "hunches," all of which may nourish the roots of the finest productions of the creative writer.

Scientific observation differs not only from the kind of observation made by creative writers, but also from the casual observations of everyday life. A simple illustration will serve to highlight these differences. Suppose in the course of a conversation three questions are raised: "Do opposites attract?" "Are college men more intelligent than college women?" and "Is success in college related to success in life?" Now all of these questions could very well serve as starting points for scientific research. In fact, a really accurate answer would in each case necessitate such a study. But most of the members of the group in which these questions are raised will have opinions even in the absence of scientific data. These opinions will probably differ from one person to the next,

[1] A. D. Sertillanges, O.P., *The Intellectual Life,* trans. by Mary Ryan (Westminster, Maryland, The Newman Press, 1948), p. 101.

METHODS OF PSYCHOLOGY

but the reasons behind them will, in general, follow a similar pattern. Typically, you will hear such remarks as: "I know a tall woman who is married to a very short man. That's why I think opposites attract." "I remember two girls in my mathematics class in college. They always got the highest marks. No one else in the class ever came near them in pulling down grades. I think that demonstrates feminine superiority." "My boss flunked out of Harvard but he makes more money than any Phi Beta Kappa I ever knew. I don't think success in college has anything to do with success in life."

Note the following characteristics of the above remarks: (1) The opinions grow out of the individual's personal and necessarily limited experience. (2) They are based upon the observation of only one case or of a very few cases. (3) No attempt is made to ascertain whether the people observed are typical or whether they are marked exceptions to the rule. We have a tendency to notice what is unusual but to ignore the commonplace. In the above examples it is clear that the people observed were markedly different from people in general. The tall wife and short husband, for instance, attract more attention than other married couples because of their conspicuous differences in height. The two girls in the mathematics class would stand out as exceptional in any group, whether of men or of women. And lastly, the "boss," too, is atypical, since he is in an executive position and most men are not. No statement is made as to whether this man secured his position through his own efforts or through family influence.

How would the psychologist go about finding a scientific answer to these three questions? (1) He would try to eliminate personal bias by going beyond his own limited experience and systematically collecting all available evidence. (2) He would include in his study a sufficiently large number of cases to warrant drawing conclusions about people in general. (3) He would carefully select a representative sample, since obviously he could not include everybody in his study. And (4) before drawing conclusions from his data, he would apply the appropriate statistical formulae for analyzing the significance of his findings. In short, he would observe the rules of procedure that prevail in scientific method. We shall describe these rules in the following section.

II. SCIENTIFIC METHOD

The word *science* means "knowledge," and, broadly conceived, the term applies to any systematized body of knowledge, irrespective of the way in which its basic data were acquired. Contemporary psychologists, however, tend to restrict the term to a particular method of investigation, the scientific method. This method is characterized by definite canons of procedure which are the same for all sciences, although the specific techniques may vary from one field of knowledge to another. Astronomy, for instance, is one of the most exact of the sciences, as measured by the accuracy of its predictions. Astronomers, however, do not and obviously cannot conduct experiments on the stars and planets. Bacteriology, on the contrary, is almost entirely an experimental science. Yet the general rules governing scientific studies in both of these fields (and in psychology, too) are the same. These rules prescribe that we carry out the following steps in conducting a scientific study:

1. We Draw Up a Design for Our Research

A building is usually constructed according to definite plans and blueprints. These plans are drawn up before the materials are ordered and before any of the construction work begins. The blueprints give detailed instructions on how to proceed. Similarly, before undertaking any scientific research, we must draw up a plan or design for our study. We must decide ahead of time what we are looking for and must have an adequate plan to guide us in finding it. We must also determine beforehand the principles which will direct us in the interpretation of the data we collect.

2. We Make Systematic Observations

Once we have decided what to observe and under what conditions we will make our observations, we begin collecting data. We make these observations carefully, keeping an accurate record of the conditions under which they were made. Complete written records are essential because scientific studies require further verification before theories or laws can be formulated. A scientific study can be verified only if all of the conditions of the original study can be reproduced. Often, too, conditions that seemed unimportant at the time of the study are later found to be crucial. Written records, moreover, are a protection against bias both at the time of the observations and later. It is an accepted principle of psychology that forgetting is selective; people have a tendency to forget what they do not want to remember. Darwin is reported to have said that whenever he made an observation contrary to one of his theories, he had to write it down or he was sure to forget it. But, if the observation confirmed his theories, he had no difficulty in remembering it.

3. We Arrange Our Data in Some Meaningful Order

When a sufficient amount of data has been accumulated, we classify these data according to some meaningful system. In doing so, we reject irrelevant material and select and organize the significant material. For instance, in seeking an answer to the question raised above, "Is success in life related to success in college?", we need some criterion of success to guide us in collecting our data. Suppose we have decided to use two such criteria, one objective, the other subjective. The objective criterion of success is income; the subjective criterion is reputation for success among colleagues. Before we can interpret the data collected we must first classify them separately for each of the criteria. In classifying according to the objective criterion, we limit ourselves to measures of income. We reject as irrelevant the subjective estimates of success. Similarly, when using the subjective criterion, we reject the data on income as irrelevant. In this way we can make a precise statement as to the conditions under which our observations are true. We are enabled, in other words, to summarize our data separately for each of the two criteria of success.

4. We Formulate a Hypothesis

After carefully scrutinizing our accumulated data, arranged in a meaningful order, we formulate a hypothesis or tentative generalization concerning the significant interrelationships of the data. A *hypothesis* is a shrewd guess made on the basis of a limited amount of evidence. It does not become a scientific theory or law until further confirming observations have been made. It serves as a temporary explanation of the findings and as a guide to further research. In the case cited above, for instance, we may find that college grades are related to income but not to reputation among colleagues. Our hypothesis may be stated as follows: "Grades in college are significantly related to economic success in later life but unrelated to reputation for success as judged by colleagues."

5. We Conduct Further Experiments

Finally, we subject the hypothesis to further verification by repeated studies. If, after repeated observation and study, the hypothesis is found to apply to a great many other cases or to a large number of related phenomena, it acquires the status of a *theory*. When, upon further study, the relation of the phenomena studied, as defined in the theory, is found to be invariably present, the theory becomes a scientific *law*.

III. THE SCIENTIFIC EXPERIMENT IN PSYCHOLOGY

A scientific experiment is a trial or special observation made to confirm or disprove a hypothesis. It differs from the observations of a field study, as described in the next section, in that all of the conditions are artificially *controlled*.

A controlled experiment is one in which the situation is so prepared by the experimenter that he can account for all the factors which may influence his results. Each of these factors is called a *variable*. Psychological experiments are designed to show the effect of an *independent variable* on a *dependent variable*. The *dependent variable* is the psychological response or behavior of a person or group of persons being studied. The *independent variable* is the factor which is systematically varied to determine its effects upon the dependent variable. You set up an experiment in the following way:

Suppose you wish to find out whether a person's reactions to stimuli can be speeded up or slowed down under varying conditions. You begin by guessing that certain factors, such as directing attention to the stimulus to be received (sensorial attitude) or toward the movement to be made (motor attitude), will affect reaction time (RT). The independent variable is the attitude adopted; the dependent variable is the reaction time. Then you secure an instrument which accurately measures reaction time. Ordinarily, you would use a chronoscope, a timing device which gives accurate measurements of intervals up to 1/1,000 of a second. The chronoscope is wired in circuit with a telegraph key and an electric light. When you turn on the light, the chronoscope starts recording time. As soon as your subject sees the light he lifts his finger from the depressed telegraph key and the chronoscope stops. The interval elapsing between the appearance of the light and lifting the finger from the telegraph key is thus recorded by the chronoscope. This interval is the reaction time. Now keeping all other conditions constant, you vary one factor at a time systematically. First you instruct your subjects to adopt a sensorial attitude, that is, to concentrate on the incoming stimulus. Then you vary the instructions by asking your subjects not to think at all of the sense impression but to concentrate on the response to be made (motor attitude). Because there is a practice effect, you will not make all your measurements of sensorial or of motor responses successively, but will vary them in such a way that the practice effects are approximately the same for both. For instance, let us designate the sensorial attitude as A and the motor attitude as B. To compensate for any practice effect, we might arrange the trials in an ABBA or ABAB order. Thus, our results would show the effect of the independent variable (sensorial or motor attitude) on the dependent variable (RT) with the practice effect, so far as possible, held constant.

You will have noticed by now that the independent variable bears to the dependent variable something like the relation of cause to effect. We do not call them cause and effect, however, because as yet we are not sure that one is truly the cause of the other. Both could be caused by a third, anterior, event which requires the independent variable as a *sine qua non,* or necessary condition of its effectiveness. For instance, you may note that the butter in your refrigerator has melted and that the cream is sour. After this happens on a number of different occasions you note that invariably when the butter melts the cream also turns sour. In other words, you have discovered a perfect positive correlation between the two variables, melted butter and sour cream. Does this mean that the melted butter causes the cream to turn sour or that the sour cream causes the butter to melt? Obviously not. Both the sour cream and the melted butter result from a third variable, heat. This third variable results from the defective functioning of the refrigerator.

Ideally, there should be but one independent variable. When it is not possible to eliminate other independent variables in an experiment, statistical methods are often used to hold the other variables "constant." The independent variable is introduced into a situation where all other factors are constant to determine what effect it has upon the dependent variable.

It is usually difficult to account for all of the factors influencing experimental results. To be sure that all factors have been adequately accounted for, a *control* is introduced. In studying the effects of variables on groups of persons, a *control group* should always be used. The control group is like the experimental group in every respect save one—it is not subjected to the influence of the independent variable. The differences in the behavior, responses, or personality development exhibited by the two groups in a very carefully conducted experiment can then be attributed to the influence of the independent variable.

The following example will illustrate the use of a control group in psychological research:

Suppose we want to know what effect a series of weekly lectures on "How to Study" has upon the honor-point ratio of college students. It is not enough to take a group of students whose honor-point ratio we know, expose them to lectures on "How to Study," and then note whether the honor-point ratio goes up or not. If, under such circumstances, the honor-point ratio were to go up, this would not necessarily indicate that the lectures were responsible. Other factors in the college environment, such as the approaching end of the term, or factors within the students themselves, might have been responsible. Since these other factors or variables are not known, we cannot eliminate them from the situation. But we can "correct" for their influence by using a control group. The control group will be like the experimental group in respect to every variable, other than exposure to the lectures, that could reasonably be expected to influence the results. Thus, we would have to be sure that the control group was "equated" to the experimental group in intelligence, age, curriculum followed, and the like. This is what is meant by the phrase "holding all other variables constant." One way of equating for intelligence would be to see that both groups are of the same average intelligence and show the same amount of variability in intelligence. Another way of doing this would be to "match" each student in the experimental group with one in the control group. For example, if in the experimental group we have a student whose percentile rating on an intelligence test is 60, we should also have to put in the control group a student whose percentile rating is 60. In like manner we would match all of the students in the experimental group with students having the same intelligence test ratings and thus make up our control group. The same thing would be done in regard to age or curriculum followed. It is probable, for example, that age and maturity might have an influence upon the students' ability to apply knowledge derived from lectures. It is also quite possible that the lectures might throw more light on improving study habits in the sciences, let us say, than in the fine arts or in music. Therefore, the type of courses taken, and those upon which the honor-point ratio is based, must be controlled.

Let us suppose, further, that the average HPR (honor-point ratio) of our experimental subjects is 1.00 before the lectures. Let us suppose, too, that at the end of the semester following the lectures, the HPR has gone up to 1.60. This means that the average grade has gone up from C to B—. It is obvious, then, that students subjected to the lectures on "How to Study" have improved in scholarship. It is not so obvious, however, that this improvement is the result of the lectures. We can determine the effect of the lectures by comparing the gains in scholarship of the experimental group with the gains of the control group. When we discover that the average HPR of the latter group has gone up to 1.45, we realize that factors other than the "How to Study" lectures have been operating to improve scholarship. True, there is still a difference between the two groups, and this difference may be attributed to the beneficial effects of the lectures. But in any event, it is only after we have compared the gains of the experimental and the control groups that we can be said to be responsibly conservative in our estimate of the probable effects of the "How to Study" lectures.

Because of the impossibility of isolating a single independent variable in the study of the total personality, most investigators have been content to study more or less limited aspects of behavior. In consequence, many carefully controlled laboratory experiments, on learning, for example, contribute little to our understanding of the total personality. Learning as it takes place in daily life is complicated by attitudes resulting from a multitude of previous experiences throughout the life history. Some experiments, nevertheless, have yielded valuable information which can be applied to the betterment of human life, provided the experimental results are viewed in the light of the total stimulating situation. The following examples will illustrate this statement:

Watson in a famous experiment showed that it is possible to have "conditioned" fears. Albert B. was a stolid baby who showed no fear of normal environmental stimuli. He showed signs of fear only when (1) support was suddenly taken away, or (2) a loud noise was made. Albert, when first confronted with a rabbit, showed a liking for it. Watson then presented the rabbit and struck a steel bar making a loud noise behind the boy's head. The boy then showed signs of fear. The experience was repeated again and again. Each time the rabbit appeared, a simultaneous noise was made which produced fear. Finally, after several such experiences, the sight of the rabbit alone was enough to cause the baby fear. Albert had been "conditioned" to show fear at a stimulus that at first had not been adequate to cause it.

Another investigator conducted an experiment known as *reconditioning*. Her subject, Peter, was an active child of three years with numerous acquired fears, among which was a fear of furry objects. The purpose of her experiment was to associate a furry object with the pleasurable activity of eating and thus eliminate the fear of furry objects. The experiment required great skill because the food could easily have become a conditioned stimulus to the fear response and have resulted in disturbed eating responses. Peter was seated at a low table in a room about 40 feet long. Just as Peter began to eat his candy a caged rabbit was brought in. When the rabbit was placed on a table four feet away, Peter began to cry and insisted that the rabbit be taken away. He did not stop crying until the rabbit had been placed at the safe distance of 20 feet. Even then, although he started eating the candy again, he insisted, "I want you to put bunny outside." Later, he burst into tears again, and the rabbit was removed. The next day, the rabbit was again brought in, but placed at some distance from Peter. Gradually, on each successive day, the rabbit was brought just a little closer as Peter was eating his candy. Eventually the rabbit was placed on Peter's table and even on his lap without arousing any protest in him. At the end of the experiment, Peter was eating with one hand while stroking the rabbit with the other. The child's previously acquired fear of other furry objects had also disappeared. In this way, Peter's fear of furry objects had been *reconditioned*. This experiment throws light upon the way in which some human fears, at least, may be eliminated. It is an interesting example of the use of the experimental method in the study of personality. Yet the findings of an experiment such as this must be supplemented by clinical data embracing the whole life situation of a subject before generalizations can be made as a basis for predicting and controlling human development. Some children are easily conditioned or reconditioned; others are not. Apparently, the child's constitution, his past experience, and his emotional adjustment at the time of the experiment have an influence upon his reactions.

IV. FIELD STUDIES IN PSYCHOLOGY

A *field study*, unlike an experiment, is made in the natural setting in which the phenomena to be observed occur. The conditions under which such a study is made cannot be artificially controlled as they are in an experimental situation, and ordinarily the coöperation of the subjects is not required. Field studies are very common in the biological sciences. Ornithologists, for instance, make studies of birds in their natural habitats. The observation of fossil remains and members of living species upon which Charles Darwin based his theory of evolution was made as a field study. Darwin did not try to alter the characteristics of living creatures by experimentation. His method was empirical but not experimental. Mendel's study of inheritance in garden peas, on the contrary, was a controlled experiment. He varied the conditions systematically in order to determine the relative influence of different hereditary factors. In general, it is easier to make a simple observational field study than to set up controlled conditions in an experiment, although this is not invariably true. Field observations sometimes suggest problems for experimentation.

Psychologists often have recourse to field methods when it is not feasible to isolate a single independent variable for study. The *time-sampling* technique, in which the frequency of selected items of behavior is recorded, is a case in point. This technique consists of observing children or adults in natural situations during a series of definite time intervals, either on the same day or on successive days or weeks. The frequency with which the behavior under study appears is recorded for each period of observation. At the end of the series of observations these frequencies for each individual are averaged. It is possible, then, to treat these measures of frequency like any other scores. Comparisons within the group or from group to group can easily be made.

In general, time-sampling techniques are useful for establishing the frequency of certain types of behavior under given conditions. They are of more value in industrial situations, for example, as a basis for designing equipment and eliminating inefficiency, than they are in studying personality development. Child psychologists who formerly used the method have now, in most instances, abandoned it as they have come to realize its limitations. The most important limitation of this method is that it calls for careful interpretation before the frequency can be accepted as a *significant* measure. Thus, any given bit of behavior, to be psychologically significant, must be interpreted in the light of the whole personality (that is, in relation to the "meaning" which the behavior has to the person studied). Again, the social and cultural setting in which the behavior occurs must be considered (that is, its relation to the standards of value and the pressures to conform which society presents to the individual whose behavior is being studied).

In other words, a mere count of the frequency of occurrence of an external action is not necessarily psychologically significant; the same external action might have a different meaning for two different individuals or in two different cultural milieus.

Field studies, like scientific experiments, differ from the casual observation of everyday life in that they follow the canons of the scientific method. Before any observations are made, the observer defines the conditions of his study: (1) he decides how many cases or instances of behavior he will have to report in order to secure a reliable record; (2) he decides on the kinds of behavior he will record; and (3) he sets up a technique for recording his observations accurately.

V. LIFE HISTORY METHODS

Life history methods consist of biographies and autobiographies. They involve intensive and often long-range studies of individuals. In their simplest form they are "Baby Books" in which fond parents record the successive stages of their offspring's development. More comprehensive studies have been published as infant biographies. In general these *infant biographies* have been valuable for two reasons: (1) they have suggested important problems for scientific research in child development, and (2) they have focused attention upon the individual child rather than upon children in general. As we shall demonstrate in the next chapter, the study of individual children over a period of time in order to trace growth patterns is superior to studying groups of children at different ages. On the other hand, infant biographies suffer from the following limitations:

1. Since the observers are generally parents or relatives, they are likely to be biased in their reports.

2. Since individuals differ greatly, it is necessary to have a relatively large sampling of biographies from which to draw generalizations. Often generalizations about child development have been based upon too few biographical records.

3. The writers of infant biographies are a selected group. Since these writers are often related to the children whose development they are reporting, the children will also be highly selected.

4. Unlike the scientific experiment, it is not possible to use an experimental check to verify the observations reported in a biography.

Similar objections can be made to *biographical studies of adults*. And, in addition, adult biographies are often written in retrospect; their basic data have not been recorded at the time they occurred. Many of the most important details of the adult's life are inaccessible to the biographer or lack the dramatic quality necessary to attract his attention. Nevertheless, biographies, when cautiously interpreted, often yield valuable clues to the student of human nature.

Personal histories or autobiographies are valuable not only for what they directly display, but for the indirect clues they give for interpreting the motivation and "inner world" of the writer. Some autobiographies offer us source material that cannot be obtained in any other way. Autobiographies in which the authors describe their own mental breakdowns are of great value and interest to the psychologist, although he cannot take all of the statements of the writers at their face value.

VI. CLINICAL OR CASE STUDY METHOD

The clinical or case study method is used to discover the origin of personality problems or peculiarities. It makes use of all available sources of information—personal and family history, interviews, test ratings, questionnaires, school history, teachers' judgments, and the like. Originally used by the psychiatrist and the social worker as a prelude to treatment, the case study is currently being used as an effective means of discovering the sources of personality difficulties and the underlying principles of psychological development. In many instances, hypotheses derived from clinical studies have served as guides for extensive experimental research.

VII. VALIDITY OF GENERALIZATIONS BASED UPON CLINICAL OBSERVATIONS

Many generalizations upon which applied psychologists operate have not been, and possibly cannot be, verified by scientific experimentation. They have grown out of clinical experience, and because they have proved useful in predicting behavior, in guiding personality development or for treating maladjustments, they have become a part of psychological "lore" and are more or less taken for granted. There is, of course, no objection to acting upon generalizations derived in this way, provided we keep in mind their tentative nature and the fact that they are for the most part hypotheses or theories and not laws. As new clinical observations are made and new techniques of study are invented, many of these generalizations, we may suppose, will have to be modified or even discarded. Meanwhile, in psychology as in medicine, since some action is demanded of us and the problem cannot be held in abeyance until absolutely certain knowledge is available, we act upon tentative hypotheses. Let us suppose, for example, that a young mother is seeking advice on how to rear her children. She is able to nurse her babies and we advise her to do so. Upon what grounds can we justify such advice? Ideally, we would be able to draw upon the results of controlled experiments. An experiment might be set up, for instance, in which a number of identical twins are used, and in which one of each pair is nursed. A comprehensive follow-up study might later be made to compare the personalities of the pairs of twins. If other factors have been properly controlled, and if nursing in infancy is an important variable in personality development, a study such as this should reveal a more wholesome personality development in the twin who had been nursed. Since clinical observations already suggest that there will be a difference, however, we would probably be loath to set up such an experiment and thus deprive one child of each pair of the desirable type of handling. Furthermore, a forbidding amount of time would be consumed in waiting for the children to mature and so to complete the experiment. We must be content instead with certain limited studies, the accumulated results of which are very suggestive, but not necessarily conclusive. Several army studies yield interesting suggestions. In one comprehensive study, in which data on early childhood were collected, a significantly higher number of recruits discharged for psychoneurotic conditions were found to have been bottle-fed than recruits in general. There were other disturbing factors in the family background of the psychoneurotic men, too; and these factors undoubtedly contributed to the situation. We are perhaps justified in assuming that bottle feeding is an important factor, even though it does not operate in isolation from other influences. As we study the other factors related to personality disturbance, we make generalizations concerning the role they play, and in giving advice we try to deter people from rearing children in situations in which such unfavorable factors may have full sway.

VIII. PAPER AND PENCIL DEVICES

Various paper and pencil devices are used in conjunction with experiments, field studies, life history and clinical methods. They include rating scales, inventories, tests, and questionnaires. Since the first three of these devices are described in detail in Chapter XIX, we shall limit our discussion at this point to questionnaires.

The *questionnaire* as a method of studying human development was first used extensively by G. Stanley Hall. Hall's questionnaires were given to adults, who were required to reminisce about the "thoughts, feelings, ideas, and observations" of their childhood. Hall used the responses to his questionnaires as an important foundation for his psychology of childhood. Psychologists would today place little faith in the results of such questionnaires. Apart from the selective nature of forgetting, the accuracy of remembering decreases with time. Though the reminiscences of adults concerning their childhood are therefore likely to be erroneous, the form of those distortions may be interesting to a clinical psychologist.

Since Hall's time questionnaires have been used to a considerable extent in other fields of psychology as well as in developmental psychology. Studies of attitudes and their development, the effect of films and radio programs on emotion and behavior, are typical examples of the use of this method. Despite many criticisms of the method as a scientific tool, questionnaires continue to be used, and a whole science governing their construction and the interpretation of their results has been built up.

In general, questionnaires calling for opinions do not yield as reliable information as questionnaires calling for facts. Even when experts are asked to give their opinions as to what certain persons do, the returns are less accurate than statements describing actual observations of behavior. When the persons whose opinions are being solicited are not experts, the mere increase in number of opinions collected does not increase accuracy.

The scientific trustworthiness of questionnaire studies is affected by:

1. The extent to which the people receiving the questionnaire are representative of the total group about whom information is sought. If, for example, you want to determine the attitudes of mothers toward disciplining children, you would probably not get a representative opinion from only one section of the city. Questionnaires would have to cut across different socio-economic and ethnic groups to get an adequate "sample" of the population.

2. The extent to which the people who return the questionnaire are typical of the group about whom information is sought. Some questionnaires, for instance, will be returned by educated people more frequently than by the uneducated. Similarly, people who are intensely interested in the questions asked are more

likely to respond than people who are lukewarm in their interest. As a result, the questionnaires tend to be filled out and returned by a selected sample of the total group.

3. The clearness with which the questions are stated. You are less likely, for example, to elicit the correct response from the question, "At what time do you terminate the illumination?" than from, "When do you turn your lights out?"

4. The way in which the results are summarized and interpreted. For instance, in some studies it makes a difference whether you refer to the "arithmetical mean" or to the "median" when speaking of the "average." The mean may be considerably lower (or higher) than the median, as we shall show in a later chapter; and if the person reading the report is unaware of these differences, he may misinterpret the results.

Sociometric techniques, of the pencil and paper variety, are questionnaires used for determining an individual's status in the group and his personal characteristics, as viewed by his companions. They provide a choice of such statements as, "Here is someone that I respect very much," "This individual is a careless workman," and "Here is a man who is usually unhappy." The person filling out the sociometric questionnaire is required to write a name after each of the statements.

Sociometric analysis can be used to yield data concerning the person-to-person attractions and repulsions in groups, or may give valuable information as to the way in which groups are formed and how they function. When used over a period of time, sociometric techniques throw considerable light upon the development of personality and particularly upon the progressive social development of individuals in groups. The science of measuring such attractions and repulsions is called *sociometry*.[2] Its use as a method of studying personality development is based upon the recognition that man is a social being, and does not develop his personality in a social vacuum. The use of sociometric techniques is described in detail in the chapter dealing with the social development of the adolescent.

[2] J. L. Moreno, *Who Shall Survive?* (Washington, Nervous and Mental Disease Publishing Company, 1934).

IX. STATISTICAL ANALYSIS

Statistical techniques are tools for the analysis of quantitative data. They enable us to extract significant truths from masses of numerical data and to make judgments concerning the population from which the data were collected. Whenever it is feasible to do so, the psychologist reports his findings in quantitative terms. He then applies the appropriate statistical formulae to his data as a prelude to determining what these data mean.

The statistical measures most commonly used are three in number: (1) central tendency, (2) variability, and (3) correlation. It is the purpose of measures of central tendency to show us where a number of scores (which may be large) tends to cluster. A *measure of central tendency*, therefore, is the most representative measure of a group of measurements. A *measure of variability* shows us the extent to which the scores or measures of the group tend to disperse or vary from the average. The scores of two groups, for instance, may have the same average and yet differ widely in their dispersion, as we have illustrated graphically in Figure 1. The average score for both groups is the same, but

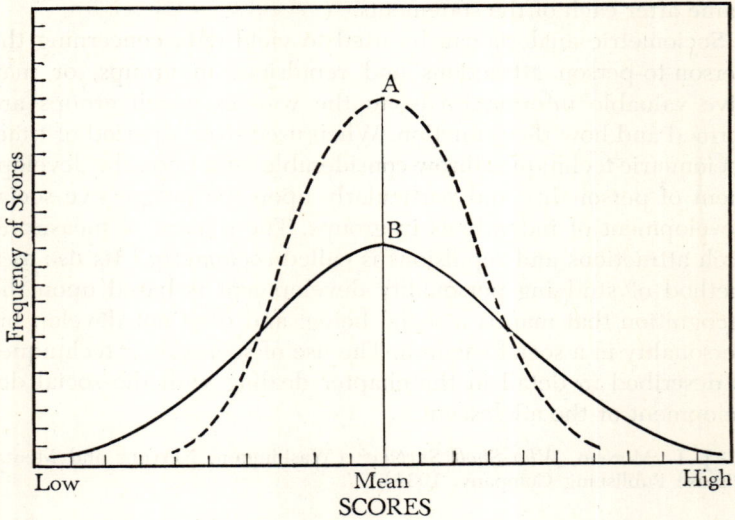

Fig. 1. Distribution of Scores for Group A and B. Both groups have same mean but differ greatly in variability.

METHODS OF PSYCHOLOGY 37

the variability of Group B is nearly twice as great as that of Group A.

When we want to determine the extent to which two sets of measures vary together, we use correlation techniques. A *coefficient of correlation* is a mathematical measure of the degree of relationship between two or more variables. It is designated as r or ρ, depending upon the particular formula used. We shall have occasion throughout this book to refer to psychological studies based upon methods of correlation. For that reason you will have to know a few principles of interpretation, which Figure 2 will help you to grasp. First of all, a coefficient of correlation may vary from $+1.00$ to -1.00. It is not a percentage. When the two sets of measures are perfectly and positively correlated, $r = 1.00$. When the two sets of measures are perfectly but negatively related, $r = -1.00$. In this second case, there is a complete reversal

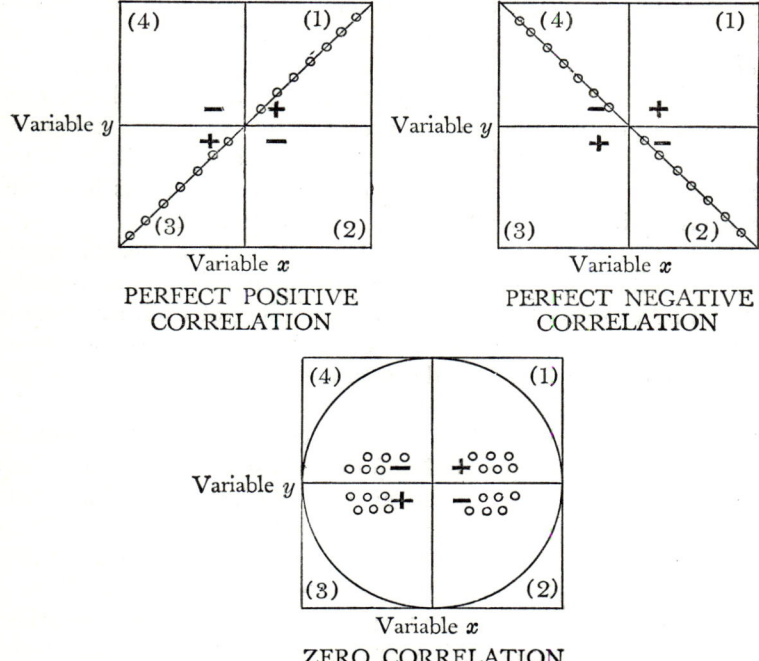

Fig. 2. Scatter Diagrams Showing Perfect Positive, Perfect Negative, and Zero Correlations.

of the two sets of scores; that is, a high score on one variable is associated with a low score on the other. And conversely, a low score on one variable is related to a high score on the other. Perfect correlations are very rare. Intermediate values of the coefficient of correlation are usually interpreted as follows: .80 or above indicates a marked relation; .60 indicates a fair relation; .40 indicates a small relation; .20 or below indicates a very low relation; and .00 indicates no relation.

Let us return now to a consideration of the three questions: "Do opposites attract?" "Are college men more intelligent than college women?" and "Is success in life related to grades earned in college?" A scientific answer to any of these questions will require the use of one or more of the statistical tools described above. In finding the answer to the first question, you will have to decide upon the particular characteristics you want to measure. Let us suppose that you have decided to use height in your study. You proceed to get accurate measurements of the heights of a representative sampling of husbands and wives. When you have collected a sufficient number of measurements, you work out a coefficient of correlation. When you find that $r = .50$ you know that there is a positive relation between the two variables, height of husband and height of wife, but it is far from perfect. In other words, there is a tendency for likes to attract as far as height is concerned, but there are exceptions to the tendency.

Perhaps the best starting point for answering the second question (whether college men or college women are more intelligent) would be to select a representative sampling of each sex from a representative sampling of colleges. Then you could administer intelligence tests and find the average score and variability for men and women.

Suppose you find that the average score for the two groups is the same but that the variability for men is somewhat greater than it is for women. (Here stated as a purely hypothetical assumption.) How will you interpret your data? You will be justified in saying that although on the average men and women do not differ, there are more men who are relatively stupid and more men who are relatively gifted than there are women in these categories.

In seeking a solution to the third question (how success in college grades correlates with success in life), you would first have to find quantitative measures of your criterion of success and compare them with college grades, which are also quantitative measures. If you chose income as the criterion, of course, this would present no difficulty except to get the figures. If you decided to use ratings of success by colleagues, however, you would have to use a somewhat different technique. Since ratings are not real numbers, you would not have a continuous series of values from which to work out a coefficient of correlation. You would have to find ρ, which is the coefficient of correlation used when data for one or more variables are in the form of ranks. *Rho*, ρ, is called the rank-order coefficient of correlation. You interpret its significance as you would r.

The accuracy of any statistical study depends, ultimately, upon whether the sample studied is a good representation of the population from which it is drawn. In answering the first question, "Do opposites attract?", we limited our study to married couples. Theoretically, we could have made measurements of *all* married couples, but practically, of course, this was out of the question. We had to content ourselves with measuring only a part of the total possible number of cases. When all of the individuals of the group are measured, we say that the *population* has been measured. Ordinarily, however, we select from this total population a *sample* which we hope is representative of the entire population of which it is a part. Statisticians have worked out elaborate sets of rules for securing samples which adequately represent the total population about which data are required. Typically, two kinds of sampling techniques are used in psychology: (1) random sampling, and (2) stratified sampling.

A *random sample* is a sample selected in such a way that every individual in the whole population from which it is drawn has an equal chance of being selected; and this selection is in no way dependent upon the selection of other individuals in the population. A sample secured in this way is said to have been selected by "chance." Obviously it would be difficult to secure a random sample of the human race because of the tendency of people with similar characteristics to congregate in the same place. For this reason, many samples, supposedly random, are biased because of "selective factors." To obviate the many difficulties involved in securing representative samples of human beings psychologists often resort to stratified sampling.

A *stratified sample* is obtained by dividing the total population into appropriate categories, and then selecting for the sample the same proportion of individuals in each category as are found in the total population. For example, we know that socioeconomic status is significantly related to scores obtained on intelligence tests. In working out norms for such tests, we might discover that it is extremely difficult, if not impossible, to find a group of children which is a cross-section of the total population available for testing. If we have census data, however, we can classify the total population according to occupational level, which is just one way of classifying them according to socioeconomic status. If we were to find that 3 per cent of the population belong to Class I in occupational level, then we would select for our sample 3 per cent from this same group. Similarly, if 15 per cent of the population belong to Class II, we would select the same per cent from this group for our sample, and so on for the other classes. In this way we would secure a stratified sample which, in the characteristic to be studied, would adequately represent the population from which it was drawn.

X. OBJECTIVE AND SUBJECTIVE OBSERVATION

Scientific psychology is one of the youngest of the sciences. It began in Germany as late as the second half of the nineteenth century. The first laboratory devoted to psychological research was established at the University of Leipzig in 1879 and was directed by Wilhelm Wundt. For Wundt the subject matter of psychology was consciousness; its method that of introspection. *Introspection*, as the early experimental psychologists understood the term, is a scientifically controlled method of observing one's own mental processes. These psychologists devised elaborate rules to govern the use of the method and for training subjects to make subjective observations. "Untrained" introspection they rejected as unscientific. The "trained" observer only could be relied upon to give an accurate description of his mental "content."

The American school of Behaviorism, which began in 1912, rejected introspection as a scientific method of observation. The Behaviorists insisted that objective observation alone is scientifically sound. *Objective observation* is the observation of behavior

METHODS OF PSYCHOLOGY

in animals or in persons other than oneself, and for this reason Behaviorism came to be called the psychology of the "other one," i.e., the other person whose behavior you observe. A psychologist who holds this view has been said to be consistent only if he avoids the conventional morning greeting, "How are you?" and instead announces to his friend, "You are fine, how am I?"

Both objective and subjective observation have limitations as well as advantages. Objective observation often leaves out what we really want to know about a person—how the situation appears to him, how he feels, and what motives inspire him to behave as he does. The overt behavior of two people may be identical, yet their motivation may be very different. One of the advantages claimed for the objective method is that environmental conditions under which the observations are made can be rigidly defined and controlled. But the human being himself—his sense organs, muscles, and nerves, as they have been modified by previous experience—is a part of the environment, and this aspect of the total environment is not open to objective observation.

Introspection is by its very nature inaccessible to verification by another person, and in this sense it does not meet one of the canons of scientific method. Furthermore, it is impossible to obtain valid introspections from young children or from stupid or uneducated adults. Another limitation, highlighted by research in clinical and abnormal psychology, is that much of human behavior is motivated by factors of which the individual is not consciously aware. Introspection obviously is limited to conscious mental content.

Today in experimental studies of human beings, even though the major observations are objective in nature, an introspective report is generally included. In this way one method can be used to compensate for the limitations of the other.

All of the various methods of study available to the psychologist —experiments, field studies, life histories, clinical studies, paper and pencil devices, objective and subjective observation—can furnish valuable insights into man and the conditions which foster or retard the wholesome development of his personality. In subsequent chapters we shall present some results obtained by the use of these methods. In evaluating these results it is well to keep in mind the method by which the particular information was obtained, for method can limit as well as facilitate research.

We turn now to a general consideration of psychological development, with special emphasis upon the environmental and hereditary influences that foster or retard human development.

PART II

Constitutional, Environmental, and Personal Factors That Influence Psychological Development

Human personality development is influenced by man's heredity, his environment, and his own free choice.

III

The Developmental Approach to Psychology: Introduction

Nativity, once in the main of light,
Crawls to maturity, wherewith being crowned,
Crooked eclipses 'gainst his glory fight,
And time that gave doth now his gift confound.
—SHAKESPEARE, Sonnet LX

I. WHAT IS INVOLVED IN A DEVELOPMENTAL STUDY?

Every human being first sees the light of day from a given geographical place on this planet, in a particular historical epoch, and within a given family and social setting. Long before his conception, dynamic historical and cultural forces have been at work which will profoundly influence his development. An American child born in the far West, for example, will find himself in a region which has the highest standard of living in the United States, and perhaps in the whole world. Consequently, he has greater opportunity to develop physically than children in less privileged areas. Yet, even in such a section, he may be a member of an underprivileged class or caste. Some communities in the United States are relatively isolated from the rest of the world by reason of cultural or physical barriers. Regardless of his hereditary potentialities, the child growing up in such a community is likely to be stunted in his intellectual and personal growth because he lacks the stimulation necessary to actualize his potentialities. He will be more ready to look upon the mores and folkways of his own community as the one "right" way of living than will a child reared in a more cosmopolitan environment, and to reject legitimate experiences which would enrich his personality because they conflict with the conduct norms of his social milieu. Certain communities in the United States, such as the Dunkards and Mennonites, are set apart from their neighbors because of religious beliefs. Islands off the main coast and settlements in certain mountainous regions of the United States, where communication facilities are primitive, are geographically isolated from the larger world. Then, too, within large cities there are certain "disorganized communities" which have developed their own code of behavior which is more or less opposed to the mores and code of laws of the larger community. Children born into such neighborhoods are much more likely to become delinquents or criminals in the eyes of the law than children born into families living in more "respectable" neighborhoods.

A complete developmental study of personality will include all of the geographical, social, historical, and cultural variables mentioned above, as well as the biological constitution of the individual person and the particular pattern of family relationships within which he grows up. It will show the effect of body build, personal appearance and strength, the influence of birth order, of childhood training, and of ways in which the adolescent is inducted into the adult society. It will of necessity go beyond psychological studies and include what historians, sociologists, economists, anthropologists, philosophers, and theologians have to say on the subject.

Needless to say, it will not be possible in a book of this size to make a complete analysis of all the myriad factors which enter into the development of human personality. In fact, it would not be possible for one person to master so broad a field of knowledge. We must content ourselves with describing certain representative studies, remembering that there is a great deal more to be said on each subject.

II. WHAT IS THE PSYCHOLOGY OF DEVELOPMENT?

The psychology of development treats of the entire life history of the human being, from the moment of conception until death. It is not limited to childhood or to adolescence. All human beings go through stages of anatomical and physiological development which are characteristic of the species, although individual dif-

DEVELOPMENTAL APPROACH: INTRODUCTION 47

ferences are marked at any one of these stages. Similarly, people appear to go through more or less characteristic phases of psychological development, including periods of growth, maturity, and decay. The application of psychology to human problems involves the recognition that people feel, think, and behave differently at different phases of the life cycle.

Developmental psychology has tended to concentrate more upon children than upon adults, partly because children are more available for study than adults. Then, too, children can more easily be helped to change for the better than adults, and this fact has, until recently, influenced research foundations to appropriate money for the study of children's problems in preference to the study of adult problems. With the changing ratio of children to adults in our population, however, this emphasis upon children is shifting. Present trends in our culture make it desirable to know more about the psychology of both early and late maturity. Medical science, on the one hand, has greatly increased the average life expectancy during the past few decades. Technological improvements, on the other hand, have shortened the period of industrial usefulness (so-called "industrial old-age"). This has created a span of the life cycle in which the individual is no longer a useful cog in the industrial machine and yet is a considerable way off from senility and death. This period is for many people in our culture a time of great frustration and bitterness. Contemporary research in this period of developmental psychology (gerontology) is being directed to a study of this adult group. In time, the results of such studies should contribute to the happiness and usefulness of older people and should provide some of the insights necessary for effective social planning and legislation.

III. REASONS FOR STUDYING THE PSYCHOLOGY OF DEVELOPMENT

A. Continuity of the Life Cycle

The human being, possessing a spiritual soul, is a "person" from the moment of conception. His soul, however, has knowledge only potentially; his bodily senses must provide it with material upon which to work. As time goes on, the bodily structures and functions gradually mature, and the individual interacts with the situations in the environment. This progressive inner growth and development, together with the accumulated experiences of life, bring about those changes that we observe in the person. These changes we refer to as the development of personality.

The development of personality is a continuous process, and every phase of it is profoundly influenced by the changes which have taken place in a previous phase. The adjustments which a school child makes to his new environment and companions are a result, at least in part, of the previous adjustments which he has made in his own home. The adjustment that an adolescent makes to the problems precipitated by his bodily maturity are similarly related to the earlier adjustments of his childhood. And often, the whole pattern of an adult's adjustment to life is the result of his experiences and the choices he made during adolescence. The entire cycle of life forms a pattern. Although there are distinct phases of life, each of these phases is intimately related to the phases which preceded it.

William Ellery Leonard, one-time professor of English at the University of Wisconsin, suffered for years from a serious neurosis which kept him from traveling beyond a radius of a mile from his home. The following lines, taken from his autobiography, illustrate his recognition of the continuity of the life cycle. They also show his recognition of the fact that human effort and will work with heredity and environment in shaping personality and character.

> You tell me (you in life and books well read):
> "Let your Past die with all its grief and riot!"
> *Let* the Past die!—The Past is never dead!
> Not at high noon! Not in the starry quiet!
> My Past is gesturing in this limp you pity,
> And whitens in this scar against the blast,
> And not a tree, a book, a song, a city,
> But has today its meaning from my Past.
> There is, good friends, scant wisdom in this "letting";
> I *am* my Past so long as I **am** I;
> And in the brave reshaping, not forgetting,
> Is my one hope and action not to die:
> The Past that might have killed me if it could
> I sternly mold to art and hardihood.[1]

[1] William Ellery Leonard, *The Locomotive God* (New York, D. Appleton-Century Company, Inc., 1942), pp. 295–296.

DEVELOPMENTAL APPROACH: INTRODUCTION

B. The Importance of Infancy, Childhood, and Adolescence

The importance of infancy and childhood in the genesis of adult personality can scarcely be overstressed. All psychologists, no matter what their theoretical leanings, are agreed upon this point. Many of them hold that early childhood is the most important period of life; others contend that early childhood and adolescence are of equal importance in the development of adult personality. It will be interesting to consider some of the reasons why infancy and childhood are so significant in the human life cycle.

1. From the standpoint of physical development

a. Nutrition. In the growth of a child, as in chemical reactions, there are both reversible and irreversible changes. An example of an irreversible physico-chemical change is that of boiling an egg until it is hard. Before the egg was boiled it had many possibilities—it could have been poached, scrambled, fried, or mixed raw in an eggnog. Once the egg has been immersed in boiling water for a short time, however, the future culinary possibilities of the egg become extremely limited.

It is possible that certain early experiences of the child, particularly those which occur early in his prenatal life, are similarly irreversible. Malnutrition, we know, either before birth or during early childhood, may cause irreparable damage to the developing organism. Such damage, when it occurs in the developing nervous system of the child, may go unnoticed until he has reached school age. Often it cannot be perceived by means of medical examination and is revealed only in the behavior of the child as he takes an intelligence test or attempts to learn school subjects. The fact that a low IQ in the early years of life is predictive of low IQ in the later years is often cited as evidence that mental ability is inherited and is relatively uninfluenced by environmental factors. It is also possible, however, to interpret such constancy in IQ rating as the result of an irreversible change occasioned by or released by early environmental factors. Although conclusive evidence on this point is not now available, it would seem prudent to suspend judgment on this problem until more facts are known. Studies of the effect of Vitamin B_1 complex and to some extent

Vitamin A on the functioning of the nervous system, for example, give promise of throwing light upon this important question.

b. Injuries and infections. Physical injuries suffered in early childhood may have a lasting effect upon the personality. Not only may they influence the child's future health and achievement, but they also influence his attitude toward himself and toward other people. Many of such injuries are the result of accidents which might have been avoided. Consequently, the child's attitude toward his parents or the persons who, however unwittingly, permitted the accident, may be charged with hostile emotions and feelings.

Physical peculiarities and defects of any kind tend to produce in a child a feeling of deprivation. This is true even when the child is born with the defect and when it cannot be blamed on the persons responsible for his welfare. Other children, instead of sympathizing with the handicapped child, often ridicule and penalize him, and thus deprive him of a sense of "belonging" to the group. The devastating effects of a clubfoot upon the personality adjustment of a school boy are vividly portrayed by Somerset Maugham in the following lines from his autobiographical novel, *Of Human Bondage:*

> He [Philip] never ran if he could help it, because he knew it made his limp more conspicuous, and he adopted a peculiar walk. He stood still as much as he could, with his club-foot behind the other, so that it should not attract notice, and he was constantly on the lookout for any reference to it. Because he could not join in the games which the other boys played, their life remained strange to him; he only interested himself from the outside in their doings; and it seemed to him that there was a barrier between them and him. Sometimes they seemed to think that it was his fault if he could not play football, and he was unable to make them understand. He was left a good deal to himself. He had been inclined to talkativeness, but gradually he became silent. He began to think of the difference between himself and others.[2]

Alfred Adler, the late Viennese psychologist, concluded from his study of mental abnormalities in adults that all neurosis has its origin in "organ inferiority." "Organ inferiority" refers to either a real or an imaginary physical defect. Adler affirms that the presence of such a defect produces in the child an "inferiority com-

---

[2] W. Somerset Maugham, *Of Human Bondage* (New York, George H. Doran Co., 1915), p. 45.

plex," and this complex is the root of his subsequent personality disorders. While Adler's theory, surely, does not adequately account for all neurosis in adults, it does, at least, point to a contributing factor in many cases of adult neurosis.

The child who is handicapped is more likely than other children to be either overprotected by parents or teachers or to be rejected by them. The deleterious effects of such treatment are discussed in Chapter V.

Certain physical weaknesses, such as calcium deficiency, produce irritability in a child. If the condition persists for a long time, a bad habit of behaving irritably may be developed. This habit, developed as are all habits by repetition over a period of time, may be difficult to break. It may persist even after the physical condition which originally produced it has been cleared up.

2. From the standpoint of social and emotional development

A child's experiences in his own home have an important and permanent though not determining effect upon his personality. During his early years the family educates the child in the following important ways:

a. It produces in him a lifelong tendency toward either emotional stability or instability.
b. It gives him his start toward a lifelong attitude either of acceptance or rejection of legitimate authority.
c. It produces in him a more or less permanent feeling of personal worth or inferiority. And, as a consequence, the child tends to look upon life either as a series of challenges or as a series of evils to be avoided.
d. It teaches him to accept or to reject religious principles and values.
e. It helps or hinders a child in the acceptance of the appropriate masculine or feminine role in life. And as a result of this training he acquires either a favorable or an unfavorable attitude toward marriage and its responsibilities. This attitude may persist through adolescence, maturity, and old age.
f. It prepares the child to be accepted by and to coöperate with persons of his own age group or to be rejected by them and to reject them in turn.
g. It furnishes the setting for the development of attitudes towards parents and siblings which may later be transferred to teachers and classmates.
h. It transmits to the child the demands of society.
i. It influences the child's affective life by means of the methods it

uses in establishing such habits as those of feeding and elimination.

An explanation and clarification of each of the above factors is reserved for later chapters.

The study of adolescence is, in a sense, a key to the psychology of personality. Adults are profoundly influenced throughout life by the attitudes, goals, and self-evaluations which, by a combination of circumstances, were built into their personalities during the formative years of adolescence.

C. The Social Significance of the Child

Children are socially significant because they are potentially adults. As adults they will determine the direction of social change, the kind of world in which human beings will live. Men and women do not, upon reaching the legal age of maturity, suddenly acquire the attitudes, ideals, and habits which will govern their adult conduct. Their psychological characteristics have been in the making throughout their whole developmental history. If we wish to perpetuate a culture or bring into existence a "brave new world," we must begin by educating the children. This education, to be effective, must be directed to the whole personality of the child; it must begin long before the child goes to school; it must be based upon a deep knowledge of the psychology of his development.

D. Professional Reasons for Studying Psychology From a Developmental Point of View

Many of the professions embraced by college graduates deal directly or indirectly with children or adolescents. This is true for teaching, law, social service, library work, nursing, medicine, and the dental profession. Such professional contacts are greatly enriched by a knowledge of the psychology of human development.

Professional people are often called upon to influence the environment of other people, either in their specific professional capacity or in their capacity as citizens with more than average education. Often they are called upon for advice or help in providing conditions which will make for optimal child and adolescent growth and development. Sometimes they are called upon to help remove obstacles to growth. And frequently they counsel

DEVELOPMENTAL APPROACH: INTRODUCTION 53

parents and other persons who deal with children and young people. The adequacy with which the professional worker meets such demands can be greatly increased by his knowledge of the psychology of human development.

IV. CROSS-SECTIONAL AND LONGITUDINAL METHODS OF STUDYING DEVELOPMENT

Psychological development can be studied by either cross-sectional or longitudinal methods. When the cross-sectional method is used, groups of people at different age levels are studied and the average differences between one age level and the next are contrasted and compared. We assume, for example, in comparing a group of six-year-old children with a group of ten-year-old children, belonging to the same population, that the differences between them are the results of age. We infer from our study that, given the same environment, the six-year-old children will, in four years' time, become like the present ten-year-old children. Such a technique has been used extensively in medicine. For example, typical norms for height and weight have been established in this way. This technique is much more economical of time than is the longitudinal technique, since conclusions can be drawn from it without waiting for the children being studied to grow up. Sampling errors, however, can easily creep into studies of this kind.

The method most in favor at the present time is the longitudinal method. This method consists in studying the same people over a period of time and noting the changes that take place. Sampling errors are ruled out by this procedure. The results, however, are not necessarily more conclusive than the results obtained from the cross-sectional methods if only group statistics are employed to analyze the results. The superiority of the longitudinal over the cross-sectional approach is demonstrated only when an analysis of individuals is made.

For instance, most studies of growth, whether of anatomical or psychological characteristics, show that there is on the average a gradual increase from year to year. This result is obtained when average growth for any given characteristic is computed either for different individuals at successive age levels or for the same children studied at different ages. Group averages, in other words, whether derived from cross-sectional or longitudinal data, show this gradual increase from year to year with no marked spurts or retardations of growth at any age level. There is another way of studying the same children, however, over a period of time. Instead of using the group statistics, previously described, an individual graph of successive measurements of the same children can be made. Typically, none of these individual graphs of growth follows the pattern of the graph derived from group averages. In almost no characteristic do we find that growth takes place in this gradual, non-fluctuating pattern suggested by the group averages. The best picture of growth, it seems, can be obtained from longitudinal data in which the individual patterns of growth have not been obscured by the use of group statistics.

We have discussed the nature and importance of developmental psychology and have mentioned a few of the methods it employs. The remaining sections of this chapter are devoted to some of the most important factors influencing personality development throughout life.

V. PSYCHOLOGY OF DEVELOPMENT AND SOCIAL CLASS

A characteristic interest of American psychologists from the beginning of the experimental period to the present has been the scientific study of individual differences by means of psychological tests. Early studies dealt with differences in reaction time, sensory discrimination, and other simple sensory and motor processes. Later, when the construction of more complex tests made possible the "measurement" of higher mental processes, psychologists turned their attention to the analysis of individual differences in general intelligence. Gradually they discovered significant differences between the average measured intelligence of different kinds of groups in the general population. The average intelligence of different occupational groups, for instance, showed marked and consistent differences. Certain ethnic and racial groups were also distinguished in this manner. Groups of persons differing in income showed significant differences in average measured intelligence, although the differences within any of these groups—particularly the ethnic, racial, and economic groups

DEVELOPMENTAL APPROACH: INTRODUCTION

—were always found to be greater than the average differences between any two groups.

Because of these observed differences in groups, psychologists adopted the practice of designating the kind of group from which their subjects were recruited whenever they reported the results of psychological research. They might, for instance, point out that the subjects were all "native born, white, and predominantly middle class." In using the term *middle class* they were referring to a group distinguished from the lower or the upper class on the basis of occupational status and income. They could determine this status by comparing the occupations and incomes of the people they were studying with census data for the population at large. Classifications of this type can be made with a certain amount of objectivity. The psychologist can make the classification himself without asking the members of the group to assign status either to themselves or to others in the group. These classifications are best designated as "socio-economic" groups rather than as "social classes." Unfortunately, the term *social class* is used in a variety of ways and it is not always possible to determine the basis upon which the classification has been made. The terms *lower class, middle class,* and *upper class* sometimes refer to different economic groups and sometimes to "status groups." Although status is correlated to some degree with income, the relationship between the two is far from perfect. Some persons, for instance, prefer to be poor while keeping their upper-class status by remaining unemployed. Others may be wealthy and still retain lower-class status, particularly if their wealth has been acquired in a dubious way as, for example, by smuggling or by operating a gambling establishment.[3]

We do not have a satisfactory definition of social class because there is as yet no criterion of class structure upon which all social scientists would agree. The following definition, however, appears to be generally accepted:

A social class is the aggregate of persons having essentially the same status in a given society. Where societies are composed of social classes, the social structure generally resembles a truncated pyramid, with the lowest social class at the base and the other social classes arranged

[3] An inherited fortune acquired by such means does not carry with it the same stigma. In America today some of the "first" families are living on inherited fortunes which were originally acquired by so-called "robber barons" who resorted to dishonest and otherwise disreputable methods.

above it in a hierarchy of rank and distinction. The fundamental attribute of a social class is thus its social position of relative superiority or inferiority to other social classes.[4]

The above definition tells us what a social class is but it does not give us the specific information we need for assigning individuals or families to the appropriate social class. Lloyd Warner and his colleagues have worked out an elaborate technique for assigning the individuals in a whole population to as many as seven distinct social classes. Their criteria, however, are so nebulous that it is difficult for other people to verify their work or to apply their norms in studying other social groups. The great difficulty in assigning status rankings is that the sorting is done by the persons immediately concerned and not by the investigator. The task of the investigator is that of interpreting what members of the group say and think about themselves and others. This is a much more difficult task than that of arbitrarily assigning ranks on the basis of the objective criterion of income.

The psychologist's interest in social class stems from his increasing awareness of the influence of the social environment on the development of human personality. Certain types of behavior are rewarded in some social classes but punished in others. A value inculcated in one social class may have no significance whatever in another.

Social classes occupy, as it were, "private worlds." They live apart and they live differently. As a result of such segregation and isolation, social classes develop, in various aspects of life, additional traits and characteristics which set them off from one another. The cockney dialect of the lower-class Englishmen, for instance, helps to mark them off from the products of Eton and Harrow. . . . Each class comes to have its special culture.[5]

Since motivation plays an extremely important role in human learning and personality development, anything which throws light on motivation is of interest to the psychologist. And since motivation differs from one social class to another, the psychologist must be cognizant of social class differences.

Throughout this book we shall be describing studies made of people in different social classes. As far as possible, when the criterion of social class is economic, we shall refer to it as socio-

[4] W. F. Ogburn and M. F. Nimkoff, *Sociology* (Boston, Houghton Mifflin Company, 1940), p. 309.
[5] *Ibid.*, p. 315.

economic. If the criteria are those of Lloyd Warner and his school of thought, we shall refer to that fact in a footnote. In all other cases, we shall simply report the facts as given by the investigator without attempting to clarify the concept of social class that is implied.

The contemporary interest of social scientists in the subject of social class has been stimulated to a marked degree by the spread of communism. Marxists tend to stress the differences in social classes and the conflicts to which such differences lead. The Christian social scientist, on the other hand, while recognizing the existence of social classes, tends to stress their complementary and coöperative functions. The Catholic psychologist finds that what all men have in common, namely, their common human nature and the fact that all men are either actually or potentially members of the Mystical Body of Christ, is more important than accidental differences of race, nationality, social class, or caste.

VI. PSYCHOLOGY OF DEVELOPMENT AND CULTURE

Since people grow up within specific cultures we shall have occasion from time to time to discuss the influence of the culture pattern upon personality development. It will be well, then, to explain at this point what we mean by the term *culture*. Culture is defined as a

. . . collective name for all behavior patterns socially acquired and socially transmitted by means of symbols. . . . It includes all that is learned through intercommunication. It covers all languages, traditions, customs, and institutions. As no human groups have ever been known that did not have language, traditions, customs, and institutions, culture is the universal, distinctive characteristic of human societies. . . . The essential part of culture is to be found in the patterns embodied in the social traditions of the group, that is, in knowledge, ideas, beliefs, values, standards and sentiments prevalent in the group. . . . The essential part of culture seems to be an appreciation of values with reference to life conditions.[6]

In our psychological study of human beings we are concerned particularly with the last part of the above definition: the sense of values which a given culture embodies.

[6] H. P. Fairchild (ed.), *Dictionary of Sociology* (New York, Philosophical Library, 1944), pp. 80–81.

VII. HEREDITY, ENVIRONMENT, AND FREE CHOICE

In the course of development, mature personality and character is produced through the interaction of three factors: (1) heredity, (2) environment, and (3) free choice. All three factors, however, do not necessarily always operate in the production of any given human trait or characteristic. A man cannot change his reaction time, for instance, just by willing to do so. Certain bodily characteristics and traits are largely, if not wholly, determined by the interaction of hereditary factors and internal and external environmental conditions. The ability to walk, for example, is the outcome of such interaction and is said to result from maturation. Such a characteristic will just naturally develop through inner growth, while others will require training and education. In the next chapter we shall try to show you how heredity operates, how the environment interacts with hereditary potentialities, and how the specifically human power of freely choosing ends and means is interwoven with heredity and environment in the total process of personality development.

SUGGESTED READING

BÜHLER, C., *From Birth to Maturity* (London, Kegan Paul, Trench, Trubner and Company, Ltd., 1937), Introduction.

DAVIS, A., "American Status Systems and the Socialization of the Child," *Amer. Soc. Rev.*, 6 (1941), 345–354.

FRENKEL, E., "Studies in Biographical Psychology," *Character and Personality*, 5 (1936), 1–34.

RIBBLE, M. A., *The Rights of Infants; Early Psychological Needs and Their Satisfaction* (New York, Columbia University Press, 1943).

SCHRODES, C. J., GUNDY, R. W., and HUSBAND, R. W. (eds.), *Psychology Through Literature* (New York, Oxford University Press, 1943), Part I, "The Formation of the Personality."

IV

Role of Heredity, Environment, and Human Freedom in Psychological Development

God speaks:
I know man well. It is I who made him. A funny creature. For in him that freedom is at work which is the mystery of mysteries.—PÉGUY [1]

I. INTERACTION OF HEREDITY, ENVIRONMENT, AND HUMAN FREEDOM

No two human beings are ever exactly alike. Even identical twins, who have the same heredity, are no exception to this rule. Little children of the same age differ considerably in the progress they have made toward anatomical and physiological maturity. They vary greatly in such traits as height and weight, body build, eye and hair color, strength, aggressiveness, energy output, motor skill, and in the effectiveness with which they express themselves. Some of these differences, such as weight, are already present at birth. Other bodily characteristics, such as hair color, appear only gradually. Newborn babies differ tremendously in the amount of activity they display, even under the same conditions of temperature and humidity. These differences persist and often increase as the children grow older.

Children, then, differ from each other almost as much as adults do in physical traits. But as regards character and personality, the situation is reversed. Little children in the same milieu resemble each other in goals and in ethical values much more than adults do, because children have had experience with simpler

[1] Charles Péguy, *God Speaks* (New York, Pantheon Books, Inc., 1945), p. 24.

environments and have not yet developed intellectual convictions of right and wrong, good and bad. The goals of little children are all more or less alike: they seek such things as the approval of parents or the acquisition of an ice cream cone. They seek specific, individual, and immediate ends because they lack the maturity to visualize or to plan for more remote goals. Adults, on the contrary, show their greatest differences in the goals they set for themselves and in the ideals they pursue. They choose among the various alternatives offered by their environment the goals which they judge to be most suitable for them. The particular choices which a man makes are not forced upon him; he chooses freely according to the light provided by his intellect.

The question we are attempting to answer in this chapter, in so far as it can be answered, is: To what extent are human characteristics the result of heredity, of environment, and of the choices and activity of the person himself? It seems obvious, at the start, that certain traits are largely of hereditary origin, as for instance, eye color and body build. Yet it is equally obvious that without appropriate environmental conditions these traits would never have developed at all. From the very beginning of life the environment must provide food for the organism, or no hereditary potentialities will ever come to fruition. Other characteristics are apparently acquired through environmental stimulation, such as the ability to speak or to ride a bicycle. Yet children in the same environment differ greatly in the rate at which they acquire these abilities and in the proficiency that they finally show in them. The "limits" or "ceiling" placed upon a child's ability to learn appear to be determined by constitutional factors operating through the biological mechanisms of heredity.

Some unlearned characteristics appear long after birth. Sex characteristics which develop at adolescence are an example. The rate at which these traits appear shows family resemblances, and consequently we infer that a constitutional factor is operating in producing it. Walking is another example of a function which begins at a certain age through maturation without having to be learned. Maturation refers to the state of readiness of the organism, achieved through the interaction of heredity and the internal environment of the body, so that it has reached a state of development at which certain types of activity, not previously possible, can now take place. Walking, for instance, does not

HEREDITY, ENVIRONMENT, AND FREEDOM 61

appear until the child's muscles and nervous system have matured sufficiently for him to take his first steps. Once he has taken a few steps, however, he strengthens his walking by exercise. The skill he develops in walking is thus the combined product of his maturation and of his learning.

As the child progressively matures, he takes more initiative in his own development. In the light of his intelligence he chooses courses of action for himself. Adolescent boys and girls are often heard to say, "I'll decide that for myself," and "I know what to do; you don't have to tell me." Often, of course, these choices are not the best ones that could be made. But they are usually the best that a particular adolescent can make because of his limited experience and knowledge. The human being, once his intelligence has matured sufficiently, is capable of weighing motives and freely choosing between the good and the bad or between the greater and the lesser good. These choices, made over the entire life cycle, are the ultimate determiners of what will become the adult personality and character. Not every trait, of course, is influenced by such free choices. A person cannot, by willing to do so, change the color of his hair or eyes. But the total personality and character are profoundly influenced by such choices. In short, the mature personality and character of the human being result from the interaction of these three factors: (1) heredity, (2) environment, and (3) man's own free choice.

Let us consider now in more detail how these three factors interact.

Each human being starts life as a single cell (the *zygote*) formed by the union of two germ cells from the parents. The *sperm* from the father unites with the *ovum* of the mother in one of the fallopian (uterine) tubes. At first the sperm, which is much smaller than the ovum, attaches itself to the wall of the ovum. Next it penetrates the wall of the ovum, and the nuclei of the two cells come together. At this point, heredity is complete; the zygote, which is the individual, contains all of the hereditary potentialities he will ever have. Immediately, the environment of the mother's body begins to have an important influence upon the development of the body, including especially the nervous system, upon which the functioning of intelligence depends. The social heritage, too, is already determined to some extent, since from the beginning of life the individual belongs to parents of a certain nationality, race, religion, social class, economic class, and historical epoch. His parents' attitudes toward him are being formed before his birth. The love or lack of love between mother and father, their desire to have or not to have a child, their preconceptions as to what the child will be—boy or girl, beautiful, or bright—all will have an influence upon his developing personality and character.

Every cell of the body is derived from the zygote. The zygote divides into two cells, each of which receives the same hereditary potentialities as the first. These cells, in turn, divide, and the daughter cells produced in this way also divide, until eventually billions of cells are formed. At first these cells all look alike, but gradually they differentiate into nerves, blood vessels, bones, and other specialized kinds of cells.

How does the environment influence the developing embryo and fetus? It affects both physical and mental characteristics, we know, but the precise nature of such influences we do not know. Psychologists generally reject the popular notion that experiences of the mother during pregnancy, such as listening to beautiful music, or being frightened by a snake, leave an impression upon the fetus. There is no connection between the nervous system of the mother and the nervous system of the fetus through which psychological impressions can be transmitted. Worry, shock, or fright on the part of the mother will influence the fetus, however, very indirectly and only if they injure the health of the mother and so interfere with the proper nourishment of the fetus.

Loud noises may cause the fetal heart to beat faster, and it is even possible to set up conditioned reflexes to sound stimuli before birth. Furthermore, to the degree that the mother's fears modify the function of her endocrine glands and cell metabolism, the composition of her blood is changed. This change in blood might sometimes prove irritating to the fetus and increase his bodily activity. If stimuli of this sort continue over long periods of time, the fetus might spend most of his intra-uterine life in a state of irritability and hyperactivity. After birth his muscular activity would remain high, and he would be prone to exaggerated bowel activity and a higher fluctuation of heart rate than most infants. Often such a child does not tolerate his feedings, and is more irritable and cries more than other children of his age.

HEREDITY, ENVIRONMENT, AND FREEDOM 63

Thus, the prenatal environment may lessen the adaptability of the infant to his new environment at birth and render him less able to utilize food in a healthy manner. As a result he is a "problem" to his mother and becomes less desirable in her eyes.[2]

Some prenatal conditions influence the developing embryo and fetus directly. Early exposure of the embryo to x-rays or to radium may result in feeblemindedness. Microcephaly (a clinical type of feeblemindedness) sometimes appears to be caused by such exposure.[3] A condition brought about in the mother by lead poisoning may prevent normal brain development of the fetus. Since this condition is present in the mother's blood it is easily transmitted to the child. The resulting feeblemindedness, though present at birth and therefore congenital, is not inherited.

Syphilis and other venereal diseases may injure the germ cell of the developing embryo in such a way as to produce permanent mutilations, although not all mutilations are caused in this way. Occasionally, a child is born with a body part missing, such as a finger or toe, a foot, a hand, or part of an arm. These abnormalities are not caused by heredity but appear to be the result of inadequate circulation. The cord may become wrapped around the wrist, arm, or ankle in such a way that circulation is cut off.

Often the question is raised as to which is more important, heredity or environment. This is an artificial question, however, to which no answer can be given. Every physical and mental characteristic, as well as the whole personality, results from the interaction of both. In this respect Woodworth[4] has compared development to the area of a rectangle, of which heredity is the width and environment is the length, or vice versa, as indicated in Figure 3. In some cases heredity may be more important, and thus be compared to length; in others, environment may be compared to length. To ask which is more important in determining the area of a rectangle, length or width, is to raise an artificial question, since without both length and width there is no area. Similarly, without both heredity and environment there is no development.

[2] L. W. Sontag, "Some Psychosomatic Aspects of Childhood," *The Nervous Child*, 5 (1946), 296–304.

[3] D. P. Murphy, M. E. Shirlock, and E. A. Doll, "Microcephaly Following Maternal Pelvic Irradiation for the Interruption of Pregnancy," *The American Journal of Roentgenology and Radium Therapy*, 48 (1942), 356–359.

[4] R. S. Woodworth and D. G. Marquis, *Psychology*, Fifth Edition (New York, Henry Holt & Company, Inc., 1947), pp. 158–159.

Let us address ourselves now to the crucial question: Are we completely the product of our heredity and environment or do we ourselves have a part in developing our own personalities and characters? We raise the question at this point because in this chapter and in the next we shall be describing in detail the effects of heredity and environment upon human development. Heredity and childhood experiences do limit what we can and cannot do. We are not free to become anything whatever; we are free only to develop the potentialities which have been given to us. Heredity and environment furnish the raw material from which we freely shape our personalities and characters. But we freely make ourselves only when we are mature enough to distinguish evil from good and the lesser good from the greater good. As we shall show in detail later on, freedom of choice depends upon intellectual apprehension, which, of course, the little child does not have. Moreover, as we progressively make choices throughout life, we are shaping ourselves in such a way that some choices become easy and others more difficult. For instance, if I refuse to make the effort required for study, it becomes more and more difficult for me to study. I am, consequently, less free to develop a habit of study than I was before I made this choice of not studying. Hence, although my freedom has now become restricted, it is *I* who have freely brought about such a limitation to my own freedom.

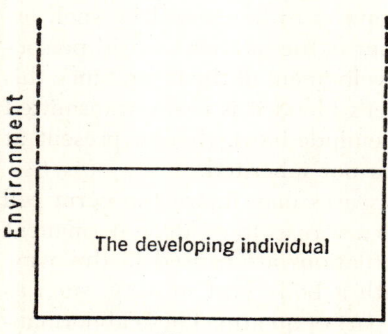

Fig. 3. The Individual a Product of Heredity and Environment. Increase the environmental stimulation (height of the rectangle) and you increase the area, but the hereditary factor (width) remains as important as ever. [From R. S. Woodworth and D. G. Marquis, *Psychology*, 5th ed. (New York, Henry Holt & Company, Inc., 1947), p. 158.]

What a man eventually becomes, then, is not just the result of his heredity and environment. The kind of personality and character which he will develop results from the free choices he makes within the limitations set up by his heredity and environment. The rectangle pictured above does not tell us the whole story of human development since it is lacking in one dimension. A better illustration is the solid pictured in Figure 4, in which the capacity is the product of length, width, and depth. The capacity here, as the area in Figure 4, represents human development. The length, too, represents heredity, and the width, environment. But the third dimension, the dimension of depth, symbolizes man's freedom of choice. The total development of human personality and character, therefore, results from the interaction of heredity, environment, and man's free choices.

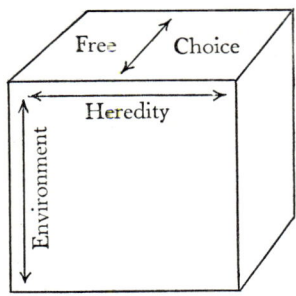

Fig. 4. Schematic Representation of the Interaction of Heredity, Environment, and Free Choice.

II. THE BIOLOGICAL BASIS OF HEREDITY

Since heredity is mediated by biological processes, familiarity with these processes and with the terms used in describing them is a help in studying psychology. If you are already so familiar with these processes and terms that you do not need even to review them, you can skip this section and proceed immediately to page 71.

A. Germ Cells and Chromosomes

The whole human body is made up of cells. Some of these cells are specialized for reproduction. These are the germ cells. As we have already shown, the male germ cell is called a *sperm;* the female germ cell is called an *ovum*. The union of a mature sperm and ovum produces a new human being. This union is called *conception,* and the one-celled organism produced by the union is called a *zygote*.

The germ cells, like other cells of the body, consist of two main parts. The outer part is called *cytoplasm;* the inner part is called the *nucleus*. A typical cell is pictured in Figure 5.

For a long time biologists believed that the nucleus alone was concerned with the transmission of hereditary characteristics. More recently, however, data have been accumulating which show that the role of the cytoplasm has probably been underestimated,[5] and it seems probable today that the cytoplasm as well as the nucleus contains particles which help to shape the organism's heredity. Little is known, however, as to the exact nature of these particles and how they operate.

A great deal is known about the role of the nucleus in the transmission of hereditary characteristics.[6] The hereditary factors transmitted by specialized structures within the nucleus of the germ cells are known as chromosomes.[7] These chromosomes are threadlike bodies which can be seen through a microscope when an

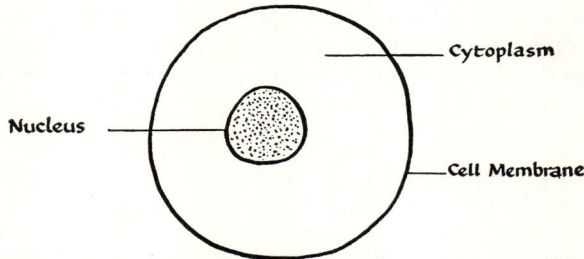

Fig. 5. A Typical Cell

appropriate stain is used. Each cell of the body contains the same number of chromosomes. The number of chromosomes, as well as their shape and internal makeup, differ considerably from one species to another. The number is constant for any one species. Thus, in man, there are always twenty-four pairs, or

[5] T. M. Sonneborn, "Partner of the Genes," *Scientific American*, 183 (November, 1950), 30–39.

[6] "The new discoveries about the genetic role of the cytoplasm leave untouched the vast accumulation of evidence that the nuclear genes do control nearly all the hereditary differences thus analyzed. They merely emphasize what has long been realized: that the gene is not in *exclusive* control of heredity. It operates not in an ivory tower but in the organic unity of the cell, and the rest of the cell has some voice in the directions that are given." —*Ibid*.

[7] In reading this section it will be well to remember "that the nuclear genes and self-perpetuating cytoplasmic mechanisms work jointly in determining heredity. When nuclear genes are the variable, they control heredity; when cytoplasm is the variable, it too controls the hereditary differences, apparently even the same differences."—*Ibid*.

HEREDITY, ENVIRONMENT, AND FREEDOM 67

forty-eight chromosomes, whereas the fruit fly always has only eight.

Chromosomes within the human ovum or sperm differ considerably in their chemical properties. These differences are greater when the germ cells come from different individuals than when they come from the same individual.

Each chromosome is made up of smaller units called *genes*. These genes are distributed over the entire length of the chromosome, and are linked together in definite patterns. They are arranged like beads on a string, and each has its own unique function in inheritance. The genes appear to be extremely tiny protein molecules, and they supposedly influence development through chemical processes. It is the genes which carry the different hereditary characters. They are the bearers of such hereditary traits as eye color, facial features, and the like. They do not operate independently in their influence upon development, but cooperate one with the other and with the environment. Each inherited characteristic, such as eye color or body build, requires the action of many genes. Each gene of a chromosome transmitted by the mother is paired with a corresponding gene of the chromosome contributed by the father, as illustrated schematically in Figure 6. Corresponding genes on the paired chromosomes always affect the same bodily parts or functions, but not necessarily in the same way. For example, one gene may contain the potentiality for blue eyes and the corresponding gene the potentiality for brown eyes.

B. Maturation of Germ Cells

During childhood the germ cells are already present, but they are relatively dormant and incapable of functioning. At the age of sexual maturity, however, these cells undergo modifications, the end result of which is a reduction of the number of chromosomes by one-half. Before the sperm and ovum are ready to unite they go through a series of changes. At the beginning of this process each germ cell contains forty-eight chromosomes. Then by "reduction division" this number is reduced by one-half. The union of the twenty-four chromosomes of the sperm and the twenty-four chromosomes of the ovum results in a zygote which has forty-eight chromosomes.

68   PERSONS AND PERSONALITY

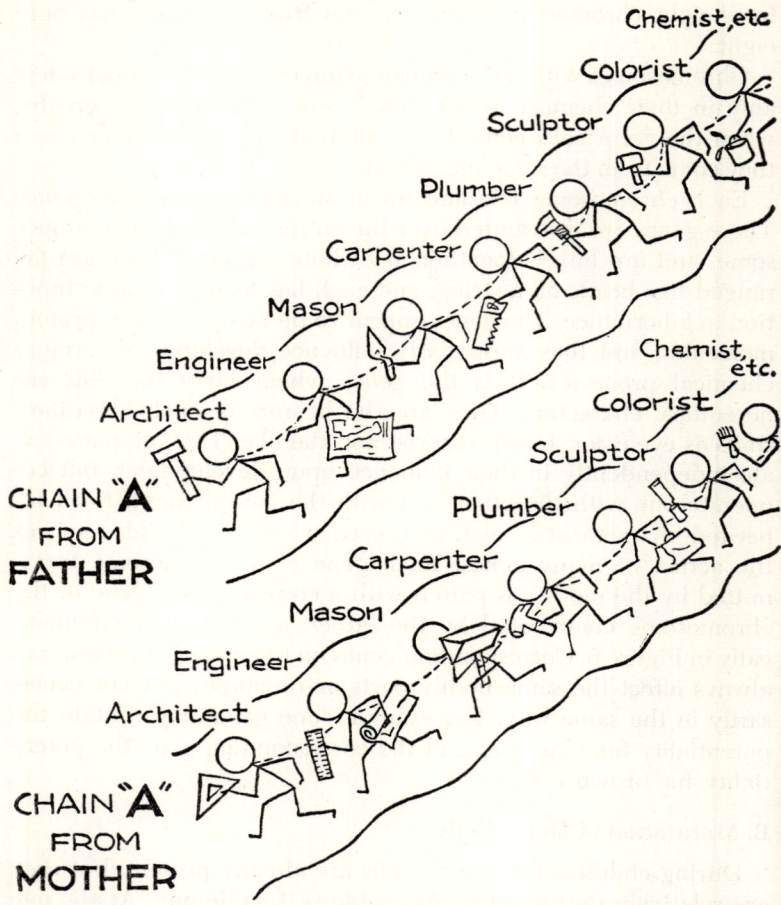

Fig. 6. Our "Chain-Gangs." [From *The New You and Heredity*, copyright, 1939, 1950, by Amram Scheinfeld, published by J. B. Lippincott Company, p. 61.]

C. Fertilization

When the ovum is fertilized by the sperm, the nuclei of the two cells unite, and eventually the chromosomes of both cells line up in pairs, and the new organism formed by the union has its full complement of chromosomes. One-half of each pair of chromosomes is received from the father and one-half from the mother. This pairing of the genes of the chromosomes exercises a protective

HEREDITY, ENVIRONMENT, AND FREEDOM 69

effect on human heredity. Since defective genes are usually recessive, when a defective gene on one chromosome is paired with a normal gene on the other chromosome, the defect does not show up in the offspring.

The differences as well as the similarities of related individuals are the result of the genes, since, except in the case of identical twins, no two individuals with the same parents ever receive exactly the same combinations of genes.

Identical twins differ to a slight but consistent degree throughout their life histories, and these differences cannot be attributed to differences in inheritance, since identical twins develop from one cell. Those that appear early are more likely the result of early prenatal environment. The twin who has the more favorable intra-uterine position and has readier access to nutritional substances may possibly start life with an advantage over the other. The fact that these differences are present not only at birth but persist throughout life tends to highlight the importance of early environment.

D. Sex Determination and Sex-Linked Traits

There are many popular theories to the effect that prenatal experiences of the mother may influence the sex of her child, but none of these theories has been substantiated. Sex is determined at the moment of conception by the chromosomes which the zygote receives.

The functional ovum and sperm, it will be recalled, each have twenty-four chromosomes. When the ovum is fertilized by the sperm, a new organism, possessing twenty-four *pairs* of chromosomes, is formed. One of these pairs of chromosomes determines the sex of the child. If the child is a female, all twenty-four chromosomes received from the mother are matched by chromosomes received from the father. It is said to possess two X chromosomes. If, on the other hand, the child is a boy, it receives only one X chromosome, and this chromosome comes from the mother. The father contributes a small, rudimentary chromosome which is called a Y chromosome. Sex is therefore always determined by a chromosome received from the father, since the father has both X and Y chromosomes, whereas the mother has only X chromosomes. The "sex-gene" balance is illustrated in Figure 7.

Certain human characteristics are known to be sex-linked. The

70   PERSONS AND PERSONALITY

recessive gene that causes red-green color blindness, for example, is located on the X chromosome. For this reason, a color-blind father will have normal children if the defective X chromosome which he transmits to his daughters is balanced by a normal X

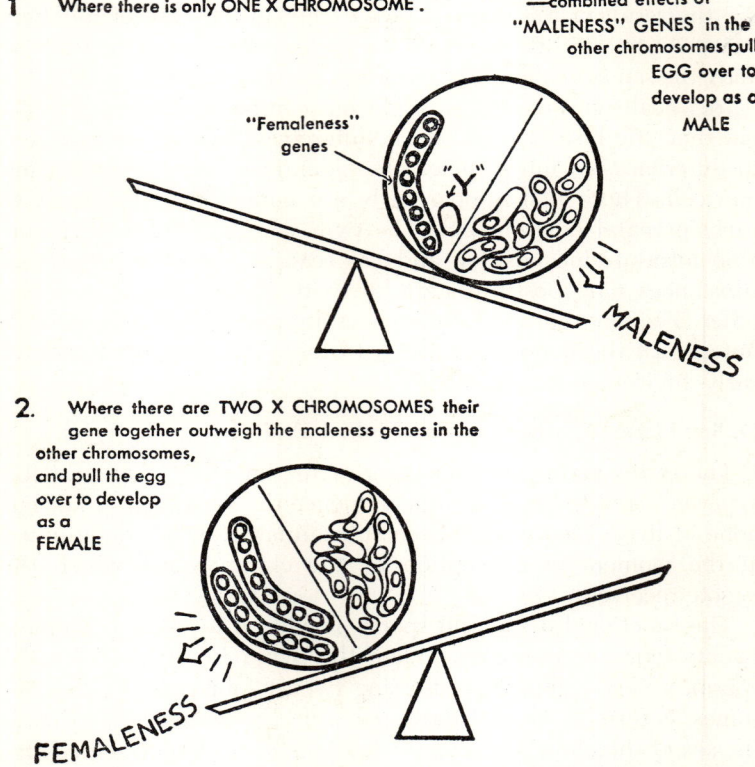

Fig. 7. "Sex-Gene" Balance. [Reproduced by permission from Amram Scheinfeld, *Women and Men* (New York, Harcourt, Brace & Company, Inc., 1944), p. 16.]

chromosome from the mother. All of his daughters, however, will be carriers of the defect. If his daughters marry normal men, none of their daughters will have the defect but one-half of their sons will. One-half of their daughters, however, will be carriers of the defect. There are very few color-blind women because it rarely happens that a defective X chromosome is received from both parents. The male exhibits the defect because he does not have a normal X chromosome to balance the defective one. Until recently, all sex-linked characteristics were thought to be transmitted by X chromosomes only. We now know, however, that certain of such characteristics may be carried by a Y chromosome. Growth of hair in the ears appears to be one such character.

E. Mendel's Law

The Austrian monk, Gregor Mendel (1822–1884), conducted cross-breeding experiments with different varieties of peas. He found that when he crossed a wrinkled pea with a smooth pea, the next generation of peas was all wrinkled. Similarly, in crossing a tall strain of pea with a dwarf strain, only the tall characteristic was observed in the offspring. Mendel called the character which appeared in the offspring *dominant* and that which did not show up, the *recessive*. In crossing these hybrids, however, all of which exhibited the dominant characteristic, he found that the recessive trait appeared in some of the offspring. By carefully controlled experiments in which accurate measurements were made, Mendel arrived at his famous law. This law states that in the second filial generation (F_2), or grandchild generation, three offspring will show the dominant characteristic for every one that exhibits the recessive characteristic. This is referred to as the *3:1 ratio*. Only one of the four, however, will be pure dominant, that is, will have no recessive characters to pass on to its offspring. The other two which exhibit the dominant character will also have recessive characters which they may transmit to their offspring. The one exhibiting the recessive trait possesses no dominant characters at all, and consequently can transmit to its offspring only recessive characters.

In general, when a trait is transmitted in accordance with Mendel's law, it is said to be hereditary. Yet, as we shall see in a moment, even "inherited" characteristics may be significantly modified or distorted by early environmental influences.

III. INTERFERENCE WITH THE NORMAL ENVIRONMENT OF THE EMBRYO AND YOUNG ANIMAL

The fact that a given characteristic is inherited does not mean that it is immutable. On the contrary, traits which are known to follow the laws of Mendelian inheritance can sometimes be radically altered by interfering with the environment in which the young organism normally develops. "Instinctive" behavior patterns, too (that is, unlearned behavior patterns which are characteristic of the species), can be changed if environmental modifications are introduced early enough. Even such human behavior as walking upright after infancy rather than on all fours apparently will not take place if the environment is unfavorable to it. We shall present at this point some of the evidence upon which these statements are based.

Normally, the fish *fundalus* has two eyes. This is a species characteristic. However, if the eggs are placed early enough in water with a high magnesium content, this basic characteristic is altered. The fish develops not two eyes but one, and this eye is located halfway between the places where the two eyes would normally develop.

A number of experiments on lower organisms show that startling alterations in the normal growth and differentiation of body parts can be produced by interfering with the environment in which the embryo develops. In one such experiment, the cells of sea-urchins were separated by a loop of hair when they were in the two-cell, four-cell, and eight-cell stage. The separated cells of the two-cell and four-cell organisms each developed into whole and perfect organisms. These sea-urchins were smaller than usual but their proportions were normal.

In an experiment on tritons, double monsters of various types were produced by constricting the egg in the two-cell stage with a loop of hair. A very deep constriction produced a monster having two perfect heads, two pairs of forelegs, and longitudinally divided nearly as far back as the root of the tail. A lesser degree of constriction produced a head slightly compressed in the middle, with two pairs of eyes, but with a single body.

Both of the above experiments were performed on very simple organisms and do not, therefore, throw any direct light on human embryonic development. The human embryo is relatively protected from violent mechanical or chemical assaults which would interfere with its normal development. Presumably, however, hereditary characteristics could be significantly altered if the early prenatal environment were greatly changed.

In popular discussions of "instinct" as well as of hereditary traits, there is often the implied assumption that if a characteristic is "instinctive," it must therefore be unchangeable. The following experiment disproves this statement. There is a species of moth which always lays its eggs on hackberry leaves even when a number of other potential host plants are present. This behavior is classed as "instinctive," since it occurs invariably and is constant for the species. But it can be altered experimentally. When the eggs are removed from the hackberry leaves and transferred to apple leaves, the larvae develop normally. When these larvae have grown to maturity the adult females behave differerently from those raised on the hackberry leaves. When these adult females are given an opportunity to deposit their eggs on various host plants, a large proportion of them select apple leaves in preference to hackberry leaves. In other words, an instinctive characteristic has been modified by manipulation of the environment![8]

All of the experiments so far reported were performed on animals, since, obviously, human beings cannot be subjected to experimental conditions which might retard or damage their development. Occasionally, however, a "natural" experiment comes to our attention. The following study, reported by Arnold Gesell, is one such natural experiment.

Gesell has written a fascinating narrative of the life history of an Indian girl supposedly taken by a wolf to her lair and raised with the wolf's own cubs. The details of the child's background are not very clear. All that is definitely known is that she was in a very wild state when discovered by a missionary and his wife, about the time that she was eight years old. The pictures indicate the types of adjustment which she had made to her non-human environment. The little girl, whom the missionaries named Kamala, had a number of anatomical peculiarities, and Gesell suggests that these were modifications produced by her abnormal childhood environment. Her hands and feet were decidedly longer than average, probably because she had been walking on all fours. Her arms were exceptionally muscular and extended from broadened shoulders almost to her knees. The child's hip and knee joints were inflexible from muscular contractions which greatly limited her motion. The joints of the

[8] Frank A. Beach, "The Snark Was a Boojum," *Amer. Psychol.*, 5 (1950), 115–124.

jaws, however, were exceptionally flexible, and the jaws opened wider than is usual. Her teeth were longer and more pointed than is normal. At first, the child prowled about at night and howled in an unearthly manner. She could make her way around very well at night, and it is reported that in darkness a glow emanated from her eyes. Her social development, too, was greatly retarded, and it was only after ten months in the orphanage that she would take a biscuit from the hand of a human being. By the time of her death, about nine years after she had been taken to the orphanage, she could speak enough to be understood, coöperated in the work of the orphanage, took care of the babies, and showed signs of grief when the children went to market without her. Although she walked on two feet at this time, her anatomical peculiarities persisted, and occasionally she would run on all fours, a mode of locomotion which was much more speedy than walking on two feet. This study shows that "original nature" can perhaps sometimes be modified by early environmental experiences.

IV. ARE ACQUIRED CHARACTERISTICS INHERITED?

We have previously noted that nothing is inherited which is not contained in the germ cells which form the zygote. The question we raise now is: Are the characteristics which parents acquire during their own lifetimes inherited by their offspring? If they are, then they must somehow bring about changes in the germ cells.

The French zoologist, Lamarck, formulated the theory that characteristics acquired during the lifetime of an individual can be transmitted to his offspring. This theory enjoyed popularity for some time, since it appeared to offer an explanation of the way in which evolutionary processes took place. The theory stimulated a great deal of research, the bulk of which has led to its refutation.

There are many lines of evidence which indicate that characteristics not present in the genetic constitution but acquired during life cannot be transmitted to the offspring. During the war, many service men lost their eyes, or an arm or a leg. Yet their offspring, conceived after these losses, were born with normal eyes, arms, and legs. French war babies brought up in this country had as much difficulty learning French in school as do children whose ancestors were English or Norwegian.

For centuries, up until modern times, Chinese women had their feet bound as infants, and as a result their feet did not grow normally. If this acquired characteristic had been transmitted genetically, it would not have been necessary to bind the feet of successive generations of girl babies to prevent foot growth. The first generation of Chinese women who were not subjected to foot binding exhibited a normal foot development both in size and in shape. Also, Jewish infants have been circumcised since the time of Abraham, yet such circumcision has had no effect upon the anatomical structure of their descendants. Further evidence that acquired characteristics are not transmitted to the offspring is seen in the fact that generations of cattle have been dehorned, but their offspring always have horns. And the tails of fox terriers have been repeatedly cut off, yet this has not produced a generation of tailless fox terriers. In one laboratory study the tails of twenty-one generations of white mice were cut off, but each successive generation still had tails. In short, characteristics acquired by parents are not transmitted biologically to their offspring. The children of a family line in which all the men were blacksmiths would undoubtedly develop bigger forearms, on the average, than normal men, but this would not be because their ancestors had exercised their arms so much.

V. STUDIES OF THE RELATIVE EFFECTS OF HEREDITY AND ENVIRONMENT ON SPECIFIC TRAITS

No human trait or aspect of development can be attributed to either heredity or environment alone, since, as we have previously shown, both factors must be present for any growth at all. Yet some psychologists have seen fit to study the *relative* contributions of each of these factors to certain specific traits, as, for instance, to height and weight or to intelligence. In studying inheritance in human beings, investigators have been confronted with special problems of method which are not encountered in the study of animals. What these difficulties are, how psychologists have tried to get around them, and the results obtained by methods devised for studying man alone will constitute the subject matter of this section.

The ideal way to study heredity and environment would be to set up carefully controlled experiments, as Mendel did, and systematically vary one factor at a time. But this method does not lend itself as readily to the study of human heredity and environment as it does to the study of plants and animals. The study of human beings is more difficult for the following reasons: (1) Human beings choose their marriage partners on considerations other than genetic constitution, except in the case of marked defects. (2) It is impossible to isolate for study a single independent variable, since there is no pure strain in human beings. (3) The human life span is so long that only a generation or two can be studied by one investigator. (4) Human dignity requires that we respect the right of an individual or of a family to privacy and, in making investigations, if people do not want to answer questions, neither a private investigator nor a government specialist can compel them to do so. (5) From birth onward, human development is influenced profoundly by social and cultural factors which obscure hereditary characteristics. And, lastly, (6) the significant psychological traits of human beings are very complex, and many phenomena which at first seem to be hereditary can often be interpreted equally well in terms of social and cultural environment.

Since controlled experiments were out of the question, psychologists in studying mental traits have had to rely to a considerable extent upon statistical studies. In general, two methods have been utilized: (1) family history studies, and (2) comparisons of likenesses and differences in people of differing degrees of biological relationship. The latter type of study is usually considered to be the more valid of the two. It has been employed in the following situations: (1) comparisons of foster children and foster parents with true children and parents, and (2) comparisons of twins, siblings, and unrelated children. We shall discuss each method in turn.

A. Family History Studies

Family history studies are not experiments; they are based upon the compilation of significant statistics. One of the earliest

HEREDITY, ENVIRONMENT, AND FREEDOM 77

of these studies was made by Sir Francis Galton, who carefully examined the biographies of 977 fairly eminent men, each of whom ranked in his opinion as about one to 4,000 of the general population. Galton tried to discover if eminence tends to run in families. Among the eminent men he studied were judges of England from 1660–1865, statesmen of the time of George III, premiers for 100 years prior to 1865, commanders, literary and scientific men, poets, painters, musicians, divines, modern scholars, oarsmen, and wrestlers. Galton inquired as to whether these men had a greater or smaller number of eminent relations than the population in general or than statistical estimates would accord them. The following table illustrates the results of this study:

Table 1

GALTON'S STUDY OF EMINENCE

Eminent Men	No. of Eminent Relations of 977 Eminent Men		Total No. of Eminent Relations of Eminent Men	Expected No. of Eminent Relations in General Pop.
977	Fathers:	94		
	Brothers:	123	362	1
	Sons:	145		
	Grandfathers:	50		
	Grandsons:	42	212	3
	Uncles:	54		
	Nephews:	66		

Adapted from Francis Galton, *Hereditary Genius* (New York, The Macmillan Company, 1925), p. 308.

Since the eminent men had a very exceptional number of eminent relations as compared to the general population, and since the number of eminent relations was significantly greater the closer the degree of kinship, Galton concluded that eminence (and the genius which he assumed to underlie such eminence) was inherited. This conclusion, however, does not grow out of his data, since no controls were used and no analysis was made of similarity of environment and motivation. The data as they stand prove nothing about heredity, since the resemblances may also have resulted from similarity of environment. Eminent people are in a better position than average persons to secure advantages for their relations. Eminent relations, too, are a socially important part of the environment. These relations, we may presume, are often held up to the young child as models for imitation. Other people may also expect more of a child coming from such a family. In other words, the level of aspiration of children growing up in families in which some members have attained eminence may differ considerably from that of children coming from mediocre families.

Terman made a study of the occupational status of the fathers of 560 children who had IQ's of 132 or above. The purpose of his study was to discover whether gifted children differed significantly from children in general in the occupational levels of their fathers. Since occupational level bears a known and predictable relation to average IQ, as demonstrated in Chapter XII, if gifted children tended to come from the higher occupational levels, the assumption was that their parents were more gifted than the parents of children in general. The results of Terman's study are summarized in Table 2. This table shows that the fathers of gifted children are to an extraordinary degree found in the upper occupational levels. Terman concluded from this study that the IQ is largely a matter of inheritance. Again, there is considerable doubt that such a conclusion is wholly justified by the data, since environment was not held constant. In short, demonstrated family resemblances and relationships do not tell us anything about how they were caused.

Terman made a follow-up study twenty-five years later of 1,400 gifted children selected like those described above. At the

Table 2

OCCUPATIONAL STATUS OF FATHERS OF 560 CHILDREN TESTING AT IQ 132 OR ABOVE

Occupation	Percentage Among Fathers of Gifted Children	Percentage in Population of Los Angeles and San Francisco 1910	Percentage of Quota Among Fathers of Gifted Children
Professional	29.1	2.9	1003
Public Service	4.5	3.3	137
Commercial	46.2	36.1	128
Industrial	20.2	57.7	35

Reprinted from L. M. Terman, *Genetic Studies of Genius*, Vol. I, p. 63; with the permission of the author and of the publishers, Stanford University Press.

HEREDITY, ENVIRONMENT, AND FREEDOM 79

time of the follow-up study they were, for the most part, in their early thirties. These adults, he found, were healthier than the average American citizen and were less apt to become insane or commit suicide. Their incomes were above average, and a considerably greater number had entered the learned professions than was true for the population as a whole. However, at this age, none of the gifted group had as yet attained real eminence. Thus, contrary to Galton's view, Terman concluded that, "In achieving eminence, much depends on chance." [9]

Studies of degenerate families have also been made and, in all of them, degeneracy was found to run in families. Typical of such studies is that of Goddard who studied the Kallikak family (1912). Martin Kallikak supposedly started two families, one of which had a normal mother and the other a feebleminded mother. Goddard, starting with a contemporary feebleminded Kallikak, traced as many relations, living and dead, as could be found. Wherever he found the relations of this feebleminded Kallikak, whether in remote mountain regions, prosperous rural districts, or in city slums, and whether they were of the second or the sixth generation, there was an appalling amount of mental defectiveness among them. Goddard, at the time of his study, attributed these findings wholly to the potency of heredity. Later, however, he repudiated this extreme conclusion, and recognized that the results could not be interpreted in this way since, as in the studies previously reviewed, environment had not been held constant.

In conclusion, it can be said that family history studies throw light upon degrees of family resemblance in various traits and characteristics. Of themselves they do not, however, reveal whether these resemblances are primarily the result of heredity or environment. For information on this problem we must use methods described in the next section. In passing, we may note here that just as physical science theory, in becoming gradually more adequate to physical reality, tends to improve methods of research in physics, so, in a similar manner, as psychological theory advances it may become apparent that a certain method does not do what we thought it did; or even, in the extreme, that it does nothing psychologically useful at all.

[9] L. M. Terman, *The Gifted Child Grows Up* (Stanford University, California, Stanford University Press, 1947).

B. Resemblances in People of Differing Degrees of Biological Relationship

You have often noticed family resemblances in facial features and other physical characteristics. Eye color, color and texture of hair, body build, height, weight, and activity level are among the physical characteristics that are said to be inherited. Yet members of the same family do not resemble each other perfectly in any of these characteristics. The degree of family resemblance in any of these measurable physical traits can be determined by computing the coefficient of correlation. You can, for instance, find the average height of both father and mother by combining them into one measure known as height of *mid-parent*. The average height of adult children of these parents is secured in the same way. By doing this for a sufficient number of parents and offspring, and computing the coefficient of correlation for the two sets of measures, a mathematical measure of the degree of parent-child resemblance is obtained. In most studies of this kind, r equals .50. This is true not only for height but for other physical characteristics as well. A similar degree of resemblance in physical characteristics is found between siblings. The assumption is made that these physical resemblances are largely the result of inheritance.

We next find the degree of resemblance for people paired at random, that is, for unrelated pairs of individuals. When this is done, the resulting coefficient of correlation is zero. We now have two reference points to use in our study of mental inheritance, namely, $r = .50$ for related individuals, and $r = .00$ for unrelated individuals. Thus, if for any mental trait r is found to be .50, we conclude that that particular mental trait is inherited to the same degree as are physical characteristics. If, on the other hand, r is zero, we infer that the trait is not inherited. If the coefficient of correlation is .20, however, we assume that it is inherited to some extent, but not nearly to as great a degree as are physical characteristics.

The studies reported in the following sections in which foster children, siblings, and twins were compared, are largely based upon coefficients of correlation. This method can be used to show degrees of resemblances, but unfortunately it can tell us nothing concerning the precise mode of inheritance of the measured traits. Then, too, it tells us only what is true of people in the mass; it will

HEREDITY, ENVIRONMENT, AND FREEDOM 81

not enable us to predict what will happen in a given individual case.

1. Studies of foster children

In studies of foster children, correlations are made to determine the degree of mental resemblance of parents and true children as compared with mental resemblances of foster parents and foster children. The average correlation for true parents and true children in intelligence has been found to be .50. In other words, it is as high a resemblance as that for physical traits. Intelligence test scores of foster parents correlated with scores of foster children, however, yield an r of only .20. This finding has been interpreted to mean that environment plays a relatively small part in determining the score a child will get on an intelligence test. Even this r of .20, it is suggested, may be spuriously high, since social workers try to match children and foster parents in both physical and mental characteristics. Matching of this kind would naturally produce a positive coefficient of correlation.

Let us note here that this low correlation between the intelligence of foster parents and foster children does not, of itself, indicate that the environment does not influence intelligence. All that it shows is that the environment does not wipe out relative differences in intelligence of parents and foster children. All foster children, for example, might improve in intelligence as a result of being placed in superior homes without, however, increasing the correlation between their intelligence test scores and those of their foster parents. To determine the absolute effect of environment, averages would have to be used. By this method it is possible to find out whether or not the average IQ of all foster children has gone up after placement in foster homes.

Studies based on averages rather than on correlations indicate that a superior environment will raise the IQ on the average from seven to ten points. Only in exceptional cases will it raise the IQ as much as 20 points or more. When these exceptions occur, either the environmental changes have been extreme, or something was wrong with the child's reported IQ in the first place. There is good reason for believing, therefore, that heredity places a "ceiling" on intelligence that even the most favorable environment cannot raise. This does not mean, however, that hereditary potentialities will be realized in the absence of appropriate environmental stimuli.

82 PERSONS AND PERSONALITY

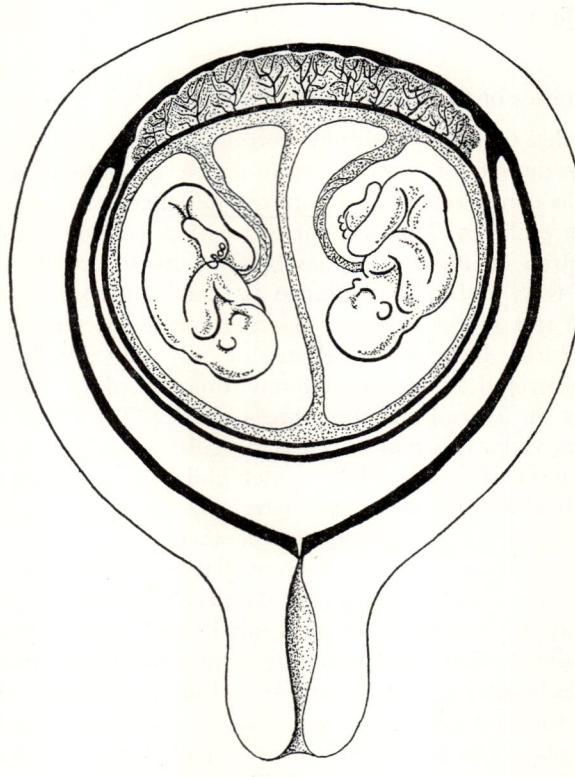

One-cell Twins

Fig. 8a. Origin of Identical (One-Cell) Twins.

2. Comparisons of twins, siblings, and unrelated children

You will recall that there are two kinds of twins: fraternal and identical. Fraternal twins are no more alike genetically than ordinary siblings, since they result from the fertilization of two germ cells. They may be of the same or opposite sex. Identical twins, however, have identical heredity, since they originate in one germ cell. The differences in origin of identical and fraternal twins are illustrated in Figure 8. The study of identical twins constitutes a natural experiment, because in this one instance we are able to hold heredity constant. In the case of unrelated children reared in orphanages, we have another example of a natural

HEREDITY, ENVIRONMENT, AND FREEDOM 83

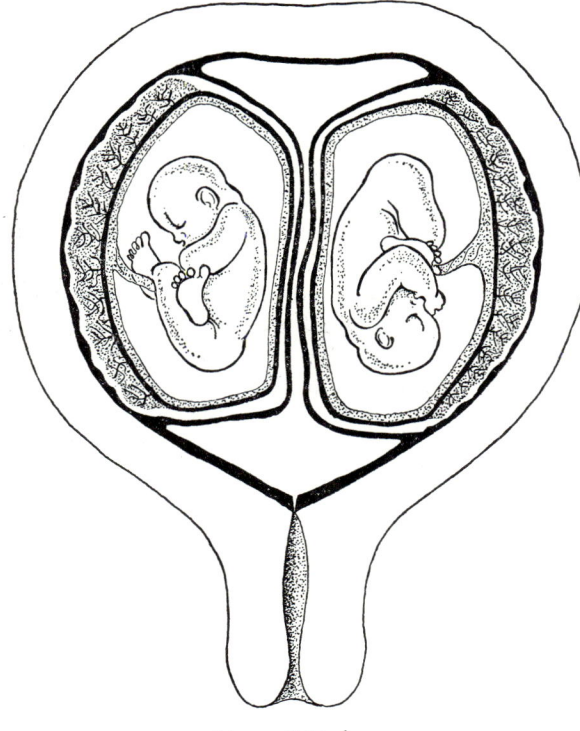

Two-cell Twins

Fig. 8b. Origin of Fraternal (Two-Cell) Twins.

experimental setting. Although these children have different heredity, their environment is supposedly the same. We shall review for you at this point some of the data which have been laboriously amassed and statistically treated to throw light on the different degrees of resemblance found in twins, siblings, and unrelated children. We shall then try to seek out the implications of these data for an understanding of the relative contributions of heredity and environment to human development.

First, let us consider the studies made of identical twins. These twins, we know from our own observations, are physically almost indistinguishable. When coefficients of correlation are worked out to determine the degree of their resemblance in such characteristics as height and weight, head measurements, and other physical characteristics, r is always .90 or above. In other words there is an almost one-to-one correspondence in physical traits of identical twins reared together. Although, in the instances we are citing, the identical twins grew up in the same home, we usually attribute these physical likenesses to heredity, since they are not present in fraternal twins reared in the same environment. The corresponding r for fraternal twins of like sex is usually about .60 and unlike sex somewhat above .50. Identical twins who have been reared apart and compared after they have reached maturity show a similar resemblance in height. In weight, however, the correlation tends to be somewhat lower, although it is still about .88, which is very high indeed. Let us see to what extent identical twins reared together resemble each other in mental as well as in physical traits. We shall do so by reviewing a case study of identical twin girls, the results of which are typical of those derived from studies of identical twins.

An early study of identical twin girls, who were extremely superior throughout their developmental history, revealed no pronounced deviations in physical measurements.[10] Both twins had tiny pigmented birth moles on the upper lip. Their hand and foot prints were remarkably alike. They differed in height not more than one-fourth inch and in weight not more than one pound. Both belonged to the same blood group and the degree of maturity of their bones and teeth at each stage of their development was the same. More surprising still, however, was the degree of resemblance they displayed in mental traits. A variety of tests of intelligence and achievement were given and observations of personality characteristics were made. Both twins not only had the same IQ, namely, 183, but even on the subtests of the intelligence test, their scores were remarkably similar. On the achievement tests they received similar scores in reading, writing, arithmetic, spelling, and drawing. They also expressed similar likes and dislikes. In short, the results of these tests and observations "revealed a consistent similarity with respect to general alertness, intensity of attention, deliberation, coöperativeness, sense of humor, and emotional reactions."[11] The investigator con-

---

[10] A. Gesell, "Mental and Physical Correspondence in Twins," *Scientific Monthly*, 14 (1922), 305–331.

[11] A. Gesell, *loc. cit.*

HEREDITY, ENVIRONMENT, AND FREEDOM 85

cluded that the "consistent similarity between these two children is based upon a fundamental, inherent similarity in endowment." [12]

In another study, made of nineteen pairs of identical twins reared apart, comparisons were made on a large number of physical, mental, educational, and temperamental characteristics.[13] Similar comparisons were made of the resemblances of fifty pairs of identical and fifty pairs of fraternal twins reared together. The average difference in IQ for identical twins reared together was only three points and for those reared apart, six points. The largest difference in IQ found between identical twins was 24 points, and in this instance the differences in education were striking. One of the twins had grown up in the backwoods and had had only two years of formal schooling. The other twin had received a college education. In the six cases out of the nineteen in which marked differences in schooling were noted, the average difference in IQ was 13 points. Identical twins reared apart but whose formal education was similar, differed only slightly from identical twins reared together. The results of this study may be summarized as follows: (1) The most marked resemblance in physical traits is for identical twins reared together or apart. (2) Identical twins reared together show nearly as great resemblance in mental traits as in physical traits, but identical twins reared apart do not. (3) Identical twins reared apart resemble each other in mental traits much more closely than do fraternal twins. (4) Identical twins reared together resemble each other in mental ability more than the same individual will resemble himself on two different occasions. As a result of these various tests and observations, the investigators concluded that physical traits are least influenced by the environment; mental ability and achievement are somewhat more influenced by the environment; and personality is most influenced by the environment.

Further light is thrown on this problem by the results of a study of a number of physiological functions which are regulated by the autonomic nervous system. These functions are collectively referred to as "autonomic constitution." They include rate of

[12] *Ibid.*
[13] H. H. Newman, F. N. Freeman, and K. F. Holzinger, *Twins: A Study of Heredity and Environment* (Chicago, University of Chicago Press, 1937).

breathing, pulse pressure, skin resistance, and rate of heart beat. Calculation of resemblances in these functions between identical and fraternal twins, siblings, and unrelated children was made. The correlations for the pairs of twins were highest, for the pairs of siblings second, and for the unrelated children about zero. These results suggest that "autonomic constitution" is much more a matter of heredity than of environment.[14] These facts will take on more meaning when you come to the study of psychosomatic illness. Psychosomatic diseases are regulated to a considerable degree by the autonomic nervous system. In this study we seem to have a clue as to why psychosomatic illnesses tend to run in families.

It remains to summarize the results of studies of orphanage children having different heredity. Presumably, if environment is the more important factor, these children should be relatively uniform in IQ. When tested, however, this assumption is not verified. Orphanage children differ as much among themselves in IQ and in personality as do other children in the average community. There is some evidence that a very superior environment can improve the IQ's of most of the children, although the relative differences among them will remain the same.

VI. MATURATION AND LEARNING

We have previously noted that the rate at which an organism develops or matures is constitutionally determined; that is, it results from the interaction of hereditary potentialities with the internal environment of the organism. The term *maturation* refers to growth and development which result from inner stimulation. We use it in contrast to *learning*, which is growth and development resulting from exercise. An important psychological problem is that of determining the relationship between maturation and learning. Can learning hasten maturation? Is it profitable to attempt learning or teaching before the organism has reached the appropriate stage of maturation? Let us consider some of the studies that throw light upon these questions.

[14] H. Jost and L. W. Sontag, "The Genetic Factor in Autonomic Nervous System Function," *Psychosomatic Medicine*, 6 (1944), 308–310.

A. Co-Twin Studies

Gesell and Thompson studied maturation and learning in identical twins.[15] Beginning at the age of forty-six weeks, one twin was coached in ladder climbing and in manual manipulation, whereas the other twin was left without training during the experimental period. Later, at the age of fifty-three weeks, the twin who had been deprived of training was given the opportunity to learn the same skills. The coached twin was somewhat superior during the coaching period, but with brief training at a later maturational level the other twin soon caught up. The investigators concluded from this finding, and from their other studies, that maturation is of more importance than coaching in motor and manipulative development.

B. Studies of Maturational Sequence

Studies of motor development show that in general all infants go through the same *sequence* of motor development, although the individual time at which a baby achieves each of the different stages may vary considerably.[16] This invariability in sequence suggests that it is a species characteristic, and may be compared to the developmental sequence in a plant. In a plant, the bud always appears before the blossom and is a necessary prerequisite for the appearance of the blossom. Special coaching and encouragement does not hasten the time at which a child first walks alone.

Studies of infants' reactions as they handle a red cube and studies of prehension show, too, that all children go through the same *sequence* of behavior, but at *different* rates. The sequence of development of prehension is shown in Figure 9.

A study of the reactions of Albanian babies to maturational tests has also been made.[17] The Albanian babies had been reared under environmental conditions which were very different from those of the infants upon whom the test norms were based. Dur-

---

[15] A. Gesell and H. Thompson, "Learning and Growth in Identical Infant Twins: an Experimental Study by the Method of Co-Twin Control," *Genet. Psychol. Monogr.*, 6 (1929), 1–124.

[16] M. M. Shirley, *The First Two Years, a Study of Postural and Locomotor Development* (Minneapolis, University of Minnesota Press, 1931), Vol. 1, *Twenty-five Babies*.

[17] C. Bühler, *From Birth to Maturity* (London, Kegan Paul, Trench, Trubner and Company, Ltd., 1937).

ing the first year of life, the Albanian babies were denied free movement and were strapped into their cradles by means of bandages. The infants were removed from their cradles only when necessary for keeping them clean or for feeding. When the bandages were removed from the babies, they at first showed

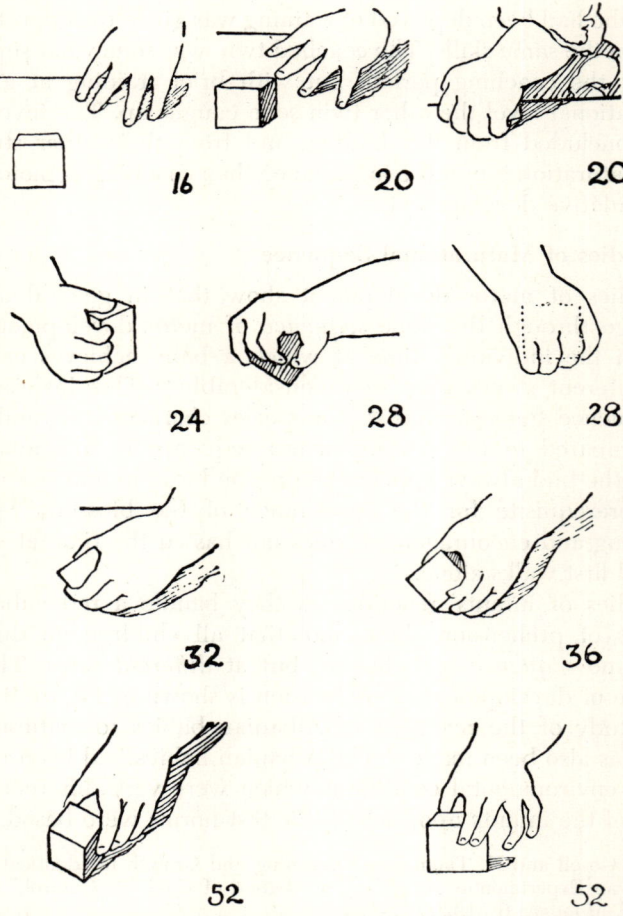

Fig. 9. Sequence of Development of Manual Prehension in Infancy. [Adapted from H. H. Halverson, "An Experimental Study of Prehension in Infants by Means of Systematic Cinema Records," *Genet. Psychol. Monogr.*, 10 (1931), 107–286. Used by permission of the publisher.]

HEREDITY, ENVIRONMENT, AND FREEDOM

very little reaction. Their first reactions were those of infants considerably younger than themselves. Several hours after restraints had been removed, normal grasping reactions appeared. Within a few hours, these babies went through all of the stages of behavior which other children go through over a period of months, and in the same sequence.

A similar pattern of development was found in an American girl reared in isolation during the first six and one-half years of her life.[18] This girl, Isabelle, was the illegitimate child of a woman who was a deaf-mute. The mother and Isabelle had spent most of their time together in a dark room shut off from the rest of the mother's family. As a result, Isabelle had no chance to develop speech; when she communicated with her mother it was by means of gestures. The specialists working with her believed that she was feebleminded, since her first score on the Stanford-Binet test was 19 months; and even on non-verbal tests her performance was so poor as to offer little hope for the future. She reached an age level of two and a half years on the Vineland Social Maturity Scale. Nevertheless, an attempt was made, through pantomime and dramatization suitable to an infant, to teach Isabelle to speak. After one week of intensive training, Isabelle made her first attempt at vocalization. Gradually she began to respond, and

. . . went through the usual stages of learning characteristic of the years from one to six not only in proper succession but far more rapidly than normal. In a little over two months after her first vocalization she was putting sentences together. Nine months after that she could identify words and sentences on the printed page, could add to ten, and could retell a story after hearing it. Seven months beyond this point she had a vocabulary of 1,500–2,000 words and was asking complicated questions. . . . She covered in two years the stages of learning that ordinarily require six.[19]

By the age of fourteen she had finished the sixth grade in a public school and participated in school activities as normally as other children. It should be noted here that Isabelle, unlike most isolated children, had been isolated with her mother. The fact that she was able later in life to respond to other human beings and to learn from them as readily as she did may be related to this fact.

---

[18] Reported by Kingsley Davis in "Final Note on a Case of Extreme Isolation," *Amer. J. Soc.*, 52 (March, 1947), 432–437.

[19] Davis, *op. cit.*, p. 436.

A series of studies on Hopi Indian children [20] has led to similar conclusions as to the importance of maturation. These children, like the Albanian babies, are bundled up soon after birth in such a way as to prevent almost all movements of hands and legs. For the first three months of life they are unbound for only about an hour a day. Some Hopi parents, however, as a result of exposure to the white culture, do not bind their infants in this manner but allow them the customary freedom enjoyed by white infants. A comparison was made of the age of walking of 63 Hopi children who had been bound in infancy with 42 children who had not been bound. The average age of walking did not differ significantly for the two groups. These results indicate that the restriction of activity in early infancy did not have a retarding influence upon the motor development of Hopi children. Our conclusion from this and other studies is that maturation or inner growth is a more significant factor in motor development than learning. Other studies show that both physical and mental development take place through environmental stimulation only when the organism is mature enough to respond to such stimulation.

VII. HUMAN FREEDOM

We have previously stated that man's heredity and environment limit his freedom of choice. Obviously, if he has inherited Negroid physical characteristics, he cannot change them no matter how much he might will to do so. As a result of this one biological trait, the environment becomes different for him from what it is for a white man. Personality development will therefore be different. If in early childhood a person loses his arms, he cannot become a violinist or a priest, no matter how much he might will to do so. These facts are obvious. But let us take a few examples that are not so clear as these.

Let us suppose that an infant is fed very irregularly and is in other ways mistreated and neglected over a long period of time. Early in life, long before he has reached the age of reason, he has acquired the "attitude" that life is hard or that people cannot be relied upon. Clinical data suggest that even in later life

[20] Wayne Dennis, "Does Culture Appreciably Affect Patterns of Infant Behavior?" *J. Soc. Psychol.*, 12 (1940), 305–317.

HEREDITY, ENVIRONMENT, AND FREEDOM 91

this individual will be influenced in his relations with other people by such early experiences. He may unconsciously, and without "willing" to do so, strike out at people in self-defense, even when there is no necessity for defense. His behavior is analogous to that of a soldier who has returned from the battle front. The soldier, hearing a tire explode, dives into the mud at the side of the road. A moment later he emerges and looks sheepishly at his muddy clothing, hoping that no one has observed him. He knows that his behavior has been unreasonable. Eventually, he may conquer this automatic response. But, even though his behavior may become better adapted to the situation, his feelings of fear may recur. Obviously, the man does not "choose" to fear or behave in this way. He cannot help it. His behavior illustrates the fact that,

Only man's will, in its deliberate and conscious decisions, escapes the law of psychic determinism. . . . But all the rest, our emotions and our moods, our habits and our attitudes, our images and our thoughts, our feelings and our sentiments, insofar as they are not under voluntary control, are indeed determined in their causes.[21]

Many other examples of impulsive acts determined in this way could also be cited. The point, however, is this: Man is always free to choose heaven or hell. He can always say "Yes" or "No" to God. Therefore, his eternal destiny is in his own hands. Man is not always free, however, to choose *how* he will attain heaven or hell. One man may never be tempted to be angry with his brother. Another may be continually struggling against anger. In spite of his firm determination not to lose his temper, he does so over and over again. This man attains heaven by saying "No" to the temptation of anger. He is not free, however, to attain heaven in exactly the way that he would like to do so, namely, by never feeling angry.

The view that man is entirely the product of his heredity and environment is known as *determinism*. Determinists deny that man has any freedom of choice. They hold that what appear to be free choices are really acts which are "determined" by factors of which the individual is not aware. There are three kinds of determinism: (1) biological, (2) psychological, and (3) physical.

1. *Biological determinism.* The biological determinist holds

[21] J. Donceel, "Second Thoughts on Freud," *Thought,* 24 (1949), 466–484.

that man's behavior is the necessary outcome of his biological structure. According to this theory, a man cannot help behaving as he does because of his inheritance, his body build, his physical peculiarities, or the functioning of his glands.

2. *Psychological determinism.* Psychological determinism holds that man's choices are the necessary outcome of his life experiences, often of those occurring in infancy or in early childhood. This kind of determinism is a basic tenet of Freudian psychoanalysis. It is also a basic principle of Behavioristic psychology. Behaviorists claim that man's environment alone makes him what he is, and they deny the importance of heredity, the existence of instincts, or the power of free choice. In the words of J. B. Watson, the founder of the Behavioristic school of psychology, "Give me a dozen healthy infants, well-formed, and my own specific world to bring them up in, and I'll guarantee to take any one at random and train him to become any type of specialist I might select— doctor, lawyer, artist, merchant-chief, yes, even beggar-man and thief, regardless of his talents, penchants, tendencies, abilities, vocations and race of his ancestors." [22] This is an extreme example of psychological determinism. It is not only a denial of biological determinism; it is also a denial of man's freedom of choice.

3. *Physical determinism.* Physical determinism, like biological and psychological determinism, is the logical outcome of the view that all things are material. This view is essentially a fatalistic one. For those who hold it, every event in the universe, including the choices which men make, is the inevitable result of the mechanical and physical movements and changes which have gone before. Such factors as movements of the planets or the tides predetermine the choices man will make. Thus, freedom of choice is nothing but an illusion. As one of Shakespeare's characters puts it,

> This is the excellent foppery of the world, that, when we are sick in fortune,—often the surfeit of our own behavior,—we make guilty of our disasters the sun, the moon, and the stars: as if we were villains by necessity; fools by heavenly compulsion; knaves, thieves, and treachers by spherical predominance; drunkards, liars, and adulterers, by an enforced obedience of planetary influences; and all that we are evil in, by a divine thrusting on.[23]

[22] J. B. Watson, *Behaviorism* (New York, People's Institute Pub. Co., 1924; Revised Edition, New York, W. W. Norton & Company, Inc., 1930).

[23] William Shakespeare, *King Lear*, Act I, scene ii, 129–138.

HEREDITY, ENVIRONMENT, AND FREEDOM

Certain criminal lawyers today plead for their clients on the basis of deterministic theories. These lawyers plead that their clients should be acquitted because they could not help killing, or stealing, or setting fires. Their argument is that no guilt is involved because the client was forced, either by reason of his biological constitution or his psychological background, to perform the act of which he is accused. While in many instances it is true that such criminal acts are the result of mental disease and the amount of guilt is inversely proportionate to the severity of the disease, this is not always the case.

The logic of this reasoning, incidentally, works two ways. One member of a jury, after listening to such a plea, voted "Guilty" nevertheless. When asked if he had not been impressed by the lawyer's plea, he remarked, "Yes, I was tremendously impressed by it. And I realized how impossible it was to formulate a just judgment. By reason of my own biological constitution and life history, I had to declare the man guilty!" [24]

Out of the deterministic conception of man has grown an exaggerated humanitarianism, based upon the notion that human progress and betterment will automatically take place if the environment is changed. Without minimizing the importance of the environment, the Christian psychologist will not expect men to become perfect as a result of slum clearance, old age pensions, or separation from a nagging wife. What makes man unique is the fact that he is never wholly determined by heredity and environment, but that to some extent he always remains free. This truth has been grasped and presented by the great novelists and playwrights throughout the ages, and works of art that have endured are those that present the human struggle as the struggle of good and evil within the soul of man, the final outcome of which depends upon his own free choice.

[24] In this connection it may be of interest to note that the widespread acceptance of existentialism in France, as represented by the work of Sartre, followed upon a long period in which naturalistic determinism held sway. Sartre has unduly emphasized the complete freedom of the individual and has violently repudiated the naturalistic dogma of determinism. The interest of the younger generation in France in the existentialism of Sartre, with its emphasis upon the doctrine that man can "freely make himself," comes as a reaction against the deterministic view at the other extreme which was cherished by their elders.

SUGGESTED READING

GESELL, A., *Wolf Child and Human Child* (New York, Harper & Brothers, 1941).
SCHEINFELD, A., *The New You and Heredity* (Philadelphia, J. B. Lippincott Company, 1950).

V

The Role of the Family, School, Community, and Cultural Milieu in Personality Development

*There was a child went forth every day,
And the first object he looked upon, that object he became,
And that object became part of him for the day or a certain part of the day,
Or for many years or stretching cycles of years.*
—WALT WHITMAN

I. INTRODUCTION

With only a few exceptions, every human being begins life as a member of a family group. Typically he remains in that group until at least the age of puberty. The structure of the family differs considerably from one culture group to another, and in some groups the ties which bind children to their parents are much stronger than in others. The relationships that exist between father and mother, parents and children, brothers and sisters, exercise a profound influence upon the developing personality of the child. Most particularly they will influence the patterns of intimacy which will govern his life.

Within each cultural group children are subjected to different learning experiences. Some of these experiences are provided formally by the school and church; others, informally by the cultural milieu in which the child finds himself. Learning is perhaps the most significant process which scientific psychology investigates.

II. GENERAL PRINCIPLES OF SOCIAL LEARNING

A. All Learning Is Interrelated

Any situation which confronts a human being must be seen in relation to the whole of his life. The family, the neighborhood, the school, and the church do not act in isolation upon the personality of the child, adolescent, or adult. The influence of any one of these factors is dependent upon all of the others. The individual's personality, as we have previously shown, is the result of (1) his biological constitution, (2) the interaction of stimuli coming from all of the social groups in which he participates, and of (3) his conscious and voluntary responses to such stimuli. The extent to which these several social groups reinforce or conflict with each other is an important factor in personality development.

B. Learning Is a Result of Environmental Demands

1. *The culture pattern and learning.* Human beings learn in order to satisfy their needs, and the way in which these needs are satisfied varies with the culture. In ancient Sparta, for example, it was unlikely that a child, however gifted, would grow up to be a disinterested scholar. It was much more likely that he would devote his time to bodily perfection and physical prowess. In Athens, on the other hand, intellectual pursuits were an accepted value of the culture. A child growing up in Athens would consequently be more highly motivated than one in Sparta to become a scholar.

Motivation is the most important factor in the determination of what and how well a child learns. But motivation is a much broader concept than is generally implied in books on educational psychology. It does not refer merely to the specific incentives used by the teacher or the parent to induce a child to learn his lessons. It refers, rather, to the entire psychological "field" of forces which impinge upon the child. The prevalent values of the twentieth-century world, the western hemisphere, the United States, and the particular part of the United States in which a child grows up provide the materials from which his own sense of values will emerge. These values, for the most part, come to the child through identification with his parents, but these in turn are transmitting the values of the culture in which they are immersed and of the social institutions that have influenced them.

2. *The sub-cultures.* In addition to the over-all culture in which everyone is immersed, each individual participates in a number of sub-cultures. These sub-cultures include the social class, age group, occupational group, ethnic group, and social clique to which he belongs. Within a given social class, an individual may find himself interacting with several sub-cultures, the demands of which are sometimes antagonistic.

City and town life in America, our democratic myth to the contrary, is stratified in greater or lesser degree into social classes or different status groups. Although there is mobility from one class to another, such mobility often requires unusual powers of adaptation and learning. Often it is accompanied by frustration and anxiety. Historically, most immigrants in our country have been socially mobile. Mobility into a higher social class, if not too rapid, is a normal and desirable state of affairs, since it gives the family socio-economic status consonant with its contribution to society. Downward social mobility, however, is commonly associated with anxiety and frustration. Upward mobility is all the more necessary in the United States since the middle and upper classes are not reproducing themselves. The school as a social institution is a powerful influence in producing such mobility.

Warner, in his study of Yankee City,[1] has delineated seven social classes, each of which is distinguished from the others by a more or less distinct code of behavior. Other investigators [2] have shown that a similar stratification exists in Negro society. In Natchez, for example, they were able to distinguish seven social classes, each of which had its own set of values as well as its own code of behavior.[3] They have shown further that adult attitudes toward schooling and toward the value of an education vary with social class. The lower-class child, by identifying emotionally with his parents, may accept their attitudes and values uncritically. If his parents belong to a lower-class group

---

[1] L. Warner, *Yankee City* (New Haven, Yale University Press, 1943).

[2] R. L. Sutherland, *Color, Class and Personality* (Washington, D.C., American Council on Education, 1942).

[3] A. Davis and J. Dollard, *Children of Bondage* (Washington, D.C., American Council on Education, 1940). Also, A. Davis, "American Status Systems and the Socialization of the Child," *Amer. Soc. Rev.*, 6 (July, 1941), 345–354.

that looks upon the school only as an evil, to be evaded whenever possible, the child may learn from them this pattern of values and reject the values of his middle-class teachers, particularly if these teachers do not "belong." Religious teachers, for example, though coming from a different social class, may, because of the value pattern of the group, have high status and may exert an influence impossible for one not wearing a religious habit. The influence of middle-class teachers who have themselves been mobile may make the lower-class child mobile, too.

The child learns from his class group his attitudes toward health and nutrition, toward law and order, and the means of satisfying his basic needs in the class-approved way. If the school stands for values different from those of the neighborhood, it is the school rather than the neighborhood which generally loses out. When the standards of the school reinforce the standards of the home, as they do more often in the upper than in the lower economic groups, the child apparently has fewer conflicts and less difficulty in developing a consistent set of values. Corroboration of this statement is found in a study of elementary school children.[4] In this study the investigators found that children in the lower socio-economic groups showed no increase in consistency of moral behavior as they grew older. Children in the upper economic groups, however, increased steadily in consistency of behavior.

Within a given social class a person may be simultaneously motivated by the demands of different, and often antagonistic, sub-cultures. A child's parents may represent one set of values, his peer group another, and his teachers still another. Correlation analysis shows that the child's attitudes are most closely related to those of his parents; to a less extent to those of his peers; and to a considerably less extent, to those of his teachers. It is even probable that the low correlation between pupils' attitudes and those of their teachers would be even lower if there were not some overlapping between parents' and teachers' attitudes. Such studies reveal the fallacy of expecting the school to be the chief educator of morals and attitudes, when actually the home has the greatest influence.

The peer group at first sight appears to be next in influence.

[4] H. Hartshorne, M. A. May, and F. K. Shuttleworth, *Studies in the Organization of Character* (New York, The Macmillan Company, 1930).

Some psychologists, however, doubt that the child's companions have as great an effect upon his sense of values as these correlations suggest. They hold that the child seeks companions who are already like himself. Because their attitudes correlate with his, he finds the group congenial and joins himself to them. Deeper emotional attachments usually exist between children and their parents and the members of their gangs than between children and their teachers.

C. Learning Directed Toward a Goal

Gestalt psychologists claim that all learning is goal-directed. This is probably an over-generalization, however, since some learning has been demonstrated in situations in which it is difficult to discover a goal. An interesting case in point is that of Burtt's child who had Greek passages read to him over and over at the age of two. Later, at the age of eight, the child was given two different selections in Greek, one of which had been read to him six years earlier, and one of which was new. The child learned the selection to which he had previously been exposed in a significantly shorter time than he did the new passage. Evidently, learning had taken place at the age of two even though there was no apparent goal toward which the learning was directed. A similar line of evidence is presented in Chapter XI, in which we discuss the phenomenon of "latent" learning.

The most useful forms of learning, nevertheless, are goal-directed; they are means to the satisfaction of basic human needs. Learning how to hold a knife and fork, how to dress in a certain approved way, how to speak correctly, are originally learned as a means of retaining the love of parents. Later, they enable the child to take his place in a larger social group than that of his own home.

The individual is not always conscious of the goals toward which his learning is directed. When in the course of growing up the individual is constantly frustrated in trying to satisfy his needs in the normal way, he may unconsciously learn undesirable and unhealthy ways of satisfying these needs. He may, for example, learn to "fail" in school, even though he has the ability to succeed. Or, he may learn to be ill when the demands of the situation are too much for him. Both of these learnings represent unwholesome adjustments, and on the surface they may seem to deprive him of the goal toward which he is supposedly striving. Yet, on deeper analysis it becomes apparent that these learnings, too, are directed toward a goal, but not the same goal as most people would be striving to achieve in a similar situation.

III. THE MARGINAL PERSON

The term *marginal man* was usefully employed by the sociologist, R. E. Park, to designate the man who has been initiated into two or more racial groups, languages, religions, moral codes, political loyalties, social classes, or historic traditions. Typically, the life history of the marginal person embraces three phases: (1) a phase in which the individual is unconscious of the conflict of cultures or loyalties; (2) a phase in which he consciously experiences the conflict; (3) a phase in which he makes, or fails to make, more or less permanent adjustments to the situation.

In any period of widespread migration, there will be a great increase of marginal persons. The United States has always had a great many of such people, but today the problem has been greatly intensified all over the world as a result of World War II. "Marginal" status is psychologically important because it frequently exercises a disintegrating influence upon the personality.

Probably the most difficult "marginal" situation is that of the person whose mother is of one race and whose father is of another. Hardly ever, especially in the United States, will the two races be accorded equal status. The child ordinarily becomes conscious of these racial differences during his first few years at school. But only in adolescence does the conflict become intense in his life. Because of the different prestige accorded the two races, the child naturally wants to identify with the "superior" group. But in doing so, he must to some extent reject the parent of the other racial group. Furthermore, social pressure may force him to identify with the "inferior" group. In America, for example, a person may be predominantly white, and yet be classified as "Negro" if his skin is dark. The intense anguish and the almost insurmountable handicaps of a person who is a racial hybrid are vividly portrayed by Johnson in his book, *Autobiography of an Ex-Colored Man.*[5] At the end of this chapter we have listed

---

[5] J. W. Johnson, *Autobiography of an Ex-Colored Man* (New York, Alfred A. Knopf, Inc., 1927).

several autobiographies and biographies, the reading of which will lead to a deeper understanding of the marginal person than will a psychological or sociological analysis of the situation. These personal histories illustrate the variety of ways in which human beings adjust to conflicts of this kind.

Adopted children, orphan children, or half-orphan children are sometimes placed in a "marginal" situation. Such children may not be at all clear as to their status. A happy, secure child who suddenly learns that he has been adopted finds the ground slipping from under his feet. His unhappiness and insecurity may persist for years, perhaps even to the end of his life. Foster parents can, however, by acquainting a child from his earliest years with the fact that he is adopted, do much to forestall such anxiety and grief.

Perhaps the most unfortunate situation is that in which a mixed marriage prevents the child at adolescence from developing a clear notion of his own role and status. When the child is equally drawn to identify with his mother and his father, the conflict may be so intense as to "pull him apart," and thus result in a psychosis or even in suicide.

In a society permeated by Christian values, of course, conflicts of this sort would never become disastrous. Although our American culture is sometimes labeled "Christian," that label is certainly a misnomer as judged by the racial inequalities and injustices which are commonly sanctioned in the United States today. Idealistic young people who witness these injustices are understandably in revolt against a social order that permits such inhumanity to man. Many of them are ready to identify themselves with revolutionary movements which promise the creation of a new and better world, a world in which all men can walk with dignity. Sometimes, because they have never come into contact with real Christianity and have seen only perversions of it, or because they have known only nominal Christians, young people are tempted to conclude that Christianity has failed. But, as Chesterton pointed out many years ago, "The Christian ideal has not been tried and found wanting. It has been found difficult and left untried." [6] The Christian revolution in American society is yet to come.

[6] G. K. Chesterton, *What's Wrong with the World* (New York, Dodd, Mead & Company, Inc., 1910), p. 48.

IV. INFLUENCE OF THE FAMILY

One of the most decisive factors in the personality development of the child is the relationship which exists between his parents. At the present time, when one out of three marriages terminates in divorce, it is evident that this relationship is, in an alarmingly large number of cases, a disturbed one. Marriage relationships vary from one culture to another and within a given culture from one social class to another. In some groups, for example, matrimonial ties are typically very fluid. In other groups, family ties are very strong and the children are as a rule emotionally secure within their family groups. This is true even when the group as a whole constitutes a "problem" neighborhood within the larger community and when the percentage of juvenile and adult delinquency within the group is fairly high. The extent to which the generalizations contained in this chapter apply to the social classes at either extreme of the scale of socio-economic status has not been determined. A sufficient number of studies of middle-class families has been made, however, to warrant generalizations concerning the relationship of husband and wife as it affects the personality development of their children within a middle-class group.

A. Attitudes of Parents Toward Each Other

1. *The culturally accepted attitude toward the husband-wife relationship.* In a culture which does not permit divorce or remarriage or which punishes divorce by social ostracism, husband and wife will marry with the conviction that their union is permanent. The realization that they cannot change marriage partners will profoundly influence their attitudes toward each other.

The approved marriage pattern in twentieth-century America is supposedly that of monogamy. Yet divorces are easy to obtain, and remarriage is extremely common. Outside of genuinely Christian communities, there is distressingly little stigma attached to divorce and remarriage. As one writer has put it, "Simultaneous polygamy is illegal in the U.S., but successive polygamy is legal." The legalization of "successive polygamy" creates, in the first place, an attitude unfavorable to having children at all; and, in the second place, it encourages an attitude of irresponsibility as far as children are concerned.

2. *Religion.* The deepest union possible between two human beings is the marriage relationship. Ideally, it represents a complete union of wills and sharing of ideals. The physical relationship of marriage is symbolic of a deep spiritual union. When marriage partners differ in religion, there can never be a complete sharing of each other's lives. The relationship must of necessity remain on a superficial level.

It is not only the agreement on religious matters that makes for a happy marriage, although agreement is important. Marriage and the rearing of a family in the true Christian tradition call for great personal sacrifice. In the words of Gerald Vann,

> There will be times when the tension of living many lives in one will wear you down. There will be tension between your selfishness and your love; there will be tension between the love of man and woman and their common love of the family; there will be tension between either or both of these and the demands of the world; and always the wicket swings and human love is in danger of rivalling God. You can become wrapped up in your human happiness and forget your need of God; or you will find at times that your human love wants to be its own master and challenge the will of God—you will be in danger of the primal sin. . . . But it is just for these difficulties that a special sacrament is given us.[7]

The happiness of the family, and with it the welfare of the children, depends upon willingness to sacrifice. Often the sacrifices demanded are so difficult as to require the special help of God. It was to supply this help that the sacrament of matrimony was instituted. This sacrament is not received if one or both of the parties is unbaptized, and the deep supernatural union which should bind husband and wife will consequently be lacking.

3. *Preparation for marriage.* Preparation for marriage includes supernatural aids, such as prayer and the sacraments, and natural factors, such as (1) the example of one's own parents, and (2) an understanding and acceptance of the responsibilities of marriage.

Terman[8] has shown that disturbed marital relations run in families. Considerably more of the unhappily than of the happily married people whom he studied reported that their own parents

---

[7] Gerald Vann, *The Heart of Man* (London, The Centenary Press, 1944), p. 109.

[8] L. M. Terman, *Psychological Factors in Marital Happiness* (New York, McGraw-Hill Book Company, Inc., 1938).

had been unhappily married. They also reported that their childhood had been unhappy; and, in general, they reflected an embittered attitude toward life. Terman attributes much of the unhappiness of these marriages not to the objective factors listed by the unhappy spouses, but to a predisposition to unhappiness on the part of one or both partners, a predisposition which had its origin in childhood and adolescent experiences.

4. *Temperament of the two parties.* There is a tendency for people to marry within their own social, economic, and educational level. The king's son apparently marries the scullery maid only if he is in revolt against his parents. There is a significant correlation between the intelligence of spouses and a positive but much less significant correlation in height. There does not seem to be a similar correlation, however, in temperament. "The reserved dignified person with a marked sense of privacy tends to marry the outgoing extroverted person whose major satisfaction comes in shared experiences." [9] These differences in temperament often result in misunderstanding, since people have a tendency to interpret the feelings of others as they would feel if they were behaving the same way. Moreover, some families are more demonstrative than others. If a girl grows up in a home in which father and mother show outward signs of affection in the presence of their children, she may feel that her husband does not love her if he does not do the same thing. Her husband, however, may be oblivious to the fact that his wife feels hurt, or, if he does notice it, he may not understand why she feels hurt. He is simply imitating his own father's behavior which is according to a less demonstrative standard than his wife would prefer.

5. *Differences in attitudes and habits built up in the parents' home.* Misunderstanding between husband and wife results from the different attitudes and practices of their own parents, which they have more or less taken for granted as the right thing to do. Commonly they involve attitudes toward (1) finances, (2) household routine and management, and (3) rearing children. Let us suppose, for example, that the wife comes from a home in which the father turned his pay check over to his wife and carried heavy life insurance as a protection for his family. Let us sup-

---

[9] J. W. Macfarlane, "Inter-Personal Relationships within the Family," *Living*, 3 (May, 1941).

pose, too, that the husband comes from a home in which the father doled out money to his wife as she needed it, and considered life insurance a foolish extravagance. The husband, imitating the practices of his own father, cannot understand why his wife is disturbed at his behavior. The wife is unhappy at his behavior not merely because she considers it wrong in principle, but because she has the uncomfortable feeling that if he really loved her he would behave as her own father had behaved toward her mother.

Similarly, no two parents ever agree perfectly on disciplinary measures for their children, partly because they differ in temperament and partly because they have been subjected to different kinds of treatment by their own parents. Husband and wife must learn to understand and to adjust to these differences if they want their children to be happy and well-adjusted.

B. Parents' Attitudes Toward Children

Parents may consciously or unconsciously adopt attitudes toward their children which interfere with the normal development of the children's personalities. Particularly unwholesome are (1) rejection, (2) overprotection, (3) rivalry for the child's affection, and (4) overambition.

1. *Parental rejection.* Many parents reject their children psychologically, even though they show great solicitude for their children's physical well-being and progress in school. The rejecting parent may, indeed, show signs of compensatory oversolicitude in order to hide from himself, as well as from others, his basic attitude toward the child. Often it is difficult to distinguish rejection from overprotection for this reason. Many forms of undesirable behavior in children are the outcome of parental rejection, either obvious rejection, or vaguely sensed but nevertheless real rejection. For this reason, all professional people who work with children should be alert to recognize the symptoms and clues which lead to a diagnosis of rejection.

The following clues are helpful in making a diagnosis of rejection: (1) The parent is apt to depreciate the child's assets. He will resent it when you praise the child and will either "freeze up" or will contradict what you say. (2) Often he will compare the rejected child with a more favored child. This other child may be a sibling or a child belonging to one of the neighbors. Sometimes the parent compares his child unfavorably to himself when he was the same age. (3) Cruel and harsh discipline is often used. (4) The parent will make dire predictions for the future, even when there is evidence to the contrary. (5) The rejecting parent likes to repeat over and over again that no one is more eager than he to do everything possible for the child. He is likely to stress the sacrifices which he has made for the child. (6) Less frequently, the parent lavishes gifts on the child. In financially secure families, the rejected children often have larger allowances and more toys than other children in the neighborhood. In such instances, parents seem to salve their consciences by giving their children material things rather than their company and themselves.

Parents reject children for various reasons. A parent may reject a child because he does not meet the preconceived ideas he had of what this child should be like. A professional man may want his son to enter the same profession and if, like most professions, it requires exceptional scholastic ability, the father will expect the boy to excel others in school. When the boy does not succeed in school, his father may reject him. Sometimes parents have set their hearts upon having a boy and are disappointed when a girl is born to them instead. Or, parents may be ashamed of a child who does not come up to their expectations. In our culture, many mothers have an ambiguous role to play. They have been educated like men and have been prepared for the same occupations as men. They continue to work after marriage until a child comes along and then their way of life changes. They resent having to care for a child and a home because they have not been prepared for these duties, and since there is no monetary reward for these services, many women feel that such activities are beneath their dignity. This is most particularly true of the college-educated woman. Even when she loves her child she often has ambivalent feelings toward him, since his birth has resulted in many frustrations.

Often the rejecting parent himself is immature and treats the child as if he were his own sibling. In our individualistic culture, a child is often looked upon as a threat to "living one's own life." Public school education which has eliminated the teaching of religious and moral values has tended to accentuate this trend, a trend which is closely linked to the increasing divorce rate. Since

ROLE OF THE CULTURAL MILIEU

children today, except in farm areas, are not an economic asset, a culture which places material values above spiritual ones will increasingly depreciate children.

The way in which a child will react to rejection depends upon his temperament. The aggressive child may resort to attention-getting behavior, annoy other children, tear his clothes, steal, develop enuresis, or become delinquent. The submissive child usually withdraws into fantasy, daydreams, and self-pity. This latter is the most unfortunate pattern of behavior, since it is a background factor in the most serious kind of mental disease.

2. *Overprotection.* Most psychologists distinguish between rejection and overprotection, although some [10] claim that overprotection is just a special form of rejection. Certainly the overprotecting parent does not accept the child's basic need to be an individual in his own right, but tries to force him into a pattern of his own. Overprotection is an exaggerated anxiety over a child's well-being, and it may be so intense that the parent actually tries to live the child's life for him. No one symptom is diagnostic, but a combination of symptoms and clues must be used. The early history of overprotected children often reveals that they were breast-fed longer than most babies. Their mothers dressed and bathed them long after most children have learned to do these things for themselves and, in general, they were either not allowed or not required to do things for themselves. Characteristically, the overprotected child tries to make other people solve his problems. He finds fault with the teacher, and the parent is prone to find fault also. He lacks a sense of responsibility even at an age when most children have acquired it. He is egocentric and wants his own way in everything, frequently resorting to temper tantrums when he is not able to get it. He sees only his own needs and is late in recognizing the rights of others. In fact, without outside help he may never get over his childish selfishness. The overprotected child wants to be the center of the stage; he is frequently jealous of siblings or schoolmates, and tends to fall into annoying attention-getting devices. He is likely to be overly concerned about his health and will run to the school nurse for no reason at all. Often he is hypersensitive to pain, will avoid any roughness, and is afraid to eat certain foods. He is unwilling

[10] D. M. Levy, *Maternal Overprotection* (New York, Columbia University Press, 1943).

to take chances, and, even if he is physically strong, he will do almost anything to avoid getting into a fight.

Three main clues help in the diagnosis of overprotection: (1) The parents' discipline is lax; they make threats which they never carry out, and they constantly give in to the child's whims. (2) The parents express the desire that the child always remain a baby, and often they dress him in a style suitable to a younger age. (3) They are abnormally involved in every situation that affects the child. They choose his friends for him; they pry into his pockets and notebooks; they do his school tasks for him. They do not complain about the sacrifices they make for the child, as does the rejecting parent, and for this reason the child feels guilty if he tries to rebel.

Parents may overprotect a child for a variety of reasons, among which the following are characteristic: (1) The death of another child may have led them to center all of their hopes in this child. (2) The parents may be compensating for the hardships of their own childhood by trying to save their child from similar difficulties. (3) One parent may overprotect a child as a compensation for the overstrictness of the other parent. (4) One or both parents may have inadequate emotional outlets, as a result of which the child has to be everything in life to the parent. (5) The parent may fear that the child has inherited character defects from him, or (6) he may be compensating for a feeling of guilt. This may be the case when the parent feels that his own inadequacy or carelessness has caused his child or family to suffer. (7) Lastly, a child may be overprotected simply because one or both of his parents is the "managing type."

The overprotected child may go through life with an overwhelming sense of his own importance. His own pains and difficulties, the trivial events of his everyday life may well become his entire universe. He may never become an adult in the full sense of the word; his relations with people remain selfish and superficial.

3. *Rivalry for the affection of the child.* A child whose parents are jealous of each other or who are rivals for his affection will have great difficulty in attaining emotional stability. The child, pulled first in one direction and then in another, may be in a chronic state of conflict. A family situation of this kind is often in the background of adults who are temperamental or impul-

sive, or who are characteristically indecisive. At its worst, the child learns to play one parent against the other and becomes a calculating egotist.

4. *Overambition.* Parents often try to compensate through their children for their own shortcomings and disappointments. Sometimes they set their standards so high that a child cannot possibly attain them. Such standards are not adopted for the good of the child but for the glorification of the parents' ego, and they frequently result in serious maladjustment.

C. Family Resemblances in Attitudes and Personality Traits

Children resemble their parents in attitudes on specific questions as well as in personality traits. Parents and children were studied to determine the correlation of attitudes toward the church, war, and communism.[11] The correlations obtained were respectively: .63, .44, and .56. There was evidence, too, that when the attitudes of parents were highly consistent, those of the children tended to be consistent also.

In another study [12] the behavior of children whose parents were subject to periodic headaches and fainting spells was analyzed. The children whose parents were subject to fainting spells or who in childhood had had episodes of breath-holding or head-banging, tended to have episodes of fainting, breath-holding, or head-banging as well. The children whose parents had periodic headaches tended to have the same difficulty themselves.

One investigator studied the seriousness of children's behavior problems as compared to the stability of their mothers' personalities. The mothers as well as the children were rated on a three-fold scale by competent clinical psychologists. The coefficient of correlation between ratings for mothers and children was .83, and indicated a very high relationship between the seriousness of maladjustments in mothers and in their children.

D. Family Discipline

Children at all ages need discipline, and discipline necessarily involves unpleasantness. Since parents administer discipline, and

[11] R. Stagner, *Psychology of Personality* (New York, McGraw-Hill Book Company, Inc., 1937), pp. 319–320.
[12] D. M. Levy and H. L. Patrick, "Relation of Infantile Convulsions, Head Banging, and Breath-Holding to Fainting and Headaches in the Parents," *Arch. Neurol. Psychiat.*, 19 (1928), 865–887.

since the most important influence in the child's life is his relation to his parents, the administration of discipline is far from being a purely academic problem.

Punishment in and of itself does not socialize the child. On the contrary, if it is not accompanied by love and affection it may have exactly the opposite result. The fact that punishment may be injudiciously administered does by no means militate against its use entirely.

One of the most traumatic experiences in the life of a child is harsh and unmerited punishment. The life histories of adult criminals and psychoneurotics are filled with instances of arbitrary and unwarranted acts of cruelty, usually committed under the guise of punishment. Nothing is better calculated to produce a hard, callous, antisocial personality than such treatment at the hands of a parent or a teacher.

Punishment is of its very nature frustrating to a child, and frustration often tends to stimulate aggression. The aggression may be overt, in the form of revolt, or implicit, in the form of a smoldering resentment under the cover of a submissive exterior. Or, because the child loves the punishing parent and feels guilty about his feelings of hostility, he may repress his aggressions toward his parents. In such a case, the aggression may be turned inward upon the child himself. Frequent accidents, self-torture —such as obsessive fears and anxieties, depressions of such severity that failure in school and in social life results—all may be the unconscious outcome of repressed hostility toward adults.

Inconsistency of discipline tends to result in fear and anxiety. All fear, of course, is not destructive of personality. There are some things which both children and adults should fear, since only by fearing danger will the proper precautions be adopted. But the fear engendered by inconsistent discipline cannot be mastered by intellectual control, since the child cannot foresee the consequences of his acts and cannot predict ahead of time which acts will be punished and which acts will not. When discipline is inconsistent the child becomes emotionally unstable. He learns, not to govern his behavior by standards of right or wrong, but to be unduly concerned about how people will react to his behavior. He thus acquires the neurotic behavior pattern of behaving at all times with an eye toward what people will think of him. He becomes a slave to the opinions of others.

E. Sibling Relationships

The attitudes which a child develops within his family group are the roots from which his attitudes toward other groups develop. Attitudes originally developed toward parents and siblings carry over into his relations with his teachers and classmates. A boy who is competing with a brother for status at home may be excessively competitive in school or on the playground.

Although rivalry is common among young children in a family, the primary reaction of a child to his sibling is not rivalry or hostility.[13] The appearance of sibling rivalry, in other words, depends on the total family situation in which it appears and not just upon the child himself. For example, the mere fact of being the younger child in the family does not necessarily define the individual's role. If the older sibling is kind and protective the younger child may find life relatively easy while he is still very young. But, as he grows older, he may find it hard to relinquish his childish dependency and learn to stand on his own feet. Or, again, a younger boy may always play an inferior role with respect to achievement when compared to an older brother. He may develop attitudes of inferiority and inadequacy, and these attitudes may persist throughout life. If the older sibling is an aggressive and teasing girl, the younger boy may struggle in vain to hold his own with her. As an adult he may have a deep-seated resentment against women, a resentment engendered for his sister and later broadened out to include women in general.

Birth order, too, apparently has an effect on personality. In a summary of the findings of the California Guidance Study we read ". . . we have found first-born children on the whole having more difficulty in establishing easy, friendly and intimate relationships with people even outside their home, than either only or later born." [14] The reasons for this situation are not very clear. One logical explanation is the fact that first-born children have greater difficulty in adjusting to the appearance of another child than do later-born children. This difficulty of adjustment may set the pattern for adjustments to people outside of the home.

[13] M. B. McFarland, *Relationship Between Young Sisters as Revealed in Their Overt Responses,* Child Development Monog., No. 23 (New York, Bureau of Publications, Teachers College, Columbia University, 1938).

[14] J. W. Macfarlane, "Family Influences on Child's Personality Development," *Childhood Education,* 15 (October, 1939), 55–59.

F. The Child Without a Family

The best institution for children is usually a poor substitute for a home, even though physical care may be on a much higher level in a children's home or orphanage than in a boarding or foster home. The entire environment, too, may be child-centered and adapted to the children's needs. Yet this very adaptation of the environment to children cuts off valuable learning experiences which are present daily in a typical family situation. In the average home, father and mother carry on a conversation in the presence of their children, a conversation which is often of such a nature that the child cannot participate. All that he can do is listen. Yet in listening, he gradually builds up a store of information which is of inestimable value to him later on. Father, for example, tells mother at the breakfast table that he is going to take out an endowment insurance policy in her name. Both parents then discuss the advantages and disadvantages of such an insurance policy in comparison with other insurance policies. The child not only drinks in these ideas, but he is learning about our present-day society, ways of protecting one's future by denying oneself today, money and banking, and many other things which he could not learn nearly as effectively in school. Or father is out on "strike" and is discussing the policy of the labor union with his wife. His children listen breathlessly to his recital because it affects them personally. On another occasion, father sits down to dinner and reports that he has just signed a contract with Joe Smith, and "the old fool signed on the dotted line without even suspecting the rotten deal he was getting!" Mother approves of father's cleverness, and the child is just that much closer to becoming a crook himself; that is, if he identifies with his parents.

It is difficult to teach institutional children to be kind and considerate of each other, since appropriate models of such behavior are frequently lacking. They do not often observe adults in their relations to each other. When they do see two or more adults together, the adults are likely to be concerned with the children's problems rather than their own. Little children in an institution learn much from the older boys and girls, particularly from those who are appointed to help care for them. This situation presents difficulties, too, since the older children are also underprivileged children as far as human relations are concerned. Often they find release from their own inner tensions by persecuting younger children or demanding homage from them. A spirit of intense competition rather than coöperation may easily develop in institutional children.

The illegitimate child suffers intense anguish when he reaches adolescence. If he knows nothing whatever of his parentage he is not thereby spared the anxious questioning and inner conflict of this stage of development. Everyone has a need to know who he is, and if he does not have access to true sources of information, he will indulge in endless conjecturing and daydreaming. Sometimes a professional worker tries to avert anxiety by telling a child to forget about his parents, that nobody knows anything about them. But such a treatment generally boomerangs. It is not possible for any normal adolescent to be unconcerned about his parentage. He must establish in his own mind his relation to his own biological family, and the professional worker must often help him to do so. It is often less traumatic for a child to learn that he is illegitimate than it is for him to have no information at all. In breaking such news to a child, the worker should explain that she is going to tell him the truth because she believes that the child has a right to know. Always she should try to identify with the erring parents, minimizing their defects as much as possible, and emphasizing their good points. If the child's mother, for example, had shown any reluctance to parting with her baby, this fact should be stressed by the worker. She may say, for example, "Your mother was very young and inexperienced when you were born. She loved you very much and wanted to do everything she could for you. But she had no home for you. She knew it would be unfair to keep you with her, even though she knew that she was going to miss you very much. It was awfully hard for her to part with you. She did it only because she knew the Children's Home (or boarding home, etc.) could provide for your needs better than she could. Nothing would make her happier than to know that you are growing up to be a fine, honest boy." The worker should make it possible for the child to discuss his parents whenever he feels the need to do so. Even when it is desirable to prevent contact with parents, the need to think about them and to talk about them must be recognized. Periodic discussions of this kind may prevent a child from developing a serious neurosis.

V. THE ROLE OF THE SCHOOL IN PERSONALITY DEVELOPMENT

A. The Teacher

Teachers have the same basic human needs as other people and they become maladjusted if these needs are not satisfied. Generally speaking, they must have a sense of personal worth and must feel that their work is significant if they are to give the best that is in them to their young charges.

A teacher's characteristic pattern of behavior in the classroom has an emotional as well as an intellectual basis. In some classrooms, for example, routine and fidelity to assignments and arbitrary rules become ends in themselves, all out of proportion to their educative values. The enforcement of these rules may help the teacher to hide her personal limitations and failures. It saves her from facing her pupils in a person-to-person relationship in which she feels insecure. The teacher who is rigid in her discipline, and who cannot adapt rules to meet the needs of individual children, will usually resist any attempt on the part of administrators or parents to change her behavior. "The teacher who protects an anemic personality with the armor that c-a-t is cat or that $2 + 2 = 4$, can ill afford that you take that covering from him." [15]

Some teachers derive great satisfaction from the authority they wield over children in the classroom, and this satisfaction compensates for frustrations in other school and out-of-school situations. A teacher may "let off steam" and punish the children because the principal has just called her on the carpet. Such impatience has an effect upon the children's attitudes toward school in general as well as toward the teacher personally.

If a teacher does not genuinely like her pupils, and does not really believe that they are entitled to her affection and respect, the children will invariably sense it. "We teach what we know, whereas we show what we feel . . . we do not impatiently teach patience, nor anxiously teach courage, nor falteringly call for faith." [16]

The American public school system all but forces a teacher to be "amoral" in her teaching. In its emphasis on neutrality in re-

---

[15] J. Plant, "Psychiatrist Looks at Today's School Child," *Educational Record*, 23 (January, 1942), Supplement No. 15, 72.

[16] Plant, *op. cit.*, p. 73.

ligious matters, it has inevitably become irreligious. The teacher is expected to refrain from any religious indoctrination. She may, it is true, try to develop in children personal and social attitudes which are not necessarily incompatible with Christian principles, and which, for the most part, reflect the historical importance of Christianity in our culture. Yet she may not teach her pupils the religious sanctions upon which Christian ideals of conduct are based. The sincere Christian, teaching in a public school, must carefully repress her deepest convictions, and must teach children to direct their lives by natural means alone, when she knows that supernatural grace is also necessary if life is to have meaning for eternity. This is a frustrating situation for the Christian teacher.

Many school systems, particularly in small towns, place restrictions upon teachers which make it impossible for them to live as normal, independent adults. Some communities are scandalized if the teacher is seen at a theater or other place of recreation on any except Friday and Saturday evening. And often the teacher who dresses attractively and is interesting to men is thoroughly suspect by the elders of the community. When such restrictions exist, young people who because of their wholesome personalities would make the best teachers are repelled at the thought of teaching. Maladjusted, inferior women, who do not object too seriously to being treated as adolescents, tend to be recruited for such positions, with unfortunate if not disastrous consequences for the children.

B. The Social Organization of the Classroom

A realistic discussion of motives in learning must deal with the total "field" or situation in which learning takes place. In a given classroom, for example, where a child is ostensibly learning arithmetic he is also learning to adjust to his teacher, to his classmates, and to his own impulses which often run counter to the demands of the situation. The nature of these concomitant learnings is often of greater importance in the child's personality development than is the learning of the specific subject matter. A teacher's attitude toward a class and her manner of handling it have a profound influence not only upon the degree to which the subject matter is mastered, but also upon the children's attitudes toward her, toward authority in general, and toward their classmates.

One of the studies which illustrates this principle is that of

Lewin, Lippitt, and White [17] at the University of Iowa. These investigators compared the behavior of ten- to eleven-year-old boys under three types of male leaders, namely: (1) autocratic, (2) laissez-faire, and (3) democratic. While these were volunteer groups, meeting after school, and therefore not comparable to the classroom situation, yet the results are suggestive of what may happen in a classroom setting under different kinds of teachers. Under the autocratic leader the work progressed speedily, without any friendly give-and-take among the boys. When the leader left the room, however, pandemonium broke loose. Not only did the work cease promptly, but a certain amount of hostility toward their comrades was manifested in a number of the boys. In the laissez-faire group, in which the adult took no initiative or responsibility whatever, nothing much happened. This was of all three groups the least effective. In the democratic group where the leader shared the responsibility of making plans, carrying projects forward, and cleaning up at the end of the session, a friendly, informal atmosphere prevailed. The work did not progress as rapidly as in the autocratic group and there was much horseplay on the side. When the leader left the room, however, the work continued without any change and, unlike the autocratic group, there was no manifest hostility among the boys. While the findings of this study must not be over-generalized, it does seem reasonable to suggest that similar psychological factors may operate in the classroom. Certainly, there is a demonstrated relationship between frustration and the impulse to be aggressive. Under an authoritarian teacher, leader, or parent, there is probably a greater amount of individual frustration than under a more democratic adult. This frustration may give rise to aggressive impulses which, by reason of the situation, cannot be taken out on the adult. These impulses are consequently vented against one's own peers, since aggressive acts of this nature are not as dangerous as acts of aggression against adults. Moreover, in punishing the same persons as the adult tyrant is punishing, the child gains added control of his latent urge to rebel against the adult. By identifying with the leader on the basis of fear he becomes like that leader in attitudes and ideals.

[17] K. Lewin, R. Lippitt, and R. White, "Patterns of Aggressive Behavior in Experimentally Created 'Social Climates,'" *J. Soc. Psychol.*, 10 (1939), 271–299.

ROLE OF THE CULTURAL MILIEU

In evaluating psychological studies such as the above, care must be taken not to over-generalize. Lewin was working with only one culture group—midwestern middle-class U.S.A.—and with only one age and sex group—preadolescent boys. We are not justified, on the basis of these studies, in assuming that democratic leadership is most effective for other social classes, other cultures, other age and sex groups. Certainly, the effect of the English public school system upon personality development might well challenge such an assumption.[18] Moreover, democratic teachers going into a community where there is rigid paternal authority might conceivably be somewhat ineffective. The psychological climate of a club, attendance at which is voluntary, is also very different from that of a classroom. Children are not free either to attend or not to attend school. Rather early in life they realize that their parents are not free to send them or not to send them to school. This situation is in itself authoritarian in nature and will undoubtedly play a part in the child's reaction to the kind of leadership exercised by the teacher.

In evaluating the outcomes of learning in the classroom the total personality of each child and his relation to the group should be considered. Subject matter which has been mastered at the cost of wholesome human relations may be very dearly bought.

The kind of teacher attitude and the way in which a class can best be handled will vary with the age level of the children, possibly with sex also, and with the family and community culture which prevails in the group.

C. The Curriculum

The curriculum influences the lives of children in the following ways:

1. It may be too difficult for some children, and thus produce maladjustment.

2. It may omit some important branch of knowledge, and thus indirectly convey the impression that such knowledge is unimportant. This happens in public schools where religion is omitted.

3. The teaching materials may be unintentionally biased. For

---

[18] In the English "public school" (which we would call a private school), the boy does not really "belong" until he has been publicly whipped by someone in authority and has demonstrated that he can "take it." The "meaning" of corporal punishment in such an authoritarian situation determines its effect.

example, readers or geographies, after presenting certain advantages of American life, sometimes conclude with, "Aren't you glad that you live in America?" Unintentionally they create in the child the attitude that his country is far superior to any other country. Our arithmetic textbooks, for instance, characteristically contain problems which deal with concepts of capitalism and familiar commercial practices. Perhaps children would develop very different attitudes were they presented with such problems as, "If a family needs $20 a week for food, but receives $7 on a public works job, what will be the percentage of undernourishment or malnutrition?" [19]

4. The teaching materials may be intentionally biased. For example, Nazi textbooks in Germany were designed to develop progressively in children paranoid delusions of persecution by the repetition of such statements as, "The world will not trade with Germany!" or, again, their references to the "decadent democracies" produced in children a feeling of national superiority which helped their morale considerably when they later became soldiers.

5. The curriculum may be so remote from the daily lives of the children that it has almost no effect upon them.

VI. INFORMAL LEARNING

Informal learning refers to learning which takes place outside of formal school situations. Among the more important sources of such informal learning are radio and television, movies, and comics.

A. Radio and Television [20]

On the average, children listen to the radio several hours a week, although there are great individual differences in this respect. Children in the upper socio-economic classes listen less frequently than do those in the lower classes.[21] Radio surveys of

[19] E. Freeman, *Social Psychology* (New York, Henry Holt & Company, Inc., 1936), pp. 264–265.
[20] At the time of writing, television appears to be much more influential than radio, although careful research studies pertinent to learning have not yet been made.
[21] K. H. Baker, "Radio Listening and Socio-Economic Status," *Psychological Record*, 1 (1937), 99–144.

ROLE OF THE CULTURAL MILIEU 119

adult listening habits have revealed, further, that there is a negative correlation between the amount of time spent in listening to the radio and intelligence. For the less intelligent adult, the radio is likely to be the chief means of entertainment and recreation. For the more intelligent adult, however, radio must compete with cultural interests, such as reading and attending concerts.

Surveys of children's preferences among radio programs have revealed that about one-third of the best-liked programs were not designed for children but for adults. Among the children's programs, there are distinct age trends in preference. Young children enjoy make-believe and fantasy, nursery rhymes and adaptations of folk tunes and musical classics. At about the age of eight or nine, the popularity of these programs declines, and comedy of the more subtle kind, drama, and news broadcasts gain in interest. Boys show more interest than girls in programs involving crime and violence, although some radio serials of this type rank just as high with girls as with boys. Girls are more interested than boys in programs involving crooners, movie stars, girl or child heroines, and domestic dramas. Girls listen to programs especially designed for boys much oftener than boys listen to programs designed for girls. Both boys and girls, but especially boys, prefer programs in which the majority of actors are adult and in which the child characters are older than themselves.

Radio and television have a powerful influence upon attitude formation and upon producing conformity in tastes, feelings, and buying habits in people widely separated by geographical and cultural barriers.[22]

Every time a child listens to the radio or watches a television screen, some incidental learning takes place. New words, colloquialisms, "wise cracks," advertising slogans, and the like are picked up by the child as a part of his cultural inheritance. What a child learns at home, through any medium, tends to become associated with the emotionally toned attitudes he has toward his parents and siblings. Radio and television programs, including commercial advertising, may become emotionally toned learnings and have a profound, but often unconscious, influence upon attitudes and ideals; they may become a part of what the child takes

---

[22] At the time of writing, young-fry all over the country are decked out in Hopalong Cassidy cowboy outfits, a visible index to the psychological influence of a television program.

for granted in his world. Efforts to dislodge such attitudes later in life may meet with great resistance.

B. Movies

A great deal of incidental learning is picked up through commercial films. To date, the most extensive studies of the influence of films upon children have been those of the Payne Fund. These studies are reported at length in several references at the end of this chapter, and no attempt will be made to cover them here.

The research of Peterson and Thurstone is unique among the Payne studies in two respects: (1) it deals with the effect of single motion pictures upon specific attitudes, and (2) it assesses changes in attitude by means of highly reliable and valid attitude scales. Unlike several of the Payne studies, the assumptions underlying the research were not ambiguous and the data collected could be easily interpreted.

The study of Peterson and Thurstone [23] reveals the effectiveness of films in engendering attitudes in children. A scale measuring attitudes toward the Chinese was given to a group of high school students before they had seen the film, *Son of the Gods*. The next day these students saw the film, in which Chinese life was depicted very favorably. The attitude scale, administered the day after the film was seen, showed a distinct shift in the direction of favorable attitudes toward the Chinese. One group of these students was again tested five months later and another group nineteen months later, and the favorable attitudes were found to persist. Even after nineteen months, 62 per cent of the immediate shift toward a favorable attitude remained. These findings suggest that parents and teachers cannot afford to be ignorant of the kinds of films their children see and should probably exert pressure upon film producers to provide the kind of movies that they want their children to see.

Other of the Payne studies attempted to answer the following questions:

1. How much do children remember of what they see in films?
2. How do movies influence social conduct and attitudes?
3. How are emotional responses related to moving pictures?
4. How do motion pictures affect children's sleep?
5. How do motion pictures influence conduct?

[23] R. C. Peterson and L. L. Thurstone, *Motion Pictures and the Social Attitudes of Children* (New York, The Macmillan Company, 1933).

ROLE OF THE CULTURAL MILIEU

The answers which the research workers of the Payne study gave to these questions have been quoted extensively in textbooks and periodicals, and have been presented in popular form.[24] Many of the conclusions drawn from these studies, however, go way beyond the data and rest on value concepts rather than upon scientific data.[25] Yet the studies purport to be scientific investigations, and the truth of their conclusions must rest upon scientific evidence rather than upon opinion. In many instances the methods of securing data may be seriously questioned. For example, in one study, delinquent children were asked to tell if, and to what extent, films had influenced them in their delinquent behavior. A high percentage of the children affirmed that films had been responsible for their antisocial conduct. The investigators did not hesitate to conclude from the statements of these children that films had had a bad effect upon them, a conclusion which is psychologically unsound. A child in trouble will naturally seek for an acceptable explanation of his conduct. A leading question may easily suggest to the child a plausible rationalization of his conduct. Then, too, delinquent children are a selected group with respect to personality difficulties. If the films actually did determine the direction of their delinquency, there is no reason to suppose that, in the absence of the film, the delinquency would not have occurred even though it might have taken another direction. A control group of normally adjusted children would have to be used before a conclusion could be drawn as to the good or bad effects of films on children's behavior. In the absence of such a control group, the data cannot be interpreted one way or the other.

In one study 1,100 junior high school pupils were asked to keep records of their recreational activities.[26] These children lived in west side New York and 75 per cent of them were of foreign-born parentage. The activities most common among the group were listening to the radio, attending the movies, reading, and outdoor play. No analysis of the individual radio programs to which the children listened was made. But a study of the movies seen by

---

[24] H. J. Forman, *Our Movie Made Children* (New York, The Macmillan Company, 1933).

[25] Mortimer Adler, *Art and Prudence* (New York, Longmans, Green & Company, 1937).

[26] R. Robinson, "Leisure Time Activities of New York's Lower West Side," *J. Educ. Soc.*, 9 (1936), 484–493.

these children revealed that 84 per cent of them were considered undesirable for children in the opinion of competent judges. Their reading, too, was considered unwholesome. It was, for the most part, limited to nickel magazines, books of lurid adventure, and to tabloid newspapers.

Even films which are not immoral may insinuate un-Christian patterns of values. Luxury is flaunted on the screen even when the people living in such luxury are supposedly poor. In one popular film, for example, a young couple with apparently no source of income, retire to a simple country cottage. But the grounds on which the cottage stands are beautifully landscaped and the cottage is complete with all conveniences and comforts. To secure such a home in present-day America would require an income considerably above that of the majority of our population. Yet children who see films of this kind week after week and year after year learn to think of such luxury as a normal and desirable thing. A subtle discontent with their own status in life may thus be engendered, and they may be encouraged to pursue money as a major goal in life. Typically, too, movie heroines wear beautiful clothes, a fact which arouses in some adolescent girls the intense desire to be similarly clothed. The desire to own beautiful clothes, and movie suggestions as to how they may be obtained, may be a factor in the delinquency of adolescent girls.[27] Nearly half of the adolescent girls who are sex delinquents report that the stimulus for their behavior came from the movies. A considerable proportion of delinquent boys, too, report that they got suggestions from the movies which determined the particular direction of their delinquency.

C. Comics

Most of the comics which children read today are not hilariously funny but have as their main attraction adventure and excitement. They offer the child an escape from an uneventful and, at times, unpleasant life situation. Comics have their good as well as their bad features. There is some evidence, for example, that they may increase reading readiness in young children. This advantage, however, is usually offset by the crude art and inferior literature of the medium in which it is presented. Many comics have a sadistic and malicious tone and, like films and advertisements,

---

[27] Forman, *op. cit.*

ROLE OF THE CULTURAL MILIEU

many of them insinuate an un-Christian attitude toward sex and toward different racial groups. Comic strip villains, for example, are almost always Orientals, Indians, and half-castes.

If comics are to serve the function of helping children to read, their printing and format should be consistent with the best principles of visual hygiene. This means that there should be a maximum of contrast between background and print. Lower case letters should be used rather than capitals, and the printing should be sufficiently large. Lower case letters give form to words since some of them project below and above the main body of type. The perception of whole words and phrases is aided by the use of such type, whereas capitals encourage a child to read letter by letter.

VII. ENVIRONMENT AND THE HUMAN ORGANISM

Human personality from birth to maturity develops as a whole rather than in segments. The direction which such personality development will take is to a considerable extent the result of (1) attitudes developed in the family, (2) culturally accepted values which are assimilated into the individual personality, (3) formal learning experiences provided by the school and church, and (4) incidental learnings acquired in living with other people or provided by media such as films, comics, radio, and television.

The human being is influenced by the world about him because he has sense organs which open out upon the world and a nervous system which coördinates and stores the information thus provided. He responds to the many influences operating upon him by means of his muscles and glands. In short, the human being is both influenced by and influences his environment. The bodily organism which makes this interaction between the person and the environment possible will constitute the subject matter of the next two chapters.

SUGGESTED READING

ADAMS, E. L., *Dark Symphony* (New York, Sheed and Ward, Inc., 1942).

CLOTHIER, F., "The Psychology of the Adopted Child," *Mental Hygiene,* 27 (1933), 222–230.

HARRIMAN, P. L. (ed.), *Encyclopedia of Psychology* (New York, Philosophical Library, 1946), pp. 491–496.
JOHNSON, J. W., *The Autobiography of an Ex-Colored Man* (New York, Alfred A. Knopf, Inc., 1927).
SANTAYANA, GEORGE, *Persons and Places: The Background of My Life* (New York, Charles Scribner's Sons, 1944).

PART III

The Human Organism

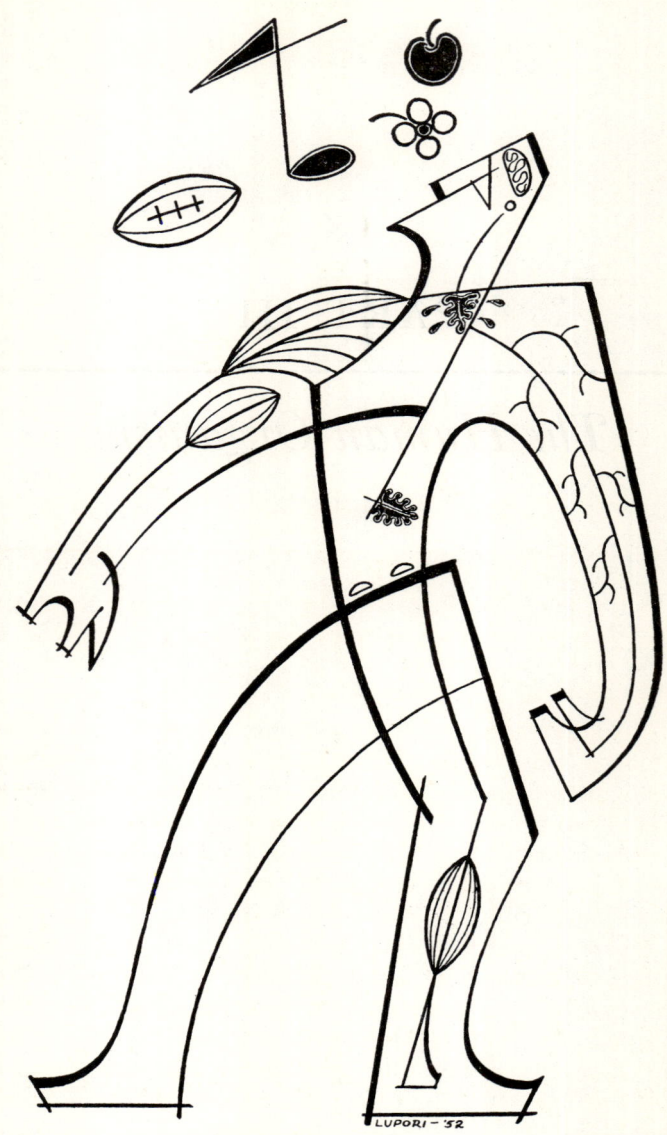

The human being is influenced by the world about him because he has sense organs which open out upon the world and a nervous system which coördinates and stores the information thus provided. By means of his muscles and glands he responds to the many influences operating upon him.

VI

Receptors, Sensory Experience, and Effectors

The colours of the world are in our eyes;
The music of the world is in our ears;
And only when the microcosmic mind
Of man has made its own swift synthesis,
Does it reflect, in moments of strange light,
Whether in art or science, beauty or truth,
The macrocosmic harmonies of God.
—ALFRED NOYES [1]

I. RECEPTORS AND SENSORY EXPERIENCE IN GENERAL

A. Sense Organs

Much of your activity is a response to some kind of stimulation acting upon a sense organ. For example, you may be resting comfortably, completely relaxed, until of a sudden, a bee stings you. At once you spring into action. The sting of the bee is the *stimulus* to your activity. A stimulus is a form of energy which acts upon a sense organ and must be converted into nervous energy before a response will take place. In all complex biological organisms, including man, sensitivity to stimuli is mediated by sense organs, the essential part of which is known as a *receptor*. The *adequate stimulus* for a given sense is the stimulus to which that sense is especially adapted; thus, the skin is sensitive to pressure and pain. Light waves are adequate stimuli for vision; sound waves for hearing. Usually at any one time most of our sense organs are being stimulated. Even during sleep a loud noise may stimulate the receptors for hearing or excessive warmth may stimulate the receptors for warmth. As a result, even though we

[1] Alfred Noyes, *The Last Voyage* (New York, Frederick A. Stokes Company, 1930), p. 29.

are unconscious, we may react by turning or by throwing off the covers.

Because the human being is sensitive to certain kinds of stimuli he gets to know the world about him. The external world of people and things makes contact with his senses and in this way influences his development and learning. People are not equally sensitive to all kinds of energy, nor are all parts of their bodies equally receptive to all kinds of stimuli. Consequently, much energy of the external world remains unsensed and undetected, unless techniques are used for bringing these elusive forms of energy into effective contact with a sense organ. The use of x-rays, radio tubes, and microscopes, for instance, greatly extends the sensitive powers of the human organism.

Very early in life human beings exhibit great individual differences in their sensitivity to various kinds of sense stimuli. Some individuals react quickly to certain kinds of sense stimuli, others relatively slowly. Some require much more intense stimulation to elicit a response than do others. And, what is probably more importantly psychologically, individual differences in sensory interests appear as early as infancy. Some little children, for instance, are fascinated by lights and colors. Others derive an almost ecstatic joy from the "feel" of velvet, silk, wool, finger paint, sand paper, and other textures. Still other children are enraptured by various combinations of sound or taste and seek to prolong experiences with stimuli of these kinds long after other children have lost interest. Upon these initial differences in the feeling-tones engendered by different sense stimuli, many nuances of adult personality are based.

In general, psychologists recognize three main classes of receptors: (1) exteroceptors, (2) interoceptors, and (3) proprioceptors. *Exteroceptors* receive stimuli from the external environment. They mediate sensations of pressure, temperature (warmth and cold), smell, taste, common chemical sense, pain, hearing, and vision. *Interoceptors* are located in the internal organs of the body. They are responsible for sensations of hunger, thirst, internal pain, and perhaps other sensations the origin of which we do not understand very well as, for example, nausea. *Proprioceptors* are located in muscles, tendons, and joints, and in the inner ear. They include the kinesthetic sense (sense of muscular movement) and the static sense (sense of equilibrium).

B. Sensation

The first conscious response to a stimulus is a *sensation*. A sensation is the particular quality of awareness that comes when a sense organ is being adequately stimulated. Sensation must be distinguished from another kind of knowledge also mediated by the senses, namely, *perception*. Sensation refers merely to the qualities of awareness evoked when a *stimulus* is impinging upon a sense organ. Perception is awareness of the object or thing or objective state of affairs in the external world that *produces* the stimulation. In this chapter we are limiting our discussion to sensation. The closely allied subject of perception is dealt with at length in Chapter XI.

In general, sensations vary in three ways, according to (1) modality, (2) intensity, and (3) duration. By *modality* we mean the kind of sense organ involved, such as the ear, eye, skin sense, or nose. In other words, the stimulation of each sense organ gives rise to a quality of sensation which is different from that elicited by any other sense organ. Differences in *intensity* vary from weak to strong, and differences in *duration* extend from short to long.

C. Actions and Reactions

Not all behavior is dominated by sense activity. As Hebb points out, the notion that "behavior is a series of *reactions* (instead of actions), each of which is determined by the immediately preceding events in the sensory systems . . . is not altogether consistent with recognizing the existence of set, attitude, or attention. . . ."[2] On the contrary, "The brain is continually active in all its parts, and an afferent sensory excitation must be superimposed on an already existent excitation."[3]

II. VISION

A. Structure and Functions of the Eye

The human eye is often compared to a camera since, like a camera, it is a light-proof structure with a small adjustable opening in it which permits light to enter. In a camera, the amount of light that enters is controlled by a diaphragm; in the eye, this

[2] D. O. Hebb, *The Organization of Behavior: A Neuropsychological Theory* (New York, John Wiley & Sons, Inc., 1949), p. 3.
[3] *Ibid.*, p. 7.

function is controlled by the iris. The *iris* is the muscle which controls the size of the pupil of the eye, and it is the part of the eye that gives it its color. When the light is very bright, the iris contracts and the pupil of the eye becomes smaller. As a result, less light enters the eye than if the pupil were larger. When the light is dim the iris expands and the pupil of the eye becomes correspondingly larger. In going directly from a very bright room to a dark one, or from a very dark room to a light one, vision is dimmed for a minute or two while the iris is making the appropriate adjustments.

The picture taken by a camera is imprinted on a sensitive plate or film at the opposite end to the hole through which the light has entered. This sensitive plate is the film. The corresponding structure in the eye is the retina. When light strikes the film in a camera it produces chemical changes which result in a partial decomposition of the film. Apparently, a similar chemical reaction takes place when light strikes the retina. The retina contains two kinds of sensitive receptors for vision, namely: (1) *rods*, which are sensitive only to colorless (achromatic) stimuli, and (2) *cones*, which are sensitive particularly to color (chromatic) stimuli. The rods are used only in night or twilight vision. The cones are used chiefly in daylight vision, and in daylight vision they are sensitive to both chromatic and achromatic stimuli. Each of the cones is connected with the brain by a single fiber of the optic nerve, whereas large clusters of rods are connected by a single nerve fiber. Consequently, the rods do not provide for as clear image vision as do the cones.

The lens of the eye, like the lens of a camera, brings the rays of light to a focus on the retina. The way in which the lens of the eye brings an object into focus, however, is different from the way in which the lens of the camera does so. In focusing a camera, the lens is moved toward or away from the film. In the eye the distance between the lens and the retina is fixed and a clear focus is obtained by changing the thickness of the lens rather than by moving it closer or farther away from the retina. The degree of reflex contraction of the ciliary muscles permits the lens to bulge or grow thicker. The lens of the eye also serves as a color filter to some extent. The normal person with an intact lens does not see ultraviolet light. But people who have lost their lenses through an operation for cataract, and who have had their lenses replaced by clear glass lenses have excellent vision for ultraviolet rays. It is of interest to note that because of the curvature of the lens, the optical image is impressed upside down upon the retina. But our vision is of an external world, not vision of the processes going on in our eyeball, so we are not confused by or even aware of the upside down image.

A cross-section of the human eyeball, with all parts labeled, and a corresponding view of a camera is shown in Figure 10. Although as an optical system the human eye and a camera are very similar, there are a great many respects in which they differ. A study of the physics of vision alone cannot tell us why the eye behaves as an eye though it will tell us why a camera works as it does.

The eyeball is composed of three layers of tissue as shown in Figure 10, the inner one of which is the retina. The middle layer is the *choroid coat* which prevents light from entering the eye except through the pupil. It is richly supplied with blood vessels and provides the retina, lens, and vitreous humor with nutrient materials. The outer layer is the *sclerotic coat*. Its chief function is that of furnishing the strength necessary to keep the eyeball in shape and sufficiently rigid to permit the external muscles of the eye to function properly. In the front, this coat is modified to form the *cornea*. The cornea transmits and refracts light waves and protects the lens and iris.

Other structures of the eye, shown in Figure 10, are the fovea, conjunctiva, suspensory ligament, and the ciliary muscles. The *fovea* is a depression in that part of the retina in which there is the greatest concentration of cones. In daylight it is the point of clearest vision in the eye. This is not true for night vision, since rods are used at night and there are no rods in the fovea. In trying to see a very faint star at night, therefore, we would do better to focus just a little to the side of the fovea. The *conjunctiva* provides a smooth surface for the gliding of the lids over the eyeball and a sensitive protecting surface to the front of the eye. The *suspensory ligament*, to which the ciliary muscles are attached, exerts tension on the lens and makes it relatively flat. When the *ciliary muscles* contract, they release the tension exerted by the suspensory ligament and permit the lens to bulge.

The eyeball contains two fluids which serve to keep it taut: the *aqueous humor* which is a watery, transparent fluid between the cornea and the lens, and the *vitreous humor* which is a jelly-like substance filling the eyeball back of the lens.

There are no rods or cones at the place at which the optic nerve

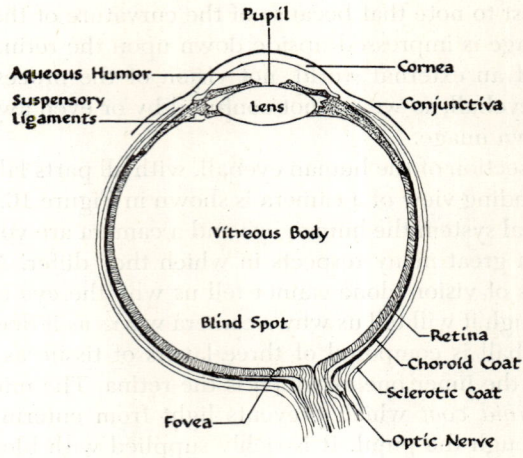
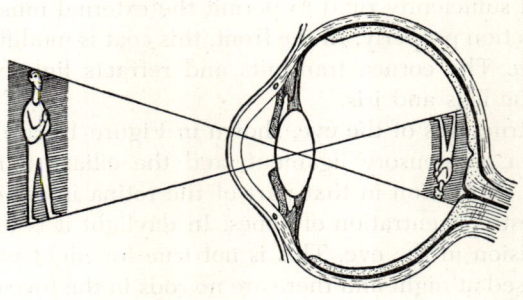
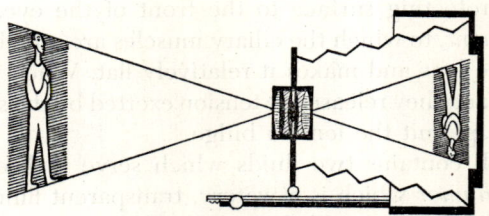

Fig. 10. Cross-section of Human Eyeball, and
Comparison of Eye with Camera.

RECEPTORS, SENSORY EXPERIENCE, EFFECTORS

enters the eye, and, consequently, nothing is seen if it is focused at that point. This point, known as the *blind spot*, is indicated in Figure 10.

B. Projection of Nerve Fibers

Before a sensation of any kind is experienced, nerve impulses must travel from the sense organ to the appropriate sense area of the brain. For visual stimuli, the sense area of the brain is in the occipital cortex, in the back of the head and at the base of the

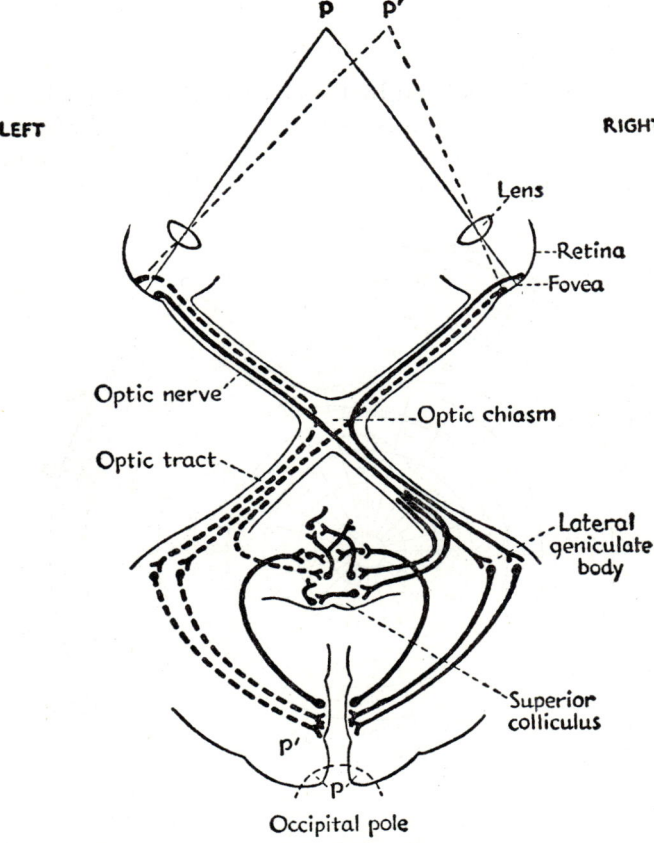

Fig. 11. Route of the Optic Fibers to the Brain. [Reproduced from S. R. Hathaway, *Physiological Psychology* (New York, Appleton-Century-Crofts, Inc., 1942), p. 99.]

134 PERSONS AND PERSONALITY

skull. Nerve impulses from the retinas of the eyes are conducted to the occipital cortex by way of the optic chiasma, as shown in Figure 11. Note that the nerve fibers from the left half of each retina go to the visual center in the occipital lobe of the left hemisphere of the brain. In doing so, the nerve fibers from the right eye cross to the other side of the optic chiasma. Similarly, the nerve fibers from the right half of each retina go to the visual center in the right hemisphere of the brain, and in doing so, the nerve fibers from the left eye cross to the other side at the optic chiasma.

C. Color Vision

Color vision is mediated by the cones of the retina. The retina, however, is not uniformly sensitive over its entire surface to all colors. Its zones vary in their sensitivity to different hues. The normal eye typically has three such zones: (1) a center zone which

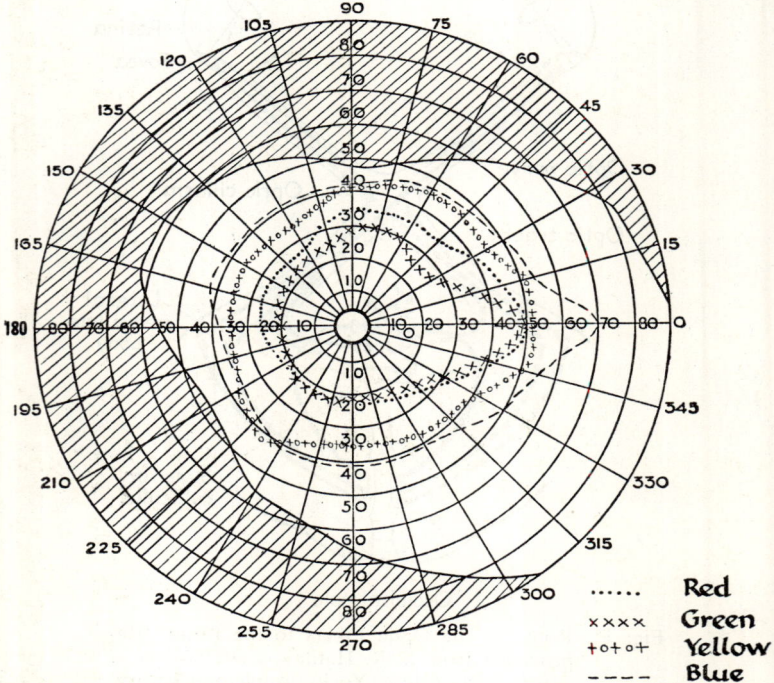

Fig. 12. Color Zones of the Retina.

RECEPTORS, SENSORY EXPERIENCE, EFFECTORS

is sensitive to all hues; (2) an intermediate zone which is sensitive to blue and yellow, but not to red and green; and (3) an outer zone which is sensitive only to achromatic stimuli. Figure 12 indicates the limits of these zones in the retina of a young woman. Color zones are mapped by means of a visual perimeter.

D. The Stimulus for Vision

The physical stimulus for vision is light, and light is a form of radiating or reflected electromagnetic energy. Several different theories of light have been proposed, the most important of which are the *wave theory* and the *quantum theory*. According to the wave theory, light travels out from its source in continuous pulsating waves. These pulsations result from periodic fluctuations in the intensity of the light. Sunlight consists of waves pulsating at different frequencies; and, when it is passed through a prism, each of these different waves is separated in such a way as to produce the visible spectrum, as shown in Figure 13. The dif-

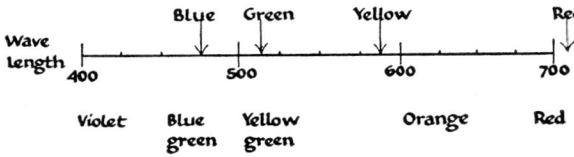

Fig. 13. Visible Spectrum.

ferent colors seen in the spectrum are characterized by different wave lengths, and these wave lengths are bent differently as they go through the prism. The longer wave lengths, seen at the red end of the spectrum, are bent less than the shorter ones at the violet end. In Figure 14 is shown a schematic representation of a light wave. The distance between two successive pulsations, as indicated by line *a*, constitutes the wave length. The amplitude is one-half the distance between the crest of the wave and the trough, as shown by line *b*.

The chief difference between the wave theory and the quantum theory is that in the latter light is assumed to be given off in separate bundles of energy and is not continuous. Each of these bundles of energy vibrates with a characteristic frequency and travels outward with a constant velocity. The bundles or *quanta* of energy are given off in such enormous numbers that even at great distances from the source there are no appreciable gaps between them.

Practically, it makes little difference to the psychologist which theory is adopted. Although recent research indicates that the quantum theory is the more adequate, for all practical purposes we continue to think of light as continuous at all points in the space through which it passes. It is only when the intensity of

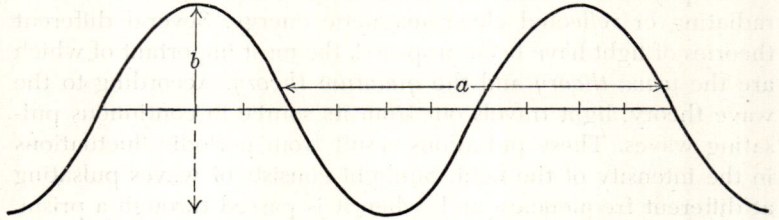

Fig. 14. Schematic Representation of a Light Wave.

the light is so weak that the action of the individual quanta become appreciable in relation to the total light received that the quantum theory must be applied.

E. Visual Experiences

Visual experiences are classified as either achromatic or chromatic. Achromatic experiences differ only in brightness, not in hue, and range from pure black to pure white with various shades of gray in between. Achromatic experiences can be arranged in a one-dimensional series, each adjacent member of which is "just noticeably different" from the one on either side of it. A psychological unit of measurement, the JND, or just-noticeable difference between one sensation of brightness and another just brighter, is used to determine the brilliance value of any achromatic experience. Usually the JND is defined as the difference that can be discriminated about 50 per cent of the time. In determining the brilliance value of any gray, we count the number of JND's which intervene between it and some arbitrarily chosen black.

Chromatic experiences vary in three dimensions: hue, saturation, and brightness. Light waves, as we have previously shown, vary in wave length and in amplitude. By *hue* we mean the different colors, such as red, green, blue, yellow, and the colors intermediate between them. Hue is determined chiefly by the wave length of light. Rays coming from the sun consist of a mixture of wave lengths, but not all of these wave lengths fall within the normal range of human vision. The average human eye is sensitive to wave lengths falling approximately between 400 and 700 $\mu\mu$.[4] These are the wave lengths found in the visible spectrum. Wave lengths shorter than 400 $\mu\mu$ are ultraviolet rays and cannot be seen by the human eye. They include x-rays. Wave lengths of 800 $\mu\mu$ or more are called infra-red, and they are sensed not as light but as heat. Radio waves are much longer waves included in this same series. Within the visible spectrum when all wave lengths of light are mixed, as they are in sunlight, a white light results. When this white light passes through a prism to a sheet of white paper, a band of colors is reflected ranging from red tinged with yellow with a wave length of 700 $\mu\mu$, through yellow at approximately 580 $\mu\mu$, through green at 510 $\mu\mu$, blue at 486 $\mu\mu$ and violet at 396 $\mu\mu$. Objects viewed in sunlight in which there is a mixture of all wave lengths have characteristic colors which result from their differential absorption or reflection of wave lengths. An object that absorbs almost all wave lengths and reflects almost none is black. If it reflects almost all wave lengths and absorbs almost none it is white. Red objects absorb almost all wave lengths except that of red; blue absorbs almost all wave lengths but that for blue, and so on for the other colors.

Saturation depends upon the amount of hue present. For example, when red is diluted with a mixture of white, pink results. Pink is a red of low saturation.

Brightness depends chiefly upon the intensity of the radiant or reflected energy, although it does bear some relation to wave length, too. The yellowest possible yellow, for instance, is brighter than the bluest possible blue.

A chromatic series, unlike an achromatic series, must be represented on a three-dimensional continuum, as illustrated by the color solid shown in Figure 15. Notice that the color circle in the center of this solid represents the different hues. Brightness is depicted on the line running through the center of the solid, and saturation by a line running from the hue designation on the periphery of the circle to the gray center of the circle. The

[4] $\mu\mu$ is the abbreviation for "millimicron(s)." One millimicron is a millionth of a millimeter.

PERSONS AND PERSONALITY

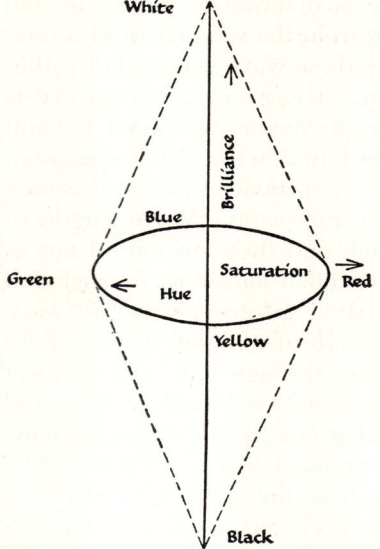

Fig. 15. Color Solid.

brightest colors are close to the white at the top of the solid; the dullest are close to the black at the bottom. The least saturated colors are in the center of the solid, and the most saturated are at the periphery.

F. Color Mixing

When you mix pigments, such as blue and yellow, a green color is reflected. But when you mix blue and yellow on a color wheel, gray results. Retinal color mixing is accomplished not by mixing the colors themselves but by placing interlocked color discs on a wheel that can be made to revolve with great rapidity. When the color wheel rotates, the retina is stimulated first by one color and then by the other. This takes place so rapidly that the colors appear as one hue instead of two or more.

There are three laws of retinal color mixture, the first two of which were formulated by Sir Isaac Newton. These laws are as follows:

1. The law of complementaries states that for every color stimulus there is another color which, when mixed with it in the right proportions, will cause the hue to disappear and be replaced by a neutral gray.

2. The mixture of colors that are not complementary produces colors that resemble the component colors to the degree that each component is present in the mixture.

3. A mixture of color mixtures that match will match either of the original mixtures provided the light conditions remain constant.

If we want to determine the complement of any given color all that we have to do is draw a straight line from the point on the color circle in the center of the color solid through the center of the circle. The complementary hue will be that point on

RECEPTORS, SENSORY EXPERIENCE, EFFECTORS 139

the circle which falls in a direct line with these two points. A line drawn from yellow, for example, and extended through the center to the periphery of the circle on the opposite side leads to blue. This indicates that blue is the complement of yellow.

G. After-Images

After the eye has been subjected to an intense stimulus for some time, a positive after-image of the stimulus is sometimes seen for a few seconds after the stimulus has been removed. This positive after-image is soon replaced by a negative after-image. The positive after-image has the same color as the stimulus had. The negative after-image, on the contrary, is complementary to the stimulus in color. If the stimulus was blue, for example, the negative after-image would be seen as yellow. Negative after-images persist for a much longer time than positive after-images. The more distantly they are projected, the larger they get.

H. Abnormalities of Vision

Some of the commonest abnormalities of vision are as follows:

1. *Nearsightedness (myopia).* A person is nearsighted if his eyeball is too long or if his lens has too great a curvature, as illustrated in Figure 16. The condition is corrected by wearing glasses which have a concave lens.

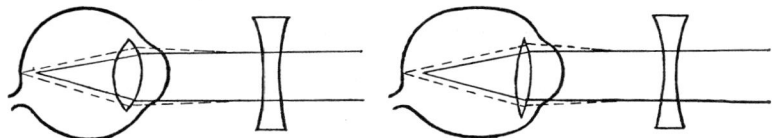

Lens too convex   Eyeball too long
Condition corrected by concave lens

Fig. 16. Nearsighted Eye.

2. *Farsightedness (hyperopia).* A person is farsighted if his eyeball is too short, or if his lens has too slight a curvature as indicated in Figure 17. The condition is corrected by a convex lens.

3. *Astigmatism.* Astigmatism is a blurring of vision which results from an unequal curvature of the different refracting portions of the eye. If it is not too marked it can sometimes be corrected by lenses.

4. *Strabismus (squint or cross-eye).* Strabismus is a condition

in which the two eyes do not focus upon the same point because of a muscular imbalance. The person who suffers from this disorder cannot look another person in the eye, and may, consequently, be thought of as "shifty-eyed" or deceitful.

5. *Color blindness (Daltonism).* Color blindness is the inability to distinguish one or more of the primary colors. Total color blindness is very rare, although red-green color blindness is found in approximately 7 to 8 per cent of the male population. It can be discovered by means of color tests, such as the Holmgren Woolens, the Ishihara Test, or the Pseudo-Isochromatic Plates of the American Optical Company.

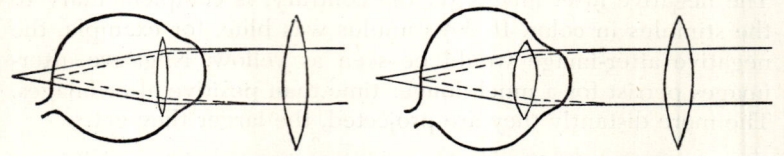

lens not convex enough Eyeball too short
Condition corrected by convex lens

Fig. 17. Farsighted Eye.

As in other characteristics, people vary considerably in their ability to discriminate colors. Therefore, color sensitivity must not be looked upon as an all-or-none affair. There are almost innumerable gradations in color sensitivity and color weakness, not just several distinct types.

6. *Half-vision.* Half-vision is a condition in which there is blindness for one-half the field of vision in one or both eyes. It results from a destruction of the optic nerve somewhere between the retina and the visual center of the cortex. Figure 11 is a schematic representation of the course of the optic nerve. If the nerve is injured between the retina and the optic chiasma, only one eye will be affected. If the injury occurs between the optic chiasma and the visual center of the cortex, blindness in one-half of each eye results.

III. HEARING

A. Structure and Functions of the Ear

The ear is made up of structures which not only make hearing possible, but which mediate equilibrium as well. The three main portions of the ear are (1) the *outer ear*, which picks up sound waves, (2) the *middle ear*, which amplifies and transforms the sound waves into lymph vibrations, and (3) the *inner ear* which contains the sensitive receptors for sound, and which transforms lymph vibrations into nerve impulses. The Eustachian tube, which leads from the middle ear to the throat, equalizes the pressure on the two sides of the ear drum. The structure of the ear is shown diagrammatically in Figures 18 and 19.

Sound waves first enter the outer ear and pass through the *auditory canal* to the *ear drum* (tympanic membrane). The sound waves then set up vibrations in the ear drum which are transmitted to three tiny bones (the auditory ossicles) known as the *hammer* (malleus), *anvil* (incus), and *stirrup* (stapes). Vibrations of the stirrup cause the membrane of the *oval window* to move in and out. This sets up vibrations of the liquid in the *vestibular canal* and in the *tympanic canal* of the *cochlea*. Within the cochlea are the auditory receptors. These receptors are tiny hair cells, located on the *organ of Corti*, which, in turn, rests on the *basilar membrane*. The sense fibers are longest at the apex of the cochlea and shortest at its base. Movements of these hair cells give rise to nerve impulses which travel along the auditory nerve to the thalamus and are then relayed to the auditory area of the brain.

Deafness may result from (1) injury of the structures which pick up, transform, and transmit vibrations to the sensitive receptors, (2) destruction of the sense receptors, (3) destruction of the auditory nerve, or (4) destruction of the auditory areas of both hemispheres of the brain. When the injury involves the structures listed under (1), it is still possible to hear by bone conduction with the help of hearing aids. When the cochlea is partially destroyed, the type of deafness will depend upon which part is destroyed. If the injury is at the base, there will be deafness for high-pitched tones. If the injury is at the apex, there will be a deafness for low-pitched tones. Injury to one or more portions of the cochlea results in *tonal islands,* or deafness for particular frequencies of sound vibrations.

Sounds differ in (1) loudness, (2) pitch, and (3) timbre or tone quality. Loudness depends upon the amplitude of the sound wave, pitch upon the frequency of vibration, and timbre upon the complexity of the vibration.

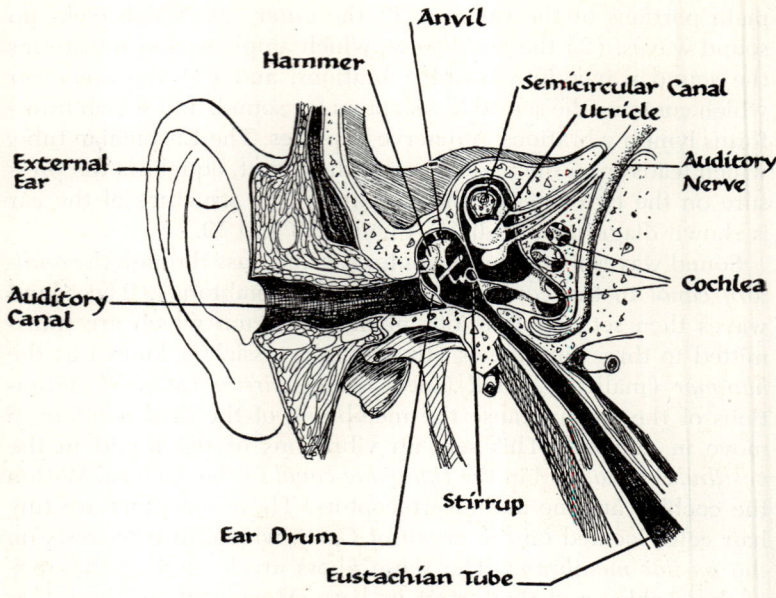

Fig. 18. Schematic Diagram of the Ear.

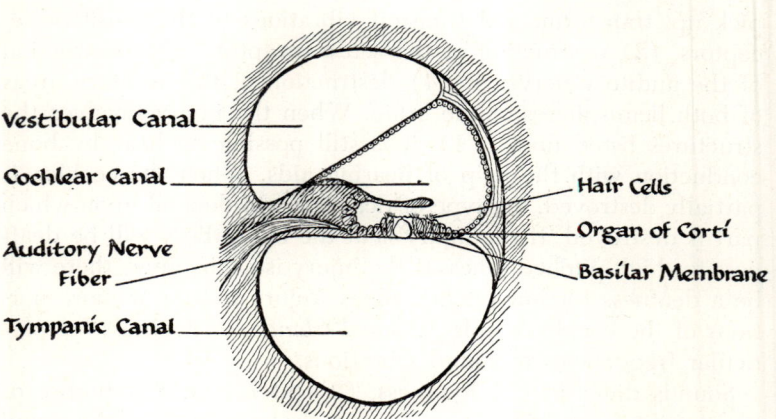

Fig. 19. Cross-section of the Cochlear Canals.

B. The Stimulus for Hearing

The adequate stimulus for hearing is energy in the form of a sound wave. Sound waves result from the vibrations of a sounding body, as, for instance, the vibrations produced in a violin string by drawing a bow across it. These sound waves can be transmitted only through a material substance, such as air, water, or metal. You can demonstrate this fact by ringing a bell in the vacuum of a hermetically sealed jar. The bell will be seen to "ring" but will not be heard. When air is pumped into the jar, the vibrating bell can be heard as well as seen.

Sound waves consist of alternate condensations and rarefactions of the substance through which they travel. The adjacent particles of the substance through which the sound wave travels are alternately crowded together and then spread out because of the oscillation of the individual particles. The wave length of a sound wave is the distance between the successive points of maximum compression of these particles. Tones result from relatively smooth and regular vibrations; noises result from unsteady and irregular vibrations.

C. Theories of Hearing

Theories of hearing attempt to explain the physiological bases of our experiences of pitch and loudness. Among the more important of such theories are (1) the *resonance* (place or piano) *theory* of Helmholtz, (2) the *frequency* (telephone) *theory* of Rutherford, and (3) the *volley theory* of Wever and Bray.

Helmholtz assumed that the hair cells of the basilar membrane act analogously to the wires in a piano; that is, that each cell, like a string in a piano, is attuned to a special frequency of vibration. When a tone of given pitch is sounded near a piano, the piano string tuned to that pitch will vibrate in sympathy. Strings not attuned to the same frequency will not vibrate. Similarly, a tone of a given frequency of vibration will, according to this theory, arouse a sympathetic response in the hair cell attuned to the same frequency of vibration. In this way, the analysis of pitch takes place within the ear itself rather than in the central nervous system. The loudness of a sound is attributed to the amount of spread of vibration over the basilar membrane. On vigorous stimulation, a band of fibers responds, and the part responding most vigorously determines the pitch.

There are several lines of evidence which support Helmholtz' theory. One line of evidence is that of tonal islands. Some people are deaf only to tones of certain pitches but not to tones of other pitches, and thus exhibit "islands" of deafness. Post-mortem examination of such persons has revealed deterioration in selected portions of the basilar membrane. The deteriorated portions correspond to the portions which, according to this theory, should mediate tone sensations of the pitches to which the individual was deaf.

Another line of evidence has been derived from experimentation with animals. Guinea pigs were subjected to tones of a given pitch over a period of from 50 to 60 days. At the end of this period, the animals were deaf to tones of this pitch. The guinea pigs were then killed, and a post-mortem examination of the basilar membrane was made. A widespread deterioration of the basilar membrane was discovered, a deterioration which was not confined to just a few fibers but which extended over about $\frac{1}{20}$ of the membrane. However, the deterioration was in the general locality where according to the Helmholtz theory we should expect it to be.

The human ear is capable of discriminating 11,000 different tones. It is hard to account for such discrimination on the basis of Helmholtz' theory, since the longest fibers on the basilar membrane are only three times as long as the shortest ones. To meet this objection, it has been assumed that the fibers of the basilar membrane have different degrees of tension, as the result of tissue loadings.

The *frequency theory* of Rutherford, unlike the resonance theory of Helmholtz, assumes that the analysis of tone takes place in the auditory area of the brain rather than in the sense organ. The ear itself is compared to the disc of a telephone receiver. Sound waves of a given frequency of vibration produce within the auditory nerve similar frequencies of vibration, and these frequencies are analyzed when they reach the auditory area of the brain. Pitch, according to this theory, depends upon the frequency of nerve impulses which reach the brain. Loudness is attributed to the number of fibers activated in the auditory nerve.

The chief objection to this theory is that it cannot account for vibration frequencies above 1,000 per second. Yet we know that human beings can respond to vibration frequencies as high as 20,000 per second. According to Rutherford's theory, the auditory nerve would have to conduct nerve impulses at the rate of 20,000 per second to account for high pitches. This rate of conduction is 20 times as fast as the most rapid nerve impulse ever measured. Individual nerve fibers cannot possibly conduct nerve impulses at this rate because, after a nerve impulse has been discharged, there is a refractory phase of $1/1,000$ second during which another nerve impulse cannot be elicited.

The *volley theory* of Wever and Bray assumes, as does the frequency theory of Rutherford, that the vibration frequency of the stimulus is reproduced in the action current (nerve impulse) of the auditory nerve. It does not assume, however, that the vibration frequency of the stimulus is reproduced in each individual fiber of the auditory nerve. Wever and Bray experimented with cats by placing electrodes on the auditory nerve and connecting these electrodes with a radio amplifier, to which was attached a telephone receiver in another room. The cat's ear was then subjected to sound waves of various kinds, including both tones and speech. Listeners in the other room found that these vibration frequencies were carefully reproduced. This result was interpreted to mean that the vibration frequency of the stimulus was reproduced accurately in the action current of the auditory nerve.

Later experiments, in which the auditory nerve responses were carefully isolated from cochlear responses, indicated that the auditory nerve did indeed reproduce the stimulus frequency up to about 3,000 vibrations per second. This shows that, although an individual nerve fiber will not discharge more than 1,000 nerve impulses per second, the auditory nerve as a whole will discharge as many as 3,000. Wever and Bray suggested that the nerve fibers work in squads, that is, that certain groups of fibers would discharge at one time, and other groups, which were in a refractory phase while the first group were discharging, would discharge at another time. The pitch of a tone would depend not upon the frequency of nerve impulses within individual fibers but upon the frequency of volleys of nerve impulses. As the intensity of the stimulus is increased, more nerve impulses are set off, and loudness is increased.

IV. THE SKIN SENSES

The cutaneous or skin senses, located in the intermediate layer of the skin, are four in number: pressure, pain, warmth, and cold. The adequate stimulus for pressure is the application of force to the skin in such a way as to deform it. The adequate stimulus for intense pain may be any mechanical, thermal, or chemical stimulus that tends to or actually does destroy or injure the skin. The adequate stimulus for warmth is, within limits, a temperature above the physiological zero of the skin. The *physiological zero* is usually around $33°$ C. As the surrounding temperature rises above this point, at first a sensation of warmth is felt, then a sensation of heat. Above $52°$ C. the sensation of heat combines with that of pain. As the surrounding temperature is lowered below the physiological zero, at first there is a sensation of cold, then of burning cold, and finally at about $0°$ C. a sensation of pain is added.

Besides the physiological zero there is also a psychological zero above which and below which one may experience a sensation of cold or warmth. If you immerse your hand for about five minutes in warm water the skin temperature will be changed. This produces a *psychological zero* which is higher than the true physiological zero. Stimuli a little warmer or cooler than this psychological zero will be experienced as either warm or cold. Furthermore, the skin adapts itself readily to temperature changes if these changes are not too great. You can demonstrate this for yourself by preparing three bowls of water, one at skin temperature, one hot, and one cold. Place one of your hands in the cold water and the other in the hot water for about thirty seconds. Then plunge both hands in the "neutral" temperature bowl. The hand that has been in the hot water will feel cool and the hand that has been in the cold water will feel warm even though both are now immersed in water of the same temperature.

V. THE GUSTATORY SENSE

The sensory receptors for taste are in the taste buds. There are only four tastes: sweet, bitter, salt, and sour. The wide variety of food flavors is vastly greater than the number of different tastes for they are the results of the various combinations of taste and smell. Cutaneous sensations, too, add to the palatability of foods.

The "taste" of lukewarm coffee, for example, is different from that of a steaming hot cup. The adequate stimulus for taste is a bitter, sweet, salty, or sour substance dissolved in a liquid. Solid substances are tasted only after they have been dissolved by salivary secretions in the mouth.

The tongue is not equally sensitive in all parts to each of the four tastes. It is most sensitive to sweet at the tip; to sour at the edge; to bitter at the back; and to salt at the edge and tip. Some psychologists claim that there is an identifiable relationship between the position of the tongue in sensing each of these tastes and the corresponding facial expression. A "sweet" expression, for instance, is supposedly one in which the tip of the tongue is pressed against the roof of the mouth. A "bitter" expression is one in which the rear of the tongue is placed in a suitable position for dislodging a bitter substance!

Taste receptors are distributed differently in the adult than in the child. The child has taste buds over the entire upper surface of the tongue and on the insides of its cheeks. The adult, however, does not have taste buds in the middle of the upper surface of his tongue or on his cheeks. The difference in anatomy may account in part for the greater pleasure children get from stuffing their mouths with food.

Old people often complain that food does not "taste good," even when young people have no complaint about the same food. The older person's complaint may result from reduced sensitivity of his taste buds. However, it probably results more from the fact that his sense of smell is becoming less and less acute.

VI. THE OLFACTORY SENSE

The human olfactory sense seems to play a less important role in adjustment among civilized peoples than among primitive peoples. It is useful as a defense against noxious air and food, although we quickly become adapted to any odor, thus lessening its effect after it has had its chance to serve as a signal either of danger or of the presence of desirable foods. Other animals, and especially the dog, have a more acute sense of smell than man. This observation prompted Chesterton's dog "Quoodle" to say,

>They haven't got no noses
>The fallen sons of Eve

Even the smell of roses
Is not what they supposes.[5]

The sensitive receptors for smell are embedded in the mucous membrane that lines the nasal cavity. The *adequate stimulus* is an odorous substance in gaseous form.

Various investigators have attempted to classify odors according to the chemical structure of their stimulating substances but without too much success. Probably the best classification that we have is that of Henning, who experimented with about 400 different odorous materials. Henning's sixfold classification of odors is as follows: spicy, flowery (fragrant), fruity, resinous, burned, and foul. For each of these odors, Henning claims, a more or less typical chemical structure is responsible. He admits, however, that there are notable exceptions to this rule.

Loss of the sense of smell is not a great psychological handicap except in certain types of situations when gases must be detected, as in warfare, though its loss does result in a failure not only to perceive odors but to enjoy the full flavors of foods. Because of this last disability aged persons may eat less than they should.

VII. THE KINESTHETIC SENSE

The sensitive receptors for the kinesthetic sense are in the muscles, tendons, and joints. The adequate stimulus for kinesthesis is a mechanical stimulus provided by the action of the body itself. This sense provides information about muscular movement. It is this sense, for example, that enables you to write fairly well even in the dark, though you are unable to see the pencil and the characters you are writing. The kinesthetic sense functions in both reflexive and voluntary movement. If you were to slip on a bit of ice, your kinesthetic sense, in collaboration with your sense of equilibrium, would initiate reflex acts which—you might hope! —would help you to maintain balance.

In certain diseases, such as *tabes dorsalis*, the dorsal horn of gray matter in the spinal cord degenerates, and incoming sensory nerve impulses from the muscles do not reach the brain. As a result, a peculiar tabetic or unsteady gait appears. The person suffering from *tabes dorsalis* cannot walk without watching his

[5] Reprinted by permission of Dodd, Mead & Company from *The Flying Inn* by G. K. Chesterton. Copyright, 1914, by Dodd, Mead & Company.

legs because vision alone tells him the position of his muscles. Even with his eyes open, however, each step is too long, and to retain balance, he must quickly jerk his foot back.

VIII. THE SENSE OF EQUILIBRIUM (STATIC SENSE)

The sensitive receptors for equilibrium are located in the vestibule and semicircular canals of the inner ear, as shown in Figure 18. This sense enables the person to orient his bodily movements and posture with respect to gravity and thus maintain bodily equilibrium. When, as sometimes happens, a disease of the inner ear destroys this sense, unsteadiness of movement results. The reflexes for maintaining upright position are lost, and if the person slips on a piece of ice he will almost invariably fall. A loss of this sense unfits a man for service as an airplane pilot, since he will not sense whether he is in an upright, upside-down, or intermediate position, although his sense of vision will help him to maintain his equilibrium. The sense of equilibrium is strongly stimulated when the person suddenly ascends or descends in an elevator or in a plane, when he turns somersaults, swings, or is whirled about in space.

IX. THE ORGANIC SENSES

The receptors of the organic senses appear to be located in the linings of the internal organs of the body. From the psychologist's point of view, the most important of these senses are hunger and thirst.

A. Hunger

Experiments by Cannon and Washburn and by Wada show that contractions of the stomach musculature are associated with the conscious experience of hunger. Experiments by other investigators, however, have shown conclusively that hunger "pangs" or contractions of the stomach are not essential to the craving for food, although they may be a part of the normal stimulus pattern. One experimenter,[6] for example, has reported

[6] F. Hoelzel, "Central Factors in Hunger," *Amer. J. Physiol.*, 32 (1927), 665–671.

the case of a human patient whose stomach was removed surgically and whose esophagus and intestine were connected. The patient reported a periodic desire for food which is characteristic of normal persons. Experiments with rats are even more revealing. A number of experiments were performed with rats whose stomachs had been removed.[7] These rats were as hungry as normal rats and, like normal rats, they showed great activity around feeding time. They also got as high scores as normal rats in the obstruction box when hunger was used as the drive to be tested. (The obstruction box is a device used for measuring strength of drive in animals and is described in Chapter VIII.) Other experiments with rats show that when the sensory nerves that normally conduct impulses from the stomach to the brain are severed, the animals show normal behavior in respect to eating. Strength of hunger drive as measured by the obstruction box was no different from that of normal rats. Rate of learning in the rats without stomachs was not different from that of normal animals even when food was used as the incentive to learning. It seems probable, in the light of the above experiments and other observations, that the main stimulus for hunger is a chemical substance and that this chemical normally produces contractions in the stomach muscle. The absence of the stomach, however, does not seem to interfere with the other phenomena normally associated with hunger.

B. Thirst

We do not know the physiological basis for thirst, although a great deal of experimentation has been carried on in the attempt to determine it. According to Cannon, thirst is stimulated by dryness of the mucous membrane of the tongue, mouth, and throat. Cannon was able to demonstrate experimentally that the sensation of thirst is alleviated by moistening the mouth without necessarily taking liquid into the digestive system. The conscious experience of thirst, he found, disappeared when the surfaces of the mouth and throat were made insensitive to the stimulus of dryness by the injection of cocaine. Thirst was also reduced by chewing gum which stimulates secretion of the salivary glands.

[7] Y. C. Tsang, "Hunger Motivation in Gastrectomized Rats," *J. Comp. Psychol.*, 26 (1939), 1–17.

RECEPTORS, SENSORY EXPERIENCE, EFFECTORS

Although the conscious experience of thirst may in part depend upon dryness of the throat, this conscious experience does not regulate the water intake of the body. A number of experiments show that in the absence of any local stimulation of the mouth or throat, animals will regulate their water intake with a high degree of accuracy in relation to their tissue needs. It is possible that a change in water content or other condition of the blood may affect the nervous system in such a way as to regulate the intake of water.

Organic sensations are important psychologically because of the role they play in the motivation of behavior. The relation of physiological states to motivation is discussed more completely in Chapter VII.

X. THE SENSES: THEIR TREATMENT IN CONTEMPORARY PSYCHOLOGY AND IN THE TRADITIONAL PHILOSOPHY

In contemporary psychology the senses are classified on the basis of the location of their sense organs. In other words, they are classified as exteroceptive, interoceptive, or proprioceptive, depending upon the location of their receptors. In the traditional psychology of Aristotle and St. Thomas, however, senses are classified under two headings: (1) external senses and (2) internal senses. This latter classification is made upon a different principle from that of contemporary psychology. Therefore, the external senses recognized by the philosopher cannot be equated with the exteroceptive senses of the scientific psychologist. Nor can the internal senses recognized by the philosopher be equated with the interoceptive senses of the scientist. All of the senses discussed in this chapter, whether exteroceptive, interoceptive or proprioceptive, would be classified philosophically as external senses, since all of them have sense organs which come into direct contact with the material world.

The traditional philosophy recognizes four internal senses, namely: (1) the common sense, (2) imagination, (3) memory, and (4) estimative sense (in animals) or cogitative power (in human beings). These internal senses do not come into direct contact with the sensible world but must rely on the external senses for their knowledge of the external world. Their function is that of refining the knowledge presented by the external senses in such a way that it can be presented to the intellect. These four powers are classified as senses because they provide knowledge on a sense level of experience. Unlike the intellect, they do not give us a knowledge of universals; they give us knowledge only of particular things.

Aristotle and St. Thomas recognized only five external senses: vision, hearing, touch, smell, and taste. Today we know that there are twice as many. The recognition of more than five senses is the result of scientific knowledge which was not available to Aristotle or St. Thomas. These new findings, however, do not invalidate the "perennial philosophy" of St. Thomas since it is irrelevant to his system whether there be five or eleven sense organs.[8]

XI. THE EFFECTORS

The responding mechanisms of the human body are the muscles and glands. They are called effectors because they produce effects which change the individual's relations with the environment.

A. Muscles and Muscular Activity

Within the human body there are three kinds of muscles: (1) *striated* (striped, or skeletal), (2) *non-striated* (smooth), and (3) *cardiac* (heart muscle). The actions that we observe in people, such as walking, driving a car, threading a needle, or sawing a log, result from the functioning of the striated muscles. Be-

---

[8] As Rudolph Allers points out:

". . . We have at least eleven external senses. Their existence and differences are absolutely sure; we know that there are as many different end-organs, each of a different structure; we know from anatomical, experimental and clinical evidence that each of these senses sends impulses by different nervous pathways to different centers.

"Does this new conception of sensory organization impair in any way the psychology of St. Thomas? Not in the least. The Thomistic conception remains exactly the same whether there be five or eleven external senses. A refusal to accept the uncontrovertible evidence furnished by exact observation is as contrary to sound scientific methodology as it is indicative of an insufficient understanding of Thomistic philosophy."—Rudolph Allers, "The Integration of Psychology and Philosophy," Workshop on Catholic College Integration (Washington, D.C., Catholic University of America, June 15, 1949), 22–23. Mimeographed.

cause these muscles are typically attached to bones, they are called "skeletal" muscles. The bones of the skeleton are arranged in a series of levers. The action of the muscles attached to these bones manipulates these levers in such a way as to change the position, posture, or movements of the body. The striated muscles can be manipulated at will, although they also function reflexly or involuntarily. Muscular activity consists of *contraction* (tensing or shortening) or *relaxation* (relaxing or lengthening). Muscles are never completely relaxed in a healthy organism but are in a partial state of contraction known as *tonus*. Individual differences in the posture and general bodily tension that people exhibit is related to the degree of tonus characteristically present in their skeletal muscles. When a nerve impulse reaches a striated muscle the muscle does not contract immediately. It does so only after a short interval known as the "latent" period. After that, the muscle begins contracting at first slowly, then rapidly, then slowly again, until it finally relaxes. The energy changes produced in a muscle as a result of a nerve impulse are known as the *innervation* of that muscle.

Motor abilities and skills depend upon the activities of the skeletal muscles, and particularly upon their coördinated or teamwork activity. Individual differences in precision, speed, and strength of muscular activity are of great psychological significance. In childhood, adolescence, and to a lesser degree in maturity, status in the group is based upon the ability to excel in (or at least to hold one's own in) motor activities such as athletics or dancing. In maturity these motor abilities are also important in making occupational adjustments.

Non-striated (smooth) muscles are located in the hollow viscera of the body (veins, arteries, stomach, intestines, urinary and genital passages, bronchial tubes), in the iris and ciliary muscles of the eye, and attached to the roots of hair. In general their function is that of maintaining vegetative processes of the body, although they also play an important role in emotional responses. Non-striated muscles, unlike the striated muscles, are not ordinarily under voluntary control. Their action is slower than that of the striated muscles.

The *cardiac* muscle is in a class by itself. It is striated in appearance but it is not under voluntary control. Its periodic contractions and relaxations (systoles and diastoles) are not dependent upon the activity of nerve impulses. For example, the cardiac muscle of a frog or chicken, if cut out and placed in a suitable physiological salt solution, will continue to "beat" for days and sometimes for weeks. Heart activity, however, may be increased or inhibited by nerve impulses from the autonomic nervous system.

B. Glands and Glandular Activity

Glands are made up of cells which are specialized for the function of secreting or excreting. They take certain substances from the blood stream and isolate them or use them for manufacturing a new substance. These substances are then delivered to other tissues of the body. If the gland is a *duct gland* it will pour its secretion onto the surface of the body or into some body cavity. If it is a *ductless* or *endocrine* gland it will pour its secretion directly into the blood or lymph stream. The endocrine glands are much more closely related to psychological processes than are the duct glands. When a gland oversecretes it is said to be hyperfunctioning; when it undersecretes it is said to be hypofunctioning.

The secretions of endocrine glands are called *hormones* or *autacoids*. They are carried by the blood stream to all parts of the body where they have an effect upon other tissues including nervous centers. The secretion of any one of these glands is dependent upon the functioning of the others, and a malfunctioning of one may result in a malfunction of all or some of the others. The location of the endocrine glands is shown in Figure 20. We shall discuss the functions of the thyroid, pituitary, adrenal, pineal, and the gonads or sex glands.

1. *Thyroid gland.* The thyroid gland, located in the base of the neck, secretes a hormone called thyroxin. About 60 per cent of this hormone is iodine; and if there is not enough iodine in the diet, a thyroid deficiency results. The thyroid hormone regulates the metabolism of the body. Too much thyroxin speeds up metabolism and leads to hyperactivity and irritability. Too little thyroxin slows down metabolism and leads to sluggishness and inertia. The energy output of an individual is, to a considerable extent, under the control of the thyroid gland.

2. *Pituitary gland.* The pituitary gland, located in the center of the head, is composed of two parts, a posterior and an anterior

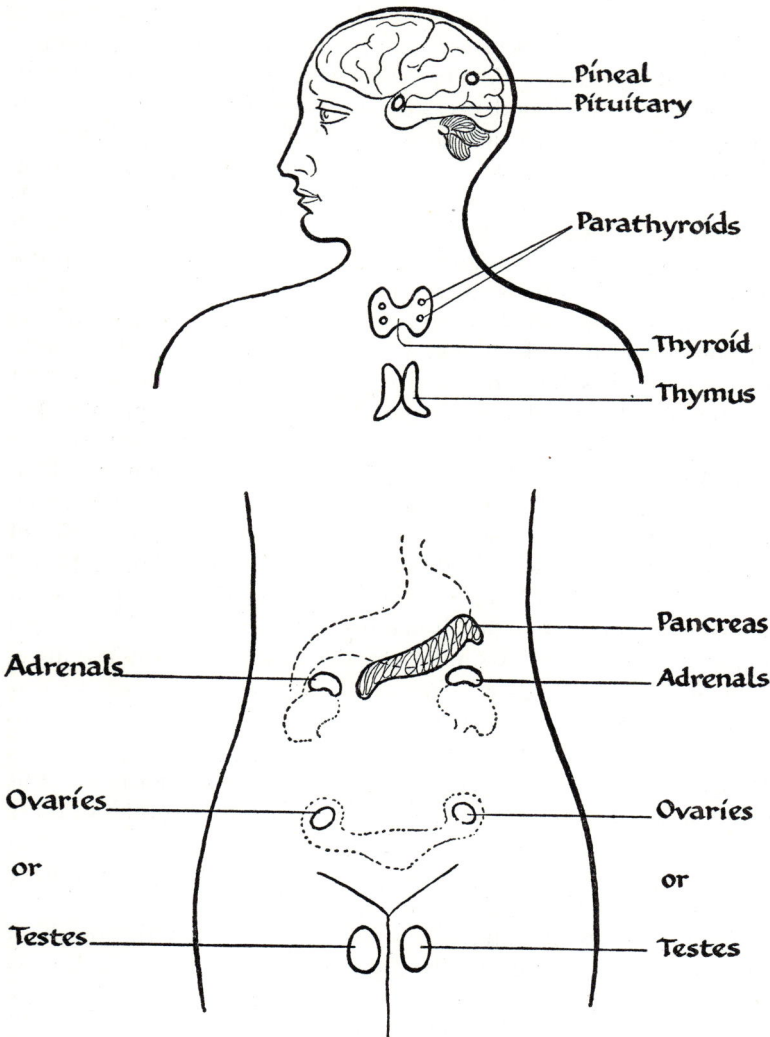

Fig. 20. Location of the Endocrine Glands.

lobe. The posterior lobe plays a part in the tonicity of the smooth muscles, and for this reason it can be used clinically for contracting the uterus after a delivery. When the secretions of this lobe are deficient, the blood pressure is extremely low and the kidneys excrete excessive amounts of water. In some of the lower animals, striking changes in skin color have been produced by injecting extracts of the posterior lobe.

Two important hormones of the anterior lobe are the growth hormone and the sex-regulating hormone. A deficiency of the anterior lobe secretions results in (1) failure to grow normally, (2) a lack of sexual development, and (3) a deficiency of the thyroid, adrenal, and sex glands. Recently, a great deal of medical research has been devoted to the pituitary hormone ACTH (adreno-cortico-trophic hormone). This hormone stimulates the cortex of the adrenal gland to manufacture hormones, one of which is cortisone. Research on ACTH and cortisone is still in its early stages, but it holds great promise of throwing light on mental disease and reactions to physical and mental stress of various kinds. Studies of fatigue and stress made during World War II showed that normally the body responds to stress by increasing its production of adrenalin—a hormone from the medulla of the adrenal gland. A similar reaction is produced by the injection of ACTH. There is some evidence that in the mental disease known as schizophrenia, this stress mechanism is absent. Although schizophrenic patients have, under ordinary circumstances, a normal amount of cortical adrenal hormone, this amount is not increased in a stress situation. Other studies of these hormones suggest that the whole idea of distinct compartmentalized diseases, which is prevalent in medicine today, may have to be relaxed if not abandoned.

Abnormalities of human development are often the result of very slight imbalances of glandular secretions. There is, for example, a very close relationship between the growth hormone and the sex hormone. Evans was able to speed up sexual development by implanting anterior pituitary grafts. When he gave the growth hormone at the same time, however, this accelerating effect was prevented. Acromegalic women, that is, women suffering from pituitary oversecretion, usually fail to menstruate and generally lose capacity for sex desire.

3. *Adrenal glands.* The adrenal glands are located on the tops

of the kidneys. They each consist of two principal parts: (1) the outer (adrenal cortex) and (2) the inner (adrenal medulla). The hormone produced by the medulla is called *adrenalin* (epinephrine) and the chief hormone produced by the cortex is known as *cortin*. Adrenalin plays an important part in initiating and sustaining strong emotions of anger and fear. The cortex produces several chemically distinct hormones. Besides cortin, it produces small amounts of androgenic hormones, the physiological effects of which are similar to those of the sex glands. A tumor on the adrenal gland or an excessive amount of the cortical hormones will lead to a reversal of certain secondary sex characteristics in the adult woman. It may, for example, result in a deep masculine voice and the growth of a beard. Cortin, among other functions, controls the sodium and water content of the body. A deficiency of this hormone will cause dehydration and lessen normal nervous excitability, and is accompanied by exhaustion and depression. A marked deficiency will lead to coma and death.

4. *Pineal gland.* The pineal gland is located near the base of the brain. Not much is known about its effects upon behavior and personality. Descartes held, erroneously of course, that the soul had its bodily seat in this gland.

5. *Gonads.* The primary function of the sex glands is the development of the reproductive cells. But in their secondary or hormonal function they influence the secondary sex characteristics, and are responsible for the strength of the sex drive. The male sex hormone is secreted in the *testes;* the female hormones are secreted by the *ovaries.* Male hormones are called *androgens,* and the androgen of most psychological significance is *testosterone.* Female hormones are called *estrogens.* Two of the most important ovarian hormones are *theelin* and *progestin.* Theelin is secreted constantly until the menopause; progestin is secreted periodically. Theelin brings about the development of the primary and secondary sex characteristics in the female. Progestin regulates the menstrual cycle.

It is of great psychological importance to note that androgens and estrogens are secreted by the glands of both men and women. The difference between masculinity and femininity is not absolute, therefore. The masculinity or femininity of a given individual of either sex depends primarily on the nature of the chromosomes that unite to form the zygote, but the relative amounts or strengths of androgens and estrogens produced by the endocrine glands influence the strength of the sex trends of a person. Masculine women and feminine men may have more than the average amount of the hormone of the opposite sex. During the life cycle the relative amounts of these hormones often change, and a corresponding change in personality characteristics can be noted. The male temperament of youth and early adulthood, for instance, is usually more masculine than that of later maturity and old age.

SUGGESTED READING

BORING, E. G. (ed.), *Psychology for the Armed Services* (Washington, D.C., The Infantry Journal, 1945), Chapters I–VII.

VII

The Human Organism: The Nervous System

> . . . ev'n so did nature's hand
> To certain species of external things,
> Attune the finer organs of the mind:
> So the glad impulse of congenial pow'rs,
> Or of sweet sound, of fair-proportion'd form.
> The grace of motion, or the bloom of light,
> Thrills thro' imagination's tender frame,
> From nerve to nerve: all naked and alive
> They catch the spreading rays: till now the soul
> At length discloses every tuneful spring,
> To that harmonious movement from without,
> Responsive.
> —AKENSIDE [1]

In the previous chapter we demonstrated that much of human activity can be traced to stimuli that act on the organism either from within or from without. That is why we call the activities of the organism *responses*, although, strictly speaking, not all activities are responses. A stimulus must be of sufficient intensity and duration to bring about a response in a sense organ. A stimulus which is just barely intense enough to arouse a sense organ is called a *threshold* or *liminal stimulus*. Below this intensity it is called a *subliminal stimulus*.

Sense organs, such as the eye or ear, have complicated accessory structures as well as receptors for their particular kind of stimuli. The essential part of a sense organ, as we explained in Chapter VI, is its *receptor*. Each receptor has nerve fibers attached to it which connect it with the centers in the nervous system. Activity in the receptor causes a discharge of nerve impulses in these at-

[1] Akenside, *Pleasures of Imagination*, I, 113–123. Quoted by Marjorie Hope Nicolson, in *Newton Demands the Muse* (Princeton, N.J., Princeton University Press, 1946), p. 87.

tached fibers. These nerve impulses travel to nerve centers in the spinal cord or brain, and ultimately out to a muscle or gland. As a result, the muscle contracts or relaxes and the gland increases or decreases its secretion.

I. NERVOUS TISSUE

The essential part of the nervous system is a special kind of tissue that conducts nerve impulses when it is excited or irritated. It consists of billions of tiny neurons, each of which is a functionally active cell, and these are supported and nourished by neuroglia cells, which are functionally inactive so far as conduction is concerned. The *neuron* is an individual nerve cell body with thread-like branches which extend from it, as shown in Figure 21. Nerve cells vary greatly in size; the largest ones are just barely visible to the naked eye; the smallest ones are no larger than a red blood corpuscle and have a diameter of only about .005 millimeters.

The thread-like branches which extend out from the nerve cell body are of two kinds: dendrites and axons. Dendrites carry nerve impulses *toward* the cell body; axons carry impulses *away* from the cell body. Although the majority of neurons are minute in

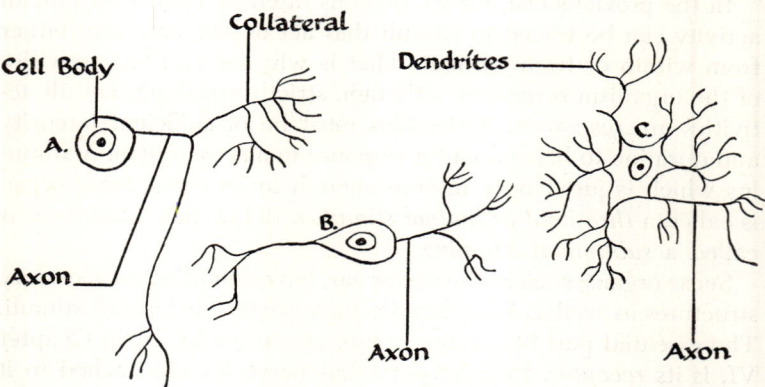

A. Unipolar Neuron
B. Bipolar Neuron
C. Multipolar Neuron

Fig. 21. Typical Neurons.

THE HUMAN ORGANISM: NERVOUS SYSTEM

size and have short branches, the longest neurons have dendrites extending from the toe to the cell bodies located in the rootlets of the spinal nerves in the person's back. The dendrites of such neurons may be more than a yard in length. The axons of some of these neurons extend without interruption to the medulla oblongata at the base of the brain.

The neurons themselves are gray, although many of their axons are surrounded by a white layer of fat known as the *myelin sheath*. For this reason it is possible to refer to cell bodies and dendrites as *gray matter* and to axon fibers as *white matter*. Most of the neuron cell bodies lie in the brain or the spinal cord. (A smaller number lie near it, and these have special functions.)

There is almost no correlation between the size of the brain and measured intelligence. This fact is not surprising when we consider that the brain is made up not of neurons alone but also of neuroglia cells, blood vessels, and a small amount of connective tissue associated with the blood vessels. No one knows exactly what the relative space occupied by nerve cells and neuroglia cells is. But some psychologists have suggested that defective intelligence may at times result from a lack of proper balance between neurons and neuroglia cells. In fact, this is the common explanation given of the clinical type of feeblemindedness known as *macrocephaly*, described in Chapter XV, in which the dominant symptom is an enlarged head.

Neuron cells do not multiply after birth. If a neuron in the brain is destroyed, it will be replaced by neuroglia cells rather than by nerve cells. If neuron fibers in the brain or spinal cord are destroyed they will not regenerate either. Injured nerve fibers outside of the brain and spinal cord, however, may regenerate under proper conditions. These fibers are part of the "peripheral nervous system" which brings impulses to and relays them outward again from the central nervous system.

Neurons of the peripheral nervous system that carry nerve impulses from the sense organ to a nerve center (spinal cord or brain) are called *sensory* or *afferent*. Those which carry impulses from the nerve center to muscles or glands are called *motor* or *efferent*. Neurons within the spinal cord or brain which provide connections between sensory and motor neurons are known as *association* or *connecting* neurons. They also make connections with other association neurons.

II. NERVES

A *nerve* is a cable or bundle of nerve fibers bound together with connective tissue and serving a particular function; it does not contain nerve cell bodies. A nerve that conducts impulses from the periphery into the nerve center is a sensory or afferent nerve. A nerve that conducts impulses from the nerve center to the periphery is a motor or efferent nerve. Nerves which contain both sensory and motor fibers are *mixed nerves*. Most nerves are mixed. For example, a nerve that activates a large muscle may have about 60 per cent motor fibers and 40 per cent sensory fibers. The sensory fibers of such a nerve conduct impulses from the kinesthetic sense organs located in the muscles and tendons.

III. THE NERVE IMPULSE

The exact nature of the nerve impulse is unknown, although we can measure it, like electricity, with a high degree of accuracy. The nerve impulse is usually described as an electrochemical wave motion traveling along a nerve fiber.

Any stimulus capable of arousing a nerve fiber to conduct at all causes it to conduct to its maximum extent. This is known as the *all-or-none law* of nervous activity. The nerve fiber may be compared in this respect to a firecracker. It makes no difference whether the fuse of the firecracker is lit by a great torch or by a tiny match. The explosion is the same in each case. The strength of the explosion results from the powder within the firecracker and not from the strength of the stimulus that sets it off.

Because neurons do not discharge beyond their capacity it is not possible for nerves to become fatigued. The explanation of so-called "nervous fatigue" must, so far as we now know, be sought elsewhere.

IV. THE SYNAPSE

The point of junction between the axon of one neuron and the dendrites of another is a very tiny space known as the *synapse*. The nerve impulse appears to be slowed down as it "bridges" this gap. Exactly what happens to a nerve impulse when it reaches a synapse is not known. Two theories commonly advanced to

THE HUMAN ORGANISM: NERVOUS SYSTEM 163

explain what happens are (1) the humoral theory and (2) the electrical theory. According to the *humoral theory*, when the nerve impulse reaches the end of an axon it causes a chemical substance to be produced. As soon as this substance reaches a high enough concentration in the synapse, it stimulates the dendrites of the next neuron so that a nerve impulse is aroused in it. According to the *electrical theory*, the nerve impulse from one neuron directly stimulates the adjacent neuron just as a sufficiently strong electrical current will jump across a gap between two wires even though the two pieces of wire are in no way connected. Nerve impulses travel across a synapse in only one direction—from the axon of one neuron to the dendrites of another.

A nerve impulse of relatively low intensity will not of itself cross the synapse and activate the dendrites of the adjacent neuron. But if a number of impulses from different fibers converge on the same synapse their combined intensity will enable them to cross. This phenomenon is called *spatial summation*. Similarly, when a given impulse is too weak of itself to bridge the gap, a succession of nerve impulses in the same fiber will often be able to do so. This phenomenon is called *temporal summation*.

V. OVERVIEW OF THE NERVOUS SYSTEM

The nervous system is the chief integrator of the behavior of the total organism. The nervous system as a whole may be classified according to two different principles: (1) anatomically, as (*a*) the central nervous system, and (*b*) the peripheral nervous system; and (2) functionally, as (*a*) the somatic nervous system, or (*b*) the autonomic nervous system. The *central nervous system* is comprised of the brain and spinal cord. The *peripheral nervous system* includes all of the nerve cells and fibers outside of the brain and spinal cord. The *somatic nervous system* includes chiefly those parts of the central system which are concerned with reporting sense data from the outside world and transmitting impulses to the striated or skeletal muscles. The *autonomic nervous system*, on the other hand, includes chiefly those nerves of the peripheral system which regulate the motor activities of the viscera, blood vessels, and glands.

VI. THE CENTRAL SOMATIC NERVOUS SYSTEM

The central nervous system may be regarded as a somatic nervous system since it is primarily concerned with the relation between the organism and the external world. It is composed of the brain and spinal cord and is pictured schematically in Figure 22. Both the brain and spinal cord are relatively "soft" substances and are protected from injury by being encased in bony structures. The brain is encased within the *cranium* which is composed of

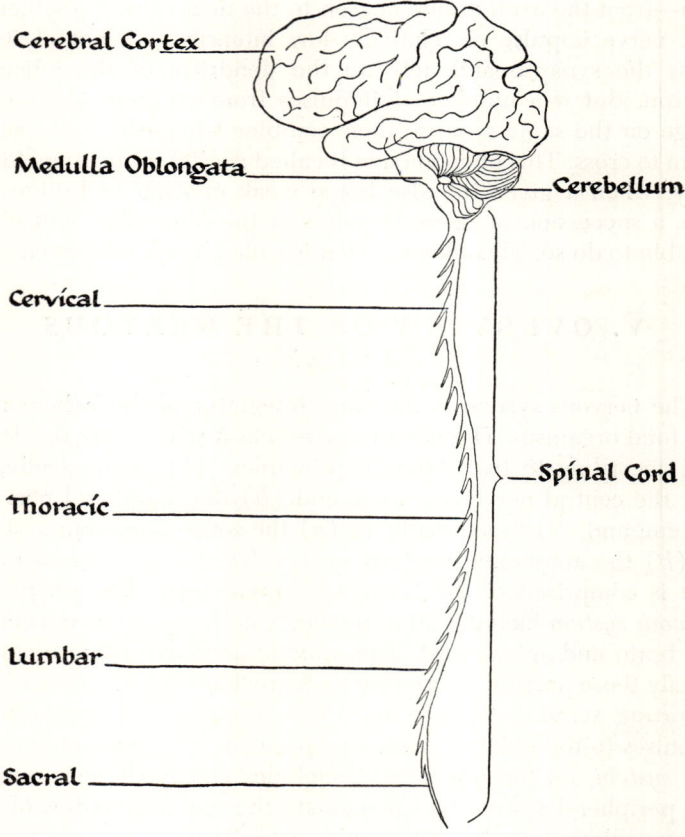

Fig. 22. Schematic Diagram of the Central Somatic Nervous System.

THE HUMAN ORGANISM: NERVOUS SYSTEM

eight bones connected together. The spinal cord is encased within the spinal column, a column made up of 33 bony segments known as *vertebrae*.

A. The Brain

The brain is the most important center of integration in the nervous system. Its three main anatomical structures are (1) the cerebrum, (2) the cerebellum, and (3) the brain stem.

1. The cerebrum

a. Anatomy of the cerebrum. The cerebrum is the largest mass of nervous tissue in the human brain. It is the only part of the brain that is visible when viewed from the top. The cerebrum is divided into two symmetrical sections by means of a deep crevice known as the *great longitudinal fissure*. These sections are called *cerebral hemispheres,* and one is the mirror image of the other. The outer portion of each cerebral hemisphere, known as the *cerebral cortex,* is made up of gray matter and in man this part of the cerebrum constitutes about one-half of the entire weight of the nervous system. The gray matter of the cortex is not a smooth surface but has many convolutions or folds. Each groove or crevice formed between two of these convolutions goes by the name of *sulcus* or, if large, *fissure,* and each ridge between two such grooves is called a *gyrus*.

Beneath the cortex each cerebral hemisphere contains white matter made up of nerve fibers which connect the cortex with lower parts of the brain. Beneath the cerebrum one hemisphere is connected with the other by a tract of fibers known as the *corpus callosum*.

Three kinds of nerve fibers are found in the brain: (1) *projection fibers,* (2) *association fibers,* and (3) *commissural fibers*. *Projection fibers* connect the cerebral hemispheres with the rest of the nervous system. *Association fibers* connect one area with another in the same hemisphere, and *commissural fibers* connect one hemisphere with another by means of the *corpus callosum.*

b. Lobes and areas of the cortex. The cortex is roughly divided into four lobes. A schematic diagram of the left hemisphere of the cerebral cortex is shown in Figure 23, and the four lobes can be distinguished on this diagram. The *frontal lobe* is the most anterior lobe. It is separated from the *parietal lobe* by the *fissure*

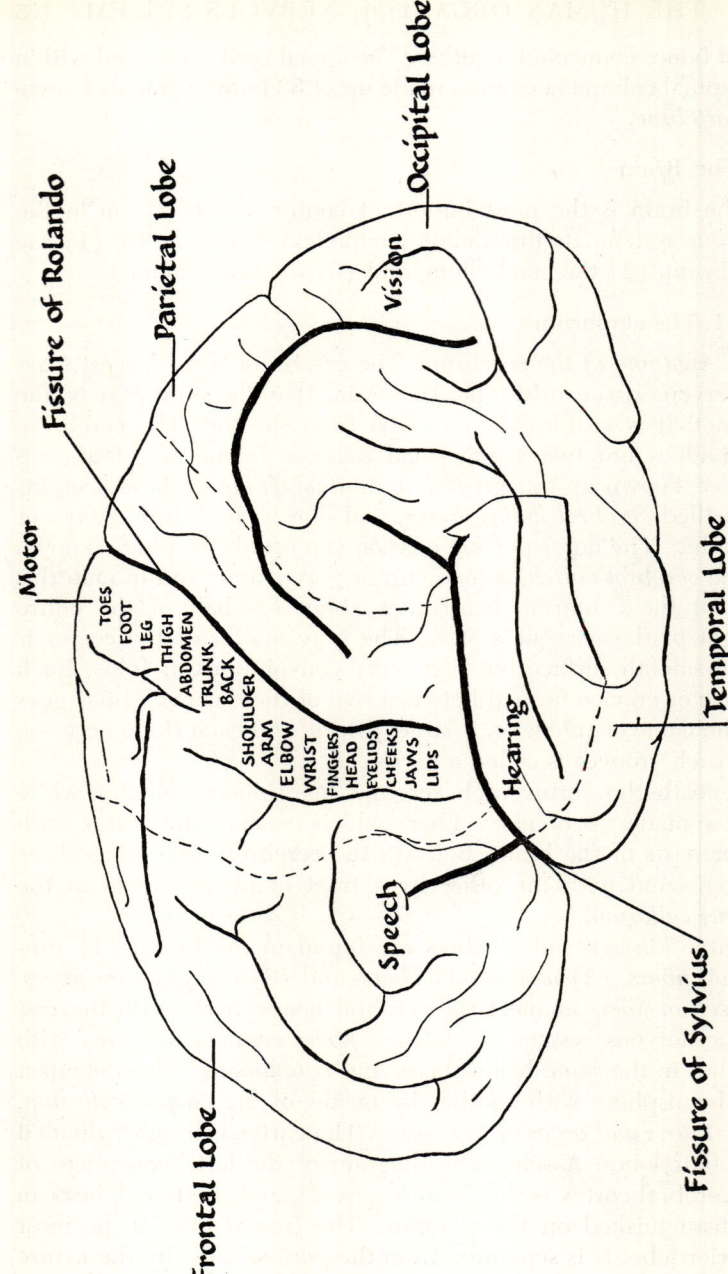

Fig. 23. Schematic Diagram of the Left Hemisphere of the Cerebral Cortex.

THE HUMAN ORGANISM: NERVOUS SYSTEM 167

of *Rolando* and from the *temporal lobe* by the *fissure of Sylvius*. The motor area, the motor speech area, and various association areas are contained in the frontal lobe. The parietal lobe contains the somesthetic area, in which the senses of pressure, heat, cold, and pain are localized, and the temporal lobe contains the center for hearing. The *occipital lobe* is the most posterior part of the cortex. It contains the visual area.

Although we usually refer to localization of senses in the brain, it is not strictly correct to do so. The senses are *functions,* and in order to function, the soul must be vivifying the body. In a dead body there are eyes but there is no sense of sight. Consequently, reference to the sense of pain as localized or located in the brain must be understood as meaning that a certain brain area mediates the sensation. The term *localization* on this and the following pages is understood to be used with this qualification.

c. Methods of studying the brain. The relation of the brain to behavior and the localization of function in the cortex has been studied by five methods: (1) the removal (technically, extirpation) of nervous tissue in animals (under anesthetic) followed by an analysis of the effect this operation has on the animal's behavior, (2) the comparison of human behavior before and after a brain operation, (3) post-mortem studies (autopsies) of the brains of people whose behavior had been abnormal, (4) the tracing of nerve fibers, and (5) direct stimulation of the cerebral cortex by electrical stimulation. More recently, a sixth method has been introduced, the method of studying electroencephalograms or "brain waves."

(1) *Extirpation studies.* The most significant pioneer experiments on animals by means of the extirpation method were made by Franz and Lashley. Franz taught cats to escape from puzzle boxes, after which he anesthetized the animals and severed their frontal lobes from the rest of their brains, thus preventing the functioning of these lobes. (He did not, however, remove the severed frontal lobes from the skull.) As soon as the animals had recovered from the operation, they were put into puzzle boxes from which they had previously learned to escape. None of them had retained the habit of escape. Franz found by performing similar operations on monkeys that they, too, lost their recently acquired habits.

Later experiments by Franz showed that when only one frontal lobe was severed the animal did not lose the recently acquired habit, although he was slower in its performance than before the operation. When both parietal lobes were severed the habits were unaffected. Highly trained habits of less recent origin functioned almost as perfectly after the operation as before. Cats trained for the first time after their frontal lobes were severed learned the escape habit as well as normal cats.

Lashley studied the effect of brain destruction upon habits [2] of brightness discrimination and motor behavior, such as running a maze. He found that the habit of brightness discrimination was retained even when a considerable portion of the animal's cortex had been destroyed. The loss of maze learning habits was not dependent upon the specific part of the brain destroyed but upon the extent of the injury. Lashley concluded that learned acts are not located specifically in definite brain areas or nervous pathways, but that the functioning involves large sections of the brain. When one part of the brain is injured, apparently other parts of the brain take over its functions. Lashley thus spoke of the *vicarious functioning* of brain areas and of the "equipotentiality" of different brain areas to produce the same behavior.

The reëducation of human beings whose brains have been partially injured shows that they can, with persistent effort, relearn lost habits. Since brain tissue does not regenerate, this fact would seem to indicate that other parts of the brain take over the functions of the diseased portions and that "equipotentiality" is characteristic of human as well as of animal brain tissue.

Other extirpation studies have been designed to determine the effect of extirpation upon learning of certain kinds for the first time. One investigator, for example, removed the entire cerebrum

[2] Contemporary psychologists use the term *habit* to designate learning in both animals and human beings. This use of the term may be confusing to a student who is acquainted only with the use of the term in the traditional philosophy of St. Thomas Aquinas. St. Thomas limits the use of the term *habit* to human learning, and in doing so he stresses the role of reason in the acquisition of habits. The intellectual virtues (knowledge, understanding, wisdom, art, and prudence) are referred to as "habits" of intellect; the moral virtues (justice, temperance, fortitude) are "habits" of the will. Obviously, the word *habit* in this connection means something different from the same word used in describing a maze learning "habit" in a rat.

In keeping with the general aim of this book to provide material for a synthesis of science and philosophy in the study of man, a section has been inserted in Chapter IX which clarifies the use of the term *habit* in the two disciplines.

of a dog to see what effect this removal would have upon the learning of a conditioned response to sound. Another destroyed different parts of the frontal lobe and studied the effects of such lesions upon learning of different degrees of complexity, such as discrimination problems and delayed reactions.

(2) *Brain operations.* The study of human behavior before and after a brain operation may be compared to the extirpation method used with animals. Several investigators have found that large portions of the frontal lobes can be removed without a disturbance of mental functioning. One brain surgeon, in fact, operated on a woman in her early thirties who suffered from failing vision, headache, a general weakness of the left side of the body, and convulsive seizures. He found that the removal of the entire right hemisphere of the brain, while it relieved her abnormal symptoms, did not impair her normal mental functioning in any noticeable way. Twenty months after the operation he was able to describe her as follows:

> The patient walked quite well without support. She was able to go up and down stairs without aid. She stated that she frequently went shopping and that her endurance was good. About her home she was able to assist with the cleaning. She washed dishes and clothes in spite of the fact that the left arm was useless. Relatives and friends could discern no alteration in her personality or intellectual abilities.[3]

(3) *Post-mortem studies (autopsies).* Autopsies have also yielded valuable information about the localization of cortical function. After death the brain of an individual who has exhibited abnormalities of behavior is examined for destructive lesions and degeneration of nerve fibers. After a number of such studies has been made, generalizations concerning the correlation of nerve degeneration and behavior anomalies can be drawn up. As long ago as 1861, Broca made an autopsy of the brain of a patient who had suffered an almost complete loss of speech. Broca's patient could communicate by means of gestures and signs but could not talk. Moreover, he had control over the various muscles which control the speech mechanism and appeared to be intelligent enough to talk. When Broca performed an autopsy on this man he found that a portion of the frontal lobe was destroyed just above the fissure of Sylvius. Broca concluded that this portion of

[3] W. J. Gardner, "Removal of the Right Cerebral Hemisphere for Infiltration Glioma," *J. Amer. Med. Assoc.,* 101 (1933), 825.

the cerebral cortex is the center for speech. Subsequent studies of other persons suffering from disturbances of speech and having similar brain degeneration have tended to confirm Broca's conclusion that the left hemisphere contains a speech area. This area, pictured in Figure 23, is known as Broca's area. Following Broca, Wernicke discovered that destruction of a portion of the temporal lobe was associated with the inability to understand spoken language. This portion of the brain is known as Wernicke's center or the auditory area, and is pictured diagrammatically in Figure 23.

(4) *Tracing of nerve fibers.* By tracing the nerve fibers which extend from different parts of the cortex to various muscles, we discover the parts of the brain which act as higher motor centers for each muscle or muscle group. If the nerve fibers are healthy, it is very difficult to trace them. If, however, the nerve fibers are severed from their cells, the nerve fibers degenerate. When cross-sections of a degenerate nerve fiber are placed on a microscope slide and stained, the degenerate fiber stands out clearly from the rest of the cell. By using a series of cross-sections, the path of the fibers can easily be traced.

(5) *Electrical stimulation.* Human beings as well as animals have been studied by the method of electrical stimulation. During a brain operation when the brain is exposed, a weak electrical current can be applied without injury to the patient. When the motor area of the frontal lobe is thus stimulated, a muscle or group of muscles will twitch. The particular location of the muscles thus affected depends upon the portion of the motor area stimulated, as indicated in Figure 23. Sometimes the surgeon carries on a conversation with the patient during the stimulation and gets further information from the patient's introspective reports.

(6) *Electroencephalography.* Brain cells, as we have already noted, are continually active even in the absence of external stimulation. This activity is accompanied by electrical changes. The electrical changes taking place during brain activity can be recorded by means of an electroencephalograph and the resulting record is known as an electroencephalogram or, more simply, the EEG. "Brain waves" recorded in this way vary from person to person, although there are certain characteristics common to all people under given circumstances. During sleep, for example, and while under the influence of a general anesthetic, the brain waves

THE HUMAN ORGANISM: NERVOUS SYSTEM 171

are large and slow. During alert activity and during excitement, on the contrary, the waves are relatively small and rapid. At as early an age as three months, a brain wave pattern characteristic of the individual is established and from that time on it is never lost. The frequency of brain waves increases rapidly during the first year of life and then increases more and more slowly until about the age of 12 at which the adult level is reached.

The psychological significance of brain wave patterns is not too clear, but certain interesting facts have been established. The pattern of waves is highly consistent for a given individual. Brain wave patterns of identical twins are as similar as other physiological and anatomical characteristics. There is a high degree of similarity for members of the same family. People who have epilepsy have a characteristic pattern of brain waves, a pattern which is present even before the first epileptic attack has taken place. Epilepsy can usually, therefore, be diagnosed by means of the EEG. "Brain waves" are illustrated in Figure 24.

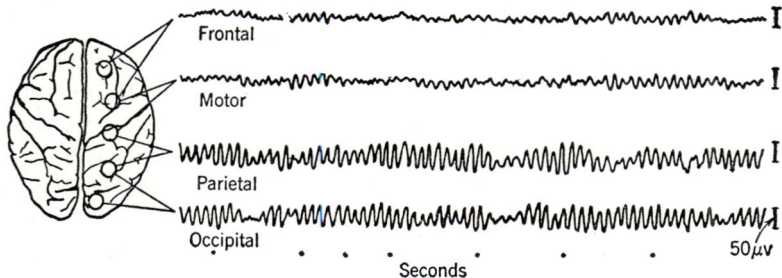

Fig. 24. Electroencephalographic Tracings from a Normal Subject. [Reproduced by permission from *Methods of Psychology*, T. G. Andrews, ed. (New York, John Wiley & Sons, Inc., 1948), p. 448.]

d. Localization of function in the cortex. The human cortex has areas that are specialized for certain functions. The psychologist is interested especially in the following areas:

(1) *The motor area.* The motor area is in front of the fissure of Rolando in the frontal lobe. This is the center for voluntary muscular action. Destruction of tissues in this region of the brain leads to a more or less widespread paralysis of movement. The motor area contains large nerve cells that are shaped like pyramids, and consequently these cells have been labeled *pyramidal cells.* The axons of these cells cross to the opposite side of the body

in that region of the brain stem known as the medulla oblongata. Because of this crossing, the left hemisphere controls the voluntary movements of the right side of the body and the right hemisphere controls the left.

(2) *The speech area.* The motor speech area is in the lower portion of the frontal lobe, just above the fissure of Sylvius. Unlike other areas of the brain it is found in only one hemisphere—usually in the left. In left-handed persons it is commonly found in the right hemisphere.

(3) *The auditory area.* The auditory area is located on the top convolution of the temporal lobe, and mediates sensations of hearing.

(4) *The visual area.* The visual area is at the back of the brain in the occipital lobe. When this area is destroyed in both hemispheres, complete blindness results.

(5) *The somesthetic area.* The somesthetic area or body sense area registers sensations of both the muscle (kinesthetic or proprioceptive) and the skin senses—touch, pressure, warmth, and cold. It is located in the anterior portion of the parietal lobe.

(6) *The olfactory and gustatory areas.* The olfactory area appears to be located just beneath the temporal lobe, and is the center for sensations of smell. The gustatory area, most investigators believe, is located close to the olfactory area. However, there is some evidence that taste is a highly developed kind of touch sensation, and that its center is near the somesthetic area where sensations from the tongue are registered.

(7) *The association areas.* In a sense, the whole brain is at work during complex mental activity, and no one area can be distinguished as the association area. A lesion of the association areas in the frontal lobe may change the activity level of the organism so affected, usually increasing locomotion considerably. These findings suggest that one function of these areas is the inhibition of motor activity. When these areas are injured or destroyed to any great extent, marked changes in personality and behavior may occur.

e. Cerebral dominance. In most people, during the course of development, one of the two hemispheres of the brain becomes dominant over the other; that is, it develops more rapidly and more completely. The hemisphere which becomes dominant determines the "sidedness" of the body. Most of the sensory and motor nerve

THE HUMAN ORGANISM: NERVOUS SYSTEM 173

fibers cross before they reach the brain. Those from the right side of the body go to the left hemisphere of the brain and those from the left side go to the right hemisphere of the brain. An individual whose left hemisphere is dominant will therefore be right-handed; an individual whose right hemisphere is dominant will be left-handed. Cerebral dominance plays an important part in some theories of stuttering, reading difficulties, and left-handedness.

2. The cerebellum

The position of the cerebellum in relation to the cerebrum is shown in Figure 22. Like the cerebrum it consists of two hemispheres. Each is below its half of the cerebrum and behind the parts of the brain stem known as the pons and the medulla oblongata. It is concerned with equilibrium and the involuntary coördination of bodily movements.

3. The brain stem

The brain stem can be subdivided into several anatomical divisions, of which we will mention only the medulla oblongata, hypothalamus, and thalamus. In general, the brain stem is a distributing point for fibers connecting the brain and spinal cord, although it also has nerve centers of its own. The brain stem is responsible both for somatic and for autonomic functions, and cannot strictly be classified under the heading of "somatic" system.

The *medulla oblongata* is the bulb at the top of the spinal cord, and is just above the place where the first spinal nerve emerges. It is the lowest part of the brain stem and is about a little over an inch in length. It is the lowest part of the brain encased within the cranium. The medulla serves as a relay station for all nerve impulses passing from the brain to lower centers in the spinal cord and from the lower centers to the brain. It is also an important reflex center for many vital functions—respiration, heart beat, blood-pressure control, swallowing, and vomiting. The medulla is essential to life; and when it is injured, breathing and heart activity fail.

The *hypothalamus* is beneath and anterior to the thalamus. Activities regulated by the hypothalamus are also controlled by lower centers in the medulla and in the spinal cord. The hypothalamus, however, integrates these activities into patterns which adjust the internal environment of the organism. It regulates temperature control, endocrine secretion, blood pressure, and sexual functions. It plays a major role in the metabolism of fats, carbohydrates, and water. Psychologically, its most important center is that which controls emotional behavior.

The *thalamus* is the great relay station between the cerebral hemispheres and the lower centers of the brain and spinal cord. Its chief function is that of transmitting sensory impulses to the appropriate area of the cortex. Like the hypothalamus, it plays an important role in emotional reactions and expressions.

B. The Spinal Cord

The spinal cord is a tapering structure, continuous with the brain, and extending downward to a level slightly above the hips. It is enclosed in the bony case of the vertebral column in which it is surrounded by cerebrospinal fluid. Unlike its location in the brain, the gray matter of the spinal cord is in the center and the white matter outside. A cross-section of the spinal cord is shown in Figure 25. In this diagram you can see that the gray matter is arranged in the form of a winged butterfly figure, in the center of which is a small opening. This opening is the *central canal* and it contains *cerebrospinal fluid*. In cross-section the spinal cord is about one-half inch in diameter at its largest (upper) portion.

A spinal reflex is a response mediated by the spinal cord alone, without the coöperation of higher brain centers. Theoretically, the simplest response possible would involve only two neurons between the receptor and the effector, a sensory and a motor neuron. Actually, an association neuron intervenes between the sensory and the motor neuron, and probably no response is so simple as to involve only one sensory and one motor nerve fiber, though a hypothetical simple response, mediated by only one sensory and one motor fiber, is called a *reflex arc*. The actual knee jerk reflex, for example, involves the discharge of thousands of parallel nerve fibers. Characteristically, in a spinal reflex the nerve impulse travels from the receptor along the sensory nerve fibers to the dorsal portion of the spinal cord. The cell body for this sensory neuron is in a ganglion outside of the spinal cord. The impulse travels through the cell body in the spinal ganglion and out along the axon which enters the dorsal horn of the gray matter in the spinal cord. Here the sensory neuron comes into synaptic contact with the dendrites of an association or connecting neuron. The

THE HUMAN ORGANISM: NERVOUS SYSTEM

association neuron conducts the impulse to the ventral horn of the gray matter. Here the end-brush of the axon of the association neuron comes into synaptic contact with the dendrites of a motor neuron. The cell body of the motor neuron is in the ventral horn of the spinal gray matter. The impulse travels from the dendrites of the motor neuron through the cell body and out along the axon to a muscle which it activates.

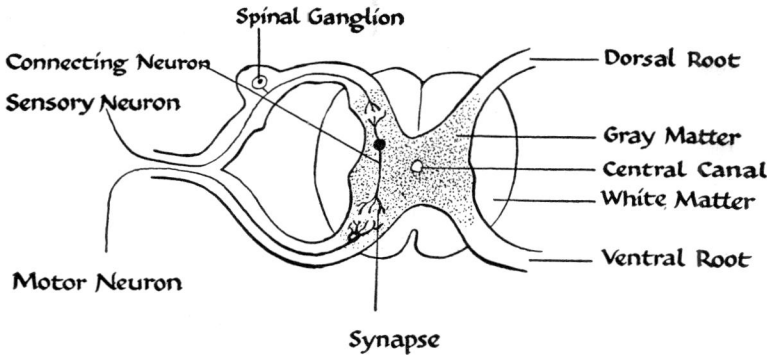

Fig. 25. Cross-section of the Spinal Cord.

In addition to this spinal reflex, connecting fibers within the spinal cord may carry the impulse to lower or higher centers of the brain. If the impulse reaches the cortex, the person may become aware of the stimulus and may exercise some voluntary control over his responses to it.

VII. THE PERIPHERAL SOMATIC NERVOUS SYSTEM

The peripheral portion of the somatic nervous system is composed of nerves and clusters of nerve cell bodies (ganglia) outside of the brain and spinal cord. The motor fibers of the peripheral system have their cell bodies inside the central nervous system, but the sensory fibers have their cell bodies in ganglia outside of the central nervous system. The nerves of the peripheral somatic system are classified as cranial or spinal, depending upon the part of the central nervous system from which they originate. In the human being there are 12 pairs of cranial nerves and 31 pairs of spinal nerves. The motor portions of the spinal nerves control the activity of the striated muscles of the arms, legs, and body, with the exception of head and neck. The sensory portions of the spinal nerves come from the different sense organs of the body and mediate sensitivity in most of the body except the face. The cranial nerves mediate these same functions in the head and neck.

VIII. THE AUTONOMIC NERVOUS SYSTEM

The autonomic nervous system plays an important part in that behavior through which emotional states are experienced and revealed. Structurally, it differs from the central nervous system in that its cell bodies and synapses are located not within the spinal cord, but in clusters outside of the spinal cord. These clusters of nerve cells are called *ganglia*, as shown in Figure 26. Most of the autonomic nerve cells are to be found in two columns of connected ganglia which run parallel to the spinal cord and slightly in front of it. Other cells are located near the organs they innervate.

The autonomic nervous system is divided into three main divisions: the cranial, the thoracico-lumbar, and the sacral, as shown in Figure 26. The thoracico-lumbar division is also known as the *sympathetic nervous system.* In general, the physiological processes activated by the sympathetic division are opposed to those activated by the parasympathetic, composed of the cranial and sacral divisions. For example, activation of the sympathetic system inhibits the peristaltic movements of the intestines, whereas activation of the parasympathetic system causes the peristaltic movements to function in the physiologically normal way.

By definition, the autonomic system is entirely motor. This does not mean, however, that no afferent nerve impulses are received from the visceral organs. Afferent fibers are mixed in with the autonomic fibers, but their roots are not in the autonomic ganglia but in the spinal cord. These afferent sensory fibers, like the other afferent fibers of the central nervous system, run into the dorsal horn of the spinal cord. Their cell bodies are in the spinal ganglia.

The processes mediated by the autonomic nervous system are not ordinarily under direct voluntary control.[4] These processes, however, are influenced by nerve impulses which come from the

---

[4] In Yoga, however, they often do come under voluntary control.

THE HUMAN ORGANISM: NERVOUS SYSTEM 177

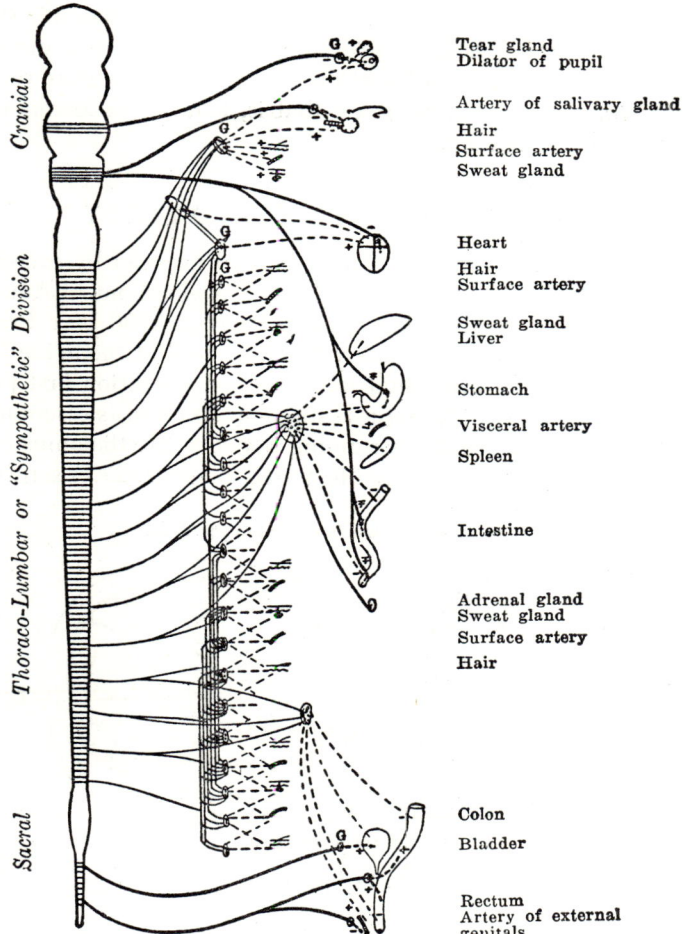

Fig. 26. Schematic Drawing of the Autonomic Nervous System. [Reproduced by permission from W. B. Cannon, *Bodily Changes in Pain, Hunger, Fear, and Rage* (New York, D. Appleton–Century Company, Inc., 1929), p. 23.]

brain and spinal cord. The autonomic system innervates the glands and smooth muscles of the body. These smooth muscles, as we have shown, are located in the viscera, lungs, blood vessels, and other organs whose function is automatic. In general, these smooth muscles of the viscera function spontaneously, provided they receive the necessary materials and conditions. The autonomic system does not cause these muscles to contract since they are already in a state of partial contraction. The autonomic system regulates the *tonus* of smooth muscles; that is, it raises or lowers the level of their functioning.

IX. PREFRONTAL LOBOTOMY

Psychosurgery, or the treatment of mental disorder by excising portions of the brain, is a relatively new development in American medicine, although it was used as early as 1890 by a Swiss psychiatrist.[5] Contemporary interest in this field of medicine has tended to center on prefrontal lobotomy, an operation first performed in 1935 by two Portuguese surgeons. It consists essentially in disrupting the nerve fibers running between the thalamus and the frontal lobes of the cortex as illustrated in Figure 27. A scrutiny

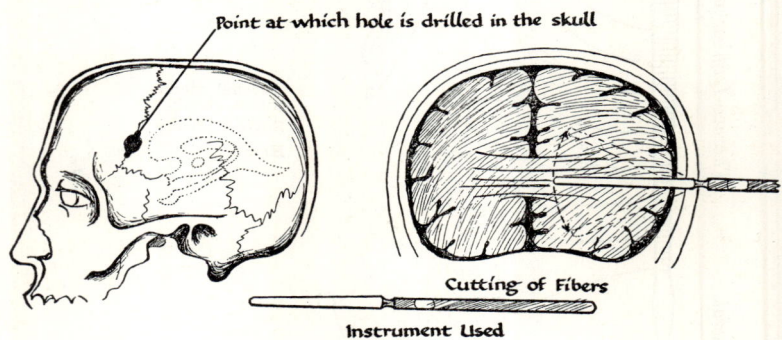

Fig. 27. Psychosurgery.

of the after-effects of such operations throws light upon the normal functioning of the brain.

In many instances, prefrontal lobotomy has produced significant changes in the behavior of mental patients. It has, at times, helped to clear up symptoms of depression and neurosis where other treatment, such as shock treatment or psychotherapy, has failed. Agitated persons lose their anxiety and overactivity. Unfortunately, however, the results are not uniformly positive. Lobotomized pa-

[5] Kurt Goldstein, "Prefrontal Lobotomy: Analysis and Warning," *Scientific American,* 182 (February, 1950), 44–47.

tients may lose all initiative, foresight, and any creative ability they might have had. The power of abstract thinking may be seriously impaired, and in some cases there is a progressive deterioration of intelligence as measured by intelligence tests. Because of these serious limitations, the operation is by no means a panacea for mental disease. Most responsible surgeons look upon its use as a last resort.

X. DEVELOPMENT OF THE NERVOUS SYSTEM AND BEHAVIOR

From the beginning of life the nervous system takes precedence over other bodily systems in growth. The brain in particular grows very rapidly during the prenatal period. By the time of birth, all of the main divisions of the brain have become differentiated. The enormous size of the head of the fetus as compared to other parts of its body results almost entirely from brain growth. In childhood, the brain reaches its adult size, but complete development, as reflected in behavior, goes on until maturity. As the nervous system matures, new and more complicated behavior patterns appear, and the child's physical and social horizons are correspondingly expanded. The interaction of the growing organism with the physical and social environment from birth until the end of adolescence will be the subject matter of later chapters. But first, we shall consider the driving or motivating forces of human nature and the role they play in human adjustment.

PART IV

Dynamics of Human Adjustment

Man shows many types of emotional expression and adjustment. His emotionalized attitudes toward people may involve: the tendency to go toward people, against people, or away from people.

VIII

Emotions, Motivation, and Patterns of Adjustment

. . . not feeling but the reasons of feeling, not the subjective state of mind but its correlated objective, not the strength of will but the goal will is aiming at, are of decisive importance.—RUDOLPH ALLERS [1]

I. AFFECTIVE EXPERIENCES

In general, the term *affective experiences* refers to the subjective aspects of mental life; it deals with feelings and desires rather than with knowledge. It is an inclusive term referring to feeling qualities of varying degrees of intensity, and in which the intellectual contents are vague and generalized. You may, for instance, experience a mild feeling of unpleasantness and yet seek in vain for an explanation or cause. Or, you may, by reviewing the various things that have happened to you in the course of the day, remember an unpleasant experience and realize that it was the source of your present feeling of unpleasantness. Affective experiences include emotion, feeling, and mood, and often temperamental characteristics as well.

Scientific and clinical psychologists, except those who belong to the psychoanalytical school, use the terms *emotion* and *feeling* in much the same sense as St. Thomas used the word *passion*. These psychologists tend to restrict the term *passion* to violent and uncontrolled emotion, just as the man-in-the-street does today. In contemporary psychology, feelings are distinguished from emotions in the following respects:

1. Feeling is more of an elementary experience than emotion; that is, it involves affective processes alone. Emotion, on the con-

[1] Rudolph Allers, *Self-Improvement* (New York, Benziger Brothers, Inc., 1939), p. 239.

trary, is a complex experience; it involves both affective and sensory experiences. For example, an emotion may include such sensory experiences as "goose pimples" or "chills running up and down the spine" as well as affective experiences of pleasantness or unpleasantness.

2. Feelings are less intense than emotions in their physical manifestations. Feelings are limited to two dimensions: pleasant or unpleasant. Emotions, on the contrary, are multidimensional experiences. They are conscious, vehement, stirred-up states with such varied dimensions as anger, elation, grief, and terror. Emotions are characterized by a wide pattern of sensations within the body and are usually accompanied by intense motor expression.

II. EMOTION

A. The Role of Emotions in Human Life

Feelings and emotions give zest to human life; without them life would be dull and tedious. Every normal human being experiences feelings and emotions, and it is just as abnormal to feel no emotion (apathy) as it is to be in a continual state of emotional excitement (as in euphoria, or even in extreme mania; or, in other instances, depression or anxiety). Emotions often help a person make the effort necessary to effect a wholesome adjustment to life. Ideally, however, emotions should be subservient to the intelligence which can channel all life into the pursuit of goals. They should not be permitted to become in themselves the sole goal of human activity.

In the emotionally disturbed person, the use of intelligence may be suspended. That is why, as a rule, you cannot reason with emotionally upset people. Emotion is not directly dissipated by an appeal to the reason. Consequently, if you try to reason with someone who is angry, you generally succeed only in making him more angry. Or, if he is afraid, and you try to reason away his fear, he may disguise his fear from you, but that does not mean that his fear has gone. All that it indicates is that he feels you do not understand and, as a result, you are likely to lose contact with him. Ordinarily, the best thing to do for an emotionally disturbed person is to let him "talk himself out," provided he is basically normal. Eventually, after he has aired his feelings, he will again be amenable to tactful persuasion and reason. Psychologists who work with emotionally disturbed people usually find that intelligence is not free to function until emotional tensions have been released, and in their treatment of such persons they generally make some provision for the dissipation of emotional tensions. One popular system of psychotherapy, the "non-directive" or "client-centered technique," is based almost entirely upon the assumption that once emotions and feelings have been ventilated and clarified, the person has gone a long way toward gaining the inner control necessary to work through a solution of his personal problems.

B. Bodily States and Emotion

The most characteristic physiological accompaniments of emotional states are (1) changes in the tonus of smooth muscles, (2) changes in the secretion of both duct and ductless glands, and (3) changes in the skeletal (voluntary) muscles, such as trembling in fright, clenching the fists, and tensing up for an attack in rage. A sudden strong emotion, for instance, will cause the digestive churning movements of the stomach muscles and peristalsis of the intestines to cease, and will result in an increased secretion of the adrenal glands. Changes in duct glands result in the flow of tears, dryness of the mouth (inhibition of flow of salivary gland), and increased sweat secretion during emotional excitement. All of these changes, and many others, are brought about by the functioning of the autonomic nervous system.

Certain physiological changes which accompany emotional excitement are readily apparent to anyone witnessing the scene and require no special apparatus or techniques for their detection. The sudden pallor or flushing, the gasp for breath, the involuntary scream, the clenched fist—all are overt signs of inner changes. Physiologists and psychologists have studied these and other changes, and in the next few paragraphs we shall summarize their major findings.

1. Changes in respiration

One of the simplest methods of studying respiration changes is by means of a *pneumograph*, shown in Figure 28, and a recording tambour. The pneumograph is a piece of coiled wire encased in a rubber envelope and connected at one end with a rubber tube which leads to a recording tambour. The pneumograph is strapped about the chest of the person whose responses are being studied. As he inhales, the rubber expands, and air is sucked in. This causes the piece of rubber covering the recording tambour to be pulled down. Sealed to this piece of sheet rubber is a metal pointer, the tip of which is in contact with the smoked paper of a revolving kymograph. When the air is sucked in, this pointer goes up. When the subject exhales, the air is pushed out and the sheet rubber is pushed up. This causes the pointer to go down. Since the drum of the kymograph revolves at a constant speed, it is possible to determine from the record scratched by the pointer (1) the length of inspiration, (2) the length of expiration, (3) the duration of the entire respiratory cycle, as well as (4) the amplitude of breathing at any moment in time.

The ratio of inspiration to expiration, or I/E, can be used as an

Fig. 28. Pneumograph.

index of emotional excitement. Another method is that of determining the *I-fraction*, the proportion of the total time of respiration taken up by inspiration. Since all of the air used by the organism is taken in during this inspiration phase, we would expect the relative length of this phase to change when the organism is in a state requiring a greater amount of oxygen. The I-fraction does, as a matter of fact, change under different psychological conditions. In laughter, for example, it averages 0.23. In excitement it registers 0.60, and in sudden fright, 0.75.[2] Changes in rate and depth of breathing also accompany emotional excitement.

2. Galvanic skin response

The galvanic skin response or GSR is an electrical change which takes place in the skin when the subject is experiencing an emotion. At one time this reflex was thought to be specific to emotional stimulation but we now have evidence that it also occurs, but usually to a lesser degree, during manual or physical work.

[2] R. S. Woodworth, *Experimental Psychology* (New York, Henry Holt and Company, Inc., 1938), p. 264.

Since the GSR always occurs during a time of emotional upset, however, it is used as a rough measure of the degree of emotional upset.

The GSR is measured by means of a psychogalvanometer which registers changes in electrical resistance of the skin. These changes result from sweat gland activity through the mediation of the autonomic nervous system. Just how the sweat glands produce a GSR we are not sure, but one simple explanation is that electrical resistance to the passage of current is lowered when the skin is moistened by sweating. An exhaustive survey of the literature on the subject leads to the conclusion that "Actual sweating goes along with the GSR, but the electrical change appears to occur before the secretion." [3]

A favorite laboratory device for studying the galvanic skin response is the administration of a free association test in which the subject is asked to respond to each stimulus word by giving the first word that comes to mind. On certain words, the GSR goes up, and these words are often found to be associated with emotionalized meanings. In college classes, a student may be asked to think of a number from one to ten and try to keep the experimenter from finding out what number he is thinking of. The subject says "no" to each word suggested by the experimenter, but after several trials, it is usually possible to tell from the greater deflection of the psychogalvanometer needle what number the subject has selected. The senior author of this book has never failed to determine the name of a student's fiancé when his name is one of ten or twelve used as stimuli and the subject has been instructed to deny being interested in any of them. However, in a more complicated situation it is necessary to make interpretations cautiously. Sometimes two names evoke an equally great GSR. In such instances, both names have evoked emotion in the subject, and perhaps one detects in this way a "has been" or a "hoped for" object of affection. In one instance, a married woman had a high response for the names "Richard" and "Robert." Her husband's name was Richard. Upon questioning her we discovered that she and her husband had decided just that morning to name their baby "Robert."

[3] R. A. McCleary, "The Nature of the Galvanic Skin Response," *Psychol. Bull.*, 47 (1950), 113.

3. Visceral and vascular changes

The presence of a strong emotion is associated with an increased secretion of adrenalin, a hormone produced by the adrenal glands. When adrenalin is sufficiently concentrated in the blood, many physiological changes take place. A strong emotion causes the rhythmical peristaltic movements of the stomach and intestines to cease and diminishes the flow of salivary and gastric secretions. In short, it brings about a cessation of digestive processes. This is one reason why mealtimes should not be used for disciplining children or for airing family grievances. Emotional disturbances associated with eating may set up a lifetime habit of inefficient utilization of food. Some studies show that although the emotion in general may not inhibit the digestive movements, it may cause an increase of hydrochloric acid, even to the point where, if the situation continues or is repeated over a period of time, an ulcer may be formed. In children and in animals, emotion is often accompanied by the emptying of bowel and bladder. Young children, too, may react by vomiting.

In one experiment, a cat was fed and a fluoroscopic picture of her stomach and intestines was taken. While she was contentedly digesting her meal, a dog barked fiercely at the cat. The cat strained to be released, arched her back, and bristled. Thereupon the digestive churning movement stopped until about fifteen minutes after the dog had been taken away.

Emotion also causes changes in blood pressure, in pulse rate, and in the distribution of blood to different parts of the body.

C. Theories of Emotion

1. Darwin's theory

Charles Darwin formulated three principles for interpreting emotional behavior in human beings. These principles stress the (1) utility value of emotions, (2) their antithetical character, and (3) the presence of useless and excessive responses during emotional excitement. Each of these principles will be explained briefly.

a. Utility. According to Darwin, emotional expressions in human beings are "vestigial" acts. "Vestigial" acts have no present utility but, at an earlier stage of evolution, were useful or necessary to survival. In anger, for example, a man will frown, raise

EMOTIONS AND PATTERNS OF ADJUSTMENT 189

his lips, and show his teeth. In a more primitive state, these actions were preparations for fighting. By frowning, the eyes were protected from the direct rays of the sun, thus providing clearer vision. Baring the teeth was a preparation for seizing or biting an opponent with the teeth. In civilized life, when anger is not expressed by physical attack, these emotional expressions are of no value to the organism and may be as harmful as racing an automobile engine with its clutch thrown out. Their presence can be understood only in the light of evolutionary processes.

b. Antithetical character of emotion. Darwin's theory of antithesis is described in the following lines:

> Certain states of the mind lead to certain habitual actions, which are of service. . . . Now when a directly opposite state of mind is induced, there is a strong and involuntary tendency to the performance of movements of a directly opposite nature, though these are of no use; and such movements are in some cases highly expressive.[4]

Darwin goes on to show that the bodily set of a dog preparing for a hostile attack is the exact antithesis of the bodily set of friendliness. In the first instance, the dog walks stiffly, his tail erect and rigid. His hairs bristle, his ears are directed forwards, and his eyes have a fixed stare. In the second instance, the body is not stiff, but flexible; the tail is lowered and wagged from side to side; the ears are depressed and drawn backward; and the eyes no longer stare. Darwin regarded antithetical expressions such as friendly behavior as useless, except in so far as they might communicate friendliness to other animals. Modern psychologists find a further usefulness in such expressions; namely, that they serve to release tensions.

c. Useless and excessive responses. Excessive activity is observed in both pleasant and unpleasant emotional states. In extreme pain or agony, there are useless movements such as grinding the teeth, clenching the fists, and changes in respiration and circulation. In extreme joy, too, there are excessive movements such as clapping of hands, shouting, dancing about, or jumping. These activities in themselves, according to Darwin, have no biological utility. They can be explained only in terms of the way in which the nervous system functions.

[4] C. Darwin, *The Expression of Emotion in Man and Animals* (London, John Murray, 1872), p. 28.

2. The James-Lange theory

An almost identical theory of emotions was proposed independently by James in America, and Lange in Denmark, and is known as the James-Lange theory. The gist of the theory is contained in James' words: "We do not cry because we are sad, but we are sad because we cry." In short, emotion is the awareness of a bodily state. Today there is more evidence against the James-Lange theory than there is for it.

Two investigators hypnotized subjects and then suggested to them that they were experiencing pains, bad smells, or pleasant tastes. These suggestions apparently "took," and the subjects showed emotional expressions appropriate to the suggestions. At the same time, changes in blood volume were recorded by a plethysmograph and changes in respiration by a pneumograph. The bodily changes did not appear until a definite time *after* the suggestions were made.

Subjects in the waking state were also subjected to sensory stimuli of pain, bad smells, and pleasant tastes. Both plethysmographic and pneumographic recordings were made. The bodily changes came *after* the sensory stimulation. The interval that elapsed between the sensory stimulus and the cardiovascular and respiratory changes was approximately the same as that which occurred between the suggestion and the bodily changes. In the hypnotized subjects there was no bodily condition which could have produced the emotional expression. The only possible cause was a mental state. There was every evidence, however, that the bodily reaction and emotional expression were the same under both conditions. Since the bodily changes were not suggested, but only the emotions, we conclude that the suggested emotions produced the bodily changes. According to the James-Lange theory, however, the situation should have been reversed: the bodily changes should have produced the emotional expressions.

Another psychologist [5] injected adrenalin into human subjects and produced in them the physiological symptoms commonly observed when a strong emotion is experienced—cold hands and feet, trembling of voice, arms, and legs, and rapid pulse. Most subjects reported that they felt "on edge" or "as if anticipating an

---

[5] H. Cantril, "The Roles of the Situation and Adrenalin in the Induction of Emotion," *Amer. J. Psychol.*, 46 (1943), 578–579.

emergency of some sort," but had no true emotions. This experiment, like the one reported earlier, repudiates the James-Lange theory.

3. Cannon's emergency theory

The bodily changes which take place while strong emotions are being experienced are favorable to vigorous muscular effort, although (with the exception of delight and elation in any ordinary degree of strength) they suppress the rhythmic contractions of the alimentary tract which are necessary for digestion. Strong emotion releases adrenalin, which in turn causes the heart to beat rapidly, the liver to release more sugar, the bronchial tubes to distend, and the blood to shift from the abdominal region to the voluntary muscles. All of these changes give the body strength to meet an emergency which calls for fighting or running away. These facts led Cannon to conclude that such emotions have the function of helping people to meet physical emergencies.

D. Emotional Expression and Gesture

The unlearned character of strong emotional expression is shown in the fact that it is almost identical in a deaf-blind child to that in a normal child. Since the deaf-blind child can neither see nor hear others, she cannot imitate their behavior. Her emotional reactions of fear, anger, and pleasure, must therefore be the result of maturation rather than of learning.[6]

Nevertheless, many of the milder emotional expressions and gestures vary with the culture pattern and cannot be looked upon as "instinctive" or unlearned. Anthropologists working in cultures different from their own have often made serious mistakes in interpreting the unfamiliar expressions of emotion on the part of the natives. At times they have even endangered their lives by acting upon a clue, the meaning of which was just the opposite of what they expected it to be. The simple gesture of nodding in affirmation has sometimes been looked upon as universal, and someone has suggested that it originates in the infant's motion of "yes" in seeking the mother's breast, and its opposite, "no," in refusing the breast. Yet a forward nod of the head to imply "yes" and a rotation of the head from right to left to indicate "no"

[6] F. L. Goodenough, "Expression of the Emotions in a Deaf-Blind Child," *J. Abnorm. Soc. Psychol.*, 27 (1932), 328–333.

are by no means universal. In at least one culture, these gestures mean just the opposite of what they do to us. Similarly, although laughter is an unlearned expression of pleasure, it may express other emotions as well. In Africa, Negroes laugh to express surprise, embarrassment, wonder, and discomfiture, but seldom to express amusement. We will not be able to understand these people if we attribute to their expressions and gestures the same meanings they would have for us. Among the Japanese, a smile is not necessarily a spontaneous expression of amusement; it is a silent language which children are taught to cultivate from their tenderest years. In Japan, etiquette demands that a person smile, even in pain and distress, to avoid inflicting his suffering upon others. Weeping and wailing do not universally imply sorrow, as illustrated by a curious custom of the Andaman Islanders of the Gulf of Bengal. Among these Islanders, when friends or relatives greet each other after an absence of some time, one sits in the lap of the other, they throw their arms around each other's necks, and weep and wail for several minutes.

III. CYCLES OF MOOD

In addition to the terms *affective processes, feelings,* and *emotions,* psychologists use other terms for emotionalized states and attitudes which, while overlapping in their meanings some of the terms above, have come to take on rather specific meanings of their own. One such term is *mood,* defined by Warren's *Dictionary of Psychology* as follows: "an enduring but not permanent emotional attitude." Here attitude, or tendency to emotion, is to be contrasted with a violent emotional outbreak. While it is difficult to put into words the exact difference between mood and emotion, the emotion is usually more intense and does not persist as long as a mood. Sometimes a mood is the aftermath or "tail end" of an emotional response. We all know the person who keeps a cheery, participating active attitude in almost every situation, and also the sluggish, passive, not so outgoing person. Neither are mood and temperament synonymous. *Temperament* is a permanent characteristic of the person, and Warren defines it as "the general affective nature of the individual as determined by his inheritance and life history." It includes such characteristics as rhythm, quality, and intensity of moods, and susceptibility to emotional stimulation.

Common sense looks upon emotion as a reaction to the varying vicissitudes of life. When we see someone crying or looking depressed we are inclined to ask, "What is the matter?" We assume that something has happened to bring on his unhappy state of mind. If we get a response to our question, it is usually some plausible explanation; the person we ask usually attributes his state of mind to a situation which might reasonably give rise to sadness. Yet just possibly the same situation, experienced at another time, might not result in depression at all, but in determination and an exhilarating feeling of being challenged. In such a case the mood which is evoked occurs independently of the nature of external situations. Our emotional reactions to the situations of life appear to be superimposed upon our dominant mood at the time they occur.

We do not mean to deny, of course, that some emotions and the moods which follow them are reactions to cognitive appreciations of an experience or situation, because there is plenty of evidence that they very often are. What we mean is that these cognitive experiences do not affect the person in isolation from the state of his whole organism. The intensity and quality of emotion may surely be related to the meaning of the situation to the person. For this reason animal and human emotion are not directly comparable since the animal is not capable of the intellectual insight which gives to human affective experience its peculiar pungency or poignancy. But certainly there is also evidence that moods fluctuate in regularly occurring cycles, independently of external situations, possibly in accord with obscure changes in endocrine functioning. In one study [7] this cycle was seen to vary from three to a little over nine weeks on the average and was present in both men and women. In women, it should be noted, the cycle varied independently of the menstrual cycle. A study of the individuals in the group showed that no one varied more than one week from his average, in spite of family difficulties, exceptional success or failure, or other external events. These events, no doubt, aroused emotion, but did not significantly alter the individual's

[7] R. B. Hersey, *Workers' Emotions in Shop and Home* (Philadelphia, University of Pennsylvania Press, 1932).

unique and characteristic cycle of moods. Other investigators have found that the moods of college students vary with the hour of the day, the day of the week, and with the month of the year. It is not clear, however, to what extent these moods relate to climate, amount of sleep, and other factors which were not controlled in these studies.

Extreme fluctuations of mood which are so intense and uncontrollable that the individual is incapable of performing his ordinary duties are pathological. Such mood cycles are characteristic of manic-depressive psychosis, a condition which appears to run in families.

IV. MOTIVATION IN HUMAN LIFE

A. Basic Human Needs

All people have certain basic needs in common, the satisfaction of which helps and the frustration of which hinders normal personality growth. Roughly, these needs have been classified (by Prescott) in three overlapping categories: (1) physical, (2) social-emotional, and (3) ego-integrative. Psychologically, these needs are mutually complementary, as, for instance, when an emotional crisis interferes with digestion or precipitates a heart attack. Included in the first category are the need for food, water, air, sex, and for a balance between rest and activity. In the second category are the needs to be treated as a unique individual, to be emotionally secure, to have a sense of personal worth and value, to feel that one "belongs," to give and receive affection, and to be reasonably successful in accomplishing the tasks of life. And in the third category are the religious and philosophical needs which come to the fore in late adolescence and maturity: the need for a sense of purpose and meaningfulness in life, and the need to define one's role in life in the light of such meaning.

Obviously, these needs are interrelated. A person who achieves satisfactorily or who gives and receives affection may have a heightened sense of personal worth as a result of such need satisfaction, although this is not necessarily true. To a limited degree only can the frustration of one need be compensated for by the satisfaction of another. When one or more of these needs is constantly frustrated the person usually becomes maladjusted. This is true especially when he cannot see any "meaning" in these

EMOTIONS AND PATTERNS OF ADJUSTMENT

frustrations, as, for instance, in the case of infants, children, and adults whose sense of values cannot encompass deprivations. In the course of life, people learn different ways of satisfying their basic needs; some of these ways are healthy, others unhealthy. Behavior which results in the satisfaction of a need is said to be reinforced or rewarded. Such reinforcement is an important factor in determining what and how well a person will learn.

Specific ways in which basic needs are satisfied and frustrated at different stages of life are described in later chapters of this book. Physiological needs, common to man and other animals, are often referred to as drives, as illustrated in the following section.

B. The Study of Drives

Since it is difficult to study the relative strength of different drives (or needs) in human beings with any degree of scientific accuracy, many psychologists have preferred to study animals instead. The experimental investigation of animal drives is, of course, a legitimate subject of research, irrespective of whether or not it can throw light upon human behavior. But animal psychologists in general have not been content to limit their generalizations to animals alone. Most of them, starting with the postulate that man is essentially no different from animals, even though he has the most complex nervous system of all the animals, assume that their studies of animals can throw more light upon human motivation than we soberly thoughtful persons are willing to credit them with. The following experiment of Warden is usually cited in support of this assumption, and we shall try to evaluate its significance for an understanding of human motivation.

Warden[8] used an obstruction box to test the relative strength of basic drives in rats. The apparatus, shown in Figure 29, places a painful obstruction, namely, a grid of wires through which an electric current may be sent at will, between the animal (at A) and the goal of his drive (at E). Warden tried to control conditions in such a way that all drives, except the one being measured, were relatively satisfied. He also attempted to test the drive at its maximum intensity. If these conditions could be fulfilled, then

[8] C. J. Warden, *Animal Motivation* (New York, Columbia University Press, 1931).

the number of times that the rat would cross the grid to reach each kind of goal, within a specified time limit, could be taken as a relative measure of the strength of the drive. Thus, if the animal crossed the grid fifteen times for food but only five times for a sex goal, we could conclude that the hunger drive was considerably stronger than the sex drive. When the hunger drive was being measured, the animal was taken from a cage which had a continual supply of water but in which, for a certain length of time, no food had been placed. When the thirst

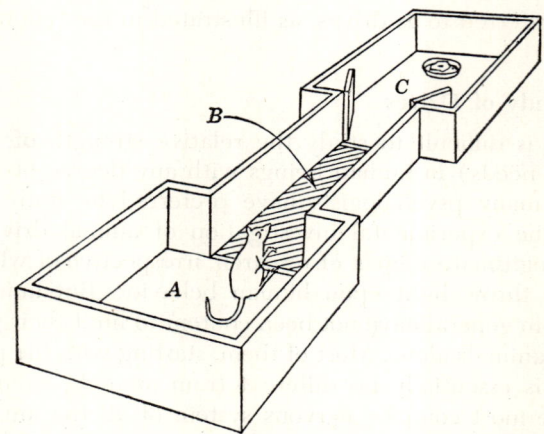

Fig. 29. Obstruction Box. [Reproduced by permission from *Methods of Psychology*, T. G. Andrews, ed. (New York, John Wiley & Sons, Inc., 1948), p. 328.]

drive was being measured, the animal was taken from a cage supplied continuously with food but no water. In this way, Warden hoped that he was testing each drive independently of the other. It seems probable, however, that thirst was not completely separated from the hunger drive since it is doubtful that a thirsty animal would eat its fill of dry food.

The measurement of the sex drive was somewhat more complicated. The peak of the drive could be determined in the male only by observing the number of times he would cross the grid after different periods of deprivation. The drive reached its maximum 24 hours after the last copulation. The female rat goes through an œstrus cycle which lasts on the average from

EMOTIONS AND PATTERNS OF ADJUSTMENT 197

four to five days. There are five distinct stages in this cycle, each of which is evidenced by characteristic changes in the vaginal mucosa, uterus, and follicles. Warden found that each of these stages was correlated with different kinds of behavior. His behavioral analysis may be summarized as follows:

1. First stage (pre-œstrum), lasts approximately 9 to 21 hours. It is characterized by vaginal congestion and a relative lack of sexual behavior.
2. Second and third stages (œstrum), last approximately 27 to 51 hours. During the initial period the animal actively solicits mating and shows greatly increased activity. At this time the sex drive is at its peak. It was at this stage that the drive of the female was measured. During the second half of this period, the animal usually refuses to mate.
3. Fourth stage (metœstrum), lasts from 3 to 15 hours. The animal shows a disinclination to mate.
4. Fifth stage (diœstrum), lasts from 42 to 75 hours. The animal does not mate during this period.

Warden also studied the maternal and exploratory drives by means of the obstruction box. The former drive was analyzed by separating a mother rat from her recently born litter, and the latter drive by offering the rat an escape from a narrowly confining cage.

By comparing the number of times the rats would cross the grid under the influence of these five drives, Warden concluded that maternal behavior was the most persistent, and that thirst, hunger, sex, and exploratory behavior were next in order.

Some investigators have looked upon Warden's study as a refutation of the Freudian postulate that the dominant human drive is sexual. This conclusion, however, is, in a sense, a *non sequitur*. The basic physiological drives of human beings cannot be compared to those of animals since in human beings all of these drives have been elevated and refined by the action of a spiritual soul. This is particularly true of the sex drive, the expression of which is an integral function of the whole personality —including basic attitudes, feelings, and ethical ideals.

Unlike most elementary text books in psychology, this book has little to say about the Norwegian white rat, the animal most commonly used for laboratory experiments in psychology. Animal psychology, of course, like animal biology, is a legitimate field of research. It can, if its findings are interpreted with appropriate discretion, throw light upon problems of human adjustment. Studies of animal drives, of the effects of drugs upon learning or the functioning of the nervous system, the effects of endocrine deprivation or oversecretion, of the behavior effects of localized brain excisions—all provide insights to the psychologist who works professionally with human beings. But unless proper cautions are observed in the interpretation of animal data, generalizations drawn from animal studies can be very misleading. Human beings, in common with the white rat, guinea pig, and the chimpanzee, have drives which are activated by biochemical changes within their bodies. It is important to know what these drives are, how they originate, and how much frustration of these drives can be tolerated by an organism. The study of rats in competition for food tells us something of the degree of punishment the animal will take to satisfy his hunger drive. And, in some respects, we are willing to concede, the animals do resemble a crowd of children around a picnic table from which the food is giving out! But that is not the whole story—at least, not as far as the youngsters are concerned. During the depression of the thirties, children as young as ten years of age were observed to go without lunch rather than stand in a line leading to free lunches for children whose families were on relief. The desire for prestige, the need to protect their families from the social stigma of being less capable of providing for their children than other families, was powerful enough in some children to make them go hungry. Yet, so far as we know, no proud and independent white rat has ever refused to take the food pellets provided by a generous appropriation of the state legislature for university research!

In an earlier epoch of psychological study, there was a tendency to read human characteristics into animal behavior. This *anthropomorphism* went so far beyond the data on hand that Lloyd Morgan in his *Introduction to Comparative Psychology* (1894) issued his famous "canon of parsimony": "In no case may we interpret an action as the outcome of the exercise of a higher psychical faculty, if it can be interpreted as the outcome of the exercise of one which stands lower in the psychological scale." At the present time there is a curious reversal of this anthropocentric tendency. There is a tendency called "animalism," to interpret human characteristics in terms of characteristics of lower animals. Perhaps we now need a canon such as this: "In no case may a human psychological characteristic be interpreted as nothing more than animal behavior unless it can be clearly shown that man's spiritual soul had no influence on elevating, refining, or modifying the behavior."

C. Unconscious Motivation

1. Unconscious motivation in everyday life

Clinical psychologists and psychiatrists, and especially psychoanalysts, have emphasized the importance in human life of unconscious motivation. Unconscious motivation is often the source of psychoneurotic symptoms, slips of the tongue or pen, errors of hearing or of reading, and of automatic or ritualistic acts. An adolescent boy, for example, suffers from a hand-washing compulsion and finds himself compelled to wash his hands several times an hour, much to his distress and his parents' and teachers'. A psychological diagnosis reveals that this washing has symbolic meaning. It is a defense against impurity. As the boy receives help in meeting the problem of impurity, the hand-washing compulsion disappears. The unconscious motivation has been dissipated. A significant slip of the tongue is reported of a Washington hostess, who for political reasons had to invite to her home a diplomat whom she heartily detested. During the reception, she went up to him to offer him a seat and to her amazement found herself saying, "Mr. A, may I show you to the door?" Freud, in his *Psychopathology of Everyday Life*, gives numerous examples of this kind. And while one may well disagree with Freud's most extreme interpretation of these cases, most psychologists would agree that Freud has here hit upon a most significant psychological principle. As Freud expressed it:

When I set myself the task of bringing to light what human beings keep hidden within them . . . by observing what they say and what they show, I thought the task was a harder one than it really is. He that has eyes to see and ears to hear may convince himself that no mortal can keep a secret. If his lips are silent, he chatters with his finger-tips; betrayal oozes out of him at every pore. And thus the task of making conscious the most hidden recesses of the mind is one which it is quite possible to accomplish.[9]

[9] Sigmund Freud, "Fragment of an Analysis of a Case of Hysteria ('Dora')," *Collected Papers*, Vol. III, 1905, p. 94.

The phenomenon of post-hypnotic suggestion is probably one of the most convincing evidences of unconscious motivation. In order to clarify this whole subject, as well as to evaluate research in which hypnotic techniques have been used, it will be necessary to describe hypnosis in some detail.

2. Hypnosis

a. Description of hypnosis. The phenomenon of hypnosis has been observed for centuries, but only within recent times has it been subjected to scientific scrutiny. Mesmer, in the latter part of the eighteenth century, used hypnosis as a means of therapy. He did not, however, have any clear notion as to what he was using. *Mesmerism,* as this method of therapy was called, was thought to result from the passage of a magnetic fluid from the body of the therapist to that of the patient. At first, Mesmer came into direct contact with his patients and thus supposedly caused the "animal magnetism" to flow to his patient. Later, he discovered that such direct contact was not necessary but that he could magnetize a steel rod or some other object, such as his famous "baquet," and that this magnetized object could, in turn, cure his patient. Mesmer had made an important psychological discovery but his interpretation of it was wrong. Mesmer and later students of the subject were violently persecuted by their medical colleagues and denounced as quacks. With the French physician, Charcot, sometimes referred to as the "father of clinical psychology," the subject took on a certain amount of scientific respectability. By the time of Charcot the phenomenon had been labeled *hypnosis,* a term which in its origin means "nervous sleep." Charcot, using hypnosis in his clinic at Nancy, concluded that it was an abnormal phenomenon, characteristic only of hysterical patients. Bernheim, on the other hand, claimed that it could be induced in normal people, a conclusion that has been substantiated by later research.

A variety of techniques can be used to induce hypnosis, but all of them have certain elements in common. The following description of the induction of hypnosis will illustrate the principles involved. The case is fictitious, and although all of the things here described *can* occur, they do not happen to *any* volunteer; they probably would not occur the *first* time, and it is unlikely that a psychologist would carry the experiment to the lengths described here. We are purposely writing an exaggerated description in order to illustrate the several phenomena that can be demonstrated in hypnosis under varying circumstances.

A young man named William volunteers to act as subject for a demonstration of hypnotism in a clinical psychology class, although he expresses certain doubts about the procedure. The psychologist reassures him and explains that he will not be required to do anything foolish or humiliating during the session. William is then seated at a table and is quietly instructed to put his two hands flat upon its surface. The psychologist then holds up his hand at some distance and slightly above the subject's eyes and asks him to fixate his gaze on the first two fingers. Then he begins to suggest quietly and with monotonous repetition, "Your eyes are getting heavy. Your eyes are getting heavy. Your eyes are getting very heavy." Or, "You are getting sleepy. You are getting sleepy." And, finally, "You are asleep. You are asleep, you are asleep. No matter how hard you try, you cannot wake up. You are sound asleep." When the psychologist is convinced that the subject is really asleep, he then challenges him with the words, "Try to wake up. You see that you cannot wake up. No matter how hard you try, you cannot wake up. You are sound asleep. Although you are sound asleep, you will still be able to hear my words and answer my questions. But you cannot wake up. You are sound asleep." By this time William's eyes are closed and his breathing is as heavy as if he were in a very deep sleep. Then the suggestion is made that although he will continue to sleep, he will be able to open his eyes. Immediately he opens his eyes. Five pieces of chalk are placed before him. William is asked to count them and to point to each piece as he counts. This task he accomplishes without any error. The suggestion is then made: "There are now only four pieces of chalk. Count them." This time William points to the first four, counts to four and then stops. It is as if he does not now see the fifth piece of chalk. Next, he is asked to write his name and he does so. The writing and spelling is normal although it takes him a little longer to write than when he is awake. Then he is told: "You do not know any of the vowels. Write your name." This time he writes "W," then hesitates and seems agitated and perturbed. The psychologist says: "Go on. Write your name." Then, painfully, William writes, "Wllm." He has written consonants only, omitting the vowels.

William is next told that he is a little boy about four years of age. A grin comes over his face. When asked what he is doing he replies, "I am going down a slide." He is then asked to write his name again. He shakes his head uncomprehendingly. When urged, he finally replies, in the voice of a four-year-old, "I can't. I don't know how to write yet." He is then told that he is a small baby, after which he does not talk but only babbles in response to questions. A sterile needle is then brought out and William is told that he will not be able to feel anything in his hand. The psychologist then stretches the skin of William's hand between his thumb and index finger and runs the needle straight through it. William gives no evidence that he feels pain. But when the suggestion is given that he feels great pain in the hand, he writhes in agony. William is told that after the experiment, when the class is still going on, he will get up and open all of the windows when the instructor turns to the blackboard and writes the word *psychology*. Finally, he is told that he will not remember anything that transpired during the trance; that he will awaken feeling well and rested. Then the suggestion is made that at the count of ten he will awaken. When the psychologist gets to "ten," William opens his eyes, is dazed for a moment or two, and then awakens completely. He resumes his seat, opens his notebook, and the instructor goes on with the lecture. Fifteen minutes later, the instructor writes *psychology* on the blackboard, and William stands up. After a moment of hesitation, he goes to the first of the five windows and opens it as far as it will go. It is a cold day, and both William and the other students begin to shiver. Nothing daunted, William goes on and opens a second and a third window. At this point the instructor asks, "What are you doing? It is cold enough in here already without opening any more windows." William replies that it is very stuffy. The instructor tells him to return to his seat, but William proceeds to open the remaining two windows. The instructor asks, "Why are you freezing us out?" William replies, "It is warm in here and we were all falling asleep. We need some fresh air." His task completed, William shows signs of embarrassment as he returns to his seat. He obeys promptly now when the instructor asks him to close the windows and shows evident symptoms of relief when this job is accomplished. William is apparently unaware of what transpired during the trance.

EMOTIONS AND PATTERNS OF ADJUSTMENT   203

The above example illustrates a number of hypnotic phenomena. (1) It shows the way in which a trance state is typically induced, namely, (a) the attention of the subject is fixated on some immobile object, (b) an appropriate emotional relationship is established between the subject and the hypnotist, (c) sensory intake (the object which he perceives) and motor output (his actions) are limited, and (d) a continuous patter of monotonous stimulation is kept up. (2) It illustrates the characteristic feature of all hypnosis, that of *exaggerated suggestibility*. (3) Hypnotic *regression* is shown in the subject's reactions to the suggestion that he is a little boy or a baby, in that he behaves appropriately to the age level suggested. This phenomenon suggests that we can compare the "growth of personality to the growth of a palm tree, in which layers are preserved although they are all integrated into the whole tree."[10] It is this feature of hypnosis which makes it a valuable tool in the treatment of certain neurotic conditions in which treatment requires the unearthing of buried or repressed memories. (4) Hypnotic *anesthesia* is illustrated in the subject's lack of pain even when a painful stimulus is applied. (5) *Amnesia* for what transpired during the trance is illustrated. Had the psychologist suggested to the subject that he would remember what had gone on during the trance, however, it is probable that he would have remembered it. Some psychotherapists, in fact, suggest to their patients under hypnosis that they will remember in a waking state the buried memories which they were able to recall only during hypnosis and will be able and eager to discuss the psychological material brought out during the trance. In such instances, the hypnosis itself does not constitute treatment; it is merely a helpful adjunct to treatment. (6) *Post-hypnotic suggestion* is shown in the fact that the subject carried through the suggestion that he open the windows even though there was no necessity for doing so. It is interesting to note that the subject gives reasons for his behavior which, evidently, are not the real reasons. In World War I, hypnosis was used to get rid of symptoms of "shell shock" or hysteria through post-hypnotic suggestion. The symptoms disappeared as a result of hypnotic suggestion but, interestingly enough, other symptoms appeared. Hence, nothing much was

[10] Werner Wolff, *What Is Psychology?* (New York, Grune & Stratton, Inc., 1947), p. 306.

gained by the use of hypnosis alone and its use for therapy was abandoned. Neurotic symptoms are ways of meeting needs, and we cannot cure the neurosis without in some way meeting the need that the symptoms were adopted to satisfy. Current use of *hypnoanalysis* in the treatment of nervous disorders is based upon the recognition that hypnosis can be of value if at the same time therapy is directed to the removal of the cause of the neurotic condition. (7) A phenomenon of hypnosis which was not illustrated in the above case is that of *catelepsy*. In a hypnotic state, it is possible for a person to maintain a given posture for a much longer time than he could in a waking state. This is of particular interest in view of the fact that in a certain type of mental disease, catatonic schizophrenia, this same symptom is very prominent.

b. Experimental studies. Most studies of hypnosis have been made with abnormal subjects in clinical situations with a view to diagnosis and treatment. A marked exception is Hull's work.[11] Hull studied normal subjects with a view to determining the basic principles of hypnosis and the interrelationships of suggestive and hypnotic phenomena. Beginning with the assumption that hypnosis is a state of exaggerated suggestibility, Hull set out to investigate direct waking suggestion by means of some ingenious experiments. In one experiment he blindfolded his subject and fastened a pin in the collar of his coat at the back without the subject being aware of it. Attached to this pin was a thread which ran backward to a pointer which recorded each movement of the subject on a revolving smoked drum. Hull then brought another person into the room and instructed him to assume certain strained postures. Although the blindfolded subject could not see the other person, he could hear the instructions which he was receiving. Under such conditions, Hull found that his subject had a tendency to go through the same movements as were suggested to the other person, as indicated by the record left on the smoked drum. He found similar but more marked responses when the subject was asked to imagine that he was taking the postures suggested or when he whispered to himself that he was taking such postures or when he received such suggestions from another person or from a phonograph record.

Hull found that, contrary to general opinion, direct suggesti-

[11] C. L. Hull, *Hypnosis and Suggestibility* (New York, Appleton-Century-Crofts, Inc., 1933).

bility is not a mark of stupidity. On the contrary, he found a zero or slight positive relationship between direct suggestibility and intelligence. There was a slight hint, too, that suggestibility is positively related to a group of traits characterized by "general amiability." [12] Women, he found, were more susceptible to both suggestibility and hypnosis than men. There was a positive correlation between all forms of direct verbal or prestige suggestion with each other and with susceptibility to hypnosis. Alcohol did not increase suggestibility, although a drug called scopolamine did increase suggestibility in those subjects who normally showed positive responses, but not in those who did not ordinarily give a positive response to suggestion. Delinquent girls in a reformatory were far more negatively suggestible than ordinary girls. Susceptibility to both suggestion and hypnosis appeared to be distributed in the adult population symmetrically.

Hull's research has confirmed the clinical observations concerning the recovery of lost memories during hypnosis. He found, however, that recently acquired material was remembered no better in the hypnotic trance than in a waking state, although remote memories were. Hull's studies also confirmed the clinical observation that successive repetitions of the hypnotic trance facilitated its performance. The curve for hypnotizability with practice was similar to the learning curve ordinarily obtained in the learning of motor habits.

Hull's experiments suggest that hypnosis is something quite different from ordinary sleep, not only because rapport with the hypnotist is maintained, but also because the response to reflex stimulation is different in sleep from what it is under hypnosis. In sleep, the knee jerk reflex disappears; under hypnosis it does not. It is interesting to note an observation made of two college students and a psychiatric patient who were placed in a hypnotic trance. Under the suggestion that they were infants they regressed to the infantile level as did the subject whose case we cited earlier. But more than that, the experimenter claims, when the soles of their feet were stimulated, they responded with infantile plantar reflex responses!

Hypnosis is not a pathological phenomenon; it can be induced in perfectly normal people and appears to be nothing more than an exaggerated state of suggestibility. After conducting exhaustive

[12] *Ibid.*

research in this field, Hull concluded that no phenomena were produced in hypnosis that could not be produced to lesser degrees by suggestions given in the waking state.

In view of the fact that hypnosis is a useful tool in the treatment of personality problems, it might be well to raise a final question at this point: What is the attitude of the Church toward hypnosis? Officially and formally, the Church has not condemned hypnosis, although eminent moral theologians have been careful to point out the dangers of its irresponsible use. The position taken by these moral theologians has been summarized as follows:

> . . . it seems that when the hypnotist is a qualified and conscientious physician or psychologist; when the proper moral precautions are taken and all danger of abuse is excluded; then, for a proper medical and curative purpose, hypnotism may lawfully be used. But, and the theologians are insistent on this, both for the sake of the hypnotist and the patient, one or more witnesses should be present when the hypnotic state is induced.[13]

V. PATTERNS OF HUMAN ADJUSTMENT

Human beings, as we all know, are constantly facing situations which call for some kind of adjustment on their part. The kinds of adjustments which will become more or less habitual differ from one person to another. Even young children differ greatly in the way in which they react to a situation which is threatening or challenging. Size, strength, vitality, and other aspects of the physical constitution play a role in determining the kind of adjustment which will be the most satisfactory. The family pattern, the way in which the child is handled, and the success or failure associated with early experiments with different types of reactions—all have a part in the formation of the relatively stable and predictable habits of adjustment which gradually come to characterize the individual personality.

People react in various ways when their egos are threatened. The direct way, and perhaps the healthiest way, is to acknowledge and accept one's limitations and defects and to try, in so far as one is able, to eradicate the defects. But people are often unable to do this, and they adjust indirectly by means of defense reactions. *Defense reactions* are patterns of behavior which a per-

[13] *The Catholic Mind*, 39 (February 8, 1941), 95.

son adopts either consciously or unconsciously, to disguise from himself or from others some aspect of his personality or some real or imagined inferiority which it is too painful for him to accept or acknowledge. Psychologists refer to these typical patterns of adjustment as "mechanisms" or "dynamisms" of adjustment, depending upon their theoretical point of view. Most of the terms used to label these mechanisms came into use through the Freudian school of psychoanalysis, and to use these terms as Freud did would mean to accept the Freudian theory of motivation and of personality development. Most psychologists today, however, use these terms in a less restricted sense than do the Freudian psychoanalysts. It is in this less restricted sense that we are using the terms in this textbook, and in thus using terms taken from psychoanalysis, we are not accepting the Freudian theory of mental life.

A. Rationalization

Rationalization, as applied to adjustment problems, does not mean the use of reason and logic to solve a problem. It means, rather, the perversion of reason to disguise the nature of the problem and to conceal from oneself or from others one's real motives. The person who rationalizes finds acceptable reasons, "props," to explain his behavior; and in doing so, he usually conceals even from himself the unworthy motives which are the real reasons for his behavior. Often the real reasons are more apparent to others than they are to the person himself. Among the commonest and most human kinds of rationalization are two which custom has labeled the (1) *sour grapes* mechanism and the (2) *sweet lemon* mechanism, respectively. The first kind receives its name from the famous fable of the fox and the grapes in which the fox, after vainly trying to secure the grapes, declared that he did not want them anyway because they were sour. It consists in finding reasons for being satisfied with your unhappy lot by persuading yourself that a change would undoubtedly be even worse. A college girl, for instance, set out to make it very clear to the other girls that she was glad a boy friend had not asked her to the prom but had asked her roommate instead, because he was "such a poor dancer" and "often stepped on my feet!" Of course, this statement might conceivably have been true, but it is of interest to note that the girl apparently became aware of it only after the boy in question had transferred his affections to another girl.

The sweet lemon mechanism, in a case such as this, would be illustrated if the girl insisted that there was nothing she liked to do better than to stay in of an evening when everybody else in the dormitory was out, for then one of her greatest desires, having a quiet evening at home to study, would be realized! Another example, taken from a nursery school, is that of a little boy who was being disciplined by being forced to stay indoors and play with picture puzzles when the other children went out to the slides and swings. The practice teacher who stayed with him heard him say in the midst of his tears, "There's nothing I like better than picture puzzles."

An example of rationalization which all of you will no doubt recognize and which will convince you that even normal people indulge in rationalization is that which accompanies "spring fever." Suppose you have a long assignment to do and a limited amount of time in which to complete it. The warm sun is shining outdoors and the birds are singing in the trees. You will be able to work much better and get a lot more done, you say, if you go out and get some fresh air for the next hour or two. In fact, your health demands it. There is really no point to slaving for a college degree if you are going to be an invalid for the rest of your life. And so—out of doors you go!

B. Withdrawal and Daydreaming

Withdrawal from the real world and from people and taking refuge in daydreaming is a very unhealthy type of adjustment. A child who tends to meet problems in this way should be helped in every way possible to externalize his conflicts. A habit of excessive daydreaming and withdrawal is frequently seen as a predisposing factor in the development of a schizophrenic psychosis.[14] Daydreaming, of course, may serve as a shock absorber for many unpleasant experiences, and normal people indulge in it on such occasions. It is not abnormal unless it is indulged in too frequently. At times, too, it is the "nursery of accomplishment" and a way of foretasting the delights that come from effort. It is a symptom of a serious disorder, however, when it

---

[14] Described in Chapter XIV.

EMOTIONS AND PATTERNS OF ADJUSTMENT

gradually takes the place of real living, and the person lives more and more in an inner world of his own, a world that cannot be and is not shared with anyone else. It is much more difficult to treat a child or adolescent who has withdrawal symptoms than to treat one who is aggressive, because the withdrawn person often will not or cannot let down the barrier to his inner world of dreams.

Two common types of daydreams experienced by normal as well as by abnormal people are (1) the *suffering-hero* dream and (2) the *conquering-hero* dream. In the former type, the daydreamer takes pleasure in imagining the chagrin of someone who has hurt, humiliated, or slighted him by imagining that person's grief upon learning that he has been injured or killed. A child who has been scolded by his mother may imagine that he has walked into the street and been struck by a passing automobile. His lifeless body is brought into the house and he can see his mother wringing her hands and groaning, "Oh, why was I so unkind? Why didn't I love him more? Oh, if I only had it to do over again!" In the conquering-hero dream, the person imagines himself to be in a very superior position over that of someone who has humiliated him. A schoolboy who has been punished by a teacher may find consolation in imagining that he is now grown up and has become president of the United States. He imagines, further, that he is returning to his home town and that everyone has turned out to meet him—brass band and all! Among the admiring throng, and now penitent and ashamed, is the offending teacher. The conquering-hero is then the soul of graciousness to everyone, with one exception. When his old teacher comes up to shake hands with him he snubs her. At this point in the dream you will see a big smile of satisfaction spread over his face as he imagines the grief of his teacher and hears her moaning, "Oh, why didn't I see what a wonderful boy he was?"

C. Compensation

Compensation is a way of disguising or making up for a real or imagined inferiority. It may be direct or indirect. It is direct if the person strives not only to overcome the defect, but actually to excel others in that area by vigorous effort, in spite of the odds against him. The famous story of Demosthenes is an example of direct compensation. Demosthenes, you will recall, had a serious speech impediment. He attacked this defect vigorously, so the legend goes, by practicing speaking with pebbles in his mouth. Demosthenes not only eliminated his speech impediment; he became one of the most famous orators of all time. Indirect compensation takes place when a person, feeling inferior in one area of life, gives up trying to compete in that field and develops instead some other characteristic to which he assigns great prestige, at the same time belittling the importance of the trait, characteristic, or performance in which he is inferior. A physical weakling may develop his intellectual or artistic skills as a compensation for his inability to compete successfully with other boys in games and sports. Or, lacking the ability to compensate with a performance of some social significance, he may learn to wiggle his ears more vigorously than anyone else in his classroom. And not only that, he may take to belittling people who cannot wiggle their ears.

D. Projection

Projection is a mechanism by which a person ascribes to someone else unworthy attitudes, motives, and feelings which he has repressed in himself and of which he is not conscious. In its simplest and less dangerous form it consists in blaming others for our failures and limitations. In its more dangerous manifestation it is a symptom of the psychotic condition known as *paranoia*, and characteristically leads to delusions of persecution and of grandeur.

E. Identification

Identification involves such a strong and complete emotional tie with a person or group that the person unconsciously takes on the attitudes, values, and behavior patterns of those with whom he is identifying; he becomes, in a sense, one with them. In doing so, he vicariously enjoys the prestige of the people with whom he is identifying and in this way derives consolation for his personal inferiority. A child who has been defeated by another may rise up and exclaim, "My father can lick your father," and thus, through identification with his father, he regains some of his injured self-esteem. Physical weaklings become football fans, and from the safe location of the grandstand they contract their puny muscles, clench their fists, and shriek themselves hoarse with cries of "tackle him," "kill him," "strangle him!" It is obvious to anyone who is not himself so completely identified with the players that he does not see the audience, that the little man in the grandstand is living vicariously the success of his favorite player out on the field. And the great interest in movie and television stars is an example par excellence of identification. The young girl who collects pictures of her hero is absorbed in even the homeliest details of his life—what he eats for breakfast, what brand of toothpaste he uses, where he buys his socks! All of these little intimate details help her mentally to construct the world in which she, as his beloved, shares in all the details as well as the triumphs of his life. She identifies, too, with the leading lady who appears with him and, so far as she is able, duplicates her wardrobe, her mannerisms, and her speech—often with ludicrous effects.

F. Regression

Regression is a type of withdrawal behavior in which a person, finding the problems of his present-day life too challenging, reverts to a type of behavior which brought satisfaction in the past and which was suitable to an earlier level of development but not to the present stage. It may be adopted only temporarily as a release from tension as, for example, when a father spends Christmas morning playing with his son's trains. This is a normal manifestation of regression and all of us have observed instances of it in everyday life. Some adult parties are perfect examples of it. Many song hits derive their popularity from the regressive tendencies of large portions of the population. Over and over again these songs echo the themes, "Make me a child again just for tonight," or "Tie me to your apron strings again." At an even more deeply regressed level, baby talk is used. And so, we have such favorites as "Twee widdo fiddees" or "I Tot I Taw a Puddy Tat." In singing these songs, grown up men and women temporarily find release from the unbearable tensions of their adult existence. Extreme regression is a symptom of mental disease and may take very bizarre forms. An elderly woman, for example, may act like a small child, talking baby talk and playing with dolls, and be completely out of contact with reality.

G. Sublimation

Sublimation consists in substituting for a blocked or unworthy motive a socially acceptable one which gives some vicarious satisfaction. An unmarried woman, for instance, may direct her "mothering" needs into teaching or child welfare. Aggressive responses to personal frustration may be directed toward removing the source of these frustrations both for oneself and for others. A man who cannot secure appropriate housing for his family, for instance, may dissipate his energies by making futile and puerile verbal attacks upon government officials whom he blames for the situation. Or, he may sublimate these aggressive impulses by directing his energies to organizing an intelligent attack upon the housing problem and thus indirectly solve his own problem and that of others. Certain kinds of artistic and intellectual achievement may be the result of sublimation, although it is probable that the greatest artistic and intellectual achievements are direct rather than indirect responses to motives.

This completes our description of the different patterns of human adjustment. We turn now to a consideration of the adjustive process itself. In the next chapter we shall discuss the meaning of adjustment, what constitutes a "good" adjustment, the different levels of adjustment and their interaction, the role of habit in adjustment, and lastly, the psychology of adjustment in the light of the Christian vocation.

IX

The Problem of Human Adjustment

Of all strong things none is more strong than man;
Man that has learned to shield himself from cold
And the sharp rain; and turns his marvelous arts
Awhile to evil; and yet again to good;
Man that is made all-glorious with his city
When he obeys the inviolable laws
Of earth and heaven; but when, in subtle pride,
He makes a friend of wrong, is driven astray
And broken apart, like dust before the wind.
—ALFRED NOYES [1]

I. THE MEANING OF ADJUSTMENT

Whenever anyone becomes more favorably related to the total situation of which he is a part or to one or more aspects of it, he has made an adjustment. An adjustment is some kind of a change for the better in an individual's relation to his environment of people, things, and his own body. Adjustments of the whole person are made in two ways. The person may (1) adjust himself to the environment or (2) adjust the environment to himself. Both kinds of adjustment can be illustrated by assuming that a person is living in a cold drafty house. Unless he makes some adjustment he is liable to become ill. Several possibilities of adjustment are open to him, two of which highlight the differences in the above types of adjustment. He may, on the one hand, go to bed and wrap himself up in heavy blankets, and thus avoid taking cold. In doing so, however, he limits his freedom of action. He may, on the other hand, adjust the environment to himself by having the house weather-stripped or by installing a new furnace. In the second instance more intelligence is called into play than in the first and the adjustment is on a more human level. The second type of adjustment leaves him free to perform

[1] Alfred Noyes, *Book of Earth* (New York, Frederick A. Stokes Company, 1925), pp. 38–39.

various activities about the house; it gives him more freedom to behave as a human being. But in either case, the person's relation to his environment has been changed for the better—either alternative is better than freezing!

II. CRITERIA OF ADJUSTMENT

The problem of human adjustment is a focal point toward which philosophy, theology, and science converge. *What* constitutes a good adjustment is a question for theology and philosophy. *How* it is achieved is a question for philosophy, for theology, and for science. Science in itself has no resources for determining what "ought" to be or what "should" be; it can only tell us what is or what probably will be under certain given observable conditions. To a limited extent only can science tell us how a good adjustment can be achieved since the ends and the means in human adjustment are very intimately related.

Three different meanings of *normal* adjustment are found in psychological literature and each is based upon a different criterion. They are (1) the pathological, (2) the statistical, and (3) the normative views. According to the first of these views, the *pathological,* a person is normal so long as he does not have an illness or peculiarity which incapacitates him for everyday living. This criterion is used in medicine as well as in psychology. A man may, for instance, have distorted hearing and still be considered normal if he somehow manages to get along in everyday life in spite of his defective hearing. Similarly, he may have many defective teeth, but if he can eat and speak without difficulty, he is considered normal.

According to the second view, the *statistical,* a person is normal if he tends to be like the average man in the population. The specific criterion commonly used is that the normal man falls within the middle 50 per cent of his group. The further away a man is from the central tendency of the group, the less normal he is according to this criterion. For instance, if the average ten-year-old has three decayed teeth, a ten-year-old with three decayed teeth is considered normal and one with five decayed teeth is considered abnormal. This criterion, like the pathological, is often used in medicine as well as in psychology. Normal weight, for example, is often thought of as that which is the average for one's height and years. Anything markedly above or below this average would be considered abnormal, even though the deviation might be in harmony with one's body build and entail no obvious disadvantages.

According to the third or *normative* view, a person is normal in proportion as he has progressed toward a given norm or ideal of perfection. This criterion, obviously, can be used only when the norm has been clarified. This leads us to a consideration of values. Since science of itself does not determine values, psychologists who use this criterion differ greatly in their notions of what constitutes a good adjustment. And since the means of achieving values are so closely related to the kind of value pursued, the recommendations psychologists make for achieving adjustment will necessarily vary with their ideas of what constitutes a "good" adjustment. Commonly, two goals of satisfactory adjustment are presented in psychological literature: (1) the satisfaction felt or expressed by the individual as to the manner of life he is pursuing, and (2) the degree to which the individual's behavior conforms to the expectations of society. It may be questioned, of course, whether this second goal falls into the normative category since it also appears to accept a statistical criterion. Implicit in the statistical criterion is the value judgment that what is characteristic of people in general is "normal." Both of the above goals are relativistic; that is, they are not based upon any objective and absolute criterion of what constitutes the "good." According to the first criterion, good adjustment is whatever the individual himself likes; his own subjective attitude of satisfaction is the norm. Nothing is right or wrong, good or bad unless the individual thinks or feels it is.[2] According to the second view, a person is well-adjusted in so far as he does not deviate from the rules of conduct approved by the social group of which he is a member. Poor adjustment would be a deviation sufficiently great to arouse social disapproval. This view is commonly accepted by social psychologists and sociologists.[3]

The Christian need not quarrel with the above norms of adjustment since they do not conflict with his own. But for him

---

[2] L. F. Shaffer, *The Psychology of Adjustment* (Boston, Houghton Mifflin Company, 1936), p. 138.
[3] E. R. Mowrer, *Disorganization, Personal and Social* (Philadelphia, J. P. Lippincott Company, 1942), p. 32.

these criteria are not enough. His religion gives him an absolute norm toward which all of his efforts to adjust must be directed. The Christian goal is to become an "other Christ," and in the pursuit of this goal everything that does not help or which positively hinders its attainment must be ruthlessly jettisoned. What he likes and what other people like about him matter only secondarily. The Christian can never be smugly complacent and content with himself as he is, because, no matter how far he has progressed along the path to Christian perfection, he always has a long way to go. He may express satisfaction with the way of life he has chosen in which to pursue his goal; he must never express satisfaction with the spiritual stature to which he has attained. He may be making a satisfactory adjustment as a Christian and be either accepted or rejected by the group. Provided his intention is good, the fact of acceptance or rejection may be irrelevant. What is important is that the Christian use all of the circumstances of his life, the pleasant and unpleasant, acceptance or rejection, to foster his spiritual growth rather than to hinder it.

The problem of adjustment is more complicated for man than for other living organisms because man must adjust simultaneously on several different levels. Naturally, the human being lives on three different levels of being: (1) the vegetative, (2) the sensitive, and (3) the rational. Supernaturally, he must make the appropriate adjustment to God. Whether he is aware of it or not, a human being is continually making adjustments at all of these levels. Other animals are called upon to make only the first two natural adjustments, adjustments at the vegetative and sensitive levels.

III. NATURAL LEVELS OF ADJUSTMENT

A. Vegetative Level

The lowest order of living beings is comprised of vegetables or plants. Man shares with these organisms the capacities for nutrition, growth, and reproduction. These powers have as their end the preservation of the individual and the species. Vegetative functions in the human being merge with the activity and functioning of the whole person. Adjustments at this level consist in maintaining the proper balance in biochemical functions within the body. This balance or equilibrium has been called

THE PROBLEM OF HUMAN ADJUSTMENT 217

homeostasis. In the following paragraphs we shall attempt to show why homeostasis is essential to human life and how it is achieved.

The human body is a complex organism, composed of different organs with specialized functions. These organs, in turn, are made up of tissues, and these tissues are composed of body cells. Each cell of the body is made up of a highly specialized system of chemical substances, mostly carbon, oxygen, hydrogen, and nitrogen. There is a constant exchange of materials going on in each body cell, a process known as *metabolism*. All parts of the body are functionally related, and the organism acts as a unitary system for the conversion and expenditure of energy. Because the rate of metabolism varies from one organism to another, there are great individual differences in the amount of energy released. These differences in energy output account in part for differences in the "social stimulus" value of people; leaders, for instance, are almost always people with a great amount of energy available. The metabolic rate is higher in infants than in older persons, and it decreases steadily up to the onset of puberty. At all age levels, however, from infancy to old age, there are great individual differences.

Metabolic changes keep the human body in a constant state of flux; yet throughout all of these changes, from birth to death, the body maintains a stability favorable to its life and growth.

> In an open system, such as our bodies represent, compounded of unstable material and subjected continually to disturbing conditions, constancy is in itself evidence that agencies are acting, or ready to act, to maintain this constancy.[4]

Ultimately, of course, the agency responsible for homeostasis in the body is the soul, or what makes the body live. But the more proximate principles of homeostasis constitute an important field of scientific research. Physiologists have conducted many investigations to determine just how the equilibrium in the body is maintained, and a brief description of their studies will be given at this point.

Since the environment of all the cells in the body is a fluid, the content and reactions of this fluid have been studied most intensively. Two kinds of regulation of the fluid matrix of the body

[4] W. B. Cannon, *The Wisdom of the Body* (New York, W. W. Norton & Company, Inc., 1932), p. 299.

take place: (1) regulation of *materials*, and (2) regulation of *processes*. Hunger and thirst, storage of food material, and the overflow of superfluous material keep the material of the body constant. Various complex mechanisms in the nervous and glandular systems carry on such vital processes as keeping the body at the optimum temperature or maintaining the proper rate of metabolism. Whenever an event occurs which disturbs the physiological balance of the organism, compensatory activities are spontaneously set up within the body to restore the balance. The internal temperature is held constant by the compensatory activity of sweating. The blood content of water, fat, calcium, oxygen, protein, and sugar remains fairly constant so long as the individual eats the foods necessary for obtaining these substances. White blood cells normally restore injured tissues. These are a few examples of homeostasis, the process whereby the body maintains a relatively constant internal physical and chemical state under changing environmental conditions. Minor failures of homeostasis are reflected in unhealthy states of body and mind.

Some contemporary psychologists consider homeostasis the basic physiological concept in terms of which psychological processes can be interpreted and clarified. They point out that homeostasis permits us as persons to rise above the immediate needs of the body and to explore, enjoy, use, and improve our environments of people and things. The key concept here, they claim, is adjustment through learning, and such adjustment is made possible because homeostatic mechanisms take care of adjustment at a lower or subhuman level.

B. Sensitive Level

Man shares with other animals, in addition to the vegetative powers listed above, three further capacities at a higher level: the capacities for (1) sense knowledge, (2) emotion, and (3) movement. In the philosophy of Aristotle and St. Thomas, the distinction between plants and animals is made on the basis of these powers. In general, the distinction holds, although there are some very simple organisms which it is difficult to label as either plant or animal on the basis of these criteria. Creeping vines and various disease producing organisms, such as viruses, for instance, are hard to classify. And one investigator (Sir Jagadis Chandra Bose) claims, as a result of his ingenious system of meas-

THE PROBLEM OF HUMAN ADJUSTMENT

urements, that plants are capable of "sensation"; they appear to be elated or depressed by favorable or noxious substances, and even seem to shudder or writhe in a way suggestive of feeling.

People differ greatly in their capacity for sense experience, and these differences are reflected in their relations with the world of people and of things. They differ also in their voluntary muscle activity through which movement is carried out. These differences appear early in life and are, to a considerable extent, unlearned. In any nursery school, during the "rhythm" activities, you will see some children who are completely absorbed in expressing their reactions to the music through rhythmic movements of their bodies. Others fail to keep time, engage in awkward movements, and participate in the rhythmic activities of the group only under compulsion. Differences in the adult personality structure and in the expression of emotions and feelings grow out of these initial differences in sensory and motor enjoyment.

Man's sense appetites (to use the term of Aristotle and St. Thomas) operate at the second level of experience. The term *sense appetite* is not used in contemporary psychology but its nearest equivalent seems to be *drive*. Warren defines the term *drive* as "an aroused reaction tendency characterized by the fact that activity of the organism is directed towards or away from some specific incentive, such as food, water, or animal of the opposite sex." [5] Ordinarily the term is not restricted to organic conditions, such as hunger, thirst, or sex, but is broad enough to include the desire for a particular object or "good," or a mental set which activates human behavior. It "refers either (*a*) to persistent behavior which is goal-directed or (*b*) to the internal stimuli which release such behavior." [6] It is a less inclusive term, however, than *motive*. A *motive* is any goad to activity, and is broad enough to include everything from the simplest physiological drives to the highest type of intellectual ideals. Motives, in other words, may operate at the vegetative, sensitive, or rational level of adjustment, whereas drives are limited to the first two. The term *motive* may be used synonymously with either

[5] H. C. Warren (ed.), *Dictionary of Psychology* (Boston, Houghton Mifflin Company, 1934).

[6] Article on "Motivation" by P. T. Young in *The Encyclopedia of Psychology*, edited by P. L. Harriman (New York, Philosophical Library, 1946), p. 385.

sensitive or rational appetite, depending upon the amount of intellectual insight involved. As used in modern psychology, the term differs in meaning from its use in ethics. In ethics, a motive is either right or wrong, good or bad. It deals with a value judgment. Ethically, a motive must be conscious, because the rightness or wrongness of a choice depends upon the extent to which it conforms to right reason. The person making a choice which is ethically right or wrong, that is, according to a right or wrong motive, must be intellectually aware of the issues involved. In contemporary psychology, however, a motive does not necessarily involve a judgment of value. A motive may be either conscious or unconscious.

The term *incentive* may be equated with the philosophical expression, *objective good*. By incentive, we mean the "good" outside of the person toward which the motivated behavior is directed. It is different at the sensitive level from what it is at the rational. At the sensitive level, water, for example, is an incentive to a person motivated by a thirst drive. At the rational level, objective knowledge may be an incentive to a person whose ideal is the attainment of truth.

C. Rational Level

Adjustments at the rational level are peculiarly human. By means of his rational powers of intellect and will, man is able, to some extent, to "freely make himself" into the kind of personality he wants to become. By means of his intellect he is able to know not only absent things, but also spiritual reality. He is able to know *what* things are (to define them), to reason about them, and to judge whether they possess or lack a given quality. In fact, everything that exists can be known in some degree by the human intellect. This is not the same as saying that any man does know everything. It merely means that in the intellect itself there is no intrinsic block to knowing any one thing or any sort of thing. The intellect is made precisely to know being, and everything that has being can be known in so far as it has being. Because some things have more perfect being than others, they are more knowable, and the intellect can recognize differences in perfection among various things. Thus, we can know the real definition of man, "rational animal," but we do not know the *philosophical* difference between dog and cat—the difference that causes their

THE PROBLEM OF HUMAN ADJUSTMENT 221

anatomical differences. This is so because man is more perfect in his being than a dog or cat.

The will is the appetite of man on the rational level—the power of choosing the things known by the intellect. On the sense level, the appetites of love and hate are immediately aroused by the object presented by the senses. But because the intellect is capable of much broader knowledge than the senses, it can always see not only the *good* in things, but also their limitations or what is bad about them. The will seeks the good, but on this earth goods are always and by nature limited, and therefore not perfect good. The will, however, could only be determined, *forced*, by the perfect good. It follows that the will cannot absolutely be forced by any one good presented to it. The will is therefore free.

Of course this freedom is limited in many ways—by education, environment, previous choices, and so on. But in optimum conditions, people have the power, if not to choose between two things, at least to refrain from acting at all.

Man, who stands at the peak of the material universe, is often referred to as a "microcosmos." He possesses virtually all of the powers of minerals, plants, and other animals, as well as those powers which are peculiarly his own—intellect and will. He is the connecting link between the material and the spiritual universe—higher than all other animals and "a little lower than the angels." Whatever affects any of man's powers affects him as a whole, since man is a unity. His vegetative, sensitive, and rational powers, although distinct in themselves, are interrelated in the economy of the whole person. Adjustments on all three levels are constantly being made by a human being while he is awake. Adjustments on the first level, and to a lesser degree on the second level, are also made while he is asleep. The physical adjustments called for on the first two levels are made more or less unconsciously by the healthy organism. It is only when the adjustments required are extraordinary, as, for example, when a disease germ produces severe illness, or when eardrums are shattered through an explosion, that physical adjustments must be mediated through the use of reason.

Many psychologists do not make a clear distinction between man's sensitive and rational powers as we are doing in this book. The failure to make such a distinction springs from a materialistic bias which makes it impossible for them to conceive of any mental process whatever as essentially spiritual in nature.

Unless we accept the essentially rational nature of man, there is no valid explanation of human freedom, for man's will functions properly only in proportion as the intellect is enlightened. Yet some scientists have, while accepting the fact of human freedom, tried to account for it in terms of Heisenberg's *principle of uncertainty*.[7] A scientific hypothesis like the Heisenberg principle, however, cannot account for an immaterial reality like human freedom. Others try to maintain that there is utter indeterminism in the world, to say that the will acts freely because it has no motive or goal. This position is diametrically opposed to the whole idea of the will's freedom in virtue of an intellectually recognized good.

There are others who deny that the will is free. They view human beings as determined by inexorable laws of nature, or by their own inner compulsions. Various attempts have been made to show that, given certain environmental situations or stimuli, human behavior is as predictable as the behavior of a metal when subjected to a given temperature. Yet none of these attempts has ever been completely successful. (We are speaking here of complex acts, not of reflexes. Reflex acts, common to both man and animal, are highly predictable and involuntary.) The most that we can say is that, in given circumstances, human beings have a *tendency* to act in a certain way but they are not *bound* to do so. Some people, of course, do not use intelligence in meeting the situations of life, and for them the psychological generalizations may very well hold. But that is a different thing from saying that no human being is free to determine his own behavior by using his intelligence and power of volition.

It is important to note that essentially the problem of free will does not concern external acts but is limited to the internal acts of the will. A person may make a very strong and vigorous resolution and still be unable to execute it. This is not a denial of free

---

[7] The principle of physics announced by the German physicist Heisenberg, that it is impossible to measure at the same time the position and velocity of a particle, and that the more accurately the one is measured, the less accurately will the other be. This makes it impossible for the physicist to discover the exact state of affairs in small-scale phenomena, and hence impossible to predict the behavior of individual units, although predictions can be made of average behavior of large groups of particles.

will. The person was free to make the choice and did so. The fact that the resolution was not put into effect does not deny the reality of the choice. A German psychologist performed an experiment which throws light on this problem. He trained his laboratory subjects to respond to a series of nonsense syllables by giving the word which had been associated with it in a paired-comparison presentation. After these responses had been practiced to the point at which they occurred automatically and without reflection, the experimental conditions were changed. The subjects were told to respond to each of the nonsense syllables used in the previous experiment by giving a word that rhymed with it rather than the word with which it had previously been associated. The subjects found that, in spite of their resolution to give words that rhymed, they were repeatedly giving the paired associates which they had previously learned. Some of them were very much chagrined at their failure to give rhymes and made vigorous efforts to overcome the previous habit. But in spite of the intensity of their efforts, they frequently responded according to the habit which had previously been so well developed. This experiment, we believe, illustrates that a resolution may be freely made and be ever so strong, and yet may not be carried into execution because of interfering conditions. The fact that this occurs, not only in the laboratory, but under the conditions of everyday life, does not mean that we are unable to make choices. What it does mean is that the *execution* of our choice is dependent upon a number of physical and psychological conditions, some of which are not under our direct control. In the above experiment, the laboratory-formed habit could be overcome by the subjects only by great concentration of attention and effort, usually accompanied by bodily postures indicating intense expenditure of energy. Theoretically, a habit can be broken by fixating your attention on an antagonistic course of action and repeatedly practicing the opposed habit. In everyday life the problem of substituting good habits for bad ones is not so simple as it looks on paper. The problem is that of concentrating the attention sufficiently to perform the antagonistic action. Bodily cravings, unconscious gestures and movements, the unconscious association of ideas, emotional states, and other factors, all interfere with the directing of attention necessary to carrying out a resolution to break a habit by substituting for it a new habit. Certain pathological conditions will do the same thing. Obsessions and compulsions are cases in point. Persons suffering from such disorders characteristically do not *will* to behave or to think as they do. They are resolved not to do the things which they do. Yet they still possess free will, the freedom to *choose* to do the right thing, but not necessarily the freedom to *do* the right thing. Under such circumstances the person is not responsible for his actions. But he is responsible for his freely chosen intention.

IV. SUPERNATURAL LEVEL OF ADJUSTMENT

The human being, baptized in Christ, becomes the adopted child of God and the brother of Christ. He begins at baptism a life of union with God which he cannot of himself merit, but which he can lose through his own deliberate choice. The supreme maladjustment in the supernatural life is sin. A sin is a rejection of God for something that is less than God. The gravity of this maladjustment is measured not by how guilty the person "feels" about his sin, but by the dignity of the God who is offended and by the amount of malice with which the sin was committed. The supernatural life begun at baptism is normally a life of growth. Failure to grow spiritually is an even greater maladjustment than failure to grow physically. Failure to grow physically is a handicap only in time; it does not, unless the person deliberately allows it to, become a handicap for eternity. Failure to grow spiritually, however, is a handicap for all eternity; nothing can ever compensate for a defect of this kind.

Spiritual writers and theologians have throughout the centuries developed criteria for the understanding of the self at its deepest levels. These spiritual writers have been preoccupied with man in his relation to God and they have been careful to point out that self-knowledge, apart from a knowledge of God, may have a disastrous effect upon the personality. They distinguish between man in his natural state and man in a state of supernatural grace, that is, man as he has been raised to share in the divine life of God. They unanimously agree that the most important thing to know is the state of man's interior life, and not his external disposition or temperament or even his superficial motivation.

Garrigou-Lagrange points out that,

THE PROBLEM OF HUMAN ADJUSTMENT

As soon as a man ceases to be outwardly occupied, to talk with his fellow men, as soon as he is alone, even in the noisy streets of a big city, he begins to carry on a conversation with himself. If he is young, he often thinks of his future; if he is old, he thinks of the past . . .[8] This intimate conversation which a man holds with himself is the key to his interior life.

If a man is fundamentally egotistical, his intimate conversation with himself is inspired by sensuality or pride. He converses with himself about the object of his cupidity, of his envy; finding therein sadness and death, he tries to flee from himself, to live outside of himself, to divert himself in order to forget the emptiness and the nothingness of his life. . . . The intimate conversation of the egoist with himself proceeds thus to death and is therefore not an interior life. His self-love makes him wish to make himself the center of everything, to draw everything to himself, both persons and things. Since this is impossible, he frequently ends in disillusionment and disgust; he becomes unbearable to himself and to others, and ends by hating himself because he wished to love himself excessively. At times he ends by hating life because he desired too greatly what is inferior in it.[9]

As a man becomes less selfish, his inner conversation is about others—his wife, his children, or his friends and their welfare.

If a man who is not in a state of grace begins to seek goodness, his intimate conversation with himself is already quite different. . . . He begins to love himself in a holy manner, not for himself but for God; he begins to understand that he must pardon his enemies and love them, and to wish eternal life for them as he does for himself.[10]

What then is "the interior life"? "The interior life is precisely an elevation and a transformation of the intimate conversation that everyone has with himself as soon as it tends to become a conversation with God."[11] This conversation is called prayer. As a man perseveres in this conversation he progressively knows himself and God. He does not necessarily know "about God" in the sense that the theologian does from his studies, but he "knows God" as a living reality, shares in His life, comes to love God more and more and to love all men as brothers because of their common Father, God. The Christian who has reached a state in which he is habitually united with God, even while conversing with his

---

[8] R. Garrigou-Lagrange, O.P., *The Three Ages of the Interior Life* (St. Louis, B. Herder Book Co., 1947), pp. 40–41.
[9] *Ibid.*
[10] *Ibid.*
[11] *Ibid.*

fellow men, has lost his egotistic self-love and is living an interior life in this world which is the prelude to eternal life in heaven. This is the supreme adjustment required of the Christian.

V. THE WHOLE PERSON ADJUSTS

The philosophy of St. Thomas, while distinguishing between different levels of human life, has emphasized the unity of human personality; it is man who acts and makes adjustments, not just man's glands or muscles or intellect. An ever increasing number of physical illnesses are being attributed primarily to mental rather than to organic causes. Such illnesses are called *psychosomatic;* the *psyche* referring to mind or soul, and *soma* referring to the body. Psychosomatic disease illustrates the truth of St. Thomas' contention that the soul and the body are intimately related; that nothing affects the one which does not also influence the other.

The fact that mind affects body and body affects mind is a commonplace of everyday experience. An attack of indigestion may leave us depressed; a cup of strong coffee may increase our mental alertness. Conversely, a bit of bad news may cause us to lose our appetite, or lead to such voracious eating as to make us ill. A feeling of shame may produce the physical act of blushing; the sight of a snake may send cold chills through our bodies. Such relationships between mind and body are recognized by everyone.

What we have not known until recently, however, about the relationship of mind to body is that diseases which are clearly organic in nature may have their origin in emotional conflicts. Peptic ulcer, a common disease among aggressive, independent executives, is of this nature. The sufferer from this disease may appear on the surface to be emotionally adjusted. Typically, he holds his emotions in, seldom betraying emotional excitement. But inwardly the emotions are causing havoc in his stomach. When strong emotions of fear or rage are present, the stomach is engorged with blood and becomes inflamed. The flow of acid digestive juices is increased at the same time. These juices cause the inflamed stomach to "digest itself." This eating away of the stomach lining produces an ulcer, as illustrated in Figure 30.

Other illnesses which seem to be psychosomatic in nature are

THE PROBLEM OF HUMAN ADJUSTMENT 227

bronchial asthma, hay fever, high blood pressure, arthritis, certain rheumatic conditions, allergies, and menstrual disturbances. Even the common cold, it appears, may be psychosomatic. The English prime minister Gladstone, it is said, often managed to have "diplomatic colds" which prevented him from seeing people or attending meetings which were likely to be unpleasant. The colds

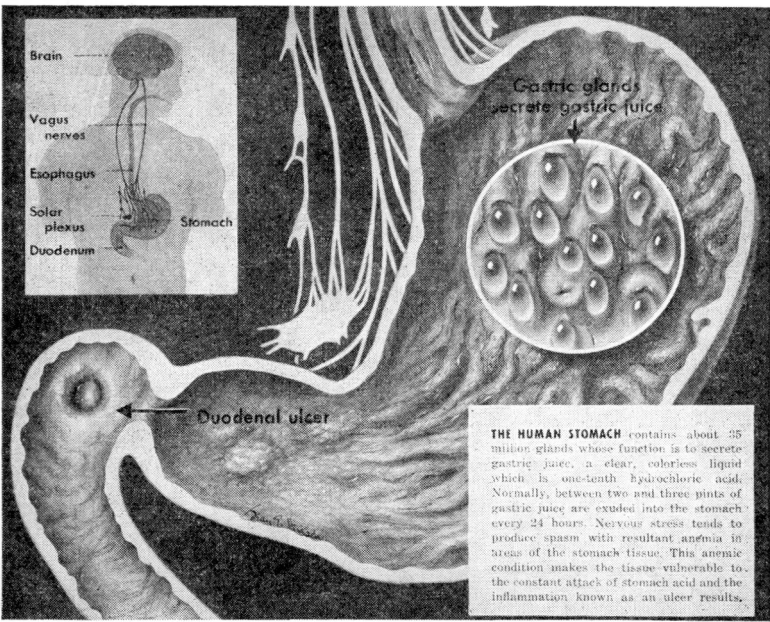

Fig. 30. Formation of a Stomach Ulcer. [Courtesy Northwestern National Life Insurance Company, Minneapolis.]

were real colds, but, significantly, they occurred only at crucial times.

Many popular expressions reflect an awareness of the relation between psychological and physiological processes, a relationship which in many instances is borne out by research findings. We express fear, for example, in the words, "I'm getting cold feet!" Actually fear and anxiety are related to circulatory changes in the extremities. The volume of blood in the feet can be measured by a plethysmograph. When a relaxed person is required to perform a task under conditions which produce anxiety lest he fail, the plethysmograph registers a diminution in the volume of blood in the foot. This diminution of blood results in a sensation of "cold feet."

Further evidence of the unitary functioning of body and soul is seen in various kinds of hypnotic experiments. Hypnosis, as we pointed out in Chapter VIII, is a state of exaggerated suggestibility, in which if you suggest to the subject that he sees red, he actually reports that he sees red. In certain individuals, the effects of this suggestibility are even more marked. Cases have been reported, for instance, in which the hypnotized subject, being told that he is out in the snow and is wearing nothing but a bathing suit, will show a rise in metabolism. Similarly, when the subject was taken to a cold room and told that he was taking a sun bath on a hot day in summer, the rise in metabolism that would ordinarily occur as a result of the cold did not take place. In at least one instance, the suggestion to the hypnotized subject that he was eating a particular kind of food called forth gastric secretions that varied in ferment content with the kind of food suggested. The subject could not, of course, either in a waking or in an hypnotic state, voluntarily control his gastric secretions.

Binet and Feré studied visual phenomena in hypnotized subjects by suggesting that certain visual stimuli were present which were not actually there. They found, interestingly enough, that suggested images of color stimuli followed the laws of color mixture and of retinal rivalry, even though the subjects of the experiments were not aware of these laws. In other words, these suggested sensory states had the same effects as they would have had if they had been real sensations. They are not, then, the effects of an imaginative power acting in isolation from the rest of the human organism. The human being acts as a whole, and imaginary visual sensations lead to the same reflexes as actual sensations.

Let us consider a few other illustrations of this fact that when a human being adjusts to any situation of life he does so as a "whole" being, body and soul. The mental apprehension of danger, for instance, immediately produces physiological changes which will enable the organism to meet the threatening situation effectively. These physiological changes take place automatically, they are not willed. At the same time as these bodily adjustments are being made, the person may also be making an adjustment at a higher level. He may by a free act of the will, for instance, keep his explosive emotions in check and try to reason about the situation. He does not, of course, always succeed in doing so, but the fact that on occasion he does, suffices to show that he has this power.

Clinical psychologists, beginning with Freud, have been greatly impressed by the irrational character of adjustments made by mentally unbalanced people. By studying these disturbed persons they have learned much about normal people and their adjustments to life. In abnormal people we see the exaggeration of many behavior patterns exhibited by normal persons, and thus by studying the abnormal we gain insight into the motivation and behavior of normal people. From the study of abnormal people many generalizations as to cause and effect relations in human behavior have been formulated. One such generalization is that frustration is invariably followed or accompanied by aggression or by "substitute-activity" of some kind,[12] rather than by reasoning. This hypothesis does have a substantial basis in fact. The child who is punished "takes it out" on the cat. The employee who is called on the carpet goes home and finds fault with his wife's cooking. Or, he suppresses criticism of his wife and directs the aggression toward himself by "accidentally" cutting himself with the carving knife. All of us have witnessed adjustments of this kind. Yet most of us, too, if our attention were called to it, could observe situations in which frustration does not precipitate aggression. These situations, of course, are much less dramatic than those giving rise to aggression, and we are consequently not as likely to notice or to remember them.

Generalizations drawn from animal studies, as we have previously shown, must be applied with caution to the normal human being. Similarly, generalizations which hold true for normal persons cannot be applied without qualifications to abnormal people, as, for example, generalizations concerning the role of reasoning in human life. The normal is not, as Freud assumed, a special example of the abnormal, even though many, perhaps all, normal people do on occasion exhibit some abnormal behavior symptoms. Valid generalizations about normal people must show how normal people characteristically react, not how they behave in their "off moments."

[12] J. Dollard, *et al.*, *Frustration and Aggression* (New Haven, Yale University Press, 1939).

Several studies which throw light on the role of reasoning and intelligent behavior in the solution of problems of adjustment which are emotionally toned will be reviewed at this point.

A study of refugees from the Nazi persecutions revealed that aggression was not the most conspicuous or natural outcome of frustration.[13] On the contrary, the most common response to Nazi aggression was increased planning and problem solving. There were also, of course, many aggressive responses. And, in addition, other common responses were "defeat and resignation, regression, conformity, adoption of temporary frames of security, changes in standards of evaluation, lowering of levels of aspiration, heightened in-group feeling," and "increased fantasy and insulation." But in spite of the intense frustration that these people were experiencing, they were more rational than irrational in their behavior and attitudes.

An experiment designed to test the frustration-aggression hypothesis led to similar conclusions.[14] The frustration in this experiment was prolonged loss of sleep. The experimenters assumed that prolonged loss of sleep on the part of college students would be sufficient to elicit aggression if the frustration-aggression hypothesis were true. Accordingly, they set up an experiment in which two groups, each consisting of six college students, were deprived of sleep for twenty-four hours. The members of Group I were permitted to spend the evening studying or reading. They were promised that when they got bored with their work, one of the experimenters would arrive with cards and games. They were allowed to smoke until midnight and then were told rather curtly that smoking from that time on would be taboo. The experimenters, however, continued to smoke in their presence. At three A.M. the experimenter who was supposed to have brought the games arrived, but explained that he had "forgotten" to bring the games and cards. Previously, the subjects had asked for food and were promised a hot breakfast at five A.M., but the experimenter who went out to get it failed to return. The members of Group II were not promised anything, but were led to expect almost anything from the experimenters during the night. The

---

[13] G. W. Allport, J. S. Bruner, and E. M. Jandorff, "Personality under Social Catastrophe," *Character and Personality*, 10 (1941), 1–22.

[14] Nicholas Pastore, "A Neglected Factor in the Frustration-Aggression Hypothesis: A Comment," *J. Psychol.*, 29 (1950), 271–279.

THE PROBLEM OF HUMAN ADJUSTMENT 231

members of Group I showed a great deal of hostility and aggression, most of which was directed at the experimenters. The members of Group II showed almost none, although the physical conditions to which they were subjected were as distressing as those of Group I. The differences in the groups suggest that the *meaning* of the situation for the subject is more important than the mere fact of frustration. Aggressive responses were elicited not so much by frustration as by the unreasonableness and unfairness of the situation. The group which had not been promised anything could assimilate the various frustrations of the night into their understanding of the meaning of the situation whereas the other group could not.

The findings of this experiment and the study of reactions to persecution, which we described above, both lend support to our view that man is essentially a rational creature. In short, the human being when confronted with a problem can adjust at a vegetative, sensitive, or rational level. Typically, adjustments at all three levels are made simultaneously. In the mentally healthy or normal person, adjustment to the total situation is controlled or guided by his intellectual apprehension of what the situation means.

VI. THE ROLE OF HABIT IN ADJUSTMENT

Suppose you have been told by a competent doctor that you must stop drinking coffee if you want to preserve your health. And suppose, too, that you are a coffee "addict" and cannot imagine yourself facing a day without the support of at least one cup of strong black coffee. What are you going to do? In this situation there is really only one reasonable solution and that is to stop drinking coffee. But to discontinue a firmly ingrained habit, such as this one, is not an easy matter. You probably will not be able to do so unless you establish a counter-habit in its place. In other words, it is not enough to tell yourself that you will not drink coffee. You must start at once to develop a taste for another harmless beverage, as, for instance, weak tea, hot milk, or orange juice. Every time you crave coffee, then, you will deliberately drink one of the above liquids. Eventually, after many repeated (and at first distasteful) experiences, the counter-habit gets established and you no longer have to fight the craving for coffee. This adjustment has been made not just by eliminating something from your life (a more or less negative adjustment) but by actively substituting something to compensate for what you are giving up (a positive adjustment). In general, a positive approach is much more effective than a negative one.

The term *habit*, as it is used in scientific and clinical psychology, denotes any learned response which, through repetition, has become automatic and predictable. Obviously, adjustment to many life situations will be facilitated by the acquisition of good habits. An important aspect of all child guidance is that of helping the child acquire useful habits and to avoid or eliminate those which are harmful. Yet, habit training must not become a fetish. Helping human beings to form habits is not the same as training animals. Habits "learned" in an atmosphere of hostility and resentment toward the "trainer" may, and often are, dramatically rejected by people, once the trainer is no longer a threat. Habitual attitudes are as important as habitual ways of doing things. In helping people to form good habits, therefore, a healthy emotional "climate" should be created and with increasing maturity, more respect must be paid to the liberty of the learner. The permanence of the habit is in part a result of the emotionalized attitudes associated with its acquisition and the intellectual appreciation of the value of forming the habit.

The word *habit*, as used in contemporary psychology, differs in meaning from the way in which it was used by St. Thomas. Current scientific usage of the term is in some respects broader, since it includes learned responses at the vegetative and sensitive levels as well as at the rational level of adjustment. The two different notions of habit are supplementary, not contradictory. For St. Thomas only learned dispositions that had their origin in the intellect could be properly classed as habits. Animals left to themselves, he pointed out, do not develop habits; they do so only when they are trained by man. In short, the source of the animal's habit is the intellect and will of man. Thus when placed in a maze in which there is no food, a rat will not run efficiently to the goal. But when the human experimenter places food in the maze as an incentive, a marked change begins to appear in the animal's behavior. He begins to eliminate the blind alleys and gradually learns to take the shortest and quickest path to the goal. He acquires the "maze habit." St. Thomas says that such animal "habits" differ from those of men in that in animals the element of will is lacking—"for they have not that power of using or refraining which seems to belong to the notion of habit."

In the philosophy of St. Thomas good habits are referred to as "virtues" and bad habits as "vices." Two categories of good habits or virtues are recognized: (1) the intellectual virtues, such as understanding, science, wisdom, and prudence, and (2) the moral virtues: justice, temperance, and fortitude. The acquisition of these virtues perfects man's powers and enables him to make an adjustment to life on the highest possible human level. The intellectual virtues alone, however, do not perfect the whole man; they merely perfect his intellect. The moral virtues, on the other hand, perfect the whole man. These habits are acquired by the repetition of acts, and a man is said to possess a virtue when he performs the acts specified by that virtue easily, promptly, and consistently.

The current emphasis of clinical and child psychologists upon the importance of helping a child or an adult with a disturbance of personality to develop wholesome mental attitudes rather than to stress the mechanical acquisition of certain routine acts is, in some respects, similar to the traditional notion of the way in which virtue is acquired. In the traditional philosophy, all the natural, moral virtues are acquired habits. Originally, virtuous acts were consciously performed in the light of reason and with great effort of the will. With repetition, however, the amount of attention necessary to elicit the virtuous act is diminished, and the effort required of the will becomes significantly less. In fact, the act becomes, in a sense, "second nature." The term *habit*, as used in Thomistic philosophy, would seem to embrace both of the current psychological terms, *mental attitude* and *habit*. It would add to these two notions, moreover, a concept which is ignored to a considerable extent in modern scientific and clinical psychology, namely, the concept of *freedom* in making one's own personality because of the capacity for making *free choices*. The Christian principle that "man freely makes himself" by voluntarily choosing his habits in the light of reason is conspicuously absent in many current psychological discussions of human adjustment.

VII. PSYCHOLOGY OF ADJUSTMENT AND THE CHRISTIAN VOCATION

In the Christian view of life, the greatest of all evils and the most distressing is sin. Life is a period of probation in which the human person is gradually transformed into the image of Christ by voluntarily using all of the events of life as God wills that they be used. Every event of life is either willed by God or permitted by Him to enable each person to reach his eternal destiny. The world is a battlefield in which the Christian struggles each day with the forces of good and evil. Success or failure as the world judges them are of little importance. What matters is not the external events of life but the way in which the human being reacts to these events—what they contribute to the development of his character. For the Christian the norm of good is God's will for him. And the hero or heroine of God not only resigns himself to God's will; he ardently embraces it. He is not unduly elated by success nor cast down by failure. Like holy Job he exclaims, "The Lord has given and the Lord has taken away. Blessed be the name of the Lord." He knows that before he is acceptable to God his soul must be tried in the crucible of suffering.

For the Christian, therefore, the goal of adjustment can never be safety, security, or comfort. For him the good life is the "true" life, not the comfortable life. He looks upon mental suffering not as a problem to be eliminated as soon as possible, but as a "cross" to be borne in union with Christ for as long a time as God wills. The vocation of the Christian is to become an "alter Christus" or an "other Christ." He attains this end, as a rule, not by any dramatic or spectacular acts (such as martyrdom) but by carrying his cross daily in imitation of Christ and in union with Christ. The measure of his stature as a Christian is the degree of his participation in the sufferings of Christ—the agony in the garden of Gethsemane as well as the crucifixion on Calvary. For the Christian as for the non-Christian, suffering in itself is an evil. But suffering willed or permitted by God and accepted as coming from God is a necessary means of spiritual growth.

An adequate adjustment is an adjustment made to the whole of reality, not to some isolated aspect of it. The goal of adjustment for the Christian is to bring his own subjective estimates of value into harmony with objective truth and goodness. Neither his own

THE PROBLEM OF HUMAN ADJUSTMENT 235

likes and dislikes nor the mediocre values of the group can slake his thirst for the ultimate objective good, which is God. Nor can his social aspirations find fulfillment in conformity to the group, in a superficial "live and let live" relationship to other people. The Christian is commanded to love all men, those whom he likes and those whom he does not like. He must be united to them in the depths of his being, not just on the surface. And he can do this only by seeking objective truth and goodness outside of himself, for

> That which satisfies me alone, which bears only upon my own enjoyment, isolates. The world of authentic values, on the contrary, unifies. And God, the deepest theme of each of us, the highest Good, is at the same time the most general theme, of which we cannot be absolutely conscious unless we are also conscious of our ultimate deepest communion with all men.[15]

Adjustment on the natural plane alone, therefore, is not sufficient for the Christian. His practical judgments, the decisions of his everyday life, will be based not only upon reason, but upon the inspirations of the grace of God. For the baptized person, nothing, not even the satisfaction of basic physiological needs, is a morally indifferent act. All of a baptized person's natural powers have been refined and elevated because they are possessed by someone who shares in the divine life. Bodily appetites and their satisfaction, common to both man and animal, are very different in the human being from what they are in the animal. The dog, being only dog, unconsciously gives glory to God in satisfying these impulses. Man, on the contrary, must consciously and intentionally perform these acts for the glory of God. And in performing these acts day by day for the glory of God, under the inspiration of divine grace, he progressively comes closer to his final goal—union with God for all eternity—the beatific vision. This is the ultimate criterion of good adjustment—the degree to which it leads a man toward or away from his eternal goal. The Christian who is making a proper adjustment to his role of "alter Christus" will carefully weigh all of the factors which enter into his everyday life, and subordinate lesser values to greater ones. This will be true not only for the great decisions of human life, such as the choice of a vocation, the selection of a professional

---

[15] Dietrich Von Hildebrand, *Liturgy and Personality* (New York, Longmans, Green & Company, 1943), p. 44.

field, or the choice of a marriage partner, but for the smaller and seemingly less important decisions which must be made every day. These include his daily behavior toward members of his family, coöperation in performing household tasks and sharing the inevitable burdens of social life, the time of retiring and the hour of rising (whether he will look at television far into the night, for instance, and sleep late in the morning, or retire at night and go to Mass in the morning). The kind of person he will eventually become and the quality of his adjustment to the whole of reality will be determined in large measure by the *voluntary* choices that enter into his everyday life.

PART V

Human Activity and Adjustment

Human culture and achievement result from the use of man's power to perceive, to learn, and to think. They are the product of man's creative thought. Mental disorder accompanies the subordination of reason to emotion.

X

How People Perceive the World

What is the Shape, that from a body flies?
What moves, what propagates, what multiplies
And paints one Image in a thousand Eyes?
When to the Eye the crowding Figures pass,
How in a Point can all possess a Place,
And Lye distinguished in such narrow Space?
—BLACKMORE [1]

We have followed the thread of discussion through the driving forces of human nature (goads to action) and have given you a brief introduction to the *why* of human adjustment and to the many factors which influence man's psychological development. But since man is a many-sided creature, it is not enough to know why he adjusts as he does. We must also know something about the tools he possesses for making adjustments. One of these tools or "service mechanisms" by which he comes to know and interact with his environment is that of *perception*. Perception involves "noticing" things and situations. Sometimes a person makes a poor social adjustment because he does not perceive the reactions of others about him. Or again, he cannot remember an individual's name because he failed to "hear" it when he was introduced to him. The difficulty here is evidently not one of faulty memory but of faulty perception. The fundamental facts and principles of human perception will be the subject matter of this chapter.

In our discussion of the sense of vision in Chapter VI, we pointed out that the eye is very similar in its structure to a camera. Such a statement, however, does not at all explain how

---

[1] *Creation*, VII, 128–133. Quoted by Marjorie Hope Nicolson in *Newton Demands the Muse* (Princeton, N.J., Princeton University Press, 1946), p. 101.

people "see" as human beings. Several people may enter a room at the same time and see very different things. You may observe that the hostess has large circles under her eyes and that her eyelids are inflamed. You "perceive" that she either has a cold or has been crying, and the way in which you participate in the conversation and the social role that you adopt is influenced by that observation. Another person present at the same time may be completely unaware of the physical or emotional state of the hostess. He may, however, be aware of parts of the room that other people do not at all perceive. He may, for example, note that a small object on an end table is a priceless bit of hand-carved ivory. He may then proceed to note all of the art objects in the room and make some judgment as to the artistic taste or the probable wealth of the owners. Another person may "see" only the tea table and note that the food is either meager or plentiful. Still another person may observe all of these things and, in addition, "perceive" the psychological interactions of the people present, such as the relative ease or tension exhibited by members of the group. How and what people perceive is an important factor in their adjustment to the environment.

Perception is an experience easier to describe than to define. If we analyze the example in the paragraph above, we shall find out some of the main characteristics of perception.

First of all, perception involves getting to know *things*. This means that perception is a process in which you concentrate on some *object* or other and not just on the immediate sensory experience you have of it (its qualities) and by which you learn of its existence. This object may be anything in the world—a table, another person, a painting, a part of your own body. In this characteristic of being object-centered, perception differs essentially from sensation. In a sensation, light simply strikes the retina of your eye evoking a train of consequences, psycho-physical in nature, which enables you, for example, to become aware of blueness. In a perception, on the contrary, you know the hostess, or the table, or some other *object through* the light seen coming from it. In a sensation, sound waves strike your ear drum and a nerve impulse travels to the brain; but in a perception, you know a person through his conversation. Another way of saying that you perceive objects is to say that you perceive *wholes*.

From the example above you can also discover another impor-

HOW PEOPLE PERCEIVE THE WORLD

tant characteristic of perception: it is influenced by past experience and by values and needs. What each person with normal sensory equipment perceives in a given situation will depend on what he is *attending* to, what he *expects* to see, what he is *used* to seeing, and often on what he *wants* to see.

Before you perceive anything, you must *attend* to it. You may, for instance, be looking in the direction in which a traffic accident occurs. When you are asked to report the details of the accident, however, you may be at a loss to do so. Although you were looking in the right direction, you did not really "see" what was happening. You failed to perceive what was happening because your attention was not focused in time upon the scene of the accident. Attention is important as a preparation for perception; we shall therefore begin by considering some basic facts about attention.

I. SOME BASIC FACTS ABOUT ATTENTION

A. What Does Attention Involve?

If you were addressing a group of people you would be able to tell from their general attitude whether they were paying attention to you or not. Among the clues that would give you this information would be the general muscular set or tension of their bodies. Ordinarily, the person who is attending to you will turn in your direction or will at least look toward you. When you finish a sentence or make an important point he may nod with a gesture of understanding or he may raise a question pertinent to what you have been saying which indicates that he has been listening or attending. Let us see what is involved in the process of attention.

First, you must be *conscious* in order to pay attention. Consciousness is characterized by different degrees of clearness. Normally, people lose consciousness in sleep, although this loss of consciousness may not be total but only partial. A partial loss of consciousness is referred to as *stupor* if it is quite deep, or *clouding of consciousness* if it is lighter. A temporary loss of consciousness resulting from a toxic cause such as an insulin injection, diabetes, or an excess of alcohol, is called a *coma*. If the loss of consciousness takes place immediately after a blow on the head or a fall, and is regained after a brief interval, the condition is known as *concussion*. Anything that interferes with full consciousness also interferes with attention and perception.

Second, to pay attention you must be in a condition of readiness to perceive a given stimulus or class of stimuli. This state of readiness is called *set*. This is a complicated affair. First there must be a set of *receptors* in a condition to receive stimuli. For example, the eyes must be open to see the stimuli and the head placed in a position most favorable for seeing, or for hearing, as when a person who is deaf in one ear turns his good ear in the direction of the speaker. Attending also involves a *muscular* set, in that the muscles of the eyes must keep them properly focused, or postural body muscles must keep the body in a state favorable for reception of the stimulus (as when an athlete is prepared to make a quick start when he hears the starting gun). A *mental* set may also be present, as, for example, when in an association experiment, you are instructed to react to the stimulus word by giving its opposite. The particular set of the moment has an influence upon what you will or will not perceive in your environment. If you are set to write an important letter to a friend, you may be barely aware that people are talking in the room but may not at all "hear" what they are saying in the sense of following what they are saying. Sleight of hand tricks are based upon this principle. The spectators are gullibly led to adopt a false set, that is, one which is unfavorable to perceiving the phenomena that the magician (who also has deft and practiced fingers) is trying to conceal. An inappropriate set is distracting and prevents people from perceiving what is taking place before their eyes. When you are fully conscious and alert and have adopted a motor or mental set favorable to perceiving a given sensory stimulus, we say you are in a state of attention.

B. What Arouses Attention?

When your attention is being attracted to something, you are being influenced by both internal and external stimuli. Your desires and needs—in a word, your motivation—provide an inner condition of readiness to attend to some stimuli and to disregard others. The smell of steak frying may cause you to spring to attention if you are ravenously hungry. If, on the contrary, you are nauseated or satiated, you will quickly get out of the way of such a stimulus or ignore it completely. All of us are more or less permanently set to attend to some kinds of stimuli because of motives that are continually present. An artist, for example, may habitually notice the lights and shadows of landscapes and the variegated hues of nature because he is interested in painting such scenes in water color. An industrialist, viewing the same scene, might miss the subtle nuances of light and color and be aware only of the nearness of the site to a potential source of water power or the suitability of the land for laying railroad tracks. Attention of this kind which grows out of rather enduring interests and attitudes is called *habitual attention*.

Attention may be *voluntary* or *involuntary*. Voluntary attention grows out of our interests, attitudes, goals, and aspirations. Involuntary attention takes place in spite of ourselves and is often the result of some striking change in the perceptual scene or field. At all times, except when we are completely unconscious, we are continually being bombarded with a variety of stimuli, only a small portion of which ever reach the focus of our attention. There is a natural limit to what we can "take in" or apprehend at any given moment in time. This can easily be demonstrated by the use of a tachistoscope, an instrument devised to expose objects, pictures, letters, words, or digits for various controlled durations of time, as shown in Figure 31. In a typical experiment, the exposure time is sufficiently short to prevent eye movements and may be as short as .01 second. When a series of unrelated letters is flashed upon a screen for this brief interval, most people are able to apprehend about eight of them. If words are used instead of the letters, however, a greater number are perceived. For example, a person who can perceive only eight letters isolated like these: H G O M E G O N, can easily perceive the nine letters in these two words: G O I N G   H O M E. When a meaningful sentence is used, the amount perceived is greater still. The number of items of any sort that can be recognized and named from a single brief exposure is called the *span of visual apprehension*. Sometimes the term *span of attention* is used, but strictly speaking this is not correct. Attention refers to the vividness or clearness of the mental process. Apprehension involves something more. It involves the ability to recognize and report upon what has been seen. It is also possible to determine the span of apprehension for sensory modalities other than vision, such as the tactual or auditory sense.

Fig. 31. Tachistoscope. [Courtesy C. H. Stoelting Company, Chicago.]

In general, the conditions listed below are important determiners of what will arouse attention:

1. *Location.* An object directly before us has an advantage over one located at the periphery, particularly if it is isolated in some way from its surroundings.

2. *Change or movement.* Objects that change in any respect, such as intensity, or move, arouse attention more easily than those that are unchanging or stationary. For instance, lights that

HOW PEOPLE PERCEIVE THE WORLD

flash on and off at intervals attract more attention than those that are on continuously; a fire siren attracts attention because of its constantly changing pitch.

3. *Novelty.* An unconventional or strikingly different combination of sounds, colors, or other stimuli, arouses attention more readily than stimuli that are common in our everyday environment.

4. *Intensity.* Strong stimuli, other things being equal, have an advantage over weak stimuli in arousing attention.

5. *Repetition.* Within limits, the repetition of a stimulus is a help in securing attention. It also helps in remembering the stimulus.

6. *Interest.* Interest, unlike the factors listed above, is an internal determiner of attention. People have a tendency to notice stimuli that have some bearing upon their habitual interests. A mother, for instance, will notice a display of children's clothing but may not attend to an adjacent display of hunting equipment.

7. *Need or interest of the moment.* Need is also an internal determinant of attention. If you are hungry, a restaurant or lunch counter will arouse your attention more readily than it would if you were not hungry.

C. Can Attention Be Given to Two Tasks at the Same Time?

Some people appear to be adept at doing two things at the same time. Students, for example, often claim that they can study and listen to the radio at the same time. A number of carefully controlled experiments have been performed to see if such a thing really takes place. The results are overwhelmingly negative. What happens when a person is ostensibly attending to two things at the same time is that his attention is rapidly shifting from one stimulus or task to the other. In most instances of this kind there is a considerable loss of efficiency in both of the tasks. In other words, efficiency is considerably below 50 per cent for each of the tasks attempted. The amount of inefficiency, however, is related to the kind of tasks performed.

D. What Effect Does Distraction of Attention Have Upon Efficiency of Performance?

Some people are able to keep their attention on their work in spite of surrounding noise and distractions while others are not. The difference is partly a function of differences in motivation or in personality and partly the result of the kinds of tasks attended to. In one experiment subjects were required to punch keys, corresponding to a code, on a specially designed typewriter. The task was one which required a high degree of concentration. As the subjects began to work, distractions in the form of bells and buzzers were introduced. At first the work was slowed up, but very soon the subjects regained the efficiency they had shown before the distractions were brought in. But this efficiency under distraction was attained through a much greater expenditure of energy than when the distractions were not present. The subjects pressed the keys of the typewriter harder and tended to speak the letters out loud. When the noise of the bells and buzzers subsided, there was again a momentary slowing up.

E. Fluctuations of Attention

Years ago a German scientist discovered that if a watch is placed in a position at which its ticking can just barely be heard, its ticking will alternately be heard and not heard.

A similar fluctuation can be demonstrated with cutaneous stimuli, such as that of a weak electric current or light corks resting upon the skin. People differ in the rate at which these fluctuations take place and the rate is not always constant for any one person. A visual phenomenon somewhat similar, but more complicated, was described by a Swiss naturalist who discovered that if you look at a cube, such as that pictured in Figure 32, one surface will be the front at one time and another surface will suddenly become the front at another time.

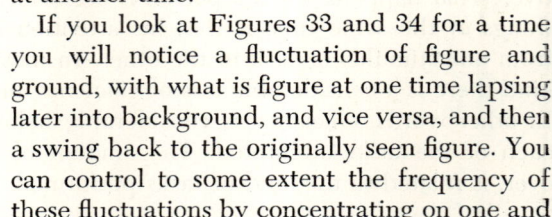

Fig. 32. Necker Cube.

If you look at Figures 33 and 34 for a time you will notice a fluctuation of figure and ground, with what is figure at one time lapsing later into background, and vice versa, and then a swing back to the originally seen figure. You can control to some extent the frequency of these fluctuations by concentrating on one and trying to hold it as long as possible. The fluctuations will still take place, in spite of your efforts to prevent it, but they will take place less frequently.

Fluctuations of the type that we have just described should

HOW PEOPLE PERCEIVE THE WORLD

probably not be classified as genuine fluctuations of attention, since they are not shifts from clearness to unclearness but the simpler ones are shifts from awareness to unawareness, and the more complicated are shifts of perceptual structuralization.

A number of theories have been introduced to account for the phenomena of fluctuation. Visual fluctuations,

Fig. 33. Fluctuation of Perspective. [Courtesy Marietta Apparatus Company.]

we know, are related to the following physiological conditions: changes in the adaptation of the retina or in the visual area of the occipital lobe, changes in respiration, and changes in the circulation of the blood. Gestalt psychologists stress in particular the importance of changes in the neural organization of the brain, or changes in what they call "brain dynamics," in accounting for the figure-ground reversals.

F. Central Factors in Attention

Attention as a state of readiness is controlled by the set or adjustment of receptor, effector, and central nervous mechanism. Under certain conditions, the mental set controlled by the central nervous system may successfully block attention even when the recep-

Fig. 34. Figure and Ground. [Courtesy Marietta Apparatus Company.]

tors are attuned to the stimuli involved. For example, a person may be put into a hypnotic trance by the repetition of monotonous stimuli. This condition is one of exaggerated suggestibility. While the subject is in the trance, the experimenter may suggest to him that although he is going to be burned with a match, he will feel no pain. This then actually happens, and even though the subject is burned rather severely, he may show no evidence of attending to or feeling pain, especially if he is a person with a certain group of personality traits. Similarly, as we have already indicated, if the experimenter suggests that the subject will see only two pencils, and subsequently puts five pencils before him and asks the subject to count them, the subject will count only two. These findings suggest that a central mechanism is responsible for the set to attend or not to attend to stimuli. The fact, too, which you have probably noticed, that when you are preoccupied with your thoughts even very strong stimuli may escape your attention, points in the same direction. People have sometimes accidentally cut themselves or even broken bones when absorbed in some skilled or creative activity, and later have had great difficulty in determining just how or when the accident occurred.

Once you have begun to pay attention, you are in a position to begin perceiving. We now turn from the subject of attention to a consideration of visual perception, sound perception, and general characteristics of perception.

II. VISUAL PERCEPTION

A. The Retinal Image

We are able to see objects only because light falls upon them and is somehow reflected, absorbed, or modified by them. The light which comes from different parts of an object reaches different points on the retina, as shown in Figure 35. Ordinarily, the rays of light reflected by objects travel in a straight direction from the object to the retina. Consequently, the object is projected point for point upon the retina. This correspondence of the retinal image to the actual direction of the object enables us to perceive the direction of objects. You will note, however, that the image of the object is projected upside down upon the retina and reversed right and left; yet we perceive it in an upright position. In an effort to determine how it is that we perceive objects right side up and in their correct position, right or left, Stratton invented a system of lenses which caused the images of objects to be projected right side up on the retina and reversed right and left. He wore these lenses constantly for a week except during the night when he was blindfolded. The effect of these lenses was that he "saw" everything upside down and "backwards." For this reason he found at first that he was greatly handicapped in orientating himself in space and that he was constantly making false movements. Gradually, however, he was able to perform manual activities with much less strain and to move about the house in a normal manner. He was able

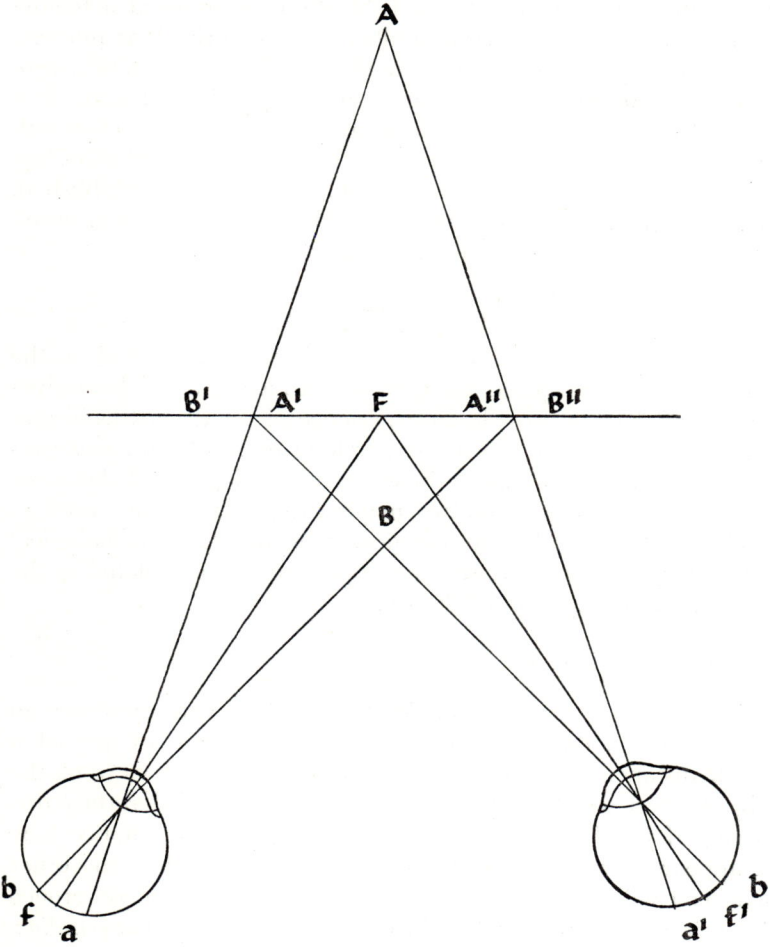

Fig. 35. Inverted Retinal Images and Non-Corresponding Retinal Points. Crossed and uncrossed images are determined by the retinal points that are stimulated. F is the fixation point, which is seen singly. Image of more distant point, A, falls upon points a and a', non-corresponding parts of the retina, and is seen double.

to readjust in this way because he had become accustomed to treating visual cues as he would normally have treated their exact opposite. At no time during this experiment did objects appear to him to be right side up. At the end of the experiment, when the glasses were removed, Stratton experienced a feeling of relief at being again in a familiar spatial world. It is interesting to note, however, that even this brief training period produced effects upon his eye-hand coördination. Placed again in a normal visual situation, Stratton showed some signs of bewilderment and false movements. In a few hours this confusion had entirely disappeared and the old habits were fully reëstablished. The results of this experiment suggest that an integration of vision and movement is responsible for what we see.

B. The Perception of Depth and Distance

The rays of light coming from an object are projected on the surface of the retina as on a plane surface and of themselves are insufficient to provide an experience of depth, just as a wire seen exactly end-on may be either long or short, and you cannot tell which. How, then, do we perceive depth and distance? In general, we recognize two major categories of cues used in such perception: (1) physiological cues and (2) psychological cues. In everyday life these cues appear to be interrelated in the perception of depth and distance.

1. Physiological cues

You perceive depth in part because each of your eyes sees an object from a different direction. Because your eyes are set a small distance apart, each gets a slightly different view of the object upon which they are focused. This is called *retinal disparity*. If you focus on a fairly near object and then notice how it appears to move when you shut first one and then the other eye, you will have an example of this. The apparent difference in position from one view to the other is called *binocular parallax*. The fact that two flat pictures of the same scene, taken at a distance apart just a little more than the distance between the two eyes, can be fused into one picture with the added and somewhat exaggerated dimension of depth, is illustrated by the *stereoscope*. The stereoscope, as shown in Figure 36, is a device for projecting two such flat pictures to the portion of each retina that would have been stimulated by them in viewing the actual scene. A sliding holder carries the card upon which are printed the two pictures. Light rays from these pictures are projected through prisms that throw the images to the outer portions of

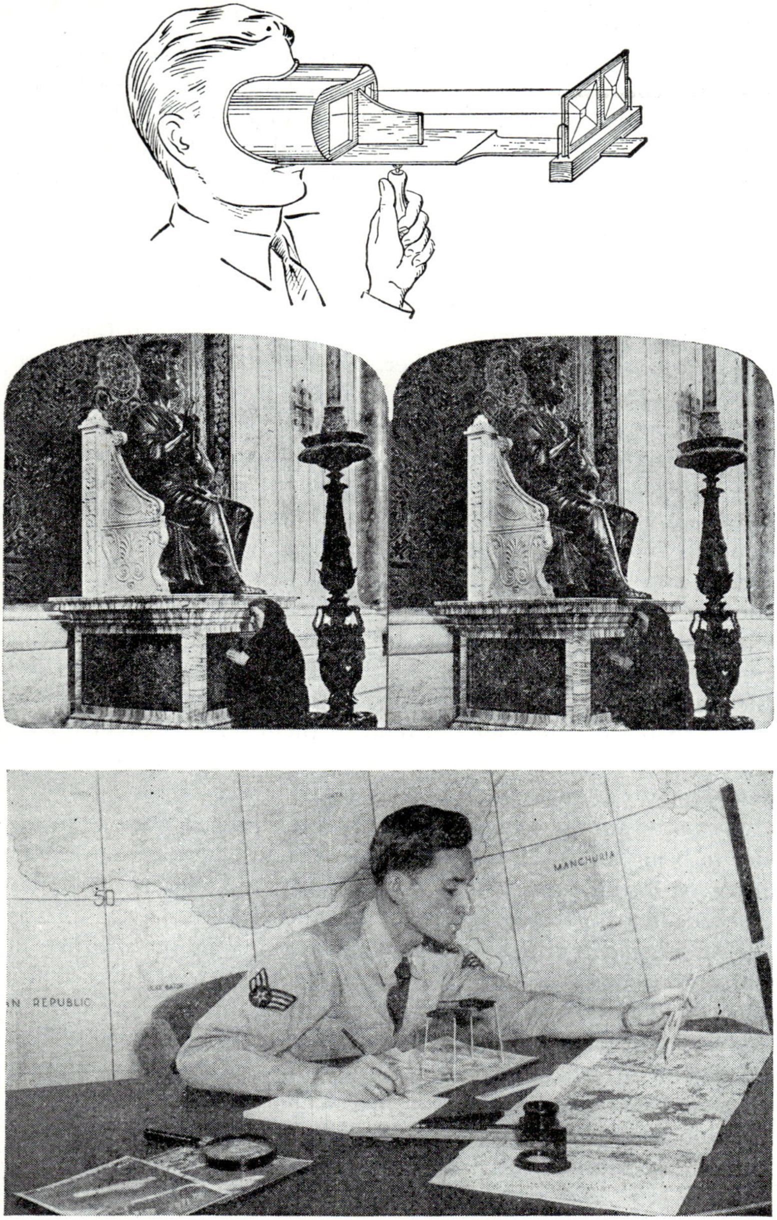

Fig. 36. Stereoscope, Stereoscopic Picture, and Stereo-Viewer Used for Study of Aerial Reconnaissance Photographs. [Stereoscope reproduced from N. L. Munn, *Psychology: The Fundamentals of Human Adjustment,* 2nd ed. (Boston, Houghton Mifflin Company, 1951); stereo-viewer, U.S. Army photo.]

the retinas. The small screen between the two prisms prevents the right eye from seeing the picture intended for the left eye and vice versa. The simultaneous views of these slightly different pictures are fused in the brain in such a way that depth is perceived. If the pictures have been taken from two separate positions at a distance apart, greater than that between the eyes, they will, within limits, be perceived with an exaggerated stereoscopic depth. When the disparity between the two retinal images is too great, fusion does not take place and a condition of *retinal rivalry* takes place. By retinal rivalry we mean that first one object is seen, then the other, in alternation. The objects are not at any time seen as one fused whole.

Other cues to distance and depth perception are double images, accommodation, and convergence. If you place your right index finger about three inches in front of your eyes and your left index finger at some distance beyond it in the same direction, you will find that if you fixate on the finger nearer to you, the one farther away will appear double. If you fixate on the farther finger, the one nearer will appear double. The reason for this is that the distant object stimulates the retina at non-corresponding points, as shown in Figure 35. Ordinarily we disregard these double images because they are outside the range of our attention. Only when we deliberately attend to them do we perceive that they are two. Double images are probably one of the unconscious cues that we use in estimating distance.

Accommodation is an adjustment of the lens of the eye in order to bring an object into sharp focus. The muscular movement involved in this process is thought to be a cue, either monocular or binocular, for the perception of distance.

Convergence normally works with accommodation to bring an object to a focus on corresponding parts of the two retinas. If the objects to be perceived are within about three hundred feet, convergence may be a help to the perception of distance. When an object to be viewed is placed close to the eyes, the muscles that turn the eyes inward contract while those which turn the eyes outward relax. The nerve impulses sent to the brain from these tense muscles serve as cues to the distance perception.

HOW PEOPLE PERCEIVE THE WORLD

2. Psychological cues

The psychological cues to distance perception are (1) linear perspective and relative size, (2) interposition, (3) light and shadow, (4) aerial perspective or distinctness, (5) relative rates of apparent movement, and (6) fixation.

By *linear perspective* we refer to the fact that objects become smaller as their distance from the perceiver is increased and larger as the distance is decreased. Artists who wish to depict a third dimension in their flat pictures utilize this principle, as illustrated in Figure 37.

Figure 38 illustrates the effect of *interposition* on the perception of depth. The picture, of course, is a plane surface, but because one object is placed in a position where it partially obscures the other, it is perceived as nearer.

In looking at an object we implicitly assume that the light striking it comes from above because this is the direction from which light usually comes. The position of *highlights* and *shadows*, then, gives a further clue to the perception of depth. In Figure 39, you will see an interesting example of this principle. Viewed right side up, the dents are perceived as dents. If you turn the picture upside down, however, the dents disappear and are perceived as mounds. In nature, the highlights appearing on convex surfaces are near the top and the shadows are below. On concave surfaces the highlights appear below and the shadows above.

The *aerial perspective*, or the distinctness with which objects are perceived, is also a clue to distance, although at times it is a deceptive one. In mountainous areas a distant peak will sometimes jut out with great clearness, and the uninitiated visitor from the flatlands will mistakenly think that it is near and try to walk to it. In general, the intensity of light is greatest near the object from which it is being reflected, and as light travels through the atmosphere it becomes progressively dimmer. Consequently, the sharpness of outline of the objects from which the light is being reflected decreases with distance. Objects that appear hazy to our vision we perceive as farther away than those that appear clear.

As you look out of the window of a swiftly moving train, the objects close to you appear to pass by speedily and those far away

Fig. 37. Linear Perspective.

at a greatly diminished rate. Furthermore, the objects close to you appear to be moving in a direction opposite to that in which you are traveling, whereas those at a big distance (like the moon) seem to be going in the same direction. These relative rates of *apparent movement* are clues to the perception of distance.

Fig. 38. Interposition.

C. Perceptual Constancy

Just as the hue of objects looks the same under different intensities of illumination, so the size and shape of objects is perceived as constant even though the retina is stimulated in different ways. If you see a man in the distance, his image as projected on your retina will be very small. You do not, however, "see" him as a "Lilliputian" but as a human being of normal dimensions at some distance. Similarly, if you bring your pencil up close to your eyes, the retinal image will be considerably larger than if you view it at arm's length. Yet in both positions you see the pencil as the same size. This phenomenon we refer

Fig. 39. Highlights and Shadows. [Courtesy C. H. Stoelting Company, Chicago.]

to as *size constancy*. There is also *form constancy*; that is, we see objects as having essentially the same form no matter at what angle they are presented to us. A square top table, for instance, is still perceived as square even though we are viewing it from the side in such a way that the retinal image is in the shape of a diamond. In short, we perceive the external situation and not our retinal images.

D. Reduced Cues in Perception

Because perceptual experiences are patterned they can sometimes be revived by only part of the stimuli which originally aroused them. This is particularly true for experiences that have become habitual. In reading proof, for instance, you may overlook missing letters and misspelled words because you perceive them as you expect them to be and not as they are. In other words, you have learned to respond to reduced cues. This tendency of a part of a perceived situation to arouse the total pattern of the situation is called *redintegration*. The concept that a part

HOW PEOPLE PERCEIVE THE WORLD

is not an isolated element of experience, but that there is always an attempt to see things integrated into wholes, is a principle underlying all aspects of Gestalt psychology, although Gestalt psychologists use different terms in which to express this idea.

E. How the Environment Influences the Ability to Perceive

We have just shown that objective facts are perceived or take on meaning when they can be related to something already known. In other words, what is perceived here and now is determined to a considerable extent by an individual's previous experiences. There is, however, a more subtle way in which the environment influences visual perception. Language, for instance, seems to be very important, as the following example will illustrate. The Eskimos, unlike ourselves, have several different words for "snow." Snow that melts as it falls is "akkilokipok," snow that freezes as it falls is "koalerpok," and snow falling straight down is "sakketovok." Because his language makes this distinction the Eskimo child must perceive snow more sharply than a child whose language has only one word to designate all kinds of snow.[2]

There is some evidence, too, that early experience with visual patterns is necessary to the development of normal visual perception. This, of course, is true also for visual sensation. Animals reared in darkness usually have difficulty in making an adjustment to the light when they are mature. In fact, parts of their visual cortexes atrophy because of lack of stimulation. Experiments with chimpanzees raised for 16 months in the dark show that in the absence of stimulation by visual patterns, the animal requires "hundreds of hours of active utilization of the eyes to develop its vision to the stage where it can adequately guide locomotion and complex manipulations."[3] Presumably, this condition would also be true of the human infant deprived of an opportunity to see visual patterns for any length of time.

Some of the characteristics of visual perception, such as the use of reduced cues, are found in sound perception also. Sound perception, however, presents special problems in that the sense of hearing is not so limited in direction or distance as is the sense of sight. These special problems are treated in the next section.

---

[2] Paul Grabbe, *We Call It Human Nature* (New York, Harper & Brothers, 1939), p. 71.

[3] A. H. Reisen, "Arrested Vision," *Scientific American*, 183 (1950), 19.

III. SOUND PERCEPTION

A. Localization of Sounds

Human beings do not localize sounds as easily as do animals that have muscles enabling them to prick up their ears and focus in the direction of a sound. The human being must either move his whole head in the direction of a sound, or, if he wants to be very accurate, he may use some kind of mechanical direction finder, such as that pictured in Figure 40. Localization is better

Fig. 40. Sound Locator. [U.S. Army Photo.]

in the horizontal than in the vertical plane and is better with two ears than with one. Among the factors commonly believed to influence localization are the following:

1. Differences in the time required for the sound to reach the two ears. The time difference may be very short, and yet be long enough to serve as a cue in determining the direction from which the sound has come.

2. Differences in the phase of the sound wave that strikes each ear. Sound waves, as we pointed out in Chapter VI, consist of alternate compressions and rarefactions in the air. The compressions produce high pressure in the air and the rarefactions pro-

HOW PEOPLE PERCEIVE THE WORLD 259

duce low pressure. Since the two ears are located at different points in space, the sound may be in a different phase as it reaches each ear.

3. Since the intensity of sound is diminished the further it gets from its source, the ear that it strikes first will be stimulated with the greater intensity.

Young devised a pseudophone, as shown in Figure 41, which caused the stimuli which would ordinarily enter the right ear to go into the left ear and vice versa. The subjects who wore this apparatus for the week found that there was a complete reversal in the localization of sounds. Sounds coming from the left were perceived as coming from the right and sounds coming from the right were localized at the left. There was also a considerable reversal of sounds coming from the front and back. When the subjects were able to see the source of the sound they were able to adjust to its direction, although the sounds still seemed to come from the opposite direction.

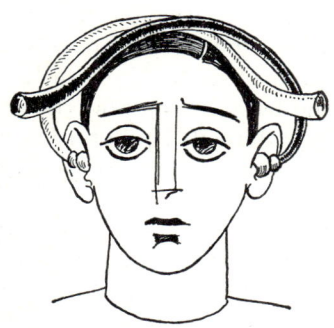

Fig. 41. Young's Pseudophone.

B. Perceiving the Distance of Sounds

The two cues used in determining the distance of a sound are (1) loudness, and (2) tone quality. Ordinarily, the nearer the sound is, the louder it is, and conversely, the further away it is, the weaker it sounds. Moreover, as sounds travel through space, the timbre or tone quality changes. The higher overtones are lost first. These changes in tone quality enable us, with experience, to determine with more or less accuracy the distance from which the sounds are coming.

This ends our discussion of visual and auditory perception. We shall next present some general facts about the process of perception.

IV. GENERAL FACTS ABOUT PERCEPTION

A. Perception Is Patterned

The law of Prägnanz

Gestalt psychologists hold that all perception is governed by a guiding principle that they have labeled the law of Prägnanz. The experimental results appear, in general, to support this point of view. The term *Gestalt* means "form" or "pattern," and the basic notion underlying all Gestalt theory is that experience is patterned. The term *Prägnanz* cannot be accurately translated; perhaps the nearest English equivalent is "compact but significant." According to the law of Prägnanz, perceptual organization tends to move toward a good Gestalt, that is, toward a state of regularity, simplicity, and stability. Under this general law are four subsidiary laws proposed by Wertheimer. These laws may be summarized as follows:

The law of similarity: the principle that, other things being equal, similar items will tend to be grouped together in perception. For example, in Figure 42, the circles will tend to form a Gestalt or pattern.

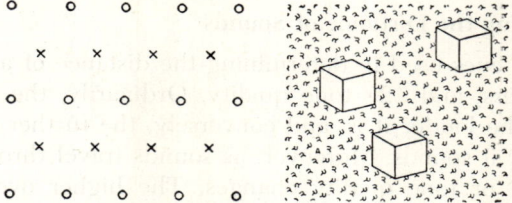

Fig. 42. Similarity Facilitates Grouping. [Reproduced by permission from *Foundations of Psychology* by E. G. Boring, H. S. Langfeld, and H. P. Weld, published by John Wiley & Sons, Inc. (1948), p. 221.]

The law of proximity: the principle that items that are placed close together tend to form groups against a background of empty space, as illustrated in Figure 43.

The law of good continuation: a principle meaning that perceptual organization tends to perpetuate a straight line as a

HOW PEOPLE PERCEIVE THE WORLD 261

Fig. 43. Proximity Facilitates Grouping. [Reproduced by permission from *Foundations of Psychology* by E. G. Boring, H. S. Langfeld, and H. P. Weld, published by John Wiley & Sons, Inc. (1948), p. 221.]

straight line, a line forming an incomplete circle as a circle, or any other figure that is predominant in a visual field. Several illustrations of this principle are shown in Figure 44.

The law of closure: a fundamental principle of Gestalt psychology, one that has been applied not only to perceptual theory, but also to learning and motivation. It means that closed areas form patterns in perception more readily than do open figures,

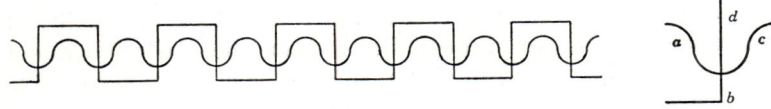

Fig. 44. Good Continuation Facilitates Grouping. [Reproduced by permission from *Foundations of Psychology* by E. G. Boring, H. S. Langfeld, and H. P. Weld, published by John Wiley & Sons, Inc. (1948), p. 221.]

and that perceptual organization tends toward "closing" areas that are partly or wholly "open." A good example of this tendency is the way in which we overlook typographical errors when we are reading for meaning. In a tachistoscopic experiment, too, incomplete letters can be exposed momentarily and the subject perceives them as whole letters. In other words, he has closed them to form familiar meaningful patterns.

B. Perception Is Influenced by Past Experience

With the possible exception of certain geometrical-optical illusions, that which is perceived will depend upon one's past experience. If you look at Figure 45, you will see it *not* as a number of isolated circles but as a cross. Another person with a different past experience might see it as a kite, an anchor, or some kind of primitive tool. For all observers the perception is

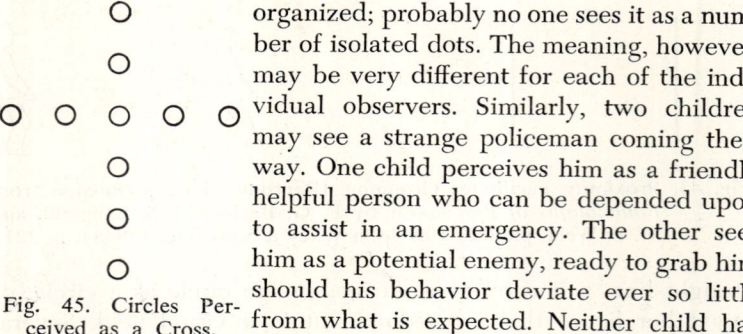

Fig. 45. Circles Perceived as a Cross.

organized; probably no one sees it as a number of isolated dots. The meaning, however, may be very different for each of the individual observers. Similarly, two children may see a strange policeman coming their way. One child perceives him as a friendly helpful person who can be depended upon to assist in an emergency. The other sees him as a potential enemy, ready to grab him should his behavior deviate ever so little from what is expected. Neither child has seen this policeman before, but the perceptions of both are profoundly influenced by their past experience with policemen, either directly or through references to them in words.

Past experience plays as important a role in tactual, olfactory, gustatory, and auditory perception as it does in visual perception. An experienced buyer, for instance, can "feel" the quality of materials which pass through her fingers; she can tell without looking whether the cloth she is handling is nylon or heavy silk. A connoisseur of fine perfumes may be repelled by perfumes which delight another woman. The gourmet, with a highly refined taste for cheese, perceives differences in the tastes of cheeses which are not at all apparent to the uninitiated for whom cheese is just cheese. And when it comes to music, there are those for whom a Beethoven symphony is just noise, or who perceive modern music as such a mass of hideous and jumbled sounds that they cannot endure listening to it. Ordinarily, the perceptual tendencies built up in childhood are difficult to change after maturity; we have a tendency to reject the new and cling to the old. We "perceive" musical themes and combination of tones as "music" if our ears have become accustomed to them. That is one reason why middle-aged and aged people may prefer old song and art favorites to modern music and art.

C. Perception Is Influenced by Values and Needs

Some recent research studies suggest that perception is not only profoundly influenced by internal factors such as past experience, which we have already mentioned, but also by personal needs and values. These studies indicate that there are both *uni-*

versal determinants of perception and *individual* determinants. The universal determinants include most of the factors which affect the perception of the "average" human being as he is studied under ideal laboratory conditions, free from distraction and deep emotional involvement. They reflect directly the characteristic electrochemical properties of sense organs and nervous tissue. Universal determinants of perception account for such visual phenomena as optical illusions, color contrast, and perceptual contrast. They account for all of the highly predictable aspects of human perception.

These universal "laws" of perception, derived from formal laboratory studies, are valid laws and can be used for prediction within the limits of a laboratory set-up. Laws of color contrast, factors of advantage in spacing type and pictures, for example, can be applied by a magazine editor, since all people can be expected to react to these factors in more or less the same way. But such laws do not enable us to understand the human being as he perceives his environment in situations that are psychologically significant, that is, in situations that involve his whole personality, including his system of values and his needs. The traditional laboratory studies of perception describe perception in real life "about as well as the Laws of Color Mixture describe one's feelings before an El Greco canvas." [4]

Individual determinants of perception are those which influence perception under the conditions of everyday life outside the laboratory. They include the beholder's temperamental characteristics, such as introversion and extroversion, social needs, attitudes, and motives. Several investigators [5] have worked out new scientific techniques for studying the influence of motivation upon perception. They presented young children with the task of estimating the height of a number of three-inch toy figures. The children were then given the toys with the understanding that they could keep them. The experimental group, however, was later deprived of the toys while the control group was permitted to retain them. When the children were subsequently asked to estimate the size of the toys again, the experimental group overestimated the size but the control group did not. In

---

[4] J. S. Bruner and C. C. Goodman, "Value and Need as Organizing Factors in Perception," *J. Abnorm. Soc. Psychol.*, 42 (1947), 33–44.
[5] *Ibid.*

another experiment with children a comparison of the difference between judgments of cardboard discs and identically sized coins was made. The coins, of course, were more valuable in the eyes of the children than the cardboard discs. It is interesting to note that the coins were characteristically judged larger in size than the gray discs and that the greater the value of the coin the greater was the deviation of the *perceived* size from the *actual* size. Apparently, then, the meaning an object has for a person has a notable influence upon the way he perceives it. The old saying that the grass is greener in the neighbor's pasture seems to state an important principle in perception. At any rate, these findings constitute a new, highly suggestive lead to further work which is needed in this field.

D. Perception Is Influenced by Context

The context in which an object or an event is presented will influence perception. The context in which a geometrical form appears, for instance, may be either an aid or a hindrance to discovering it. If you look at Figure 46, you will see that the first form is

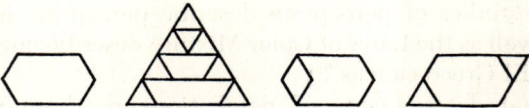

Fig. 46. Context and Perception of Form. [After Gottschalt, reproduced by permission from N. L. Munn, *Psychology*, 2nd ed. (Boston, Houghton Mifflin Company, 1951), p. 409.]

reproduced in each of the diagrams but in a different geometrical setting. It is easier to perceive the form in one of the settings than it is in the other two.

Because perception is influenced by context, values, needs, and past experience, and because perception is patterned, it is possible for us to perceive things as other than they really are. In the next section we shall discuss various kinds of inaccurate or abnormal perceptions.

V. INACCURATE AND ABNORMAL PERCEPTION

A. Illusions and Hallucinations

Both illusions and hallucinations are false perceptions, but we generally think of illusions as normal phenomena, common to all people, whereas hallucinations are almost always abnormal manifestations of perception. *Illusions* are false or inaccurate perceptions. They differ from hallucinations in that they are always false interpretations of sensory stimuli actually present to the senses.

A *hallucination,* on the other hand, often takes place in the absence of the sensory stimuli which the person thinks he is receiving. If you were to smell sweet peas and interpret the odor as the odor of roses, that would be an illusion. If you were to smell roses in the absence of any pronounced odor, that would be a hallucination. Illusions are normal phenomena; certain geometrical-optical illusions are universally experienced. Hallucinations, however, as a rule are not. An important criterion for distinguishing a hallucination from an illusion is the self-reference of the hallucination. For the mentally sick person, the man-shaped juniper tree which becomes a lurking aggressor on a dark night, may be diluted farther and farther from *really* looking like a man until it becomes hallucinated as a fully detailed fiend. Hallucinations typically occur in mental disease, in drug or alcoholic poisoning, and in the delirium of a fever. We shall first discuss illusions and then hallucinations and other abnormal perceptions.

B. Illusions

Illusions may occur in any sensory modality, although we probably know more about visual and auditory illusions than we do about others. Study the visual illusions shown in Figure 47 and read the captions below them. These are the commonest visual illusions.

A motion picture is a good example of the illusion of apparent motion, or what Gestalt psychologists refer to as the *phi-phenomenon.* In a moving picture you see what seems to be steady, continuous movement on the part of the actors. This impression of steady movement, however, is produced by the actual exposure of many single still pictures. A moving picture is made up of a

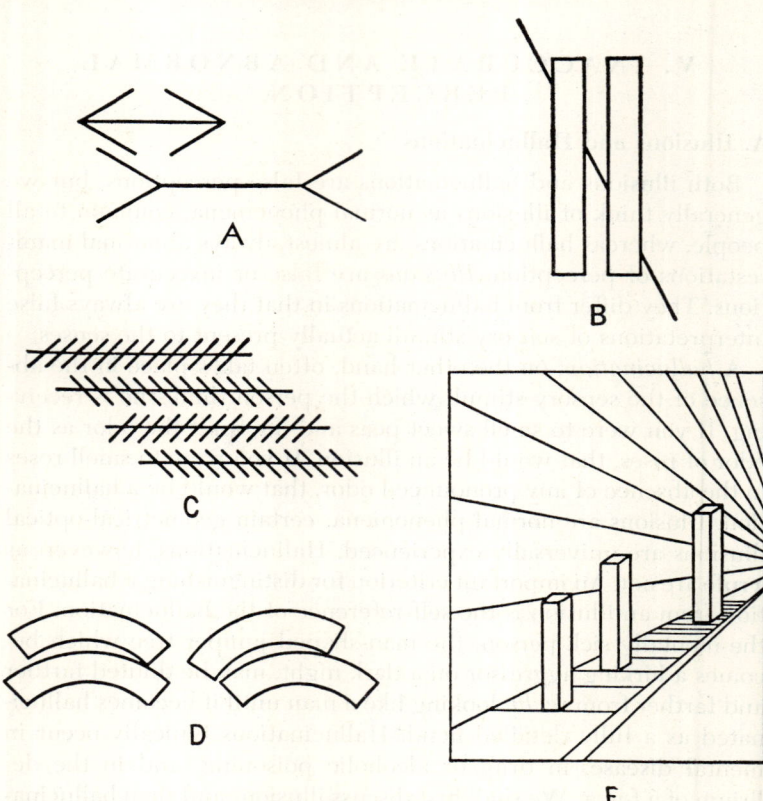

Fig. 47. Visual Illusions. (*a*) Müller-Lyer Illusion. (*b*) Poggendorff Illusion. (*c*) Zöllner Illusion. (*d*) Ring Segments (*e*) Perspective. [Reproduced by permission from J. F. Dashiell, *Fundamentals of General Psychology*, 3rd ed. (Boston, Houghton Mifflin Company, 1949), p. 463.]

great number of separate picture frames, each one of which exposed briefly, is only slightly different from the preceding one. After each frame is exposed, it is covered by a shutter and the next frame moves into place. Only when a picture is still is it exposed. When these frames succeed one another at appropriate and very brief time intervals, we do not see them as many still pictures but as portraying a succession of integrated movements. When the rate of movement is too fast, the pictures are jerky or blurred. If the rate is too slow, we see a flicker or in extremes a series of still pictures instead of movement. A similar phenomenon is often ob-

HOW PEOPLE PERCEIVE THE WORLD 267

served in electrical advertising signs, as, for example, one in which the contents of a bottle of milk are progressively poured into a glass. The "milk," of course, does not really move but it appears to do so because different portions of the sign are successively lighted at appropriate distances and at proper time intervals.

C. Hallucinations

A hallucination is usually experienced as an actual perception even though there are no external stimuli to account for it and it has no relation to reality. Hallucinations should be distinguished from delusions, in that hallucinations are false perceptions, whereas delusions are false beliefs. A hallucination is a response to one's own fantasies and is mistakenly attributed to an objective source outside.

Hallucinations may occur in any mode of sensory experience, although in mentally disturbed persons auditory hallucinations appear to be the most common. Often the hallucinations are complicated perceptions involving vision, smell, hearing, and tactual sensations. Certain kinds of drugs predispose toward the development of hallucinations. Cocaine produces hallucinations of vision and touch, usually in the form of small parasites creeping on the skin. Similar hallucinations occur in *delirium tremens*, a pathological result of alcoholism. In delirium tremens the hallucinations are often elongated moving objects, such as wires or sprays of water. This false perception of continual motion sometimes becomes outright "seeing snakes."

D. Synesthesia

A relatively rare abnormality of perception, known as *synesthesia*, is a condition in which the sensation from a particular sense organ has some of the perceptual qualities of a different modality of sensation from the one being stimulated. Musical tones, for example, are immediately perceived in terms of color while they are also perceived in terms of sound. In other words, the tone is actually perceived as a color; it does not just remind the subject of a certain color. Many examples of synesthesia are found in the novels of Balzac. In the first seven of the last ten lines of Charles Baudelaire's sonnet *Correspondences*, quoted below, we find an interesting literary example of synesthesia. The first four lines give the theory and the next three lines show the application.

> Like prolonged echoes mingling far away
> In a unity tenebrous and profound,
> Vast as the night and as the limpid day,
> Perfumes, sounds, and colors correspond.
>
> There are perfumes as cool as children's flesh,
> Sweet as oboes, as meadows green
> —Others, triumphant and corrupt and rich.[6]

Special problems in perception are involved in the consideration of eidetic imagery and the perception of time. We shall therefore treat each of these subjects in a separate section.

VI. EIDETIC IMAGERY

Most psychologists today distinguish between *eidetic imagery* and hallucinations. According to Jaensch, who invented the term, eidetic images differ from both after-images and memory images. Although they resemble hallucinations in their vividness, they are not the same thing. And, unlike dream images, they are more directly associated with actual perceptions. People who claim that they experience eidetic images say that they resemble the original percept in both completeness and vividness. Jaensch claims that eidetic images, like after-images, are actually *seen*, and that they occupy an intermediate position between sensations and images. Eidetic imagery is common in children, less common in adolescents, and rare among adults.

How do we know that there is such a thing as eidetic imagery? What objective evidence is there besides introspective reports? The most convincing objective evidence is that obtained from young children who have not yet learned to read, or, for that matter, to discriminate the forms of different letters. Cases have been cited in which a card containing printed words has been presented to a small child for a brief interval of time and the child has "traced" with his finger the shapes of the letters after the card has been removed. Behavior of this kind has been demonstrated even when the exposure time was so short that, had the child been able to read, he would not have been able to read all of the words exposed.

[6] From the translation by C. F. MacIntyre (Berkeley, University of California Press, 1947).

VII. THE PERCEPTION OF TIME

Time, though in one sense not real, does, however, have a certain basis in reality, in that it is the measure of the change of real things. Every experience we have takes place during an interval of time, and the passage of time can be perceived only as it is marked off by distinct events that go on in time.

People differ greatly in their ability to estimate intervals of time. In estimating time the most common external cue is the cycle of day and night. In an artificial environment in which these changes cannot be perceived, internal physiological rhythms are more likely to be utilized. Habits of eating at given intervals often provide us with internal "hunger clocks," and pressure in the bladder informs many people that morning has come, even though, as in winter, it may still be very dark outside. Some people show a remarkable facility in awaking at the same time every day without having to be called or without using an alarm clock; though often when this is reported they are only responding to external stimuli of which they are not fully aware, such as the whistling of the newsboy or the arrival of the milkman.

When we are bored, time seems to "drag" and when we are deeply interested it seems to "fly." Moreover, intervals that are "filled" with some continuous activity are usually estimated as longer than intervals of the same length when they are "unfilled." Much depends upon the way in which the interval is filled. Commonly, intervals of less than one second are overestimated and those of more than a second underestimated. The sound of a word appears to last for a shorter time than a noise which objectively takes up the same amount of time. Meaningful sentences are estimated as having a duration shorter than that for a series of nonsense syllables which lasts for the same amount of time. Time intervals that are marked by some striking beginning and end are estimated as longer than those having no marked boundaries.

VIII. EXTRA-SENSORY PERCEPTION

Normal perception, as we have thus far described it, is based upon the stimulation of definite sense organs. There is no disagreement among psychologists about this fact. The possibility of extra-sensory perception, however, is still a moot question. Extra-

270   PERSONS AND PERSONALITY

sensory perception, or ESP, is defined in the glossary at the back of every issue of the *Journal of Parapsychology* as "response to an external event not presented to any known sense." The phenomenon has been demonstrated experimentally time and time again, yet no one seems to know what causes it, and scientists generally are extremely reluctant to accept the findings of research studies in this field, even though they can find nothing wrong with the experimental techniques or the statistical analyses used in such studies. There is something weird and uncanny in the whole notion of mental telepathy or extra-sensory perception. We tend to dismiss as fantastic the claims which people often make that they received a mental "message" from a friend or relative and later learned from a letter or telegram that the "message" was correct. We have no way really of verifying these casual reports, but we do have a way of verifying experimental studies. A typical experiment on ESP will be described.

J. B. Rhine at Duke University uses for his experiments on ESP a standard deck of 25 cards. Five different designs are used on these cards, as shown in Figure 48. Five cards of each design are included in the deck. The subject, O, and the experimenter, E, work in different buildings, usually facing in opposite directions, and with no means of communication. They work with synchronized watches. At a time previously agreed upon, E begins the

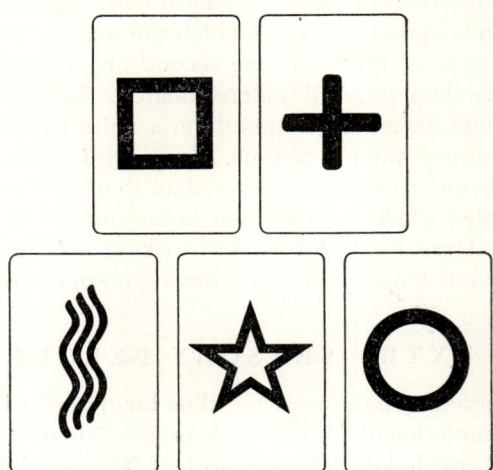

Fig. 48. Designs Used in ESP Experiments.

HOW PEOPLE PERCEIVE THE WORLD

experiment by turning up the first card and recording its symbol. At the same time, O records his guesses. The other cards are turned up at one minute intervals and the same procedure is repeated until all 25 cards have been used. The extent to which O has responded better than "chance" is then computed. On the basis of chance alone, five responses should be correct. The experiments of Rhine and of others have shown repeatedly that responses significantly above chance do occur over and over again. As yet, however, no one knows how to account for these results.

IX. PERCEPTION IN RELATION TO OTHER PSYCHOLOGICAL PHENOMENA

In the last analysis it is not the eye nor the ear nor any of the senses or powers of man that perceive; it is the human being himself. The human being is a composite being; that is, he is composed of body and soul. Body and soul are related as two mutually complementary principles, and it is the soul that gives life to the body and makes every kind of human activity possible. Although proximately the sources of human activity are to be found in the several powers of man, ultimately their source must be traced to the human soul.

Perception enables the human being to know his world and is accordingly a basic factor in his adjustment to the environment. It influences the amount, the direction, and the rate of his learning. It is a component of intelligent behavior and has an important role to play in the initiation and control of emotional states. It is an essential prerequisite of all creative thought. As such, the discussion of perception is an appropriate beginning for this section on "Human Activity and Adjustment" since it is a basic factor in all psychological phenomena which we shall describe under this general heading.

XI

How People Learn and Remember

Without memory we could not learn, and without learning we could not live.—WERNER WOLFF [1]

I. THE PROBLEM OF LEARNING

The challenging environment in which the human being finds himself forces him to make many complex adjustments. Most of these come about through *learning*. Unlike other animals, man has few ready-made "instinctive" responses to the environment. It takes the human being longer to mature than other animals, and a much greater proportion of his life is spent in learning. To survive and live as a human being, man must be able to *learn*.

Human learning varies from the very simple to the very complex. It includes such varied activities as bladder control, speaking, driving a car, voting Republican, and nervously biting one's fingernails under stress. Some learning, apparently, affects only part of the organism, as for example, learning to ignore a ringing telephone that does not concern you, or unconsciously pulling out a cigarette after coffee has been served. Such learned behavior, in itself, may have little significance for personality development, inasmuch as it is not directed to a psychologically significant goal. It is only a part activity of the organism.

In contrast to such part learning, psychologically significant learning is directed toward a goal which is sought by the organism as a whole. This goal-directed learning is said to be *motivated*. A *motive*, as the psychologist defines the term, is a goad to action of some kind. It is directed to some specific satisfier in the environment. The term *motive* is a hypothetical construct which the psychologist uses to account for behavior that is directed toward

[1] Werner Wolff, *What Is Psychology?* (New York, Grune & Stratton, Inc. 1947), p. 90.

a goal; the fact that a motive is not something that can be seen need not puzzle anyone if he remembers how easily it can often be inferred and identified. When a man snatches a sandwich and wolfs it down we are in no doubt that he is acting from the hunger motive, or, as we shall more precisely label it, the hunger drive.

We use the term *drive* to designate an inner condition or activity of the organism which acts as a stimulus to a particular kind of behavior. Usually, it refers to mass activity on the part of the organism and, unlike a motive, it is directed more to a general class of stimuli than to a specific satisfier.

In the present chapter we shall consider a few of the most important phases of the vast subject of learning and memory. Before we turn to the actual study of problems and theories of learning, however, something should be said about two important tools used by psychologists in studying learning: (1) animal research and (2) the learning curve.

It will perhaps seem strange to you that psychologists use animals in their study of learning even more often than they use human beings. In fact, the major theories of learning in contemporary psychology are based almost entirely on animal studies. Psychologists who study learning in animals, however, are usually not interested in animals as such. Rather, they try, by studying organisms simpler than man, to arrive at basic principles of learning that can also be applied to man. How well they have succeeded you will be in a better position to judge after you have become acquainted with the crucial experimental studies.

Since many experimental studies of learning can be interpreted only after some measurement of the rate of learning has been made, we introduce you next to the learning curve.

II. THE LEARNING CURVE

The *learning curve* is a graphical means of representing improvement by plotting measures of successive performances. The measures are in units such as time required for a performance, number of errors in the performance, number of tasks performed per unit of time, et cetera. Or, to take one instance, if you want to see how much an individual has learned over a period of time, you draw a graph on which you plot the time required for his performance in successive trials, as illustrated in Figure 49. Notice that time required per performance is plotted on the *ordinate,* which is the vertical axis of the graph. Successive trials are plotted on the *abscissa,* which is the horizontal axis of the graph. The learning curve shown in Figure 49 shows the rate of learning a form-digit substitution performance. It indicates that the fastest

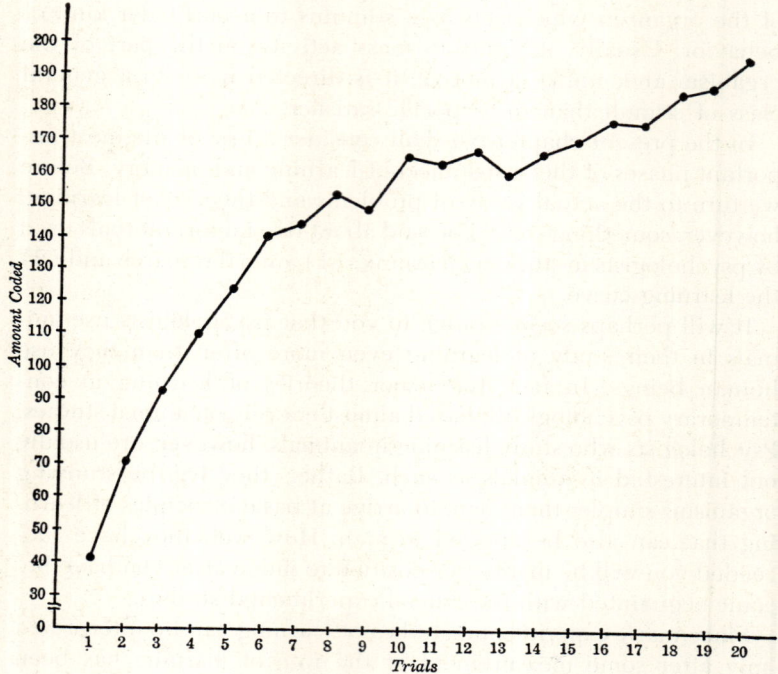

Fig. 49. Learning Curve Depicting Progress in Form-Digit Substitution. [Reproduced from M. A. Tinker, *Introduction to Methods in Experimental Psychology* (New York, D. Appleton–Century Company, Inc., 1947), p. 41.]

learning took place in the early trials and that as learning progressed the amount of improvement became less and less with each successive trial. Such a curve is said to be negatively accelerated. A *negatively accelerated* curve is one which ascends most rapidly at the beginning and rises more and more slowly with each successive performance until it stretches out into a line parallel to the base of the graph. This straight line is said to be

HOW PEOPLE LEARN AND REMEMBER 275

asymptotic to the base and it indicates that no further progress is taking place.

Speed of performance is not the only indication that learning is taking place. Another criterion is increase in accuracy, which can be expressed as either (*a*) a decrease in the number of errors made in a given period of time or for a specified amount of work done, or (*b*) an increase in the number of units of work done or of time-per-error.

When speeding up of performance is used as the criterion of efficiency, progress is recorded either as (*a*) a decrease in the time necessary to accomplish a given amount of work, or as (*b*) an increase in the amount of work done during a given unit of time.

Learning curves vary according to the kind and complexity of the materials learned. The most common learning curve is *negatively accelerated*. Negatively accelerated curves are usually obtained for the learning of sensori-motor activities, such as typewriting, ball-tossing, maze learning, telegraphic sending and receiving, and for the memorization of simple material, such as columns of syllables and words.

The type of learning curve obtained may be, at least in part, a function of the complexity of the material. Simple memory material results in a negatively accelerated curve; but as the complexity of the material is increased, the curve may assume the properties of an S-shaped curve. With a further increase in the complexity of the material, a positively accelerated curve may be obtained. These results are shown in Figure 50.

Many learning curves show periods in which no apparent learning is taking place. These periods are called *plateaus*. There is probably no one explanation that holds for all plateaus. Some writers have suggested that plateaus are the result of effort wrongly applied, or of emotional upset or fatigue. One investigator, as a result of his studies of ball-tossing, typewriting, and learning Russian, came to the conclusion that plateaus are the outcome of three factors: (1) a diminution of the learner's effort and enthusiasm, (2) the experimenter's inability to

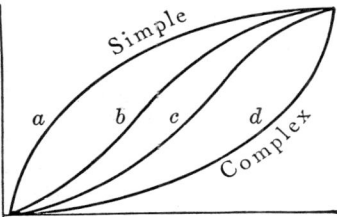

Fig. 50. Complexity Influences Form of Learning Curve. [After Stroud.]

measure the real progress taking place, and (3) the fact that the learner must perfect certain responses before he can proceed to a higher level of efficiency. Others have explained the plateaus in curves for learning telegraphy as follows: (1) a plateau occurs in the receiving curve because the subject is acquiring a "hierarchy" of verbal habits, which means that the learner must perfect the "letter-habit" before he can perfect the "word-habit," and the "word-habit" before the "phrase-habit"; and (2) the sending curve shows no plateau because, as in the early part of the receiving curve, the various habits are acquired simultaneously.

Most people, in developing skills, never reach the utmost limit of performance of which they are capable. In technical words, they do not reach what has been called their *physiological limit*. When the learning curve flattens out and becomes parallel to the abscissa, it may look as if the learner has reached the physiological limit of his performance. But often, when added incentives are introduced, the curve again rises, and it is then apparent that the physiological limit had not been reached.

III. KINDS OF LEARNING PROBLEMS

A. Conditioning

In the early 1900's, Ivan Pavlov, a Russian physiologist, began his experiments on the "conditioned reflex" in animals. One of his first experiments was that of reflexly producing a flow of saliva in a dog at the sound of a bell. The biologically adequate stimulus for producing a flow of saliva is the presence of food in the mouth. By repeatedly ringing a bell just before food was given to the dog, a *conditioned reflex* was gradually set up. From this time on the sound of the bell alone caused the flow of saliva. Pavlov found, however, that if he continued to ring the bell without reinforcement or rewarding the response with food, the conditioned reflex disappeared. He called this phenomenon *experimental extinction*. Later, the so-called "extinguished" conditioned response was easily restored by only one or two reinforcements. By *reinforcement* we mean presenting the primary unconditioned stimulus (meat powder, in Pavlov's experiment) at the time or shortly after the conditioned response stimulus (bell) is also presented. Also, if the animal was allowed to rest for a while, a *spontaneous recovery* took place; that is, the conditioned response reappeared. Unless the response was again reinforced, however, extinction took place more rapidly than before.

Pavlov discovered, too, that if, in the training series, the substitute stimulus precedes the primary stimulus by a definite interval of time, the reaction to the substitute stimulus will take place after the same time interval. This phenomenon Pavlov referred to as a *delayed reaction*. *Trace reactions* were also noted, but these were very weak. If, during the interval between the ringing of the bell and the presentation of food, the bell did not ring continuously, a response would occur, but it was much less intense than the delayed reaction and was therefore called a trace reaction.

The newly learned conditioned response was not specific to the original stimulus alone but was susceptible to *irradiation* or generalization. This means that the dog did not react only to the particular bell of a given pitch which was used in the training series but would respond indiscriminately to bells of other pitches. With further training, however, the dog could learn to *differentiate* or distinguish between different pitches. By gradually reducing the difference between two pitches, reinforcing one and withholding reward from the other, a point was eventually reached at which the dog could no longer discriminate. At this point the animal salivated in response to any stimulus, struggled to get free, and was unfit for any further conditioning experiments. Pavlov labeled this type of behavior *experimental neurosis*.

Conditioned reflexes or responses can also be produced in human beings, both children and adults. One investigator,[2] for example, by touching a child's arm when a piece of candy was put in his mouth, found that in time the child opened his mouth as soon as the arm was touched. She found, too, that in normal children the response was conditioned and extinguished more rapidly than in mentally deficient children. There are several other research studies, however, which suggest that this relationship between intelligence and speed of conditioning does not always hold. One psychologist, for instance, obtained a negative correlation between the speed of forming a conditioned withdrawal reaction and intelligence.

The pupillary reflex, by means of which the eye adapts to different intensities of light, has also been conditioned. By ringing a

[2] N. Munn, "Learning in Children," in L. Carmichael (ed.), *Manual of Child Psychology* (New York, John Wiley & Sons, Inc., 1946), p. 379.

bell and flashing light into the eye of a man, it was found that after approximately 400 trials the pupil of the eye contracted to the sound alone. In a further study the reflex was first conditioned to the bell, then to the verbal command of the experimenter, then to the subject's own subvocal command, and finally to the subject's *thought* of the word *contract*. Some psychologists claim that in this experiment we have a clue to the origin of voluntary action. When words were employed in a conditioned response experiment, the responses did not become extinguished as rapidly as when non-verbal material was used as either the stimulus or in the response. Furthermore, salivary responses which had been conditioned to meaningful words were not extinguished as readily as salivary responses to nonsense syllables.

An interesting difference between human and animal conditioning is shown in the kind of irradiation that takes place. A dog, for example, may respond to a tuning fork at 256 vibrations by producing 8 drops of saliva per minute and to a tuning fork at 260 vibrations by producing 6 drops of saliva per minute. Because the physical stimuli are similar the responses too are similar. This is not so for the human being; at least, it is not so when words are used as stimuli. When a human being has been conditioned to salivate to the word *bell*, he does not salivate when the words *bill* or *ball* are substituted. If, however, the words *gong* or *ring* are substituted, he often salivates as much as he did to the word *bell* itself. In other words, he responds to meanings rather than to the formal physical similarities in the stimuli. Conditioning of this type is called *semantic conditioning*.

The principles of conditioning have been applied to the solution of a number of practical problems among which is the cure for alcoholism. The "conditioning" of the odor or taste of liquor to the response of nausea and vomiting is an important feature of many "liquor cures." Some clinical psychologists, too, have found the conditioning technique a successful means of treating nocturnal enuresis. For instance, an ingenious device is sometimes used for conditioning bladder tension to the response of getting out of bed. A thin bed pad is so wired that when a drop of liquid touches it an electrical current starts which rings a bell. The bell awakens the sleeper before the bladder is empty. After a number of repetitions, the bladder tension alone, without the bell, awakens the sleeper before he has wet the bed. And, as we have previously shown, the conditioning method of removing fears has also been successful in the treatment of human beings. It should be stressed, however, that the conditioning of human beings is not identical with the conditioning of animals. What happens to the human being in a conditioning experiment depends to a great extent upon his feelings, attitudes, and willingness to be conditioned. In experiments with adult human beings, conditioning is by no means the predictable response it was with Pavlov's dogs. Conscious attitudes toward the experiment or the experimenter, systematically produced by the experimenter, markedly affect the results. One experiment suggests that unconscious attitudes are also important. A variation of Pavlov's experiment was set up in which mint candy was used as the unconditioned stimulus for a salivary response. The conditioned response was a nonsense syllable. The responses of the experimental subjects could, it was found, be classified into three general categories: (1) prompt conditioning similar to that of Pavlov's dogs; (2) no evidence of any conditioning at all, and (3) conditioning in "reverse," that is, responses which showed a reduction in the flow of saliva. An analysis of the individual subjects giving these responses showed that their attitudes toward the experiment and the experimenter were different. It was obvious that the kind of response elicited was influenced greatly by the condition of the organism as a whole.

Some psychologists have tried to explain the acquisition of personality traits as the outcome of "conditioning" in different life situations. They account for such observed differences in people as aggressiveness or submissiveness in terms of early conditioning or association of responses and their reinforcement by a reward. Young children, for example, struggle to escape or free themselves when their movements are restrained. If such persistent "fighting back" produces further restraint or punishment rather than freedom, the child may become passive. If passive behavior is rewarded or "reinforced" in some way, it will tend to be repeated on subsequent occasions. Any person or object present during the original struggle tends to become associated with the situation. These persons or objects are "conditioned stimuli" and come to act as primary stimuli in the formation of other conditioned responses. Conditioning of this type is known as *higher order conditioning*. It consists essentially of setting up a new conditioned response by using as the "primary" stimulus a previously conditioned stimulus. The notion of higher order conditioning plays an important role in theories which attribute personality development and personality traits to conditioned responses. The more higher order conditioning there is, the more remotely is the learning associated with the biologically adequate stimulus from which it originally derived. Unfortunately, there is not much evidence to support such a theory. Pavlov and others found it difficult to establish higher order conditioning. This difficulty increased as the learning became more remote from the original stimulus.

B. Trial-and-Error

1. The problem box

In one of his earliest experiments, Thorndike placed a hungry cat in a puzzle or problem box, outside of which food was placed, and made careful observations of how the cat got out. The box was so constructed that when the cat manipulated a latch, a concealed mechanism would cause the door to open and permit the cat to secure the food outside. On the first trial, the cat took a great deal of time to get out, meanwhile clawing, biting, and dashing about. On succeeding trials, the time gradually and irregularly became less and less, until finally the cat made no mistake in going directly to the latch. There was no evidence that the cat "caught on" to the solution. According to Thorndike, the cat learned to get out by trial-and-error. In other words, the successful responses were "stamped in" and the unsuccessful responses were "stamped out." The responses were made directly to the sensory stimuli without any mediation of ideas.

Let us consider for a moment what is involved in this type of learning. First, the cat was hungry. That means that he was motivated to find a solution to the problem. Second, there was no obvious way for him to reach the goal. Third, he tried one solution after another until eventually he hit upon one that *worked*. And, fourth, with each successive trial, he made fewer errors and took less time in reaching the goal until at length he invariably got out without any extraneous movements. The animal had learned where to work (place learning) and how to manipulate the latch (tool learning) in order to get out.

Trial-and-error is not limited to animal problem solving but is also characteristic of many kinds of human learning. Typically, a

HOW PEOPLE LEARN AND REMEMBER   281

man solves a mechanical puzzle by manipulating it in various ways until it "accidentally" comes apart. Usually, he does not know how it came apart, and has just as much difficulty in getting it together again as he had in taking it apart. But with successive trials, he gradually eliminates false movements until, like the cat in the puzzle box, he performs the correct movements unerringly. Often, however, a human being suddenly "sees" the solution, after a certain amount of trial-and-error, at which point he is said to have obtained "insight." Insight, as we shall show in a later section of this chapter, can be demonstrated in some experiments with animals as well as with man.

2. Maze learning

Another device commonly used in studying both animal and human learning is the maze. Mazes are of various kinds: some are simple, others more complex; some are enclosed, others elevated. Mazes used with human beings often require the subject to trace a path with a stylus or with a pencil, as shown in Figure

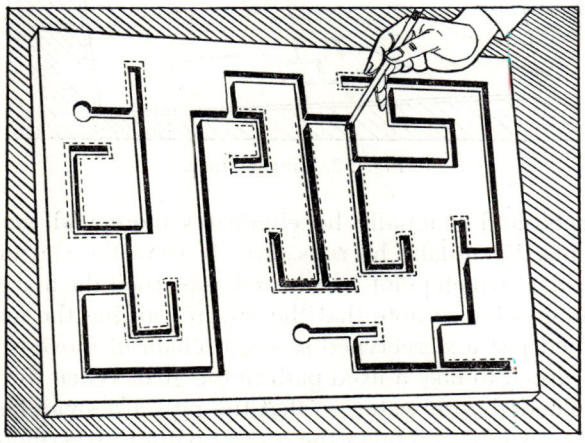

Fig. 51. Stylus Maze.

51, or they require the blindfolded subject to trace a path with his finger as shown in Figure 52. All mazes consist of a series of complicated pathways and blind alleys. By working his way through the maze the subject eventually reaches his goal. This goal may be food, drink, escape, or some other incentive sufficient to motivate the subject to learn.

The hungry rat, put in a maze for the first time, does not know, of course, that there is food to be found there. His hunger makes him restless enough to explore the maze, and in the course of this exploration, he finds the food. If, after this discovery, he is taken out and put again at the starting point, he does not go directly to the food, but again goes into many of the blind alleys. But now that he is going toward a definite goal he is less leisurely in his

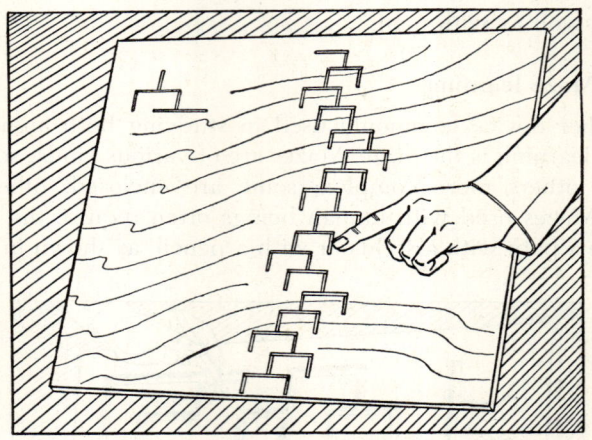

Fig. 52. Finger Maze.

movements, and gradually he eliminates more and more false movements. Eventually he runs directly from the starting point to the goal, at which point we say he has learned the maze.

It is interesting to note that the rat, in learning the maze, has not learned just a stereotyped series or chain of movements, nor has he learned to take a fixed path to the goal. When the learned maze is flooded with water, so that the rat must swim instead of run to the goal, he still takes the correct path. Furthermore, when the blindfolded rat is placed in a maze that he has learned to run, but from which certain partitions have been removed, he does not traverse the usual pathway, but takes a shorter route to the goal. Human maze learning, like that of animals, is accompanied by much trial-and-error. But human beings have certain advantages over the animals, the chief of which is verbalization, the spontaneous expression of intellect. The subject sometimes gives the experimenter clues as to how he is learning the maze by saying, for instance, "turn twice toward the right, then once left, then twice right," and the like. Nevertheless, the curve for human maze learning is very similar to that for the white rat.

C. Insightful Learning

Köhler's pioneer experiments with hens, and later with a three-year-old child, illustrate insightful or relational learning. The hens were presented with two paper-covered boards, one of which was covered with a lighter colored paper than the other. Both boards were sprinkled with grain. When the hens pecked at grain upon the lighter of the two papers they were shooed away; but when they pecked upon the darker paper, they were allowed to eat. The hens were prevented from acquiring position habits by a frequent shifting of the colored papers from one side to the other over a period of several hundred trials, until the hens eventually learned to respond only to the darker paper. Then the stimuli were modified in such a way that the darker paper, to which the hens had learned to respond, became the lighter of the two stimuli. If the hens had acquired a "bond" between the specific stimulus paper and the response of eating, they should have pecked at the same paper as in the preceding series of trials. In 70 per cent of the trials, however, the hens did not peck at the paper to which they had previously responded but pecked instead at the new stimulus which was the *darker* of the two papers. This finding indicates that the hens were responding to a brightness *relation* rather than to a specific stimulus.

A similar experiment was set up in which a three-year-old child learned to select candy from the brighter of two boxes. The child, in a relatively small number of trials, learned to select the brighter of two boxes rather than the specific box in which it had previously found candy. The child, like the hens, reacted not to colors as isolated elements of perception, but to the relations between them. Gestalt psychologists claim that behavior such as that described above cannot be called a conditioned response since it is not specific to a given stimulus. Yet the experimental results do not necessarily rule out the possibility of conditioning. It is extremely difficult to teach an animal to react to a specific shape or color.[3] Yet it is quite simple for the animal to discriminate relative size or intensity of stimuli. The conditioning, in other words, may be made to "brighter" or "duller" rather than to the individual stimulus, although the customary explanation given of this phenomenon is that of the Gestalt school.

Experiments with apes often show "insight" or an "aha!" experience during the course of learning. A chimpanzee was placed in a cage, outside of which food was placed just beyond his grasp. After trying in vain to reach the food with his hands and with a stick, the animal apparently abandoned the problem. Shortly afterward, however, while he was playing with two bamboo poles, he suddenly fitted one into the other, hurried to the side of the cage, and raked in the food. This sudden "grasp" of the solution is known as insight.

On another occasion, food was hung from the ceiling, and two boxes were placed rather close to each other and about four meters away from the food. After trying in vain to reach the food by standing on one box, the chimpanzee rushed at the other box and began venting his rage upon it. Suddenly, however, he quieted down, pulled the second box up to the first one, placed it upright upon the first one, and then climbed up the shaky structure to get the food. Again, the suddenness with which the solution came and the lack of apparent trial-and-error leads to the conclusion that the animal solved the problem by insight.

D. Negative Adaptation

Learning in which the learner "gets used to" a stimulus which proves to be harmless is known as *negative adaptation*. A white rat placed in a new cage for the first time may, for instance, show signs of fear by struggling to escape or by cowering in a corner. On subsequent days, when the rat is placed in the cage, however, these fear responses disappear. Similarly, a spider that is spinning its web will at first drop down when a vibrating tuning fork comes into contact with the web. As the stimulus is repeated without producing any harmful effects, the spider learns to "ignore" it; he has become negatively adapted to the tuning fork. In these

---

[3] D. O. Hebb, *The Organization of Behavior: A Neuropsychological Theory* (New York, John Wiley & Sons, Inc., 1949).

HOW PEOPLE LEARN AND REMEMBER 285

two instances, the fear responses were not reinforced by anything harmful in the situation and consequently they disappeared.

Human beings as well as animals learn by negative adaptation. A child who is threatened with punishment may at first be frightened. But if the threats prove harmless he learns to pay no attention to them. Or, a newcomer to a city may awaken for a few nights after his arrival whenever a streetcar passes by. In a short time, however, he no longer notices the streetcars and does not awaken when they pass his house. He has become negatively adapted to harmless stimuli.

E. Rational Learning

Rational learning is treated in detail in Chapter XIII on "Thinking and Creative Imagination," and we mention it here merely for the sake of completeness. Certain types of problem solving are common to both man and animal. But problem solving which requires thinking is limited to man alone. Rational learning experiments involve the least complex of thinking tasks.

Rational learning transcends the world of sensation and perception upon which trial-and-error and certain kinds of "insightful" learning depend. It involves the apprehension of the problem in an abstract manner. In other words, rational learning is a spiritual function not intrinsically dependent upon material stimuli. The insightful learning of the chimpanzee, in which bamboo poles are fitted together in such a way as to provide a tool for raking in a banana, requires that all of the objects used be in a single optical field. It is intrinsically dependent upon the material stimuli of the learning situation. Rational learning is not. Then, too, although the chimpanzee can learn to pile boxes one on top of another, the boxes must be ready for him to move. If the boxes are filled he does not empty them to make them light enough to move.

F. Canalization

All human beings appear to be born with the same general needs—such as the need for food, for drink, and for physical activity. But, as they grow older, their needs become specific through learning. One child learns to be hungry for whale blubber, another for roasted snails, and another for cheese. The child who learns to like cheese is likely to be disgusted with whale blubber or snails. Similarly, the child who has learned to like such delicacies may be repelled by cheese.

The need for fluid is also a biologically universal need. The way in which it is satisfied, however, is determined within limits by the culture. One person will learn to drink tea, another wine, and still another, coca-cola. These particular beverages are habitually consumed not just because of an acquired taste but because of their social significance. "Coke" belongs, and certain liquors are always drunk by "men of distinction." Even within a given culture, however, people may learn to differ markedly in their tastes for the beverages commonly provided.

All children enjoy rhythms, yet the particular kind of music and the particular kind of rhythmical games they play differ from one part of the world to another. As they become accustomed to one kind of music, one kind of activity, one kind of food, and one kind of drink, they reject or are dissatisfied with other alternatives. In short, because their needs have been satisfied in certain specific ways, they develop needs for the specific means which have previously satisfied their more universal needs. Their needs have been *canalized* into specific channels. The term *canalization* denotes the process by which drives toward a general class of stimuli tend to become satisfied only through certain specific stimuli of the general class because of repeated satisfaction of drives through such specific stimuli. In other words, canalized responses have been repeatedly *reinforced*. Canalization is a psychologically significant kind of learning, and is illustrated in the following anecdote:

A piano teacher decided to give a big party for all of her pupils shortly before the end of the school year. Most of the children (to whom she was donating lessons) were first and second generation Americans of European descent. They lived for the most part on farms and came into town on a school bus. As soon as school was over, the bus took them back to their farms. Consequently, they had few social contacts with each other. The teacher wanted all of the children to be at her party, and succeeded in building up a joyous anticipation of it. "Be sure to come," she said. "We're going to have a party just as you have at Christmas time. There'll be everything good to eat!"

On the day of the party, caterers provided roast turkey, dressing, yams, mashed potatoes and gravy, fruit salad, hot rolls with butter, ice cream, nuts and raisins, and milk. The teacher, surveying the tables, felt very much pleased. She was surprised, however, to find that after the children were seated, nearly half of them were not eating. Two little ones were actually crying. "What is the matter?" asked the teacher. "Oh," sobbed one of the children, "you said it was going to be a party, and it isn't!" "Why, what do you want that you haven't got?" she inquired. "We thought we would have gefüllte fish," he sobbed. The children were unhappy because their canalized needs were not being met.

Acquired tastes are canalized responses. They differ in several important ways from conditioned responses, although we know less about the processes basic to learning of this kind than we do about conditioning. (1) Canalized responses are not extinguished as easily as conditioned responses; once a person has learned to want something he goes on wanting it. Every experience with it is reinforced. (2) A conditioned response modifies an activity "preparatory" to the satisfaction of a need, whereas a canalized response modifies "consummatory" behavior. In other words, an acquired taste or canalized response is *essentially* related to a need. A conditioned response, on the contrary, is only artificially or *accidentally* related to a need. The dog, conditioned to a flow of saliva at the sound of the bell, for instance, has undergone a modification of his preparatory response to eating. He does not, however, learn to satisfy his hunger by eating and digesting the bell.

Canalization is an important aspect of human learning since it occurs in all the major kinds of motivation. The desire for certain types of activities, food preferences, esthetic interests, persons liked, and things valued—all fall under this heading.

IV. TRANSFER OF LEARNING

An important practical problem for human learning is that of discovering what effect the learning of one activity, skill, or habit will have upon another. Learning is said to "transfer" when the acquisition of one kind of learning has an effect upon the acquisition of another kind of learning. If the earlier learning helps in acquiring later learning, the transfer is *positive;* if it interferes, the transfer is *negative*. Negative transfer of sensori-motor skills is known as *habit interference*.

E. L. Thorndike and others conducted a series of experiments to test the doctrine popularly known as *formal discipline*. According to this doctrine (as Thorndike and his collaborators understood it), it does not matter what a person learns provided the subject is difficult enough. The mind, like a muscle, grows with exercise. The particular subject matter upon which it is exercised is important not for its content but for its difficulty. Mathematics and Latin, for example, are better subjects for training the mind than the social studies because they require more effort in learning. Thorndike and his collaborators, in scrutinizing the results of their experiments, concluded that these experiments provided no evidence to support the doctrine of formal discipline. They discovered a positive transfer from one type of learning to another only when there were overlapping elements in the two. This led them to formulate the theory that learning transfers from one situation to another only when there are *identical elements* in the two situations. For example, the learning of mathematics transfers to the learning of physics because the same mathematical formulas and processes are involved in both.

A rival theory, the *theory of generalization*, was proposed by Judd and has considerable evidence to support it. Judd trained two groups of boys to throw darts at underwater targets. Group I was given instruction in refraction before shooting at the targets. Group II was given no preliminary instruction. Both groups then practiced shooting at targets twelve inches under the water and both improved at about the same rate. Preliminary instruction which acquainted the boys of Group I with the necessity of correcting for the refraction of light apparently gave them no advantage over the boys who had not had such instruction. Later, however, when the target was removed to a position four inches below the water, the boys in Group I learned very quickly to readjust their aim. The boys in Group II, however, had to fumble just as they had previously done with the target twelve inches below the water. Judd concluded that transfer is facilitated by the learner's *cognitive grasp* of the situation, that is, by his understanding of the principles involved in the two learning situations. This theory, unlike that of Thorndike, does not look upon transfer of human learning as a simple mechanical process. Thorndike's view might well hold, however, for animal learning and for the

HOW PEOPLE LEARN AND REMEMBER 289

simpler types of human learning. But it is doubtful that it explains transfer of more difficult types of human learning.

This completes our description of the basic phenomena upon which learning theories are based. We shall now turn our attention to the major learning theories in contemporary psychology.

V. THEORIES OF LEARNING

All of the learning problems described in this chapter point to the central importance of motivation in learning. The conditioned response, you will remember, is acquired and retained because it is periodically reinforced or rewarded. Trial-and-error learning, too, occurs because the learner is rewarded for correct responses and punished for or frustrated by incorrect ones. Both insightful and rational learning lead to a goal. Even negative adaptation is motivated in the sense that useless responses drop out because they are not reinforced by noxious or harmful stimuli. And lastly, needs and drives tend to be canalized because in the life history of the organism the particular object or kind of stimulation that has habitually satisfied a need gradually becomes more and more satisfying. In short, all of these different kinds of learning take place because the learned responses are reinforced.

The one apparent exception to the rule that responses are learned because they are reinforced is found in *latent learning*. Latent learning seems to be unmotivated, although a drive to some kind of activity must precede it, as we shall illustrate by the following maze experiment.

Three groups of hungry rats were run in a maze under different conditions of reinforcement. One group was rewarded by food at the end of the maze; a second group was not rewarded at all; and a third group was not rewarded until the eleventh day of the experiment, at which time food was placed at the end of the maze. The results of this experiment are pictured graphically in Figure 53. Note that the rewarded rats progressively reduced their number of errors on the successive trials. In contrast, the rats that were not rewarded reduced their errors only slightly. The most interesting learning curve is that of the rats that were not rewarded until the eleventh day. Until the reward was introduced, they learned very little. But immediately after the reward was given their error scores dropped suddenly, which indicates that learning had taken place during the "unmotivated" trials even though it could not be measured. This unmeasurable learning is called *latent learning*. As we shall see in a moment, the interpretation of latent learning experiments plays an important role in contemporary theories of learning.

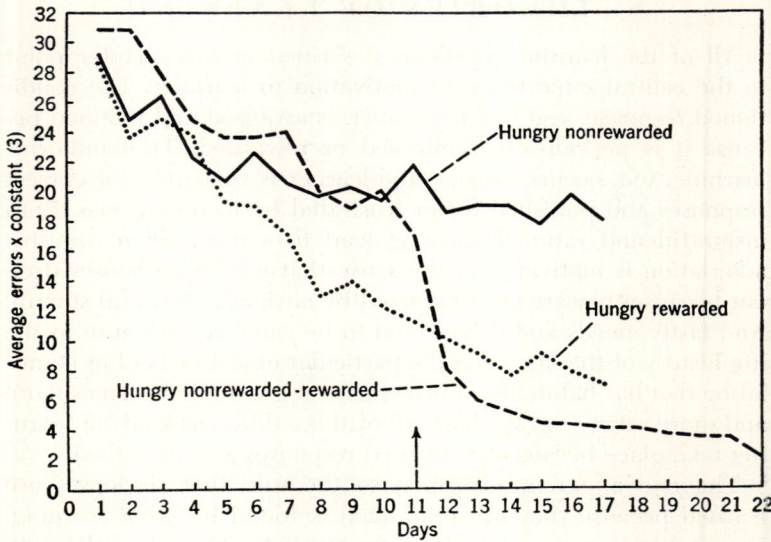

Fig. 53. Evidence for Latent Learning. Curve of errors for HNR (hungry non-rewarded), HR (hungry rewarded), and HNR-R (hungry non-rewarded-rewarded) rats. Arrow indicates the introduction of reward for the HNR-R group. [Reproduced by permission from N. L. Munn, *Psychology,* 2nd ed. (New York, Houghton Mifflin Company, 1951), p. 145.]

There are today two major sorts of theories of learning. We shall cite one outstanding instance of each. (1) Hull's stimulus-response theory, and (2) Tolman's field-expectation theory. The basic experiments upon which each of these theories rests have been performed on white rats. According to Hull's *S-R theory,* learning or habit formation consists essentially of building up connections between stimulating conditions and responses. A habit is established when the stimulus, the response, and a reinforcing state of affairs occur close together in time. Reinforcement may be either primary or secondary. *Primary reinforcement* relieves a basic tissue need of the organism; *secondary reinforcement* is a reward that was originally neutral but which, because it has previously been associated with the satisfaction of a drive, now serves as a reinforcing agent in its own right. According to Hull, the strength of a habit increases at a decelerating rate as the number of reinforcements increases. The *principle of stimulus generalization* has been formulated to account for the spread of the effects of learning from one situation to another not identical with it. It states that the habit strength attached to one particular stimulus will generalize or transfer to similar stimuli, in proportion to the degree of similarity of the stimuli. These principles, in a much more developed form than they are given here, are supposedly adequate to account for all learning—from the most simple to the most complex—and to hold for human as well as animal learning.

In contrast, according to Tolman's *field-expectation theory*, specific stimuli are not connected directly to specific responses through contiguity in time and reinforcement. Learning is explained, rather, in terms of "cognitive maps" or insights which immediately organize the relationships between stimuli and responses. These cognitive relationships occur through togetherness in time and space and through the brain's organizing property; they do not require reinforcement. Transfer of learning depends upon how limited or comprehensive the cognitive maps are, a factor which is influenced by the state of the brain, environmental cues, repetition of training, and motivating conditions within the learner. Unlike Hull's theory, Tolman's theory does not claim to cover all types of learning. Tolman recognizes that different laws may well hold for different kinds of learning.

VI. HUMAN LEARNING

The evidence for the learning theories described in the barest terms above comes from carefully controlled research upon animals, but psychologists apply these theories to human learning as well. The question we now raise is this: Is it legitimate to generalize from animal to human learning, and if so, to what extent?

First of all, it is easier to conduct research on animals than upon human beings because all of the conditions affecting them can be controlled. Then, too, parts of the animals' bodies, such as nervous tissue or glands, can be removed to discover what effects such operations have upon behavior. The offspring of laboratory animals can be studied for a number of generations, a fact which makes it possible to study the inheritance of learning ability. Obviously, in many respects it is easier to study rats, chimpanzees, and guinea pigs than it is to study *Homo sapiens,* and many psychologists have done just that. Let us now try to evaluate the importance of these studies for human psychology.

The use of animals in psychological research serves the same purpose as it does in medical research, and no other. In medicine, new drugs or operative procedures are first tried out on animals whose physiological makeup is similar to that of human beings. Such research is usually a preliminary step in the standardization of a drug or a technique. If the drug or operative procedure injures the animal, it is then abandoned without applying it to human beings. If, however, the effects are good, the procedure is then cautiously applied to human beings. In pharmacology, generalizations as to the effect of drugs on human beings are made only after considerable research has been made with people as well as with animals. This is a wise precaution since some drugs do not have the same effect upon people as they have upon animals. Where psychosomatic illnesses are involved, results of animal studies may, in fact, have only a limited application to human beings.

We have previously noted that a basic concept in learning theory is that of motivation. All animal learning, with the possible exception of latent learning, results from reinforcement. The reinforcement used in experimental studies of animals is the satisfaction of some basic physiological drive, such as hunger, thirst, sex, or exploration. To keep the animal motivated, feeding or drive reduction is usually postponed until the experiment is over each day. What relation does motivation of this type bear to human motivation in the ordinary learning situations of everyday life?

Human beings, of course, have physiological drives like other animals. They seek food, drink, and mates. But the life of civilized man is not dominated by such drives. His most important learnings, those upon which his culture is based, come after he has learned to secure the basic necessities of life and so to free himself to live and to learn as a human being. Some people never really experience hunger; they live according to a schedule by which they anticipate hunger and eat before a biological need is intensely felt. In mastering problems of real significance, people often become indifferent to their bodily needs. Madame Curie, for instance, was scarcely conscious of hunger or even of grave illness while working on her radiation research. For human beings, learning is controlled to a considerable extent by its personal *meaning* for the individual. As we shall show in detail later on, one of the most important things to know about a person is his idea of himself. What and how well he learns is dependent upon the amount of ego-involvement present—a factor which is not present in animal learning. Animals and very young children may well learn according to similar laws, in so far as their motivation is similar. But adult human beings are guided by a much more complex motivational system than the animal, and one that is profoundly linked up with the intellectual apprehension of values. Since animal motivation, then, is so different from that of man, animal studies have a very limited application to human learning. They must of necessity deal with only the most peripheral and psychologically least significant of human learnings.

Psychologists have, unfortunately, not always been too cautious in applying generalizations based upon animal research to human psychology. Tolman, for instance, has tentatively applied his findings on rats to human learning in interpersonal and group-to-group situations. He recognizes, of course, that the human situation is different from the animal, and has added to his theories derived from animal experimentation a number of theoretical formulations from clinical psychology concerning motives and drives.[4] The result of adding together principles from such widely dissimilar fields of research is a highly ingenious theory of human social psychology. It is logically consistent, the facts upon which it is based are correct, and yet it is doubtful if its theoretical principles really "explain" anything. An adequate explanation of human behavior can probably never be derived by a process of adding up observations of isolated aspects of behavior and tying them together with a thread of theory, since every part or aspect of learning merges into a total situation and

[4] E. C. Tolman, *Drives Toward War* (New York, Appleton-Century-Crofts, Inc., 1942).

derives meaning only from the whole situation of which it is a part. The "whole" situation of an animal is necessarily and *essentially* different from that of a human being. Many psychologists, of course, do not recognize this *essential* difference between animal and man. They view all animal life as a continuum from the most simple to the most complex, with man at the highest point of the complex end of the scale. In our view, however, man is essentially different from all other animals, not in his receptors, effectors, or nervous system, but in the possession of a spiritual soul, a soul which elevates and refines his bodily functions. For this reason we hold that generalizations of a psychologically significant nature about human learning can be derived from animal research only to a limited degree.

The generalizations drawn from animal studies and applied to human social learning seem very naïve to the Christian psychologist who approaches the study of human growth and learning from a different "frame of reference." The theoretical assumptions from which modern experimental and comparative psychologists proceed in their research are incredible to him unless he understands the historical and philosophical roots from which they have sprung. We do not have space in this book to discuss or trace these roots, but the serious student of psychology can acquire such knowledge from other sources. In general, contemporary trends in the psychology of learning derive from an acceptance of the theory that man's "mind" and body have evolved from those of lower animals and the materialistic view encouraged by Darwin's theory of evolution. The word *mind* is put in quotation marks to indicate that these theorists do not actually accept the reality of mind or a spiritual substance.

VII. LEARNING AND MEMORY

The total process of learning consists of three facets: (1) acquisition, (2) retention, and (3) recall. Memory, therefore, is one aspect of the whole procedure of learning. In the following sections, we shall describe the methods of studying memory, discuss the most important facts and principles of memory, and then develop some general principles for effective learning and retention.

VIII. THE METHODS OF STUDYING MEMORY

The first experimental study of memory was published by Ebbinghaus in 1885. Previous to that time no "higher" mental processes had been subjected to experimentation, and in this respect Ebbinghaus' research was a pioneer contribution.

In testing memory you may require your subject to recall, recognize, or relearn something. You may, for instance, be interested in determining his *immediate memory span*, or the number of items that he can immediately reproduce after they have been presented to him only once. Or, you may give him a *paired associates test*. This consists of presenting your subject with a number of stimuli in pairs, usually words, and having him learn them in pairs. Later you present him with the first item of each pair and ask him to give the item with which it was associated. When this technique is used the items are often presented through a slot in a memory drum, as pictured in Figure 54, since in this way associations with other pairs are minimized. Both of the above methods call for rote or verbatim learning. Recall can also be tested by asking your subject to retell a narrative in his own words. When this is done you measure his recall by the number of distinct ideas or phrases which he reproduces. The theme and succession of events, rather than the exact words, are required for passing this test.

Fig. 54. Memory Drum.

With young children and animals, recall is often tested by the delayed reaction technique. For example, an interesting stimulus may be presented to the child, and then covered, and only after a delay is he allowed to reach out for it. If, when he is free to reach for the stimulus, he goes to the place where he saw it covered, we conclude that he recalls. Several adaptations of this technique have found their way into intelligence tests for children. In the Stanford-Binet Test, for instance, the child is shown a card upon which are glued a number of objects which he is asked to name. Then, while he closes his eyes, one of the objects is covered by a small box. The child is asked to tell which object was covered. In the Bühler Baby Tests a rubber ball is pressed in order to make a chicken pop out. The infant is given sufficient time to observe the chicken before it is taken away. Other tests are then given for several minutes. Later, a ball like the first one except that it has no chicken to pop out is shown to the infant. The child indicates his recall by giving some evidence that he misses the chicken, as, for example, by looking for the hole, poking with his finger or looking questioningly at the examiner.

A recall test familiar to every student of history is one which requires the subject to put a series of items into the appropriate order. A list of historical events may be given, and the subject then arranges these events according to their chronological order.

Tests of recognition are usually easier than tests of recall and require less effort for passing. Students, for instance, report that true-false tests (requiring to a great degree only recognition) are less difficult than completion tests (requiring recall). A recognition test used to ascertain the memory value of different advertisements will serve to illustrate this kind of test. The subjects page through a new magazine and look at the advertisements. After they have had an opportunity to look at all of the advertisements in the magazine, the magazines are put away and some other activity is pursued for a time. After a suitable interval, the experimenter presents the subjects with a series of advertisements, half of which were in the magazine they recently perused, and half of which are new. The subjects are asked to indicate which ones were in the magazine they had just looked through. An analysis of results from experiments of this kind helps us to understand the factors which influence the remembrance of advertisements.

The *savings method* of Ebbinghaus calls for relearning and is probably one of the most accurate methods we have to measure memory. It consists of learning the material to the point of mastery and then allowing a period of time to elapse in which no review takes place. Later, when a stage has been reached in which neither recall nor recognition is possible, the subject relearns the material. The difference between the amount of time required for learning the first time and for relearning is the amount saved. It is encouraging to note that when this method is used the amount of saving is usually considerable. Probably many of our past learnings which we think have been totally forgotten have left permanent traces and can be relearned more economically than they were learned the first time if the need should arise.

IX. FORGETTING

A. Ebbinghaus' Curve of Forgetting

Ebbinghaus, in tracing the course of forgetting, drew up a curve showing the rate of forgetting over a period of time after the learning. He found that in all of his experiments the general pattern for the curve of forgetting was the same, although the gross amount of forgetting varied with the kind of learning involved and with the thoroughness with which the material had originally been learned. Forgetting was relatively more rapid and complete when the material was learned only to the point of one correct repetition. When the material was *overlearned,* that is, when it was repeated over and over again immediately after learning, the amount of forgetting was considerably less.

B. Meaningfulness of Material Learned

In general, the more meaningful the materials are to the learner, the more readily they are recalled. In one experiment, for example, college students were required to learn a number of match puzzles. One group of students learned the tricks by memorizing the solutions. The other group learned the principles involved in solving the tricks. Both groups were later tested for retention, with the result that the first group (which had memorized the solutions but not the principles) forgot very rapidly. The second group (which had memorized the principles involved) showed almost perfect retention when tested at intervals up to one month after the learning period.

In rote memorization, nonsense syllables are forgotten most rapidly, then prose learning, and lastly, poetry. Memory for poetry is facilitated by its rhythm as well as by meaningfulness.

C. Rhythm and Memory

Rhythm and cadence in a selection to be learned not only facilitate the learning but aid in retention. Sometimes when a series of unrelated items is to be memorized, it helps to impose upon them some sort of artificial rhythm. College students studying German, for example, have found it a help to learn the several series of prepositions which govern the different cases by imposing upon them an artificial rhythm.

D. Reminiscence

Reminiscence is a curious exception to the general rule that rapid forgetting takes place after learning. It is, in fact, the opposite of forgetting. By *reminiscence* we mean that after a period of time the subject sometimes remembers more than he did immediately after the learning took place. What causes reminiscence is a matter of conjecture; no adequate explanation is known. Some psychologists suggest that an unconscious review is going on within the subject; others suggest that factors which inhibit or interfere with remembering disappear with the passage of time.

E. Influence of Interruption on Retention

Laboratory studies show that, in general, people remember interrupted tasks better than those which they completed. But not all interrupted tasks are remembered; and the cases which do not follow the general trend suggest that in this matter central personality factors are at work and not merely memory. Some interrupted tasks which are remembered are not readily resumed. Best-remembered interrupted tasks are those that are interesting to the person. Uncompleted tasks that are of slight significance to the person, or those whose completion does not satisfy some ego-involved need, tend to be forgotten.

F. Role of the Emotions in Memory and Forgetting

Forgetting is not just a matter of disuse or the result of physiological changes which take place within the organism over a period of time. Forgetting in everyday life is selective; it is a means of resolving internal conflicts and of satisfying important emotional needs. Memories are assimilated into the personality

HOW PEOPLE LEARN AND REMEMBER

and become integrated with its aspirations and strivings. When memories cannot be so assimilated, when they present too great a threat to the personality, they tend to be "forgotten." Two lines of evidence support this view: (1) experimental studies, and (2) clinical data. A brief review of both lines of evidence is presented below.

1. Experimental studies

A number of experiments have been conducted with a view to determining the effect of pleasantness or unpleasantness on retention. The results of most of them confirm the hypothesis that pleasant experiences are remembered better than unpleasant experiences. A typical experiment is one in which the retention of 132 college students was studied the day after they had returned from their Christmas vacation. They were asked to list and to write a brief description of all their experiences during the vacation. Pleasant experiences were labeled "P"; unpleasant experiences were labeled "U." Of the 2231 experiences reported, 62.43 per cent were reported pleasant as compared with 37.37 reported unpleasant. Six weeks later, without any previous warning, the experiment was repeated. The results were substantially the same. The percentage of pleasant experiences retained after six weeks was 53.03 per cent as compared with 39.75 per cent unpleasant. It may, of course, be that college students actually have more pleasant than unpleasant experiences in their lives, and consequently a greater proportion of pleasant memories to report.

2. Clinical data

Clinical data as well as everyday experience reveal disturbances of memory which are intimately related to emotional experiences and needs. These disturbances will be discussed briefly under the headings of (1) retrospective falsification, (2) amnesia, and (3) exaggerated memory.

Retrospective falsification is the process of filling in gaps in a story, the details of which have been forgotten. The person telling the story is usually not aware of the fact that he is adding fictitious details and is not consciously lying. In general, the false details added make the story more acceptable to the ego of the teller. If the story concerns himself, for instance, the teller is usually represented in an improved light. In the young child retrospective falsification is quite obviously inspired by the child's needs and desires and reveals the difficulty the child has in distinguishing between reality and imagination. In old people retrospective falsification is also motivated by needs and desires. The elderly person, too, uses this device to disguise from himself and from others the fact that his memory is failing.

Amnesia is a pathological disturbance of memory characterized by an unusual form of partial or total loss of the ability to recall or recognize past experiences. It is not simple forgetting but loss of ability to recall something, due to injury, excitement, or repression. A common precipitating factor is a deep and unconscious emotional need to forget. It is usually more complete than ordinary forgetting and includes items of experience that the normal person never forgets, such as his name, his address, or his occupational and marital status. There is abundant clinical evidence that amnesia is not forgetting; specialized therapeutic techniques and devices, such as hypnosis, crystal gazing, automatic writing, and narcoanalysis frequently revive such memories. Often the amnesia disappears spontaneously. An amnesia which embraces all of the events occurring over a given period of time is said to be *localized*. An amnesia for all of the experiences relating to a given subject or complex of ideas, regardless of time, is said to be *systematized*.

Exaggerated memory or *hypermnesia* is a pathological disturbance of memory which results from fever or from great emotional stress. Some people, for example, report that under great emotional stress as a result of threatened drowning or burning to death, their entire lives passed before them in review. Occasionally people under the influence of an anesthetic or in a fever *delirium* will speak in a language which they learned in childhood but could not consciously recall or recognize in their normal state.

In everyday life our problems of learning and remembering are, of course, not as dramatic as those we have just described. The chief problem for most college students is that of attaining greater efficiency in learning, which automatically leads to greater efficiency in remembering. Learning requires study and study takes both time and energy. If you can acquire better methods of study, you will have more time for other important activities and probably have more fun in college.

HOW PEOPLE LEARN AND REMEMBER

In later life, too, either as a parent or a professional person, you will undoubtedly be faced with the problem of stimulating others to learn. The principles of efficiency in learning and remembering which we shall discuss in the next and last section of this chapter should therefore prove useful to you both now and later.

X. EFFICIENCY IN LEARNING AND REMEMBERING

A. Distributed Practice Is Usually More Effective than Massed Practice

In learning skills and tasks made up of many independent units, such as the memorization of dates or spelling items, less time and effort is required if your practice is distributed over a number of short periods rather than "crammed" into a few longer periods. Remembering improves if you review each subject for some time each day in addition to reviewing it just before examinations. Long-time retention more than immediate retention is favored by such spacing of study. Shorter learning periods are conducive to more intensive work; and when a subject is uninteresting, this is often the only way you can learn it at all. On the other hand, if the learning requires a complex train of associations, as it often does in advanced courses, the study period must be long enough to permit these associations to develop. Such tasks as reasoning problems in mathematics and creative writing fall into this category. In the elementary school, there are relatively few tasks of this nature. In college, however, such tasks are very common.

B. The Intention to Remember Influences Retention

The intention to learn and remember not only increases the efficiency of learning, but also determines the direction which learning will take. Experiments have shown that without the intention to learn even intelligent people fail to recall associated materials to which they have been subjected hundreds of times. Bankers and merchants, for example, who handled money all day long, were found to be as inaccurate in estimating the size of a dollar bill or in selecting circles of the same size as a cent, nickle, dime, quarter and half-dollar as were people who had

had considerably less experience in handling money. Experiments made with groups equated for ability show a marked difference in retention for the group having the intention to remember. The retention of the group which did not have the intention to remember was decidedly inferior.

That a definite intention to remember influences retention is demonstrated in an experiment in which 24 subjects learned two lists of syllables under different kinds of instruction. The first list was to be learned by paying special attention to their pronunciation while reading. The second was to be learned by making a definite effort to remember and reproduce the syllables. An average of 10.8 syllables was recalled by the group concentrating on pronunciation and 15.9 syllables by the group concentrating on remembering. These results are even more striking than they seem, since several subjects who did well on both lists admitted that while concentrating on pronunciation they were also attempting to remember.[5]

C. Whole Learning Is Usually More Effective than Part Learning

The statement that whole learning is usually more effective than part learning applies only to "wholes" which are genuinely meaningful units and in which the parts are systematically related in some way. In the learning of nonsense syllables, the whole method does not seem to have much of an advantage. It has been demonstrated that the progressive-part method is superior to the whole method in learning relatively short lists of nonsense syllables. However, since much of the learning which goes on in school is of a meaningful nature, it is probably better as a rule to learn by wholes than by parts.

D. Recitation Is an Important Aid to Remembering

Memory is greatly facilitated if you recite to yourself. This is true at all age levels, from the primary grades through college. A psychologist selected as subjects for an experiment seven or eight children in grades three through eight and a number of adult subjects. He had them learn nonsense material and meaningful material found in biographies. The results of this study are summarized in Table 3. You can easily see that a combination of

[5] J. G. Jenkins, "Instruction as a Factor in 'Incidental' Learning," *Amer. J. Psychol.*, 45 (1933), 471–487.

reading and recitation was superior to reading and rereading both for immediate and more remote retention.

Table 3
RECITATION VERSUS REREADING

Material Studied	16 Nonsense-Syllables, Per Cent Remembered		5 Biographies Total of 170 Words, Per Cent Remembered	
	Immediately	After 4 Hours	Immediately	After 4 Hours
All time devoted to reading	35	15	35	16
⅕ time devoted to recitation	50	26	37	19
⅖ time devoted to recitation	54	28	41	25
⅗ time devoted to recitation	57	37	42	26
⅘ time devoted to recitation	74	48	42	26

Adapted from A. I. Gates. "Recitation as a Factor in Memorizing," *Arch. Psychol.*, No. 40 (1917). Reproduced by permission of publisher.

The value of recitation as a method of learning appears to result from the following factors: (1) In reciting, you are necessarily active and alert; (2) by reciting and prompting yourself with the printed material, you can discover your mistakes and correct them before recitation in class or before the examinations; (3) in reciting, you are studying as you will later have to perform—answering questions; and, (4) recitation provides you with an immediate goal for achievement.

E. Interpolated Learning Influences Retention

Forgetting is not just the result of disuse or the fading out of impressions but is also the result of an active process of interference. New learning, by interacting with previous learning, may interfere with the retention of the latter. This process is called *retroactive inhibition*. A typical experiment to determine the factors which make for such interference is as follows:

1. Two groups of subjects equated for ability are required to learn some original material.

2. Group I (experimental group) is then given some further material to learn. This is the "interpolated" activity.

3. Group II (control) is allowed to rest, sing, or relax.

4. A test of retention of the learning of the original materials is then given to both groups.

5. By comparing the amount of forgetting of Group I with that of Group II, the effect of the interpolated learning upon retention is determined.

The factors which affect retroactive inhibition are as follows:

1. The greater the similarity of original and interpolated learning, the greater is the interference with retention.

2. Activities interpolated immediately after the original learning or just before its recall cause more interference than others.

3. The better the original material is learned, the less likely it is that the interpolated learning will cause interference.

4. Interpolated activities which are not well learned cause more interference than when they are well learned.

5. The more previous experience the learners have had with both the original and the interpolated learning, the less interference results.

6. Meaningful materials are less subject to interference than nonsense materials.[6]

An example may help to make clear how the above factors work out in practice. Let us suppose that you are just starting college. You have just come from the first session of your first class. It is a French class and this is your first acquaintance with French. Is it likely that you will remember much about what happened in your first French class?

To some extent the answer to this question depends upon what you do next. If you decide to go swimming, clean your room, or go for a walk, then according to principles 1, 4, and 5 above this should help you remember the material you just learned. If instead, however, you go immediately to another class just as new to you as French, there should be more interference than there would have been in the first case.

Principles 3, 5, and 6 indicate that since French is utterly new to you, subsequent learning can easily interfere with it.

Principle 2 seems to imply that the best way to let your French "soak in" is to go off and take a rest right after class.

F. Knowledge of Results Stimulates Learning

Experiments to determine the effect which a knowledge of results has upon learning show that such knowledge is an effective

[6] A. I. Gates, A. T. Jersild, T. R. McConnell, and R. C. Challman, *Educational Psychology* (New York, The Macmillan Company, 1942), pp. 413–414.

HOW PEOPLE LEARN AND REMEMBER

stimulus to further learning. Two groups of college students were given learning problems which involved canceling letters, multiplying two-place numbers, and translating series of digits into letters. The members of Group I were instructed to count their scores after each practice and to compare them with previous scores. They were also told to be on the watch for better methods of work. The members of Group II, on the other hand, had no knowledge of their scores. Group I showed decidedly more improvement than Group II, as shown in Figure 55. When

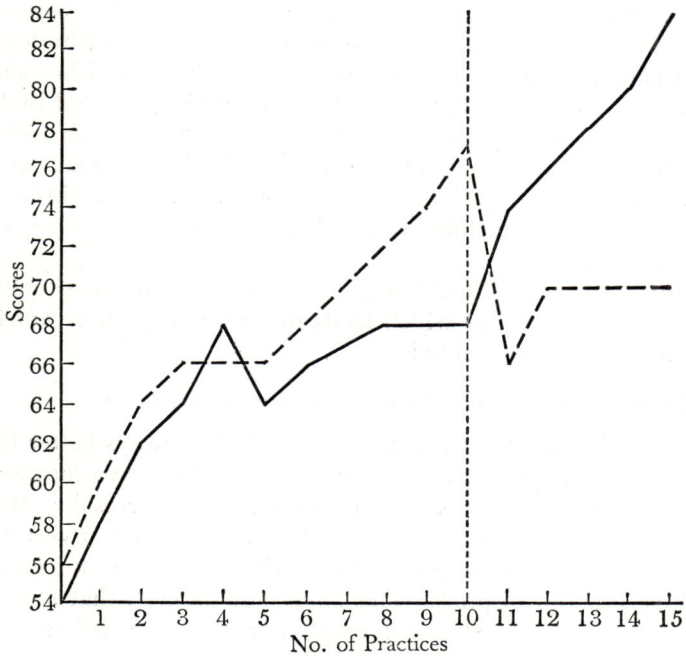

Fig. 55. Knowledge of Results Facilitates Learning. Solid line is curve for Group II, which received no knowledge until trial 10. Dotted line is curve for Group I, which received knowledge until trial 10. [Redrawn from Book and Norvell, *Pedagogical Seminary* (1922), p. 29.]

the experiment was about half-way over, the instructions for Group I and Group II were reversed. As a result, Group II now forged ahead and Group I fell behind. This study, the results of which are summarized in Figure 55, shows how important a knowledge of results is to further learning.

G. Reward and Punishment Both Increase Efficiency of Learning

Human learning, like animal learning, is facilitated by either reward or punishment or by a combination of both. Here, as in all questions of human motivation, however, the problem is not merely one of immediate incentive. A child, for example, may learn his arithmetic or learn to wipe the dishes without being asked because, when he has completed these tasks, his father gives him money. This child has learned not only to do the socially-approved thing, but to do it for the wrong motive. Rewards given to a child for doing something which in common decency he should do are liable to result in faulty attitudes. A child can reasonably be expected to help with the dishes since he himself has shared in the family meal and has profited by the use of the dishes. An intrinsic reward growing out of this situation is the greater sense of "belonging" and of personal worth which result from making a social contribution. Extrinsic rewards may destroy a child's sense of values and retard his progress toward maturity.

Punishment, too, should ideally be intrinsic to the situation. Above all, punishment which leads to intense and disorganizing emotion should be avoided.

H. Praise Is, in General, More Effective than Blame

As an incentive to learning, praise is almost always better than blame. In comparing the relative values of these two incentives for school children, it was found that praise universally stimulated better work than reproof. The brighter children, it was true, responded better to reproof than the duller children, but not so well as they did to praise. This study also showed that it is not a single occurrence of praise or of reproof which differentiates the two incentives, but the cumulative effect of either one or the other which produces very different results.[7] Apparently most people can take an occasional reproof in their stride, whereas they become discouraged if they are continually blamed.

[7] E. B. Hurlock, "An Evaluation of Certain Incentives Used in School Work," *J. Educ. Psychol.*, 16 (1925), 145–169.

XI. LEARNING AND MEMORY IN RELATION TO THE WHOLE PERSONALITY

Learning and memory play complementary roles in the economy of the whole organism. Both are governed by psychological laws which hold for people in general and are therefore highly predictable. Both are greatly influenced, too, by individual factors of need, desire, interest, and motive. What and how well a person learns and remembers is, in the last analysis, determined by his goals, as shown by the fact that learning and remembering are facilitated by meaningfulness, intention to learn and remember, interests, and by the relation of the materials of learning and memory to "ego-involved" needs.

Ability to learn and remember is partly hereditary and partly environmental. People differ greatly in this respect. One important factor to be considered in this connection is general intelligence. We turn next to a discussion of intelligence.

XII

Intelligent Behavior

> ... *Intelligence is not the same as an accumulation of knowledge. Even a person who has an encyclopedic knowledge need not be intelligent, for intelligence depends on what use he makes of his knowledge, how he interrelates it and how he applies the data.*—WERNER WOLFF [1]

I. THE HUMAN INTELLECT

The terms *intellect* as used by philosophers and *intelligence* as used by scientific psychologists do not mean the same thing. The former refers to a spiritual power which does not depend intrinsically upon a bodily organ and therefore cannot be subjected to measurement. The latter term refers to a combined power of body and soul and is indirectly measured by intelligence tests. When we compare the IQ's of two individuals, for example, we say that the person with an IQ of 140 is "more" intelligent than the one with an IQ of 100. By this statement we mean that the person with an IQ of 140, when placed in a test situation, responds to the test items in a more appropriate way than the individual with an IQ of 100. From an analysis of behavior in a situation which calls for concentration, problem solving, adaptability, and the like, we arrive at an estimate of "functional intelligence"; that is, an appraisal of how an individual behaves in situations calling for ingenuity, problem solving, and similar mental functions. We do not, however, measure "intellect" as such. Nor can we derive from intelligence test scores comparative measures of the "amount" of intellect present. "Intellect" and "intelligence" as used in this chapter, are not synonymous terms.

---

[1] Werner Wolff, *What Is Psychology?* (New York, Grune & Stratton, Inc., 1947), p. 209.

II. INTELLIGENCE

A. Popular Notions of Intelligence

All of us have ideas about intelligence long before we study psychology. It is common for first-graders to know who are the "smart" and who are the "dumb" members of their classes. Even such euphemisms as "daisy group," "pansy group," or "butterfly group" do not escape their vigilant notice, and very young children make judgments as to the relative status of such ability groups.

The man-in-the-street, too, has his own ideas as to what constitutes intelligence. He carefully distinguishes it from "book learning" or from any isolated intellectual accomplishment, such as the ability to learn Latin and Greek easily, if it is not accompanied by evidence that the person lives his life generally on a high level of efficiency. Popularly, intelligence refers to the total adjustment of a human being to his life situation, and not just to one limited aspect such as his rating on an intelligence test. The college teacher, for example, who said of a certain student, "She has brains but no sense," was reflecting this point of view. Jokes and cartoons about the so-called "brain-trust" and the familiar caricatures of the absent-minded professor are other illustrations of the same idea. These examples imply that intelligence, thought of as the ability to do well in school tasks and as measured by psychological tests, and intelligence, thought of as the ability to meet successfully the situations of everyday life, may be two different things.

It is certain, however, that the test movement would not have developed to anything like its present proportions if tested ability were not related to socially significant behavior in life situations. The routine testing that goes on in schools, in the armed forces, and in industrial organizations represents the investment of large sums of money and effort and these would not be available in support of a program that had not pretty well sold itself. Industrial executives certainly curtail expenditures which do not pay off in increased efficiency and, before long, in dollars and cents. Yet the tendency today is in the direction of more rather than less testing in industry, a fact which testifies to the usefulness of measurement.

Of course, the counseling psychologist who uses intelligence tests as one tool of diagnosis in making recommendations to and about his clients does not base his judgment on intelligence tests alone. Like the man-in-the-street, he considers the total adjustment of the person. He takes into account the client's personality, motivation, general appearance, character, and educational and social assets. However, it is a very practical component of his analysis, as he distinguishes the several different factors which enter into life adjustments, that he should be able to obtain measures of his client's intelligence which are relatively independent of the other factors involved in adjustment.

B. The Concept of "General Intelligence"

"Mental tests" were first used in the United States, not for any practical reasons, but to extend scientific knowledge of the nature and extent of individual differences in people. Cattell,[2] as early as 1890, published an article in which he demonstrated by means of coefficients of correlation that there was almost no relationship between scores on mental tests and the academic achievement of college students. The "mental tests" which he used, however, had little in common with what we know today as intelligence tests. Cattell's tests measured sensory discrimination, reaction time, and other "simple" psychological functions which do not correlate highly with what psychologists today call "general intelligence." As long as investigators were testing "simple" rather than "complex" mental functions, attempts at measuring intelligence were not very successful. It was not until the French psychologist, Binet, conceived of intelligence as a number of "complex" mental functions, that the concept of "general intelligence" began to develop. The revolutionary opinions of Binet and his collaborator, Simon, regarding the nature of intelligence, which pointed the direction for contemporary intelligence testing, are summed up in the following quotation:

. . . in intelligence there is a fundamental faculty, the alteration or the lack of which is of the utmost importance for practical life. This faculty is judgment, otherwise called good sense, practical sense, initiative, the faculty of adapting oneself to circumstances. To judge well, to comprehend well, to reason well, these are the essential activities of intelligence. A person may be a moron or an imbecile if he is lacking

[2] J. M. Cattell, "Mental Tests and Measurements," *Mind*, 15 (1890), 373–380.

in judgment; but with good judgment he can never be either. Indeed, the rest of the intellectual faculties seem of little importance in comparison with judgment. . . .[3]

Following Binet, a number of psychologists contributed their own definitions of intelligence. Some of them stressed the biological aspects of adaptation, or adjustment of the organism to the environment. An example of such a definition is that of the German psychologist, Stern (inventor of the concept of the "intelligence quotient"), who viewed intelligence as "the general capacity of an individual consciously to adjust his thinking . . . to new problems and conditions of life." Others, less influenced by evolutionary theory, have emphasized the peculiarly human ability to think abstractly. Terman, for example, points out that, "An individual is intelligent in proportion as he is able to carry on abstract thinking." But whatever the definition, since the time of Binet, no one has conceived of intelligence as a series of simple sensori-motor functions. All psychologists today agree that intelligence is a complex mental function.

The testing of intelligence was not postponed until psychologists could agree upon a satisfactory definition of intelligence. The psychologist may be compared in this respect to the physicist who succeeded in measuring electricity with a high degree of accuracy and harnessed it for practical purposes, without knowing exactly what electricity was.

C. The Measurement of General Intelligence

1. Historical development of individual tests of intelligence

Psychological measurement originated in Germany shortly after the middle of the nineteenth century under the influence of two independent workers, Fechner and Weber. The type of measurement they introduced is known as "psychophysical measurement," and it exerted a profound influence upon the establishment of experimental psychology in Germany. Psychophysical measurement, like the German experimental movement which it stimulated, was not at all concerned with individual differences. Its object was to determine psychological "constants" similar to the "constants" which we find in handbooks of physics, as, for

[3] A. Binet and T. Simon, *The Development of Intelligence in Children*, trans. by E. S. Kita (Baltimore, Maryland, The Williams & Wilkins Company, 1916).

example, coefficients of expansion of metals under standard conditions of temperature. These constants would presumably hold for men in general. Subsequent research, with its repeated discoveries of individual differences in every conceivable psychological variable, has blasted all hope of determining psychological constants for human beings.

In England, Sir Francis Galton established an anthropometric laboratory in 1885 for the purpose of studying individual differences. Galton was not interested in tests as such, although he did devise tests for studying degrees of imagery, for discriminating weights, and for discriminating pitches. The Galton whistle devised for discriminating pitch differences is still used in psychological laboratories. Galton is important in the history of testing, however, not for the tests he produced, but for diverting emphasis from the study of the generalized mind to the study of individual differences, for the development of statistical methods used in testing, and for his statistical studies of the inheritance of mental traits.

The great genius in the history of intelligence testing was Alfred Binet (1857–1911), a Frenchman who, interestingly enough, had taken his university degree not in psychology or in medicine, as might be expected, but in law. Binet's interest in the experimental measurement of individual differences began in 1886, when he was but twenty-nine years old, and continued until his death in 1911. During this period of twenty-five years, he wrote more than fifty articles on the subject. In 1904, Binet was appointed to a national committee charged with the task of investigating retardation in French schools. This assignment stimulated him to construct the first individual test of general intelligence. Binet, in collaboration with Theophile Simon, published his first scale of intelligence tests in 1905. This scale consisted of thirty tests arranged in the order of increasing difficulty. It included items such as completing sentences, finding rhymes, defining abstract terms, comparing two lines of different lengths, following a moving object with the eyes, recognizing objects in a picture, and repeating sentences presented verbally. In 1908, and again in 1911, Binet revised his tests. With the 1908 edition Binet introduced the now familiar concept of *mental age* (MA) and divided the tests into age groups suitable for children of each age from three to eleven years. In the 1911 edition, Binet

(1) included five tests at each age level except the four-year level, (2) extended the scale [4] to the adult level, (3) excluded all items which appeared to be tests which would require special schooling in order to be able to answer them, and (4) included fifty-four items in the total scale (as against the original thirty-item scale). It was this scale which served as the basis for intelligence testing in America. In it Binet included tests which he believed represented the three phases of behavior in which intelligence was primarily shown, namely: (1) the ability to take and maintain a given mental set; (2) the capacity to make adaptations for the purpose of attaining a desired end; and (3) the power of self-criticism.

Before the Binet-Simon tests could be used with American children, it was necessary to translate them into English, and to revise and adapt them in various ways. The first such adaptation for American children was made in 1910 by Goddard, who was at that time director of the Vineland Training School for defective children. Goddard's revision was used widely for a few years after its appearance, chiefly to detect mental deficiency and to distinguish between various degrees of mental deficiency. At that time the tests were used for the purpose that Binet had set himself, to detect feeblemindedness. It was some time later before tests were used as they are today to distinguish varying degrees of normal intelligence.

The most widely used revision of the Binet-Simon scale was made by Lewis Terman and published in 1916. This scale, known as the Stanford Revision of the Binet-Simon Scale,[5] became the standard measuring instrument in psychoeducational clinics throughout the United States. For many years this test served as a basis for determining whether other tests were measuring intelligence or not. For example, when it became evident that children with language handicaps or sensory defects were penalized on the Stanford-Binet, performance tests were constructed to meet their needs. The two performance tests most commonly used in America were the Pintner-Paterson, and the Arthur Scale of Performance Tests. Both of these tests were "validated" against

---

[4] The term *scale* is used when test items are arranged according to the degree of difficulty.
[5] Known as the Stanford Revision from Stanford University with which Terman was connected.

the Stanford-Binet Scale; that is, they were considered "good" tests because they correlated significantly with the Stanford-Binet. They did not correlate perfectly, however, and thus to some extent were measuring different aspects of intelligence.

In 1937, Terman, in collaboration with Maud Merrill, published a new revision of the Stanford-Binet, and this revision has gradually superseded the earlier edition. The new revision is published in two forms, Form L and Form M, and it is thus possible to give the test at frequent intervals without spuriously raising the score as a result of the practice or coaching effect. The 1937 edition contains tests that extend it down to the two-year-old level and also contains materials for the lower age levels which are much more interesting to young children than were the materials in the 1916 edition. It also includes many more items at the upper age levels.

Sample items from Form L of the 1937 Stanford-Binet are given below:

Year VI.
1. Vocabulary. (Child must define five words in vocabulary list.)
2. Copying a bead chain from memory.
3. Mutilated pictures. (Child must tell which part is missing.)
4. Number concepts. (Child must place twelve, three, nine, five, and seven blocks upon a sheet of white paper.)
5. Pictorial likenesses and differences. (Child identifies the one picture on each of six cards which is unlike the others.)
6. Maze tracing.

2. What is an intelligence test?

An intelligence test is a series of carefully selected situations calling for some kind of a reaction on the part of the subject. If the subject reacts appropriately, that is, if he gives the response corresponding to the test key, he gets a positive score on that item. The person who gets many positive scores is assumed to be much more intelligent than one who gets mostly negative scores. Yet no test contains more than a sample of the many situations to which an individual might react "intelligently" or "stupidly." In constructing the test the psychologist assumes that the items he includes are an adequate sample of all of the possible items to which his subjects might respond. The psychologist is interested not so much in devising an instrument which will measure the complete intellectual ability of any one person as he is in devising an instrument which will differentiate individ-

INTELLIGENT BEHAVIOR 315

uals of different abilities upon a single continuous scale. For this reason, intelligence tests could not be said really to measure "genius"; they merely show that a given individual scores at or near the top when compared with other members of his age group.

The measurement of an individual's degree of intelligence is not made directly, but is inferred from an analysis of his behavior under test conditions. In this respect, psychological measurements are similar to measurements made in the biological and physical sciences. The biologist infers from measuring the number of white corpuscles present in a sample of blood that a serious infection is present in the body. He does not measure, for example, scarlet fever directly. The physicist measures the amount of electrical current by observing the angle through which an armature carrying the current is turned in a magnetic field; he determines the temperature by observing the length of a column of mercury in a thermometer. All of the above measurements make it possible to infer rather than directly observe some variable. This limitation, however, does not prevent either the physicist or the psychologist from taking many practical steps, armed with his measurements.

3. Individual and group tests of intelligence

In psychological clinics tests of intelligence are almost always given individually. This person-to-person testing situation helps the psychologist to know his client better and provides him with more opportunities to set the client at ease. A condition of rapport must exist if the client is to do his best on a test. By "rapport" we mean that an emotional relationship favorable to maximum coöperation exists between the examiner and the examinee. With a few notable exceptions, rapport is easier to establish in the individual situation than it is in the group situation. Furthermore, a disturbed person often finds that the presence of a group intensifies his emotional problems and distracts him from the task at hand. And lastly, the experienced clinical psychologist gets valuable insights into the personality of his client by observing his behavior during the testing.

In spite of the advantages noted above, individual testing is an expensive procedure and is unnecessary for most kinds of routine testing, as, for example, when tests are to be given to all the children in a school, or to men in industry, or in the armed forces for purposes of classification and guidance. It was the problem of selecting and classifying recruits in World War I that led to the construction of group intelligence tests. The experience of the armed forces with group tests suggested that such tests might also be used successfully in other situations, such as school and college classes, and with employees in industry and business.

Psychologists constructed two group tests of intelligence to be given to the armed forces in World War I, the Army Alpha for soldiers who could read and write, and the Army Beta for illiterate soldiers or for men whose acquaintance with the English language was limited. The success of these tests in the classification of army personnel led to their widespread civilian adaptation and use in schools, colleges, offices, and industrial plants. In World War II, the Army General Classification Test superseded the Army Alpha.

4. Linguistic and performance tests

Tests of intelligence may be linguistic tests, performance tests, or a combination of both. In general, however, if a test calls for oral or written responses or if the directions, at least in part, require an understanding of language, it is classified as linguistic. The use of linguistic tests presupposes that the persons to be tested know the language and, what is sometimes overlooked, that they have had approximately equal opportunities to learn its fundamentals. Obviously, however, there are both children and adults for whom this assumption does not hold. At the time of World War I, for example, Army psychologists discovered that about 30 per cent of drafted men were unable to write letters home. These psychologists, therefore, constructed a performance test, the Army Beta, which did not require the use of language either in giving the test or in taking it.

A simple example from a performance test is reproduced below:

Fig. 56. Sample Item from a Performance Test. [From Terman, McCall, and Lorge, *Non-Language Multi-Mental Test,* Form A (New York, Teachers College, Bureau of Publications, Columbia University).]

The directions for this test are given in pantomime. The examiner gets attention by rapping on the desk with a pointer. He points for a moment to each of the five pictures, then looks at the class questioningly. After a short pause, he makes a gesture of sudden comprehension. He then points to each eye of the first face, holds up two fingers, and nods approvingly. He repeats this for the second, fourth, and fifth face. He points to the whole eye of the third face and then taps the incomplete eye several times while shaking his head to express "no." He then crosses out the third face with his pointer. He points again to each of the complete faces and nods affirmatively. He then points to the third face, taps the unfinished eye three times in rapid succession, and shakes his head to express "no," after which he crosses out the third face with chalk. He then indicates that the subjects are to do the same thing on their test copies, both with the sample test, described above, and with other similar items. Other wholly different test items are presented in the same general way until the entire test is administered.

One of the first performance tests was the Sequin Form Board which was used for classifying the feebleminded. This test requires the subject to place a number of differently shaped objects in the appropriate holes, as shown in Figure 57. One of the useful performance tests for children is Form I of the Arthur Point-Scale of Performance Tests. This Form has proved itself as valid for both deaf children and Indian children. Form II, of which the stencil design test shown in Figure 58 is a part, is available for retesting.

Performance tests, in spite of their usefulness, do not always correlate too well with verbal tests. Some performance tests, notably the Porteus Maze Tests, appear to measure quite different mental functions from verbal tests. In general, they appear to measure "concrete" intelligence rather than "abstract" intelligence. It is sometimes desirable, in appraising a child's mental ability, to administer both a linguistic and a performance test. Discrepancies on the two types of tests often have clinical significance.

5. Criteria of a good intelligence test

In judging whether a given test is a good test of intelligence or not, certain criteria or standards of judgment are used. The most important of these standards are those of (1) validity and (2)

318   PERSONS AND PERSONALITY

reliability; others are (3) objectivity and ease of scoring, and (4) adequate standardization. A test should not be used unless there is evidence that it meets the requirements generally agreed upon.

Fig. 57. Sequin Form Board. [Courtesy C. H. Stoelting Company, Chicago.]

a. Validity. A test is said to be valid if it measures what it purports to measure. Thus if a test claims to measure "general intelligence," it must not measure special aptitudes or skills or traits which vary considerably with training or experience. Ordinarily, the validity of an intelligence test for children is determined (1) by the criterion of chronological age, and (2) by comparing test results with other criteria of intelligence.

The chronological age criterion presupposes that intelligence increases as a child grows older and that the distribution of intelligence among groups selected at random is approximately the same from year to year. This criterion is met if an increasing percentage of children pass the test at each age level from the lower to the higher ages. An item, for example, which is passed by 15

INTELLIGENT BEHAVIOR 319

per cent of seven-year-olds, 15 per cent of eight-year-olds, and 15 per cent of nine-year-olds, would not be discriminating. When the percentage of increase from one year to the next is small, the test item has too little discriminative capacity and is not included in the finished test.

In addition to using the criterion of chronological age, which in a well-constructed test is never adopted as the only criterion of

Fig. 58. Dr. Grace Arthur Administering Stencil Design Test.

its validity, we generally assume that a test is valid if it discriminates between two groups known to differ in intelligence. Thus, intelligence tests are expected to correlate somewhat with teachers' judgments of ability, with school achievement, and with other tests measuring intellectual ability. Sometimes the grade location or the chronological age of pupils within a given grade is also used.

Intelligence tests are not equally valid in the prediction of achievement for all kinds of people, although it is sometimes difficult to isolate the disturbing factors in a given case. If a psychologist measures the ability of only one or two children in a given neighborhood or from a culture group different from that used in the standardization of the test, he may attribute all failures on the test to the stupidity of the child. As he continues to work in the neighborhood, however, and to observe the children in other than test situations, he often begins to doubt the significance of his test results. A sister psychologist working in Boston found that children consistently reacted to the Stanford-Binet vocabulary item "roar" with the words "not cooked." It is easy to see that this response was culturally determined by the idiosyncracies of pronunciation in that particular part of the country. Accordingly, she quite properly gave the children full credit for the response even though it was not listed on the key. In World War II, the Wechsler-Bellevue test designed for use in the army at first contained a cutout puzzle of a house. The subject was required to assemble this house. Strangely enough, this test appeared to have no relation whatever to ability. But when a face to be assembled was substituted for the house, the test was found to be significant. Apparently, soldiers who came from regions in which houses such as those shown in the picture puzzle were uncommon were handicapped in solving the puzzle, even though they did have normal intelligence. In both of these instances it was relatively easy to see what was happening to invalidate the tests. But it is more than probable that other cultural influences invalidate some test items in ways that the examiners have not been alert enough to detect.

b. Reliability. A test is reliable if it measures consistently and accurately whatever it measures. This means that if a test is repeated, the individuals should rank in approximately the same order upon second testing as they did the first time. The fact that a test is reliable, however, is no indication that it is also valid. While it is true that a test cannot be valid unless it is reliable, it is also true that a test can be reliable without being valid.

Some of the common ways of determining test reliability are the following:

(1) *Equivalent forms.* Perhaps the best method of determining the reliability of a test is to give two equivalent forms and work out of the coefficient of correlation between the two sets of scores. The resulting coefficient of correlation is known as *reliability coefficient*. Equivalent forms of a test are carefully constructed by giving a large number of items to a sample population. The difficulty level of these items is then computed. The two equiv-

alent forms are constructed by carefully selecting and balancing the items which will go into the two forms. Items of the same level of difficulty but which are nearly identical should not be included, because the practice effect on such items may spuriously or falsely raise the score on the second test.

(2) *Split-half technique.* In this technique, two separate scores are computed for the test, and the coefficient of correlation between them is computed. There are two ways of doing this: (1) separate scores may be derived by totaling separately the even-numbered items and the odd-numbered items. Or, (2) separate scores may be derived from the first half of the test and then separately from the second half. The second way, however, cannot be used when the test items have been arranged according to difficulty. In using the split-half technique, we assume that we are correlating equivalent or comparable forms. Since the reliability of a test varies with its length, this method of using a score based upon only one-half of the items needs to be corrected before we can determine the reliability of the whole test. A statistical correction, known as the Spearman-Brown formula, is used for this purpose.

The split-half technique usually yields a higher reliability coefficient than does the equivalent-form technique. Because the two scores are obtained at the same sitting, chance factors, as, for example, a temporary physiological condition of the subjects, will influence both scores in the same direction. These errors, then, are correlated, and the resulting reliability coefficient is spuriously or falsely high.

c. *Objectivity and ease of scoring.* In addition to validity and reliability, an intelligence test should be scored as objectively as possible. By objective scoring, we mean that the items are scored in such a way that all persons correcting the test would have to accept or reject the same answers. In other words, everyone scoring the test would come out with the same result. Test scores are more likely to be accurate if the test has been constructed in such a way that scoring is objective, and if the spaces for answers are so placed as to make scoring easy.

d. *Adequate standardization.* An individual score on an intelligence test is interpreted by comparing it with published norms for that test. The norms for an intelligence test are averages obtained by testing large groups of children, and these averages are used as standards for comparison. If age norms are used, it is necessary that they be derived from random or systematic samplings of children at each age. If selective factors have been present in the groups upon whom the test has been standardized, then the norms are not adequate standards of comparison.

6. Mental age and intelligence quotient

When Binet set about to arrange the tests in his scale according to age levels, he had to test each of the items in the scale empirically. He tested children at different age levels and analyzed the results of these tests to determine the age at which children could actually pass the tests. Binet assumed that if a given item was passed by all children of a certain age, then the item was too easy for that age level. If no children at a given age passed the item, it was obviously too difficult for that age level. He finally decided that if about 75 per cent of children at a given age passed an item of his scale, then that item was appropriately placed at that age level. For example, if 75 per cent of six-year-old children could repeat four digits backward, then that test was placed at the six-year level of difficulty.

In the 1937 revision of the Stanford-Binet Scale, each form of the tests contains 129 items, arranged in order of difficulty from age two to the superior adult level. The number of tests which a given individual passes is compared with the norms for the whole scale in order to determine his mental age. Mental age norms are based upon studies of what children at different ages will do with the tests. If, for example, we test a ten-year-old boy and find that he passes the same number of tests that the average seven-year-old child passes, we say that the boy's mental age (MA) is seven. Since his chronological age is ten, the boy is mentally retarded three years. The MA, unlike the intelligence quotient, is referred to as an *absolute measure* of intelligence.

When tests were first used the extent of mental retardation or acceleration was determined by finding the difference between the chronological age (CA) and the mental age (MA). This procedure, however, was not too accurate, since the meaning of the difference between CA and MA varies with the age level at which it is determined. A four-year-old child, for example, who is two years retarded is feebleminded. A twelve-year-old child who is mentally retarded two years is not feebleminded but merely dull.

Terman, following a suggestion of Stern that the ratio of mental to chronological age be used in interpreting test results, adopted the now commonly used concept of intelligence quotient (IQ). The IQ is obtained by dividing MA by CA (chronological age) and multiplying by 100 in order to eliminate decimal points. Thus, the average IQ is 100. If a child's MA is 10 and his CA is 8, his IQ is 125. The IQ, unlike the MA, is a *relative measure* of intelligence; it is an index of brightness, not a measure of the level of intellectual development. Since the IQ has the same meaning at all age levels, it is far more useful than MA as a quantitative measure of mental retardation or acceleration.

III. ACHIEVEMENT AND THE IQ

The use of intelligence quotients by teachers who have not been trained in psychology has led to a number of abuses which may be harmful to children. A score on an intelligence test, like a measure of any of the components of personality, must be interpreted in the light of the whole personality and the life situation of the individual tested. Teachers sometimes say when the results of tests are made available to them, "Well, that settles it! That's the last time I'll accept poor work from him. He can do better. He's just not trying!" Or, "Now I have something to show to his mother to prove to her that he can't learn. She thinks we're just not teaching him anything." The second remark was overheard when it was made about a boy with an IQ of 88 in a school in which the average was 108. The point we want to stress is that in both of the instances cited, the IQ did not in itself justify the proclaimed conclusion. A judgment as to whether a child can learn to do the work of a particular grade or not or whether he is working to capacity must be based upon a study of his total situation. Not all children (and adults) have the same amount of energy to expend. The amount of available energy is a biological characteristic which an individual cannot change at will. It is determined by a complex of many interacting factors—nutrition, metabolism, and hereditary constitution—to mention only a few. Human beings differ as much in energy as in other physiologically conditioned characteristics, and the same expenditure of time and effort should consequently not be expected of everyone. Two children may have the same amount of intellectual ability as measured by tests, they may both be in perfect health, and, what is more important, they may both be putting forth their best efforts in school; yet the amount they achieve may be quite different. These differences in achievement do not necessarily indicate that one child is conscientious and the other lazy. They may indicate nothing more than that the two children differ physiologically in something, perhaps rate of metabolism, which influences their respective work output.

IV. EDUCATIONAL AND OCCUPATIONAL LEVEL IN RELATION TO THE IQ

The rate at which children progress through school as well as the final level of education that they reach is significantly related to the IQ. Terman, as early as 1919, discovered that children of low IQ were almost always in grades lower than those of their chronological age mates. In fact, he found that the simplest way of finding the brightest child in a given classroom was to pick out the youngest child in the group. Often when Terman had pointed out the brightest child in the classroom, the teachers were surprised at the choice because the child in question had not impressed them as being as intelligent as the tests indicated. In this respect, Terman's study corroborated an earlier observation of Binet that teachers were highly inaccurate in their judgments of children's intelligence. Teachers, in judging intelligence, do not usually consider the age of the child. The bright child who is accelerated in school is competing with children older than himself and consequently does not stand out as being different from the group. In a class of children his own age, his superior ability would be much more apparent. Terman [6] noted also that if the MA alone were taken as the index of ability, then the dull child was usually not as retarded in school as one would expect, nor was the gifted child as accelerated as one would expect. Although Terman regretted that this state of affairs should be so common, it was probably better at least in some ways than to have a bright child placed in a class in which physical immaturity would set him apart from the group and thus subject him to isolation from or rejection by his peers.

Not only is the rate of progress through school roughly commensurate with mental ability, but so is the final grade level at-

---

[6] L. M. Terman, *The Intelligence of School Children* (Boston, Houghton Mifflin Company, 1919).

tained. In general, the lower the IQ, the lower the grade at which the individual drops out of school. For that reason we say that the school selects children on the basis of IQ. The average IQ of children in the eighth grade is higher than that of children in the first grade; the average for high school seniors is higher than that of freshmen. In college a similar relationship is seen, but not to so great a degree. A student may fail in college because of lack of ability and yet be quite a bit above the average of the general population in IQ!

Occupational level and educational achievement are related in the sense that preparation for certain types of occupation requires a longer and more exacting kind of study than for other types of occupations. The professions require more formal schooling than do clerical, business, and trade jobs. But even within the professions, there are differences in ability levels. In World War I an analysis of occupation in terms of scores on the Army Alpha test yielded information which has since proved of considerable value to psychologists who do vocational guidance.

A recent study made to determine the general intellectual aptitude required for the Ph.D. degree confirmed the results of an earlier study in finding that the median IQ of Ph.D.'s, if translated in terms of the 1937 Stanford-Binet Scale, was 139. If the Ph.D.'s received in one field were eliminated, the median would be 146. A follow-up study was made of graduates of the University of Minnesota High School who subsequently received advance degrees. Table 4 is an abbreviation of the findings which shows the median IQ of those who went into the various professions.

Table 4

1937 STANFORD-BINET INTELLIGENCE QUOTIENTS OF UNIVERSITY HIGH SCHOOL GRADUATES OF 1941–1942 WHO HAD BEEN GRANTED ADVANCED DEGREES

Degrees beyond the Bachelor's	Number	1937 Stanford-Binet Median IQ
D.D.S.	11	115
M.D.	24	131
LL.B.	17	135
M.A. and M.S.	62	135
Ph.D.	13	139
All advanced degrees	127	134

Adapted from C. G. Wrenn, "Potential Research Talent in the Sciences," *The Educational Record*, 30 (January, 1949), 12.

V. THE DISTRIBUTION OF INTELLIGENCE IN THE POPULATION

Intelligence, like most of the bodily characteristics of human beings, such as height or foot length, is distributed in the general population according to the normal probability curve, as shown in Figure 59. This curve indicates that there are as many intellectually gifted as intellectually retarded people in the general population. The great majority of people tend to cluster in the middle ranges of intelligence. The more extreme the level of intelligence, the fewer people there are who reach it.

VI. INTERPRETATION OF IQ'S

In the manual for the 1916 Stanford Revision of the Binet Test, Terman suggested the IQ equivalents indicated in Table 5.

Table 5

IQ EQUIVALENTS FOR 1916 STANFORD-BINET TEST

Descriptive Terms	IQ's
Near genius	140 and above
Very superior	120–140
Superior	110–120
Normal	90–110
Dull	80–90
Borderline	70–80
Moron	50–70
Imbecile	25–50
Idiot	0–25

Adapted from L. M. Terman, *The Measurement of Intelligence* (Boston, Houghton Mifflin Company, 1916), p. 79.

Terman's interpretation of IQ's has been quite generally adopted by American psychologists, but with certain reservations. Terman's use of the term *genius,* for example, to designate children with IQ's of 140 or above was surely unfortunate. Other characteristics besides general intelligence contribute to genius, among which energy, character, originality, and the like would certainly be included. Many college students and professional people have IQ's above 140 and yet make no great social or intellectual contribution to the society in which they live. Leta Hollingworth who, like Terman, has made extensive studies of children with

INTELLIGENT BEHAVIOR

superior ability, prefers the term *gifted child* or *exceptional child* to the term *genius*. She considers a child with an IQ of 180 or above a potential genius, but even then believes he has but one or two chances in ten of making a contribution sufficiently great to warrant the use of the word *genius*.

At the other end of the scale, the diagnosis, *feebleminded*, is not merely a statistical concept; it is also a social one. The determination of feeblemindedness must, therefore, not be based upon a test score alone. This subject is discussed more fully in Chapter XV.

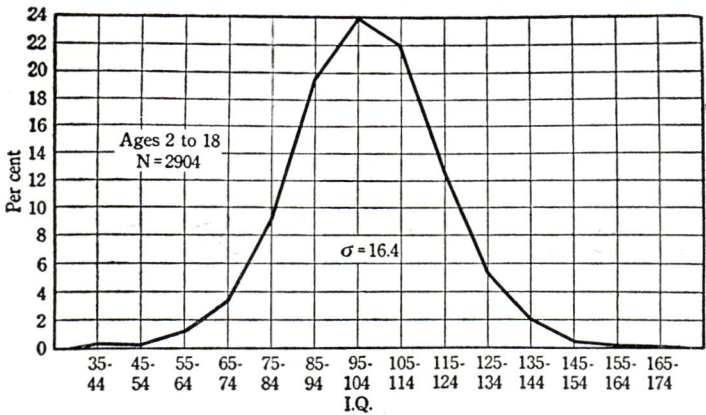

Fig. 59. Distribution of IQ's of Standardization Group for Revised Stanford-Binet Test, Forms L and M. [Reproduced by permission from L. M. Terman and M. A. Merrill, *Measuring Intelligence* (New York, Houghton Mifflin Company, 1937), p. 3.]

VII. RACIAL, NATIONAL AND CULTURAL DIFFERENCES IN INTELLIGENCE

Differences in average scores on intelligence tests have been noted for different national and racial groups in the United States. These trends have been summarized as follows:

> . . . as compared with the white American norms which serve as a basis for comparison, relatively poor scores are obtained by American Negroes, American Indians, Mexicans, native Hawaiians, and immigrants from Italy, Portugal, and Poland. Scores at or near the American norm are reported for the Chinese and Japanese, Germans and

Irish, whereas Jews, English and Scotch, Swedes and Norwegians tend to surpass the American norms to a slight degree. These results are found both in the case of adults and children, although considerable variation is shown in the scores made by the same ethnic group according to the sample studied and the test used.[7]

The presence of such differences in tested intelligence must be interpreted with great caution. With our rapidly increasing knowledge of anthropology and sociology, our greater realization of the lifelong effects of early environment and experience, and our greater awareness of the assumptions underlying the use of intelligence tests, we are less likely to conclude that there are genuine ethnic differences than we were several decades ago. Brigham, on the basis of Army test results in World War I, claimed that these results gave definite proof of the superiority of North Europeans to the Alpines, who in turn were somewhat superior to the Mediterraneans. He also concluded that the whites were definitely superior to the Negroes. As a result of further study of the method of validating the Army Alpha test, however, Brigham later (1930) repudiated his earlier conclusions, saying that the "study with its entire super-structure of racial differences collapses completely."[8]

Other investigators of racial intelligence, too, have become more conservative in the interpretation of their findings as new evidence has accumulated concerning the factors which influence test results.

Among the factors which may be responsible for apparent ethnic differences are those of (1) language, (2) motivation, (3) socioeconomic status, (4) amount and quality of education, (5) selective sampling, and (6) rapport with the examiner.

Of particular interest in this connection is a study in which 325 six- through eleven-year-old children of different Indian tribes were tested on the Goodenough Draw-a-Man Test.[9] The Draw-a-Man Test is supposedly a culture-free test, in that children of all cultures have had equal opportunities of observing people. In

[7] H. S. Jennings, *et al.*, *Scientific Aspects of the Race Problem* (Washington, D.C., The Catholic University of America Press, 1941, and Longmans, Green & Company, 1941), pp. 254–255.

[8] C. C. Brigham, "Intelligence Tests of Immigrant Groups," *Psychol. Rev.*, 37 (1930), 159.

[9] R. J. Havighurst, *et al.*, "Environment and the Draw-a-Man Test: the Performance of Indian Children," *J. Abnorm. Soc. Psychol.*, 41 (1946), 50–63.

this test the child is given a pencil or crayon and a piece of paper and asked to draw a man. The test is scored according to the number of essential details included. In the white, urban, American culture this test gives a valid measure of intelligence for ages up to ten. Goodenough obtained an *r* of .75 between IQ's on the Draw-a-Man Test and the 1916 Stanford-Binet for a group of white, midwestern American children.

The results of these Indian studies show that the Draw-a-Man Test is not nearly so culture-free as one might suppose. These results are summarized in Table 6.

Table 6

SCORES OF INDIAN CHILDREN ON THE GOODENOUGH DRAW-A-MAN TEST COMPARED WITH MIDWEST WHITE CHILDREN

Indian Tribe	Mean IQ, age 6–11		
	Boys	Girls	Total
Zia	116.4 (N = 17)	101.9 (N = 15)	109.6 (N = 32)
Zuni	122.1 (N = 18)	104.0 (N = 24)	111.7 (N = 42)
Hopi (Oraibi)	120.5 (N = 24)	99.5 (N = 22)	110.5 (N = 46)
Hopi (First Mesa)	126.7 (N = 15)	108.6 (N = 17)	117.1 (N = 32)
Navajo (Shiprock)	110.1 (N = 20)	109.4 (N = 27)	109.7 (N = 47)
Midwest (whites)	98.3 (N = 28)	103.4 (N = 38)	101.2 (N = 66)

Adapted from R. J. Havighurst and others, "Environment and the Draw-a-Man Test: the Performance of Indian Children," *J. Abnorm. Soc. Psychol.*, 41 (1946), 50–63.

These results show (1) that Indian children of all tribes are superior to white children, (2) that boys are superior to girls in most of the Indian groups, and (3) that sex differences were negligible in the Navajo tribe.

Both boys and girls in the Navajo culture have similar experiences and opportunities in learning to draw, and neither sex is encouraged to produce graphic art. In the Zia, Zuni, and Hopi cultures, on the contrary, boys are encouraged from infancy to draw and are given many more opportunities and much more encouragement than girls to engage in art activities. Zia boys, for example, are expected to paint animals on the walls to encourage fertility, and to paint masks, altars, and other ceremonial objects. Girls, however, rarely draw except in school. They are not encouraged to draw or paint human or animal forms but limit their painting to conventional designs used on pottery. The general superiority of Indian over white children is a reflection of the different value and emphasis placed upon drawing in the two cultures. Apparently, cultural influences have a profound effect upon intelligence as measured by the Draw-a-Man Test. If this is true for a non-verbal test, it is probably even more true for tests requiring the use of language.

VIII. RURAL AND URBAN DIFFERENCES

Rural children tend to score lower on intelligence tests than urban children. This is probably not a genuine intellectual difference between farm and city children, since in most instances intelligence test items appear to favor the city group. If more items were selected from the everyday experience of farm children, it is likely that the scores of city children would drop.

IX. THEORIES ABOUT THE NATURE OF INTELLIGENCE

A. The Organization of Intelligence

1. The bi-factor and multi-factor theories

There are two main theories as to the organization of intelligence, those of Spearman and Thorndike. According to Spearman's bi-factor theory of intelligence, all mental abilities may be resolved into two components or factors, namely a g-factor and an s-factor. The g-factor is found to some extent in all mental abilities, although the amount may vary from ability to ability. Spearman compares the g-factor to the steam generated in a locomotive. Much of the steam is used for propelling the locomotive. A lesser amount is used for blowing the whistle. Yet it is steam (g-factor) in both cases. It is the g-factor which is responsible for the positive correlations that are found between various abilities. The s-factors, on the other hand, are more or less specific to particular abilities or activities, such as musical or artistic talent or mechanical ability. Traits or abilities which are made up largely of these s-factors are said to be loosely organized. The correlations between tests of such abilities are low.

An alternative to Spearman's theory is Thorndike's multi-factor theory. Thorndike holds that we have intelligences rather than intelligence, and that intelligence should be defined in terms of the kind of tasks that are performed. He distinguishes three varieties of intellectual tasks or intelligences, namely, abstract, mechanical, and social.

2. Factor analysis

Often one finds two people with identical IQ's or percentile ratings on intelligence tests who differ markedly in their approach to intellectual problems. One of the explanations of such differences is that the component factors which go to make up the rating of intelligence are of relatively different weights in the two cases. On the A.C.E. test for college freshman, for example, two main "factors" are isolated for measurement: (1) a quantitative factor, assessed by means of a Q-score; and (2) a linguistic factor, assessed by means of an L-score. Two students, A and B, receiving total percentile ratings of 60 might have the following factor percentile ratings:

	Student A	Student B
Q - score PR	50	10
L - score PR	10	50

Obviously the "kind of intelligence" which A has is different from that of B.

Thurstone and others have developed statistical techniques for determining the "dimensions" of an individual's abilities and the interrelationships among these abilities. The general term for these techniques is *factor analysis*. Thurstone found that some tests correlate among themselves much more highly than others and concluded that to the extent that they correlate, such tests were measuring the same abilities. Other tests, however, do not correlate so highly, and these he concluded were measuring relatively different abilities. By a series of statistical manipulations, Thurstone found seven kinds of tests which were apparently measuring different "factors" of intelligence. An inspection of the test items from which the factor analysis was made led him to name the factors as follows: (1) verbal understanding, (2) word fluency, (3) number facility, (4) space thinking, (5) perception, (6) reasoning, and (7) shape recognition.

Another important consideration in interpreting intelligence tests has been expressed as follows:

> Although two persons might have the same final scores—e.g., concerning vocabulary, memory, comprehension, and reasoning—they may be widely different in their general intelligence, because it is not the sum of separate points which decides, but the interrelationship of items and their organization.[10]

[10] W. Wolff, *What Is Psychology?* (New York, Grune & Stratton, Inc., 1947), p. 217.

B. Gestalt Point of View

Koffka, one of the pioneer Gestalt psychologists, claimed that mental growth involves much more than the addition of new increments; it involves rather a complete reorganization of the entire mental structure as new abilities are added. This point of view has been widely accepted by American psychologists. Its implications for mental testing, however, have not always been clear. Some psychologists think that if this Gestalt idea were accepted it would "outlaw the current conceptions of quantitative differences in intelligence, and the attempts to express the growth of intelligence upon a continuous scale." [11] Others, however, do not consider this a real difficulty in testing, since test constructors have always assumed that their tests increase in complexity from the early to the late chronological ages. They believe that as long as we know that our quantitative measures of intelligence involve hierarchies of abilities, no logical difficulty is involved.

X. ATTRIBUTES OF INTELLIGENCE

Three attributes of intelligence which have been traditionally measured by intelligence tests are: altitude (or power), range (or breadth), and speed. Altitude refers to the difficulty level of the test items, range to the number of items at any given level of difficulty, and speed to the number of items completed in a given period of time. More recently the following have been added: (1) abstractness, (2) adaptiveness to a goal, (3) social value, and (4) the emergence of originals. Each of these attributes will be explained briefly.

The attributes of intelligence are entirely in the world of the abstract. Mental activity "takes place in symbols and fragments; it is once removed from the physical, the explicit, the concrete." [12]

The attributes of adaptiveness to a goal and social value tend to merge and indicate that "intelligent behavior is never busywork. It is always geared to a problem, a project, a goal, a need." [13] Besides being able to perform speedily difficult and complex tasks, the intelligent person must have a goal and "apply his mental

---

[11] K. S. Lashley, *Brain Mechanisms and Intelligence: A Quantitative Study of Injuries to the Brain* (Chicago, University of Chicago Press, 1929), p. 3.

[12] George Stoddard, *The Meaning of Intelligence* (New York, The Macmillan Company, 1943), p. 15.

[13] *Ibid.*, p. 24.

processes . . . to whatever is believed by the social group, rightly or wrongly, to be contributory to general welfare."[14] Not much attention has been paid to the "emergence of originals" in intelligence tests. In the light of this attribute, growth of intelligence is not just more of something already there; it is something new and different. For example, in engineering it may manifest itself in the discovery of a new principle or design.

XI. INTELLIGENCE AND PERSONALITY

In the early days of intelligence testing, it was not uncommon for psychologists to make far-reaching recommendations on the basis of MA's or IQ's alone. Terman, in his pioneer book, *The Measurement of Intelligence,* suggested that grade placements, promotions, and similar adjustments be made on the basis of intelligence tests alone. This point of view has been completely discredited.

Any complete diagnosis of personality, of course, requires the accurate measurement of intelligence. Standardized intelligence tests, measuring altitude, range, and speed, or divisible into factors such as linguistic or quantitative, help us to see the individual in relation to others of a group. But they do not give us a picture of the way in which intelligence functions in the life of the person whom we are testing. The *kind* of intelligence a person has, the *availability* of his intelligence, i.e., the degree to which his intellect interacts with his motives, and controls or is controlled by his emotions, is one of the most significant aspects of personality. Traditional intelligence tests do not give this picture of the total personality. The nearest approach to this problem appears to be that of the Rorschach investigators. The Rorschach Test gives us a picture of the intelligence of the subject in the light of his total personality. The fact that Rorschach ratings do not correlate too highly with traditional intelligence tests does not necessarily invalidate the Rorschach. On the other hand, the Rorschach should not be used as a substitute for the carefully standardized intelligence test. One of these measures, it would seem, complements the other. Each has something to contribute to an understanding of the whole personality. In making recommendations for any given individual, one must not lose sight of the total picture.

[14] *Ibid.,* p. 22.

Neurotic and psychotic people may receive high scores on intelligence tests and yet function badly in life situations because of emotional problems. The criminal psychopath often has an amazing excess-cargo of uncoördinated and useless information. "Even when absolute measurements disclose a 'high' intelligence, so far as its applicability to the routine tasks of life and the special activities of the moment are concerned, its function as a mediator and regulator is absent." [15] We generally think of intelligence as a control mechanism, as a restraining tool in the adjustments of life. But the psychopath's behavior is characteristically free from restraint and takes no account of consequences.

Psychologists working with the Rorschach and other projective tests are not the only ones who have criticized the use of standardized tests as the only basis for assessing the intelligence of people. Others have commented upon the fact that intelligence tests are constructed after the pattern of the formal interview. The ability to answer set questions, they point out, is psychologically different from meeting reality. What we need, in addition to intelligence tests, is a method of testing which is patterned after a life situation.

XII. A CLARIFICATION OF SOME STATISTICAL TERMS COMMONLY USED IN THE MEASUREMENT OF PSYCHOLOGICAL CHARACTERISTICS

Statistical facts, as we have previously noted, are quantitative expressions of knowledge. Statistical techniques enable us to extract significant truths from masses of numerical data and to make inferences concerning relationships among them which tell us something about the population of things counted or measured (the population from which the data are drawn).

In Chapter II we presented a brief overview of the statistical tools most commonly used in psychological research. At this point, we are going to present a more detailed analysis of them.

You will recall that the statistics most commonly used in psychology are classified into three categories: (1) measures of central tendency, (2) measures of variability, and (3) measures of

---

[15] R. M. Lindner, *Rebel Without a Cause* (New York, Grune & Stratton, Inc., 1944), p. 5.

INTELLIGENT BEHAVIOR

correlation or relationship. In the first category we classify statistical methods which give us a single value most typical or representative of a population. In the second category we put statistics which tell the extent to which the measures obtained differ from the average. In the third category we put statistics which show the tendency of two or more sets of measures to vary together. An elementary knowledge of each of these three categories of statistical devices is necessary for reading psychological literature and for that reason we are explaining them in the paragraphs that follow.

A. Statistical Techniques

1. Measures of central tendency

Any statistical average is a measure of central tendency. A measure of central tendency is defined as the best representative measure of a group of measures. It always represents a *point* on a scale. The most common measures of central tendency are (1) the *arithmetical mean*, and (2) the *median*. A less commonly used measure is (3) the *mode*. The arithmetical mean is a *computed* average, the median a *counted* average, and the mode an *inspectional* average. The arithmetical mean is obtained by adding up all of the measures taken and dividing by the number of cases. The formula for doing so is $\Sigma X/n$, where Σ means "the sum of," X the individual measures, and n the number of cases. The median is defined as that point on a scale above and below which there is an equal number of cases. The mode is the measure which occurs with the greatest frequency, or the point on a scale at which there is the greatest number of cases. When the measures are distributed according to a bell-shaped or "normal" curve, all three measures of central tendency fall on the same point of the scale, as shown in Figure 60.

In general, the mean is the most accurate measure of central tendency, but there are occasions in which it is preferable to use the median. If, for example, there are a few very extreme measures in the group, the mean would be unduly affected by them. For example, if a few men with very high incomes live on a street, the median might give a more representative picture of central tendency than the mean.

2. Measures of variability

Measures of variability are always *distances* on a scale. They give us a picture of the *spread* of scores on a scale. Three commonly used measures of variability are (1) the *range*, (2) the *standard deviation*, designated by σ, and (3) *quartile deviation*, designated by Q. The *range* is an inspectional measure and is defined as the distance between the lowest and the highest score in the distribution. It is a rough measure of variability which is greatly influenced by extreme scores. It is never used in careful scientific work.

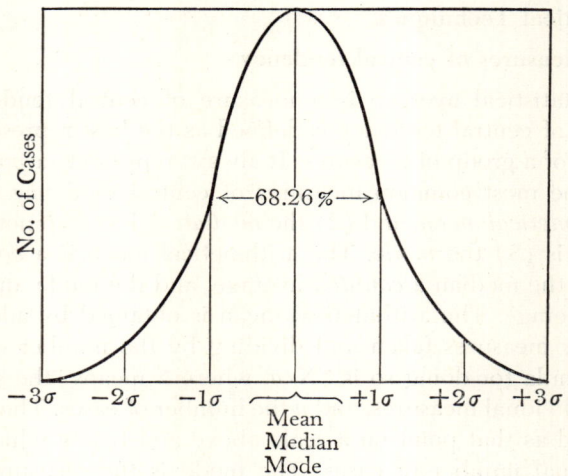

Fig. 60. Normal Distribution Curve. Mean, median, and mode are identical.

The *standard deviation* (σ) is a calculated measure of variability and is used whenever the mean is used as the measure of central tendency. Its use presupposes that the measures are distributed according to the normal curve. When this condition is fulfilled, the distance on the scale from a point one standard deviation below the mean to a point one standard deviation above the mean comprises 68.26 per cent of the measures, or, roughly, two-thirds the total range.

The *quartile deviation* (Q) is a counting measure of variability and is used as a measure of dispersion whenever the median is used as the measure of central tendency. Like standard deviation, its use assumes that the measures are "normally" distributed. The distance between a measure one quartile below the median and a measure one quartile above the median comprises the middle 50 per cent of the total distribution.

3. Determining relationships

Sometimes we are interested in finding out whether people who rank high in one trait or ability also rank high in another trait or ability. The way to ascertain this fact is to compute the statistical measure known as the coefficient of correlation, or r. Let us suppose, for example, that our problem is that of determining the relationship between intelligence and the appreciation of visual art. We would first give our subjects an intelligence test and then give them a test, the scores on which would yield a reliable and valid measure of art appreciation. Our results might look somewhat as follows:

	Score on Intelligence Test	Score on Art Appreciation Test
Mary	98	34
Jane	36	20
Margaret	49	23
Helen	63	35
Laura	34	21
Patricia	96	33
etc.	82	29

It would be difficult to tell from inspection alone whether the two scores were related, and if so, to what degree. But it would be possible to discover the relationship by computing the coefficient of correlation. The *coefficient of correlation* is defined as a mathematical measure of the degree of relationship between two variables. The "variables" in the above example are intelligence and art appreciation. If we should find that $r = .43$, we could conclude that the two variables do tend to be related to some extent. The relationship, however, is so low that we could not possibly know, if we had only the score on one test, what the person's probable score on the other test would be.

When two sets of scores or measures are perfectly related, $r = 1.00$. This means that the person who received the highest score on one test also received the highest score on the other test. It means, too, that the person who received the second highest score on the first test received the second highest score on the second test, and so on. Such a perfect correlation is very seldom obtained.

When the scores are negatively related, such that the person scoring highest on test 1 scores lowest on test 2, and vice versa, r is always preceded by a minus sign. If the negative relationship is perfect, $r = -1.00$. Such a correlation indicates that the higher a person's score is on one test, the lower it will be on the other test. Such correlations between desirable mental functions have never been obtained. Usually, desirable traits are positively correlated, although they seldom correlate perfectly.

When there is no relationship whatever between two variables, $r = .00$. Perfect positive, perfect negative, and zero correlations were pictured in Figure 2, page 37.

When we do not have actual measurements of the two variables to be studied but know only their rank order, the relationship is computed differently. In such instances, the Spearman rank-order coefficient of correlation is used. This measure is designated as ρ (rho).

B. Holding Variables "Constant"

Another problem which we frequently face in psychological research may be illustrated as follows:

Let us suppose that we want to find out if scores on tests of interest in academic subjects are related to the grades which students receive in such courses. For example, let us suppose that we are trying to find out whether a student who scores high on a test of interest in science gets higher grades in science courses than students whose scores on the "science interest test" are lower. Let us also suppose that, by computing r, we find a rather high relationship. Can we infer that high interest in science is probably responsible for the high grades? Before we can draw such an inference, we must find out to what degree intelligence and grades in science are related. Since we know that intelligence alone, apart from interest, is an important factor in securing high grades, we must determine the extent to which intelligence alone is related to grades. Then, by applying the appropriate statistical formula, we can find out to what extent interest and grades are related when the complicating factor of intelligence has been ruled out. In such a case we would be able to determine how much science interest scores are related to grades in science when intelligence is held "constant." Another way of summarizing our results would be: science interest scores and science grades are positively correlated when intelligence has been "partialed" out. The latter term derives from the formula used for holding intelligence "constant," namely, the "partial correlation" formula.

XIII. INDIVIDUAL DIFFERENCES AND THE STUDY OF THE INDIVIDUAL

We must distinguish between the psychology of individual differences and the psychology of one individual. The study of individual differences makes use of such statistical measurements as those of central tendency and variability. Typically, in the study of individual differences, a large group of people is measured in respect to one or more specific characteristics, traits, or aspects of development, and a frequency distribution is made of the findings. If the group studied consists of a random sampling of the total population from which it was drawn, the resulting curve showing the distribution of the measurements usually approaches that of a normal curve. Averages and measures of variability are then computed. Often when the measurements are tests of intelligence or personality, percentile ratings or standard scores are worked out. To determine how any given individual stands in comparison to the group as a whole, his score is superimposed on the graph showing the total distribution. If his score is just at the middle, he is said to be average or "normal"; he is looked upon as the "typical" individual. Yet in respect to other qualities not tested he may be very "atypical." Generalizations applicable to particular human beings in life situations cannot be made from such studies without many qualifications because they ignore the fact that at any moment it is the whole person who is reacting and not just an isolated segment of his personality. The psychology of individual differences has no meaning apart from group norms. Interestingly enough, it does not tell us nearly as much about the individual as we would like to know, but only how he differs in one or more respects from other members in the group.

We have reason to believe that many anatomical, physiological, and psychological generalizations made about people in the past have been misleading because the statistical techniques used in analyzing the data were not adequately adapted to the problem. Statistical methods, as traditionally applied to groups, often obscure rather than highlight the important facts of development. In the Harvard growth study, for example, data collected over a long period of time on the same individuals were analyzed by averaging the data for each age level and computing measures of variability. The statistical techniques commonly employed in the analysis of cross-sectional data were applied to the analysis of these longitudinal data. No observable relationship between age of maturing and stature growth was shown by such analyses. Shuttleworth,[16] however, demonstrated by using the same data that the routine procedures of statistics, such as the calculation of averages, measures of variability, and correlation, are inadequate for the analysis of longitudinal data. The use of such techniques does not exploit the advantages of longitudinal methods of study over the cross-sectional. Shuttleworth, instead of finding the gross average size at each age level, and taking the difference in gross size from one age level to the next as the basis for computing growth increments, computed the growth increment from one age to the next for each individual. He then plotted individual growth patterns and found a high degree of uniformity in the growth patterns of the children who matured early, of those who matured late, and of those who matured at about the average age for the total group. The growth pattern for each of these groups was different from the others, but within the group itself there was a high degree of uniformity. The presence of such uniform growth patterns was not revealed by the statistical computations used by Dearborn in the Harvard study.

The study of individual growth patterns rather than that of group averages from one age to another makes it necessary for us to revise many of our generalizations regarding the growth of physical and mental characteristics. The older medical charts of growth in height, for example, show a smooth, negatively accelerated curve. The inference that is usually drawn from the scrutiny of such a curve is that growth is a steady, non-fluctuating process, which gradually slows down until maturity is reached. Yet the pattern of growth for any individual shows marked fluc-

---

[16] F. K. Shuttleworth, *Sexual Maturation and the Physical Growth of Girls Age Six to Nineteen* (Washington, D.C., Soc. for Res. in Child Development, National Research Council, 1937).

tuations at different points in the life cycle. The statistical techniques upon which the group curve is based tend to smooth out all individual irregularities. It is obvious, however, that a generalized growth curve that reveals a pattern different from that of any individual in the group must be in error. If and when we begin making studies of intellectual growth by studying the growth patterns of individuals instead of groups, it is possible that we may have to revise some of our supposedly well-established generalizations about the curve of intellectual growth, just as we have already done in the study of anatomical growth.

The intelligence of man is revealed most especially in his thinking and creative imagination. We shall discuss these subjects at length in the next chapter.

SUGGESTED READING

HOLLINGWORTH, L. S., *Gifted Children, Their Nature and Nurture* (New York, The Macmillan Company, 1936).

XIII

Thinking and Creative Imagination

> . . . *imagination, which in truth*
> *Is but another name for absolute power*
> *And clearest insight, amplitude of mind,*
> *And reason in her most exalted mood.*
> —WORDSWORTH [1]

I. THE ROLE OF THINKING IN HUMAN LIFE

People modify the environment and make it serve their needs better largely because they have the power of imagining or thinking about things *as they might be*. Yet it is not solely on questions of practical importance that man thinks. Human beings do not think just when they are confronted by a practical problem to be solved. They engage in thinking for its own sake out of a natural desire to know. Often their most profound thinking takes place when they are trying to answer a theoretical question, a question the answer to which has no practical applications. People have a natural desire to know truth, to penetrate the meaning of reality. Since reality is more than the data presented to the senses, a person who would know reality must think.

Even the small child has a curiosity about his world, a curiosity which transcends mere factual knowledge of observable things. Very early in life he begins to "figure things out." When he is told to be good, for instance, he has been known to challenge adults with the question, "Why should I be good?" In other words, people think, not only because they have practical problems to solve but because they want to know, and thinking is a way of satisfying this peculiarly human need for knowledge and truth. Often the finest products of human thought flourish at a time when

[1] William Wordsworth, *Prelude, or The Growth of a Poet's Mind*, ed. by Ernest de Sélincourt (Oxford University Press, Inc., 1926), xiv, 189.

practical problems crying for solution are at a minimum. Great works of art, literature, religion, and philosophy are often produced by minds interiorly free from the insistent demands of practical affairs. The creative writer is sometimes so overcome by his need to create, to give birth to his brain child, that he becomes totally oblivious to the demands of everyday life, to the practical problems of human existence. The stereotyped notion of the poet starving in his garret may be a caricature, but it does contain a nugget of truth, since the thinker must not be enslaved by the demands of the body or of the senses if his best ideas are ever to see the light of day. He needs leisure for reflective thinking; his mind must not be diverted from its proper object by utilitarian considerations.

Strictly speaking, then, thinking need not be classified under the heading of "adjustment," although it is customary in contemporary psychology to do so. The tendency to view thinking in its utilitarian aspects only and to see it as nothing essentially different from complex sense perception springs from a philosophical bias which is deeply embedded in American thought today: the bias of "biologism" and Darwin's theory of evolution. Psychologists of a pragmatic complexion, following the lead of John Dewey and other "functionalists," hold that all mental functions, including thinking, have as their primary if not their exclusive end the purpose of helping the organism adapt to its environment. According to this view human beings think only when they are confronted by a challenge of some kind for which their previously acquired responses are inadequate. In other words, thinking is elicited not so much by an inner compulsion to know as by an external stimulus in the form of a practical problem to be solved.

Thinking, of course, does have a survival value for the human organism and the need to solve a practical problem may act as a powerful stimulus to imagination and thinking. But human beings also think because they have a natural craving to know.

II. THE MEANING OF THINKING

Sometimes when we say we are thinking we are merely daydreaming. At other times we use the word *thinking* to mean the process carried on by the creative artist. Again, thinking can mean serious reflection or scientific reasoning. It is in the last two senses that the word is used in the philosophy of St. Thomas, and that is how we shall use it in this chapter. Let us examine briefly these kinds of thinking to see what is involved in each.

In scientific thinking you start by thinking about real things. You get to know real things through *ideas.* An idea is the thing known as it exists in your mind. When you combine two ideas you make a judgment. Thus, a biologist has the idea of what a fruit fly is, and he gets an idea of the specimen before him. Then he can combine the two ideas in his mind, saying to himself, "This specimen is a fruit fly," and if he is not in error, his judgment reflects the true state of affairs. After you have made a judgment, you may be able to infer other judgments from the judgment made; or you may be able to combine two or more judgments and from them draw a further conclusion. Thus the biologist could say, "Since this is a fruit fly, it is not a mosquito." The process of drawing new conclusions from judgments already known is called reasoning. Because he possesses this power, man is called a rational animal.

When we say that man is a rational animal, we do not mean to imply that all human beings at all times meet the problems of life rationally. Far from it. Many people characteristically live their lives on a lower level; they base their choices on sense experience and emotion rather than on the light provided by their intellects. In this respect the power to reason is similar to other human powers. A man may have the power to become a great tenor, but if he lives in an unmusical environment where the ability to sing is not valued and if he receives no voice training, the power to sing may never be developed. Or, a man with good eye-hand coördination may have the power to play badminton. But unless he learns the rules of the game and practices playing badminton, he will never reach his optimal skill. So, too, the human power to reason must be cultivated and exercised if it is to reach its maximum proficiency. A man may have the power to think and yet reason very badly. He may, for instance, be ignorant of the rules of logic, which are in chief part the rules for correct reasoning. Or, he may not concentrate enough attention on the objects to be thought about because his emotions, feelings, expectations, and desires are distracting him. Clear thinking requires a concentration of attention which it is almost impossible to give in many situations of daily life because of interior and ex-

THINKING AND CREATIVE IMAGINATION

terior distractions. In all such cases, thinking will be imperfect because the conditions for its proper exercise are absent. The fact that people act unreasonably much of the time, therefore, does not prove that given the proper conditions, they could not think clearly and thus act reasonably.

Usually the process of scientific thinking is *symbolic*, at least in its more advanced stages; and it generally takes the form of solving some problem. The problem may be anything from how to put a mechanical puzzle together through how to play a hand of bridge to the complex problem of the relation one set of phenomena might possibly bear to other actual or possible sets of phenomena.

Scientific thinking is obviously a highly complex process. An elaborate preparatory process on the part of the senses is required before such thinking can take place. If we would understand thinking we must investigate not only the actual thinking process itself, but also the activities preparatory to thinking that take place in the senses. Because the higher animals have sense organs very similar to those of man, some of these preparatory processes are advantageously studied in experiments on these animals. Tests such as those of N. R. F. Maier, for instance, set up to measure "reasoning" in rats, measure the animal's ability to handle a concrete situation but they do not and cannot measure the ability to handle *abstract* materials as man does. The animals give no evidence of possessing abstract ideas.

Creative thinking probably involves a larger share of imagination than scientific thinking. The artist is essentially bringing into being a new reality, whereas the scientific thinker is comprehending the order already existing in the universe. Both scientific and creative thinking shed light on how the human being acts. In the following sections we shall show how psychologists study scientific and creative thought and what conclusions can be drawn from their studies. In section III, we shall discuss methods of studying thinking in laboratory and clinical situations, and we shall describe some representative studies made under these conditions.

III. THE SCIENTIFIC AND CLINICAL STUDY OF THINKING

A. The Introspective Approach of Titchener

The first experimental psychologists in America used "trained introspection" as a method of studying thinking. Titchener, for instance, believed that by using this method all mental "contents" could be analyzed into the elements of which they were composed. These elements, he held, were three in number: sensations, images, and affections. Titchener rejected the Aristotelian notion that thought is defined in terms of its object. Instead of defining thought in terms of its object, he defined it in terms of the mental content present when a person is thinking. Titchener's method of studying thinking was to present his subjects with problems which presumably required thinking and to ask them to describe what their states of "consciousness" were while they attempted to solve the problems. He assumed that the subject would be able at one and the same time to think and to observe his thinking, a dubious assumption which is open to many criticisms. Such a procedure requires the subject, in a sense, to "divide" himself in such a way that one part of him is thinking while the other part is introspectively watching the thinking. Whether or not people are capable of such dissociated behavior is open to question. What probably happens is that the subject in reporting his mental content is reporting what he remembers of an immediately past experience rather than the experience contemporary with the reporting.

B. Free and Controlled Association

Since the subject of free association is described elsewhere, in Chapter XIX, we shall confine ourselves in this chapter to studies of controlled association. Reasoning is controlled association in that the direction the associations take is directed by the nature of the problem to be solved. In studying controlled association, a popular task is that of asking the subject to respond to each of a series of words that represent "wholes" by giving a "part" of that whole or vice versa, that is, by asking the subject to respond to "parts" by giving "wholes." For instance, if the word *car* is given, the response might be *tire, seat, engine,* or the like. Or, if the part, such as *radiator* is mentioned, the response might be *car*, or *house*.

Both free and controlled association tests are commonly used in modern psychology. Strictly speaking, the primary laws of association (contiguity, similarity, and contrast) apply only to "free" association. The primary laws of association derive from Aristotle, but their interpretation by modern psychologists, as well as by the British associationist philosophers of an earlier day, departs radically from the way in which Aristotle used them. In his *Treatise on Memory and Recollection,* in which he presented the laws of association, Aristotle was careful to point out that the connections between objects of thought are of two kinds: (1) necessary and (2) contingent. Necessary connections are founded on the very nature of the objects; there is a logical or meaningful relation between them. Such connections exist, for instance, among the successive objects of thought involved in solving a mathematical proposition. Ideas associated in this way, Aristotle held, are the most powerful aids to memory, provided their connections are understood. The fact that it is easier to learn and to remember lists of meaningful words or sentences than it is to learn nonsense syllables or phrases substantiates this point of view. The British associationists as well as many contemporary psychologists tried to reduce all association to "contiguity," that is, to the fact that the two connected ideas had occurred together in time and place. In doing so, they rejected Aristotle's notion of necessary connections and attributed everything to the kind of association which Aristotle called "contingent." According to Aristotle, contingent associations or connections are those which exist because they have been experienced together in time or place or in immediate succession, or because they give rise in us to some far-fetched similarity or contrast between two objects, a similarity or contrast which does not grow out of the very nature of the objects. For Aristotle, these were less important in the rational life of man than were the necessary associations.

C. Rational Learning

One of the least complex of thinking tasks can be studied by the so-called "rational learning" experiment. It consists of presenting the subject with ten letters which are paired at random with ten numbers, as illustrated in Figure 61. The subject, after being told that each letter is paired with one number and that no one number is assigned to more than one letter, is asked to discover and then to remember the number associated with each letter. He must guess at first and continues guessing until he gets the right number for the first letter used in the experiment. This procedure is repeated for each of the other letters but gets progressively simpler if the subject is rational in his responses. For instance, if letter A is associated with 8, then, if the subject remembers this connection, his possible number of rational choices for the other letters is reduced by one, and so on down the list. For the last stimulus letter there can be only one response, provided the subject remembers the responses that preceded it. Once this initial series has been gone through, the order of the

M	N	O	P	Q	R	S	T	U	V
8	4	9	3	1	6	2	5	7	10

Fig. 61. Rational Learning.

letters is varied from trial to trial. The speed with which he learns the problem depends to a considerable extent upon his ability to remember. Rational learning differs from paired associate learning in only one respect; that is, the subject has to discover for himself the correct response out of a limited number of possible responses.

D. Ruger's Experimental Study of Problem Solving

In a pioneer experimental study of problem solving, Ruger [2] adapted for use with human beings some of the methods used by Thorndike in his study of animal learning. Ruger gave his subjects a number of mechanical puzzles, such as the twisted nail puzzle in which two nails are so twisted together that they can be pulled apart only by turning them exactly right in respect to each other. His subjects, he found, engaged in as many random movements as did Thorndike's animals in trying to get out of the puzzle box. His subjects worked on the puzzles not just until they were able to do them once, but until they were able to perform the manual operations involved with maximal speed as evidenced by their failure to make further improvement. Records were kept of the subject's overt behavior and his verbal comments.

[2] H. A. Ruger, "The Psychology of Efficiency," *Arch. Psychol.*, 15 (1910).

THINKING AND CREATIVE IMAGINATION

Sometimes the subject was interrupted in the middle of a trial and asked to tell what he was thinking at that moment. Ruger's data showed, in addition to the random trial-and-error behavior mentioned above, that many learning curves showed a sudden spurt of learning, often preceded by an unusually long trial. The subjects reported in about 80 per cent of these cases that at this point of abrupt improvement they suddenly "saw" the essential relation or operation required for solution. Ruger called this phenomenon *analysis,* a term which is probably equivalent to the Gestalt term *insight.* Ruger did not stress this result, however. What he considered to be the most significant outcome of his research was the large amount of trial-and-error behavior exhibited by the educated adults who served as his subjects. It appears that, given a problem the conditions of which forbid rational insight, the human being is forced to make repeated efforts in which his rational powers are not needed or of much help.

E. Maier's Analysis of Achievement in Problem Solving

Maier investigated the role of *direction* in thinking. He studied the problem of constructing a pendulum in order to see if the solution of a problem involves just the selection of the appropriate responses, or if it also requires the appropriate general approach or direction. The problem consisted of constructing two pendulums which would make chalk marks on two points indicated on the floor. The materials available for the solution of the problem are pictured in Figure 62-A. They consisted of wire, burette clamps, a table clamp, lead tubing, pieces of chalk, and four poles. The correct solution of the problem is pictured in Figure 62-B.

Maier divided the college students who were to act as subjects for this experiment into five groups, equated for ability as measured by an intelligence test. Each of these five groups received a different kind of preparation for solving the problem as follows:

Group A. The members of Group A were given instructions in making all the part responses which would be required for solving the problem and were told that these part responses included everything necessary to the solution of the problem. For instance, the experimenter showed them how two rods could be clamped together to make one long rod. He also showed them how to make a firm T-structure with two rods by placing one rod against

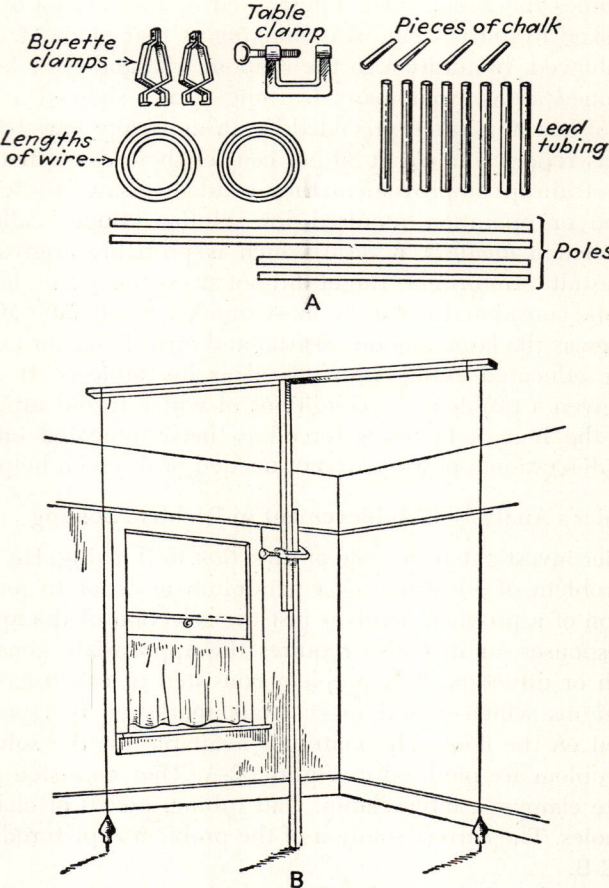

Fig. 62. (*A*) Materials Used in Pendulum Problem. (*B*) Diagram Showing Correct Solution to Pendulum Problem. [By permission from *Recent Experiments in Psychology,* 2nd ed., by L. W. Crafts, T. C. Schneirla, E. E. Robinson, and R. W. Gilbert. Copyright, 1938, 1950. McGraw-Hill Book Company, Inc.]

the vertical side of a doorway. The other rod was then wedged between the midpoint of this first rod and the opposite side of the doorway. (These rods were in the reverse position to what would be required for solving the problem. In solving the problem, the first rod would have to be placed horizontally across the

THINKING AND CREATIVE IMAGINATION 351

ceiling and the other rod would extend vertically from its midpoint to the floor.) The experimenter also demonstrated how to make a plumb line by attaching a pencil to a cord.

Group B. This group received all of the instruction which Group A had received but, in addition, the experimenter made the following comment to provide for them the proper approach or direction: "I should like to have you appreciate how simple this problem would be if we could just hang the pendulum from a nail in the ceiling. Of course that is not a possible solution, but I just want you to appreciate how simple this problem would be if that were possible." [3]

Group C. These subjects received neither set of instructions given Group A or Group B.

Group D. This group was instructed in the part responses but was not told that these responses had anything to do with the solution of the problem.

Group E. These subjects were given the direction only. They were not instructed in the part responses.

Maier's results from this experiment were unambiguous. Group B surpassed all of the other groups by a wide margin. Of the 22 people in Group B, eight solved the problem. Of the 62 people who made up the other groups, only one solved it. These results indicate clearly that it is not enough to provide subjects with the general approach or direction only or with instruction in the part responses only but that both direction and appropriate part responses are required for the solution of the pendulum problem.

F. Concept Formation

The term *concept* as used in scientific psychology has a number of different meanings, depending upon the context in which it is used. It does not mean in psychology what it means in philosophy.[4] The definition of concept formation which perhaps best applies to the situations and experiments described in this section is that it is a "Generalizing process which follows the

---

[3] N. R. F. Maier, "Reasoning in Humans, I. On Direction," *J. Comp. Psychol.*, 10 (1930), 115–144.

[4] According to St. Thomas, a concept is the essence of the thing known, existing in the mind so as to enable the mind to know the object. We are not using the term in the Thomistic sense in this chapter.

discrimination of similarities and differences among objects or symbols." [5]

A characteristic laboratory experiment on concept formation is one which calls for a kind of inductive thinking. A variety of specimens is presented in the form of words, designs, or symbols, and the subject arrives at a knowledge of the class to which each of these specimens belongs by noting similarities and differences. In one study subjects were presented with twelve consecutive series of twelve drawings each in which the problem was ostensibly that of associating each of the drawings with its name. In other words, the task appeared to involve nothing more than memorizing. Samples of the drawings used are shown in Figure 63. In the different series the same name was applied to more

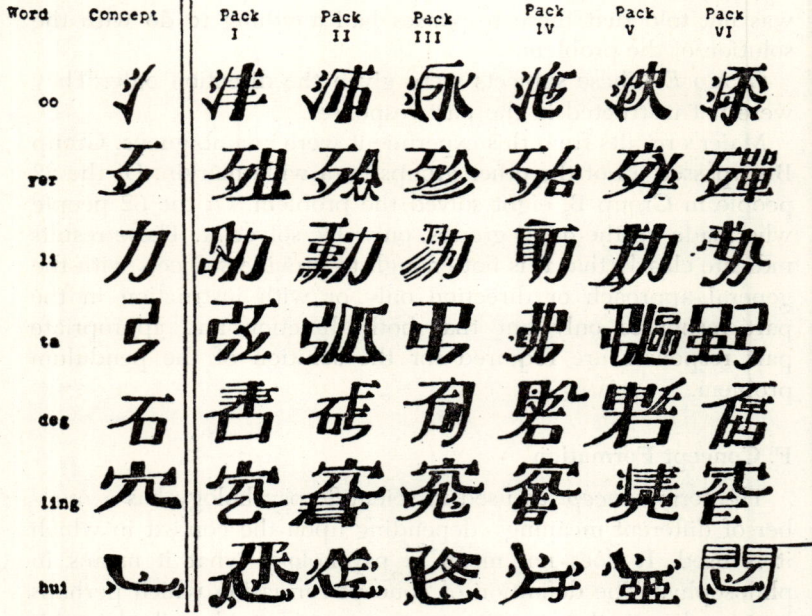

Fig. 63. Sample Drawings Used in Study of Concept Formation [Reproduced from C. L. Hull, "Quantitative Aspects of the Evolution of Concepts," *Psychological Monographs*, No. 123, Vol. 28, 1920, p. 1–86. By permission of *Psychological Monographs* and the American Psychological Association, Inc.]

[5] B. J. Underwood, *Experimental Psychology* (New York, Appleton-Century-Crofts, Inc., 1949), p. 625.

THINKING AND CREATIVE IMAGINATION

than one drawing; there were twelve different names used for all of the drawings, and each drawing with the same name had one feature in common. The subject could, of course, and sometimes did, memorize the series. However, he could, by discovering the common element, anticipate the name of a drawing having the same element. If the subject correctly named a drawing the first time it was presented, it seemed evident that he was responding to a characteristic common to two or more drawings. When this happened, the subject was said to have formed a *concept*. A variation in this method was one in which "common components" which were perceptibly the same in each instance were not used but in which the difficulty of the problem was increased by presenting non-pictorial relational patterns. For instance, one of the problems consisted of discovering, regardless of variations in size, color, and location, that a circle with one dot inside and one dot outside was always named *dax*.

G. The Hanfmann-Kasanin Test

A test of thinking which has found many clinical applications and which is based upon a classification method is that of Hanfmann and Kasanin. The test consists of 22 blocks, as illustrated in Figure 64, and the subject is asked to divide them into four groups. The blocks cannot be sorted into four groups on the basis of any one perceptual feature, as, for example, form, size, color, or height. The subject in solving the problem must construct his own concept as a basis for classifying the blocks. Beneath each block is the name. Blocks that are tall and large are *lag*, those tall and small are *mur*, those flat and small are *cev*, and those flat and large are *bik*. The examiner starts by turning up one of the blocks and showing the name to the subject. He then puts this block into one of the corners and suggests that the subject start by putting into the same corner all of the blocks which he thinks might belong to the same class. After the subject has done so, the examiner turns up one of the wrongly assorted blocks and shows the subject that this is a different kind of block. After each new attempt of the subject, one of the wrongly classified blocks is turned up, and the subject is encouraged to keep on trying. The test continues until the subject either discovers the principle of classification and sorts the blocks accordingly, or until all of the blocks have been turned up by the examiner in the process of correcting wrong responses. The subject is then asked to formulate the principle of classification, and the test is repeated to see if the subject has actually grasped the principle of the double dichotomy. Throughout the test a detailed record is kept of the subject's remarks as well as of his behavior. Emphasis in scoring the test is on the *qualitative* aspects of the subject's behavior

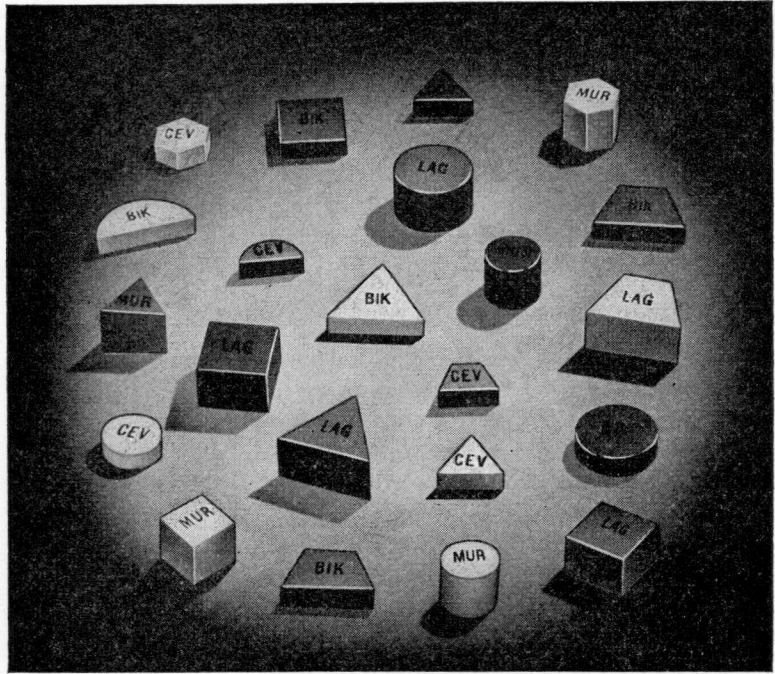

Fig. 64. Hanfmann-Kasanin Blocks. [Courtesy C. H. Stoelting Company, Chicago.]

rather than the *quantitative* results. The test has been extensively used in investigating Goldstein's theory [6] that two qualitatively different kinds of activity are required for *concrete* and *abstract* behavior, and consequently in observing the subject an effort is made to determine whether he is treating the blocks as "things" or as "categories." An interpretation of his responses is made which indicates his degree of proficiency at each of the two

[6] Kurt Goldstein, *After-Effects of Brain Injuries in War* (New York, Grune & Stratton. Inc., 1942)

levels of behavior: the concrete and the abstract. Results, in general, show that normal people are capable of both the concrete and the abstract attitude, but that the abstract attitude is impaired in serious brain injuries and in some functional psychoses, such as schizophrenia.

H. Studies of Syllogistic Reasoning

Woodworth and Sells [7] analyzed the mistakes in syllogistic reasoning made by intelligent adults. They raised the question as to why people are prone to make some errors more than others. Recognizing that training in formal logic would enable people immediately to spot invalid conclusions, they limited their subjects to educated adults who had never had any training in formal logic. Woodworth suggested that the general "atmosphere" or "global impression" of a syllogism might be a significant psychological factor leading to erroneous conclusions. A universal affirmative statement, such as "all *a*'s are *b*'s," might create an "all-yes" atmosphere and thus dispose a person for erroneously accepting the converse, "all *b*'s are *a*'s," since the converse also has an "all-yes" atmosphere. Similarly, a universal negative, such as "no *a*'s are *b*'s," might produce an "all-no" atmosphere, and thus lead the subject to accept an invalid conclusion stated in a negative way more readily than he would one stated in the affirmative. Sells constructed a test of 180 items of good or bad syllogistic reasoning, 128 of which were logically invalid. These 128 items were so stated as to provide for every possible "atmospheric" effect. Sells's data show clearly and unambiguously that Woodworth's hypothesis was correct and that the atmospheric effect has a pronounced influence upon the conclusions which educated adults come to in analyzing syllogisms. In evaluating these results, however, it is well to remember that the subjects in these experiments had not been trained in the rules of syllogistic reasoning. If they had been so trained, it is doubtful that the atmospheric effect would have been present, at least to the same degree.

Other studies show that logical thinking may be distorted by personal attitudes and unconscious biases. A test of 15 syllogisms was drawn up in two forms, one of which was stated in formal

[7] R. S. Woodworth and S. B. Sells, "An Atmosphere Effect in Formal Syllogistic Reasoning," *J. Exp. Psychol.*, 18 (1935), 451–460.

symbolic logic, and the other of which contained the same syllogisms stated in emotionally toned words. Highly significant differences in responses on the two forms of the test were found for a group of 98 college students. There was a much higher percentage of error for the emotionally toned items than for the symbolic items, even though the logical (or illogical) construction of the statements was the same. A further analysis revealed that the most frequently accepted wrong conclusions were those which represented current newspaper, radio, and magazine opinion. It is interesting to note that when the emotionally toned conclusions were in line with current radio and newspaper opinion but were in the opposite direction from the "atmospheric" effect, the emotionally toned conclusions usually prevailed over those which one would expect as a result of the atmospheric effect.

IV. CREATIVE THOUGHT

The creative worker is one of the most interesting, and at the same time most baffling objects of psychological study. We cannot observe him at work because, even if he were willing to let us observe him, we could not anticipate the time of an inspiration. We cannot put him into the laboratory and use him as a subject in an experiment on creative processes without so altering the conditions of creating in real life that our results would have no meaning. For these reasons psychologists have had to resort to methods other than direct observation in their studies of creative thought. One such method is that of perusing the various drafts of the manuscript, painting, composition, or invention as an indirect means of studying the mental processes of their creator. A second method is that of studying the biographical descriptions given by friends or acquaintances who have observed the creative person at work. Most of these descriptions have, of course, not been written by psychologists, and for that reason the language must often be translated into psychologically meaningful terms. A third, and possibly the most fruitful method, is that of studying the introspective accounts of the authors, composers, artists, and inventors themselves.

The literature on creative thought is filled with references to inspirations which "seized" the person and compelled him to write, paint, compose or invent. There seems to be an urgency about creative work which, though often painful, is not nearly so painful as failure to create when the inspiration is there. In this sense, giving birth to a "brain child" may be compared to an actual delivery. Sir Francis Galton wrote, "What is generally meant by genius is the automatic activity of the mind, as distinguished from the effort of the will. In a man of genius, the ideas come as by inspiration; he is driven rather than drives himself." [8] This statement and that of other writers who stress the "inspirational" character of creative work is deceptive if taken at its face value. It may lead to the mistaken notion that ideas for creative work come "out of the blue" and that no work is involved but only "inspiration." Such a notion is entirely unfounded. The available evidence points to the conclusion that preceding the moment of inspiration there is usually a more or less prolonged period of preparation, much of which has been devoted to hard work or study. Apparently, nothing comes out when the basic ingredients for making it have not previously been put in, although the organization and form may be truly new and creative.

Creative processes can usually be broken down into four more or less distinct stages: (1) preparation, (2) incubation, (3) illumination, and (4) verification. The first stage includes all of the education of the person, as, for example, his instruction in reading, use of language or logic, or acquisition of number concepts. Obviously, no one can write who does not have a command of the language. Similarly, new mathematical discoveries are not made by persons unacquainted with numbers. All of the experiences of his life—the joys and sorrows and relations with people —are part of the preparation of the novelist, poet, and writer in general. For creative work in highly specialized fields, as, for instance, in engineering or medicine, more specific preparation is needed. The period of preparation is one in which facts are amassed, information of various sorts is acquired, and special skills are sometimes developed. Much of this preparation is undertaken consciously and deliberately although at the time of its acquisition the person may have had no inkling whatever of how he was actually going to use his preparation later. Inspirations

[8] Francis Galton, *English Men of Science, Their Nature and Nurture* (London, Macmillan & Co., Ltd., 1874), p. 233.

for creative work seldom come during such periods of hard work; usually they follow it.

After the period of preparation there follows a period of no observable progress. During this "incubation" period ideas about the creative work may come into the mind from time to time without any consciously directed effort. At this stage there is no drive to finish the work and no clear-cut mental picture as to how it is to be done. Many creative workers intentionally drop the subject when they have completed their preparation, having learned from experience that no inspiration will immediately follow the laying of the ground work.

Following the period of incubation comes the "inspiration" or "illumination." Usually the creative idea comes suddenly and often the creative writer works furiously until the inspiration runs out. Sometimes this inspiration ceases in the middle of a poem, for example, and may not return until weeks or months later. The Irish poet, A. E. (Russell), describes the experience as follows:

. . . To me it was only after long reverie that a song would come as a bird might fly to us out of the vast hollows of the air. . . . There was always an element of the unexpected in the poetry itself, for it broke in upon and deflected the normal current of consciousness. I would be as surprised at the arising within me of words which in their combination seemed beautiful to me as I would have been if a water-lily had blossomed suddenly from the bottom of a tarn to make a shining on its dark surfaces. The words often would rush swiftly from hidden depths of consciousness and be fashioned by an art with which the working brain had but little to do.[9]

and again,

These waking dreams would fall upon me at any time, while I was at work, or in the streets, or in the country roads at night. Once I was walking down a passage in the great building where I was employed over forty years ago, a passage which led from one office to another; and in that dim lighted corridor my imagination of myself was suddenly changed, and I was a child and was looking upwards to a dawn of faintest yellow behind snowy peaks made blue and shadowy by that glow. The mound on which I stood was brown and bare as if it had been baked by the heat of fierce suns. The boy I had become was gazing in adoration at the high and holy light. He was celestially transparent, pure and virgin. He chanted a divine name, and a fire that was

[9] G. W. Russell (A. E. pseud.), *Song and Its Fountains* (New York, The Macmillan Company, 1932), p. 23. With the permission of the publisher.

THINKING AND CREATIVE IMAGINATION

heaven-born leaped up from the heart, and for an instant the child was a delicate lyre whose strings quivered echoing the song of Brahma. Then all that faded and I was again at the office of Pims . . .[10]

A study of inventors revealed that a "step of the inventive process followed by nearly all the inventors . . . consists in a survey of all available information bearing on the problem at hand."[11] Nevertheless, the inventive idea seldom came during or immediately after these periods of strenuous effort. As one inventor expressed it: "Ideas often occur to me without conscious effort or concentration. It appears to be on the order of inspiration, usually when I am rested, and allow my mind to wander at will."[12] Or, as Helmholtz said, "Happy ideas came unexpectedly without effort, like an inspiration. So far as I am concerned, they have never come to me when my mind was fatigued, or when I was at my working table. . . . They came particularly readily during the slow ascent of wooded hills, on a sunny day."[13]

After the illumination, the real work again begins. Seldom is the work completed during a period of inspiration. If the creative idea has led to invention, it is now necessary to verify it and see if it will work. If the work is a poem, it must now be revised or recast before it meets the author's standards of critical judgment. This period of verification or revision, like the period of preparation, is usually time-consuming. The shortest period in the whole process of creating is that of illumination, but without the illumination, there could be no creative work. The work of verification which takes much longer is equally essential in most creative work. In the words of the French mathematician, Poincaré:

It never happens that unconscious work supplies *ready-made* the result of a lengthy calculation in which we have only to apply fixed rules. . . . All that we can hope from these inspirations, which are the fruit of unconscious work, is to obtain points of departure for such calculations. As for the calculations themselves, they must be made in the second period of conscious work which follows the inspiration, and in which the results of the inspiration are verified and the consequences deduced. The rules of these calculations are strict and complicated;

[10] *Ibid.*
[11] J. Rossman, *The Psychology of the Inventor* (Washington, D.C., The Inventors Publishing Co., 1931), p. 59.
[12] *Ibid.*, p. 70.
[13] E. Rignano, *The Psychology of Reasoning* (New York, Harcourt, Brace and Company, Inc., 1927), pp. 267–268.

they demand discipline, attention, will, and consequently, consciousness.[14]

The above quotations show clearly that the creative thinker and artist, though gifted above other men, nevertheless shares with them the common human lot of having to work for whatever good is achieved.

V. THINKING AND THE VOCATION OF MAN

Thinking is the highest of all human activities. By exercising his powers of thought for the right ends, and with a good intention, the scientist complements the work of God and reveals His laws; the philosopher and the artist help to interpret and complete creation; and every man gives honor and glory to God.

It is his spiritual power to know, to judge, and to reason that goads the human being, "divinely discontent," to search always for better ways of human living. But reason alone does not tell the whole story of human achievement. People must also want to achieve, and the driving forces of will and need must urge them to realize and bring to completion the conceptions of their creative intelligence. When these driving forces distort or interfere with rational thought, they sometimes result in the serious disturbances of personality described in the following chapter.

SUGGESTED READING

RUSSELL, G. W. (A. E. pseud.), *Song and Its Fountains* (New York, The Macmillan Company, 1932).

[14] Quoted in G. Wallas, *The Art of Thought* (New York, Harcourt, Brace and Company, Inc., 1926), p. 81.

XIV

Disorders of Personality

*O the mind, mind has mountains; cliffs of fall
Frightful, sheer, no-man fathomed. Hold them cheap
May who ne'er hung there.*—G. M. HOPKINS [1]

I. THE PROBLEM OF MENTAL DISORDER

Of all the ills that flesh is heir to, none is more distressing than mental illness. Mental illness destroys the happiness of the individual who suffers from it and causes anxiety and often anguish to his relatives and friends. The mentally ill are a serious social and economic burden to the community as a whole; the amount of money spent annually for the care of abnormal persons exceeds that devoted to the education of all the college students in the United States. Yet few communities provide optimal care and treatment for the mentally ill, and still fewer have mental hygiene facilities which are at all adequate for preventing mental disease. Over a period of years the number of people in our mental hospitals and the number receiving treatment for mental disorders have been increasing at a steady rate. This increase, however, does not mean necessarily that mental illness is on the increase. It may be, at least in part, the result of (1) better methods of diagnosis, (2) improved facilities for treating the mentally ill, (3) an increasing number of old people, (4) social conditions affecting housing which make it impossible to treat a mentally sick person in the home, and (5) an increasing knowledge on the part of the public that treatment opportunities are available.

Mental disease does not strike all ethnic groups or social classes in the same way nor is it present to the same extent in all culture

[1] G. M. Hopkins, from "No Worst, There Is None. Pitched Past Pitch of Grief," *Poems of Gerard Manley Hopkins,* Third Edition (New York, Oxford University Press, Inc., 1948), p. 107.

groups. In the United States, for instance, alcoholic psychoses are relatively more common among the Irish, epilepsy among Jews, and schizophrenia among Germans than among other ethnic groups. Certain types of mental disorders are more prevalent in one social milieu than another, perhaps because the number and seriousness of possible conflicts to be resolved differ from one group to another.

There is no one cause of mental illness; its causes are multiple. There are, first of all, *predisposing causes,* such as constitutional factors or hereditary tendencies, childhood training in running away from life, or a background of anxiety and unhappiness. Then there are the *exciting causes,* that is, the immediate situations or the conditions that set off the mental disturbance. A broken love affair or a financial disaster, for example, might be an exciting cause but *never* the only cause of a mental disease. Let us suppose several people are subjected to the same exciting cause at the same time. One of them breaks down; the others do not. The differences in such behavior under stress may be attributed to predisposing factors. Without the predisposing causes, the exciting cause may have little or no effect; it is, consequently, important to eliminate the predisposing causes. This is the major goal of mental hygiene.

II. MENTAL HYGIENE

At the present time many professional groups are interested in the problem of mental hygiene. At the beginning of the century under the influence of Clifford Beers the mental hygiene movement was begun. Interest was at this time primarily focused upon improving hospital conditions for the insane. Gradually, interest shifted to the prevention of mental disorder. With the growing realization that the conditions leading to adult mental disorders arise in childhood, more and more attention was given to the mental health of children. Child guidance clinics were established throughout the country and periodicals such as *Mental Hygiene* were published to disseminate needed information. As a result of the mental hygiene movement many reforms were introduced in the treatment of abnormal persons. People in general have become increasingly aware of the problems of mental health and

DISORDERS OF PERSONALITY

the prevention of mental illness. In this area of life it is especially true that "an ounce of prevention is worth a pound of cure."

III. TYPES OF PERSONALITY DISORDER

Moore [2] classifies "mental difficulties according to the degree to which they involve a disorder of the whole mind and the eventual disintegration of the personality" under four headings, in a roughly descending order of severity as follows: (1) psychoses, (2) psychoneuroses, (3) constitutional psychopathic states, and (4) behavior problems. We shall discuss personality difficulties in this order.

A. The Psychoses

A *psychosis* is a major mental disturbance. It differs essentially from the milder disorders (psychoneuroses) and from normal mental states in that there is a loss of contact with reality, especially social reality. Traditionally, the psychoses have been classified as either organic or functional. In the next few paragraphs we will show how these two categories differ and describe some specific psychoses which fall under each of these two headings.

1. Organic psychoses

The organic psychoses all have, as at least one cause, an anatomical or physiological basis, as, for instance, fever, lesions of brain tissue, syphilis, or brain tumor. *Senile degenerative psychosis* results from a shrinkage of the brain tissue, often accompanied by blood clots formed by a hardening of the walls of the blood vessels. Typically, there is a loss of memory, confusion, disorientation in space and time, and a loss of well-established habits, such as cleanliness. *Involutional melancholia* is another disorder of middle age and later maturity which is classed under "disturbances of metabolism, growth, nutrition, or endocrine functioning." [3] It is characterized by great agitation

---

[2] Dom Thomas V. Moore, *The Nature and Treatment of Mental Disorders* (New York, Grune & Stratton, Inc., 1944), p. 4.

[3] A. Rosanoff, *Manual of Psychiatry and Mental Hygiene,* Seventh Edition (New York, John Wiley & Sons, Inc., 1938), pp. 967–985.

and depression, accompanied by self-condemnation, general restlessness, and insomnia. The condition clears up after a time. *Paresis* or general paralysis results from syphilis of the brain. The brain condition usually shows up years after the original infection and long after the sufferer believes himself to be cured. The inflammatory degenerative process attacks the frontal and parietal lobes of the cerebral cortex with the greatest intensity. Thus there is a progressive loss of functions "localized" in these areas. Slurred speech, a tabetic gait, and a loss of critical powers are characteristic symptoms. Excitement and grandiose delusions are common. Gradually, the degeneration spreads to more and more functions until at last the patient is completely bedridden. *Alcoholic psychoses* are brought on by brain damage caused by alcohol poisoning. Different syndromes (groups of associated symptoms which serve as the basis for making a differential diagnosis) are found in the several alcoholic psychoses. Visual and auditory hallucinations and profound impairment of intellectual functions are invariably present.

2. Functional psychoses

The functional psychoses have no known organic basis, although it is possible that some day with improved instruments of diagnosis a physiological basis may be found. The two most common functional psychoses are schizophrenia and manic-depressive psychosis.

Schizophrenia is characterized by extreme withdrawal symptoms and occurs, in the great majority of cases, in late youth or early maturity. Traditionally, schizophrenic patients have been classified under one of four subtypes, although there is much overlapping and a patient may be shifted from one category to another as his symptoms change or develop. *Simple schizophrenia* is an apathetic type of withdrawal in which the patient sits and stares into space and is apparently indifferent to everything going on about him. *Hebephrenic schizophrenia* shows a marked incongruity between mood and thought. It is characterized by silly behavior and grimaces, and the patient may, for instance, giggle when presented with bad news. *Catatonic schizophrenia* is characterized by peculiar postures and by the fact that these postures may be maintained for hours. Sometimes the patient's arms, legs, or other bodily parts can be placed in the most grotesque and uncomfortable positions and he will retain such positions indefinitely. A normal person finds it impossible to imitate and hold these postures. *Paranoid schizophrenia* is characterized by delusions of reference (everything going on about the patient, he believes, refers to himself) or of persecution. The patient is convinced that two people talking at the end of a corridor are gossiping about him or plotting his destruction. The sugar on the breakfast food is not real sugar but ground glass, he will tell you, put there to kill him. This kind of patient is dangerous because he may suddenly attack an innocent bystander who he believes is threatening him. Paranoid schizophrenia is distinguished from another functional disorder known as *true paranoia*. In true paranoia there is no intellectual deterioration and the patient may be normal in all respects but one: his pathological delusion that he is being persecuted. In true paranoia the delusion has become systematized in some way and this delusional symptom dominates the person's whole life. Often the true paranoid is not recognized as a psychotic until he is sued for libel or starts legal action himself against someone whom he conceives to be persecuting him.

Manic-depressive psychosis is characterized by cycles of mood in which hyperactivity and elation alternate with periods of inactivity and depression. On the average, its first symptoms are manifested at a later age than those of schizophrenia. During the manic phase the patient is often so obstreperous that he must be restrained. He may engage in shouting, singing, back-slapping, or excessive talking. He may work hour after hour in a violent fury of ambition; nothing fatigues him. In the depressed stage, however, the picture is reversed. His pessimism and self-hatred may go so far as to prevent his eating or taking care of bodily needs. In this phase he resembles a schizophrenic in many respects. Sometimes suicide is attempted. It is of interest to note that the alternating cycles of elation (euphoria) and depression occur with more or less regularity for a given individual. In one person, the euphoric phase may last six months and be followed by a three- or four-month period of depression. In another the manic phase may last only two months and be followed by a three-month period of depression. Individuals differ greatly in the length of their cycles, but for a given individual there is a certain amount of consistency. This consistency, however, is not high enough to enable one to make accurate predictions. Although manic-depressive psychosis is functional, there must be a constitutional basis for it, because there is unmistakable evidence that it runs in families.

B. The Psychoneuroses

1. Description

The *psychoneuroses* are referred to as "benign" mental disorders. They differ essentially from the psychoses and are qualitatively different from them, not necessarily because they are less distressing, but because the psychoneurotic retains his contact with reality. The psychotic does not. The psychoneurotic has the same mental reactions as the normal person except that the unwholesome reactions which all people experience at some time or other are chronic with him. Most people, for example, indulge at intervals in self-pity or in feelings of inferiority. The psychoneurotic, however, is likely to be always pitying himself, or is habitually so overcome by his sense of inferiority that he accomplishes nothing. His reactions differ from the normal chiefly in their intensity and diffuseness of response. The psychoneurotic person is more like the normal than he is like the psychotic. The psychotic, for example, not only indulges in self-pity; he develops hallucinations or delusions of persecution. Hallucinations and delusions are never found in normal people or in psychoneurotics except during temporary deliria caused by drugs, fevers, or illness. People who are psychoneurotic seldom become psychotic because the personality structures underlying the two kinds of disorders are very different.

2. Types of Psychoneuroses

According to the nomenclature adopted by the American Psychiatric Association in 1933, the psychoneuroses are classed under the following heads:

    a. Hysteria (anxiety hysteria, conversion hysteria and sub-groups)
    b. Psychasthenia or compulsive states (and sub-groups)
    c. Neurasthenia
    d. Hypochondriasis
    e. Reactive depression (simple situational reaction, others)
    f. Anxiety states
    g. Mixed psychoneurosis

DISORDERS OF PERSONALITY 367

All types of psychoneurosis have something in common, just as different physical diseases have something in common. Malaria, pneumonia, and rheumatic fever, for example, are all characterized by an abnormal temperature. Yet the disease "syndrome" or pattern of symptoms differs sufficiently so that one condition can be distinguished from the others. Similarly, in the psychoneuroses, there are characteristic syndromes which enable the experienced psychologist or psychiatrist to distinguish one psychoneurotic condition from another, although there is considerable overlapping of behavior patterns.

a. Hysteria or *conversion neurosis.* In an hysterical neurosis the person translates his mental conflicts into physical symptoms. Once he has done so he is likely to be remarkably indifferent to his disorder, sometimes assuming the air of "the patient sufferer." Almost any function of the body may be involved. Cases have been reported of such widely different ailments as hysterical blindness, paralysis, mutism, heart conditions, and blisters. These symptoms are not consciously willed and it is unfair to call the hysterical a malingerer. The hysterical person, it is true, "wants" his symptoms but this is not the same as saying that he consciously "wills" them. The probable sequence of events in the development of hysteria is as follows: [4]

(1) The desire to escape from some unpleasant situation.
(2) Suggestion of a way of escape.
(3) Accidental escape through a suggested channel.
(4) Fear of return to the unpleasant situation with recovery.
(5) Exaggeration of the symptoms.
(6) Appearance of the symptom with no cause.

Hysterical illness, like all neurotic illness, is not imaginary but real. It is illogical to suppose that it does not have a cause.[5] The hysterical disease is definitely "caused" but not by the factors which usually bring about such physical symptoms.

The French psychiatrist, Janet, made extensive studies of hysteria from which he concluded that hysteria results from sug-

---

[4] J. J. B. Morgan, *The Psychology of Abnormal People* (New York, Longmans, Green & Company, 1945), 477–478.

[5] Mind and body are both equally "real" although one is spiritual, the other material. Any real substance can be a cause (whether mental or physical). In man, body and soul are so united that everything which happens to the one affects the other. To assume that a mental disease is not real but "imaginary" is to adopt a materialistic attitude toward human problems.

gestibility and can be cured by suggestion. He found, for instance, a very interesting cure for what he called "stocking anesthesia." Anesthesia is a lack of sensitivity to pain. It may be caused by lesions in the nervous system, in which case the anesthesia is distributed according to the affected nervous pathways. Hysterical anesthesia, on the contrary, does not follow definite nerve paths but corresponds to the layman's notion of disease. There may be an anesthesia of the hand, for instance, in which the entire hand is insensitive, but the lack of sensitivity stops sharply at the wrist. Janet labeled this condition "glove anesthesia." "Stocking anesthesia" is anesthesia of the foot and leg which stops sharply at the point above the knee corresponding to the top of a stocking; it does not follow neurological paths. Janet found that by appropriate suggestion and by applying stimuli which supposedly would cure the condition, the anesthesia could be decreased day by day just as if he were drawing off a stocking, until it eventually disappeared.

It has sometimes been claimed that all miraculous cures, such as those occurring at Lourdes or the Shrine of Ste. Anne de Beaupré, are in reality hysterical cures brought about by "suggestion." No doubt many so-called cures have been of this nature. An analysis of the certified cured, however, in the light of what we know about hysteria, should dissipate the notion that all cures are of this nature. Hysterical symptoms can be removed by suggestion, but suggestion does not result in a permanent cure. Unless the cause is removed, the patient relapses into his former condition or develops other symptoms equally distressing. To cure a neurotic ailment is a much more difficult task than to cure many physical illnesses because it involves a cure of wrong attitudes which have been built up over a long period of time. The fact that authentic miraculous cures are permanent indicates either that the disease was not hysterical, or, if hysterical, that the patient's whole mental outlook on life has been changed. This latter case would be an even greater miracle than the cure of the physical condition. Moreover, the dossiers signed by physicians at Lourdes often report cures of ailments which are ostensibly organic, and which have never been observed in hysterical patients and which, so far as we know, have never been dissipated by psychotherapy or suggestion.

DISORDERS OF PERSONALITY

There are certain external similarities between extraordinary spiritual gifts, such as the stigmata,[6] and physical symptoms which have an hysterical origin. This similarity, however, is more apparent than real. A description of any psychological phenomenon, if it is to be psychologically significant, must take into account the motivation of the subject and the total situation in which the phenomenon occurred. In determining whether or not a given phenomenon, as, for instance, stigmatization or ecstasy, is an hysterical manifestation or a genuine divine fact, certain criteria are invoked. Theologians [7] tell us that we must note "the differences: (1) on the part of the subject; (2) on the part of the phenomena; (3) on the part of the effects."[8] The differences on the part of the subject are usually pronounced. The hysterical personality is highly impressionable and suggestible, guided by emotion and feeling rather than by intellectually acceptable principles. The saint (who is the subject of mystical phenomena), on the contrary, is exceptionally stable; his emotions are controlled and directed by his intelligence. His conduct and judgment in particular situations are based on deep moral convictions and, far from being impressionable, he consistently resists the influence of the crowd which would lead him to mediocrity. It is characteristic of saints who have been favored with mystical gifts that, far from escaping difficulty and hardship through this means, they have received this favor along with the most excruciating suffering. The hysterical person's symptoms are a means of retreating from reality. The mystic, on the contrary, sacrifices everything he is and has to the attainment of reality. The mystic rejoices in suffering not because he is insensitive to it or because he is masochistic, but because he sees in suffering borne in union with Christ the means for becoming an "other Christ" and thus of attaining his eternal destiny.

Mystical phenomena and hysterical phenomena are distin-

[6] The stigmata are the marks of the wounds inflicted upon Christ in His passion. They have appeared miraculously upon the bodies of several saints and holy persons, as, for instance, St. Francis of Assisi. St. Paul is sometimes thought to have had these marks, because of his statement, "I bear the marks of the Lord Jesus in my body." Gal. 6:18.

[7] R. Garrigou-Lagrange, O.P., *The Three Ages of the Interior Life,* trans. by Sister M. Timothea Doyle, O.P. (St. Louis, B. Herder Book Co., 1948), Vol. II, 608–616.

[8] *Ibid.,* p. 608.

guished by notable differences in the way in which they manifest themselves, as, for example, in the phenomenon of ecstasy. According to Garrigou-Lagrange:

> There is absolutely no relation between so-called hysterical ecstasy and the ecstasy, for example, of Bernadette during the apparitions of Lourdes. In a real ecstasy there is no morbid excitation, no strange agitation, no entirely physical delectation, followed by depression. Ecstasy is the movement of the whole being, both body and soul, toward the divine object present in the imagination or intellect. Ecstasy ends in the calm return to the natural state, with simple regret over the disappearance of the celestial vision and the wholly spiritual joy that it gave. St. Teresa even points out in her *Life* that this new state, which should weaken the body, on the contrary, gives it new strength.[9]

The effects of mystical states, too, are very different from those of hysterical states. The hysterical is typically motivated by a "prudent morality," a morality based not upon moral principles but upon expediency. The hysterical, in other words, is honest because "honesty pays," or because trouble can be avoided by being honest. When he finds himself in a situation where honesty does not pay he has no qualms about being dishonest. His motivation is predominantly selfish and his criterion of what is good or bad is determined by what he "can get out of it." The mystic, on the contrary, shows a steady growth in disinterestedness and unselfishness. To quote Garrigou-Lagrange again:

> In true mystics and ecstatics . . . there is a growing development of the understanding of divine things, of those of the interior life, of the life of the Church, of all that touches on the salvation or the loss of souls. There is likewise a steady increase in the love of God and in devotion to their neighbor, as shown by the works they undertake and often bring to success, to such a degree that their foundations last for centuries.[10]

In this connection, it is interesting to note the care which the Catholic Church has exercised in distinguishing genuine from apparent miracles in the canonization of its saints. Pope Benedict XIV (1675–1758) in his *De Servorum Dei Beatificatione* (1749) laid down the basic principle that we must not call miraculous what can be explained by natural forces. His conclusions on this subject are in harmony with present-day thinking on psychosomatic medicine, as shown in the following translated excerpt:

[9] *Ibid.*, p. 611.
[10] *Ibid.*, pp. 611–612.

It first appears that certain diseases, springing from the imagination, can be cured naturally by the power of the contrary imagination. . . . Secondly, it appears that the imagination can often cause purgations and vomitings through which the sick man regains his health. . . . Thirdly, it appears that the natural power of the imagination can extend so far as to suppress for a time the sting of the pains that affect the body. . . . Fourthly, it appears that even in grave diseases the imagination can help along the cure which, however, will not be sudden, but gradual. . . . Finally, it even appears that perhaps at times diseases can be cured instantaneously by the power of the imagination, but that such a cure is not permanent, and that a relapse will follow.

Hysteria was once thought to be a purely feminine disorder, and the term *hysteria*, referring to the uterus, reflects this notion. The ancient Greeks believed that hysteria was the result of a "wandering uterus," a notion which bears some relation to the present-day Freudian theory as to the causation of neurosis. During World War I, however, so many soldiers suffered from hysteria that the term seemed inappropriate. Soldiers suffering from this neurotic ailment were classified as "shell-shocked." In World War II the term *shell-shock* was eliminated because of its suggestive effect, and the term *exhaustion* was used instead. Army psychiatrists attribute the permanent fixation of hysterical symptoms in many soldiers to the suggestive effect of the diagnostic term.

While hysteria is a condition which affects both sexes, it is still considerably more frequent among women, perhaps because in our culture women are encouraged to be dependent and even sometimes immature.

b. Psychasthenia. Psychasthenia includes the obsessive and compulsive neuroses, and like the other neuroses is characterized by an undercurrent of fear. In an obsessive state, the patient is troubled by a painful and persistent idea which, though unwanted, dominates his consciousness. One woman, for example, claimed that she loved her husband but was forced periodically to leave him because she was afraid she might hurt him. She was obsessed by the idea, "Someday I am going to kill him and then myself." After struggling with this distressing thought for a long time, she found it necessary to run away lest she put it into effect.

In a compulsive state the person has an irresistible urge to perform an act which he does not consciously will to do and which causes him distress. Sometimes it is a simple matter, such as the need to go back three or four times to see if the garage door is locked or to see if the matches have been completely extinguished. Back of such actions is a pathological fear of neglecting responsibilities. Religious scruples, in which the penitent insists on confessing acts or thoughts which were not sins and is apparently unable to follow the confessor's advice, are often symptoms of a compulsive neurosis.[11]

Among the more serious compulsive neuroses are *kleptomania,* or the compulsion to steal, and *pyromania,* or the compulsion to start fires. Sometimes the motivation for such acts is rather obvious, although often it is obscure. An unmarried woman in her thirties, for example, had a large collection of baby clothes. Although she might well have bought such clothes, since she had wealth enough, she stole them instead. The connection between this neurosis and the woman's frustrated maternal tendencies is not difficult to see. Another woman who had apparently been a practicing Catholic all of her life, fell in love with a divorced man. After a long struggle with herself she finally married the man, thereby cutting herself off from the Church. During the next six months things seemed to run smoothly, and in fact even later on her associates would hardly have suspected that anything was wrong. Her "husband," however, became alarmed because his wife insisted that he accompany her at night through the entire house while she checked to see that all the windows and doors were locked. Even the window in her bedroom had to be locked although it was located on the second floor. Not only was this ceremony performed every night, but it was performed several times each night. Only after hours had passed could the miserable woman finally sleep. This case is interesting because, if one did

---

[11] According to A. Wilson, C.P., the cause of scruples may be physical, psychological, or spiritual. If the chief cause is physical, Wilson says, "Unless the physical nature of the trouble is realized, the patient will tire himself by endless self-analysis and futile search for the nonexistent spiritual causes of his worries." And again, "Scruples cannot be cured until the root cause of the disease is detected and removed. Every confessor is conscious of the fact that sometimes spiritual advice does not 'register.' The reason is because there is a hindrance to understanding on the physical or the psychological plane. . . . We must not expect God to work miracles to make up for our fatuity; and to expect a spiritual cure for a physical or psychological ailment is, in reality, to expect a miracle."

—From *Pardon and Peace,* by Alfred Wilson, C.P. Copyright 1947, Sheed and Ward, Inc., New York.

DISORDERS OF PERSONALITY

not know the circumstances, the motivation would be difficult to ascertain. In the light of the woman's background, however, it seems probable that her fear of thieves is not her real fear, but is merely a symbol of her fear of hell. The condition will probably persist until she settles her problems of conscience.

c. Neurasthenia. Neurasthenia is a condition of extreme mental and physical fatigue. Unlike hysteria, it is more common in men than in women. Along with fatigue and irritability, there are usually hypochondriacal complaints. The sufferer has exaggerated symptoms in the morning, and as the day wears on these become less severe. Often his fatigue is completely dissipated by night, and he dislikes going to bed. Insomnia, general lassitude, and inability to concentrate are common complaints of neurasthenics.

Formerly neurasthenia was treated by a graduated "rest" cure known as the Weir-Mitchell treatment. It is now known, however, that, in spite of connotations of the term, namely "weak nerves," neurasthenia does not have a physiological basis. It originates in a personality too weak to face the difficulties of life, whose inadequate adjustment to them brings on symptoms of anxiety, irritation, and insecurity. Back of this disorder, as in almost all neuroses, is a childhood background of maladjustment and the failure to grow in strength of character.

d. Hypochondriasis. Hypochondriasis is a neurotic condition which, without other symptoms of a psychosis or psychoneurosis, is characterized by an abnormal concern over one's health. The dominant symptom, an obsessive preoccupation with ill-health or with the ills of various organs, is not cured by a demonstration that there is no anatomical or physiological basis for such concern.

e. Reactive depression. Under this heading are classified depressions which follow obvious external causes which naturally produce sadness, such as the death of a relative, disgrace, illness, or financial worry. The reaction differs from normal in that it is of a more marked degree and of longer duration.

f. Anxiety states. Anxiety states are perhaps the most distressing of the neuroses and are essentially non-adjustive reactions. Anxiety differs from a phobia in that it is not focused on anything in particular. Phobias are fears of specific situations. "Claustrophobia," for instance, is a fear of closed places; "agoraphobia" is a fear of open places. Anxiety is a "free-floating" fear characterized by a general perturbation of mind, in which the sufferer always expects the worst. The character structure of the person suffering from an anxiety state is quite different from that of the hysterical. Typically, he is conscientious and reliable to such an extent that he cannot possibly solve his problems by "running away."

g. *Mixed psychoneurosis.* Under this heading are included psychoneuroses, the symptoms of which do not fall predominantly in any of the above categories.

3. Prevention and treatment

A variety of means are used in the prevention and treatment of psychoneuroses. Among them are the following: (1) preventive therapy, (2) environmental therapy, (3) psychotherapy, (4) group therapy, (5) expressive therapies, (6) occupational therapy, and (7) bibliotherapy. The essential characteristics of each of these means will be briefly discussed.

(1) *Preventive therapy.* Preventive therapy aims to prevent maladjustments and mental disorder by removing the obstacles to mental health. The chief means it uses is reëducation, by which the neurotic grows out of his conflicts toward maturity and the ability to accept life's challenge with courage and enjoyment. A course in psychology, for instance, may help a student to recognize some of his own maladjustments and may lead him to seek help in overcoming his problems. Such assistance, coming at the right time, may be enough to stave off a threatening mental disorder.

(2) *Environmental therapy.* Sometimes environmental conditions make it impossible for an individual to adjust even when he has had the benefit of psychotherapy. In such instances, changes must be made in the environment before the patient's mental health can be restored. Sometimes this involves moving a child to a foster home, changing schools, or, in the case of a college student, changing roommates or courses. In recommending environmental changes one must always be careful that such changes do not enable the person to run farther from life and evade meeting major problems which he can and should work out for himself.

(3) *Psychotherapy.* Psychotherapy aims to bring about changes in the individual's attitudes and feelings, and thus to eliminate

the neurosis. This is usually accomplished by setting up a person-to-person relationship with a therapist in whom the patient has confidence. There are great differences of opinion among therapists as to the exact nature of this relationship and what treatment involves. A number of different methods of psychotherapy, however, are used with great success.

(4) *Group therapy.* Group therapy is based upon the recognition that man is essentially social in nature and that his maladjustments involve disturbed relations with other people. It is used with both children and adults. Its chief purpose is usually that of helping the maladjusted person to move from his self-centeredness to a wholesome responsiveness to other people. In the treatment of children,

> Group Therapy . . . is treatment in which no discussion is initiated by the therapist; no interpretation is given except in very rare instances and under specific conditions. Emotional reorientation comes from the very fact that the child experiences actual situations, lives and works with other children, comes into direct and meaningful interaction with others, and as a result modifies his feeling tones and habitual responses.[12]

(5) *Expressive therapies.* Expressive therapies are based upon the principle that emotionally disturbed people need outlets for ventilating their conflicts and releasing their emotional tensions. Common types of expressive therapy used with children are play therapy, art and music therapy, creative writing, and dramatics. With the exception of play therapy, the other types are also used in the treatment of adults.

(6) *Occupational therapy.* Occupational therapy is used in the treatment of normal people with physical injuries as well as with emotionally disturbed persons. It uses arts and crafts, games, educational and industrial activities, such as printing, weaving and woodworking, as means of restoring injured joints and muscles, of retraining in skills, and of reëducating patients in their personal adjustments.

(7) *Bibliotherapy.* All behavior disturbances have an emotional basis, although intellectual factors are also present. Human behavior is the result of intellectual as well as of emotional influences, and mature behavior is possible only when the emotions

---

[12] S. S. Slavson, *An Introduction to Group Therapy* (New York, The Commonwealth Fund, 1943), p. 2.

are directed and controlled by the intelligence. In the disturbed person emotions have the upper hand, and before an appeal can be made to the intelligence, these disturbing emotions must be dissipated.

There is a psychopathology of the mind that does not consist essentially in any organic defect of cognitive ability, or in the over-accentuation of any type of emotion, or in the disbalance of impulsive drives, but simply in the presence of a false principle or an unwholesome attitude of mind.[13]

For example, in asking a juvenile delinquent the question, "Who is your greatest hero?" a psychologist received as an answer, "Dillinger." So long as a child identifies with an unworthy model there is no hope of improving his behavior. The method of "bibliotherapy" is a means of supplanting unwholesome ideals and introducing in their place healthy attitudes of mind. The method consists essentially of lending a child an interesting book, carefully selected to fit his needs. When the child returns the book, he is asked how he liked it and what he learned from it. He is then subjected to a series of questions calculated to bring out in clear relief wholesome principles and ideals.[14] Such questioning is an essential part of the treatment since it clarifies ideas of which the child might otherwise be only dimly aware.

The object of bibliotherapy is to support impulsive drives by truly human conduct in which one is conscious of the end toward which one is striving, knows that it is worth while, and is determined to attain it.[15]

C. Constitutional Psychopathic States

The term *constitutional psychopathic state* or *psychopathic deviate* has no clearly defined usage among psychiatrists. Moore places in this category persons whose conduct resembles that of psychotic persons in various ways, but whose symptoms do not go on to the development of a full-blown psychotic condition.

---

[13] T. V. Moore, "Bibliotherapy in Psychiatric Practice," in B. Glueck (ed.), *Current Therapies of Personality Disorders* (New York, Grune & Stratton, Inc., 1946), p. 134.

[14] An appropriate list of books for this purpose, adapted to the preadolescent and adolescent ages, has been published by Clara Kircher under the title, *Character Formation Through Books; A Bibliography*, Second Edition (Washington, D.C., Catholic University of America Press, 1945).

[15] T. V. Moore, *loc. cit.*, p. 138.

DISORDERS OF PERSONALITY

These people show many of the symptoms of psychotics and neurotics except that deep emotional involvement is apparently absent. Typically, the psychopath is a likable person who makes a good first impression on others. He may behave in an exemplary manner and then suddenly shock his associates by shameless, erratic, and immoral behavior. When he is threatened with punishment he may shed crocodile tears and appear to be truly repentant. He is incapable of profiting by experience, however; and since he is incapable of loving anyone very deeply, he lacks motivation to change. When questioned, the psychopath is often at a loss to explain his acts. An excellent example of psychopathic behavior is shown in an excerpt from Dostoevsky's *The Possessed*. Nicolay (the prince), a very personable young man, has returned from Petersburg, where it was reported that he

had suddenly taken to riotous living with a sort of frenzy. Not that he gambled or drank too much, there was only talk of savage recklessness, of running over people in the streets with his horses, of brutal conduct to a lady of good society with whom he had a liaison and whom he afterwards publicly insulted. It was added, too, that he had developed into a regular bully, insulting people for the mere pleasure of insulting them.

Upon returning home, Nicolay made such a good impression on people that they tended to forget his reputation.

He made his appearance in society, and with unfailing propriety performed all the duties demanded by our provincial etiquette. . . . But a few months passed and the wild beast showed his claws. . . . Suddenly, apropos of nothing, our prince was guilty of incredible outrages upon various persons and, what was most striking, these outrages were utterly unheard of, quite inconceivable, unlike anything commonly done, utterly silly and mischievous, quite unprovoked and objectless.[16]

When called to account for his strange behavior, Nicolay answered,

"I'll tell what drives me to do it!" . . and looking around him he bent down to Ivan Ossipovitch's ear. . . . Poor Ivan . . . hurriedly and trustfully inclined his ear; he was exceedingly curious. And then something utterly incredible, though on the other side only too unmistakable took place. The old man felt that, instead of telling him some

[16] F. Dostoevsky, *The Possessed*, trans. by C. Garnett (New York, The Macmillan Company, 1948), pp. 33–37.

interesting secret, Nicolay had seized the upper part of his ear between his teeth and was nipping at it rather hard.[17]

D. Behavior Problems

Under this heading are placed episodes of abnormal behavior, such as stealing, alcoholism, and truancy, in a personality which is essentially sound. What distinguishes these conditions from neurotic states is their episodic character; that is, these behavior patterns are not habitual. Alcoholism, for example, when chronic or compulsive, is more than a "behavior problem"; it is a mental disease. An occasional spree, however, would come under this category. Because of the seriousness of the alcohol problem, we shall discuss it here in some detail, even though we are not limiting our discussion to the problem of "occasional intoxication."

Within recent years alcoholism has become a major social problem in the United States. It is estimated that about a million and a half people in our country are social problems because of the excessive use of alcohol.[18] The number of male alcoholics increased 43.6 per cent between the last year of Prohibition and 1945.[19] The corresponding figure for women is 12.6 per cent, although the upward trend for women did not start until 1940.

What causes the excessive use of alcohol? One explanation is that,

Every person with an alcohol problem has a personality difficulty—a neurosis. Every alcoholic is an immature, insecure, oversensitive and anxious person who is suffering from marked feelings of inferiority, unable to meet and enjoy people socially or unable to get on with his work without the support of alcohol in fairly large quantities. This sounds like a serious indictment against the alcoholic, but with rare exceptions it is a true one. The reason we do not as yet generally accept it as true is because we often see the alcoholic at his best rather than at his worst. We see him before he has drunk too much, when he is genial, friendly, often full of compliments, telling jokes and amusing people with his wit. But after he has a little more to drink his wit becomes monotonous and his stories cease to hold the center of attention, whereupon his sensitivity comes to the fore, he drinks some more in order to cover up his feelings of chagrin and finally he becomes so objectionable that he has to be removed from the scene. The use of

[17] *Ibid.*, 41–42.

[18] O. S. English and G. H. J. Pearson, *Emotional Problems of Living* (New York, W. W. Norton & Company, Inc., 1945), p. 356.

[19] E. M. Jellinek, *Recent Trends in Alcoholism and Alcohol Consumption* (New Haven, Hillhouse Press, 1947).

alcohol in large quantities is an indictment against society and shows a lack of maturity in that society.[20]

A man may drink excessively on occasion or even habitually without being classified as a chronic drinker, provided he is still able to leave it alone when the occasion requires it. However, the habitual drinker can never be sure just when he is going to cross the invisible line which separates him from the compulsive drinker. The compulsive drinker cannot ever take alcohol in any form or in even the most minute quantities without setting off his compulsion to drink. His condition is a disease, but unfortunately it cannot be treated as one. Individual psychotherapy is almost never successful. Medical treatments, such as the "Keeley Cure" or conditioned reflex therapy are effective for only limited periods of time. The only cure is that of complete abstinence, and the chronic alcoholic cannot abstain without an entire change in his attitude toward life. *Alcoholics Anonymous*, an organization composed of ex-alcoholics, has helped many chronic alcoholics to abstain when exhortation and medical treatment have failed.

Just what is at the root of chronic alcoholism we do not know. Some research workers claim that, in addition to the personality problem, the craving for alcohol has a physical basis. According to one theory, the potential alcoholic suffers a partial "genetic block," a condition which prevents him from producing the necessary enzymes unless he gets more than the usual amount of certain chemical substances. In other words, there is a lack of certain chemicals in the body of the potential alcoholic, a lack which he unconsciously strives to supply by imbibing alcohol. If, however, he abstains from alcohol completely and never acquires a taste for it, he is safe.

The young person who comes from a family in which alcoholism has appeared may, if this theory is true, find that he has inherited the "genetic block." He need not, however, become a chronic alcoholic if he abstains completely. A good suggestion would be to take the pledge at an early age and keep it perpetually. Alcohol is not bad in itself, but for some people it is poison for both mind and body. The disintegration of personality and the profound misery of the alcoholic and his family can be surely prevented, at the present time, by only one means—total abstinence.

[20] O. S. English and G. H. J. Pearson, *op. cit.*, p. 356.

Alcoholism after a long period of time may result in Korsikoff's syndrome, a psychotic disorder never completely curable. *Delirium tremens* is a temporary alcoholic psychosis not unlike some very high fevers; fortunately, it leaves no after-effects.

IV. DOUBLE OR MULTIPLE PERSONALITY

One curious pathological disturbance of personality is commonly referred to as double or multiple personality. While this disorder has something in common with the types mentioned above, it is sufficiently different from them to merit separate treatment. Stevenson, in his famous *Dr. Jekyll and Mr. Hyde*, has immortalized this phenomenon in literature. Almost equally well known and certainly as dramatic is the case of Miss Beauchamp, reported by Morton Prince. Miss Beauchamp was a respectable "old maidish" young woman of about thirty whose behavior was dignified and above reproach in every way. One day, however, in the presence of a young minister whom she was assisting, she suddenly went into an hysterical episode and behaved in a most irresponsible and childish way. This was the beginning of a series of such episodes in which a "secondary" personality who called herself "Sally" would suddenly break through. "Sally" claimed that she had always been with Miss Beauchamp but that only now was she able to assert herself. The personality of "Sally" would come and go, alternating with the "primary" personality, that of Miss Beauchamp. Miss Beauchamp had no knowledge of Sally. But Sally, even when she was not the dominant personality, was continuously aware of everything Miss Beauchamp thought and did. For this reason Sally is called a *co-conscious* personality. Finally, a third personality emerged, more mature than Sally, but also more aggressive and realistic than Miss Beauchamp. Prince identified Sally with the repressed life of Miss Beauchamp, extending over a lifetime of conflicts. Miss Beauchamp had been what we would today call a rejected child, and her childhood was one of exceptional unhappiness and bitterness. Her mother died when she was thirteen years of age, and Prince says of her, "the three years following her mother's death, when she lived with her father, were a period of successive mental shocks, nervous strains, and frights," and she became more and more "given to daydreaming and living in her imagination." [21] Prince was able after years of treatment to effect an integration of the three "personalities" by therapeutic techniques, including suggestion and hypnosis. Miss Beauchamp was gradually enabled to see "Sally" and her "third personality" as a part of herself, as the embodiment of her repressed impulses and desires. Once she was able to "accept" her whole self and not just the window-dressing aspect of her personality, there was no longer any need of repression, and consequently no further need of a secondary personality.

In referring to the above multiple states of consciousness, we do not mean to imply that Miss Beauchamp was more than one person. Strictly speaking, Miss Beauchamp had only one personality because, like every other human being, she had only one substantial and indivisible soul. This soul itself is never split, although its manifestations through the bodily organism may be. In the words of Moore, "When, for any reason, whether toxic or emotional, or both, only certain groups of materials are available in one period of the patient's existence, and other groups are available in an alternating phase, we have what is known as a change of personality, but it is a change in what may be termed the *empirical* and not in the *metaphysical* personality." [22]

V. MENTAL DISEASE IN CHILDHOOD

Functional psychoses are very rarely found in children; and when they do appear their symptoms are different from those of adults. Because of the child's lack of experience and his intellectual and social immaturity, he is more likely to have schizoid tendencies (which at the extreme become schizophrenia) than any other mental disease symptom. Schizophrenia in childhood is rarely accompanied by clearly defined delusions as in the adult. The following are the most typical and consistent symptoms of psychosis in children:

1. *Seclusiveness and social withdrawal.* This pattern is observably different from that of shy, normal children. Unlike normal children, the possibly pre-psychotic child seems to be out

---

[21] M. Prince, *The Dissociation of a Personality* (New York, Longmans, Green & Company, 1925), p. 12.

[22] Dom T. V. Moore, *Cognitive Psychology* (Philadelphia, J. B. Lippincott Company, 1939), 42–43.

of contact with the group, not interested in what they are doing or saying although he does not necessarily attempt to escape. He is "peculiar," "different" in a way that interferes with his socialization.

2. *Emotional rigidity.* The child's emotional expressions do not change with changes in the objective situation. For example, one psychotic thirteen-year-old reported every experience, both pleasant and unpleasant, as "magnificent" or "wonderful."

3. *Varying degrees of personality dissociation.* This dissociation is usually shown in defective orientation to other children, various linguistic dissociations, and concentration on a given activity to the exclusion of all other activities. For example, an eleven-year-old psychotic found it impossible to stop drawing for over an hour after the drawing period was over and the teacher had asked him to stop.

4. *Unusual attention to detail.* A morbid conscientiousness is observed. For example, one boy when asked to write his name, wrote it more than fifty times, saying that he wanted to write it carefully.

5. *Excessive daydreaming and vivid phantasy.* These children live much of the time in a mental world of their own. For example, some school children reacted to imaginary companions and conditions as if they were realities. Young children who have no social contacts with other children often have imaginary companions. Daydreaming of this kind, however, is not a symptom of abnormality until school age or later.

6. *Differential intellectual deterioration.* Although the IQ's of pre-psychotic children do not go down, capacities such as judgment and occasionally the ability to handle some specific subject matter do deteriorate.

7. *Manneristic behavior.* In many cases, mannerisms, such as the compulsion to tap on a cup or a dish, or to perform an act twice occurs.[23]

VI. CAUSES OF PERSONALITY PROBLEMS

One of the naturally most persistent questions that come to the mind of anyone considering mental illness is: what are its causes?

[23] M. Sherman and H. Jost, "Diagnosis of Juvenile Psychosis," *Am. J. Dis. Child.,* 65 (1943), 868–872.

DISORDERS OF PERSONALITY

We have mentioned above that many instances of mental disturbance can be traced to organic causes. If this is so, it seems possible that heredity may play a significant role in the genesis of mental disease. In the functional disorders, environmental factors may have as great an influence as heredity. Finally, free choices may have an effect upon the development of personality difficulties. The question as to what causes mental illness is by no means definitely answered as yet. We shall, however, consider the hypotheses offered above and summarize a sampling of the evidence in favor of each of them.

A. Inheritance of Mental Disease

The evidence on the inheritance of various mental diseases is ambiguous, and more research is needed before we can arrive at definite conclusions. We shall present here two studies which throw some light upon the problem.

Roe and Burks [24] made a follow-up study of four groups of adults, all of whom had been reared by foster parents not related to them. These adults had as children been placed in foster homes by the State Charities Aid Association of New York. Their parents were known to have had the following characteristics:

1. Twenty-five had normal parents.
2. Thirty-six had an alcoholic father. Of these children, many had mothers who were also alcoholic or promiscuous.
3. Eleven had one psychotic parent. A few had fathers who had criminal records.
4. Six had an alcoholic father and a psychotic mother.

At the time of the study, the age range of the subjects was from 22 to 40 years, with an average of 31 years. The investigators tried to find any relationships that might exist between adult adjustment and (1) parentage and (2) environmental factors. In general, their data suggested that adult adjustment was much more closely related to factors operating in the childhood environment than it was to parentage. None of the offspring of the alcoholics, for instance, was alcoholic, although two of them were seriously maladjusted. None of the children of the psychotic parents was seriously maladjusted either. Of the few girls who became sex

[24] Anne Roe and Barbara Burks, *Adult Adjustment of Foster Children of Alcoholic and Psychotic Parentage and the Influence of the Foster Home*, 1945, Memoirs of the Section on Alcohol Studies (New Haven, Yale University), No. 3.

delinquents, none had promiscuous mothers; of the few boys who became delinquent, none had criminal fathers. There was, however, a significant association between adult adjustment and (1) the childhood experience of love from the foster parents and (2) the absence of personality problems in the adults in whose home they had been reared.

Kallman,[25] with the coöperation of the mental hospitals under the supervision of the New York State Department of Mental Hygiene, studied the relative effects of hereditary and environmental factors in the development and outcome of schizophrenia. Using the "Twin-Family Method," he studied the incidence of schizophrenia in six distinct groups of blood relationship, namely: (1) identical twins, (2) fraternal twins of the same sex, (3) fraternal twins of opposite sex, (4) full siblings, (5) half-siblings, and (6) step-siblings. Kallman assumed that if heredity were of importance in the genesis of schizophrenia, there would be a higher degree of resemblance between identical than between fraternal twins in the occurrence of schizophrenia. Also, full siblings should resemble each other about as much as fraternal twins, and half-siblings, with only one parent in common, should be about midway between full-siblings and the step-siblings who had neither parent in common. The results of the study appear to verify this assumption and may be summarized as follows:

Category	Per Cent of Incidence of Schizophrenia in Both Members of Pairs
Identical twins	85.8
Fraternal "	14.7
Full-siblings	14.3
Half-siblings	7.0
Step-siblings (unrelated by blood)	1.8

Kallman concludes that the predisposition to schizophrenia depends on the presence of a specific genetic factor, but that this finding is not incompatible with the concept that schizophrenia can be prevented as well as cured. He also points out that,

over 85 per cent of our groups of siblings and dizygotic (fraternal) co-twins did *not* develop schizophrenia, although about 10 per cent of them had a schizophrenic parent, all of them had a schizophrenic

[25] Franz. J. Kallman, "The Genetic Theory of Schizophrenia," *Amer. J. Psychiat.*, 103 (1946), 309–322.

DISORDERS OF PERSONALITY

brother or sister, and a large proportion shared the same environment with these schizophrenics before and after birth.[26]

Further research is needed to corroborate Kallman's findings, however, before we can arrive at a scientific generalization as to the inheritance of schizophrenia, or of other mental diseases.

B. Culture and Mental Disorder

The study of mental disease is carried on in one of the most fascinating and also one of the most baffling areas of contemporary research. Specialists of various kinds—brain surgeons, neurologists, psychiatrists, psychologists, sociologists, and anthropologists—all are making research contributions which help to unravel the mysterious threads of mental abnormality. Yet in spite of their combined efforts, we are still just beginning to understand a few of the factors that contribute to mental disease, and we are even further away from a constructive understanding of prevention and treatment. It is true, we no longer content ourselves with diagnosing symptoms and classifying the disease into the appropriate category. Nor do we delude ourselves into thinking that because we have so classified the disorder we now "understand" the person suffering from the disease. That was the tendency for a considerable time after the German psychiatrist Kraepelin brought a little order into the study of mental diseases. We have also long since discarded the assumption of Freud that mental disease grows out of parent-child relationships which are essentially the same from one culture to another. Today we recognize that personality development is the complex outcome of many interrelated and interacting constitutional and environmental influences. Within this hereditary and environmental setting the human being apprehends and chooses those "goods" which will progressively determine the kind of person he will become. Prominent among the environmental factors which will influence him is the culture pattern with its component systems of values, taboos, rewards and punishments.

Anthropologists, psychiatrists, and educators have popularized the view that mental disease and its presenting symptoms have their origin in the conflict-producing aspects of the social and cultural environment. One anthropologist, for example, compares

[26] C. Kluckhohn and H. A. Murray, *Personality in Nature, Society, and Culture* (New York, Alfred A. Knopf, Inc., 1949), p. 69.

the "storm and stress" characteristic of adolescent personality development in our culture with the freedom from emotional tension and neurotic behavior of adolescents coming of age in Samoa, New Guinea, and other so-called "simpler" cultures. These differences she ascribes to the fact that in America adolescents are uncertain about their status and are placed in conflict-producing situations which are unknown in more primitive cultures. Another goes so far as to claim that the very concept of mental disease is relative to the culture; that is, what would be considered normal behavior in one culture would be considered abnormal in another. She illustrates this point by comparing the attitudes of the Zuni Indians toward personal initiative and drive with that of our own competitive culture. Among the Zuni Indians, if a person demonstrates greater drive and initiative than his fellows, he is likely to be looked upon as a sorcerer and strung up by his thumbs. Or, if he is acquisitive and collects possessions (a symbol of status in our society), he will certainly be branded as abnormal and queer. The Zuni Indian acquires prestige not by collecting property but by distributing it in a magnificent celebration known as "potlatch." Among some Indian tribes, children cannot be prevailed upon to accept positions of leadership because such positions entail responsibility without any rewards in the form of prestige or honor. Needless to say, this stands in marked contrast to our own prevailing culture pattern.

Among the Northwest coast Indians, existence is viewed in terms of a cultural "insult complex." If a chief is surpassed in any way by a rival chief, he arranges a "potlatch" ceremony in which goods are given to the rival, while at the same time he gives a ceremonial recital which resembles that of the paranoid psychotic with his delusions of persecution and grandeur. This is the culturally approved pattern of behavior; it is what the chief's social group expects him to do. Similarly, if his wife dies, he seeks revenge against the enemy who, he believes, has caused her death by using magic or sorcery. Such behavior is considered normal in his group, but in our culture we would not hesitate to label it pathological. We do not believe in magic; we attribute the death to bacteria or other causes which we have been taught from childhood on are the causes of death. The question arises: Are the two similar patterns of behavior—that of the Indian chief and that of the paranoid psychotic—the same psychologically? Are there any real differences between the two men themselves? Is the one normal and the other pathological just because of the different cultural valuations of their behavior?

The above questions can be answered only by considering the motivation behind the delusional behavior in the two cases cited and by ascertaining the function which the delusions play in the total personality adjustment of the two men. In the case of the Indian chief, the delusional behavior is imposed from without. The chief is acting as he is expected to act; and once he has gone through the ritual prescribed by his group, the matter is dropped. The delusions are brought out not by any imaginary crisis, but by a real crisis, even though the supposed cause of the disaster may not be the true one. The paranoid, on the other hand, defends himself against imaginary persecutors, even when there is no evidence that anyone is persecuting him and no external crisis to be faced. Psychologically, the behavior of the two men is extremely different, because the motivation is different. In the Indian culture, the behavior is *externally* determined; in the case of the paranoid, it is determined by his own needs, that is *internally* determined.[27] It is probable that even in the Indian culture, if one of the men decides that he is the chief and that the acting chief has usurped his place, contrary to all evidence, his fellow Indians will consider him just as abnormal as we consider the paranoid psychotics in our midst. In other words, a similarity of external behavior does not indicate a similarity of internal meaning. To suppose without evidence that it does is to commit the logical fallacy of an uncritical use of analogy.

Another difficulty that we face in comparing the relative incidence of mental abnormality in two or more cultures is the unconscious bias we have toward accepting our own culture as the "norm." A country which has not utilized all of its natural resources by becoming industrialized, for instance, is looked upon as "backward." Another generation or two, however, may be all that is necessary to reverse this evaluation. When our frontier is gone, our forests denuded, our coal, oil, and water depleted, we may look upon a "century of progress" as a century of irresponsibility, perhaps even of insanity. Similarly, people in our society who do not struggle to "get ahead," to "better their lot," by which

[27] Henry J. Wegrocki, "A Critique of Cultural and Statistical Concepts of Abnormality," *J. Abnorm. Soc. Psychol.*, 34 (1939), 166–178.

is meant securing a higher income or a more comfortable home, are looked upon with pity or disdain. They are the failures in life, those who have given up the struggle, those who have gone down to ignominious defeat. Yet, in the Christian scheme of life, these may be the "poor in spirit" for whom, like Lazarus, a blessed eternity awaits, and the busy go-getter may be reaping the final reward of the rich man, Dives, condemned to hell for all eternity.

Within our own culture certain conditions exist which appear to be conducive to mental disease. *Overstimulation* is one of them. Children as well as adults are bombarded by a tremendous amount of stimulation today, much more so than they were a generation or two ago. At home, there is continuous stimulation by radio and television and frequent interruption by the telephone. After school, in middle-class communities, there are scout meetings, music and dancing lessons, and other extracurricular activities to absorb almost all the minutes of the waking day. Advertisers call whatever they are selling "AN EXCITING BUY." Week-ends are spent at motion picture theaters, at which there is further excitement and overstimulation. These conditions prevent some children from quietly directing their lives toward chosen goals and assimilating their various experiences into an integrated whole, and thus promote anxiety.[28]

Another source of difficulty is the *conflicting value pattern* presented by our culture. Children are taught, on the one hand, to compete with others and to try to excel them. They are taught, on the other hand, to be unselfish and to put aside their self-interest for the welfare of other individuals or of the group. In a sense, these two values are mutually incompatible, and the person who accepts both of them uncritically will find it difficult, if not impossible, to develop a completely integrated, mature personality. Undue emphasis on competition, moreover, may produce a distorted sense of values. For instance, a person who has made a real contribution may feel that he has failed if someone else surpasses him. He may also be satisfied with and actually proud of mediocre achievement if he excels others in his group.

Unrealistic goals set up by our culture may produce intense frustration. Not so long ago the United States was a land of un-

---

[28] D. A. Prescott, *Emotions and the Educative Process* (Washington, D.C., American Council on Education, 1938).

DISORDERS OF PERSONALITY

limited opportunity and the frontier was still open. To a considerable extent, anyone with physical strength, intelligence, and the will to work could become economically secure and socially independent. Typically, Europeans coming to America bettered their lot, and theoretically anyone, if he really wanted to, could enter any occupation and even become president. Out of this historical condition came our cultural stereotype that the individual has unlimited freedom to develop or to do as he pleases. Actually, of course, this is no longer true. (In a sense it was never true.) Individual freedom is limited in many respects, as we have shown in previous chapters. Personal limitations, race, and socio-economic status restrict freedom in many important respects. These conditions, of course, are a source of frustration whether the person anticipates them or not. But if he grows up believing in the stereotype of individual freedom, his frustration is considerably greater. Social and economic conditions over which individuals have no control produce anxiety and often lead people to an abnormal preoccupation with attaining security. Business cycles, seasonal changes in availability of jobs, and changes in public taste, result in unemployment. A catastrophe serious enough to be classed as an exciting cause of a mental disorder may, when superimposed upon these predisposing factors, result in mental disease.[29]

Widespread *migration and uprootedness* are a threat to mental security since they make it difficult to make and keep lifelong friends and to establish family traditions. A child growing up in a family that moves frequently lives in an almost continuously changing world. One little girl of four, whose family had moved frequently during World War II, developed intense symptoms of anxiety. She clung passionately to each of the chairs in succession, exclaiming, "Mamma, this is ours, isn't it? No one can take it from us. Mamma, help me to hold on to it." And, on another occasion, she said, with a dreamy far-away attitude, "Nothing is ever the same ever. Nothing." This child was more sensitive than most children, it is true, but her reaction illustrates what may happen to other migrating children in a lesser degree.

Uprooted adults, too, are subjected to anxiety because there is no one to call upon in an emergency. They find it difficult to know

---

[29] In a non-materialistic culture, these predisposing factors appear to be of little importance. Only when the situation is threatening to life itself, as, for instance, in widespread famine and starvation, will mental disorders crop up.

people, to achieve status, and to acquire a sense of belonging to the group.

In short, the environmental factors associated with mental illness are multiple and complicated. But that is not all. The study of the etiology of mental disturbance is further complicated by the influence of voluntary factors as we shall indicate below.

C. The Relation of Free Will to Personality Problems

It is difficult at times to distinguish in an emotionally disturbed person the role of freedom and of compulsion in his acts. It is important to know that a free choice depends upon the proper operation of the intellect. Saint Thomas has pointed out that passion (emotion) may interfere with the operation of the intellect in a number of important ways, and hence may limit a person's freedom of choice. In general, we may summarize the relation of free will to personality problems as follows:

1. Some problems have their origin in wrong choices, that is, in the sinful use of free will. A case in point is that of the woman described earlier who suffered from a compulsive fear. Her personality disorder cannot be treated by psychological means unless the moral guilt is dissipated or, in other words, until the moral problem of her invalid marriage is resolved.

2. Some problems have their origin in a faulty organic constitution or in traumatic experiences over which the person had little or no control. For example, some obsessive and compulsive states stem from a wrong conscience built up by improper education in childhood. Some cases of scruples are of this sort. Even though the sufferer may have learned *intellectually* that his scruples are unfounded, yet the feelings and emotions built up in childhood still persist. Psychological treatment in such cases is indicated if help received in the confessional is not enough. The wise Christian psychologist, while treating a case such as we have just mentioned, will secure for his patient the help of an understanding confessor. Other cases falling into this category are acute states of depression which are often precipitated by obscure nutritional or glandular changes in the body. Cases of acute schizophrenia, for example, cannot be dissipated by any amount of persuasion but they sometimes clear for a time after insulin therapy. The insulin changes the "internal environment" upon which the proper functioning of the nervous system depends.

DISORDERS OF PERSONALITY

3. Some, and perhaps most, personality problems have their origin in a combination of factors; that is, they are partly the result of wrong choices and partly the result of factors over which the individual has no control. A rejected child, for instance, may become a thief through his own responsible choice. But his choice may be unconsciously influenced by his feeling that the world owes him something. The stealing in such a case is a compensation for a very real need and one of which the child has a right to demand satisfaction. The child's stealing is a sin, of course, but he is probably less guilty than another child who deliberately chooses to steal but whose intellect is not under the influence of such strong emotion.

In his treatment of personality disturbances the Christian psychologist or psychiatrist finds the principles of his religion a great source of insight and strength. The Christian psychologist cannot, any more than the non-Christian, adequately perform his functions without an intensive and extensive grounding in the science and philosophy of man. He needs a thorough grounding, too, in the techniques of therapeutic treatment. But more than that, he draws inspiration from his realization that all men, well or ill, are either actual or potential members of the Mystical Body of Christ, and that in serving his patients he is serving Christ. In helping people he must always maintain an attitude of reverence; his ultimate goal is not merely to help his patient become comfortable; it is to help the patient become the kind of person God wants him to become.

For the Christian, no human problem, whether it be mental illness, as we have described it in this chapter, or some of the other types of abnormalities which we shall consider next, may become a mere psychological curiosity. Human problems must be seen in the light of man's origin and destiny. The Christian psychologist, while refraining from judgment, will never look at human conduct as a purely neutral affair, but will try to see it in its relation to God's will and God's law.

SUGGESTED READING

BEERS, C., *A Mind That Found Itself* (New York, Longmans, Green & Company, 1908).
HORNEY, K., *Neurosis and Human Growth* (New York, W. W. Norton & Company, Inc., 1950).

HOUSELANDER, CAROL, *Guilt* (New York, Sheed and Ward, Inc., 1951).
KEENAN, ALAN, *Neuroses and Sacraments* (New York, Sheed and Ward, Inc., 1950).
TABOR, EITHNE, *The Cliff's Edge* (New York, Sheed and Ward, Inc., 1950).

XV

Adjustment of the Atypical Person

> *... the body is a small portion of matter to which the soul has given life. Why be surprised at its limitations and miseries?*—JEAN MOUROUX [1]

Atypical development of any kind may set up a psychological barrier between the individual and his group. The degree to which the abnormality will affect his total personality adjustment depends upon: (1) the nature of the abnormality, (2) the extent of abnormality, and (3) the value which the social group or culture places upon normality in that particular sphere.

All of the abnormalities discussed in this chapter are in themselves liabilities in our culture (with the possible exception of left-handedness). This is not true, of course, of all abnormalities. Exceptionally high intelligence or unusual artistic or literary gifts are abnormalities, to be sure, but we look upon them as assets rather than as liabilities, since the culture places a high value upon such talents and abilities.

I. BLINDNESS

Blindness may result from the destruction of (1) the retina itself, (2) the optic nerve, or (3) the optical center in the brain. It may be partial or total.

A child is classified as blind if his vision is so defective that tactual methods, such as the Braille system, must be used in his education. He is classified as partially seeing if he can be educated by visual methods but with special adaptations not required by the normal child. Such adaptations may include increased use of auditory aids, large type, and special lighting.

[1] From *The Meaning of Man*, by Jean Mouroux. Copyright, 1948, Sheed and Ward, Inc., New York.

Blind children are usually slow in acquiring motor control. As infants, they are often mistaken for feebleminded babies. They are, as a rule, less active and show less initiative than seeing children of corresponding ages. Blind and partially blind children seldom make progress in school commensurate with their intellectual ability. At every stage of their educational careers, they need special help with specially adapted methods of instruction. For example, before these children can learn reading they must learn to use Braille.

The blind are not, just because of their defect, more sensitive to sounds, touch, or vibrations than normal people. Because the visual sense is lacking, however, the other senses must be substituted for visual stimuli in teaching the blind.

Blind children must be encouraged at an early age to explore their environment and develop concepts of space and of all the common objects around them. Knowledge of familiar objects, such as plants and animals, is acquired by the blind only after many years of effort. Care must be taken to prevent the blind child from being injured but not at too great an expense to his spontaneity of movement. Fear of injury, either through previous experience or through adult oversolicitude, may retard the blind child's development. As a result he may become listless and apathetic, and suffer from low physical resistance and poor posture.

Blind people learn to read Braille by using the index fingers of the left and right hand simultaneously. One finger precedes the other over the embossed dots and does the "reading." The other finger does the "verifying."

II. DEAFNESS AND HEARING DEFECTS

A. The Problem

Deaf children, technically, are those in whom there is no residual hearing whatever. The seriousness of their defect is related to the age at which it occurred. About 50 per cent of the children in schools for the deaf are congenitally deaf; the others have usually acquired deafness as the result of infectious and contagious diseases of childhood. The most serious problems are presented by children who became deaf before they had acquired the use of speech. The normal child acquires the use of language without formal teaching by imitating older people in his environment. The child who cannot hear speech, however, remains mute until he is taught by various mechanical means to speak. Even after years of highly specialized individual training, his speech is labored and lacking in intonation and resonance. The teaching of speech to the deaf is one of the most difficult of all educational problems. The child must be taught to produce sounds artificially, and each word added to his vocabulary must be taught specifically for its meaning, pronunciation, and inflection. Each tense and each idiom must be taught separately. Other senses, such as the visual and tactile, are appealed to as a substitute for the defective hearing. Through these other senses the child gradually acquires over a period of many years the mechanics of speech, including a fair degree of volume and quality control and the control of pitch, accent, and rhythm. The acquisition of speech is tremendously more difficult for the deaf child than the acquisition of a foreign language through classroom instruction is for the hearing child.

Sign language is not the solution to the deaf child's problem. If he is to take his place among normal people, he must acquire facility in lip-reading and in vocalizing words. Instruction from the earliest years must be directed toward these objectives.

Deaf children, even more than blind children, are apt to be misclassified as feebleminded, particularly in preschool years. Deaf children are also mute children. They are mute, not because they cannot speak, but because they have never heard language. Deaf children are slow in learning to read, since their general language capacity is retarded. They suffer more as they grow older because in the junior and senior high school methods of teaching become less visual and more auditory.

In some respects, deafness is a greater liability in the development of personality than is blindness, although results of developmental studies are ambiguous in this respect. Deaf children (and perhaps blind children, too) have more fears than normal children.[2]

Among adults deafness is more *socially* disabling than blindness. Blindness cuts off only the sharply defined and clear kinds of human communication. Deafness cuts off the innuendos. As a

[2] R. Pintner and L. Brunschwig, "A Study of Certain Fears and Wishes among Deaf and Hearing Children," *J. Educ. Psychol.*, 28 (1937), 259–270.

result, the older person who becomes deaf or very hard of hearing may develop suspicious, paranoid characteristics more often than the older blind person.

B. Causes and Extent of Hearing Defects in School Children

Surveys to determine the number of school children who are deaf or hard-of-hearing have led to widely different results. These discrepancies are partly the result of different methods of testing hearing and partly the result of differences in the communities sampled. The percentage differs from community to community, and is related to socio-economic status.[3]

Hearing disabilities are the result of heredity, congenital defects, foreign bodies in the ear, and disease. About 40 per cent of the deafness of children is caused by scarlet fever, meningitis, brain fever, middle ear infections, sinusitis, typhoid fever, measles, colds, pneumonia, and whooping cough.

C. Detection of Children with Hearing Defects

The best method of testing hearing is by means of an audiometer. Below grade two, children must be tested individually; above grade two, as many as forty children can be tested simultaneously. Audiometers provide records of hearing by ear and by bone conduction and can detect whether or not a child has defective hearing at any point in the pitch range. Because of the accuracy of audiometer testing, it is possible to determine periodically whether there has been a gain or loss in hearing acuity.

Audiometers are expensive and many schools do not have them. In schools which do not have audiometers, two older methods of detecting hearing disorders are used, namely: (1) the whisper test, and (2) the watch-tick test. Both of these tests are so time-consuming that it is difficult to test entire school populations by means of them. Moreover, the watch-tick test does not reveal whether or not a child hears various ranges of speech, and a child's reaction time may be misleading when he gives the signal that he has ceased to hear. The whisper test is not too accurate, since voices, even of experienced testers, differ.

[3] A. O. Heck, *The Education of Exceptional Children* (New York, McGraw-Hill Book Company, Inc., 1938), p. 378.

III. ORTHOPEDIC DEFECTS

Crippled children tend, on the average, to score slightly below normal children on the Stanford-Binet Test of Intelligence. This may be a genuine difference in intelligence, or it may result from the fact that certain kinds of physical deformities so limit a child's experience that he cannot compete on equal terms with normal children in taking intelligence tests. Intelligence tests are based upon the assumption that all children taking the test have had equal opportunities to learn. This assumption does not hold in the case of many crippled children.

Most children suffering from orthopedic defects have had limited social experience and have been confined for long periods of time either at home or in a hospital. Special provisions must be made for them in school, such as rest periods, time out for brace fittings, physiotherapy, medical examinations, and other kinds of specialized services. Many of these children are retarded or below average for their grade level, and require highly individualized teaching. All of them need help in adjusting to their defect and in establishing wholesome relations with other people.

IV. ILLNESS AND ACCIDENT

The effects of illness and accident on the personality development of the child depend upon a variety of factors, among which the following have an important place:

1. *Attitude of parents.* If the illness or accident might have been prevented, the parents may react with feelings of guilt. As a compensation they may spoil the child and punish themselves by making unnecessary or undesirable sacrifices for him.

2. *Age.* In general, the younger a child is at the time of an accident or the onset of a chronic illness, the better he adjusts to the situation. This is not invariably true, however, since some kinds of illness and accident prevent a child from having the experiences which lead to learning.

3. *Handicap, permanent or temporary.* A relatively permanent handicap, such as a heart ailment, which involves limitation of activity, or a diabetic condition, which requires constant attention to diet, will have an effect different from that of a temporary handicap. Such conditions may so set a child apart from his

fellows that he fails to mature socially and emotionally. A deformity, such as that which sometimes follows burning, may make a child appear repulsive. People unconsciously reveal to the child the impression which he makes on them, and as a result he acquires a deep feeling of inferiority. Inferiority "complexes" at any age may result in compensatory behavior, such as withdrawal from social contacts or aggressive and antisocial reactions. Oversensitivity to criticism and an overresponsiveness to praise are often seen. A tendency to belittle others and to blame them for one's failures and limitations is also common.

4. *Length of illness.* In general, the longer an illness persists, the harder it is for the child to make a wholesome adjustment. To minimize the bad effects of illness everything possible should be done in the hospital or in the home to help the child live a normal life. The child should cut his own meat, for example, if this activity does not aggravate his illness. As soon as he is able to eat his meals at the table, he should no longer be served from a tray in bed.

Some diseases, such as encephalitis lethargica, may have a permanent effect upon the child's intelligence and behavior. The effect of encephalitis lethargica upon ultimate IQ is partly dependent upon the age at which the disease is contracted. The disease, in many cases, arrests mental growth. If a child with an MA of 6, for example, contracts the disease at six years of age, his IQ at the time would be 100. At the age of seven, one year after the onset of the disease, his MA is still 6, but his IQ has dropped to 86. The absolute measure of intelligence, that is, the MA, tends to remain arrested from the time of the onset of the disease. But since with advancing age the CA increases, the IQ progressively goes down.

In testing the intelligence of the physically handicapped child, standardized procedures must often be modified. The spastic child (who suffers from cerebral palsy [4]), for example, often presents a special problem because of his incoherent speech and lack of motor coördination. One psychologist found that although 75 per cent of cerebral palsied children could be adequately tested

---

[4] Cerebral palsy is a condition in which muscular control is lost because of a lesion in the brain. The *spastic type* is characterized by stiffness and results from a lesion of the motor area of the cortex. The *athetoid type*, characterized by involuntary motion, results from a lesion in the basal ganglia. The *ataxic type*, characterized by a lack of balance and muscular coördination, results from a lesion of the cerebellum.

ADJUSTMENT OF THE ATYPICAL PERSON 399

by the 1937 Stanford-Binet, the rest could not. Minor modifications of the test, such as using large beads instead of the standard size and disregarding the time limit, made it possible to test these children accurately.[5] Such accuracy of testing, however, occurs only when the examiner had had considerable experience with handicapped children.

V. FEEBLEMINDEDNESS

A. Occurrence of Feeblemindedness

The occurrence of feeblemindedness in the general population has been variously estimated to be from 2 to 5 per cent, depending chiefly on the standard adopted. In England at the beginning of the century it was estimated at 2 per 1,000. Later, the estimate was extended to 4 per 1,000 and still later to 10, or 1 per cent.

In the United States during World War I, local draft boards at first rejected 1.2 per cent on the basis of mental subnormality and later about 2 per cent. This did not include institutional cases which were not even registered. Surveys of school children have resulted in even higher figures, usually from 2 to 5 per cent. The discrepancies in estimation of occurrence are the result in part of different methods of making the surveys and especially of different definitions of feeblemindedness. When intelligence tests are used, the results obtained vary with the particular test used. The Kuhlman-Binet test, for example, will classify more children as having IQ's below 75 than will the 1916 Stanford-Binet.

The *White House Conference*, in 1931, reported that about 2 per cent were definitely feebleminded, and that a second group, somewhat smaller, having IQ's above 60 and below 70, could be classified as subnormal. This is probably the best estimate that we have.

B. Types of Feeblemindedness

1. Legally recognized types

The first clear distinction between lunatics, idiots, and imbeciles to be found in modern legislation appears to be the British Idiots Act passed in 1886. In 1904, a Royal Commission was appointed

---

[5] Reported at annual convention, American Psychological Association, Sept. 6, 1946, Philadelphia. K. Maurer, "Mental Evaluation of Cerebral Palsied Children," *Amer. Psychol.*, I (July, 1946), 288–289.

"to consider the existing methods of dealing with idiots and epileptics, and with imbeciles, feebleminded, or defective persons not certified under the Lunacy Laws." The Mental Deficiency Act of 1913 was the outcome of this committee's recommendations. The definitions laid down in this act, which were slightly modified in 1927, are in use at the present time. They may be summarized as follows:

a. Idiots are persons in whose cases there exists mental defectiveness of such a degree that they are unable to guard themselves against common physical dangers.

b. Imbeciles are persons in whom there exists mental defectiveness which, though not amounting to idiocy, is yet so pronounced that they are incapable of managing themselves and their affairs or, in the case of children, of being taught to do so.

c. Feebleminded are those persons in whose cases there exists mental defectiveness which, though not amounting to imbecility, is yet so pronounced that they require care, supervision, and control for their own protection or for the protection of others, or, in the case of children, that they appear to be permanently incapable by reason of such defectiveness of receiving proper benefit from the instruction in ordinary schools.

d. Moral defectives are persons in whose cases there exists mental defectiveness coupled with strongly vicious or criminal propensities, and who require care, supervision, and control for the protection of others.

In the United States the term *moron* was coined by Goddard and is used in the same way as the British use *feebleminded*. The American use of the term *feebleminded* includes all of the first three categories listed above.

2. Clinical types

The great majority of feebleminded children cannot be distinguished from normal children on the basis of physical characteristics. Nevertheless, there are varieties of feeblemindedness which result from factors which also produce physical effects. Children who fall into these categories are usually, although not always, in the lower two categories of feeblemindedness; that is, idiocy or imbecility.

a. Cretin. Cretinism results from congenital underactivity of the thyroid gland, and is characteristically accompanied by the following symptoms: dwarfed stature, bent legs, rough and dry skin, coarse and dry hair, large head in which the fontanelles close late, badly shaped teeth which are late in eruption and deficient in enamel, and a subnormal temperature. The intellectual level is usually that of an idiot or imbecile.

Cretinism can be treated with glandular products which affect both physical and mental growth. The adequacy of such treatment depends upon how early it is begun. Recent research, however, indicates that early treatment is much more successful in removing physical than mental symptoms. Two investigators found a very low correlation between the time of beginning treatment and the ultimate mental growth attained by the child. This led them to suggest that

> ... the changes in the brain which are responsible for the mental defect take place during prenatal life and are not the sequels of postnatal hypothyroidism. The common coincidence of mental defect with congenital hypothyroidism suggests that both organs, the thryoid gland and the brain are affected harmfully during the formative stage.[6]

A hypothyroid condition which develops later in life and which is characterized by mental and physical sluggishness, is known as *myxedema*.

b. *Mongoloid*. Mongolism is always present from birth and derives its name from the characteristic symptom of narrow slanting eyes which is also a characteristic of the Mongolian race. Other diagnostic symptoms are flattened face and skull, protruding tongue with deep fissures, and soft, flabby hands. One of the most striking features of the "Mongoloid" is his physical resemblance to others of the same type; it is very difficult to tell one "Mongoloid" from another. The upper level of intelligence is never above an MA of seven years. About 7,000 Mongoloid babies are born each year in America.[7] The incidence of Mongolism is about the same for all social classes. The most important causative factor appears to be the age of the mother at the time of the child's conception. Over one-half of all Mongoloids are last-born children. A comparison was made of the ages of 2,822 mothers who gave birth to Mongoloid infants, to the ages of mothers who gave birth to

---

[6] H. Bruch and D. J. McCune, "Mental Development of Congenitally Hypothyroid Children." *Am. J. Dis. Child.*, 67, No. 3 (Mar., 1944), 223.

[7] T. H. Ingalls, "Etiology of Mongolism," *Am. J. Dis. Child.*, 74 (Aug., 1947), 147–165.

normal infants in 1934. The peak maternal age of the former was found to be 41, whereas that of the latter was 24.[8]

c. Microcephalic. The microcephalic has an extremely small skull and a receding forehead. It has been suggested that this condition results from damage to the fetus during gestation.[9]

d. Macrocephalic. The macrocephalic has an abnormally large skull which results from an enlargement of the brain. His head is likely to be more square than that of the hydrocephalic, and does not show the bulging line at the fontanelle, sutures, and temples which are seen in the hydrocephalic. The brain enlargement results not from the increased growth of active nerve cells but from the abnormal growth of the neuroglia or supporting cells of the brain.

e. Hydrocephalic. The hydrocephalic, like the macrocephalic, has an abnormally large head. This condition results either from (1) a blocking of the outlets of the cerebrospinal fluid, or (2) a lack of absorption of this fluid. If the condition occurs in later childhood or maturity it may not have the same devastating effects upon intelligence that it would if it occurred earlier. Medical treatment sometimes relieves but very seldom cures this condition.

C. Diagnosis of Feeblemindedness

The clinical types of feeblemindedness described above are diagnosed on the basis of the physical symptoms presented. Most feebleminded children, however, have no physical stigma by which their defectiveness can be diagnosed. At birth, and for several months or even years later, the defect may not be suspected. Psychological tests are available by which feeblemindedness can be diagnosed or at least strongly suspected in infancy. These tests, however, are valid only when administered and interpreted by expert psychometricians who have had considerable experience with both normal and defective children. The services of such psychometricians or clinical psychologists are usually not available, except for children in institutions or children who are to be placed in foster homes. Mental defectiveness should be suspected if an infant rarely reacts socially, cries, or smiles, is very inactive and is uninterested in toys or in handling objects which

[8] A. Bleyer, "Role of Advanced Maternal Age in Causing Mongolism: Study of 2,822 Cases," *Amer. J. Dis. Child.*, 55 (Jan., 1938), 79–92.

[9] L. S. Penrose, *Mental Defect* (New York, Farrar and Rinehart, 1934), 126–128.

ADJUSTMENT OF THE ATYPICAL PERSON

most babies of the same age take delight in. Mental defectiveness is also indicated in lack of motor development, such as serious retardation in age of supporting head and trunk, walking, and particularly talking.

The psychologist diagnoses feeblemindedness in infancy by administering tests which have been standardized on a random or systematic sampling of children. He seldom makes a final diagnosis on only one test. Ideally, tests should be repeated at intervals, and the scores plotted on a graph. Since rate of development in infancy does not follow a straight line, such a graph is extremely important. It may happen, for example, that the first time the child is tested, he is at a stage in which his growth is temporarily slowed down. The next time he is tested, he may be going through a stage in which his growth is temporarily accelerated. By giving at least three tests and plotting the developmental quotients on a graph, discrepancies in the results are readily detected. The most accurate developmental quotient can be obtained by drawing a straight line which most nearly connects the three points on the graph. Prognosis of future development should be made from this line, even though its numerical value may be different from that obtained from any one of the tests. In this way, idiosyncracies in growth pattern as well as unnoticed and temporary environmental factors which affect test performance are compensated for. In spite of the typical textbook statement that development is gradual and not saltatory, experienced examiners often find discrepancies in test results on two occasions. These discrepancies rarely indicate a real change in developmental or intelligence quotient, but are the result of rhythmical changes in rate or pattern of growth and are artefacts resulting from unavoidable difficulties in testing young children. One thirteen-month-old child, for example, was tested for placement, and received a Cattell IQ of 94. By evening of the day of testing, the child had a very high temperature and other symptoms of a respiratory infection, symptoms which were not apparent at the time of testing in the morning. The only symptoms present in the morning were a lackadaisical attitude toward the test materials and a rather stolid indifference to the examiner and foster mother. Since these symptoms are characteristic of retarded children, an incorrect diagnosis might easily have been made. Two months later, when the child was in good health, he tested at IQ 117. The reported difference in IQ's is, of course, spurious (false). It would seem logical, in such a case, to accept the second rating since it is improbable that a child could surpass himself. Better still, however, would be to give a third test, and average the ratings on the second and third. The results from the first test should be discarded because of the evidence that the child was probably ill at the time of testing.

D. Treatment of Feeblemindedness

There is no cure for genuine feeblemindedness. Cases of spurious feeblemindedness, resulting from undiagnosed sensory defects or from exceptional deprivation of environmental stimuli, have been reported. These cases are extremely rare. Such pseudo-feeblemindedness can be corrected by appropriate modifications of the environment. True feeblemindedness does not respond to treatment.

In general, the IQ's of feebleminded children tend to decline with age. There is some evidence, however, that feebleminded children placed in superior environments and given special education do not suffer a decrease in IQ, and may, on occasion, even improve.

The feebleminded child, if he is not an idiot, can learn, and educational experiences commensurate with his mental ability should be provided. An imbecile, with patience and with continuous supervision and reminding, can be trained in appropriate toilet habits. He can also learn to wash, clothe and feed himself and perform simple tasks. There are fewer low-grade mental defectives in the upper than in the lower age levels, since their life span is less than that of normal people.

Idiots and imbeciles are best cared for in institutions. Under conditions of modern city life, it is often impossible to care for a moron at home since constant vigilance is usually impossible. By the age of puberty, at least, special arrangements must be made for the supervision of such children at all times. Feebleminded girls often become pregnant after this age, and feebleminded boys are prone to commit crimes against property or sex crimes. Feebleminded persons must be prevented from marrying, since they are incapable of properly rearing children.

ADJUSTMENT OF THE ATYPICAL PERSON

E. Helping Parents to Accept the Fact of Feeblemindedness

Parents find it extremely difficult to accept the fact that their child is feebleminded. If the news is broken to them too suddenly or without regard for their feelings, they may never get over the shock. Even when a parent understands the diagnosis and accepts it intellectually, his feelings and emotions often rebel. Because the feebleminded child does learn, even though slowly, the parent wishfully thinks that the child will eventually become normal. This hope is tenaciously retained in spite of expert judgment to the contrary. Sometimes the resources of an entire family are squandered on quacks who minister to the parents' need to feel that their defective child will be cured. It is, therefore, no kindness to encourage parents in the hope that their child will be normal. Since this is a situation which cannot be remedied, parents must be helped to accept it and to make plans accordingly.

The inadequacy of simply explaining the condition to the parents without giving the parents an emotional outlet is illustrated in an excerpt from Carl Rogers, *Counseling and Psychotherapy*, which reports an interview with the mother of a thirteen-year-old son who is mentally defective. In spite of the fact that a number of professional workers have carefully explained the situation to her, she has not accepted the fact of her son's defectiveness. The phonographic recording of a portion of the interview with a psychologist illustrates the advantages of non-directive psychotherapy in cases of this type:

Counselor. You feel that the whole thing rests on you, don't you? You've got to make him eat, you've got to make him learn, you've got to make him wear his brace [for a cracked collarbone], and all.
Subject. I don't know. Today, tomorrow, then what? You know, time runs away before you know it. He's grown up, and what can he do? Nothing, absolutely nothing. He tells me he'll be able to—when I say to him, "What's going to happen? You won't be able to read and write," he says, "I'll be able to drive a truck; I can fly an airplane; I can lay linoleum; I can hang window shades." He has an argument for everything to tell me what he can do. I said, "You can't fly an airplane if you can't read and write. There's numbers on the dial," and then I don't know a thing about an airplane to tell him about it.
C. You think that perhaps he can't learn some of those things that you'd like to have him learn.
S. I don't believe that he *can't*. Now, I may be blind from a mother's

point of view; understand, I may be blind, but I don't think so. I think Isaac has a little stubborn streak in him. If I could get to the bottom of that I think that he *could,* but I don't know.

C. But you've tried for quite a few years to make him learn, haven't you?

S. Maybe I haven't tried hard enough.

C. Maybe you've tried too hard.

S. I don't know. I don't know. I went to this baby specialist, and he asked me two questions, and then he said to me, "Well, take him home and let him be," and I said, "If there is something wrong with him, why don't you tell me the truth?" [Voice rises to crescendo.] I'd like to know the truth, then I would know exactly how to go about it and know that I've got to make up my mind, and I'll hire him out for a carpenter or cement mixer or something! Tell me the *truth*—!

C. [Sympathetically] Don't you know the truth already?

S. [Very quietly—very much changed] I don't want to know it. I don't want to believe it. I don't want to know it. [Tears come to her eyes.] [10]

F. Causes of Feeblemindedness

It has been customary to classify all cases of mental deficiency for which no environmental cause could be found as the result of heredity. Many undoubtedly are, but to assert that because many are, all must be, is based upon the logical fallacy of going beyond the data. It would be better, in the face of the inadequate evidence at our disposal, to acknowledge that the cause or causes of mental deficiency are in many cases unknown. The known fact that intelligence is not a unitary genetic trait substantiates this point of view. Until recently the influence of blood incompatibility (Rh-factor) [11] on the fetus was not known. Consequently, cases of feeblemindedness resulting from such incompatibility would have been classified with feeblemindedness of presumably inherited origin.

[10] C. Rogers, *Counseling and Psychotherapy* (New York, Houghton Mifflin Company, 1942), pp. 175–176.

[11] The Rh-blood factor was first discovered in the rhesus monkey and gets its name from the first two letters of *rhesus*. This blood factor is inherited. The dominant gene is designated *Rh;* the recessive gene *rh.* If a person receives the recessive gene from both of his parents, his blood is Rh-negative. If he receives Rh from both of his parents or Rh from one parent and rh from the other, he is Rh-positive. Abnormalities of development may occur when the mother is Rh-negative and the fetus Rh-positive.

VI. THE SLOW LEARNER

Slow learners are children who are below average in intelligence but are not feebleminded. They fall within the IQ range from 70 to 90, and constitute somewhat more than 20 per cent of the school population. These children are able to learn but do not do so as rapidly or attain as high a level of learning as normal children. The school subjects with which they have the most difficulty are those which involve reading or which require reasoning with numbers, words, or other symbols. Slow learners are often socially adjusted and make more progress in manual than in verbal skills. However, the fact that a child is academically incompetent does not mean that he is better equipped for manual or mechanical learning than the normal or gifted child. Desirable traits are positively correlated as illustrated by the fact that intelligence and scores on the Stenquist Mechanical Aptitude Test correlate 0.25. The slow learner, however, is often relatively better in manual and mechanical tasks than in the more intellectual activities, and for this reason is willing to give more time and effort to the former than to the latter type of learning.

Slow children often become emotionally insecure or anxious because they cannot keep up with the requirements of the ordinary classroom. Special classes, adapted to their needs, sometimes help them to make a satisfactory adjustment.

The education of the retarded child should be based upon the prediction of the ultimate mental age which he will attain. In general, he will learn more by direct experience than by verbal teaching. Excessive time should not be spent on developing skills or acquiring information which are valuable only after a degree of mastery has been attained of which he is incapable. Spelling, arithmetic, and to a lesser extent, reading, often fall into this category. The retarded child should first of all be taught those things (1) which are necessary to his health (bodily, mentally, and spiritually), (2) which will enable him to earn a living, and (3) which will help him to make wholesome social adjustments.

VII. LEFT-HANDEDNESS

Left-handedness is usually considered to be a handicap, although many left-handed adults claim that it is not. In diagnosing left-handedness, it is usually not sufficient to observe the hand with which a child writes. He may be left-handed in writing but right-handed in many other activities, so it is well to make a diagnosis of sidedness in general, not just handedness. By giving a child tasks such as putting on overshoes, combing his hair, getting into a coat, riding a bicycle, dealing out playing cards, or pitching a ball, it is possible to work out a measure of the general degree of left- or right-sidedness. Right- or left-eyedness is tested by means of a manoptoscope, a funnel-like tube. You test eyedness by asking the child to sight an object which you hold in front of you by looking through the tube with both eyes, with the large opening next to him. As you observe the child's eyes through the narrow end of the tube you will see that only one eye is really doing the sighting. This is the dominant eye.

There are several theories to account for the emergence of a preferred hand. These include (1) the hereditary predisposition to functional dominance of one hemisphere of the brain; (2) prenatal position, that is, the hand which is most free to move becomes the preferred hand; and (3) environmental pressure.

There is considerable evidence that environmental pressure alone cannot account for the emergence of handedness. White rats, for example, show a decided preference for using either the right or left paw in securing wheat germ from a narrow-necked bottle. People of all races and people living under widely different environmental conditions are predominantly right-handed. During the first 17 months of life, infants display consistent differences in the spontaneous activity of the two hands. These differences are positively related to spontaneous movements of the head, legs, and trunk. We conclude that hand preference is just one aspect of a general "sidedness" which results from the dominance of one hemisphere of the brain over the other.[12]

Left-handedness is related to school adjustment, but not to general intelligence or physical status. It is often associated with difficulties in reading and writing. The custom of reading from the left to the right of a line is easier for the right-eyed than for the left-eyed person. Left-eyed children show a greater tendency

---

[12] M. Giesecke, *The Genesis of Hand Preference*, Monog. of the Soc. for Res. in Child Development (National Research Council, 1936), Vol. I, No. 5.

than right-eyed children to reverse letters, letter pairs, and letter sequence in reading.

Mirror writing, which is a normal accompaniment of the early writing efforts of many children, tends to persist much longer in the left-handed than in the right-handed child. It is usually related to poor visual motor imagery.

VIII. SPEECH DEFECTS

Two of the most serious speech defects are stammering and stuttering. Stammering differs from stuttering in that there is no repetition of sounds but only a persistent blocking which makes it impossible to articulate speech sounds. Stuttering is characterized by a repetition of sounds, words, or phrases and is often accompanied by grimaces and general muscle tension.

In more than two-thirds of the cases, stuttering originates before the sixth year. It is more prevalent in boys than in girls, and is almost invariably accompanied by emotional disturbance. A number of theories has been advanced as to the origin of stuttering. One theory, which has been almost thoroughly discredited, is that stuttering results from a disturbance of the peripheral speech mechanism. Another point of view which leads to a very different kind of therapy is that stuttering is the result of emotional conflict. A third view, which recognizes the presence of psychological factors, attributes stuttering to a structural abnormality in the language centers of the brain. According to this theory, people with brain defects do not necessarily develop speech disorders, but they are more likely than people with normally structured brains to break down under emotional stress. A fourth theory is that speech disorders result from a lack of brain dominance or from a disturbance of dominance caused by forcing a child to write with his non-preferred hand.[13]

Johnson[14] made a study of 46 stuttering children, using as a control group 46 non-stuttering children equated for age, sex, and intelligence. The stutterers could not be differentiated from

---

[13] S. T. Orton, *Reading, Writing and Speech Problems of Children* (New York, W. W. Norton & Company, Inc., 1937); and L. Travis, *Speech Pathology* (New York, D. Appleton–Century Company, Inc., 1931).

[14] Wendell Johnson, "Study of the Onset and Development of Stuttering," *J. Speech Disorders*, 7 (1942), 251–257.

the non-stutterers on the basis of handedness or changes of handedness. Neither were they found to be retarded in development as compared with the non-stutterers. Several observations in particular offer promising leads and need to be investigated further: (1) All of the stutterers had begun to stutter at a very early age, but only after they had spent some time during which their speech was apparently normal. (2) The initial diagnosis of stuttering had usually been made by one or both of the parents. (3) The persons making the diagnosis were apparently unfamiliar with the normal hesitations and repetitions characteristic of children's speech, and had therefore misdiagnosed as stuttering what was perfectly normal for the child at that age. (4) Once the children had been "diagnosed" as stutterers, they then began to develop abnormal speech patterns to a marked degree. The implication is that the stuttering children might have remained normal except for the fact that adults began to emphasize the "fact" that they were different, and so created a tension situation around speech functions. There was evidence, too, that the parents of the stutterers not only had perfectionistic standards of speech for their children, but that their standards of behavior in general were too high for children of that age level. These perfectionistic standards extended to table manners, cleanliness, toilet training, and obedience.

Johnson's conclusion that stuttering is a response to diagnosis rather than a cause of diagnosis and results from perfectionistic standards of the parents rather than from something inherently wrong with the child is substantiated by two further lines of evidence: (1) the results of treatment based upon this hypothesis; and (2) the fact that among Indians there are no cases of stuttering; in fact, that Indians do not even have a word for stuttering. Both lines of evidence will be briefly discussed.

Johnson's treatment of stuttering children was directed toward changing the environment and thus indirectly changing the children's evaluations of their speech. In no case was any physical treatment or speech exercise given to the children. Yet, at the end of "treatment" about three out of four of the stuttering children had regained normal speech. This effect was produced by teaching parents and teachers what was happening to the children and why, and by instructing them not to compliment the children on their speech when it was fluent, but to

ADJUSTMENT OF THE ATYPICAL PERSON

compliment them when they deliberately talked non-fluently. Since stutterers, in general, become panicky when their speech is not fluent, their evaluation of fluency has to be changed before they can control the stuttering. Emphasis on speech exercises or upon any technique for increasing fluency, such as instruction to speak slowly, take a deep breath, and the like, only serve to convince the child of what a terrible thing it is not to speak correctly. Techniques directed toward changing this point of view are in the majority of cases successful if begun early enough.

In certain cases, the speech improved when more affectionate relationships were established between parent and child. Parents of stuttering children thus broke down the effects of their hypercritical and disapproving attitudes as previously evidenced by their criticism of normally hesitant speech as abnormal.

The explanation that Johnson gives for the absence of stuttering among the Indians is that their standards of training in general are very lax as compared to those of our culture; and, secondly, that Indian children are not praised or blamed for their speech. In fact, no comments at all are made about their speech. Consequently, they do not become panicky when their speech is not fluent, since they do not learn that non-fluent speech is to be feared and avoided.

IX. WHAT CONSTITUTES A HANDICAP?

Generally speaking, anything that is common to all normal men, either in the way of physical or mental endowment, social advantages, such as a modicum of this world's goods or an intact family, is looked upon as good. Anyone who is deprived of these things is said to be handicapped or placed at a disadvantage. Yet this notion, like other popularly accepted ideas, needs to be subjected to critical scrutiny.

Everything that happens to a human being occurs within a psychological framework of meaning. It becomes an advantage or a disadvantage depending upon the evaluation he places upon it. A crippled arm may be a painful limitation to a boy who gets almost all of his prestige with the group through excelling in athletic stunts. But to the boy who has no skill and is constantly being ridiculed for his clumsiness, a crippled arm may furnish a plausible excuse for not engaging in sports and subjecting himself to ridicule. It is often possible for an individual to turn a "handicap" into an asset for personality growth if he receives adequate help and guidance.

This completes our general discussion of human activity and adjustment. In the next three chapters we shall trace the psychological development of the individual from infancy to maturity as a preparation for our later discussion of the mature personality.

SUGGESTED READING

BALDWIN, M., "The Road of Silence," *Atlantic Monthly*, 120 (1917), 731–734.

CARLSON, E. R., *Born That Way* (New York, John Day Company, 1941).

JOHNSON, WENDELL, *Because I Stutter* (New York, D. Appleton–Century Company, Inc., 1930).

KELLER, HELEN, *The Story of My Life* (New York, Doubleday, Page and Co., 1905).

PART VI

Stages of Growth and Development

There are several stages on the way to maturity: intra-uterine stage, infancy, middle childhood, preadolescence, and adolescence. Typically, in our culture, preadolescent children reject members of the opposite sex. During adolescence they are attracted to each other.

XVI

The Psychology of Development: Infancy and Early Childhood

'Issues from the hand of God, the simple soul'
To a flat world of changing lights and noise,
To light, dark, dry or damp, chilly or warm;
Moving between the legs of tables and of chairs,
Rising or falling, grasping at kisses and toys,
Advancing boldly, sudden to take alarm,
Retreating to the corner of arm and knee,
Eager to be reassured, taking pleasure
In the fragrant brilliance of the Christmas tree, ...
—T. S. ELIOT [1]

I. PERIOD OF INFANCY

All aspects of a child's growth are interrelated; and his development at any moment in time is more than the sum of discrete or separate aspects of growth. We will probably be closer to the truth if we refer to the growth of the "whole" child as the "product" rather than the "sum" of his various dimensions of growth. These dimensions include (1) sensory reactions, (2) reflexes, (3) motor abilities, (4) gross bodily development, (5) social reactions, (6) emotional behavior, and (7) intellectual development. Growth in any one of these dimensions overlaps and influences the others. The use of language, for example, is at once a function of social and of intellectual development. Language development is influenced, too, by both emotional maturity and motor competence. For the sake of clarity, however, each dimension of growth will be considered separately.

A. Sensory Reactions

Since all knowledge in man comes through the senses, there is a close relationship, in early life at least, between sensory and

[1] T. S. Eliot, "Animula," *Collected Poems: 1909–1935* (New York, Harcourt, Brace, & Company, Inc., 1936), p. 129.

mental development. The way in which the senses function in the infant and young child will be presented briefly.

1. *Vision and hearing.* The newborn infant (neonate) is sensitive to visual stimuli, but probably does not actually "see." The ability to see requires more than a mere awareness of a light stimulus impinging upon the retina. It involves the capacity to discriminate between different hues, as determined by different wave lengths of light stimuli. It also requires the ability to bring objects to a focus upon the retina, an ability which the neonate lacks.

There is no unequivocal evidence at the present time that neonates can discriminate different wave lengths or stimuli of different complexity. Nor is there clear-cut evidence that they exhibit the Purkinje phenomenon after dark adaptation. The shift in brightness after dark adaptation in which blue becomes relatively more bright, for example, and red relatively less bright is apparently absent in the neonate as it is in totally color-blind adults.

The neonate's reaction to visual stimuli depends upon the intensity and duration of such stimuli. If the stimuli presented are of adequate strength and duration, he may exhibit any one of the following reflexes:

    a. Pupillary reflex (pupil of eye becomes smaller when intensity of light is increased).
    b. Ocular—neck reflex (the head bends backward when a flash of light is presented).
    c. Circulatory and respiratory reflexes.
    d. Moro and "startle" reflexes.

The neonate is able to hear, and his responses to auditory stimuli are modified by the intensity and duration of such stimuli. He does not, however, respond differently to different pitches or to stimuli of varying complexity. He may respond to sound, as he does to light, by changes in circulation and respiration, or by the Moro or "startle" reflex. He may show eyelid reflexes, and, if the stimuli continue for a long time, he will probably become less active than if the stimuli were discontinued.

After the first month of life, the infant develops certain selective "interests" in sense stimuli. At six weeks, for example, since he can only perform one action at a time, he will listen to a bell in preference to looking at yellow wool. At the end of the second month he will turn his head toward a sound stimulus, and by the end of the third month he will be able to distinguish different acoustical stimuli. At this time he is at the peak of acoustical "interest," whereas in the fourth month he is primarily interested in visual stimuli. Grasping "interests" begin in the sixth month and culminate somewhere between the eighth and ninth month. During the sixth month, for example, most infants will not be content with listening to the bell or looking at the wool, but will grasp at both. Near the end of the first year of life, the child will again show an interest in sensory stimuli but in a different way. At this stage he is no longer interested in the raw materials of life as such but in combinations of stimuli. Gradually he observes the shapes of pictures in connection with their colors, as shown by his tendency to trace with his fingers the lines enclosing geometrical forms. Still later, after about the second half of the second year, he will see a picture as a picture and will react to rhythms and melodies as such, rather than to isolated acoustical stimuli.[2]

2. *Smell and taste.* There is some evidence that neonates react to odors, but it is not conclusive. Though neonates do react vigorously when ammonia or acetic acid is placed near their nostrils, it is impossible to tell whether they are responding to the odors as such or to pain.

A baby can be trained by the seventh or eighth month to control his breathing in such a way as to perceive odors more intensely. At this age, and for some months later, odors which are unpleasant to the adult are apparently not disagreeable to the child.

The newborn infant appears to differentiate several different tastes. The sucking response is eliminated by a salt solution but is stimulated and maintained by a sugar solution. Bitter solutions seldom elicit sucking but are the occasion of facial expressions of "displeasure." Acid solutions stimulate sucking but to a lesser extent than sugar solutions. As the child grows older his sucking reactions to sugar increase. By the end of a few months he can discriminate all four of the basic tastes: salt, sweet, sour, and bitter.

Tastes, like odors, may be pleasant to the infant though un-

[2] C. Bühler, *Testing Children's Development* (London, George Allen and Unwin, Ltd., 1935).

pleasant to the adult. This makes it possible to give the child foods of high nutritive value without causing him to reject them because of taste.

3. *Temperature and pain.* At birth an infant's senses of temperature and pain are not well developed. His response to temperature varies with the part of the body stimulated. His general activity level is influenced by the outside temperature; that is, it increases when this temperature goes below his body temperature.

The newborn infant does not show the acute symptoms of pain which an adult does when undergoing a surgical operation, even when an anesthetic is not used. This lack of outward expression of pain may reflect a genuine insensitivity of the sense receptors to pain. Or, it may be that the adult's greater expression of pain results not so much from greater sensitivity as from the fears and tensions resulting from past experience with pain, and these the neonate has not had.

4. *The other senses.* The neonate is very sensitive to contact stimuli. He also demonstrates kinesthetic sensitivity and sensitivity to changes in position. His general, over-all activity is largely the result of internal organic stimuli.

B. Reflexes

A *reflex* is commonly defined as a prompt, unlearned, involuntary and therefore predictable response to a stimulus. This definition, implying as it does that a reflex is a highly specific and invariable reaction, is a little misleading in the case of the newborn. Most reflexes in the neonate are somewhat variable at first, although they quickly tend to become more specific. Sucking, for example, may at first be elicited by such varied stimuli as stroking the cheek, touching the lips, or pinching the large toe. As the infant grows older, the stimuli which evoke sucking movements become more specific. A similar growth pattern is followed by the *plantar reflex*, which is elicited by stroking the sole of the infant's foot along the median line from toes to heel.[3] In the newborn, a wide variety of responses to such stimulation, including extension of toes, fanning of toes, and flexion of toes

---

[3] K. C. Pratt, "Generalization and Specificity of the Plantar Responses in Newborn Infants. The Reflexogenous Zone: I. Differential Sensitivity and Effector-segment Participation According to the Area of Stimulation," *J. Gen. Psychol.*, 44 (1934), 365–400.

or of the foot occurs. Although more or less clearly defined reflexes are present in the newborn, generalized or "mass activity" is characteristic of this period. Gradually more specialized movements individuate from such mass activity.

The *Moro embracing reflex* is also present at birth and disappears in most infants within a few months. When the infant is stimulated by a loud noise, the arms reflexly extend out at right angles to the trunk, the trunk arches backward, the head is extended, and the fingers are extended and spread.

The *startle reflex,* like the Moro reflex, is elicited by a loud sound. Some psychologists claim that this reflex appears only when the Moro reflex has disappeared. Others,[4] however, who have made thorough studies of these patterns by means of high-speed motion picture analysis claim that the two reflexes exist side by side. The difference in the two patterns is schematically shown in Figure 65.

The *palmar* or *grasping reflex,* present at birth, is elicted by placing a sufficiently small object in the infant's palm. Many babies are able to support their entire weight for a short time while reflexly grasping a rod or an adult's fingers placed in their two hands. Reflex grasping differs from voluntary grasping in that it is performed entirely by the fingers without the assistance of the thumbs. The grasping reflex disappears in most infants after the fourth month and is later replaced by the voluntary act of grasping. The difference between reflexive and voluntary grasping is shown in Figure 66.

The fact that certain reflexes appear at birth and later disappear led G. Stanley Hall to formulate his famous "recapitulation theory." Hall, accepting the evolutionary theory of man's development, assumed that some of these reflexes had, in the history of the race, an important survival value. Thus, the grasping reflex, which enables the neonate to support his entire weight, was supposedly of value at an earlier stage of evolution when the race lived in trees. The fact that a neonate, when placed prone in water, will make coördinated swimming movements, as Hall erroneously thought, was looked upon as an atavistic survival of a response pattern which was biologically important at an earlier stage of racial development. According to the *recapitulation*

[4] C. Landis and W. A. Hunt, *The Startle Pattern* (New York, Farrar and Rinehart, 1939).

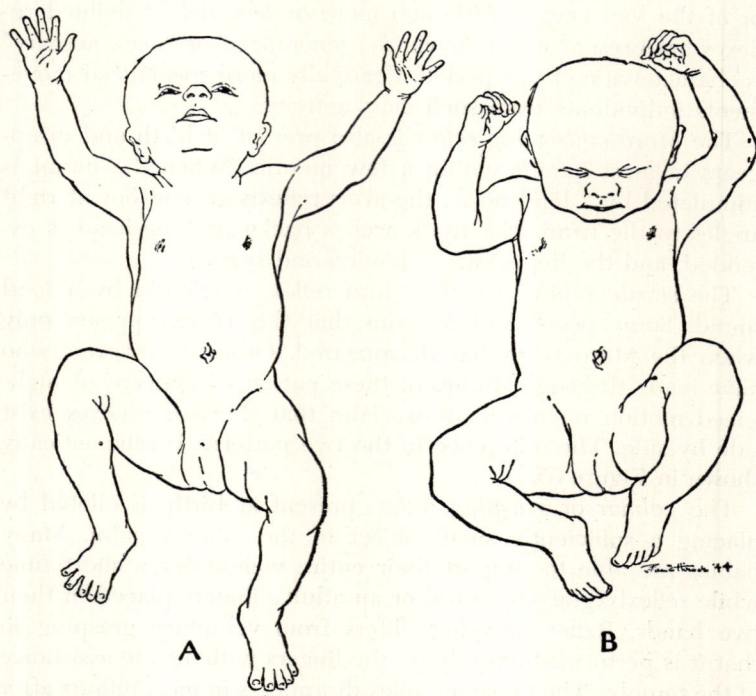

Fig. 65. Difference Between Moro Reflex (*A*) and Startle Pattern (*B*) in Infancy. [Reproduced by permission from F. L. Goodenough, *Developmental Psychology*, 2nd ed. (New York, Appleton-Century-Crofts, Inc., 1945), p. 193.]

theory, every individual in his development goes through, or re capitulates, all of the stages which the species has gone through in its long developmental history. As Hall put it, "Ontogeny recapitulates phylogeny." *Ontogeny* means the "history of the individual," and *phylogeny* means the "history of the race." Another form which this theory took was the "culture epoch theory." According to this theory, every human being in his individual development passes through all of the stages through which the race has gone in its social and cultural development. The fact that children enjoy chasing small animals, for example, was supposedly a carry-over from an historical period in which the race survived by hunting. Although the "recapitulation" and the "culture epoch" theories have now been thoroughly discredited,

INFANCY AND EARLY CHILDHOOD 421

they did for a time exercise an influence over educational theory and practice.

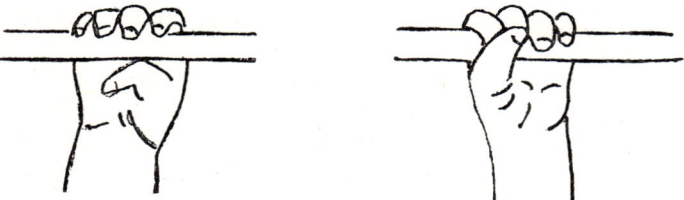

Fig. 66. Grasping Reflex of the Neonate Compared to Voluntary Grasping in the Older Infant.

C. Motor and Manipulative Development

1. *Characteristics of motor behavior during the first two years of life.* During the first three months, the movements of the child slow down. This is particularly true during the first ten days. From a comparison of the movements of neonates on the first day and on the tenth day of life, it appears that the number of movements is considerably less on the tenth day.[5]

There are great individual differences in the activity of infants from the first day of life. These differences are manifested even though environmental conditions, outside of the child's own body, are the same for all infants. The most active baby, one investigator found, was 290 times as active as the least active baby on the first day of life. Such differences appearing at birth cannot be attributed to differences in stimulation and in culture pattern. They suggest that temperament is constitutionally "determined" and is not the result of learning.

Because the newborn infant is active much of the time, even in the absence of external stimuli, his movements have sometimes been called "random." This term is no longer used because it is now evident that his movements are definitely patterned. The first movements tend to be over-all, "generalized" in nature; that is, they involve most of the body. Gradually, as the baby matures, movements become more "specific" and involve smaller segments of the body. Similar trends in development are seen in animals.

---

[5] O. C. Irwin, "The Activities of Newborn Infants," in R. G. Barker, J. S. Kounin, and H. F. Wright (eds.), *Child Behavior and Development* (New York, McGraw-Hill Book Company, Inc., 1943), pp. 29–47.

Coghill [6] has demonstrated that the earliest movements in salamanders are not simple reflexes. They are grosser movements, starting with the head and trunk, and involving the entire body. Gradually more specific movements "individuate" out of this "mass" behavior.

In general, development proceeds from the head to the tail region, and from the center to the periphery of the body. These trends have been summarized in two developmental laws, namely: (1) law of cephalocaudal progression; and (2) law of proximodistal progression. There are a few instances, however, in which the above generalizations do not hold. For example, in the grasping reflex, the distal segments develop earlier than do the proximal segments.

2. *Illustrative sequences of motor behavior.* A study of progression toward walking is pictured in Figure 67. The age at which each new type of behavior appears as shown in this graph is the average for the group studied. Individual children may, within limits, vary from these averages and still be normal. These data show that the age at which each aspect of motor development will appear cannot be predicted from the age at which previous aspects have appeared.

3. *Tests of motor and manipulative development.* Tests of motor and manipulative development, as well as of sensory development, have long been used for appraising the developmental status of infants. The common practice of designating such developmental status in terms of intelligence quotients (IQ's), however, is somewhat misleading. Results of baby tests do not correlate very highly with intelligence tests given later in life. For this reason, it is preferable to use Gesell's term *developmental quotient* when referring to the results of infant tests, and to use the term *intelligence quotient* only when the tests used measure "complex" mental functions or "general intelligence."

D. Physical Development and Body Build

1. *Social class.* A comparison of neonates from poverty-stricken environments with those from more favorable environments shows that the former are smaller in all dimensions measured than the

---

[6] G. E. Coghill, *Anatomy and the Problem of Behavior* (New York, The Macmillan Company, 1929).

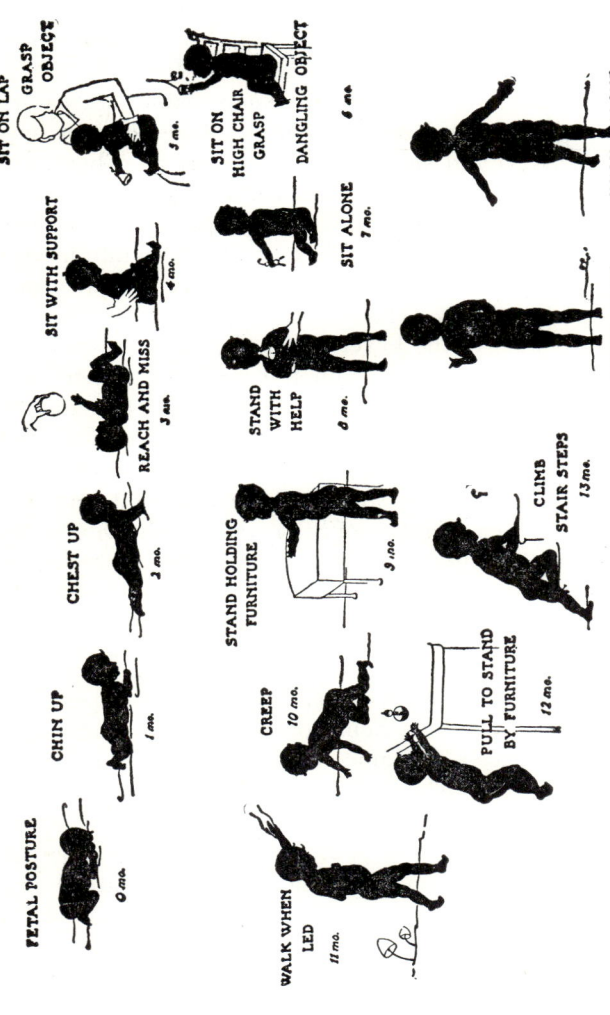

Fig. 67. Motor Sequence Chart (by Mary M. Shirley). [Reproduced by permission from M. L. Faegre and J. E. Anderson, *Child Care and Training* (University of Minnesota Press, 1947), p. 74.]

latter but are similarly proportioned.[7] These babies, however, when put under supervision in a pediatric clinic, gain in height and weight until they resemble children from homes of average socio-economic status. Apparently, physical retardation in height and weight at birth can be compensated for by a favorable postnatal environment.

2. *Racial differences.* On the average, Negro babies are smaller and weigh less than white babies. However, since Negroes have more girls than boys, and since girls weigh less than boys, this observation must be interpreted with caution. Further studies in which sex ratio is controlled may throw light on this subject. The growth of Negro babies is slower than that of white infants. Such differences may be genuine racial differences, or they may be social class differences. The great majority of Negroes in North America belong to the lower social class and are in straitened financial circumstances. Within the white race there is a substantial correlation between socio-economic status and intelligence, and it is probable that the same holds true for other races.

3. *Birth order.* A review of studies of birth weight and gain in weight during the first ten days of life revealed that weight was least for first-born children and that it went up progressively for later-born children.

E. Social Development of Infants

The human being is a social animal from the very beginning of life. The peculiarly human behavior of social smiling occurs in the infant as a primary and unconditioned response at a very early age. A "true" smile is a social response characterized by a sparkling of the eyes and the coördination of eye and mouth muscles, and it is first elicited by the sound or sight of a person. Reflex smiles, in which the mouth alone is activated, are the result of visceral changes in the child's body, such as attacks of colic, or physiological satisfaction following eating, and they are not genuine social responses.

Behaviorists have claimed that the child's basic needs are physical and that all social behavior is learned through "condition-

---

[7] H. Bakwin, R. M. Bakwin, and L. Milgram, "Body Build in Infants: IV. Influence of Retarded Growth," *Am. J. Dis. Child.,* 48 (1934), 1030–1040.

INFANCY AND EARLY CHILDHOOD 425

ing" and is not primary. According to their theory, a child smiles when he obtains food, is changed, or is relieved from any physical distress. Because the satisfaction of bodily needs is accomplished by a person, the response which was originally called forth by food or the removal of distress becomes associated with a person; that is, smiling at the sight or sound of a human being becomes a conditioned reflex. A number of investigations provide evidence that this theory is untenable. Charlotte Bühler, in a penetrating analysis of the behavioristic studies of smiling in infants, distinguishes as we have done between "true" smiles and "reflex" smiles. She writes:

> The first primitive attempts to draw up the corners of the mouth, described by *Preyer* as the sequel to a satisfying meal observed in the newly-born infant, differs radically from the drawing up of the mouth accompanied by a sparkling of the eyes that we can observe as a response to the human voice or glance from the fourth week of life. In descriptions of this nature accuracy is of greatest importance, because the expressions of satisfaction are fundamentally different from those of smiling. The first follows a state of physical satisfaction, the second is primarily the result of the psychological effect of another person. Smiling in response to the touching of the body, tickling, or other kinesthetic or tactile stimuli has not been observed in the newborn child prior to smiling in response to another human being.[8]

Bühler attributes the inability of the Behaviorists to make accurate observations of *psychologically significant* behavior, such as smiling, to the limiting effects of the Behavioristic theory. For the Watsonian Behaviorist, all that the child has with which to begin life are reflexes. Reflexes are by definition *physiological units*. *Psychological units* are much more meaningful. They consist of meaningful performances and achievements which have definite results. The Behaviorist looking for a physiological unit could not, except by accident, discover the psychological meaning of a "true" smile.

Bühler[9] has also studied the behavior of infants when first placed in a crib with another infant. She found that from about six months on most normal babies become socially active. Her

---
[8] C. Bühler, *From Birth to Maturity* (London, Kegan Paul, Trench, Trubner and Company, Ltd., 1937), p. 218.
[9] C. Bühler, "Personality Types Based on Experiments with Children," *Ninth International Congress of Psychology*, Proceedings and Papers (Princeton, N.J., The Psychological Review Co., 1930), pp. 100–102.

observations led her to distinguish three different patterns of initial reaction to another infant, namely:

1. *The socially blind child.* This infant is not influenced at all by the presence of the other baby. He makes no attempt to stimulate the other baby and, judging from his behavior, does not even see the other child.

2. *The socially dependent child.* Bühler distinguishes two very different patterns of behavior under this classification, namely:

  a. The overwhelmed or timid child. This child is so overcome by the presence of another infant that he stops everything that he is doing. He makes no attempt to touch or stimulate the other child in any way.

  b. The "tyrant." This child grabs all of the toys for himself and appears to be tremendously stimulated by the presence of the other infant. He makes no attempt to touch the other child or to offer him a toy.

3. *The socially independent child.* This child recognizes the presence of the other baby and attempts to make physical contact or offers a toy. If the other infant does not respond, however, the socially independent child will play by himself as before. This pattern of behavior is the most mature of the three. In the words of Bühler:

The social blindness, the social dependency, and independency mark three steps of development . . . for the being unorientated to the social object is the most primitive state, the being in but not master of the social situation is the second stage, and the being orientated and mastering the situation is a third stage of development.[10]

Nevertheless, the "three attitudes are types in so far as we seem to be born with the disposition more in one direction than in the others." [11] Bühler, of course, recognized that "As always in speaking of types, a concrete individual represents it only to a certain extent. The type is an abstraction to which concrete individuals approach." [12]

In the second year of life, the child becomes more independent and begins to demonstrate will. His relations with other people become more complicated. At this age the child begins to show intense emotional behavior. Often he will cling to his mother and undergo severe punishment rather than release her. He also reacts definitely with antipathy toward certain people. Often the antipathy is shown toward his father. Freud calls this situation

[10] *Ibid.*, p. 101.
[11] *Ibid.*, p. 102.
[12] *Ibid.*, p. 101.

the "Œdipus complex" and claims that it is most prevalent from ages two to four. According to Freud's theory, the small boy loves his mother and resents his father; in fact, he wants to take the place of his father. While there are serious objections to Freud's interpretation, the type of behavior upon which it is based is frequently observed in young children.

Beginning in the second year of life, and correlated with the mental development taking place at this age, a period of simple resistance occurs. The child learns that he can disobey and he uses this learning on every possible occasion. A psychologist reports that his young son marched over to his grandmother's house one morning and announced, "I won't!" His grandmother had not yet asked him to do anything, but in case she should, the child had made it quite clear what position he would take. This simple resistance is a normal developmental stage which reaches its peak shortly before the age of three years. Parents should not worry about children who are going through this phase of development, but should, rather, worry about the child who shows no such negativism. The latter is more likely to be retarded or to lack initiative.

As the child matures during the second year of life he begins to plan programs of action for himself, the precise nature of which is usually not recognized by adults. Interference with these programs meets with resistance. When the interference is such that the child cannot cope with the situation, his whole behavior is greatly disturbed. He may strike at the person who is interfering with him. He may shriek or sob violently, or show other symptoms of "temper tantrums." Such a tantrum, however, should not at this age and under such circumstances be called neurotic or problem behavior. It differs from neurotic behavior in that it is not directed at a person nor calculated to influence a person. Moreover, it is a temporary condition and not an attitude of hostility. It is simply an expression of overwhelming helplessness in the face of an intolerable situation. Some European psychologists label this specific pattern a "catastrophe reaction." This term was taken from Goldstein's writings in which he described similar behavior in adults who have suffered brain injuries and are confronted with tasks to which they are not equal.[13]

[13] K. Goldstein, *After-effects of Brain Injuries in War* (New York, Grune & Stratton, Inc., 1942).

F. Emotional Development in Infancy

Young infants differ just as much in emotional responses as they do in motor behavior. Observation [14] of infants from the second to the twelfth month revealed that many of them could be classified into three groups, as follows: (1) those who laughed or smiled easily and often; (2) those who cried or were sober; and (3) those who varied from smiling to sober. Infants classified into any of the above three groups remained true to type throughout the entire study. Consistent patterns of crying behavior have been found in observing the same children from month to month. These results suggest the presence of a constitutional factor in emotional behavior.

Watson,[15] in his pioneer study of emotions in infants, claimed that only three patterns of emotion were innate: rage, fear, and love. He also claimed that the stimuli giving rise to each of these emotions was highly specific for that particular reaction pattern. For example, fear was originally elicited by only two stimuli, a loud noise or sudden removal of support. By simultaneously presenting other stimuli with these two, fear patterns became associated with or "conditioned" to other stimuli which originally did not evoke them. More recent studies, however, have given positive evidence that other fears appear spontaneously in infants and young children even when the possibility of learning through "conditioning" has been ruled out. Moreover, more recent evidence [16] indicates that well-integrated and coördinated responses such as fear and rage are not present at birth. Watson claimed that the infant showed rage by screaming, crying, stiffening, slashing or striking with arms and hands and holding his breath. Other investigators,[17] however, failed to corroborate Watson's claim when they repeated his experiment. They found, upon restraining the infant's arms, that in most instances no response

[14] R. W Washburn, "A Study of the Smiling and Laughing of Infants in the First Year of Life," *Genet. Psychol. Monogr.*, 6 (1929), 397–539.

[15] J. B. Watson and J. J. B. Morgan, "Emotional Reactions and Psychological Experimentation," *Amer. J. Psychol.*, 28 (1917), 163–174.

[16] K. C. Pratt, A. K. Nelson, and K. H. Sun, "The Behavior of the Newborn Infant," *Ohio State Univ. Studies, Contributions to Psychology*, 10 (1930).

[17] J. H. Taylor, "Innate Emotional Responses in Infants," *Ohio State Univ. Studies, Contributions to Psychology*, 12 (1934), 68–81.

followed. Sometimes restraint had a quieting effect upon the infant. It is possible that Watson used more intense and prolonged stimulation than did the other investigators.

Fear, according to Watson,[18] was shown by a "sudden catching of the breath, clutching randomly with the hands (the grasping reflex invariably appearing when the child is dropped), sudden closing of the eyelids, puckering of the lips, then crying." This response pattern, originally elicited only by the two stimuli described above, could be elicited by other stimuli through "conditioning." Fear, as well as rage and love (the latter consisting of "cessation of crying, smiling, attempts at gurgling and cooing, released by stimulation of some erogenous zone, tickling, shaking, gentle rocking, patting and turning upon the stomach across the attendant's knee"), Watson concluded, were the only innate emotional response patterns. This does not necessarily follow, however, even if it were true that these three specific patterns, and only these, were clearly present at birth. It is now generally agreed that a response may be innate even if it does not appear at birth. Such responses occur only when sufficient maturation has taken place. Sexual responses, for which the maturational period is very long, fall into this category.

Watson's contentions were most tellingly discredited as a result of research using a series of motion pictures of emotional responses in infants.[19] When these were shown to observers who had had experience in studying infant behavior and who were asked to identify the emotions which the infants seemed to be experiencing, the observers showed little agreement in labeling the emotional patterns displayed by the infants. As a result, psychologists no longer refer to "emotions" in describing the behavior of the newborn infant. For the most part, they now agree that neonates do not show differentiated emotional responses. They show, rather, a general agitation or excitement from which specific emotions gradually differentiate. In this respect emotional

[18] *Ibid.*
[19] M. Sherman, "The Differentiation of Emotional Responses in Infants: I. Judgments of Emotional Responses from Motion Picture Views and from Actual Observation," *J. Comp. Psychol.*, 7 (1927), 265–284; and "The Differentiation of Emotional Responses in Infants: II. The Ability of Observers to Judge the Emotional Characteristics of the Crying of Infants, and of the Voice of an Adult," *op. cit.*, 385–394.

behavior exhibits a developmental trend similar to that of motor development. The development of fear behavior may be summarized as follows:

The arousal of fear depends not only upon situational changes, but also upon the individual's general level of development. With a young infant, perhaps the only changes which are fear-producing are those which substitute loud sounds for quiet, pain for comfort, or loss of support for a previous state of bodily balance. As a child develops, his intelligence innately matures, and his perceptions become enriched through experience. New things startle him because of his keener perception of the fact that they are new and unusual.[20]

G. Intellectual Development in Infancy

Tests of infant intelligence are of value in determining normality and are useful in selecting babies for placement in foster homes. However, the fact that these tests do not correlate highly with linguistic tests given later in life suggests that the results should be interpreted very cautiously. Some people claim that intelligence is essentially the ability to grasp relationships and that the first clear-cut evidence of this ability does not appear until the average age of eleven months. Therefore, tests given before that age cannot properly be called intelligence tests.

II. SEX DIFFERENCES

Sex differences in many characteristics are already present at birth. At birth, boys exceed girls in both height and weight. Girls, however, are superior to boys in skeletal development, a superiority which increases at a fairly steady rate until growth is completed. Male neonates are more reactive to stimulation than girls. Boys are larger than girls, on the average, in all body measurements.

Sex differences are present even before birth. Although the ratio differs with race, there is a consistent excess of male over female births. However, the survival ability of females is considerably greater than it is for males. For still-births, the ratio is about 130 or 135 males to every 100 females. For miscarriages

[20] M. C. Jones and B. S. Burks, *Personality Development in Childhood, a Survey of Problems, Methods, and Experimental Findings* (Washington, D.C.: Soc. for Res. in Child Development, National Research Council, 1936), p. 9. Quoted from H. E. and M. C. Jones, "A Study of Fear," *Childhood Educ.*, 5 (1928), 136–143.

INFANCY AND EARLY CHILDHOOD 431

the ratio is about two males to one female. Girl babies are also more resistant to infectious diseases than are boys. Mortality statistics of the United States show that for seventeen of the eighteen foremost causes of death during the first year of life, the mortality sex ratio is significantly lower for girls.

III. TRAINING AND PERSONALITY DEVELOPMENT

Each child is an individual who differs from everyone else. He has his own particular rate and pattern of growth. Training in the basic habits of bowel and bladder control must be based upon a study of the individual child to be trained. There is an optimal time for introducing such training. Premature training as well as delayed training is detrimental.

Training in proper toilet habits must be conducted in such a way that the child does not feel that he is being deprived of something pleasant. The acquisition of such habits is, of course, a marked advantage for the child. He is no longer a slave to his physiological functions. He does not suffer the discomfort of wetness. With proper encouragement he will be only too willing to coöperate in the establishment of such habits. Control of the muscles used in elimination is a difficult task to learn. It involves many failures along the way. Even when the habit appears to be well established, it may break down again under a slight environmental change. "Failures" may be humiliating to a child; they may be a threat to his security, for he fears the loss of his mother's love. Faulty training appears to retard or distort the personality development of the child.

IV. FUNDAMENTAL NEEDS OF THE YOUNG CHILD

The physiological and psychological needs of the young child are very closely related. It has long been known, for example, that even with the best of nutritional care and isolation against infection, infants develop poorly in institutions. This condition is attributed to the infant's loneliness and emotional deprivation, as illustrated in the case of five hospitalized infants who developed fevers lasting from three to five months.[21] The fever, in each case, fell to normal within a few days after the infants were returned to their homes. There was a significant drop in infant mortality rate at Bellevue Hospital when measures were taken to meet the infants' emotional needs. The infants did considerably better in the hospital when nurses and interns were encouraged to pick them up at every opportunity and parents encouraged to visit them. Unfortunately, in adequate amounts, such "mothering" cannot be given by professional personnel in hospitals or children's institutions because of the time and consequent cost of such service.

We see, then, that the infant and young child needs, above all, a sense of emotional security. This security in early infancy appears to be greatly influenced by the "mothering" which the baby receives and by the regularity with which his needs are met. At this age the whole body of the infant is receptive and needs the warmth and comfort of skin to skin contact with the mother or mother substitute. Breast feeding contributes greatly to the child's feeling of well-being, and the emotional effects of such experience may continue to influence behavior throughout life. When breast feeding is impossible, most psychologists believe that the baby should at least be held in the arms during feeding and be given adequate opportunity to suck. Many cases of prolonged thumb sucking appear to result from inadequate sucking and emotional starvation in early infancy.

Psychologically, an infant should be fed on a "self-demand" schedule, since he is not able at this age to make adequate adjustments to reduced blood sugar. On a self-demand feeding schedule, an infant will gradually set up his own rhythms, but will not develop the tensions which accompany a forced routine. In general, any deprivation is a threat to a small child and a source of anxiety. He needs to be reassured when he is weaned; he needs added affection and reassurance during bladder and bowel training, the time of which must be guided by his own capacity for control. Too early or too rigid toilet training is related to persistent hostilities, infantilisms, insecurities, faulty speech, and other neurotic conditions. The unfortunate personal-

[21] H. Bakwin, "Psychogenic Fever in Infants," *Am. J. Dis. Child.*, 67 (1944), 176–181; and "Loneliness in Infants," *op. cit.*, 63 (1942), p. 30.

ity patterns may persist long after the training has been completed, although they do not invariably persist, as some psychologists seem to imply.

The small child, like all human beings, needs to be treated as an individual, different from every other human being. Parents should realize that their child is a sacred trust from God and that, in the providence of God, their child will work out his salvation in his own way. Parents should study their child and try to help him to fulfill his destiny in the way in which God intends him to fulfill it. They should try to rid themselves of preconceived ideas as to the child's ability, sex, or personal appearance. They must accept their child as he is, on the basis of *who* he is rather than on *what* he can do. Otherwise the child will be insecure and may develop a warped personality by trying to meet unreasonable parental standards.

The life histories of neurotic and psychotic adults are filled with instances of psychological deprivation and traumatic experiences in childhood. It is probable that abnormalities are superimposed upon such a background. Yet it is dangerous and logically unsound to draw generalizations about normal people from a study of the abnormal. No one goes through life without some traumatic experiences. Adolescent diaries and autobiographies written by normal college students contain accounts of traumatic experiences such as are found in the life histories of people who have broken down. Why one person becomes stronger as a result of such experiences while another "gives up" is not always clear. Sometimes the explanation is found in a deep religious faith, but not always. In the light of the evidence now at hand, there is no cause for undue alarm or pessimism when we find a child whose basic emotional and social needs have not been adequately met. An eminent pediatrician, after years of experience with underprivileged children, concludes:

> There is a widespread conviction that psychologic trauma is irreparable and that injuries sustained during infancy and early childhood permanently color the personality. Though this is probably true in some instances, it is an unwarranted generalization based mainly on the clinical observation of patients with severe psychologic trauma and psychiatric disease. The persons who are permanently affected by improper training are those in whom the unfavorable treatment has continued to operate over long periods during childhood and even into

adult life. If the situation is rectified soon enough, there is every reason to believe that the effect on the personality will be without serious consequences in the large majority of instances.[22]

Perhaps it should be added that permanent injuries result not just from unfavorable treatment over a long period of time, but from the combined effect of the entire physical, social, and intellectual context in which the unfavorable treatment occurs.

V. THE PRESCHOOL PERIOD OF DEVELOPMENT

The most rapid period of child growth is the preschool period, and the most important kinds of learning take place at this age. By the time a child has reached school age, his attitudes, social and emotional adjustments, and speech have advanced to such a point that what he learns in school will be considerably influenced by them.

The normal preschool child actively searches out and explores his environment and has a wide range of interests. There are very few objects in his environment to which he reacts negatively. His energy output is extremely high, although there are great individual differences in this respect.

In guiding the development of children at any age, but particularly at the preschool level, emphasis should be placed upon balance. When one aspect of growth is greatly accelerated or retarded at the expense of or to the exclusion of other aspects of growth, great harm may be done to the child's personality.

The preschool child should be encouraged to do things for himself when he shows a readiness to do so. This does not mean that he should be held to rigid and unyielding demands which threaten his security. Usually a child's ability to perform a task, such as hanging up his clothes or putting away his toys, precedes his willingness to take responsibility for these acts.

VI. EMOTIONAL AND SOCIAL DEVELOPMENT OF THE PRESCHOOL CHILD

Bright children develop socially at an earlier age than do average children, and dull children develop at a later age than

[22] R. M. and H. Bakwin, *Psychologic Care During Infancy and Childhood* (New York, D. Appleton–Century Company, Inc., 1942), p. 5.

INFANCY AND EARLY CHILDHOOD

the average. As in motor and intellectual development, there is a definite sequence of social adjustment. Two-year-old children are solitary in their play, although they imitate the behavior of older children. This is true even when there are other children playing in the same room. By the age of three, children will already play with other children and show some beginnings of coöperation with each other. Four-year-olds are greatly influenced by the social group and are very conscious of the opinions of others.

Quarrels are extremely common among children of preschool age, but they last only a short time and are not followed by grudges. These quarrels often originate in conflicts over property. Quarrels are most common among the three-year-old children and are more common among boys than among girls. The child who becomes aggressive at an early age is more likely to be stable in personality than the dependent, unaggressive child.

Sympathetic behavior begins at this age level, but there are great individual differences in its appearance and expression. From the age of three years and up, girls are more sympathetic than boys.

VII. SEX AWARENESS AND INSTRUCTION

The normal child becomes aware of sex differences, in the sense of distinguishing between boys and girls, as early as two or three years of age. He distinguishes, however, upon very superficial bases. A study [23] was made of 128 boys and 72 girls, ranging in age between four and twelve years at the children's Psychiatric Service of the Johns Hopkins Hospital, to determine the development of their sex awareness and sex attitudes. It was found that even the youngest children (four-year-olds) made sex distinctions on the basis of hair style. Distinctions on the basis of clothes were introduced at five years, strength and general body configuration not until eight years, and gait not until nine years. Fundamental distinctions on the basis of actual genital differences are made by very young children only when they have had close contact with other small children of the opposite sex.

[23] J. H. Conn and L. Kanner, "Children's Awareness of Sex Differences," *J. Child Psychiat.*, 1 (1947), 3–57.

Ideally, the child learns sex differences very early in life (preferably before the age of four or five) by observing babies or other small children in his own family. The average child, if handled correctly by his mother or other adults when this discovery is made, accepts sex differences tranquilly and as a matter of course. Sometimes he makes the discovery when his mother is changing the baby. When this happens, the mother should accept his interest and answer his questions without becoming emotionally perturbed. She should allow the small child to observe and, on occasion, to help her to change the baby, without giving the child any reason to feel that his interest is in any way "not nice" or bad. Similarly, if two preschool children suddenly discover their sex differences, the parents may do them untold harm by showing embarrassment, shame, or horror at their interest in each other. They should take this discovery as a matter of course and not hasten to cover up the children in order to prevent further observation.

Small children may also be permitted to see their mother nurse the baby, and the mother should answer their questions about the mammary glands. Too much information should not be given, but only what is necessary to satisfy the child's curiosity. He should never be told that he must not ask such questions, nor must he be given the impression that there is something very mysterious about this subject, since that is the way morbid and pathological attitudes are developed. It is not so important *what* the child is told, although the truth should always be observed, as *how* it is told. The parent must himself have a wholesome attitude toward sex before he can transmit it to his child. The way in which an adult imparts sex information to a child is partly the result of his own emotionalized attitudes. The child senses the adult's attitudes and feelings on the subject regardless of what is said. It is not possible to lie to a child in the emotional field.

It does not seem necessary to tell the preschool child the whole story of procreation, since he will forget it anyway, and will have to be told again after he has reached the age of seven or eight. However, if the story is told simply and unemotionally, with emphasis on the wonderful and beautiful aspects of human procreation, it will do no harm. The following anecdote illustrates a characteristic reaction of preschool children to information of this kind:

INFANCY AND EARLY CHILDHOOD

It was story hour in the nursery school. The children were seated in a circle, and the teacher asked, "Who wants to tell a story?" "I do," responded four-year-old Jack. "I want to tell the story of how I came to be born." The children clapped their hands in joyful anticipation and exclaimed, "Tell us the story of how you came to be born." Only the teacher showed no enthusiasm, since she knew that Jack's mother had instructed him thoroughly in the mysteries of human procreation. Furthermore, she had a roomful of practice teachers and observers to increase her discomfiture. Jack proceeded with his story, leaving out no detail from conception to birth, and holding his audience in spellbound attention. When he finished there was a moment of silence, and then a small girl burst out with, "Fairy tales!" Whereupon, all of the other children also laughed and exclaimed, "Fairy tales!" In a few minutes, Jack himself was exclaiming, "Fairy tales!" To the children, this story was no different from that of Goldilocks or Snow White.[24]

VIII. COMMON BEHAVIOR PROBLEMS OF THE PRESCHOOL PERIOD OF DEVELOPMENT

Among the common behavior problems of preschool children, the following appear to be the most common: (1) eating difficulties, (2) faulty elimination, (3) disobedience, (4) aggressive behavior, (5) thumb sucking, (6) temper tantrums, (7) fear, (8) jealousy, (9) nail biting, and (10) masturbation.

In a study of 252 children and their families, it was found that no normal child during the preschool period escaped what is commonly labeled as "problem behavior."[25] The average number of such problems varied from four to six per child. The fact that fears, temper tantrums, and jealousy occurred in 50 per cent of the children at one age level suggests that such behavior is a normal accompaniment of the tensions of this age and cannot be regarded as symptomatic of neurosis. The children whose physical status was below par tended to have more eating difficulties, elimination problems, nail biting, overdependence and negativism, than did the healthier children. The children who were physically above par, on the other hand, had more problems of thumb sucking, lying, overactivity, and fear. Jealousy and temper tantrums were unrelated to physiological status.

[24] Told by Sister Ann, Director of the Nursery School at The College of St. Catherine.
[25] Jean W. Macfarlane, "Study of Personality Development," in R. G. Barker, J. S. Kounin and H. L. Wright (eds.), *Child Behavior and Development* (New York, McGraw-Hill Book Company, Inc., 1943), 307–328.

IX. LINGUISTIC DEVELOPMENT

Man is the only animal capable of true speech. Psychologically, the use of speech marks the transition from infancy to early childhood. Typically, the child uses only a few words from about ten or twelve to sixteen months of age, and then very rapidly increases his vocabulary in the latter half of his second year. There is a "plateau" in speech development during the time in which the child is learning to walk. At this age, a child can do only one thing at a time, and walking is more important to him than speaking. As soon as walking is well established, the child is again free to acquire language.

Studies of language development show a remarkable similarity from one locality to another even when different languages are used. A study of American children in Iowa yielded almost identical results with those obtained in Geneva.[26] The similarities of development were shown in the fact that, age for age, the average number of words for both localities was the same, and the various parts of speech were given the same relative importance.

The language development of a systematic sampling of 140 children ranging in age from 18 to 54 months was studied by one psychologist.[27] She recorded, for each child, fifty consecutive remarks which they made when they were alone with her. These remarks she analyzed for (1) length of response, (2) parts of speech, and (3) complexity of sentence structure. She found that the average length of sentence increased from 1.2 words at 18 months to 4.6 words by 4.5 years. Newly acquired words were used alone for some time before they were combined in sentences. The first few words were usually nouns in form, but they were often used as verbs. The first combination of words was usually a noun-verb. Only much later did qualifying words, such as adjectives and adverbs, and relational words such as connectives and prepositions appear. Phrases were used only by the most advanced two-year-olds. Ten per cent of the responses of 4.5-year-olds were simple sentences with phrases, 7 per cent were either

---

[26] M. E. Smith, *An Investigation of the Development of the Sentence and the Extent of Vocabulary in Young Children* (University of Iowa, Studies in Child Welfare), Vol. 3, No. 5 (1926).

[27] D. McCarthy, *Language Development of the Preschool Child*, Institute of Child Welfare Monog., No. 2 (Minneapolis, University of Minnesota Press, 1928).

compound or complex sentences, and 6 per cent were elaborated sentences, having either two phrases, two clauses, or a phrase and a clause.

Another investigator found that emotionally-toned responses decrease with age, and more emotional responses are made on the playground than when alone with one adult and with many toys.

Speech difficulties, when they occur, generally originate in the preschool period. Almost anything which interferes greatly with a preschool child's routine or his emotional adjustment may be reflected in his speech, as illustrated by the following example:

A four-year-old boy was placed in a war nursery while his parents worked in a neighboring defense plant. During the first two months his speech and general behavior were normal. His parents were working on the day shift for the first six weeks, after which they were transferred to the swing shift. This made it necessary for the child to sleep at the nursery until his parents called for him at 11:30 P.M. At 11:30 he was awakened, dressed, and taken home in a car, and then put to bed again. After two weeks of this regime, he began to stutter. The stuttering grew progressively worse and he began to show signs of extreme irritability during the hours of play. The nursery school teacher suggested to the parents that, instead of waking the child when they called for him at night, they simply wrap him in a blanket, carry him to the car, and let him sleep on the way home. The parents acquiesced and after they had been carrying out the suggestion for two weeks, the stuttering disappeared and the child's general behavior returned to normal.

Language development is related not only to intelligence, but to sex, socio-economic status, and various environmental factors. Twins, in general, are slower in the acquisition of language than are singletons, and boys are slower in speech development than girls. This initial sex difference persists as children grow older. Tests show that girls have a superior vocabulary to boys at all age levels and make fewer grammatical errors. Children from homes of unskilled laborers are retarded in speech as compared to those from homes of skilled laborers and clerical workers. These latter, in turn, are retarded as compared to children from the professional classes.

X. INTELLECTUAL DEVELOPMENT OF THE PRESCHOOL CHILD

The mental development normal for a child at each of the several preschool ages can be indicated by showing how he is expected to react to a selected number of items on the Stanford-Binet Test, Form L.

Year 2 [0]

1. *Three-hole form board.* The child at this age must place three blocks into insets for a circle, a square, and a triangle, as shown in Figure 68.

Fig. 68. Three-Hole Form Board.

2. *Identifying objects by name.* In this test the child is shown a toy cat, a button, a thimble, and a small cup, engine, and spoon. He is expected to give the correct names for four of these objects.

3. *Identifying parts of the body.* The child is shown a large paper doll and is asked to point to the hair, mouth, ear, and hands. He passes this test at the two-year level if he points to any three of these four body parts.

4. *Block building: tower.* The examiner builds a tower of blocks. The child is asked to build one in imitation of the examiner. The child passes the test if he builds a tower of four or more blocks.

5. *Picture vocabulary.* The child is shown pictures of common objects, as shown in Figure 69. He passes the test if he names at least two pictures of common objects.

6. *Word combinations.* To pass this test the child must combine at least two words, such as *Mama, bye-bye, all gone,* or *see man.*

Year 2 [6]

1. *Identifying objects by use.* Six objects in miniature are shown to the child, as pictured in Figure 70. The child must indicate the use of three of them to pass the test.

INFANCY AND EARLY CHILDHOOD 441

Fig. 69. Picture Vocabulary. [Courtesy Houghton Mifflin Company.]

2. *Naming objects.* The child is presented with a miniature chair, automobile, fork, and a box and a key. He is expected to name four or more of them.

3. *Picture vocabulary.* This is the same test as that used at age two, only the child is now expected to name nine pictures, seven more than he did at age two.

4. *Repeating two digits.* The child is expected to repeat two digits after the examiner pronounces them.

5. *Three-hole form board: rotated.* This is the same form board used in the earlier test. This time the form board is rotated and the child has to turn each of the blocks upside down and insert them to pass the test.

Year 3 °

1. *Stringing beads.* The examiner demonstrates the stringing of

beads. The child is then told to imitate the examiner. He passes the test if he succeeds in stringing four beads within two minutes.

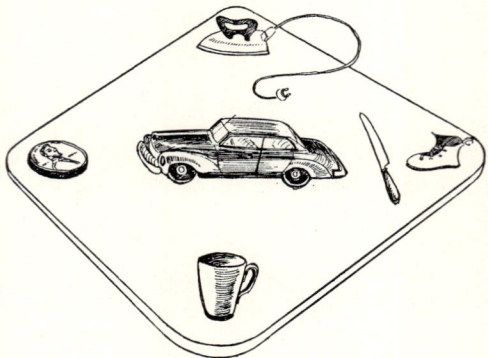

Fig. 70. Objects to Be Identified by Use.

2. *Picture vocabulary.* At this age the child must name twelve of the pictures presented to him.

3. *Comparison of sticks.* Two match sticks of different lengths are placed before the child. He is expected to indicate which of the two sticks is the longer.

4. *Response to pictures.* The child must spontaneously enumerate three objects in a picture.

5. *Comprehension.* The child must answer correctly one of two questions, such as "What must you do when you are thirsty?"

Year 4 [0]

1. *Picture vocabulary.* At this age the child must identify sixteen of the pictures.

2. *Naming objects from memory.* A number of commonplace objects are presented to the child. Then the child is asked to close his eyes. While his eyes are closed, one of the objects is covered. The child is expected to name the object that is covered.

3. *Picture completion.* An incomplete man is presented to the child, as shown in Figure 71. To pass this test the child must add one essential part that is missing.

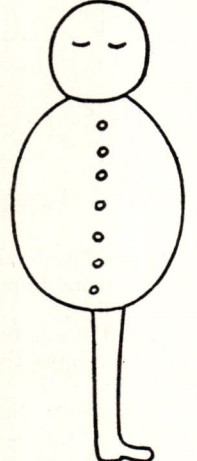

Fig. 71. Picture Completion. [Courtesy Houghton Mifflin Company.]

Year 4 [6]

1. *Esthetic comparison.* The child is asked to indicate which of two pictures of faces is the prettier.

INFANCY AND EARLY CHILDHOOD

2. *Repeating digits.* At this age the child must repeat four digits after the examiner to pass the test.
3. *Pictorial likenesses and differences.* The child is required to indicate likenesses and differences in pictures.
4. *Materials.* The child must tell what two of the following three objects are made of: chair, dress, and shoe.
5. *Three commissions.* The child is expected to execute three commissions in proper order: place a pencil on a chair, open a door, and bring a box from some distance.
6. *Opposite analogies.* The child is expected to complete two statements such as the following: "Brother is a boy; sister is a ———."

In general, the child's language development is the best single index of his intellectual development. Feebleminded children are always delayed in speech, and idiots never talk. Gifted children, as a rule, are markedly accelerated in language development. Terman, in his study of children having IQ's above 140, found that these gifted children had talked on the average at approximately eleven months. This is about four months earlier than the average child begins to talk. However, some of this gifted group did not speak until they were nearly three years of age. Other factors, besides intelligence, apparently play a part in speech development.

There are not only great individual differences in IQ among preschool children but also in the rate of mental growth among children with the same IQ.[28] The mental test scores of preschool children predict fairly well for age spans from six months to one year, as shown by correlations ranging from .71 to .78, but this prediction becomes increasingly lower with increasing age spans, as shown by the following correlations:

Age Span	r
2 years and 5 years	.32
3 years and 6 years	.66
5 years and 8 years	.70

XI. PERCEPTION

To the very young child it makes no difference whether a picture is right side up, upside down, or tilted at an angle. He perceives it equally well in any position. One investigator [29] studied the responses of children from three to five years of age to con-

---

[28] Macfarlane, *op. cit.*, p. 320.
[29] S. M. Newhall, "Identification by Young Children of Differently Oriented Visual Forms," *Child Development,* 8 (1937), 105–111.

crete geometrical forms. He placed before each child five of such forms and asked them to indicate the forms on a wall chart which corresponded with them. The children were able to identify familiar figures, such as a chair or a horse, nearly as correctly and accurately in an upside down or left-right reverse position as in a normal position. Apparently, the children were reacting to the total impression of the picture.

XII. SOCIAL CLASS AND CASTE DIFFERENCES

That children are reared differently in different social classes is clear from a number of independent observations and studies. In one study [30] a guided interview schedule was used to obtain histories of training procedures from 48 middle-class and 52 lower-class mothers.[31] There were 107 middle-class and 167 lower-class children in the groups studied. Although the results of this study show great individual differences within a given social class, there were enough significant differences between the two groups to permit generalizations. These significant differences, found in feeding practices, cleanliness training, environmental exploration and control, and age and sex roles, may be summarized as follows:

1. *Feeding.* In middle-class families, fewer infants were breast fed, and if at all, breast feeding tended to be for a shorter time than for lower-class children. Three times as many middle-class children as lower-class children were reported to be thumb-suckers.

2. *Cleanliness training.* Although middle-class parents trained their children for bowel and bladder control earlier than did lower-class parents, the middle-class children did not attain control earlier than the lower-class children.

3. *Age expectations and sex roles.* Middle-class children were expected to assume responsibility in the home earlier than were lower-class children, and to be home earlier at night. Lower-class children went to the movies alone at an earlier age, and many more of them were paid for working and for errands than were

---

[30] Martha C. Ericson, "Child-Rearing and Social Status," *Amer. J. Soc.*, 11 (November, 1946), 190–192.
[31] Lloyd Warner's criteria were used in determining social class.

middle-class children. Middle-class girls were expected to begin cooking and sewing earlier than were lower-class girls.

Similar results were obtained in a study in which a comparison was made not only of social class differences but also of Negro and white differences.[32] The results showed that middle-class parents, regardless of color, were more rigorous than lower-class parents in feeding and cleanliness training and expected their children to take responsibilities earlier. Negroes, they discovered, were more permissive than whites in feeding and weaning but more rigorous in toilet training. The social class differences within a given race were much more conspicuous than racial differences.

Underprivileged children do not become food problems since nutritious food is relatively scarce in such groups.[33] There is likely to be competition for the best kinds of food, such as the pieces of meat in a stew. The underprivileged child will prefer a gift of bread or of meat to candy since he gets more candy than does the middle-class child. Candy is about the only thing he can buy with the occasional penny that comes his way. The underprivileged child, similarly, does not develop a sleep problem since, commonly, he shares a room with adults. For him, the chief problem is that of getting enough sleep in a room where lights are on and adults are talking late into the night.

XIII. GEOGRAPHICAL AND CULTURAL DIFFERENCES

The education and socialization of children differ greatly according to geographical area, social and economic status of the family, and ethnic background. Farm children, for example, are less likely to be subjected to rigid toilet training at an early age than are city children. Their movements are not as restricted as are those of city children, and particularly of those children who grow up in apartments. While they are warned against dangers such as overturning an oil lamp, or touching a hot stove, they are less likely to be nagged for disarranging furniture or upsetting the

---

[32] A. Davis and R. J. Havighurst, "Social Class and Color Differences in Child-Rearing," *Amer. Soc. Review*, 11 (1946), 698–710.
[33] Gladys Sellew, "Problem Behavior in Children: A Comparison of Children in Different Social Classes," *Am. J. Nursing*, 41 (1941), 1–5.

neatness of the house than are city children. Farm children, too, are probably less liable to acquire the attitude that adult authority, and the punishment which follows disobeying, is purely arbitrary, as illustrated below:

> The cause and effect of a child's activities are likely to be much clearer in the farm setting. If a city child leaves open a forbidden door, arbitrary punishment may follow. If a farm child leaves open a gate, he sees the young turkeys head for the highway, and this direct experience puts meaning into the punishment that follows. Inhibitions that stem from concrete things doubtless have a different meaning from those that stem from mere words spoken by people; not only are the "do's" and "do not's" much easier for the young child to grasp in the natural-consequence setting, but it is likely that there is not the same kind of tension as that which comes from violating the arbitrary orders of older members of the family.[34]

XIV. RELIGIOUS EDUCATION

The religious education of the child begins long before he has reached the "age of reason." The attitudes which he acquires toward religious practices are "caught" rather than "taught," and, like all significant learnings, result from emotional identification with other people. The example of adults and older children, and particularly of the people whom he loves, is the most important single influence in the child's religious development. This is sometimes dramatically portrayed in a child whose parents differ in religious attitudes and practices. When the mother is Catholic and the father is not, the non-Catholic father may sincerely wish to keep his promise of rearing the children as Catholics. Yet, his male children will often reject the religious values and practices of the mother because such practices are considered "feminine." They do so, not because they reject the mother, but because they are learning to be "masculine." A boy cannot be expected to see that he must imitate his father in other things but imitate his mother in religious practices. He may, it is true, participate in his mother's religious practices during childhood because that is something expected of children. At the same time, if his father does not participate in religious ac-

---

[34] L. Levinger and L. B. Murphy, "Implications of the Social Scene for the Education of Young Children," *National Society for the Study of Education*, Forty-sixth Yearbook, Part II (1947), p. 20. Quoted by permission of the Society.

tivities, he may acquire the attitude that religion is something for women and children; and when he grows up, he readily drops his religious practices. The following examples illustrate the effect of a four-year-old boy's identification with his father:

1. Ted was the four-year-old son of a Catholic mother and a non-Catholic father. One day the mother's sister came to dinner with the family and asked Ted to say "Grace." Ted turned to her contemptuously and said, "Men don't say 'Grace!'"

2. Jerry had, from the age of two and a half years, been going to Sunday Mass with his Catholic mother and older sister. Ordinarily, his father drove them to the church and remained in the car until Mass was over. Occasionally, when the father had wanted Jerry to remain with him, Jerry had protested vigorously and insisted upon going to Mass with his mother and sister. One day, however, when he was four and a half years old, he refused to enter the church, saying, "Men don't go to church!" Only punishment on the part of his father could get him to enter a church after that.

Statistics on the religious practices of children of mixed marriages serve to substantiate this point of view. Only 40 per cent of such children practice any religion once they have reached maturity. And of this group only 20 per cent, or one out of five, remain Catholics. It is highly probable, too, that among this small group which remains Catholic there are some who are very weak Catholics at that.

In the next chapter you will find a number of specific suggestions for the religious education of young children as well as of school-age children.

SUGGESTED READING

GESELL, A., *The First Five Years of Life* (New York, Harper & Brothers, 1940).

XVII

The Psychology of Development: Childhood and Preadolescence

> The heavy burden of the growing soul
> Perplexes and offends more day by day;
> Week by week, offends and perplexes more
> With the imperatives of 'is and seems'
> And may and may not, desire and control.
> The pain of living and the drug of dreams
> Curl up the small soul in the window seat
> Behind the Encyclopedia Britannica.
> —T. S. ELIOT [1]

I. THE PERIOD OF "MIDDLE" CHILDHOOD

Middle childhood begins where early childhood leaves off and ends when preadolescence begins. It covers, roughly, the ages of six through ten years. Typically, it includes the primary school years as well as the fourth grade, although often it extends into the fifth and sixth and even the seventh grades as well. The period of middle childhood is often described as the most objective phase of development, since the child of this age is interested in the external world of events and things. At this age he is not normally preoccupied with his own emotions and is less emotional than he was during his preschool years and than he will again be at adolescence. For this reason, the period of middle childhood is usually considered an ideal period for teaching a child the basic school subjects.

A. The "Whole" Child

In most parts of the civilized world, a considerable portion of childhood and youth is devoted to formal education. In middle-

---

[1] T. S. Eliot, "Animula," *Collected Poems: 1909–1935* (New York, Harcourt, Brace & Company, Inc., 1936), p. 129.

CHILDHOOD AND PREADOLESCENCE 449

class groups, particularly, the school and the values which it represents are extremely important in the lives of both children and parents. Success in school may be synonymous with success in life for the child whose parents have a narrow scale of values. In contrast, childhood among the Alaskan Indians or on the island of Samoa is a period in which formal learning in the sense of separating children from adults for instructional purposes is uncommon. In these simpler societies, children learn what they need to know in association with adults, by participating in adult tasks. Success and failure is not determined, as in most of our schools, by a child's comparative status on academic tests of achievement. The child who performs satisfactorily, but who achieves less than other children, does not develop feelings of inadequacy as he does in the European or American school in which school tasks are competitive.

The central place of the school in our culture has sometimes led psychologists to overemphasize the importance of the school in personality development and to overlook other influences of equal importance. Developmental tasks centered around school situations are, of course, important in our culture. But they are only part of the many developmental tasks faced by children. The personality does not develop in isolated segments. At every moment it develops as a whole. Experiences on the playground and in the home, the child's bodily constitution and physical stamina, exercise an influence upon what and how well a child will learn in school. Similarly, experiences in the classroom influence the child in his relations with others on the playground and in his own home. The total maturity of the child shows a higher relationship with school success than does any one measure of maturity, as, for example, mental age, reading age, or stage of bodily development.

B. Physical Growth and Development

Throughout life, but particularly during childhood, physical and motor development are intimately related to personality development. The child who cannot compete with the group in sports or games does not develop a sense of "belonging" to the group. The boy who always gets caught when the rest of his gang has escaped after some escapade, or the one who always fumbles the ball instead of catching it, is made to feel his inadequacy on every occasion. His attitude toward himself is profoundly influenced by such experiences, and he may attempt to compensate for his inferiority in a number of unwholesome ways.

C. Attitude Toward Teachers and Toward Authority

Typically, the primary school child from a happy home accepts the teacher and her authority unquestioningly. He identifies with the teacher on the basis of love and accepts her standards uncritically. He seeks the approval of his teacher; and if he fails to get it, he is very unhappy. If another child is frowned upon by the teacher, he will frown upon that child, too. If a teacher ever so inadvertently conveys to her class the impression that she dislikes a child, the children will tend also to reject that child. It is the teacher rather than the peer group which is of central importance at this age level.

This unquestioning acceptance of authority and identification with the teacher gradually decreases as the children grow older. It changes in boys shortly before puberty, at the beginning of the so-called "preadolescent" period of life.

II. DEVELOPMENTAL TASKS OF "MIDDLE" CHILDHOOD

At each stage of life the human being faces certain problems to be solved—problems peculiar to his particular stage of development. These problems are referred to as "developmental tasks." In infancy and early childhood, for example, the child has the developmental task of gaining bowel and bladder control. If he does not perform these tasks at the appropriate period in life, he is handicapped in making adjustments at a later age. Similarly, in middle childhood American children, for the most part, face the developmental task of learning to read. If they do not learn to read in the primary grades, their progress in school is retarded, and their personality development may be disturbed.

The basic developmental tasks of the primary grades are (1) the acquisition of the "three R's," (2) the acquisition of various skills with which to meet life, (3) the formation of social interests extending beyond the home, (4) coöperation with peers, (5) fortitude, (6) the development of a right conscience, and (7) the realization that God's will is the supreme rule of life.

A. The Three R's

1. *Reading.* Mechanically, the reading process consists of eye movements and eye fixations. There is no perception during the movements but only during the fixations. The eyes move continuously along a line of print in a series of little jerks or *saccadic movements.* In the child, and in the less efficient adult reader, there are also *regression movements,* that is, backward eye movements over the line just read. In reading difficult material the number of eye fixations as well as the number of regressive movements tends to be increased.

The child who has learned to read does not perceive isolated letters, but whole words. As his skill increases, he perceives phrases as wholes rather than isolated words.

One of the commonest sources of reading difficulties is the failure to establish the left-right progression. Other things which the child looks at do not have to be approached in this systematic way. In looking at a picture, it matters little where the child first fixates his gaze. He may start in the center, at the right or left, or above or below. But in reading, he must start at the left and work directly to the right without any reversals. He must also be able to sweep back from the right to the next line on the left. This is a highly artificial situation and requires considerable practice. If the child acquires faulty habits and fails to establish the left-right progression, he may practice these faulty habits until it is almost impossible to eradicate them. As a result he may be retarded in reading during most of his school life. Reading is related to every other subject in the curriculum. It is related also to social adjustments and to the child's sense of adequacy and of personal worth. Some children are rated lower on intelligence tests than they should be as a result of faulty reading habits. Most group intelligence tests given in school, particularly after the primary grades, require reading ability.

A child whose reading is below the normal expectancy for both his chronological age and his general intelligence is classified as a case of *reading disability.* A disability of this kind does not usually result from one factor but from a combination of factors. If the child's intelligence is below that of his grade level, he will usually test low on tests of reading achievement. He is not, however, classified as a case for remedial teaching in reading, since he is likely to be retarded in everything. The general principles which apply to the teaching of slow learners apply to him. He is not singled out for specific remedial work in reading.

Reading defects result from the following conditions:

1. The introduction of reading instruction before the child is physically or mentally ready to profit from such instruction.

2. Retarded language development, usually because another language is used in the home or community, or because the child has a marked speech defect.

3. Defective vision, hearing, or nervous coördination.

4. Faulty instruction, resulting in failure to develop systematic habits of observation in reading.

5. Emotional maladjustment.

6. Interruptions in the learning process caused by frequent absence from school or by changing schools or teachers.

The choice of appropriate remedial reading procedures rests upon a careful diagnosis of the nature and causes of the difficulty. In addition to tests of reading, intelligence, and language, studies of personality are also useful. Often a complete case study must be made before suitable recommendations for treatment can be made.

The emotional problems which accompany reading disability are not necessarily the result of the disability. There is a growing body of evidence that the reading disability may be the result rather than the cause of emotional disturbance.

In one study [1a] of the emotional background of thirty children of normal intelligence who had reading disabilities, ten were found who had mothers who rejected their children and were openly critical and hostile. Another ten of the mothers were described as tense, coercive, and perfectionistic. The fathers of these twenty children were described as follows:

> Nine were away from home most of the time, four were spoken of as stern disciplinarians, three took no interest in their child whatsoever, and one was overtly hostile to his boy. One was lenient, but pushed his boy with his school work. Only two fathers were described as being fond of their sons, and one of these was a nervous, irritable man with

---

[1a] W. H. Missildine, "The Emotional Background of Thirty Children with Reading Disabilities with Emphasis on Its Coercive Elements," *The Nervous Child,* 5 (July, 1946), 257, 263–272.

CHILDHOOD AND PREADOLESCENCE 453

stomach ulcers, while the other was a thin, tense man who himself had recently suffered a psychotic episode.[2]

Four children were suffering from extreme jealousy of siblings at the time they were learning to read. With perhaps one exception, all of these children were insecure, restless, and emotionally ill as a result of disturbed relationships with some member or members of their families. Consequently:

> We must become aware of the fact that in many instances difficulty with reading is the child's way of letting us know that he is disturbed inwardly, and that he needs help in relationships which are far more important than his relationship to the printed word.[3]

Another psychologist made intensive case studies of 40 non-readers, and found that the reading disturbance was almost invariably related to other difficulties in school and at home. In a number of cases, parental rejection, parental overprotection, and sibling jealousy or rivalry were unmistakable factors in the origin and continuance of the disorder. Other children, insecure to begin with, had been subjected to traumatic experiences in their early school careers. One non-reader, for example, was a boy of eight and a half who, according to the history given by his mother, had been slapped across the face by a first-grade teacher. After the psychologist had established rapport, the child suddenly blurted out, "I'm scared of something. I'm always frightened, but I don't know of what. Sometimes that the teacher will hit me because I don't get 100, and then during the test I think that maybe she'll hit me and I forget the letters of the words that I do know. I'm not scared when I enjoy myself, but that's not much." [4]

In those cases where maternal or paternal rejection were causal factors, the children were amenable to treatment at the onset of adolescence, when the child has a natural tendency to become emancipated from his family.

These findings lend support to the theory of personality development given in Chapter III. They are another line of evidence that attitudes formed in the home toward parents or siblings

---

[2] *Ibid.*, p. 267.
[3] *Ibid.*, p. 271.
[4] D. McCarthy, "The Psychologist Looks at the Teaching of English," *The Independent School Bulletin,* Secondary Education Board, Milton, Mass. (May, 1947), 3–11.

tend to be carried over into situations outside of the home. In some of the cases described, it appears that the children failed to identify themselves with the teacher because they were already disturbed in their relations with adults. The lack of harmony between these children and their parents or siblings is carried over into a new situation. The child's inability to accept his teachers or peers, or to be accepted by them, may set up a powerful emotional block. The resulting emotional disturbance is sufficiently disintegrating to make any real learning impossible.

2. *Writing.* Learning to write is not as closely correlated with intelligence as is learning to read, nor are writing difficulties as emotionally disturbing to the child. Typically, girls learn to write more quickly than boys, and their handwriting at all age levels is more legible.

3. *Number concepts.* The names of numbers, such as *one, two, five,* etc., and the symbols which stand for these numbers are abstractions. Children may, and frequently do, learn to repeat these names, as in counting, and to read number symbols, without at the same time acquiring the basic concepts of numbers. The acquisition of these basic concepts, however, is a developmental task of the primary grades.

B. Readiness for School

Human growth is characterized by regularity and rhythm. The sequence of growth stages through which children go is highly regular for the species. But individual children have their own rhythms of growth; that is, one child will develop rapidly in reading interest at the beginning of his ninth year. Another child may go through the same stage of development at eleven years. There appears to be a family resemblance in rhythms of growth and in the age at which different phases of development are reached.

Different aspects of a child's growth may mature at different rates. For instance, a child may be more mature in his skeletal growth than in his mental growth. Each child appears to have his own design or pattern for growing. Any attempt to interfere with this pattern meets with resistance on the part of the child. Attempts to force a child to perform tasks beyond his developmental level may lead to temporary acceleration of growth. But the long-run effects are usually disastrous. Typically, periods of forced

CHILDHOOD AND PREADOLESCENCE 455

growth are followed by compensatory periods in which growth slows down. Unwholesome personality development is fostered by interfering with a child's idiomatic pattern of growth.

The best single index of a child's readiness for school is his general over-all maturity—physical, mental, social, and emotional. Some psychologists specify certain aspects of maturity in determining a child's readiness for school. We shall discuss several of these kinds of maturing as they relate to achievement in school.

1. *Work maturity.* "Work maturity" appears to be a prerequisite for successful school adaptation. Work maturity is defined as the ability to handle materials constructively. It is characterized by a task attitude in play; that is, the child sets for himself a goal and adapts his activities to the attainment of that goal. This attitude appears spontaneously as a result of inner maturation and is relatively free from environmental influences. Theoretically, the child who is able to set a task for himself is also able to receive a task from another. The average child reaches this stage at about the sixth year. The following example illustrates the difference in behavior of a small child who has not reached the stage of work maturity and an older child who has:

> The mother of two boys of 3½ and 7 years had just taken down the washing. She placed the clothes-pegs in a basket on a chair near the table in the kitchen. The elder of the boys gathered all the clothes-pegs on the table, and made a horse by putting several of them together. While working he was silent, and when he was finished he clapped his hands with joy and asked me triumphantly if I knew what it was that he had made. I answered, "A horse." He was pleased that I had recognized what he had built and then took the clothes-pegs apart again. He began to build again and there followed consecutively a horse, an aeroplane, and a motor-car. As he finished making each object he asked me to identify it. He always tried to put as many clothes-pegs as possible into each construction.
> The younger brother had at the same time arranged his clothes-pegs in two cardboard boxes and fastened the boxes to his wagon. While the older brother was building he rode several times in the kitchen, then stopped at the sofa near his brother and said: "Good day, I am the baker. Do you need anything?" The older boy answered: "Yes, give me twenty rolls." The younger boy thereupon gave him some clothes-pegs out of his boxes and said, "That costs 20 pfennigs." The older brother then pretended that he was counting out money into his brother's hand and laid the purchased clothes-pegs on the sofa. He did not, however, use them in his building, but considered them rolls. The younger boy

rode around several times, even going into the hall. He then sold rolls to his brother again.[5]

Note that the younger child can start and finish his game whenever he likes, whereas the constructive work of the older child must be brought to a conclusion. Children who have a task attitude look upon their play activities as work. For example, a small girl refused to go swimming with her companions because, as she explained, "I have to wash my babies' clothes."

The contention that 80 per cent of first-grade children who fail do so because they have not developed the work attitude in their games before entering school, suggests that observation of work maturity might help to determine a child's readiness for school.

2. *The capacity for self-criticism.* There is also evidence that the young child achieves the capacity for self-criticism very gradually and only as he begins to evaluate what he does in terms of a goal. Findings on this subject may be summed up as follows: (1) There is a primary tendency in the direction of self-praise under any and all circumstances, regardless of whether the success is the result of capable performance or an accident. (2) A child takes every opportunity to compare himself favorably with other children who are either being praised or criticized, who complete a task successfully, or who possess something. (3) There is a primary tendency to deprecate the other child. (4) When a child fails to solve a problem, the significance of the problem is belittled.

Children of ages two to seven years were presented with competitive building problems and a twofold analysis of their behavior was made. The remarks which the children made spontaneously about their own work and the work of others and the expressed opinions of their own work and the work of others when asked "Whose is prettier?" were studied. The results showed that: (1) Two- to five-year-old children rarely expressed spontaneous opinions. If they were expressed, however, they were always positive for their own and negative for the work of others. (2) Spontaneous negative self-criticism made its first appearance at six to seven years in 10 per cent of the cases, in contrast to 71 per cent

---

[5] C. Bühler, *From Birth to Maturity* (London, Kegan Paul, Trench, Trubner and Company, Ltd., 1935), pp. 117–118. Quoted by permission of the publisher.

CHILDHOOD AND PREADOLESCENCE 457

self-praise. (3) Only 4.5 per cent of opinions of five- to six-year-old children were spontaneous criticisms of others.

In general, it is only when the child is seven years or older that he begins to assume an appreciative attitude toward the accomplishments of other children and to evaluate his own work sufficiently to accept criticism. The appearance of this ability is related to the child's adjustment in school. School learning depends to a considerable degree upon the capacity to accept criticism and to profit by it.

3. *Reading readiness*. A child is not "ready" for the first grade until he is ready to read. Reading readiness implies that the child has acquired a certain degree of facility in the spoken language and has mastered the basic speech symbols. It also depends upon the child's experiences. The rural child, for example, may have difficulty in reading if the books deal with elevators, skyscrapers, and subways. The city child, on the other hand, will have difficulty if the reading material tells about cows, pigs, and harvesting. Before these unknown subjects are introduced into the child's reading he should be given opportunities for becoming acquainted with them by first-hand experiences.

4. *Organismic age*. It is possible to measure a number of different aspects of a child's growth at any one time. Anatomical and physiological measures might include height, weight, maturity of bony structure (as shown by x-rays of wrist bones) or degree of maturity of reproductive organs. Mental maturity is designated as mental age (MA); reading maturity as reading age (RA); language maturity as language age (LA); and so on. By computing the average of the various "ages" of a child, we secure the "Organismic Age" (OA).[6] Although growth in any particular dimension, such as anatomical or mental growth, may fluctuate widely from time to time, the organismic age or central tendency of growth remains fairly constant. The total achievement of a child in school is more closely related to OA than to any one measure of maturity.

C. The Acquisition of Various Skills with which to Meet Life

Among the important skills which should be developed during the primary school years are (1) self-expression through speech,

[6] W. C. Olsen, *Child Development* (Boston, D. C. Heath & Company, 1949).

music and art, and (2) facility in games and sports appropriate to this age level.

D. The Formation of Social Interests Extending Beyond the Home

The primary school child normally makes friends at school and enjoys visiting their homes and having them visit his home. If a child shows no such interest at this age, it is a sign that something is seriously wrong.

E. Coöperation with Peers

During this period of development, a child must show a progressively greater ability to put his own interests aside and to coöperate with the group. If he is developing normally, there should be evidence that he is accepted by the group rather than rejected.

F. Fortitude

The child of this age must begin to acquire fortitude or what is commonly called the ability to "take it." He must learn not to run home to his mother every time he is hurt; but, if he does, he must not be given the impression that such things should not happen to him. The mother can help, while sympathizing with the child, by showing him the necessity for meeting such problems with his "chin up." She must avoid anything that might lead him to self-pity. Maturity is attained not by running away from difficulties but by meeting them courageously. The attitude of parents and teachers toward hardships and suffering will either help or hinder the child in the development of fortitude.

G. The Development of a Right Conscience

All children do not reach the "age of reason" at the same age, but for most children it comes during the primary school period. At this age the child becomes responsible for his acts and can be taught to distinguish right from wrong. The primary responsibility for this teaching rests with the parents. The teacher merely supplements the instruction of the parent. The fact that a child is in a Catholic school does not relieve the parents of this responsibility. Parents are in a much better position than is the teacher to know what is happening in the child's life.

Great care must be taken to help the child to prepare for his first few confessions. Fear and unpleasantness must be scrupulously avoided, since early attitudes toward confession may influence the child for a lifetime. Peace of mind and confidence are necessary for the development of a right conscience.

H. Realization that God's Will Is the Supreme Rule of Life

Religious needs and the developmental tasks of each age level which must be solved in order to meet these needs are of great importance for the harmonious development of human personality. Because these needs are most acutely felt at adolescence and again in later maturity, we may possibly overlook their importance in the life of the young child. Yet with rare exceptions, the person who in adulthood develops a deeply satisfying and mature adjustment to the truths of religion is one who received appropriate instruction, good example, and help in living a spiritual life in childhood.

Early in life, long before the child is ready for school, he must be taught that he is the citizen of two worlds—the temporal world in which he will work out his salvation, and the eternal world of union with God, the life of which he begins to live as soon as he receives baptism. These two worlds are intimately related. The child must learn from his earliest years to view his life in the temporal order in the perspective of the eternal life to which he is destined. The primary responsibility for this education rests with the parents. Parents must teach the child that religion is not a matter of Sunday observance only but must permeate every thought and action of every day. The child, of course, learns this truth best through the example rather than through the instruction given by the parents. Nevertheless, assuming that good example is being given, certain specific instructions must be given at the preschool and school age if the child is to make normal progress in spiritual growth. We shall indicate briefly in the next few paragraphs what we consider to be the minimum essentials of such instruction.

First, the child must learn to pray. All spiritual growth is a growth in grace, and prayer is the channel through which grace flows. The child can and must be taught to pray long before he is old enough for school. This prayer must not be a purely verbal exercise according to set forms; it must be a real conversation with God in which the heart as well as the mind is directed to

God. The best way for a child to learn to pray is in the family group. It is not enough to "hear" a child's prayer; the parents themselves must pray with the child. Ideally, the little child should join in the family prayer as soon as he is able, even though he may not be able to follow everything, and even though he may be a distraction to the adults. Morning and evening prayer said in common by parents and children, grace before and after meals, the family Rosary, and family participation as a group at the Holy Sacrifice of the Mass and later at the Communion table are the ideal, if not the only adequate means for teaching a child to pray.

Second, the child must be taught to live in the presence of God. One excellent means of helping him to do so is to teach him to say a short prayer and to make the Sign of the Cross every time the striking clock marks the passage of time. Again, parents must perform these acts with the child when they are together. It is not enough to tell the child to do so. If the children are encouraged to do these things while adults neglect to do so, the children may believe that these are practices appropriate only for children and slough them off when they are older.

Third, the child must be taught the necessity and value of work in God's plan for him.

From the consciousness that even the smallest household task when faithfully carried out draws him closer to God, the child will derive a continuing motivation for relating all that he does to God. . . . In this way the child will have learned at home a great lesson which will make it easier for him to adjust to the demands of school life. As he takes his place in that larger community, he will do so as a responsible individual. He will see his homework, his attention in class and his participation in school activities as part of the same divine plan learned in the home whereby each action has its significance in God's eyes. This mindfulness throughout his daily life of the supernatural value of his actions will be a safeguard against the careless performance of any duty. The greater his talent, the more he will be conscious of his obligation to serve God by a rightful exercise of that talent.[7]

By encouraging a child to make his nightly examination of conscience and his weekly confession, parents help the child to use the spiritual helps necessary to develop his sense of responsibility. In this respect as in others, the example of the adults whom the

---

[7] "The Child: Citizen of Two Worlds." Statement issued by the Cardinals, Archbishops, and Bishops of the United States at their annual meeting, November, 1950. Printed in *The Catholic Bulletin*, St. Paul, Minnesota (November 25, 1950).

child loves and admires has more lasting influence than their verbal instruction.

III. STUDIES OF CHARACTER AND MORAL DEVELOPMENT

One of the most thorough-going experimental studies of character in children of school age was that of the *Character Education Inquiry*.[8] The investigators submitted children to a variety of tests in which they were given an opportunity to lie, cheat, or steal. When the same tests were given to the children a second time, those children who had lied, cheated, or stolen the first time tended to do so again. In other words, children were consistent in the way in which they reacted to the specific test situations. However, they were not consistently honest or dishonest in all situations. The child who reported a fake score on an athletic feat did not necessarily tell other lies. These findings led the investigators to conclude that there are no such generalized traits as honesty or dishonesty, and that a child's character must be described in terms of the specific situation to which he is reacting. Other experiments, in which self-control, coöperativeness, and persistence were studied, led to the same conclusion: that there were no honest or dishonest children, but only honest or dishonest acts, and that there were no traits such as coöperativeness, service, and self-control, but only people who at times act coöperatively, perform service for others, and exhibit self-control.

The above contention that there are no general traits of character has been subjected to considerable criticism and today perhaps no psychologist accepts it without qualifications. One psychologist, for example, points out that although the children showed little consistency from one situation to another, there were some children who were consistent in acting in the desired way, whatever it might be, e.g., acting honestly.

This [she points out] is a highly significant fact, for it indicates that socially desirable traits, once they have been established may become relatively stable. So we may justifiably say of an individual that he is honest or coöperative or generous or truthful with some feeling of as-

---

[8] H. Hartshorne and M. A. May, Vol. I, *Studies in Deceit*, 1928; Vol. II, *Studies in Service and Self-Control*, 1929; Vol. III, *Studies in the Organization of Character*, 1930 (New York, The Macmillan Company).

surance that his subsequent behavior will bear out our statements. But this is not true at the other end of the scale.[9]

Another psychologist has similarly criticized these conclusions and rejects the doctrine, which supposedly derives support from this study, that personality is composed entirely of specific habits. He points out that "whenever moral standards are involved the question of the *age* of the subjects is of greatest importance."[10] Consequently, even if this study could prove that in children character traits are highly specific, we would be going beyond the data in assuming that this was also true for adults. Moreover, "whether specificity or generality is found in the structure of personality depends to a large extent, not only upon the interpretation of quantitative evidence, but upon the methods used."[11] In one study[12] in which mature subjects were studied intensively by methods of individual analysis, the results entirely contradicted the specificity hypothesis. It is probable that the conclusions of many commonly accepted psychological studies, based upon mass statistics, will have to be similarly revised in the light of the newer research based on studies of *individuals,* rather than of *groups.*

The fact that a child will not cheat when taking a test under one teacher and will cheat when taking a test under another teacher, highlights the importance of human relations in the classroom. In the first instance, the child may feel that he is on his honor because his teacher trusts and respects him. In the second instance, the emotional tie between the child and the teacher is considerably less. There may even be a feeling of antagonism between them, and the child may look upon cheating as a way of getting even or of putting something over on the teacher.

IV. THE DEVELOPING CONCEPT OF SELF

The child's concept of himself is built up gradually as people express their evaluation of him. Almost every experience of life has something to contribute. A person's concept of himself and

---

[9] F. L. Goodenough, *Developmental Psychology,* Second Edition (New York, Appleton-Century-Crofts, Inc., 1945), p. 430.

[10] G. W. Allport, *Personality: A Psychological Interpretation* (New York, Henry Holt & Company, Inc., 1937), p. 252.

[11] *Ibid.,* p. 253.

[12] D. W. McKennon, "The Violation of Prohibitions in the Solving of Problems," in H. A. Murray *et al., Explorations in Personality* (New York, Oxford University Press, Inc., 1938).

of his abilities may be very different from the actual facts of the case. For example, a young man who is considerably above average in mechanical ability and manual dexterity considers himself incompetent in working with his hands. From early childhood he had been subjected to unfavorable comparisons with a brother who was superior to him. The young man's evaluation of his ability is not true to the facts but is a reflection of his family's evaluation of him. Curiously enough, he still "feels" inferior, though a psychologist has interpreted his test scores and has demonstrated objectively that the young man has superior ability.

When a child goes to school his concept of self is modified by the evaluations of his teachers and classmates. A child may achieve satisfactorily and yet feel inferior if other children are more competent than he. When comparisons are made, as they inevitably are under the marking systems which exist in our schools, the child who is usually below the others tends to get discouraged and to conceive of himself as a poor student. He learns to appraise his abilities and direct his energies to goals which he feels that he can attain. The individual goal that he sets for himself, which may be high or low, or anywhere between, and the goal for which he is willing to strive, is known as his "level of aspiration." He feels satisfied when he reaches it and discouraged when he fails. In general, when a child feels successful, his level of aspiration goes up. When he feels defeated, his level of aspiration for the immediate future goes down. For this reason any type of discipline or criticism which serves to lower a child's confidence in his ability to achieve defeats its own purpose. A feeling of success is an incentive to further success, both for children and for adults. Studies of the relative merits of praise and blame as incentives for learning corroborate this view. These studies invariably show that praise is a more potent incentive to learning and to good behavior than is blame.

William James pointed out many years ago that "With no attempt there can be no failure; with no failure, no humiliation. So our self-feeling in this world depends entirely on what we back ourselves to do." James expressed the relationship between self-esteem, success, and "level of aspiration" (pretensions) in the following formula:

$$\text{Self-esteem} = \frac{\text{Success}}{\text{Pretensions}}$$

"Such a fraction," he said, "may be increased as well by diminishing the denominator as by increasing the numerator." [13] In this formula we have a clue to the motivation behind the raising or lowering of the level of aspiration.

V. SPECIAL GIFTS OR TALENTS

A. Musical Talent and Ability

Several tests have been developed for measuring the presence of musical and artistic talents and abilities in children.[14] The problem of measurement is not a simple one, since different kinds of music require different psychological and physiological endowments. A gifted singer, for example, would usually not be at all able to compose a symphony. A violinist presumably needs a higher degree of pitch sensitivity than an organist.

Musical abilities are not correlated to any considerable degree with general intelligence. Superior musical talent has been observed in children with inferior and mediocre as well as with superior intelligence. One investigator measured the musical sensitivity of a group of children all of whom had IQ's above 135. These children, she found, did not score higher than children in general on the musical tests. It is interesting to note that one psychologist, in asking gifted children to list their easiest and most difficult school subjects, found that mathematics was frequently listed among the easiest, and music and art among the hardest. The mere fact that these children possessed superior intelligence did not help them when the subject studied required special talents and abilities not correlated with intelligence.

We should not suppose, however, that eminence can be achieved in music without superior intellectual endowment in addition to the specialized musical abilities. Directing and composing in particular would appear to depend considerably upon intellectual functions, requiring as they do an interpretation of the compositions of others and the origination of new ideas.

Musical sensitivity cannot usually be measured accurately before the mental age of ten because the test directions are too com-

[13] William James, *Psychology. Briefer Course* (New York, Henry Holt & Company, Inc., 1892), p. 187.
[14] G. Revesz, "Das Musikalische Wunderkind," *Zeitschrift für Päd. Psychol.*, 19 (1918), 29–34; C. E. Seashore, *The Psychology of Musical Talent* (Boston, Silver Burdett Company, 1919).

plex and because the tests themselves require a high degree of concentration. Perhaps the best tests to use are the "Seashore Measures of Musical Talents" which consist of two twelve-inch double-faced records, divided into two series. Series A is used for general group surveys, and Series B is intended for groups or individuals selected out for some musical purpose or function, such as choral club or orchestral groups. The tests measure six components of musical talent, namely: (1) pitch, (2) loudness, (3) time, (4) timbre, (5) rhythm, and (6) tonal memory. According to the test manual, ". . . musical talents . . . mean specific capacities or abilities involved in the hearing, appreciation, and performance of music." [15]

Ordinarily, we do not speak of musical talent in terms of the measurable variables of the Seashore Test. We limit our meaning to the demonstrated ability to play, compose, direct, or appreciate good music. When we say that musical talents tend to run in families we are using the term *talent* in this second sense. These talents appear early in life and reach their peak during early maturity. Brahms, for example, played a composition of his own in a public recital at the age of ten. Mendelssohn had composed a symphony and several operas before the end of his twelfth year, and his overture to the *Midsummer Night's Dream* before he was twenty. Beethoven performed in public before he was ten years old and published a musical composition at the age of thirteen. Haydn, Handel, and Mozart, too, all reached the peak of their talents at a very early age. Mozart, in particular, was a child prodigy who began his musical studies at the age of three. He began his public appearances at the age of six and composed a symphony at the age of eight.

B. Artistic Talent and Ability

Attempts to analyze into its separate elements the ability to draw or to appreciate art [16] have not been so successful as the

---

[15] *Manual of Instructions and Interpretations for the Seashore Measures of Musical Talents*, 1939 Revision (Camden, N.J., Educational Department, RCA Victor Division, Radio Corporation of America), p. 3.

[16] Among the most frequently used tests of artistic appreciation are the Meier (published by the Bureau of Educational Research and Service, State University of Iowa, Iowa City, 1942) and the McAdory (published by the Bureau of Publications, Teachers College, Columbia University, New York, 1929).

analysis of musical talents. Two facts stand out, however, from the studies that have been made. The first is that artistic, like musical, talent appears to run in families. In one study [17] of school children who were talented in art it was found that almost all of them had near relatives who were also artistically gifted. The second finding is that artistic talent usually manifests itself in childhood, although it matures only much later. There are, however, a number of gifted artists who began their artistic careers late in life.

VI. THE PREADOLESCENT

The preadolescent period is set off sharply from the earlier school age in a number of important respects. It appears to be very different for girls than for boys. In general, girls of this age do not present a problem to adults as do boys. Some girls, of course, do, but this is true of any age level and is not particularly characteristic of the preadolescent age. The most important psychological studies of girls at this age appear to be those which deal with the factors which make for social acceptance or rejection. We are summarizing those studies in the following chapter on adolescence in order to show the contrast between preadolescence and adolescence. In this chapter we shall limit our discussion to the preadolescent boy.

According to Furfey,

Preadolescence is a distinct period in the life of the boy. It is distinguished from the period of childhood which precedes it by the rise of the gang spirit, an awakening interest in team games and in the hostile attitude toward girls. It is distinguished from the period of adolescence which follows it, because the adolescent develops a newly independent spirit, shows less hostility toward girls and breaks sharply with preadolescent gangs. The period of preadolescence in the most typical cases begins between the eighth and eleventh birthday and it ends with puberty.[18]

Unfortunately, fewer studies have been made of this age level than of either early childhood or adolescence, and consequently, we know much less about it. For boys, the most marked symptoms

---

[17] H. T. Manuel, "Talent in Drawing: An Experimental Study of the Use of Tests to Discover Special Ability," *School and Home Educ. Monog.*, No. 3 (Bloomington, Illinois, Public School Publishing Co., 1919).

[18] P. H. Furfey, *The Gang Age* (New York, The Macmillan Company, 1928), p. 14.

CHILDHOOD AND PREADOLESCENCE 467

of preadolescence occur between the fifth and eighth grade according to school classification.

The preadolescent boy is negative in his attitude toward adults and often shows this attitude by being as rude as he dares to be toward both parents and teachers. If he has previously been a shining light in school, he now strives to hide his light under a bushel. It gives him no prestige at this age to be well liked by the teacher; in fact, it may single him out for persecution from the peer group. Physical prowess, daring, and a certain disdain for adults are characteristic of boys of this age who are held in highest regard by the group. Tidiness carries no prestige, and too much of it may be a definite handicap. Success in school and conscientiousness about lessons do not contribute to a boy's popularity. Girls are definitely rejected at this age, unless they are tomboys and can hold their own with boys in games and sports. The most marked characteristic of this age is its physical restlessness. The preadolescent boy appears to be constantly wiggling and moving. If there is a pencil on the desk he must manipulate it perpetually, often drawing his initials on the desk and then slowly but surely carving the wood with it. If he has a string he must constantly wind it around his fingers and then unwind it again. This characteristic, along with his almost complete lack of appreciation for what adults are doing for him, makes him especially obnoxious to his elders. Habits of courtesy, firmly built up at an earlier age, may break down badly. Innumerable irritations about little things fill the lives of parents and teachers who deal with preadolescent boys.

Parents and teachers are often consoled to know that this is only a transitional stage of development in which childhood patterns of behavior become disorganized in preparation for future growth which will take place during adolescence. The development of gang loyalty and the concomitant rejection of adult authority are necessary preparatory stages in growing up. Adults will get along better with the preadolescent if they keep their own egos well in the background. The preadolescent boy's assumption that adults are stupid or silly is hard to accept with equanimity, and the temptation to disprove the assumption is very great. Yet, no preadolescent changes his opinion on this subject until he is mature enough to accept his own limitations without projecting them to others. This takes time, and neither parents nor teachers can accelerate the process by being unpleasant and irritable.

Teachers of preadolescents are often unaware of the prestige factors operating within the group until some seemingly trivial incident comes up in class. One teacher, for instance, decided to make an example of a boy who had failed to do his work, and unfortunately for her, picked the boy who was for the group a "star of attraction." Any authority which she had previously been able to exercise over the group now broke down. The other boys all identified with the boy who was being disciplined and the teacher, as a result, became a "star of rejection."

By means of sociometric tests, data have been collected showing the sharp contrast between this level and the first grade level of development. In the first grade, for example, there are many boy-girl friendships, whereas in the sixth grade there are scarcely any at all. This situation continues until the age of puberty.

Leaders may emerge in the first grade, but their influence is limited to small groups. By the time the fifth grade is reached, however, a class leader may influence as many as thirty or forty children.

Some of the "rough-neck" behavior patterns of boys at this age may be masculine reactions against feminine authority both at home and in school. It is just possible that, were boys of this age taught by men, their reactions would not have to be so violent as they are under the present system where the majority of teachers are women.

In conclusion, childhood and preadolescence, like other stages of growth, present the child with developmental tasks which must be solved for healthy personality development. The adequacy with which these tasks are solved depends in part upon the experiences and adjustments of early childhood. We now turn to a consideration of puberty and adolescence where we shall again see this principle of continuity in personality development illustrated. The way in which the adolescent faces and solves the developmental tasks of this age level is influenced appreciably by the kinds of adjustments he has made at an earlier age level.

SUGGESTED READING

GESELL, A., ILG, F. L., AMES, L. B., AND BULLIS, G. E., *The Child from Five to Ten* (New York, Harper & Brothers, 1946).

OLSON, W. C., *Child Development* (Boston, D. C. Heath & Company, 1949), especially Chapters VI–XIV.

XVIII

The Psychology of Development: Puberty and Adolescence

The imagination of a boy is healthy, and the mature imagination of a man is healthy; but there is a space of life between, in which the soul is in a ferment, the character undecided, the way of life uncertain, the ambition thick-sighted: thence proceeds mawkishness.—KEATS, Endymion: Preface

1. WHAT IS ADOLESCENCE?

Adolescence is the period of transition from childhood to maturity. It begins with *puberty*, the time at which the individual is first capable of reproduction. The exact time of puberty is difficult to establish. The onset of menstruation in girls and the appearance of the male hormone in the urine, of pubic hair, or other secondary sex characteristics in boys, are usually accepted as indices of reproductive maturity. These symptoms are not exact indications, however, but are only approximate. Evidence from primitive cultures, in which mating takes place soon after the first menstruation, indicates that there is a period of sterility which lasts for a year or more after the first menstruation. During this period, pregnancy does not occur.

The period of *adolescence* is the interval between the onset of puberty and the time at which maturity is reached. In this chapter, the expression *pubescent-adolescent growth cycle* refers to the entire sequence of changes in rate of growth which marks the transition from childhood to complete physiological and anatomical maturity.

Many studies have been made to determine the average age at which the pubertal spurt in growth occurs, and the results of these studies have differed widely. Two methodological reasons for these discrepancies have been cited. The composition of the age groups selected for study is partly responsible. If measurements are made at six-month intervals, for example, the peak of growth for girls may appear at eleven and a half years. If full year intervals are used, however, the peak may not show up until after twelve years. Accurate measurement is further complicated by the fact that there are seasonal differences in growth of height in children. Unless measurements are made at least as often as at three month intervals, the results will be affected by such seasonal variations in rate of growth.

The age at which the first menstruation occurs is known as the *menarchy*. The best measures we have at the present time indicate that the average age of the menarchy in American girls is somewhat below thirteen years of age. There is a family resemblance in age of menarchy, although daughters in general mature earlier than did their mothers. Data collected over the last three generations show a trend indicating that biologically the period of adolescence is beginning earlier with each succeeding generation. Socially, it is extending for a longer period of time in American children than was formerly true, with some interesting and not wholly desirable consequences. There are marked twin resemblances in age of maturing.

The period of adolescence as we know it in our culture is not the same as it is in other cultures. Nor is it the same from one social class to another. In the upper- and middle-classes in our culture there is a greater lag between physiological and psychological maturity than in the less privileged classes or in culture groups such as those of Samoa and New Guinea.

It would be a mistake to assume that the problems of adolescence are the same from one social class, one geographical area, or from one culture group to another. They are not. In some so-called primitive cultures, the changes of puberty are accompanied by elaborate ceremonies of initiation into the adult groups. The young person on the completion of this ritual is inducted as an adult into the community and given all the rights and privileges, as well as the duties, of adults. He is in no confusion as to his status.

Obviously the adolescent in the United States, and particularly in the middle-class, faces a different set of problems. His status is not clearly defined. He is biologically mature long before he has an opportunity to earn a living or rear a family. He lives in a social group, the mores of which are rapidly changing. He must choose from a number of socially approved, but often mutually antagonistic values, his own set of goals and values. This necessity for choice may be a major factor in producing the "storm and stress" of the adolescent period. Another factor which produces anxiety is the social mobility of many families. Regardless of whether this mobility is upward or downward, it is usually accompanied by strain.

II. THE BODY IN ADOLESCENCE

A. Skeletal Growth

1. The curve of stature growth

The marked changes which take place in rate of growth in stature during adolescence were overlooked until a decade or so ago. Mothers, it is true, seemed to know that a growth spurt occurred, since it was they who had to lengthen the adolescent's clothes. But doctors and psychologists failed to observe a growth spurt because they were using faulty techniques of investigation and analysis. Typically they were using cross-sectional methods of collecting their data. In using the cross-sectional method, large groups of children at different age levels are measured at one time. The average height of the children at each level is computed, and the difference in height from one age to another is taken as the increment of growth between those two ages. The assumption underlying the use of this technique is that the older children are now what the younger children will be when they are the same age. This is true, of course, only when the groups of different age levels have been properly equated and when no selective factors are operating. However, even when the groups are adequately matched for such obviously necessary controls as racial stock, intelligence, socio-economic status, and the like, the cross-sectional method still has decided limitations. Cross-sectional growth curves fail to show any marked changes in rate of growth at adolescence. Graphs based upon group data tend to obscure what is happening in individual cases.

In the California Growth Study, conducted by Stoltz, the above-mentioned errors were avoided. Stoltz drew growth curves of individual children measured at six months' intervals over a period of six or more years. A scrutiny of these curves revealed that marked changes in rate of growth took place in each child. Moreover, there were similarities in the pattern of growth for all of the children studied. The sequence of the growth changes was the same for each child but the age at which each stage of the sequence was reached varied markedly from child to child. The growth curve of each individual child, for example, showed a dip sometime before there was a spurt in the curve. This dip indicated a slowing down of growth. By adding the ages at which this dip occurred for each child and dividing by the total number of cases, Stoltz located a point on a scale which designates the average age at which this slowing down of growth appears. The other points on the growth curve were located by the same technique.

Figure 72 is a schematic graph of Stoltz's study of the growth of individual boys.[1] This is a generalized curve and no individual

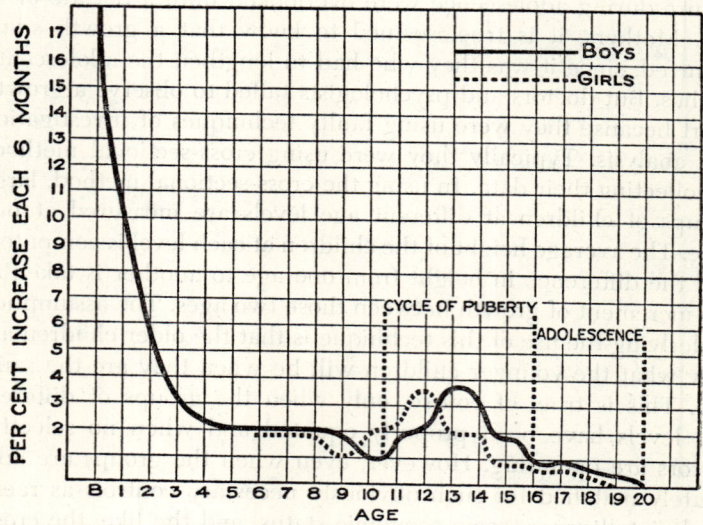

Fig. 72. Schematic Curve Showing Changes in Rate of Growth of Boys from Birth to 20 Years. Dotted line, added by authors, is hypothetical growth curve for girls. [Adapted from Lois Meek, *The Personal-Social Development of Boys and Girls with Implications for Secondary Education,* New York, Committee on Workshops, Progressive Education Association, 1940, p. 34.]

[1] L. Meek, *The Personal-Social Development of Boys and Girls with Implications for Secondary Education* (New York, Committee on Workshops, Progressive Education Association, 1940).

PUBERTY AND ADOLESCENCE

curve is exactly like it. Although Stoltz was working primarily with boys, he suggests that the growth of girls follows the same general pattern, but occurs at an earlier age. We have added the dotted line to Stoltz's curve as a hypothetical growth curve for girls.

A scrutiny of Stoltz's generalized growth curve as well as of some of his unpublished data [2] yields the following information:

1. All children undergo a marked change in velocity of growth during the pubescent-adolescent growth cycle.
2. All children show roughly the same pattern of growth, namely:
   a. Just before accelerated growth begins there is a slowing down of growth as compared with the preceding period;
   b. This initial decrease is followed by a marked acceleration in growth;
   c. At the peak of the growth spurt, the individual has achieved a rate of growth which is at least twice as great as that which initiated the pubescent cycle;
   d. Following the period of maximum growth, there is a period of deceleration which lasts, on the average, from eighteen months to two years.
3. Girls go through the cycle about one and one-half to two years earlier than boys.

2. Relation of skeletal growth to physiological maturing

During the pubescent-adolescent growth cycle there is a very close relationship between physiological development, as indicated by development of the reproductive system, and skeletal growth. This relationship is so close that if we have accurate measures of skeletal growth, we can predict with a high degree of accuracy the stage of physiological growth that the organism has reached. In his study of boys, Stoltz obtained a high correlation between measures of change in stature and the development of both external genitalia and secondary sex characteristics. He concluded that there is a common basis for both physiological and anatomical growth. Shuttleworth has shown that a similar relationship is found in girls. He found identical patterns of stature growth when he classified the girls according to the menarcheal age.

Associated with these anatomical and physiological changes are changes in interests and in motivation which are more or less

[2] On file at the Center for the Study of Human Growth and Development, The University of Chicago.

similar for all adolescents. These interests vary according to social class and economic status. In middle-class white society, for example, at the phase in which the dip in the curve occurs, and for a short time afterward, boys are rigidly intolerant of girls and girls are equally intolerant of boys. At the peak of the growth spurt, however, the normal boy or girl is vitally interested in making contacts with the opposite sex. At first these contacts are awkward and self-conscious. Much pushing and shoving behavior is observed. Gradually these clumsy beginnings of heterosexual contacts change to more mature patterns of behavior, and near the end of the decelerated half of the growth curve, boy-girl social relations have typically become smoothly established.

B. Primary and Secondary Sex Characteristics

At puberty, a number of changes take place in boys and girls, the end result of which is to make possible or to facilitate reproduction. The primary sex characteristics, the reproductive cells, develop at this time as a result of glandular changes. The secondary sex characteristics also develop at this time. In boys, these changes include growth of the beard, deepening of the voice, and changes in the skin, hair, and cutaneous glands. In girls, they involve development of the breasts, widening of the hips, menstruation, and changes in the skin, hair, and cutaneous glands.

The anatomical and physiological changes of adolescence appear to be initiated and sustained, at least in part, by two hormones produced by the anterior lobe of the pituitary gland. One of these hormones, the gonadotropic or gonad-growing hormone, is produced in sufficient quantities, just before the onset of puberty, to cause the immature gonads to grow and eventually to mature. As a result of this pituitary gland secretion, the gonads begin to produce hormones of their own. In the female, these gonadal (ovarian) hormones result in mature development of the breasts, mammary glands, uterine (Fallopian) tubes, vagina, and of the secondary sexual characteristics. In the male, gonadal (testicular) hormones bring about the mature development of the prostate gland, seminal vesicles, penis, and associated structures, and the various male secondary sexual characteristics.

The gonadal hormones exert an influence on the growth hormone of the pituitary gland. They cause a gradual reduction in either the effectiveness or the amount of the growth hormone produced and eventually cause it to stop completely. For this reason, if the gonads begin functioning too early in life, the individual may be stunted in growth or end up small in stature. If, however, they begin functioning late, growth, and particularly growth of the lower extremities, may continue for too long a time, and the individual will take on atypical bodily proportions.

C. Basal Metabolism and Energy Output

The determination of basal metabolism provides a direct measure of the rate of energy transformation in the body cells, and an indirect measure of available energy. In general, basal metabolism decreases with age, as shown in Figure 73. This curve, however,

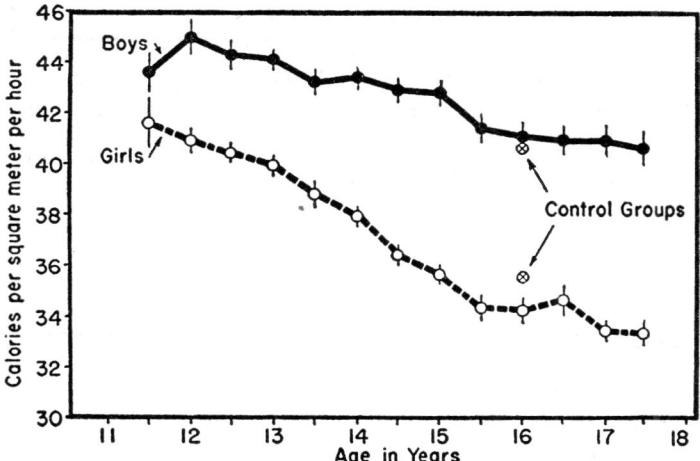

Fig. 73. Age Changes in Basal Metabolism, Repeated Tests on Same Subjects. [Reproduced from the Forty-third Yearbook of the National Society for the Study of Education, Part I, 1944, p. 62. By permission of the Society.]

suffers from the same limitations as stature curves in which group data have been averaged as previously explained. Such averaging obscures the actual changes which are taking place within individuals, as shown in Figure 74. A summary of the results of the California Growth Study indicates that only ten of the 100 cases followed the uniformly even decrease which characterized the curve based on group averages, and that over half of the subjects showed periods of rapid change as illustrated in Figure 75. Moreover, five

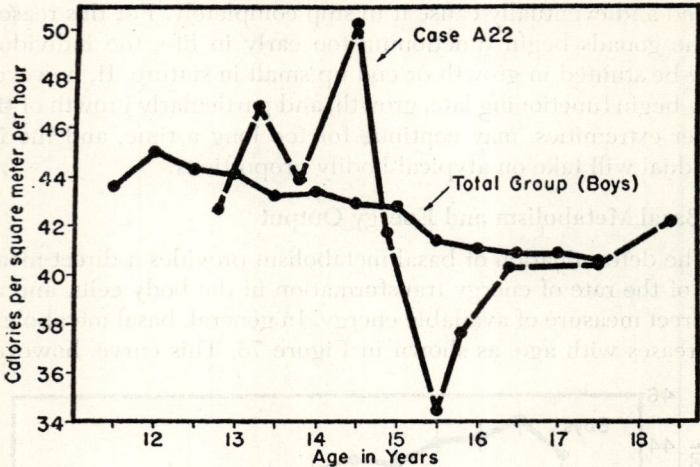

Fig. 74. Individual Growth Curve of Basal Metabolism (boy). [Reproduced from the Forty-third Yearbook of the National Society for the Study of Education, Part I, 1944, p. 63. By permission of the Society.]

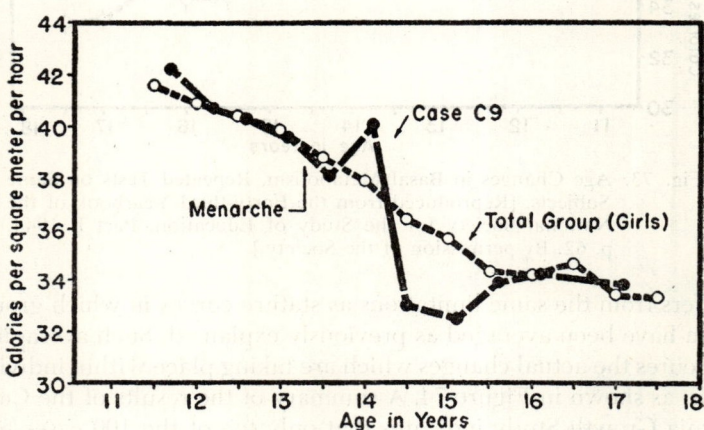

Fig. 75. Individual Growth Curve of Basal Metabolism (Girl). [Reproduced from the Forty-third Yearbook of the National Society for the Study of Education, Part I, 1944, p. 63. By permission of the Society.]

of these children showed an increase rather than a decrease in basal metabolism with age. These children also tended to be small, slow-maturing, physiologically unstable individuals, and were "frequently marked by atypical social behavior." [3]

In general, the pubescent-adolescent growth cycle is characterized by marked variability in basal metabolic rate, associated with marked fluctuations in energy output and appetite. At the end of the cycle, the basal metabolism is considerably below what it was at the beginning.

D. Pulse Rate and Blood Pressure

Growth from childhood to adulthood is also accompanied by great changes in the circulatory system. The arteries of the adult, as compared with the heart, are much smaller than they are in the child. Along with these growth changes there is a gradual decrease in pulse rate and a gradual rise in blood pressure. Figure 76 summarizes the age changes in systolic blood pressure for boys. There are significant sex differences in this respect. The changes are less marked for girls during this period, although before the age of 13.5 there is no significant difference between the

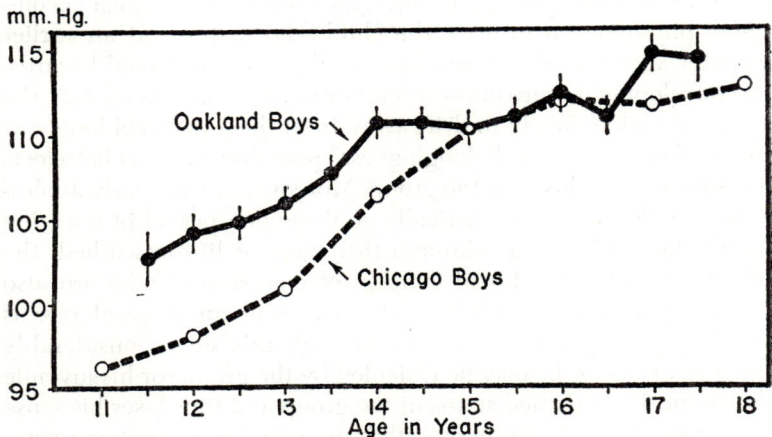

Fig. 76. Age Changes in Systolic Blood Pressure for Boys. [Reproduced from the Forty-third Yearbook of the National Society for the Study of Education, Part I, 1944, p. 60. By permission of the Society.]

[3] N. W. Shock, *Physiological Changes in Adolescence,* Forty-third Yearbook, National Society for the Study of Education (1944), Part I, Chapter V, pp. 56–79.

systolic blood pressure of boys and girls. Shock suggests that "the lower blood pressure of girls in late adolescence may be a factor which contributes to their reduced physical performance and activity during this period." [4]

E. Sexually Inappropriate Development

In boys, any deviation from typically masculine development is associated with anxiety. About one boy in ten goes through a period in which he suffers from a feminine distribution of fat or some deviation from the culturally desirable masculine pattern. During this period the boy is always emotionally upset and disturbed in his social relationships. He is often the butt of jokes and receives such nicknames as "Buttercup," "Cream Puff," or "Fatso." He withdraws from contacts with the other boys, particularly when the situation calls for undressing in their presence, as in classes in physical education or swimming. Most of these deviations from masculine development clear up spontaneously, although a few of them may require endocrine therapy.

F. Atypical Rate of Maturing

Because of the changes in interests and behavior which accompany physiological growth, the child who matures at an earlier or later age than his companions is subject to emotional hazards. By developing mature interests earlier or later than his friends, the atypical child is likely to drift away from them and feel lonely or isolated. His sense of "belongingness" may disappear as he rejects or is rejected by his own age group. Moreover, during early adolescence, children characteristically go through a period of rejecting adult standards. To go through this stage of life unscathed, the child needs the emotional support of companions who are also rejecting adults. The child who matures at an atypical rate is denied this support. If he goes through this stage considerably later than others, he may be ridiculed by the group for his juvenile behavior. He is denied status in the group and thus loses his sense of personal worth. He may withdraw, adopt unwholesome compensations, or develop undesirable defense mechanisms.

[4] *Ibid.*, p. 61.

G. The Body as the Symbol of the Self

In adolescence the child who has previously taken his bodily structure and physical appearance for granted suddenly becomes aware of both to a marked degree. He is greatly disturbed by anything which mars his physical attractiveness. Physical deformities, to which he has previously adjusted, may now loom up as insurmountable obstacles to achieving a sense of personal worth. Growing too tall or remaining too short, being too fat or too thin, having acne or moles, wearing glasses, or bands on the teeth—all are factors of personal appearance which he must accept emotionally. Failure to accept these realities of his appearance may result in such self-consciousness that social relations are seriously impaired. The overemphasis on physical attractiveness which children see in advertisements and in films serves to intensify their distress if they are not good-looking.

During adolescence, the body becomes a symbol of the self, and physical unattractiveness of any kind may threaten the child's whole life. Tolstoy, for example, says of himself, in *Childhood, Boyhood, Youth,*

> . . . moments of despair often visited me; I fancied that there was no happiness on earth for a person with such a wide nose, such thick lips, and such small eyes as I had; I besought God to work a miracle, to turn me into a beauty, and all I had in the present, or might have in the future, I would give in exchange for a handsome face.[5]

Sometimes an adolescent's anxiety over a physical blemish is symbolic of a more deep-seated maladjustment. Peter Blos [6] has written an interesting case study of an attractive adolescent girl, Betty, who was in the throes of a personality conflict. For a time Betty attributed all of her difficulties to the fact that her mother would not allow her to have a mole removed. If the mole could only be removed, she seemed to feel, her problems would disappear and she would renew her social contacts. Blos points out that the mole was actually not a disfiguring blemish, but that Betty's concern over it was symptomatic of her underlying personality conflict. Apparently, Betty found it less painful to project

---

[5] Count L. N. Tolstoy, *Childhood, Boyhood, Youth* (New York, Thomas Y. Crowell Company, 1886), p. 64.
[6] Peter Blos, *The Adolescent Personality: A Study of Individual Growth* (New York, Appleton-Century-Crofts, Inc., 1941).

her troubles to the mole than to face the problem of forming new relations with her parents and age mates.

Obesity at any age, but particularly at adolescence, may be a symptom of personality maladjustment. Obesity is occasionally the result of glandular dysfunction but more often it is merely the result of overeating. Animals do not overeat nor do well-adjusted babies, children, or adults. It is the unhappy person, the person whose basic human needs have not been met, who consoles himself by overeating. The consumption of large quantities of food is often an unconscious compensation for something of which the individual feels deprived. Food may be a symbolic substitute for affection, "belongingness," or a sense of personal worth.

Because of our cultural emphasis upon slenderness as an attribute of beauty, the normal adolescent girl is likely to err on the side of becoming too thin. The disturbed child, however, often has a compulsion to overeat. The recommendation of reduced diet in such a case is not effective unless help is at the same time given the adolescent in the solution of her emotional problems. While it is true that the adolescent girl is emotionally disturbed because she is overweight, it is even more true that she is overweight because she is emotionally disturbed.

III. DEVELOPMENTAL TASKS OF ADOLESCENCE

A. Formation of New Relationships with Adults

A major problem of adolescence is establishing new relationships with parents, teachers, and other adults. The success with which the adolescent meets this problem depends upon many factors, such as (1) his rate of maturing, (2) the wholesome or unwholesome personality adjustments of his parents or teachers, (3) his whole life history, including (a) rivalry with or jealousy of brothers and sisters, (b) overprotection or rejection on the part of one or both parents, (c) rejection of or excessive attachment to one parent, (d) his parents' expectation or demand that he achieve, and (4) his own personal assets and liabilities.

The problem of becoming emancipated from parents is much different for the underprivileged child from what it is for the middle- or upper-class child in our society. The underprivileged child, from infancy on, has greater freedom from parental restraint.

PUBERTY AND ADOLESCENCE 481

Even in very early childhood he often roams the streets alone, gets what he can to eat, comes and goes as he pleases. Frequently both parents are working and he must shift for himself. Children in poor families often take part of the financial responsibility of the family at an early age. Naturally, the boy or girl who is contributing to the support of the family will have a different attitude toward himself and toward his parents than the child who is completely dependent upon his parents for financial support. Parents, too, under such circumstances, often grant a child more freedom than he would otherwise have. This is not true, however, in certain immigrant groups, in which the father demands the entire pay envelope of his adolescent boy or girl and attempts to exercise over them a dictatorial authority characteristic of parents in the country from which he came. In America such a parental attitude inevitably leads to disturbed relations between parents and children. Commonly it results in delinquency and in a rejection of the parents and of their standards.

In middle-class American culture, as we pointed out in the previous chapter, the period just before puberty in boys is typically accompanied by a rejection of all authority, including the parents' standards and values. Characteristically, the boy adopts childish "know-it-all" attitudes and is much more concerned with what the group thinks of him than with what his parents think. Even though he has previously been well mannered, he may now go through a stage in which he is rude to adults. This is usually very disturbing to the middle-class parent. Such "symptoms," however, are normal accompaniments of this stage of growth and are, happily, of only temporary duration. In late adolescence, the normal boy will again try to conform to adult standards and values. Whether these values will be those of his parents or of some other adult model will depend upon a number of factors peculiar to his life history.

Just before puberty, girls, unlike boys, do not reject authority, but at first accept it completely. Later on, in adolescence, however, this pattern changes. Middle-class girls, in general, do not at any time appear to reject adult authority as much as do boys.

1. *Overambitious parents.* Some parents have preconceived ideas of what a child should be even before he is born. Regardless of the child's talents and aptitudes, the parents plan to rear him for a particular role in society and a predetermined career. For

example, a certain father who had tried to become a doctor and also was unsuccessful at what he did do, had his heart set on a medical career for his son. The boy did not have the requisite aptitude and interest but, out of filial loyalty, worked doggedly to get into the medical school. After six years of pre-medical school training, and after failing twice in the entrance examinations, he finally managed to squeeze through the requirements for entering medical school. At the end of the second semester, however, he failed in his examinations and was dismissed. By this time he was twenty-five years of age and felt that he was too old to start over again. He had a marked feeling of inferiority which led him to adopt a number of unwholesome compensations.

2. *Parents who "absorb" the personalities of their children.* Some parents "absorb" their children and try to train them to conceive of themselves as part of their parents' non-physical personality. Their demand extends not only throughout childhood but is projected on into adult life, perhaps even beyond the death of the parent. To a limited extent, this is even a normal desire on the parents' part. It exemplifies the normal desire for physical continuance of the family, thus making the cleavage between life and death less drastic.

Many factors may produce an abnormal desire on the part of parents to absorb the child's personality: the parents' own limited outlets for making a lasting impression in the world of affairs; extreme concentration on the affairs of this world and its overestimation; the child may be an only child and hence the only outlet for their hopes; middle- and upper-class codes of making a mark in the social world through manipulating other people's personalities; the upper-class concept that the child belongs to a long line of ancestors and must bear their family name worthily among the coming generation; and, of course, the inadequacies in the personality of the dominating parent.

Such a child may rebel against this absorption while still an infant or during the preschool period. On the other hand, he may accept it, knowing nothing else. But the catalytic factor in the situation which precipitates a problem—and it must come sooner or later—appears when the same parent expects the child who has been subordinated now to become a leader among his companions. The two roles are incompatible, and the climax of the difficulty is likely to appear in adolescence. It is more pronounced in boys than in girls, since greater dominance behavior is expected of the male than of the female. The girl may achieve dominance through her beauty or her very appealing dependence and submission to parents or their surrogates. Unless there is a conflict in the demands made upon her by her associates with those of her parents, it is possible for her to play a relatively similar role at home and away from home. But the boy is expected to achieve dominance (which his father possesses or longs impotently to achieve) among his peers, even while he is submissive to his father's outmoded concepts and techniques.

The child of the lower income group is less likely to be absorbed by his parents because those factors operating in the lives of the middle class and the wealthy to cause them to try to absorb their children are less pronounced and because other factors which tend to stand in the way of absorption are present, as, for example, the economic success achieved by the young person through his manual skill and physical strength.

3. *Parents who are too strict and rigid in their discipline.* Children at all ages need discipline, and discipline necessarily involves unpleasantness. Punishment, however, in and of itself does not socialize a child nor make him a better human being. On the contrary, if it is not accompanied in the child by an awareness of love and affection it may have exactly the opposite effect. But because some parents and teachers punish unwisely, it does not follow that all punishment is undesirable or unnecessary. The wise adult should ask himself two questions when a child's behavior seems to merit punishment: (1) Why should I punish? and (2) What permanent effect is this punishment likely to have upon the child?

One of the most traumatic experiences in the life of a child or young person is harsh and unmerited punishment. The life histories of adult criminals and psychoneurotics are filled with instances of unreasonable punishment on the part of a parent or parent substitute. It often leads to aggression which shows itself under varied forms. It may take the form of outward revolt, such as incorrigible behavior, stealing, and destructiveness. Or it may take the form of smoldering resentment under the cover of submissive behavior. An already submissive child may, through feelings of guilt, repress his anger toward his parents and unconsciously turn it inward upon himself. Certain types of illness, frequent accidents, self-torture—such as sleeplessness, obsessive fears and anxieties, depressions of such severity that failure in school and social life result—all may be the unconscious outcome of repressed hostility toward parents.

4. *Parents who are too lax.* Adolescents strive to become emancipated from their parents and resent too much parental control. A complete lack of parental control, however, does not make them happy. Fleege [7] made a study of the problems of adolescent boys enrolled in Catholic high schools. He found, interestingly enough, that not a few boys complained about parents who were too lax. He found that for almost every boy who complained that his parents insisted that he come in early at night, there was another boy who complained that his parents did not care enough about him to set up standards of conduct. The boys whose parents gave them too much freedom were not grateful but interpreted this parental laxity as a lack of love.

5. *Relations with adults other than parents.* An adolescent's relations with adults have a very important influence upon the attitudes and values which will guide his own life. Adults may help or hinder adolescents in their progress toward maturity. Some of the commonest roles in which adults function in the lives of adolescents are as follows: (1) as parent substitutes; (2) as objects of "crushes" and hero-worship; (3) as scapegoats or objects of hostility and aggression; and (4) as friendly counselors.

B. Boy-Girl Relationships

The glandular changes at puberty are accompanied by a new interest in the opposite sex. In middle-class society this interest first manifests itself in awkward, bungling attempts to make contact with members of the opposite sex. At social gatherings of both boys and girls, there is an early tendency for boys to line up on one side of the room and girls to congregate on the other side. The girls at first dance with each other, and as they do so they come closer and closer to the boys. Often, as the girls come near, one of the boys will push his pal against the girls, and both boys and girls will giggle hilariously. Later the boy will, instead of pushing his pal, pretend to trip a girl accidentally. Her characteristic comment, "Why don't you look where you're going?" is

---

[7] Urban Fleege, *Self-Revelation of the Adolescent Boy* (Milwaukee, Bruce Publishing Company, 1945).

followed by his, "Keep your big feet out of my way!" Later, when the boy asks the girl to dance, he does not say, "May I have this dance?" but "Do ya think you can dance? Well, let's see!" After that, boy-girl contacts proceed more smoothly.

The adolescent boy's prestige with other boys is enhanced if he is accepted by girls. In later adolescence, this prestige comes not just from being accepted by girls, but from being accepted by the "right" girls. Often two boys will develop a friendship on the basis of their mutual interest in the same girl. This apparently never happens among girls.

Sexual maturity is accompanied by a heightened sensitivity to many different stimuli and by an increased intensity of feeling. The adolescent "falls" in love or develops "crushes." For the time being he lives only for the object of his devotion; nothing else matters. But these first love affairs are usually temporary even though the adolescents experiencing them may expect them to last forever.

The emergence of a deep love for one member of the opposite sex, occurring as it generally does shortly after puberty, has led some psychologists to claim that "love" and "sex" are synonymous. To reason thus is to commit a logical fallacy. It is like saying that because glass is a non-conductor of electricity, all non-conductors are glass. Similarly, to hold that sexual maturity is the "cause" of love is to commit another logical fallacy. It is the same fallacy as that occurring when we assume, without evidence, that a positive coefficient of correlation indicates a cause and effect relationship. The fact, for example, that in London the viscosity of the asphalt at different times in the year is positively correlated with the rate of infant mortality, is a case in point. It would be absurd to assume, from this correlation, that the change in one of the above variables is the "cause" of the change in the other variable. Both variables are probably correlated because they are dependent upon a third variable, namely, temperature.

The boy's first love for a girl is one of adoration rather than of sexual desire. In his mind, the boy is likely to put the object of his love upon a pedestal, and cast himself, unworthy as he is, humbly at her feet. His love and his sex impulses are not directed to the same object. Even when a boy does give expression to his developing sexual impulses, his partner is never a girl whom he loves.[8] One of the big problems of adolescent development, and one upon which the integration of the adult personality depends, is the finding of a way of harmonizing physiological and spiritual desires. The solution of this problem is a necessary preparation for a complete satisfying marriage.

Many adolescents, particularly those of the middle class, have confused attitudes toward sex and are worried and anxious because of their new bodily sensations. It is a mistake for anyone to assume that sex instruction or education will remove these anxieties. Attitudes toward sex are only one aspect of a child's total attitude toward life. If an adolescent's general attitude toward life is good, and if he enjoys wholesome relations with his parents, with other adults, with boys and girls of his own age level, and is happily adjusted to his school and community, there need be no serious sex problem in his life. Maladjustment in any sphere of life, however, may be converted into a problem of sex.

The preparation for adolescence begins at the dawn of life. Attitudes toward sex are not suddenly acquired in adolescence, but have their roots in the experiences of infancy and childhood. *How* the child's first interest in sex was accepted by adults who cared for him rather than *what* they said to him may influence him for a lifetime. If, during the preschool period, the parent has hinted in any way that sex is "not nice" or "nasty," a lifelong attitude of shame or embarrassment may be the result. Even though the adolescent will have forgotten these early experiences, his emotional life will still be colored by them and may prevent him from making a wholesome adjustment to the opposite sex.

The boy-girl relationships first formed in adolescence have as their basis a generalized sex attraction. This attraction is not centered in any one member of the opposite sex nor is it directed toward a physical satisfaction. It consists of an interest in and a delight in the company of the opposite sex, accompanied by an appreciation of the distinctive characteristics of the opposite sex.

Personal sex attraction differs from generalized sex attraction in that it is directed toward a given individual and is accompanied by intense and sometimes overwhelming emotion. When associated with true friendship, it has an important role to play

---

[8] Iovetz-Tereschenko, *Friendship-Love in Adolescence* (London, George Allen and Unwin, Ltd., 1936).

in the preparation for and happy adjustment in the marriage state. It can, however, be nothing more than an infatuation, that is, a blind and unreasonable attraction to a person totally unsuitable for a marriage partner. Adolescents need guidance in determining whether or not their love is real, that is, a love based on true friendship and involving the total personality. In coming to such a decision the following criteria of true friendship will be helpful:

1. There must exist between the two persons a genuine basis of agreement on fundamental issues, an agreement which will make for lasting harmony. This does not imply that the friends cannot disagree on minor issues and have different likes and dislikes. But it does mean that they must have the same ideas of (*a*) right and wrong, (*b*) the purpose of human life, (*c*) the rights and duties of married couples, and in general, (*d*) the same religious principles and ideals.

2. The relationship must be morally helpful to both persons. True friendship or comradeship is always based upon a sincere desire to promote the other's welfare. It is characterized by a desire to share with the friend whatever of good one possesses. It may or may not be accompanied by a physical attraction, but it always implies a mental attraction. True friendship is fundamentally a love of the mind. An appreciation of the good in the other person leads to a desire for union with him.

3. Lastly, true friendship involves a willingness to sacrifice oneself for the friend. It is based upon an unselfish love of giving, not of getting. Unless this element of sacrifice is present, there is no true friendship.

True friendship, such as we have described it above, is a necessary prerequisite for a happy marriage. Unless the three criteria for judging true friendship are fulfilled, it is dangerous to consider marriage. The attraction should be carefully, even if painfully, rooted out before the infatuation becomes too great. If allowed to develop, an infatuation that cannot be rationally justified will lead to untold unhappiness and perhaps even to the loss of one's soul.

In summary, let us quote Father Gerald Kelly, S.J., who says,

> . . . the love of married people for each other is not merely spiritual, nor mere emotion, nor certainly mere passion; but it crosses

through all spheres—the mind, the heart, the body—and is thus a distinctive kind of love. Theirs is a love of the *mind,* a union of mutual esteem and appreciation which enables them to achieve harmony in the vast community of interests that make up married life; a love of the *heart,* affectionate and tender and exclusive; and a love of the *body,* through which they mutually find great joy in the utter self-giving which makes them 'two in one flesh' and enables them to bring forth children as the fruit of their love. With this three-fold bond of love they are able to achieve the full perfection of marriage. The physical provides for procreation; the exclusive attachment of the heart provides for fidelity; and the spiritual union of souls keeps them together unto death.[9]

C. Acceptance by Other Adolescents

In adolescence both boys and girls develop new relationships with members of their own age group. The personal traits and characteristics which make for acceptance or popularity in adolescence differ in some respects from those which led to acceptance at an earlier age. Acceptance by the group and the adolescent's status in the group do not, however, depend entirely upon his own personal characteristics. They depend upon the kind of group in which he participates, its sense of values, and its status in the larger community.

As children grow older, their notions of what constitutes desirable behavior in their companions undergo a change. At present, there are not enough available research data from which to draw up clear-cut generalizations concerning the factors associated with prestige at each age level, but there are several very suggestive studies. C. M. Tryon made a follow-up study of adolescent boys and girls. These children were asked to fill out the "Guess-Who" test when they were in the seventh grade and again when they were in the ninth grade. The directions for this test and some sample items are given below. At the end of the "Guess-Who" test is the statement: "Here is someone who is my best friend." An estimate of a given child's popularity or prestige is derived from his score on this item, which is the number of times he is mentioned as "best friend" by members of the group. The next step in determining what characteristics are associated with prestige is to work out scores on the other items of the questionnaire. A study is then made of the differences in

---

[9] Gerald Kelly, S.J., *Modern Youth and Chastity* (St. Louis, The Queen's Work, 1941), p. 26.

A Sample of the "Guess-Who" Test

Directions

Below are some word pictures of members of your class or school. Read each statement and write down the names of the persons whom you think the description fits. Remember:

One description may fit several persons. You may write as many names as you think belong under each.
The same person may be mentioned for more than one description.
Write "myself" if you think the description fits you.
If you cannot think of anyone to match a particular description, go on to the next one.

1. Here is someone who finds it hard to sit still in class; he (or she) moves around in his (or her) seat or gets up and walks around.

    _____   _____

    _____   _____

2. Here is someone who can work very quietly without moving around in his (or her) seat.

    _____   _____

3. Here is somebody who likes to talk a lot; always has something to say.

    _____   _____

ratings for children who apparently have prestige, as indicated by ratings on the last item, and those who do not.

The specific characteristics mentioned more frequently for the "high prestige" group are, supposedly, characteristics which have prestige value at the age level studied. The children filling out the "Guess-Who" test were all middle-class, white children living in Oakland, California. Among seventh-grade girls in this group, prestige was associated with such qualities as being friendly, quiet, tidy, and ladylike. By the time these girls had reached the ninth grade, however, their conception of the ideal girl had changed. Tryon says of this group, "In general the emphasis has shifted from being ladylike and conforming to adult standards to being a good sport and attractive to the boys." [10] Elsewhere, in summarizing her findings in terms of twelve-year-old and fifteen-year-old patterns, she points out that prestige for fifteen-year-old girls may be achieved through either of two major channels, namely: (1) through buoyant, rather aggressive

[10] C. M. Tryon, *Evaluations of Adolescent Personalities by Adolescents*, Monograph of the Society for Research in Child Development (Washington, D.C., National Research Council, 1939), Vol. IV. No. 4.

good fellowship with boys or girls, or (2) through sophisticated, glamorous qualities which attract the boys.[11]

In this same chapter, summarizing the prestige pattern for twelve-year-old boys, Tryon writes,

> There is a marked tendency for children of this age to emphasize for boys the desirability of activity of any sort; to prefer in the boy aggressiveness, boisterousness, and unkemptness, to submissiveness, reserve, and tidiness; to appreciate certain "feminine" components if they are associated in the individual with other masculine qualities; to respect above all competence in group games.[12]

Of the fifteen-year-old boys, Tryon writes,

> Attributes which are frequently considered "masculine," such as skill in games, fearlessness, and self-assertion, continue to be important determiners of prestige for the fifteen-year-old boy. However, equal emphasis is placed upon personableness and social ease, and poise in heterosexual situations. Cheerfulness and a sense of humor are important but boisterousness and hyperactivity are regarded as rather childish and unimportant.[13]

Further research on this subject is needed before we can say that this is the characteristic pattern in other geographical areas, social classes, and of other ethnic groups in the United States.

The results of the "Guess-Who" test, like all other data, must be evaluated in terms of the total personality. It is going beyond the data to assume that the person of greatest prestige in the group is necessarily the happiest and most well adjusted. On the contrary, it is possible for a boy or girl to have prestige in the group and at the same time fail to establish any warm, personal relationships with individual members of the group. Some adolescents undoubtedly sacrifice nearly everything in life to attain popularity. The struggle for prestige may be an overcompensation for a lack of love or security. An individual may have prestige in the group and still be the victim of the deepest anxiety. The normal personality is the balanced personality. The oversatisfaction of one basic human need does not make up for the frustration of another.

[11] C. M. Tryon, "Evaluations of Adolescent Personalities by Adolescents." By permission from *Child Behavior and Development*, edited by Barker, Kounin, and Wright. Copyright, 1943, McGraw-Hill Book Company, Inc.
[12] *Ibid.*, p. 558.
[13] *Ibid.*, p. 560.

PUBERTY AND ADOLESCENCE

A child's ability to make friends outside of his home and to establish relations with other people is profoundly influenced by his family background. If his parents are cold, reserved persons, he is likely to experience greater difficulty than if they have warm, outgoing personalities. The parents' ways of expressing affection, their tolerance or intolerance of others, and their attitudes toward coöperation and competition are the foundation upon which the adolescent builds his patterns of social and emotional behavior outside the home.

The social class to which an adolescent belongs determines, to a considerable extent, the social groups and cliques to which he will be admitted. During adolescence, the child becomes increasingly aware of social stratification. For the first time in his life he may be snubbed or feel that he is being avoided by people who accepted him as a child. Parents sometimes consciously, often unconsciously, bring pressure to bear on the child to confine his friendships to "acceptable" people. In the upper class or in the upper-middle-class this may be done by suggesting that a companion is undesirable because "we don't know his family," or "he just isn't our kind." If a boy or girl continues to bring an "unacceptable" friend to the home, the friend is often subtly humiliated, until in self-defense he stays away. Thus is the American status hierarchy strengthened and maintained.

Participation in the social life of a high school is limited by social and economic background. Attendance at school dances, particularly if they are formal, is often limited to the two upper social classes represented in the school. Usually none of the lower-class and few of the lower-middle-class [14] children are present at such functions. Positions of leadership, too, in the high school are more often held by children of superior social status than by those of inferior status.

One phase of high school life which would seem to be relatively free from social class influence is that of ability grouping. Yet here, too, the social class system is at work. Warner presents data showing that ability grouping in high school is made by teachers along social class lines. Warner also shows that within the large, so-called "democratic" public high school, a child's so-

---

[14] The term *class* is used here in the sense that Lloyd Warner and his co-workers use it, as described in Chapter III.

cial class determines, to a considerable extent, the curriculum he will follow.[15]

In many schools, social groupings follow definite ethnic lines, so that the Jewish children, for example, attend only Jewish social functions, Polish children form cliques made up exclusively of Poles, and Irish children reject the Scandinavians, and vice versa. These ethnic groupings are a reflection of the adult social pattern in the community, and an adolescent cannot violate the prevailing social code without incurring censure. The mere fact that all of these children attend the same high school does not insure democratic participation in social activities. High school social functions, participation in which brings the greatest prestige, may never be attended at all by adolescents from ethnic groups whose status in the community is low.

Neighborhood playgrounds may be adequate in size for all of the children, but are often dominated by one ethnic group. One Chicago playground, for example, was patrolled by several hundred Irish boys who successfully prevented any Polish or Italian children from using it.

D. Realistic Occupational Adjustments

Satisfactory vocational adjustment means that a person is not only able to earn a living, but also that he is content with the way in which he is earning a living. A great many young people, however, suffer intense disappointment and frustration when they leave school and enter the vocational world. The occupations open to them are often very different from those in which they had hoped to find employment. A marked discrepancy exists between the aspirations of youth and the possibilities which exist for fulfilling them. The situation appears to be even more serious for girls than for boys.

One reason for youth's unrealistic attitude toward job opportunities is our culturally approved acceptance of the goal of social mobility. The preferred occupations of youth have a higher social prestige value than the non-preferred jobs. Mobility is facilitated, too, by an increase of wealth. Hence, occupations which provide the best opportunity for making money are usually

---

[15] L. Warner, "Educative Effects of Social Class," in E. W. Burgess, *et al.*, *Environment and Education* (Chicago, University of Chicago, Committee on Human Development, Supplemental Educational Monograph, 1942).

preferred. They are sometimes preferred even when they involve the sacrifice of significant human values, such as leisure time to spend with one's family.

Teachers, belonging as they do to the white-collar class, may play a part in the unrealistic attitude of youth toward occupations. Many teachers have themselves been socially mobile, and even when they do not consciously urge young people to aspire to a higher vocational level than that of their parents, they often do so unconsciously.

The frustration and disillusionment of youth, once they leave school and find that the occupations they planned to enter are not open to them, may have serious social consequences. To prevent such disillusionment, teachers should be better educated to understand social and economic problems in their impact upon youth. They should also be encouraged to teach children as early as possible the realities of the situation. The Christian teacher, conscious of the dignity of all significant work, must do everything in her power to prevent children from believing that the more remunerative occupations are more "respectable" and desirable than those less remunerative. She must help them to think realistically about the social contributions of which they are potentially capable.

A young person who is sincerely Christian will not have a snobbish disdain for manual labor nor for any type of work that is necessary and useful. He will select his life work not for the money nor for the social position which will accrue from it, but for its value as a means to his eternal destiny. This implies that he will judge the value of any specific work on the following criteria: (1) the will of God, (2) the development of the human person engaged in the work, and (3) the service that can be rendered to God and to other human beings by means of such work.

Adequate vocational guidance is based upon an analysis of the needs of society and upon the aptitudes, interests, abilities, and goals of the individual who is being guided.

Many tests of aptitude have been developed which are useful in vocational counseling. General academic aptitude tests are perhaps the most frequently used, although more specific tests, such as those of scientific, artistic, or linguistic aptitude, are also commonly used. An aptitude test is used to predict what an individual is likely to do in the future, once he has acquired the necessary education and training. Typically, such tests measure a sampling of the abilities and characteristics of the person as he is at the time of testing and do not actually measure his future accomplishments. From the responses made to an aptitude test, a prediction is made of what the person is likely to do in the future. This prediction is always made in terms of probabilities only. Once a sufficient number of persons has been tested and the test results analyzed in terms of what these persons later accomplished, it is possible to estimate what the chances are that a person with a given test score will succeed. For example, if only 10 per cent of persons making scores of 30 or less later succeed in a given task, the probability that an individual getting a score as low as 30 will later succeed is extremely low. Ordinarily, it would be wise to counsel such an individual out of an occupation for which his aptitude score was so low. However, the chances are one in ten that he can succeed, and given other favorable conditions, he may decide to take the chance.

Personality traits must also be considered in making vocational recommendations. The highly competitive person who is happy only if he surpasses others may not be too happily adjusted in an occupation for which he has only an average amount of aptitude. His personal adjustment may be better served if he is counseled into an occupation for which his aptitude is exceptionally high, even if this occupation is on a lower level than another in which he could achieve mediocre success. In this way he can become "a big fish in a little pond" rather than "a little fish in a big pond."

E. Establishment of His Role in the Community

During adolescence the child's place in the community is gradually defined and crystallized. The factors of importance in defining this role are (1) his own personality; (2) his parents —their characters; educational, social and economic status; their attitude toward him; his identification or lack of identification with them; (3) the nature of the community—whether rural, small-town, or urban; whether social or antisocial; types of adults in the community who enjoy prestige.

The effect of the second of the above factors in defining the social role of the adolescent is strikingly illustrated in a study by

PUBERTY AND ADOLESCENCE

Porterfield.[16] In summarizing his findings, Porterfield has this to say:

> The data given so far indicate strongly two conclusions: first, there are great similarities in the behavior of college students and in cases that are complained about in the juvenile court; second, there is a wide difference in the extent to which the two groups are brought to court for the same offenses.[17]

The fact that one group appears in court for offenses for which the other group does not appear, Porterfield attributes to two main factors:

1. *Socio-economic status.* The college students come from more important families which, at the same time, are families that come to the rescue of the youth in trouble. The other children come from families of less social importance than the police who arrest them or the clerks and managers of five-and-ten-cent stores who turn them in for petty shoplifting. Their parents either will not or cannot come to their defense. Such children, even if they wish to reform, usually have nothing to look forward to as an incentive to good living.

2. *Family disorganization.* Only 16 per cent of the college students as compared with 50.6 per cent of the court cases from families of known status, came from broken homes. In more than 17 per cent of the court cases the fathers were dead.

It will be of interest to note here that during the great depression of the early 1930's statistics showed that the amount of juvenile delinquency in the country was less than it had been. At this time, many fathers were out of work and spending their time at home. Although these men were in a state of frustration as a result of their forced idleness, their presence at home was apparently a factor in keeping their children out of trouble.

In adolescence there is a marked increase in percentage of delinquency, although in most cases, the first delinquency occurs before the age of puberty. The factors making for delinquency are both sociological and psychological. Shaw and McKay have helped to clarify the sociological factors which lead to delinquency. They feel that efforts to treat and prevent delinquency have in general been ineffective because too much attention has been given to the individual offender and not enough to the neighborhood setting in which the delinquency occurs. In some

---

[16] A. L. Porterfield, *Youth in Trouble* (Fort Worth, The Leo Potishman Foundation, 1946).
[17] *Ibid.*, p. 45.

neighborhoods it is now quite evident that children learn to shoplift just as in others they learn to play tennis. A child who lives in a neighborhood where a gangster has prestige may accept his scale of values as easily as another child would accept those of a doctor or a lawyer. In the words of Shaw and McKay,

> Whether or not we care to admit it, most delinquent boys reflect all too accurately what they have learned in the process of living in their own communities. If we wish to have fewer delinquents, or if we wish to modify the mode of life of those who are already delinquent, a way must be found to modify those aspects of the community life which provide the appropriate setting for delinquency careers and which give to these careers the sanction and approbation on which all social behavior depends.[18]

Important as is the neighborhood in the genesis of delinquency, the family pattern appears to be of equal or even of greater importance. Almost without exception, whatever other factors enter in, the delinquent is a child whose need for satisfying relationships within his family circle has somehow been blocked.

Prescott, in a summary of the factors that tend to give rise to delinquency, lists the following:

1. A gap between desires and the ability or opportunity to achieve these desires.
2. Unbearable repression at home, at school, or both.
3. Failure to achieve a sense of personal worth and of "belongingness" in society because of racial, religious, or cultural differences, or because of personal peculiarities.
4. The loss of adequate affectional ties brought about by broken homes, or because of undesirable personal characteristics of parents or of the child.
5. An overstimulated life which results in the craving for more and more emotion.
6. An emotionally starved life which leads the child to feel that anything is better than the drabness he has experienced.
7. Unbearable tensions of a wide variety of types which are released by the thrill of a delinquent act.[19]

The adolescent's problem of adjustment to the community is partly dependent upon the type of community in which he is reared. In a farming community the adolescent takes his place as

[18] C. R. Shaw and H. D. McKay, *Juvenile Delinquency and Urban Areas* (Chicago, University of Chicago Press, 1942), p. 446.
[19] D. A. Prescott, *Emotion and the Educative Process* (Washington, D.C., American Council on Education, 1938), 152–153.

PUBERTY AND ADOLESCENCE

an adult much earlier than he does in an urban community. Economically, he is an asset to his parents on the farm, but in the city he is a liability. On the farm he can earn a living as an adult and start his own family at a much earlier age than he can in the city. Unlike the urban child, the rural adolescent is likely to be more concerned with his status among adults than among his own peer group. Today, when so many rural youth are leaving the farm for small towns and cities, their problem of social adjustment is increased. Rural youth, partly because they usually leave on the school bus immediately after school, have in general shared fewer social functions with their own age group than have urban youth. As a consequence, many of them lack the social experience necessary to cultivate poised relationships with people. When these individuals move to a larger community, they often feel isolated and lonely and experience difficulty in making social adjustments.

F. Mature Religious and Philosophical Outlook

The child accepts the religious beliefs and practices of his family uncritically just as he accepts their political views, their ways of celebrating holidays, and their general outlook on life as the "right" way. But in adolescence he begins to question these things. His questioning is a necessary part of his growing up, of attaining independence of his family. During adolescence the child must develop a religious outlook that is his "own" rather than one which has been accepted automatically and uncritically because of his parents' or teachers' views. He must think through the implications of his religious beliefs for his everyday life, and must strive on his own initiative to effect a harmony between belief and practice.

The experiences of every period of life contribute to the development of an adult philosophy of life. During adolescence, however, certain very intense experiences may profoundly alter the entire course of a life. Sometimes a "crush" on a teacher or on a football coach results in a complete emotional identification on the part of the adolescent. This identification leads the child to adopt, uncritically, the entire system of values held by the loved adult. If the adult has a nasal drawl, the child will develop one, too. If the adult dresses sloppily, so will the child. Long after the "crush" is over, the standards and values of the idol of youth may continue to govern his life as a mature person. This is one reason why it is so important to surround the adolescent with persons worthy of identification. Boys, for example, need men teachers with whom they can identify. These teachers should exemplify the best pattern of manhood in the community. Yet in many cities men teachers are not available because people do not give enough prestige to the vocation of teaching and because the community is unwilling to pay a sufficiently high salary to attract good men to the teaching profession.

In early adolescence, the child is primarily concerned with making adjustments to his changing body and to his widening social horizon. He is little given to altruism at this stage. Generosity and magnanimity require, as a prerequisite background, a satisfactory solution to these problems of physical, social, and emotional adjustment. Once these problems have been satisfactorily handled, the adolescent becomes emotionally free to plan his life in terms of meaningful goals.

The turning point of the adolescent's life occurs when he first asks the question, "For what do I want to live?" This question implies that the answer will be one all-embracing goal, in terms of which the whole life can be interpreted and evaluated.

Before this stage of development, the child's goals have been more or less specific and "piecemeal"; for example, "To be popular at this dance," "To get a larger allowance," and "To get a passing grade in this class." Earlier in life, he does not usually even raise the question of a unifying purpose, let alone attempt to answer it.

In our twentieth-century world, the adolescent is surrounded by a confusion of values. Try as he may, he may never find a satisfactory answer to his question. As a result he goes through life seeking only specific, non-related goals. And when he fails to achieve one of these goals, he often feels that he has failed in life. He is, consequently, more susceptible to mental breakdown than is the individual whose life as a whole has meaning—the one who can afford to lose individual battles provided that in the end he wins the war.

Studies of delinquent adolescents sent to reformatories throw considerable light upon the genesis of antisocial philosophies of life. Identification with an older delinquent who has status with the group and who is doing time for "pulling a big job" is a common factor. There are many illustrations of this phenomenon in the scientific literature on the subject, in autobiographies, and in fiction.[20]

IV. THE UNDERPRIVILEGED ADOLESCENT

Studies of slum cultures made during the first quarter of this century describe the environmental conditions under which underprivileged youth of that day lived. But even our slum cultures have not remained static, and today such studies are chiefly of historical interest in throwing light upon the factors which influenced the older members living in our society today. They do not describe the environment of the contemporary adolescent. These earlier studies tended to emphasize either the personality of the child himself (while recognizing, of course, the interaction of the child and the environment) or the culture of the group. Probably the best integration of the knowledge of both the individual and of the culture is found in the work of Healy and Bronner and of the Gluecks in dealing with dependent and delinquent children in child guidance clinics.

Studies depicting the contrasting factors in the lives of typical Polish families of the lower income group with youth in the American middle-class home are illuminating.[21] The Polish child is more likely to become delinquent, since delinquency lies in the culture pattern of his neighborhood. He is less likely to develop personality difficulties and neurotic traits, however, since his personality is not absorbed by his parents as so often it is in the middle-class home. Viewed in the light of ideal standards of child care, he appears to be neglected and even harshly treated. Possibly he would be better off if he were more emotionally dependent upon his parents, instead of living an independent life with his peers. The point to be stressed, however, is that certain configurations of factors in a lower socio-economic group, such

[20] E.g., in C. Shaw, *The Jack Roller, a Delinquent Boy's Own Story* (Chicago, University of Chicago Press, 1930), and *The Natural History of a Delinquent Career* (Chicago, University of Chicago Press, 1931); and Willard Motley, *Knock on Any Door* (New York, Appleton-Century-Crofts, Inc., 1947).
[21] A. W. Green, "The Middle Class Male Child and Neurosis," *Amer. Soc. Rev.*, II (1946). 31–41.

as that of the Polish immigrant family, may be more conducive to mental health than the presumably more favorable factors operating in middle-class homes.

V. DIFFERENTIAL EDUCATIONAL OPPORTUNITIES OF ADOLESCENTS

A child's progress toward maturity is helped or hindered by the presence or absence of formal educational opportunities. Such opportunities vary somewhat from one part of the country to the other. They are determined to a great extent by the economic status of the family. From several studies made in small cities of New England, the South, and the Middle West, in which the population of each city was sorted into several groups, the education of the children of each group was compared. The following broad categories emerged:

a. The upper group as regards income sends nearly all its children through high school, public or private, and about 90 per cent to college. These are professional people, owners, managers, and persons living on inherited money. Practically all of them can afford to send their children to college, but they produce only some 8 per cent of the children in the community.

b. The middle group as regards income sends about 60 per cent of its children through high school and about 15 per cent to college or some other higher institution. They are small business men, clerical and other office workers, minor professional people, foremen and a few skilled workers. They produce about a third of the children in the community. Many of these young people aspire to positions above those of their parents, and for them high school and, more rarely, college, are roads to this goal. While a good number of them have excellent native ability, their parents cannot afford to send them to college, and they must look to scholarships and part-time employment if they go. The presence of a tuition-free college nearby makes their going more likely.

c. The lower group sends about 30 per cent of its children through high school and about 5 per cent through college. It comprises the great majority of workers, skilled, semiskilled, and unskilled. They are the poor. They produce about 60 per cent of the children of the community. It is usually a sacrifice for them to keep their children in high school, and they cannot possibly pay money toward college. The minority of young people from this group who finish high school are often ambitious for better things. They take commercial and other vocational courses hoping for more security and a higher income than their fathers knew. But there is usually a limit to their hopes. Most of them will be satisfied with a step up to a slightly higher income, and the very few who aspire to college must work their way without help from home.[22]

VI. CHARACTERISTICS OF COLLEGE STUDENTS

College students tend to be a selected group intellectually and physically. The degree of selection varies with the particular college attended. In general, the average intelligence of the freshman class is lower than that of the sophomore class, and that of the sophomore class lower than that of the junior class. Since the least gifted tend to drop out of college, college graduates are an even more selected group than the college population itself.

By the time college is reached, most girls have just about completed their anatomical and physiological growth. Some bodily measurements, however, do increase slightly long after maximum height has been attained. Hip width in girls tends to increase slightly during the college years. Chest depth in college girls, as well as in boys, tends to increase.

At the college age, boys generally reach the peak of their motor abilities. This development is reflected in the interest in athletics characteristic of this age. Both boys and girls apparently reach the peak of their mental ability at this age level.

VII. ADJUSTMENT PROBLEMS OF THE COLLEGE STUDENT

College students, like people in general, need to feel that they are valued members of the groups in which they participate. But some students unfortunately are rejected by their fellows. The rejection may be based on personal characteristics, such as an unpleasant disposition, lack of sensitivity to the needs of others, or a boastful egotism. Or, it may be based upon factors over which the student has no control, such as the social class to which his family belongs or his membership in a minority group. Then, too, it may reflect a superficial sense of values on the part of the group, such that they cannot accept a person of superior worth. How the problem can best be attacked will depend upon the pat-

---

[22] *General Education in a Free Society*, Report of the Harvard Committee (Cambridge, Harvard University Press, 1945), pp. 86–87.

tern of causes which determine rejection in a particular instance.

The way in which a student will react to rejection by his classmates will vary with his temperament and background. He may resort to attention-getting behavior, chronic complaining or boasting, habitual tardiness or absence, scholastic failure, violations of regulations and rules, withdrawal and daydreaming, or compulsive "A"-chasing. If he has a sufficiently deep sense of personal worth, based upon successful achievement or affectionate and secure relationships outside of college, and a well-formulated philosophy of life, he may accept the situation as a challenge. When such is the case, he often has a better opportunity than most students to develop an independent, forceful and creative personality, and to pursue his ideals without hesitating because of what the group might think.

The best-adjusted college students are not of necessity the campus leaders, those who are most popular, or those who get the highest grades. Among these are many eminently successful students on every college campus who put on a good show of being happy and at peace, the so-called "pillars" of the college. Yet inwardly they may be seething with emotional problems and their excessive activity may be a defense against anxiety and insecurity. Their lives are unbalanced, lacking in significant purpose, and it is characteristic of them to sacrifice the most important values in life to the acquisition of prestige and success. In spite of their poise and savoir-faire they are not "mature" in any genuine sense of the word.

Some college students continually borrow on tomorrow's energy, live in a state of constant tension, yet characteristically accomplish very little. They fill their lives with unrelated activities, all of which seem to them of equal importance. They are constantly at war with time. Yet in spite of an enormous expenditure of energy, they feel frustrated and blocked. They may even succumb to a so-called "nervous breakdown," the explanation of which is not as simple as is generally implied by the familiar masking term *overwork*. The breakdown is caused not by overwork alone, since many people work extremely hard, yet do not break down. It is caused by overwork which does not result in anything significant. Typically, it results from a feeling of futility, a feeling which inevitably, in the case of gifted students, proceeds from the lack of a clearly defined, realistic, and unifying goal. It is essential to the development of an integrated personality that there be but one central goal in life, yet many college students are unable to acquire this singleness of purpose, partly because of social factors existing on the campus, partly because of the disintegrated curriculum, and partly because of their own personal limitations.

SUGGESTED READING

ALLERS, RUDOLPH, *Character Education in Adolescence* (New York, J. F Wagner, Inc., 1940).

HAVIGHURST, R. J., and TABA, H., *Adolescent Character and Personality* (New York, John Wiley & Sons, Inc., 1949).

KUHLEN, R. G., *The Psychology of Adolescent Development* (New York, Harper & Brothers, 1951).

SCHUMACHER, H. C., *The Adolescent, His Development and His Major Problems* (Huntington, Indiana, Our Sunday Visitor Press. N.D.).

SUPER, DONALD E., *The Dynamics of Vocational Adjustment* (New York, Harper & Brothers, 1942).

PART VII

Personality and Social Psychology

Human beings develop their personalities in association with their fellows. A common social milieu produces similarities in development. Yet even in the same environment each human being retains his individuality.

XIX

Human Personality

Person signifies what is most perfect in all nature.
—ST. THOMAS AQUINAS [1]

1. THE INDIVIDUAL "WHOLE PERSONALITY" IN PSYCHOLOGY

Throughout this book we have stressed the necessity of studying the whole personality rather than isolated segments of it. The reason for this emphasis is readily apparent when we consider that everything we study in psychology—sensation, perception, learning, memory, feeling, thinking—has its roots in an individual person. It is the *person* who senses, perceives, learns, remembers, feels, and thinks. Concretely and actually there is no such thing as sensation or perception or any other psychological "accident" apart from the experiencing person.

The person who acts and reacts to the environment remains the same in substance from birth to death. His personality, the sum total of all of his potentialities actualized at a given time, is constantly changing. Most of the acts of a human being take on meaning only when they are seen in relation to the whole personality of the person acting. It is for this reason that we here discuss the meaning of personality for psychology, methods of studying personality psychologically, and some of the findings of personality studies.

In contemporary psychology, the terms used in discussing personality are frequently the same as those used in philosophy, but the denotative and connotative meanings often differ. The term *person*, for instance, is typically used as a synonym for *individual* and has no deeper philosophical significance than that;

---

[1] St. Thomas Aquinas, *Summa Theologica,* I, 29, 3, c. (New York, Benziger Brothers, Inc., 1947), Vol. I, p. 158.

it does not necessarily connote a rational nature. The term *personality* is also used in a philosophically naïve sense. Its meaning differs for psychologists. The definition we are adopting is as follows: "Personality is the dynamic organization within the individual of those psychophysical systems that determine his unique adjustments to his environment." [2] In this definition, the term "organization" suggests that personality must be considered as an integrated whole and not just as the sum total of a number of unrelated traits. *Dynamic* implies that it is constantly changing. *Psychophysical* means that this personality organization is not a function just of the mind or just of the body but "entails the operation of body and mind, inextricably fused into a personal unity." [3] The word *determine*, as used in this context, indicates that "personality is not synonymous with behavior or activity" but "is what lies *behind* specific acts and *within* the individual." [4] "Unique," of course, refers to the fact that no two people are ever exactly alike; each personality is different from every other.

Let us consider briefly some of the data of psychology which can be interpreted only in the light of the personality as a whole. A number of facts presented earlier concerning perception and memory will serve for this purpose.

Perception is influenced by a number of conditions external to the perceiving person, such as proximity, continuity, and grouping. These factors hold for people in general and are a part of the body of information that makes up "general psychology." So dependable are these influences that we can predict with a high degree of accuracy what people will perceive under given controlled conditions in the laboratory. Yet needs, desires, and expectations also have an effect upon what and how well a given individual will perceive. When a lantern slide is projected with a very faint light so that the figures projected by it are barely perceptible, the individual reports of what is seen vary considerably. The hungry man may "see" a round object as an apple or orange; a small boy may see it as a baseball; still another person may see it as a picture of the world. All see the projected figure

---

[2] G. W. Allport, *Personality: A Psychological Interpretation* (New York, Henry Holt and Company, Inc., 1937), p. 48.
[3] *Ibid.*, p. 48.
[4] *Ibid.*

as an organized whole, but the "meaning" is contributed by the individual personality.

A similar thing happens in memory. There are certain laws of forgetting which hold for people in general. The fact that forgetting is most rapid immediately after learning and then proceeds more slowly with the lapse of time is a case in point. Also the fact that progressive alterations take place in the reconstruction of a drawing, such as that shown in Figure 77, is an illus-

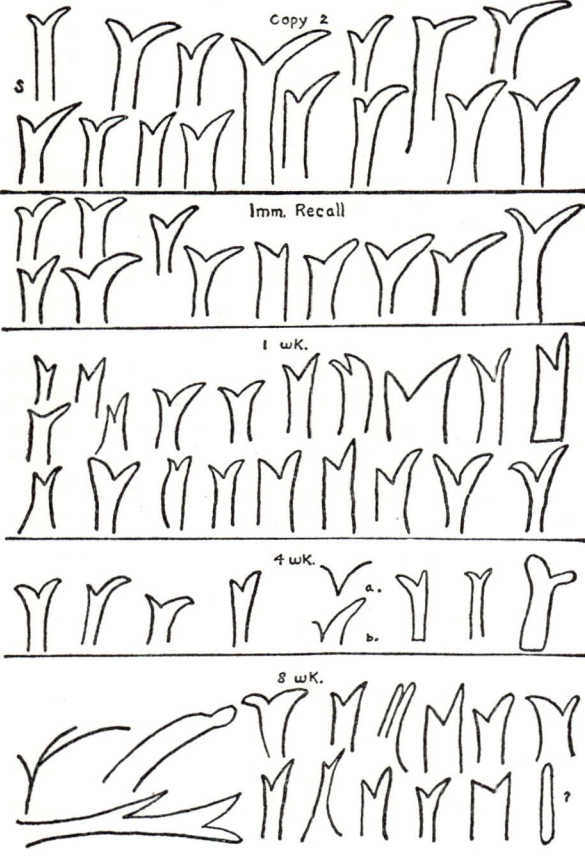

Fig. 77. Progressive Alterations in the Reconstruction of a Drawing. [Reproduced from N. G. Hanawalt, "Progressive Alterations in the Reconstruction of a Drawing," *Arch. Psychol.*, No. 216 (1937).]

tration of this principle. These are highly predictable characteristics of forgetting; they reveal general principles rather than individual idiosyncrasies. Yet like perception, forgetting is also, in part, a function of the individual personality. The insecure person may remember for years a slightly disparaging remark which a more secure person sloughs off almost as soon as he has heard it. No two people ever report the details of an accident in exactly the same way, partly because they have perceived it differently, partly because they remember it differently. The greater the amount of time which elapses between the event and the recall of it, the more the individual puts his own stamp on his description of it. This is true not only for naïve or uneducated observers but also for critical observers who are trying to be accurate in their reports.

In short, what is perceived and remembered is colored by the individual's needs, expectations, desires, past experiences, values and mood of the moment. It is inextricably bound up with his personality as a whole. For this reason, it is impossible to secure perfect fidelity of perception and recall in life situations. It is only in the laboratory under controlled conditions and in situations which have no personal relevance to the subject that perception and recall can be predicted from the general laws apart from a knowledge of the individual experiencing person. If you want to predict what an individual person will perceive or recall, you must know that person as well as the general laws of psychology, since each human being is a unique individual with his own unique life history. In other words, you must know this individual personality; you must understand the "dynamic organization" within this individual of the "psychophysical systems that determine his unique adjustments to his environment." [5] This does not mean that the general laws of psychology are invalid. It means only that the general laws and principles, if they are to be relevant to human life, must provide some insight as to how uniqueness and individuality arise. They must throw light upon the way in which each personality develops and how it responds to the stimulation of the external world.

[5] G. W. Allport, *op. cit.,* p. 48.

II. THE EGO OR SELF

Like other terms used in contemporary psychology, *ego* and *self* have specific philosophical meanings. In psychology, too, they are used with specific meanings, but these meanings grew up apart from philosophical considerations and are not the same as the philosophical ones. It is important, then, when reading on the subject of personality, to note the context in which the terms of the discussion are used. In this chapter, for instance, we are using the terms *ego* and *self* not in their specific philosophical sense but as they are used in modern scientific psychology.

Early in life every child asks himself the question: What am I? And gradually he learns that he is a being of body and soul, distinct from his mother, distinct from his clothing, distinct from his surroundings. Only gradually does he become aware of himself as a unit separate from his surroundings. Once infancy has been passed, however, he knows what is implied by the word *I*. He uses expressions such as "She thanked me," "He stepped on me," "I ate the cookie," and the like. When he uses an expression such as "He stepped on my foot," he is implicitly saying "He stepped on me." In other words, the foot is "me." It is part of the self or ego. The "I," the "self," or the "ego" is the whole human organism, body and soul.

Psychologists find it helpful to make the following distinctions when discussing the self: (1) the self as it really is, (2) the self as the individual himself perceives and understands it, and (3) the self as perceived and understood by others. The self as it really is can be known only by God, although some people acquire knowledge both of themselves and of others with a high degree of accuracy. We shall limit our discussion in this chapter to (1) the person's notion of himself and to (2) the concept he has of others.

A. The Notion of Self

The little child has only a vague uncrystallized image of himself. This image may be far removed from reality, based as it is on the interpersonal relationships he has experienced in his limited social group. An only child may, if his parents' interests are all centered in him, look upon himself as the most important person in his family, if not in the whole universe. He may with difficulty revise this notion of himself when his classmates and teachers fail to reinforce it. Gradually, through the combined action of the various experiences of his life and his maturing intelligence, he builds up a definite, more or less consistent view of himself. This view or image which the person has of himself is called his "phenomenological self." His view of himself as he would like to be is called his "self-ideal." Both the phenomenological self and the self-ideal may differ from the self as it really is. When the real-self differs greatly from the ideal-self, the phenomenological self is more likely to resemble the ideal-self, than the real-self. In other words, people whose conduct is vastly different from what they believe it should be tend to minimize the discrepancy between what they are and what they would like to be. This characteristic is found to some extent, of course, in everybody, but in some persons it is present to an exaggerated degree. An individual's self-respect is based upon his notion of the degree to which his actual attitudes and conduct conform to what he thinks they should be.

Personality becomes integrated through the unification of consistent attitudes and ideas. These ideas and attitudes, in turn, are patterned on the individual's notion of himself. All of the experiences of life do not become assimilated into the personality. The person's view of himself appears to function as a "semipermeable membrane" through which experiences are selectively filtered. Ideas and experiences which threaten this notion of self tend to be rejected, ignored, or distorted in such a way that they can be reconciled with it. Serious conflicts arise when a person is attracted to ideas or situations which are opposed to his self-image and which, if accepted, would cause him to lose his sense of personal worth and dignity.

The notion which a person has of himself is responsible for his "level of aspiration." Any attempt to raise an individual's level of aspiration and thereby change his attitudes and behavior is doomed to failure unless his image of himself can be changed accordingly. This is one of the reasons why praise is more effective in producing desirable behavior than blame. Praise heightens the individual's evaluation of himself as a person. It enables him to conceive of himself as a person capable of achievement. All great leaders have capitalized on this principle by inspiring their followers with a sense of personal worth and with confidence in their own ability. Blame and belittling have a devastating effect since they lower the sense of personal worth and tend to destroy any constructive self-ideal. An inferior notion of self can forestall worthwhile achievement. The child who has learned to think of himself as the school dunce will not and probably cannot improve until he can conceive of himself as the kind of person who can succeed in school. Sometimes, too, a specific bad habit or fault of character can be eliminated by helping an individual to see that such a trait is inconsistent in a person of his character and ideals. Similarly, a person may be inspired to acquire a new habit or pattern of behavior if he can see such behavior as fitting in with his general idea of himself as a person. As a rule, people resent and ward off attempts to change their attitudes and behavior when such changes do not harmonize with their views of themselves.

You will have observed by now that the term *ego* or *self*, as used in this psychological context, is not synonymous with the whole personality. It involves only those aspects of the personality which are related to personal status or value. A situation which is related to an individual's sense of personal worth is said to be "ego-involved." Many experiences of life do not become ego-involved; they are matters of indifference to the person. The memories of certain events, specific habits and skills, knowledge of many kinds, are components of the personality. But unless they bear some relationship to the individual's notion of himself, they do not become ego-involved.

Besides the images which people have of themselves, they also form mental pictures or ideas of other people. These notions of other people are important in all social interaction; they are a part of the environment in which personality develops. Let us consider briefly how we arrive at our ideas of other people and what barriers operate to prevent us from arriving at a true notion and evaluation of the other person.

B. The Notion of Others

The notion or "concept" of a person other than oneself is the nature we impute to him, our idea of him, based upon the way in which we see and interpret him. The idea we have of this person should not be confused with the attitudes we may take toward him, though there is inevitably a complicated network of interrelationships between the way we picture people and the attitudes that we take toward them. For example, we may be greatly attracted to a particular individual because we have a distorted or faulty idea of his personality. Or we may have a distorted concept of his personality because we are attracted to him. Our idea of the person defines the meaning of the attitude we take toward him. The attitude, in turn, influences or determines the content of our idea.

What a person "truly" is, what constitutes his real self, is very hard to determine since there are many barriers to our understanding of other people. Stereotyping and prejudice, which we shall discuss in the next chapter, are two of them. Other difficulties are the fact that (1) we can observe behavior but cannot observe motives, (2) we do not observe all of the significant behavior of any given individual, (3) social conventions regulate our outward expressions, (4) people are assigned "roles" to which they try to conform, and (5) the same gestures and expressions have different meanings in different cultural groups. Let us see how these barriers operate.

The behavior of two individuals may be similar, but the reasons behind it may differ considerably. Often we do not even ask ourselves why other people behave as they do. We assume that they think and feel as we would think and feel were we acting as they are. We tend to project our own attitudes, feelings, and motives to the person we observe, and as a result, we get a wrong notion of him. Then, too, we see only a limited part of the total behavior of most people, and thus get a very one-sided view of them. If we see a given teacher only in the classroom, we may perceive him as strictly logical and reflective in his behavior toward people and events. But if we meet the same teacher on Halloween when his car windows have been smeared with soap by some prankster, we may have to revise our notion of him. The teacher, too, because he sees a certain boy only in his classroom, may conclude that the boy is constitutionally incapable of effort or enthusiasm. Should he have the opportunity of seeing this boy play football or dance, he would probably have to change his view.

There is always a certain amount of incongruity between the outward expression of our personality and our inner attitudes, ideals, sentiments, and values. This incongruity results partly from our own reticence and partly from the fact that social conventions regulate our outward expressions. They limit or define not only what we reveal to others but also the way in which it will be revealed. Then, too, society assigns us certain "roles" to which it expects us to conform. Certain kinds of behavior are expected of people at different age levels and in different professions. Children are taught to "know their place," which, to some extent, means behaving according to an extrinsically imposed standard of behavior regardless of how they really feel or what they believe. The young teacher may be frowned upon if he goes to a prize fight; the local bartender is not. For fear of what others will think or say, people often refrain from actions which appear to be inconsistent with the roles they play in society.

Lastly, the same gestures and verbal expressions mean different things in different cultures, as we demonstrated in Chapter VIII. For this reason, it is almost impossible to form a realistic notion of an individual whose personality has been shaped by a culture psychologically different from one's own.

III. METHODS OF STUDYING PERSONALITY

Many people besides psychologists are interested in studying human personality, but their approaches differ from those of the psychologist. Creative writers—novelists and poets in particular —have given us descriptions of personality and character based upon the most penetrating observations. Beside the literary artist's description of character the psychologist's case history may look like a fumbling and uninspired product. Yet for his own purposes, the psychologist's description is of inestimable value. Unlike the creative artist, the psychologist must understand this particular individual *as he is,* not as he would like him to be or as he can imagine him to be. To aid him in his professional work with people, the psychologist has been prolific in devising methods with which personality can be diagnosed. These methods find particular applications in (1) research studies of personality and the conditions which affect the way personality develops, (2) personality diagnoses in clinics, schools, and hospitals as an aid to therapy, and (3) the formulation of psychological theory. In this section we shall describe, first, some of the illegitimate or pseudo-scientific methods that have been employed by non-psychologists in the study of personality. Secondly, we shall describe a number of methods used by psychologists in the experimental or clinical study of human personality.

A. Pseudo-Scientific Methods of Studying Personality

People who have not been trained in the methods of psychology, nor in the rigorous logic which these methods demand, often resort to short-cut methods of understanding people. Among such beguiling short-cuts we shall mention four: (1) phrenology, (2) physiognomy, (3) graphology, and (4) astrology.

1. *Phrenology.* Phrenology undertakes to diagnose personality, temperament, and character by studying the swellings or protuberances on different parts of the skull. It assumes that various mental faculties or powers are located in definite parts of the brain, and that the greater or less development of the parts of the brain is reflected in the contour of the skull. This system of studying personality and character originated with a Viennese physician, Franz Joseph Gall, about 1800. Gall and his disciple, Spurzheim, drew up charts and diagrams, such as that shown in Figure 78, purporting to show the location of such characteristics as self-esteem, firmness, cautiousness, destructiveness, and the like.

Phrenology has today been thoroughly discredited by many lines of evidence. In the first place, there are no grounds whatever for supposing that the development of the brain is related to the external surface contours of the skull. Secondly, modern neurological research throws doubt upon the localization of any complex mental function in any one small area of the brain's surface (the cortex). Thirdly, there is no evidence that the "mental faculties" basic to Gall's system of phrenology actually exist.

2. *Physiognomy.* Related to phrenology is another pseudo-science, physiognomy. Physiognomists claim that they can discover your predominant temperament and mental characteristics by studying your outward appearance, complexion, body build, and so forth. Most of them place particular emphasis upon the shape of the face and its features. One example of this type of analysis is that of Lombroso, an Italian criminologist, who claimed that criminals had certain "stigmata of degeneracy" by which they could be distinguished from non-criminals. These

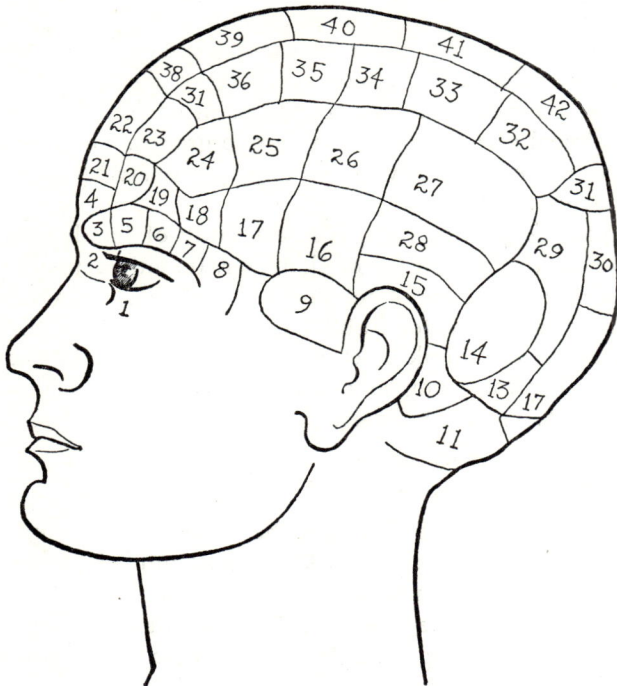

Fig. 78. Phrenology Chart, Indicating the Localization of Mental Faculties. The numbers are interpreted as follows:

1. Language
2. Form
3. Size
4. Individuality
5. Height
6. Color
7. Order
8. Calculation
9. Alimentiveness
10. Vitativeness
11. Amativeness
12. Parental love
13. Conjugality
14. Combativeness
15. Destructiveness
16. Acquisitiveness
17. Constructiveness
18. Tune
19. Time
20. Locality
21. Eventuality
22. Comparison
23. Causality
24. Mirthfulness
25. Ideality
26. Sublimity
27. Cautiousness
28. Secretiveness
29. Friendship
30. Inhabitiveness
31. Continuity
32. Approbativeness
33. Conscientiousness
34. Hope
35. Spirituality
36. Imitation
37. Agreeableness
38. Human nature
39. Benevolence
40. Veneration
41. Firmness
42. Self-esteem

stigmata included, among other characteristics, cleft lips, teeth with the molars undeveloped, ears that are long and thick, and eyebrows that are beady or scanty. The discovery that non-criminals also have these characteristics as frequently as do criminals was enough to disprove this theory.

A special type of physiognomy is *palmistry*. Proponents of this system are usually not content to read character from the palm but predict future events, such as a long or short life, or success in love or business. The lines of the palm, of course, correspond to anatomical divisions between muscle groups. There is no evidence whatever that they are in any way related to personality or character.

3. *Graphology*. Graphology is the study of handwriting as a basis for making judgments of character. Its judgments are based upon arbitrary systems of relationships between certain features of writing and character traits. Graphologists assume that these relationships are simple and can be summed up in neat little formulas. Typical examples of the arbitrary relationships which graphologists set up between personality and handwriting are the following:

a. The crossing of "t's."
   (1) If crossed like this: ㄴ , the individual is supposedly care-free, given to tardiness, and unlikely to be conscientious or anxious.
   (2) If crossed like this: ㇄ , the individual is inclined to cross his bridges before he comes to them, is anxious and pessimistic.
   (3) If crossed like this: t , the individual avoids both of the above extremes.

b. Formation of "o's."
   (1) If left open like this: ʘ , the individual is said to be openhearted, generous, and extroverted.
   (2) If closed like this: ⌀ , the person is supposedly stingy, frigid, and introverted.

The claims of graphologists, when subjected to rigid scientific tests, have never been verified.

Graphology must not be confused with experimental and clinical studies of handwriting which are now being made by highly trained psychologists and subjected to rigorous scientific tests. Such studies [6] show that there are subtle relationships between expressive behavior, including handwriting, and the individual's personality, but the relationship is not a simple one such as the

[6] G. W. Allport and P. E. Vernon, *Studies in Expressive Movement* (New York, The Macmillan Company, 1933).

"reader of handwriting" is looking for. To see the relationship at all requires considerable training in methods of observation as well as considerable clinical experience.

4. *Astrology.* Astrology is a pseudo-science (having no relation to contemporary astronomy) which, like palm-reading, does not content itself with reading character but also predicts future events. Its basic thesis is that an individual's character and temperament are determined by the particular constellation of heavenly bodies, especially the planets under which he was born.

All of these pseudo-scientific methods of studying personality have now been thoroughly discredited in scientific circles. Yet the man-in-the-street seems to find them perennially interesting. Charlatans, by exploiting these rackets, have built up lucrative businesses at the expense of gullible people.

B. Psychological Methods of Studying Personality

In the construction and selection of tools for studying personality, psychologists are guided by various theories of personality. Some, for example, are strongly impressed by the importance of *personality traits*, that is, by the distinctive and more or less permanent and predictable patterns of behavior which people characteristically display. For instance, we are familiar with persons recognized as possessing to an unusual degree such traits as cheerfulness, accuracy, stoicism, or endurance. Other psychologists put extra stress on personality as a *process*, a dynamic, continually changing interaction between the "outer" and the "inner" world of the experiencing person. It is beyond the scope of an introductory textbook to go into these and other theoretical differences in any detail, but at least one ought to be aware that there are different points of view and that these differences are reflected in the contemporary methods and techniques of studying personality.

Most of the available instruments for studying personality can be classified under one or more of the following heads: (1) paper and pencil tests, questionnaires, rating scales, and inventories; (2) situation tests; (3) free association and dream analysis; and (4) projective and expressive techniques. We shall describe some representative devices falling under each of these heads.

1. Paper and pencil tests, questionnaires, rating scales, and inventories

Typically, personality inventories and questionnaires present the subject with a series of statements or questions concerning a variety of personal reactions, attitudes, and emotions which may be experienced in life situations. The subject is asked to respond to these items so as to tell something about himself, sometimes by checking each "yes" or "no" or "uncertain," sometimes by ranking items according to what he feels to be their order with respect to feeling or value; or again by checking statements "agree," "disagree," or "uncertain." In one widely used instrument, the *Bernreuter Personality Inventory*, there are 125 questions which can be answered "yes," "no," or "?." Sample items from this inventory are as follows:

1. Yes No ? Does it make you uncomfortable to be "different" or unconventional?
2. Yes No ? Do you daydream frequently?
3. Yes No ? Do you usually work things out for yourself rather than get someone to show you?
4. Yes No ? Have you ever crossed the street to avoid meeting some person?
5. Yes No ? Can you stand criticism without feeling hurt?
6. Yes No ? Do you ever give money to beggars? [7]

The *Bernreuter Personality Inventory* has been validated [8] against other inventories supposedly measuring the same traits, and yields separate scores for (1) self-sufficiency, (2) neurotic tendency, (3) introversion-extroversion, and (4) dominance-submission.

The *Allport Ascendance-Submission Study* recognizes the fact that social situations in which ascendance or submission are called into play are different for men and women, and the scale therefore has two forms, one for men and one for women. The questions are presented in multiple-choice form as illustrated on the next page:

---

[7] Robert G. Bernreuter, "The Personality Inventory" (Stanford University, California, Stanford University Press).

[8] By "validated" we mean that evidence has been secured which shows that the test measures what it sets out to measure.

1. In witnessing a game of football or baseball in a crowd, have you intentionally made remarks (witty, encouraging, disparaging, or otherwise) which were clearly audible to those around you?
   frequently ———
   occasionally ———
   never ———
2. (a) At a reception or tea do you seek to meet the important person present?
   usually ———
   occasionally ———
   never ———
   (b) Do you feel reluctant to meet him?
   yes, usually ———
   sometimes ———
   no ———
3. At church, a lecture, or an entertainment, if you arrive after the program has commenced and find that there are people standing, but also that there are front seats available which might be secured without "piggishness" or discourtesy, but with considerable conspicuousness, do you take the seats?
   habitually ———
   occasionally ———
   never ———

This instrument, unlike the Bernreuter, was validated against an external criterion. Each student taking the test (for purposes of validation) was rated once by himself and at four different times, well spread apart, by his classmates as to his degree of submissiveness or ascendancy. His "score" was computed by averaging his own rating with those of the four classmates who rated him. The scoring key for the scale was based upon a careful scrutiny of the responses made by students who were rated as more ascendant or more submissive than the typical student. Answers typically made by the more ascendant students were taken as indicative of ascendance; those made by the more submissive students were taken as indicative of submission.

The *George Washington Social Intelligence Test* purports to measure ability to get along with people. It is divided into five parts, each of which supposedly measures a different aspect of social intelligence: (1) judgment in social situations, (2) recognition of the mental state of the speaker, (3) observation of human behavior, (4) memory for names and faces, and (5) sense of humor.

Attitude scales are usually designed to measure degrees of

attitudes upon specific questions rather than general dispositions or traits of personality. An *attitude* is defined as "the specific mental disposition toward an incoming (or arising) experience, whereby that experience is modified," [9] and as such it is an important component of personality. Carefully constructed attitude scales measuring attitude toward different races, toward religion, and toward various social issues have been published.

The *C.S.C. Religious Attitude Scale* [10] is a scale designed for women students in Catholic colleges. We shall describe this technique at length because it illustrates a number of principles involved in psychological testing. If you would like to take the test yourself, you would do well to take it now before reading any further because a knowledge of what it purports to measure will almost certainly influence your score. The items in the test are selected with the purpose of measuring a person's attitude in each of ten respects as follows:

a. Individualistic, parochial and selfish viewpoints *versus* a social attitude in worship.
b. Materialistic and merely natural values *versus* spiritual and supernatural values, "other-worldliness," and sensitivity to grace.
c. Preponderance of emotion *versus* intellect and will in worship.
d. The Church regarded primarily as an organization *versus* the Church as a living organism, the Mystical Body of Christ with solidarity of all members and diversity of functions.
e. Apathetic and indifferent attitude *versus* the apostolic spirit of Catholic action.
f. Cock-sure, more or less pharisaical attitude of strength *versus* appreciation of, and compassion for, human frailty, and understanding of the human character both of those who govern the Church and of those who are governed, and an attitude of dependence on grace.
g. Scepticism, indifferentism and subjectivism *versus* belief in our ability to know and in the objectivity of truth.
h. Prudery, lack of appreciation for the body *versus* an appreciation of the "whole man," body and soul.
i. Religion as a matter for Sundays and prayer-time *versus* religion penetrating every act of man.
j. "Getting" *versus* "giving" spirit in worship.

[9] H. C. Warren (ed.), *Dictionary of Psychology* (New York, Houghton Mifflin Company, 1934), p. 24.
[10] Sister Marie Philip Haley, "An Attitude Scale in Religion for Catholic Colleges," *J. of Rel. Instruction* (June and September, 1941); Sister Annette "Further Validation of the C.S.C. Religious Attitude Scale for College Students," *Cath. Educ. Rev.*, 46 (January, 1948), 37–42.

Items for the scale were obtained from college faculty members who were asked to keep their eyes and ears open for evidences of these attitudes on the part of students. As far as possible the items in the test were worded as students (rather than faculty members) express them. When a sufficient number of items had been collected, they were grouped according to one or more of the ten categories listed above, and twenty faculty members from four different Catholic colleges were asked to check them by marking "agree," "disagree," or "uncertain" after each item. They were also asked to check any statements which they believed to be ambiguous or which they felt did not really "measure" a religious attitude that belonged in the category under which it was listed. As a result of this scrutiny, many items were reworded, subdivided, or discarded.

This revised scale was then given to a group of students shortly before they entered college, a group which varied greatly in ability and in previous religious instruction. These students were interviewed to find out how they interpreted each of the items. In a number of instances it was discovered that the items meant something quite different to students than they did to faculty members. Such items were then eliminated. Finally, the whole scale was submitted to a theologian and, on the basis of his criticisms and suggestions, a scoring key was drawn up. At this point the scale contained only 192 items although nearly twice that number had been originally collected.

The next step was to determine the *reliability* or consistency with which the scale measured whatever it measured. By means of the Kuder-Richardson formula, it was found that this reliability was .94 when based upon measurements of approximately 300 students. This is a very high correlation and indicates that the test is sufficiently reliable or self-consistent for most purposes. The next step was to determine the *validity* of the scale. One type of validation had already been made, as described above, namely, validation by a *consensus of expert opinion*. Another type of validation used was that of *discrimination between known groups*. A number of different groups was compared, as, for example, Catholic college freshmen and postulants in a religious community of approximately the same age as the college students. The lowest score of any postulant was just at the mean for the college group. (Two of the postulants of this group went home, but unfortunately we have no way of knowing whether they scored lower than the others on the scale.) Seniors in a Catholic college were significantly higher than freshmen, and sisters enrolled in summer school classes were significantly higher than the seniors. In this connection it is interesting to note that none of the students who had ranked in the lowest 5 per cent of their freshman class on the Religious Attitude Scale remained in a Catholic college after their second year. This group comprised the greatest number of transfer students, and in no instance did one of these students transfer to another Catholic college.

A third type of validation was undertaken; but because faculty members felt that this type of validation was somewhat "snoopy," it was necessary to be content with fewer cases than one should have had to make a conclusive study. Faculty members were asked to rate freshman students as to Catholicity of behavior after they had had eight months to get acquainted with them. These ratings were made by persons ignorant of the test scores. Although all faculty members were hesitant in making such ratings, they were remarkably consistent in their ratings of the same students. The relationship between ratings and scores on the Religious Attitude Scale is shown in Table 7. The coefficient of correlation (contingency coefficient corrected for broad categories) is .82. This is suggestive only, however, since there were not enough cases to rule out the possibility of error. This third type of validation is known as validation by determining the *correlation of scores with rating of actual behavior*.

Table 7

DATA FOR COMPUTING CORRELATION BETWEEN TOTAL SCORES ON THE C.S.C. RELIGIOUS ATTITUDE SCALE AND RATINGS OF BEHAVIOR

	Total Scores on Attitude Scale		
	High	Medium	Low
High	18	9	3
Medium	2	7	4
Low	1	2	13

Rating scales are a method for assessing personality when it is not feasible to experiment or use methods requiring more technical skill. They may be used either for rating oneself or for rating other people.

In rating other people two common errors must be avoided: (1) the "halo" effect, and (2) the "central tendency of judgment."

By "halo" effect we mean the tendency of judges to rate people in respect to a variety of particular traits on the basis of some general, over-all impression which they create. Thus, if a judge is rating a person whom he likes, he tends to rate him as superior in specific traits, such as "patriotism," "pleasant voice," and so forth, even though to an impartial judge he may seem markedly deficient in these respects. One method of avoiding such an error is to require the judge to support each rating with a description of an actual observation which justifies the rating. In general, the rater tends to be more critical than he would otherwise be when he is asked to accompany his rating with a description of behavior.

Another error, the "central tendency of judgment," results from the fact that most people are loath to rate others at either extreme of a scale. On a sevenfold graphic rating scale, for example, such as that illustrated below, there is a tendency to avoid rating people as either "very inferior" or "excellent." This tendency seems to

very inferior	inferior	below average	average	good	very good	excellent

stem from the realization that in being conservative we are not as likely, as a rule, to be so far wrong in our judgments as when we rate people at one extreme.

2. Situation tests

Situation tests, unlike the paper and pencil tests mentioned above, do not require the subject to designate how he thinks or what he characteristically does. They measure his actual behavior in a life situation of some kind. In personality studies at the Harvard Psychological Clinic, for example, the subjects were observed in the waiting room before the experiments had ostensibly begun. To accomplish this purpose an observer was "planted" in the waiting room, whose role the subject had no reason to suspect. This observer, for example, dropped a box of matches and the reaction of the subject was noted. Some subjects immediately arose to help. Other expressed sympathy but did not help to pick up the matches. And still others retained an attitude of complete detachment from the scene. An enticing-looking toy, so constructed that when it was handled it would break, was placed on the table. Again careful records (this time from behind a one-way screen) were made of the subject's reactions when the toy "broke" in his hands. Some subjects carefully replaced the toy and made it look as if they had never touched it. Others set it down indifferently, leaving the pieces spread out, whereas still others became worried and even offered to pay for it.

In the Hartshorne and May studies of character, miniature life situations were set up to measure honesty, self-control, and service. In one test, the tester appeared to leave a dime inadvertently on the table after the test, and a record was made whether the child took it or not. Similarly, opportunities were presented for cheating, lying, and being of service.

3. Free association and dream analysis

When the terms *free association* and *dream analysis* are used together they generally refer to the method used by Freudian psychoanalysts to unearth emotional complexes. Both of these techniques, however, antedate Freud and their use does not obligate one to accept the Freudian theory of personality development and motivation.

a. Free association. Centuries ago, Aristotle recognized three principles which guided the associative processes of man: contiguity, similarity, and contrast. These principles are often referred to as the *primary laws of association*. According to the first of these principles, two objects or events which are presented together in time tend to become associated so that, at a later date, when one of the objects or events is presented, the other will be recalled. According to the second of these laws, the presentation of an object or event causes a similar object or event to be recalled. And, according to the third of these principles, its opposite will tend to be recalled. Psychologists of the British associationist school claimed that only the first of these laws was necessary and that the second and third could be subsumed under the first. Today, in addition to these primary laws, we recognize four subsidiary or secondary laws of association: frequency, recency, vividness or intensity, and primacy. These secondary laws were formulated to specify the conditions under which the law of contiguity operates. The laws may be summarized as follows:

(1) Other things being equal, the more frequently the associated events have occurred together, the greater will be the probability of the recall of one when the other occurs.

(2) Other things being equal, the more recent the connection, the greater is the probability that it will be recalled.
(3) Other things being equal, the more intense or vivid the association, the greater is the probability of its recall.
(4) Other things being equal, the first association of one thing with another has an advantage over subsequent associations of that same thing with others in being recalled.

Note that the laws of association apply to "free" and not to "controlled" association. The distinction between "free" and "controlled" association was first made by the English philosopher Hobbes who pointed out that in "free" association the "thoughts are said to wander, as in a dream," whereas in controlled association the thoughts are "regulated by some desire and design." It is of interest to note that Sir Francis Galton, a pioneer in the study of individual differences in people, was the first to conduct a free association experiment. It consisted of 75 stimulus words, to each of which a subject responded by giving the first two ideas that came to his mind. It was apparent to Galton that the results of this experiment revealed much more of the individual's thoughts and "mental anatomy" than he would probably care to have made public. And Galton, being a reticent English gentleman, deemed it better not to pursue this inquiry further!

Today the free association test is used as a *complex indicator.* A complex is a group or constellation of emotionally toned ideas. Ordinarily, the test is composed of a series of words, some of which are more or less "neutral" to most people, such as *chair, sky,* and the like, and certain words which are emotionally toned for most people, such as *kiss, love, snake,* and the like. The subject taking the test is asked to respond to each of the stimulus words by giving the first word that comes to his mind. His reaction time to each of the words is noted, and if his reaction is longer on certain words than on others, this is taken as a "sign" that that word is emotionally significant for him. It is not the only clue, however, since we also note any embarrassment or evidence that the first response which comes to the subject's mind has been suppressed in favor of a more neutral word which does not give so much away. If the response has no logical or apparent connection with the stimulus word, or if the reaction time has been unusually long, there is legitimate ground for suspecting that a substitution has been made, perhaps more or less involuntarily. For several free association tests, tables are available, showing the frequency of certain responses, and it is possible to determine for a given subject the "commonality" of his responses, that is, how his responses correspond to those most frequently given. Some psychologists are of the opinion that more can be inferred about emotional complexes from the stimulus word on which there is some sign of disturbance before the associated word is given than from the content of the reaction word. Research to date shows that there is no correlation between intelligence and originality of responses to the free association test. There is considerable evidence, however, that something about one's personality is revealed, although great caution must be exercised in making interpretations from a free association test, and the test should never be used alone as a single index of personality. Creative writers, for example, and especially poets, tend to give highly original responses, but this is also true of psychotics, probably for a quite different reason!

Free association tests are also used to detect "guilty" knowledge. A test is constructed in which words relating to a crime are interspersed with other words having no relation to the crime. The assumption is that the person who is involved in the crime will have both recent associations and more vivid associations with certain key words than will a person who knows nothing of the crime and who certainly did not commit it.

b. Dream analysis. Dreams, when properly interpreted, often throw light on the "inner world" of desires, frustrations, needs, and meanings, as the following examples will illustrate:

A young graduate student of psychology was working very hard in preparation for his German exams. In spite of his many hours of study, he felt that he had not mastered the subject and was afraid of failing. Shortly before the examination day he had a dream in which he saw himself standing before a display case of bakery products. A label pasted to a toothpick had been inserted into each bun, roll, and cake, and on this label was printed the price and "name" of the object. As the student leaned over to read the label he discovered to his joy that each article was priced at only a few cents and was well within his reach. Then too, he perceived that the labels all contained printed German words which he recognized as psychological terms. The student proceeded to buy the whole display and then walked out of the store triumphantly with a huge bag of bakery goods thrown over his shoulder, each item of which carried a different psychological term printed in German.

Let us consider another example before attempting an interpretation of this dream. A college girl found herself having almost the same dream for three or four nights in succession. Each time she dreamed that she was in a small and secret room in the dormitory building where nobody could possibly find her. She heard her friends calling to her and inviting her to take part in their various activities. She tried desperately to let them know where she was and to go to them but to no avail. Each time they went off without her, but even then she was unable to walk out of the room. All that was left for her to do was to sit down and study. At this point in the dream, however, she invariably woke up.

What is the meaning behind each of these dreams? Perhaps you can already hazard a guess. The symbolism of the first dream is relatively clear, since a little information has been given concerning the boy's anxieties and hopes. The rolls and cakes bought by the graduate student were symbols of the German vocabulary he was trying with indifferent success to master. In the dream he was able to "buy" this knowledge very cheaply with almost no effort on his part. It would seem that we have here a perfect illustration of wish-fulfillment in a dream.

What about the second case? Here the interpretation is not so obvious, since we do not have any information to guide us. Upon making inquiry, however, we elicit the following significant information. The girl in question has always been an "A-student" and her parents expect her to continue in this role. But recently she has come to "belong" to a college clique of high social prestige but which, for the most part, is composed of mediocre and indifferent students. The girl enjoys the prestige of being a member of this group. But since she has shared the social activities of this group, her grades have suffered. Unconsciously, the girl wishes to escape from the group and study, but consciously she wants to be with them. She suffers a conflict of values in that she wants to please her parents as well as her friends. In her dream the problem is solved for her; she does not have to make a decision. She is *unable* to do anything but study. Thus, in both dreams we see a kind of wish-fulfillment.

The significance of dreams for personality diagnosis is an important contribution of Freudian psychoanalysis. For Freud, dreams were wish-fulfillments and, as such, provided a clue to the repressed life of the dreamer. Freud distinguished between the *manifest* and *latent* content of the dream. The *manifest content*, according to Freud, is the obvious content of the dream, that is, people, animals, and rivers as the dreamer actually dreams and reports them. The *latent content*, on the other hand, is not obvious but is indirectly expressed in the manifest content. The latent content consists of the unconscious desires which find an indirect expression through being clothed in symbols which disguise their real meaning.

Other psychologists besides psychoanalysts interpret personality from dreams, but the significance of the dream symbol and the way of interpreting it vary with the psychologist's theory of personality.

4. Expressive and projective techniques

Expressive techniques, as used by psychologists, are a refinement of the methods which the layman, the artist, and the creative writer use for judging personality. They are based upon the assumption that expressive movements, such as those of writing, gait, gestures, and voice, are more than merely mechanically learned habits, and have their deeper roots in the depths of personality. If these movements were nothing more than learned ways of reacting and had nothing to do with the whole individual personality, then we would not expect to find similarities from one type of expression to another in the case of the same subject because the learning of each of these kinds of habits occurs under different conditions. Experimental studies show, however, that for a given person there is an underlying unity in these various modes of expression. Speed and decisiveness in handwriting, for example, are associated with speed and decisiveness in walking. Gestures and voice have something in common. Earlier in this chapter we pointed out that the claims of graphologists that handwriting can be used to judge character and personality are largely unfounded. This statement is true, not because handwriting does not in any sense express personality, but because the graphologists have not yet discovered the suitable techniques for diagnosing such a complex product of personality. Although handwriting is a learned reaction, individuality is so great that when signatures are written on legal documents there is almost no possibility of mistaking one signature for another. The amount of pressure, the continuity or hesitancy of writing, the meticulousness or slovenliness of writing—all are influenced by moods and by one's outlook on life.

Projective techniques are methods of stimulating imaginative processes and of helping the subject to express them in words or actions. The idea behind projective testing is that, when presented with an ambiguous situation, that is, one which can be interpreted or reacted to in several different ways, the individual will reveal his personality by the way in which he sees, describes, interprets, or organizes the materials in the situation. When he is asked, for example, to tell what he sees in a cloud picture, he "projects" his inner world of needs, desires, feelings, fears, or attitudes to the material, often without being consciously aware that he is doing so. The psychologist who has been trained to interpret such responses often learns much that the person cannot or will not express directly.

The psychologist who uses projective techniques assumes that, in responding to the test situation, the person is giving him a small-scale sample of his typical responses to life situations. He also assumes that each person has a "private world" which differs from that of everyone else. The "public world" is the same for everyone. As we walk down the street we see the same electric signs, the same sunset, or the same green grass. But the "meaning" of what is seen differs from person to person, depending upon the structure of the individual personality, mood, temperament, and above all the background of experience. One person may sadly shake his head as he watches the neon lights flash on and off. For him they may mean a tinsel cheapening of life and its values; he is struck by an aching sense of aloneness in a roaring impersonal city. Another may view these same lights with a blessed sense of relief from the drab monotony and the prying eyes of small town life. The public world of each is the same; the private world is different.

Projective tests are designed to throw light on the "private world" of the individual person. They do so indirectly by the use of materials which are more or less "structured." "Structured" materials provide more suggestions for responses than do "unstructured" ones. Cloud pictures, for instance, are relatively unstructured as compared to cartoons to be interpreted or stories to be made up about specific pictures. They provide fewer suggestions for responses than do the more structured materials and thus provide a freer setting for the play of imagination.

Ordinary test situations which are not intended to be projective techniques may, on occasion, elicit "projections" as shown in the following example:

During the depression of the 1930's, the senior author was administering the 1916 form of the Stanford-Binet test to children in an orphanage. One eleven-year-old girl, whose IQ proved to be 120, reacted to the picture of a colonial scene which most children interpret as a lovers' quarrel as follows:

She's crying because she's sick and there's nothing to eat in the house and the children are hungry. She just doesn't know what they're going to do. He's going out again to see if he can't get a job—but he thinks it's no use. These are sure hard times!

The above interpretation, which differs markedly from the "correct" and expected responses listed in the test manual, is a reflection of the child's recent experiences. The father, out of work for over a year, had tried desperately to keep his family of five together. When his wife became ill, he arranged to have his three daughters cared for in an orphanage until he could again find a job. The eleven-year-old girl's response to the test is more than an indication of her intelligence; it is a reflection or projection of her own preoccupations and of the way in which she looks at life.

Two of the most widely used projective tests are the *Rorschach* and the *Thematic Apperception Test,* commonly abbreviated, *TAT.* The Rorschach test gives us a view of the "personality skeleton," that is, of the basic structure of the personality. Its use in psychology has been compared to the use of the x-ray in medicine. It consists of ten inkblots, presented one at a time. The directions for the test are usually very simple, as, for example: "Have you ever seen children drop a blot of ink on a sheet of paper and then fold the paper and spread the ink? Well, I am going to show you some blots like that and you are to tell me what they look like to you. Since they are only inkblots, there cannot be any right or wrong answers." Then, handing the card to the subject, the examiner continues, "Tell me what you see. What might this be?" The responses to this test are analyzed not so much for content as for the subject's "original psychological experience" with the blot, that is, what aspect of the blot elicited made up about specific pictures. They provide fewer suggestions for responses than do the more structured materials and thus provide a freer setting for the play of imagination.

Ordinary test situations which are not intended to be projective techniques may, on occasion, elicit "projections" as shown in the following example:

During the depression of the 1930's, the senior author was administering the 1916 form of the Stanford-Binet test to children in an orphanage. One eleven-year-old girl, whose IQ proved to be 120, reacted to the picture of a colonial scene which most children interpret as a lovers' quarrel as follows:

She's crying because she's sick and there's nothing to eat in the house and the children are hungry. She just doesn't know what they're going to do. He's going out again to see if he can't get a job—but he thinks it's no use. These are sure hard times!

The above interpretation, which differs markedly from the "correct" and expected responses listed in the test manual, is a reflection of the child's recent experiences. The father, out of work for over a year, had tried desperately to keep his family of five together. When his wife became ill, he arranged to have his three daughters cared for in an orphanage until he could again find a job. The eleven-year-old girl's response to the test is more than an indication of her intelligence; it is a reflection or projection of her own preoccupations and of the way in which she looks at life.

Two of the most widely used projective tests are the *Rorschach* and the *Thematic Apperception Test,* commonly abbreviated, *TAT.* The Rorschach test gives us a view of the "personality skeleton," that is, of the basic structure of the personality. Its use in psychology has been compared to the use of the x-ray in medicine. It consists of ten inkblots, presented one at a time. The directions for the test are usually very simple, as, for example: "Have you ever seen children drop a blot of ink on a sheet of paper and then fold the paper and spread the ink? Well, I am going to show you some blots like that and you are to tell me what they look like to you. Since they are only inkblots, there cannot be any right or wrong answers." Then, handing the card to the subject, the examiner continues, "Tell me what you see. What might this be?" The responses to this test are analyzed not so much for content as for the subject's "original psychological experience" with the blot, that is, what aspect of the blot elicited his response. He may, for instance, have been most influenced by form, to the exclusion of color. Or, he may have been impressed by the implied movement in the blot. The test is scored for form, color, movement, and originality of response. No part of the test and no particular group of responses are interpreted apart from the whole test, and that is one of the reasons why this test is so difficult to interpret and requires special training on the part of the psychologist.

The Rorschach test, consisting as it does of ten inkblots, is not very impressive to the uninitiated. Yet there are many psychologists who hold that it is the most penetrating instrument of personality diagnosis that we now possess. Rorschach was not the first investigator to work with inkblots. Experimental psychologists had previously used them for studying imagination. But Rorschach was the first person to use inkblots in such a way as to construct a portrait of a subject's personality from his responses to them. The inkblots that he used were carefully selected from an original group of 100, later reduced to 60, and finally to the 10 blots which now comprise the Rorschach test. At first glance we might expect the Rorschach to be a highly unreliable instrument, since ten items are never enough for a reliable measure of any psychological characteristics. Each blot, however, should not be thought of as an item, since each blot presents a myriad of possibilities. Some people have been known to give as many as 200 responses to one blot alone. Reliability for a test such as the Rorschach cannot be computed as it is for the personality questionnaires and inventories which we have previously described, but requires different techniques. These techniques, like the Rorschach test itself, require so much knowledge and experience in clinical psychology that it will be impossible to go into them here. Suffice it to say, that if one accepts the assumptions underlying the use of such techniques for securing reliability, the test compares favorably in this respect with other more objective instruments. The validity of the Rorschach test, too, has been fairly well established, provided the tester and interpreter is a highly trained specialist in Rorschach techniques. Without such specialized training and experience, not even the clinical psychologist will be able to use the instrument effectively.

The Thematic Apperception Test (TAT) was developed at the Harvard Psychological Clinic and consists of 31 pictures, some of which are designated as suitable for men, for women, and for younger or older subjects. Usually the tests are given in a definite order. The subject is asked to tell a story about each of the pictures and about one blank card which is inserted in the series. No significance is attached to responses to only one of the pictures; the interpretation is based upon responses to the whole series. Unlike the Rorschach, the interpretation of the TAT is based chiefly on content.

The TAT cannot be scored objectively and there are a number of different conceptual schemes for analyzing the results. Some of the things that most investigators look for are the following: (1) the character picked out as the principal one, who is always in some sense also the character with whom the subject appears to identify himself; (2) the main theme of the story; (3) the recurrence of dominant themes; (4) the adequacy of the principal characters to their situations; (5) the conditions under which good and bad endings occur; (6) the conditions under which specific needs and desires of the characters are gratified; (7) attitudes toward parents and siblings; (8) introduction of people not shown in the picture; (9) introduction of specific objects not shown in the picture, such as water, animals, and weapons; and (10) signs of embarrassment and inhibition.

In many clinics the Rorschach and the TAT are usefully given to the same patients since the two tests supplement each other.

The results of psychological tests and instruments do not automatically interpret themselves. For this reason, no matter how objective the test, there is always a subjective element in its interpretation. Tests, such as the Rorschach, which furnish data about the total personality, are cases in point. How much enlightenment a psychologist derives from the Rorschach test depends not only on his training in Rorschach testing, but also on the depth and richness of his own personality. There is no recipe or formula available for an unerring diagnosis of personality. Diagnosis is an art and is as dependent upon the personality of the interpreter as upon his knowledge of science and technical skills.

Expressive and projective techniques are used by some psychologists who believe that personality is more than the sum total of one's traits, and that it is even more than the inclusive dynamic organization of these traits. These investigators typically hold that, even if it were possible to measure each specific trait of a person, and even if you had a complete profile of these trait measurements, you would not at the same time have a complete study of his personality. The traits would be there, but the personality would be lacking. This is often called the *holistic* or *global* view of personality, as contrasted with the *atomistic* view.

The *atomistic* approach to personality consists, in general, of isolating for analysis a number of specific traits, assigning names to these traits, measuring them by any tests available, and then manipulating the results by statistical methods. It is concerned chiefly with discovering the distribution of some trait in a population or group and then with finding out how much a particular individual deviates from the group norms. Any measurement or analysis of an individual by such methods has meaning only in so far as such analyses can be compared to group norms. Both physical and personality traits have been studied in this way. In the study of physical traits, various morphological indices and the visceral aspects of emotion have been studied. In the study of personality traits, personality tests, questionnaires, and inventories have been used; quantitative ratings on various behavior traits such as honesty have been devised; and various measures of intelligence have been constructed. By adding together a number of such discrete or separate personality measurements, or by drawing up a "profile" of test results, as shown in Figure 79, a diagrammatic picture of the personality is supposedly obtained. This view of personality is rejected by many users of projective techniques, though some projective techniques, such as the Rorschach, appear to combine the atomistic and the global approaches.

IV. DEPTH OF UNDERSTANDING

The psychologist who uses the methods of studying personality that we have just described derives from them an insight into the personality which neither the individual himself nor other persons ordinarily have. The psychologist can understand the "structure" of a given personality—how flexible or how rigid it is in adjusting to new situations—and he is, consequently, able to predict how the person is likely to react in the future. He has significant clues to the unconscious as well as to the conscious motivation of the individual he has tested. In short, the psychologist's understanding

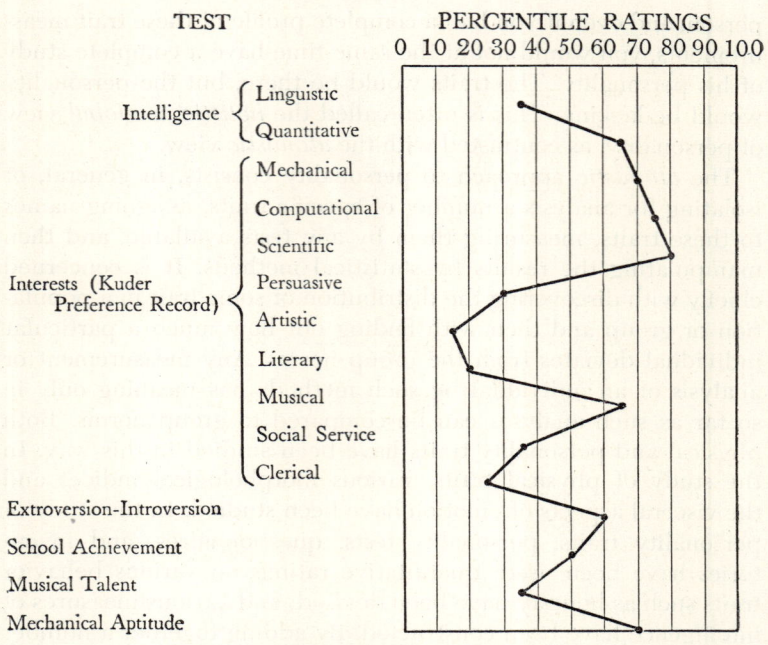

Fig. 79. Profile of Test Results.

is more penetrating than that of persons who do not have access to his specialized tools of diagnosis.

There is a depth of personality, however, which neither the psychologist nor other persons can ever sound completely. This is the deepest level of the personality; it is that which involves the man's relation to God. A psychologist cannot, with all of the tools at his disposal—inventories, situations tests, Rorschach, TAT, or dream analysis—ever form a correct judgment as to the person's relation to God. "Depth psychology," no matter how deep, does not transcend the natural order. The only way that we can ever know even remotely how a man stands before God is through his own affirmation. And even he, no matter how honest he may want to be, can still be deceived. The trained psychologist, therefore, like other human beings without his specialized training, must observe the divine injunction, "Judge not, that you may not be judged," not only because it is a precept of Christian charity, but also because there are no means at his disposal for making correct judgments in such matters.[11]

Human temperament and behavior are profoundly influenced by biochemical, physical, and environmental stimuli; temperamental characteristics and behavior are open to direct observation. The inner act of willing, however, cannot be observed; it can only be inferred. Environmental stimuli do not determine the inner act of willing however much they may affect the way in which the will is expressed. The fundamental moral decisions are made in the inmost depth of the soul, and it is at this level that the effects of right choices are first experienced. Temperamental characteristics and external behavior are affected last of all. Thus it can happen that a person genuinely turns to God and resolves to do God's will. Yet the superficial habits of impatience, hastiness of temper, or petty vanity may still be observed in him, and he may still rate high on tests of aggression and hostility. We have a tendency to judge the inner worth of a person on the basis of these characteristics that we observe in him. Yet in doing so we are judging rashly. As one writer puts it:

. . . it is precisely these more superficial traits of character and conduct which are the most socially obvious. Therefore, those who do not possess or accept the profound insight of religion are apt to measure a man's moral worth by them, because they make him socially agreeable or disagreeable. For his inner state they care nothing. And if they possess some superficial religion they expect to see first and foremost the evidence of true religion in this superficial zone, where, in fact, it makes itself felt, most slowly. For example, they condemn a man if getting up for fasting communion makes him irritable, and fail to see that his will to serve God at the sacrifice of comfort is of deeper significance.[12]

V. THE GLANDS AND PERSONALITY

Throughout this book we have stressed the influence of bodily constitution and the efficiency of the body as an organism upon human personality. Health, we believe, is a significant variable

---

[11] The Church, of course, does make such judgments in beatifying and canonizing saints. The Church has this power but no individual may claim it for himself.

[12] From *The Catholic Centre*, by E. I. Watkin. Copyright, 1939, Sheed and Ward, Inc., New York.

in the total picture of personality, yet just how it is related to personality it would be difficult for us to say. We all know of people with outstanding personalities who have spent their lives in ill health or nearly continuous pain and suffering. The amount of energy that a person has to expend, his vitality, is a more or less permanent characteristic of his temperament, and is dependent upon his basal metabolism. His basal metabolism, in turn, depends upon the functioning of some of his endocrine glands. We should, consequently, not be surprised to find both biologists and psychologists sometimes attributing specific traits and characteristics to the over- or under-secretion of certain of the endocrine glands. In so doing, they are giving us a sophisticated version of the ancient and time-honored doctrine of the four temperaments in relation to the four "humors" of the body.

Contemporary research, particularly research in the field of psychosomatic medicine, does not, however, justify our asserting that the "glands regulate personality." No one-to-one relationship between specific glandular conditions and personality has as yet been discovered. In the words of Hathaway:

After going through the experimental and clinical literature, the thoughtful reader will conclude that the effects of personality upon glands are more impressive and easier to illustrate than are the effects of the glands upon personality. To take a single example among many, it has long been recognized that individuals with hyperthyroidism or toxic thyroid have appeared to be entirely free from symptoms until some crisis occurs in their lives, causing prolonged emotional disturbances. The psychological change then reacts apparently upon the thyroid with consequent precipitation of the syndrome and characteristic histologic alterations in the gland.[13]

VI. FAMILY RESEMBLANCES IN PERSONALITY

A very fruitful type of personality research has been opened up by Wolff, some of which throws light upon family resemblances in personality. Wolff assumes that some characteristics of personality are manifested in expressive movements, such as gait, gestures, handwriting, and drawing. In one experiment, Wolff gave to each of nine of his students a pencil and a piece of paper, under which were nine carbons. He then asked these students to draw a hori-

[13] S. R. Hathaway, *Physiological Psychology* (New York, Appleton-Century-Crofts, Inc., 1942), p. 203.

zontal line upon the paper, then a triangle, then a circle, and finally to write the words "The United States of America." No other instructions were given. The same instructions were mailed to the parents of these students together with the materials necessary for the experiment. Each father and mother responded separately to the instructions and sent the records of their performance to Wolff. The pressure of writing was assessed by counting the number of carbons upon which the pattern was transferred. The performance of each student was compared with that of his father and mother and the performance of each parent was compared to that of the other. Even with such a small group of subjects the results suggest a resemblance in pressure between students and parents which cannot be attributed to chance. In length of line and size of design, the parents resembled each other more than they resembled the student. "There was identical pressure between student and father or mother in 44 per cent of the cases (equally distributed for father and mother). Father and mother had the same pressure, but different from that of the student in 33.3 per cent of the cases." [14] Unfortunately, Wolff did not use a control group of unrelated subjects with which these results could be compared.

Another highly suggestive study of Wolff's was made with a pair of identical twin sisters, nineteen years of age, and a younger sister sixteen years of age. In this study he found less resemblance in the handwriting of the twins than between one of the twins and the younger sister. This was true also for association to stimulus words; there were many similarities in the responses of the one twin and her younger sister but none in the responses of the twins. An analysis of the situation revealed that the younger sister admired one twin more than the other, and it was this admired twin (with whom she "identified") whom she resembled.

VII. PERSONALITY TYPES

A. Type Theories in General

Throughout the ages there have been attempts to classify people according to personality "type." Sometimes these types refer to the total personality, such as extrovert-introvert types, and again

[14] Werner Wolff, *What Is Psychology?* (New York, Grune & Stratton, Inc., 1947), p. 309.

they refer to rather specific functions, such as imagery types—auditory, visual, olfactory, or tactual. The use of typology in modern psychology appears to have been stimulated by the work of psychiatrists in classifying mental diseases. At times there has been an uncritical tendency to use psychiatric classifications, such as cycloid or schizoid personality, as convenient pigeon-holes for "typing" normal personalities. Although type theories are extremely attractive to people not well grounded in the science of psychology, there are many objections to them. Some of the more important objections will be discussed here.

Any attempt to classify people into two or more distinct types runs counter to results obtained from quantitative studies of personality. In general, quantitative studies of both physical and mental traits have resulted in continuous distributions, with the greater number of people in the middle, and fewer and fewer as the extremes of the distribution are reached. For example, if people are either extroverted or introverted, the results of measuring the traits which make up extroversion or introversion would yield a bi-modal curve, as shown in Figure 80. When this hypothe-

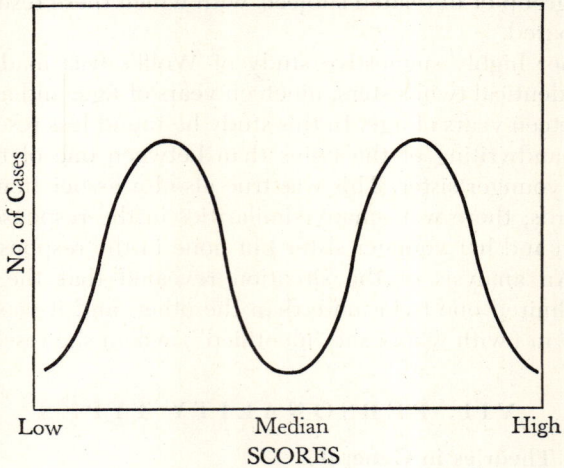

Fig. 80. Bi-Modal Curve.

sis was tested by giving an extroversion-introversion questionnaire to a random sampling of university students the results yielded a continuous distribution. A very large proportion of students, it appears, are neither introverted nor extroverted, but ambiverted.

The theory of types, as it is commonly used, is contrary to the fundamental thesis of this book, namely, that each person is a unique individual, different from everyone else while sharing with all a common human nature. Types "exist not in people or in nature, but rather in the eye of the observer." [15] The following criticism of type theories appears to be well taken:

Whatever the kind, a typology is always a device for exalting its author's special interest at the expense of the individuality of the life which he ruthlessly dismembers. Every typology is based on the abstraction of some segment from the total personality, and the forcing of this segment to unnatural prominence. All typologies place boundaries where boundaries do not belong. They are artificial categories.[16]

In spite of the limitations mentioned above, type theories do play a part in contemporary as well as in ancient psychology, and several of these theories are currently invoked in medicine and in studies of delinquency. We shall describe several of the specific type theories which have at one time or another enjoyed popularity.

B. Specific Type Theories

The classification of human beings according to body types has its roots way back in history. Hippocrates (460–370 B.C.) distinguished two such body types: the (1) *habitus phthisicus*, and the (2) *habitus apoplectus*. Aristotle (384–322 B.C.) recognized the profound relationship between mind and body although he did not set up a system of classification. In the *Physiognomica* we read, ". . . there was never an animal with the form of one kind and mental character of another: the soul and body appropriate to mankind always go together, and this shows that a specific body always involves a specific mental character." [17]

1. The four temperaments

One of the oldest type theories is that of the four temperaments, a theory ascribed to Hippocrates and modified by the Roman physician, Galen (131–201 A.D.). According to this theory, people can

---

[15] G. Allport, *Personality: A Psychological Interpretation* (New York, Henry Holt and Company, Inc., 1937), pp. 295–296.
[16] *Ibid.*
[17] According to W. D. Ross, *Physiognomica* is pseudo-Aristotelian. Although this work is not a genuine work of Aristotle, it nevertheless illustrates an ancient interpretation of the relation between soul and body.—W. D. Ross, *Aristotle* (London, Methuen and Co., Ltd., 1932), p. 12.

be classified as (*a*) sanguine, (*b*) choleric, (*c*) melancholic, or (*d*) phlegmatic. The sanguine, described as quick, active, and hopeful, but lacking in strength and stability, was thought to have an excess of blood. The choleric, quick, strong, and irascible, was thought to have an excess of yellow bile. The melancholic, slow and pessimistic, was supposed to suffer from an excess of black bile; whereas the phlegmatic, slow, stolid and weak, was thought to have an excess of phlegm. Normal personality, in terms of this theory, would be the result of a balance of all four fluids. This theory, in its emphasis upon the fluids or "humors" of the body, anticipates the modern theories of the relation of endocrine gland secretions to personality (the truth of which we have said above that we doubted) and its emphasis on "balance" as a requisite for normal personality anticipates the modern concept of integration.

2. Kretschmer's body types

Kretschmer, a German psychiatrist, published his now-famous book, *Physique and Character*, in 1921. In this book he distinguishes two principal body types, the *pyknic* and the *asthenic* (or leptosome), and an intermediate type, the *athletic*. The *pyknic* is, in general, round, heavy-set, short-limbed and short-necked. This body build, Kretschmer claims, is characteristically found among psychotics of the manic-depressive type. The *asthenic*, on the other hand, is the opposite of the pyknic in both physique and personality. He has a slender body, long limbs, and lean features. This body build is characteristic of the psychotic suffering from schizophrenia. By extending this constitutional theory to normal personality, Kretschmer claims that people of pyknic body build tend to be cyclothymic, that is, predominantly extroverted, jovial, and objective, although inclined also to be moody. Those of asthenic body build, on the other hand, are introverted, shy, and subjective. A fourth category, the *dysplastic,* is a mixture of several body types.

Kretschmer's claims have been partially substantiated with pathological subjects, but with normal subjects the evidence is inconclusive.

3. Sheldon's theory

One of the more recent attempts to classify male constitutional types and relate them to personality characteristics is that of Sheldon and his collaborators. The human body, according to Sheldon, is made up of three components: endomorphy, mesomorphy, and ectomorphy, respectively. Each of these components is present in some degree in everybody. They are described as follows:

a. Endomorphy. Endomorphy is characterized by soft, rounded contours. The head is large and round, the neck is short, and the face is broad. The hands and feet tend to be small and the limbs tend to be short. Anabolism predominates over catabolism, and by middle life the endomorphic individual becomes extremely heavy. The physique of the endomorphic person is dominated by the digestive tract.

b. Mesomorphy. Mesomorphy is characterized by a strong body structure and powerful muscles. The body contours are hard and squared. The neck is long, the face is relatively large, and muscular ridges stand out. The shoulders are broad and the waist is slender. Outstanding athletes in wrestling and football (bodily contact sports) tend to be extreme mesomorphs, since their physique is built around the large bones and muscles; but tennis players and distance runners, for example, do not.

c. Ectomorphy. Ectomorphy is characterized by a linear physique in which the contours are neither round nor hard. The trunk is narrow and relatively short, the face is small and tends toward triangularity, and the shoulders tend to droop. The ectomorph has more skin surface in relation to body mass than has the endomorph or the mesomorph. He is light in weight, quick and sensitive in his movements, and has little muscular strength. The physique of the ectomorph is built around the nervous system.

The relative amount of each component is rated by Sheldon on a scale from 1 to 7, in which 1 represents a minimum and 7 a maximum of the component. Not only are these ratings given for the body as a whole, but they may be used for rating different parts of the body. These part analyses are made in five body regions: (1) neck, head, and face, (2) thoracic trunk, (3) abdominal trunk, (4) arms, shoulders, and hands, and (5) thigh, calf, and feet.

The analyses of the relative degree of each body component

within a given individual is called *somatotyping*. An extreme endomorph is rated 711, an extreme mesomorph, 171, and an extreme ectomorph, 117.

The three body components correlate highly with temperamental patterns, which Sheldon has designated as follows:

Bodily Component	Temperamental Pattern
Endomorphy	Viscerotonia
Mesomorphy	Somatotonia
Ectomorphy	Cerebrotonia

The *viscerotonic* person is temperamentally relaxed both in posture and in movement. He reacts slowly, sleeps deeply, and loves food and comfort. He tends to be extremely sociable and amiable and greatly desires the affection and approval of other people.

The *somatotonic* person loves physical adventure, is willing to take risks, and moves in a decisive and self-assertive way. He seeks relief from trouble in physical action and feels little need to confide in others. He loves to dominate and lacks both the amiability of the viscerotonic and the love of privacy of the cerebrotonic.

The *cerebrotonic* person is more concerned with his own thoughts than with the external world. His posture and movements are tense and restrained. His reactions are extremely rapid, his physiological reactions uncomfortably intense, and he often suffers from the skin eruptions which accompany emotional disturbances. He is inhibited in the expression of his feelings, is unpredictably moody, and extremely sensitive to pain. He sleeps poorly and tends to suffer from chronic fatigue.

The theories of both Sheldon and Kretschmer attribute the personality traits associated with each of the different body types to innate constitutional factors. There is no evidence, however, to support this assumption. Even were it true that a one-to-one relationship between body build and personality traits existed (a degree of relationship which has not been proved) there would still be an alternative explanation. The child with a strong, vigorous body learns early in life to behave differently from the weak and undeveloped child. He derives satisfactions from aggressive and self-expressive activities which are denied to the youngster more fragilely constructed. He therefore has more incentives to be extroverted than the child who lacks vitality and thus tends to find substitute satisfactions by retiring into himself. A close correlation between body type and personality does not in itself, therefore, demonstrate an innate relationship between the two. It could just as readily be explained in terms of the interaction of the bodily organism with the physical and social environment.

4. Spranger's theory

According to Spranger, an individual's personality is best known by the values he holds. Spranger classifies people into six basic types, according to the kinds of values which are most important in their lives. These types include the (*a*) theoretical, (*b*) economic, (*c*) aesthetic, (*d*) social, (*e*) political, and (*f*) religious.

Allport and Vernon have devised an interesting, easily administered, and valuable personality test which is based upon Spranger's classification of types of men. The test, called *A Study of Values*, contains a number of controversial statements or questions to which the subject responds by checking among several alternative answers. The test is so constructed as to reveal the relative strength of Spranger's six kinds of values in a given individual.

5. Carl Jung's system of types

Carl Jung's system of types rests upon the notion that the basic attitude types, those of introversion and extroversion, are constitutionally determined. These types, he holds, are fundamentally opposed; they are differentiated by the characteristic attitude each takes towards objects. For the extrovert, the external object takes precedence over his own subjective processes. For the introvert, this situation is reversed; it is not the object so much as the subjective psychological processes which hold the dominant place. The introvert "sees everything from the angle of his conception, the other (extrovert) from the view-point of the objective occurrence."[18] Jung further distinguishes within these basic *attitude types* four *function types:* thinking, feeling, sensation, and intuition. Jung's system has unfortunately been greatly misrepresented in popular psychological writing, and a common error of interpretation is that of identifying the "thinking type" with introversion and the "feeling type" with extroversion. According to Jung, however, "Every one of these types can . . . be introverted or extroverted according to his relation to the object . . ."[19]

[18] C. G. Jung, *Psychological Types* (New York, Harcourt, Brace and Company, Inc., 1939), p. 12.
[19] *Ibid.*, p. 14.

Both the *thinking extrovert* and the *thinking introvert*, for instance, have a tendency to regulate their lives on the basis of intellectual conclusions. These conclusions, in the case of the thinking extrovert, are based upon objective facts or upon ideas generally accepted as valid. In the *thinking introvert*, on the contrary, the aim and origin of thinking lies not in external facts but in his subjective view of things. New "views rather than the perception of new facts" [20] are his main concern.

An interesting test designed to measure introversion-extroversion in college students is the *Minnesota T-S-E Inventory*. This inventory tests for three types of introversion-extroversion, thinking, social, and emotional, and has a certain predictive value for success in college. A high score for thinking-introversion, for instance, is correlated with high scholastic achievement, and a high score for social-extroversion is characteristic of the more successful student teachers.[21]

C. Evaluation of Type Concept

In spite of the objections to type theories, there appears to be a legitimate place for "types" if we are careful to recognize (1) that not all individuals can be classified into one or another of the categories we have set up and (2) that there are great differences among individuals who fall into the same category. A distinction can be made between ideal types and empirical types.[22] Empirical types are not spun from theoretical conceptions of "ideal" types without the support of factual evidence. Empirical types are generalizations of data gathered from controlled observation. They have the same function as all scientific generalizations in bringing meaning out of chaos, and they stand "logically between observation and the reformulation of theory." [23]

The ultimate perfection of human personality is dependent upon social participation with others. Certain psychological aspects of man's relations to others in society will be presented in the next chapter.

[20] *Ibid.*, p. 481.
[21] *Manual for the Minnesota T-S-E Inventory*. Published by Science Research Associates, 228 South Wabash Avenue, Chicago 4, Illinois.
[22] R. F. Winch, "Heuristic and Empirical Typologies: A Job for Factor Analysis," *Amer. Soc. Rev.*, 12 (February, 1947), 68–75.
[23] *Ibid.*

SUGGESTED READING

ALLPORT, G. W., *The Individual and His Religion, A Psychological Interpretation* (New York, The Macmillan Company, 1950).

VON HILDEBRAND, DIETRICH, *Liturgy and Personality* (New York, Longmans, Green & Company, 1942), Chapter II, "The Essence of Personality."

XX

The Person in Society

Does not the psychology of a group of men freely associated in the service of some great cause show entirely different characteristics from those to be observed in crowd psychology, and does not the same term "collective life" mean in the second case purely and simply fusion and in the first the exaltation of each personality?—HENRI DE LUBAC.[1]

I. MAN AND SOCIETY

Man is *naturally* a social being. He can develop neither physically nor mentally without the help of other people. Man did not invent society in order to satisfy his needs, nor can he repudiate it if it does not suit him. He can, of course, work to produce changes in the society in which he finds himself, but society itself he cannot slough off. It is an inescapable fact of his very existence.

Christian man is *supernaturally* a social being. He is united to his fellow Christians in the Mystical Body of Christ. This union is epitomized in the words of Christ, who said, "I am the vine; you are the branches." This union of man to man in the Mystical Body of Christ is thus shown to depend ultimately on an intimate union with Christ Himself; Christ is the head, all men united to Christ are branches united to each other because they derive life from the vine. If a man severs his relation with Christ, he becomes a dead branch, and in doing so he severs the deep supernatural bond with his fellow men which he had as a living member of the Mystical Body of Christ. The deepest possible union of man to man is that resulting from a full participation in the supernatural life of the Mystical Body of Christ.

Psychology deals with the natural factors only which enter into

---

[1] Henri De Lubac, *Catholicism* (New York, Longmans, Green & Company, 1950), p. 179.

man's relation to his fellows. Yet natural factors alone are not enough to explain the relation of men to one another. If you want to secure a deep understanding of human solidarity, you must not limit yourself to psychology, as we are doing in this book, nor even to the philosophical study of man in society. You must study theology as well, and particularly the theology of the "vine and the branches," of the "Mystical Body of Christ."

II. CULTURE AND PERSONALITY

Of all animals man alone is capable of social life in the true sense of the word, because man alone is capable of choosing means to an end. Many other animals, of course, are gregarious; they travel in packs, herds, and flocks. Bees show a high degree of specialization of labor; ants behave in a way that seems highly coöperative. Yet none of this group activity of insects and animals has an enriching effect upon the participants. An animal raised in captivity may be an even more perfect specimen than one that grows up with the pack. The behavior of animals in groups is strictly predictable; it works smoothly and surely toward the accomplishment of an end. But the end is not freely chosen by the animals nor is the selection of the appropriate means to its accomplishment within their power. Man alone can consciously formulate his aims and adapt the means at his disposal to the achievement of his ends. He cannot achieve these ends alone; other people must help him and he must help others. Human personality develops in society. Man codifies the rules of his society in laws, systems of ethics, and in rules of etiquette.

The extent to which a person's potentialities become actual is dependent to a considerable degree upon the kind of society into which he is born and in which he lives. In a society which has developed only the simplest number concepts, for instance, a child with a potentiality for mathematical discovery could never become a mathematician. An individual living in a society with a very primitive type of language may not have the verbal symbols necessary to express profound philosophical truths even though he may have the potentialities for becoming a philosopher. A child with a bent for artistic expression, especially in the medium of the dance or of sculpture, may, in a narrowly puritan culture, be so repressed that neither he nor anyone else is aware of his talents.

Should he try to express or develop these gifts in spite of community censorship, his personality is likely to suffer in other respects. He is liable to be ostracized or persecuted.

Today, no less than in ages past, the social group has a powerful influence upon the values, attitudes, habits of thought, level of aspiration, and the material and spiritual achievements of its individual members. It is the rare individual who will or can "rise above the crowd." The so-called "socially adjusted" person typically adopts the attitudes and standards of the group or groups in which he seeks acceptance. This is true not only of the larger communities of the world, the nation, state, or city; it is also true of communities within the community, such as a business men's association or a college campus. At Sarah Lawrence College, for instance, it was found that students typically came from families which were relatively conservative in their opinions on economic and political questions. The college community, however, tended to be much more liberal. Most students soon discovered that liberal opinions had a prestige value at Sarah Lawrence and changed markedly in that direction as they tended to identify themselves with the faculty and student body The girls who had difficulty, however, in adjusting to the college community and gaining acceptance, tended to retain their conservative views and continued seeking their security in their own families rather than in the college group. Some girls, it appears, had looked forward to college as an opportunity to escape from dependence upon their parents. These girls not only tended to be liberal but also to be radically more so than the rest of the college students. The statements which the students gave to explain their change of attitude since coming to Sarah Lawrence College showed clearly in the great majority of cases that the girls had changed because they wanted to "belong" to the group having prestige.

Since, then, the group exerts such a powerful influence upon the personality of its members, it seems reasonable to suppose that by improving the group as a whole, the individual personalities affected by the group will also be improved. This is not to deny, of course, that the status of a group can be raised by the personal improvement of each of its members. It merely raises the question as to which is the most economical way to proceed in trying to effect a desirable improvement. School administrators, teachers, business executives, statesmen, and other people in positions of leadership are often faced with a problem such as this: in order to effect a desirable change, is it more economical to focus attention on each specific member of the group in turn, or is it better to work toward improving the group as a whole? While there are advantages and disadvantages in each of these approaches, psychological studies of group psychology suggest that in many instances the individual personality has a better chance to improve if the group as a whole can be affected in such a way as to facilitate such a change. Contemporary studies in "group dynamics" promise to throw more light on this question than we now possess.

III. GROUP DYNAMICS

That individuals behave differently in groups than they do when alone is a common experience of everyday life. A boy who affiliates himself with a delinquent gang is soon enmeshed in the delinquencies of the gang even though when alone his behavior may be above reproach. A confirmed alcoholic may be powerless to help himself or even to profit from psychiatric treatment. Yet, strangely enough, he can and often does mend his ways when he becomes a member of Alcoholics Anonymous. Only recently have social psychologists recognized a distinct psychology of "normal groups," although they have long recognized the phenomena of "crowd" or "mob" psychology as a psychology different in many respects from that of any of the individuals of the group. Some of them at an earlier date even spoke mistakenly of a "group mind." There is no such thing as a group mind but only the individual minds of the specific people who compose the group and who may be different in many ways because they belong to the group. Unfortunately, psychologists, in reacting against the unwarranted postulate of a group mind, tended for a long time to the opposite error, that of attributing group psychological phenomena to the same psychological factors which had been found to operate in the individual person. Even as late as World War II, a committee of eminent and well-intentioned social psychologists drew up a set of psychological principles for enduring peace and presented them to the president of the United States and other government officials. Later, they had to repudiate these statements and admit that the generalizations they had made about groups on the basis of principles developed for individual psychology were invalid. The relatively recent field of research known as "group dynamics" is repeatedly showing that group psychological principles cannot be deduced from individual psychology alone, and that generalizations concerning individual motivation can be applied to groups only to a limited degree. The "dynamics" of groups is a field of study by itself, and we are gradually finding through research in this area that there are definite laws of group structure and function. Although research of this kind is relatively new, an impressive amount of data has already been amassed. It throws new light on many problems of social psychology related to social justice, such as improving the lot of minority groups, eliminating prejudice and scapegoating, and increasing the effectiveness of communication and coöperation among peoples of different culture groups. The scope of these studies goes far beyond that of an introductory textbook of this kind. A few illustrations of problems falling in this area, however, will suggest the importance of research in this field.

A. Communication

Human beings develop their personalities through social participation with others. This social participation and interaction is mediated by communication. Effective communication is necessary for group solidarity and for a feeling of "oneness." Anything which facilitates communication, therefore, tends to facilitate effective group interaction. Anything which interferes with effective group communication also interferes with group interaction. It is significant that in international relations we speak of having "conversations" with representatives of other nations as long as we are on friendly terms with them. When these conversations cease we are usually on the verge of war or in an actual state of war. In other words, effective communication is as necessary for social solidarity on the international level as it is on the national and local level. An increasing number of social psychologists are studying this problem. Research to date has been successfully applied, however, to small neighborhood groups for the most part.[2] Little has as yet been accomplished on the national or international scale.

[2] Saul Alinsky, *Reveille for Radicals* (Chicago, University of Chicago Press, 1946).

B. Crowd Behavior

Crowds are temporary social groups which spring into existence suddenly with little or no formal organization. Unlike the established social groups of the community, they have no traditions, no clearly defined functions, and no responsible leaders. Crowd behavior begins by the gathering together of individuals who, although they may not and usually do not know each other, have nevertheless shared a common background of experience, including common experiences of frustration, discontent, or disruption. One kind of crowd, for instance, does not act as a unit until something happens which causes everyone in the crowd to focus attention on the same object or occurrence so that all competing stimuli are for the time inhibited. If the object of attention is a symbol for common frustrations or for common fulfillment of desires, the members of the crowd tend to become emotionally identified with each other. The shouting, milling about, and gesturing of a crowd tend to enhance excitement and produce a common mood. Once this common mood is present, the crowd is ready to act as a unit.

The crowd may unwittingly become an important instrument for social change, or it may serve merely as a collective way of letting off steam. A crowd may, for example, destroy property, break windows, injure a few people, and then dissolve. Or, it may develop slogans which enable the crowd to reassemble or other crowds to assemble and which guide the individuals even after the crowd is dispersed.

Crowd behavior is exhibited in religious revival ceremonies where the ecstatic "conversion" of one or two individuals sets off a chain reaction of "conversion." These "conversions," however, do not last, since they are not based upon reasoned convictions but spring from fleeting emotions. A skillful speaker may, on occasion, inflame his audience into a crowd, as has been demonstrated repeatedly by successful evangelists. The speaker must succeed in getting the undivided attention of the group by appealing to some deep emotional need. Music, banners, uniforms, and dramatic stage effects are helpful in keeping the individual's attention away from himself and from observing how he is behaving. Singing may be introduced to produce rhythmic movements in the crowd and thus break down barriers between individuals. The more limited the space, the easier it is to form a crowd. Ordinarily, standing is more conducive to crowd formation than sitting because it allows for greater physical contact and excitement.

Certain destructive kinds of group activity, such as riots, panics, and lynchings, can be interpreted only in terms of group psychological phenomena and not in the light of principles derived from the study of individuals alone. Only a few pathological individuals behave in a way that even approximates what normal people will sometimes do when gathered together in crowds or mobs.

C. Rumor

Rumor mongering has its origin in the psychological needs of the individual although it is expressed only in a social situation. Before a rumor gets started two basic conditions must be present: (1) the theme of the story must have some personal significance to both the speaker and listener, and (2) the true facts must be shrouded in some sort of mystery. Most of us, for example, would probably not be interested in spreading the rumor that a given factory in Great Britain was going to give its workmen two weeks' paid vacations beginning with the next fiscal year. But among the workmen in the factory, rumors may be rife on the subject. Also, if a certain law has been passed which affects us personally and arouses in us strong emotions, we do not spread rumors about it. We do not need to spread rumors when all of the facts are known.

Various motives underly the acceptance and spreading of rumor. Fears, anxieties, and desires are often alleviated by giving them this indirect verbal expression. Often they serve to relieve feelings of guilt by providing people with "reasonable" motives for feeling the way they do. If a person dislikes Negroes, let us say, he may feel guilty about this dislike. If he hears rumors that Negroes cannot be trusted, however, or that they are dirty, then he can feel justified in his dislike. He is predisposed to accept the rumor. For this reason, we can often learn a great deal about the "inner world" of a person by studying the rumors which he either accepts or rejects. Sometimes, of course, there is no real malice behind rumor. A person may accept or invent a rumor because he has an insatiable need to "explain" something that needs to be made intelligible.

During World War II, a study was made of rumors relating to

waste and special privilege in the OPA (Office of Price Administration).³ A significant finding was the difference in people who admitted feeling guilt or shame over "chiseling" on their ration allowances and those who did not. Those who admitted "chiseling" but denied that they felt guilty about it tended to believe and spread the rumors relating to waste and special privilege in the OPA. Those who admitted feeling guilty about their behavior were less prone to accept rumors concerning the malpractice of others. Briefly, the spreading and believing of rumors disparaging to others seems to act as a safeguard against developing a guilty conscience ourselves.

In our world today rumors are often deliberately planted and cultivated as a means to disparage an individual or a group. An example of this is seen in the so-called "morality trials" of the Nazi government in Germany which preceded World War II by many years. They were aimed at destroying respect for and confidence in the teachers of Catholic schools in order to destroy the influence of the Church in Germany and thus eliminate a powerful opponent to totalitarianism in that country. The newspapers and radios daily carried "rumors" of immorality among the teaching brothers and sisters, and later of their trials and convictions. Many people who at first were skeptical of such rumors gradually came to believe them because of the power of repetition. The Soviet government does the same thing in trying to destroy the influence of both Catholic and Protestant churches in the countries under its control. Cardinals, bishops, and priests are convicted, not because they oppose a régime that forces God out of the picture, but because they are "traitors" to their countries. The daily reports of such accusations gradually give rise to the rumor that the Church is the enemy of the country and consequently of the people.

Within the narrow confines of our own neighborhood groups we also engage in gossiping and in spreading rumors. These rumors may do grave harm to the solidarity of the group and cause serious injustice. We can guard against listening, accepting, and spreading such stories if we understand the motivation behind such behavior. Typically, the gossip selects for his target someone whom

³ F. H. Allport and M. Lepkin, "Wartime Rumors of Waste and Special Privilege: Why Some People Believe Them," *J. Abnorm. Soc. Psychol.*, 40 (1945), 3–36.

he envies or by whom he feels frustrated. A gossip is never emotionally detached from the story he is telling, and for that reason he is almost certainly compelled to distort the facts. Notice, too, that the gossip never calls you over to whisper in your ear, "I have a juicy story to tell you! So-and-So is a wonderful person!" On the contrary, gossip is always disparaging, and that fact alone gives us a clue to the motivation behind it.

D. The Participant Observer

Study of group dynamics has brought into psychological research a number of methods borrowed from sociology and anthropology. One such method is that of the participant observer. The great variety and complexity of everyday life situations cannot be reproduced under the conditions of an experiment or a test, nor can the motivating influences of everyday life be called into play in an artificial research situation. The psychologist who uses this method moves into the community in which he intends to make his observations and becomes a part of the group that he is studying. In his capacity as "participant observer" he becomes acquainted with the people and their culture pattern, discovers the natural leaders of the group, and learns many facts about human beings which he could not learn in a laboratory or clinic.

E. Leaders and Group Functioning

Wherever people are gathered together in groups, a hierarchy of status is set up. Certain individuals have more prestige than others; certain people stand out as leaders. This status ranking is not always made consciously, and often the members of the group are not aware of it until a decision is to be made. Then it is usually apparent that the opinion of one or two individuals bears more weight than that of others. Various studies have been conducted to find out what is characteristic of such natural leaders. In some instances, sociometric questionnaires have been used, and the results have been analyzed to determine what characteristics the "overchosen" and "underchosen" persons in different types of groups possess in common. The results of one such study lead to the conclusion that the persons "overchosen," that is, those who are the natural leaders of the group, are not popular in any superficial sense. Characteristic of these natural leaders, according to the group consensus, is the fact that "they act in behalf of the about people often revolve around racial, religious, and class conflicts. Prejudice is a special problem in human relations and, like all problems in human relations, it is an attempt by an individual or by a group to satisfy a basic human need. Often, if we would understand a given prejudice, we must first answer the question: "Why does this individual or group *need* to be prejudiced?" In this connection it is of interest to note an observation by the Swedish sociologist, Myrdal, as to why Americans have adopted and persistently clung to the notion that the Negro is biologically inferior to the white man in spite of scientific evidence to the contrary. Myrdal says, "The biological ideology had to be utilized as an intellectual explanation of, and a moral apology for, slavery in a society which went out emphatically to invoke as its highest principles the ideals of the inalienable rights of all men to freedom and equality of opportunity." [6] In other words, the doctrine of biological inferiority often has its origin in the need of a people to justify itself and may be called a cultural rationalization. Prejudice usually has both an intellectual and an emotional basis, although the emotional basis ordinarily predominates. If the prejudice has only an intellectual basis, which is very rarely the case, then it can be dissipated by an increase in knowledge. The deep-seated prejudices which result in social injustice often spring from unconscious needs and cannot be removed by logic and persuasion. They serve the function of enhancing one's own status by making others appear inferior.

A. "Tabloid Thinking"

Not all prejudice is emotionally determined. Much of it results simply from the limitations of the human mind. In our complex society it is impossible for one person to know everything that is going on. All of us are confronted with problems toward which we must take some stand, even though we know that our knowledge of the subject is limited. Voting for political candidates is a case in point. To meet these practical problems we often resort to "tabloid" thinking. By "tabloid" thinking we mean reducing a complicated body of knowledge to a simple formula without any qualifications or distinctions. Most true statements about complicated matters, however, cannot be summed up in a few words.

[6] G. Myrdal, *An American Dilemma: The Negro Problem and Modern Democracy* (New York, Harper & Brothers, 1944), Vol. I, p. 89.

Tabloids are therefore inevitably biased or inaccurate statements. The slogan, "High tariffs make for high wages," which has occasionally appeared in campaign speeches, would be a case in point. Under certain conditions it might well be true, but under other conditions it would be false. The statement as it stands, however, is untrue, because it fails to define the conditions under which it would be true. Or, to take an example closer to home, "Students who make study their first objective in college will get the highest grades." This statement, too, alas, is an oversimplification of the facts. Grades in college are the result not of one or two factors acting in isolation but of the interaction of multiple factors. Good preparation in high school, exceptionally good teachers, and high intelligence on the part of a given individual may be the most important reasons for getting good grades. (In fact, there is often a low negative correlation between measured intelligence and amount of time spent in preparing assignments.) The type and difficulty of curriculum pursued would be another factor influencing grades. Some subjects are harder than others; some courses call more for special skills than they do for study. The relationship, in other words, between studying and college grades is not nearly as simple as the above tabloid statement would lead us to believe.

People are victims of tabloid thinking for the following reasons: (1) they do not have time to investigate every issue toward which they must take a stand; (2) they do not have the information necessary to think through and analyze a problem; and (3) they get a certain amount of emotional satisfaction from having come to a decision, no matter how incorrect the decision may be. Most people are uncomfortable when they have to suspend judgment. They want "closure."

Tabloid thinking is not always dishonest thinking. Often we resort to it in self-defense. It is the only way to save ourselves from having to analyze everything. Even the most intelligent person reaches the limit of his ability to understand complex situations in a limited amount of time. The college professor, for example, who has read one of his colleague's books and finds it wanting in some respects, may never read another book by the same author. Subsequent books by the same writer may be much better than the first. The professor's prejudice, however, keeps him from reading these books and changing his opinions about the writer. This prejudice is, of course, unfair to the writer. But it simplifies the professor's life in that he cannot read everything, and in the majority of cases his first judgment is likely to be the correct one. By acting upon his prejudices in this way, he saves himself time in the long run which he can put to better advantage.

B. Causes of Prejudice

1. *Causes are multiple.* The psychological factors causing prejudice do not operate in a vacuum; they are dependent upon socio-economic conditions, educational background, cultural values, ideologies, and perhaps other obscure environmental factors. Social conditions furnish the milieu in which the psychological causes of prejudice germinate. In this chapter we are limiting our discussion to psychological factors. In reading this discussion, however, it will be well to keep in mind that all of these factors operate in a group psychological atmosphere. In many respects, the "group" rather than the individual is the central problem in dealing with prejudice.

2. *Role of unresolved personality conflicts.* As we have noted before, all human behavior is an attempt to satisfy basic human needs. When behavior accomplishes its end, namely, the satisfaction of one's needs, the individual is said to have made an *adjustment*. When the behavior actually deprives the person of the good he is seeking it is called a *maladjustment*. A maladjustment may be (1) no more than a casual breakdown, such as an occasional behavior problem in a child who is usually well-adjusted, or (2) it may be more continuous and of such a nature as to be labeled *neurotic*, or (3) it may be serious enough to be called *psychotic*. All three of these maladjustments are the result of unresolved personality conflicts. All have emotional bases of more or less depth.

Prejudice, which is emotionally determined, may be compared to a behavior problem, a neurosis, or a psychosis. It is essentially a maladjustment resulting from inner conflict. The tenacity with which the prejudice is held depends upon the seriousness of the emotional conflict and the resources the person has for meeting such conflicts. Prejudice, like mental illness, is an attempt to establish emotional equilibrium. Like mental disease, however, it is socially destructive. Prejudice never really solves a problem; it merely represses or disguises the problem. It may at times be as destructive of wholesome personality as a neurosis or a psychosis.

C. Prejudice in College Students

If prejudice were nothing more than ignorance, it would not be found to any considerable extent among educated people. And this is true—at least for certain types of prejudice. The absurdity of certain prejudices held by uneducated people is obvious to the college student or graduate, and he is not likely to hold such prejudices himself. This is not to say, however, that college students (and their professors) do not have prejudices. They do. But the kind of prejudice is different from that of the unlettered. The prejudices of educated persons are in some ways more dangerous than those of the unlettered because (1) they can be defended with greater verbal skill, (2) they can be "rationalized" more completely by a kind of "pseudo-logic," and (3) these people typically hold positions of leadership in the community. The prejudices of the educated may be just as irrational and just as intense as those of the uneducated because, though they are perhaps different in kind, they spring from the same source—the emotionalized attitudes and needs, both conscious and unconscious, of the individual prejudiced person.

Several interesting studies have been made of the characteristics of college students who show marked racial prejudice. We shall describe one such study because of the light it throws upon the relation of the individual's personal adjustment and traits to his social behavior and attitudes.

A test of anti-Semitism was administered to a group of 100 university students, 76 of whom were women enrolled in an elementary course in psychology.[7] Since the women students were in the majority we shall limit our discussion to them. Test items consisted of common unfavorable stereotypes of Jews as well as suggestions that Jews be avoided, secluded, and suppressed. Although the test papers were not signed, it was possible to identify each individual's responses. The personalities of the girls receiving extremely high and low scores (upper and lower 25 per cent) were analyzed to see if there were any characteristic differences in

---

[7] Frenkel-Brunswik and R. N. Sanford, "Some Personality Factors in Anti-Semitism," *J. Psychol.*, 20 (1945), 271–291.

those most prejudiced and those least prejudiced. Eight girls receiving high scores, eight receiving low scores, and four receiving intermediate scores (these latter made up the control group) were subjected to further testing and questioning. They were given a second set of questions pertaining to public opinion, political loyalties, and membership in various groups. They were also given the Rorschach test, the TAT, and a number of "projective" questions designed to reveal indirectly the individual's goals, fears, aspirations, and identifications with people. Among the questions asked were: "What great people, living or dead, do you admire most?"; "If you knew you had only six months to live, but could do just as you pleased during that period, how would you spend the time?" Each of the girls was interviewed as well as tested.

The personality differences between the two extreme groups were striking. The most prejudiced girls appeared on the surface to be typical middle-class people, well-groomed, submissive to authority, conservative, devoted to their parents, and apparently satisfied with themselves and with their lives. A deeper analysis of their personalities revealed, however, that this outward calm and satisfaction had been attained at a great price. There was a preponderance of extremely aggressive and destructive themes in their TAT responses. They showed little interest in or knowledge of social and economic problems. They tended to support the status quo automatically without inquiring into matters of right or wrong, good or bad. These girls were extremely reluctant to talk about themselves and their affairs. Their main interest was their social standing and how they might make an appropriate marriage. They failed to recognize any primitive emotions in themselves and projected them instead to minority groups. (In a later study of 140 individuals, an r of .75 was obtained between anti-Semitism and rejection of other minority groups.) [8] These girls were not nearly so accepting of their parents as they appeared to be on the surface. The people they admired most had power and control, and in some of the girls' responses there was a suggestion of paranoid trends.

In contrast, the girls showing little or no prejudice were not as

---

[8] These findings are in line with those of D. J. Levinson and R. N. Sanford, "A Scale for the Measurement of Anti-Semitism," *J. Psychol.*, 17 (1944), 339–370. These investigators found that as the income of the father went up, so did anti-Semitism.

well-groomed or socially at ease as the prejudiced group. They had more varied interests, were willing to talk about themselves and their affairs, and expressed maladjustments openly instead of projecting them onto other people. The people they admired most were humanitarians, artists, and scientists. They made more critical appraisals of their parents, but at the same time showed more acceptance of them. There was little or no hostility shown in their responses to the TAT. The investigators felt that in these girls, religion was experienced on a deeper level and better integrated with the whole personality than it was with the more prejudiced girls.

The above study lends support to our thesis that prejudice grows out of the personality needs of the individual as well as from social factors. Presumably, then, prejudice can be diminished or eliminated by helping the individual prejudiced person to come to grips with himself and develop a more wholesome personality.

D. Origin of Prejudice in Children

Prejudice is not inherited. It grows out of the life history of the individual. Prolonged insecurity and deprivation in childhood set the stage for the personality distortions of adult life, some of which find expression in prejudiced behavior. The frustration of the need to be accepted by others, to be loved, and to be valued often results in feelings of hostility and aggression. Such hostility is seldom directed toward the source of the frustration. The source of the frustration is usually the parents or other adults who care for the child. The small child needs these people desperately. Because the child loves the person or persons who are hurting him, or because he fears that he will suffer more if he strikes back, the child may repress his aggressions toward them. Repressed aggressions often find a substitute outlet. A child who has been neglected or unloved may go through life with a chip on his shoulder. Often he will identify with the people whose favor he craves and strike at the people of whom they disapprove. In this way he handles his feelings of insecurity by strengthening his feeling that he "belongs" to the group.

The motive force behind prejudice appears to be the satisfaction or frustration of basic human needs. The direction which these prejudices take, however, is determined by economic, social, and cultural factors, the scope of which is too vast for us to cover here. We shall limit our discussion to the effects of three factors upon the development of specific prejudices in children: (1) contact with cultural stereotypes, (2) emotional involvement, and (3) imitation of parents and other adults.

1. *Contact with cultural stereotypes.* Stereotypes are "pictures in our heads" according to which we pigeon-hole people, occupations, political parties, or other socially significant aspects of reality. A stereotype is always an oversimplification; it may even be a caricature. A stereotype, like a tabloid statement, reduces the reality that it pigeon-holes to a few bold, clear-cut, unqualified characteristics, ignoring aspects and details which do not fit in with the sharply simplified "picture." When we view people in terms of stereotypes, we do not see them as individuals or as they really are, but as members of a given class, race, nationality, or occupation. For instance, if we have a mental picture of doctors as unselfish humanitarians, we may fail to observe that a given doctor is a self-seeking, lazy bluffer. Or, if we have accepted the stereotyped notion of "humorless Englishmen," we will tend to notice as "Englishmen" only those Englishmen who conform to our bias. Those who do not correspond to our mental picture may be thought of simply as persons rather than as Englishmen.

Early in life children come into contact with cultural stereotypes, such as "Uncle Tom," "Aunt Jemima," "Mammy," "Nigger," "Grasping Jew," "Bull-headed German," "Stupid Swede," or "Drunken Irishman." These stereotypes of themselves, it appears, do not cause prejudice, but they do help to determine the direction which prejudice will take. As long as the individuals accepting the stereotypes find adequate satisfaction of their basic needs and as long as the group seen in this stereotyped way does not constitute a threat, no serious injustice may be done. But when the social and economic conditions change and when violent emotions are aroused for any reason whatever, these stereotypes may suggest a channel for releasing tensions or directing aggression.

Knowledge alone, as we stated above, will not eliminate prejudice already acquired, since prejudice satisfies an emotional need. But education directed to eradicating cultural stereotypes long before the child has become emotionally involved can be effective in preventing prejudice when the child grows older. Often we naïvely assume that, once a person has come into contact with the people represented by our cultural stereotypes, he will recognize the stereotype for what it is, an unreal and unjust appraisal of his fellow man. Yet, as we know from our study of perception, this is not always true. Often because of our stereotypes we do not see people as they are; our prejudices limit what we actually see.

2. *Emotional involvement.* Perception and prejudice are related in two ways: (1) accurate perception may dissipate the prejudice, or (2) the prejudice may prevent accurate perception. People have a tendency to see what they want to see or what they expect to see, as demonstrated in the following experiment by Zillig.

Zillig asked grade school children to make lists of the children whom they liked the most and those whom they liked the least. From these lists he selected the five children who were "most-liked" and the five who were "least-liked." These ten children were then used as subjects for an experiment, the real nature of which was not known by the children. The most-liked group was instructed to do the opposite of what they were told to do when the experiment began. For example, if they were told to raise the right arm, they were expected to raise the left. The least-liked children, on the contrary, were given intensive practice in following directions and were instructed to follow them when told to do so in the classroom. Meanwhile, the children in the classroom were told that some of their members were going to perform a number of exercises in their presence and that they were to observe how accurately these children followed the directions given. Efforts were made to motivate the children to observe and report accurately. The ten children were then mixed up at random, after which they filed into the classroom and performed the exercises before their companions. The results show clear-cut evidence of prejudice. None of the most-liked children were reported to have made mistakes. All mistakes reported were attributed to the least-liked children who had actually not made any! These results, together with studies reported earlier on the relation of perception to emotion and need, suggest that prejudice cannot be eliminated just by giving prejudiced people the opportunity to correct their errors of judgment or belief by observation. Prejudice, based upon emotional involvement, prevents people from "seeing" what is actually there.

3. *Imitation of parents and other adults.* Young children identify with parents and teachers and imitate them in their prejudices.

THE PERSON IN SOCIETY 567

Some of these prejudices are taught explicitly. At first, children are aware of the source of their prejudices, but later they often forget that they were taught these things and tend to think that their prejudices are "instinctive." Sometimes prejudices are not taught directly but are "caught" from the parent or teacher. It is not always a matter of what the adult says but rather *how* he says it. The parent's raised eyebrows may convey his subtle disapproval of a playmate brought home after school. The teacher's smile of approval to the boy whose shoes are polished or who wants to be a doctor may build up or reinforce social class prejudice. Her unconscious tension or obvious disapproval of a boy who dresses "improperly," or who uses a lower-class vocabulary, or who wants to be a janitor, also conveys unmistakably the teacher's middle-class set of values.

E. Elimination of Prejudice

The cure of prejudice, like the cure of behavior problems or mental disease, rests upon a knowledge not only of symptoms, but also of the factors which cause the symptoms. If you were to complain to a doctor that you have frequent fevers, for example, he would probably subject you to a number of tests to determine the causes of the fever. He would not content himself with applying ice packs, administering cold drinks, or wrapping you in a wet blanket to remove your fever. Such measures, while they would eliminate your symptom temporarily, might only aggravate its causes. In general, the doctor's approach to your illness would be as follows: (1) he would carefully observe your symptoms; (2) he would take measures to diagnose your symptoms, i.e., to determine their causes; (3) he would direct his treatment to the causes rather than to the symptoms themselves. If his methods of treatment proved effective, the symptoms would automatically disappear.

The proper way to study a social malady such as prejudice is, in general, to begin as one would study a physical malady—by studying the symptoms. The next step (and a necessary step before selecting a treatment) is to analyze as far as possible all of the causes and their interrelationships. Ordinarily, the most effective treatment is one which aims at eliminating the causes. It is true, of course, that sometimes a symptom is treated when it is impossible to remove the cause or causes. For example, if one has a headache, he may take an aspirin tablet. But if the cause does not naturally take care of itself, the effect of the aspirin will soon wear off. Similarly, at the present time, if we cannot locate and eliminate the causes of prejudice, we can try to eliminate the symptoms. But usually the only permanent cure is one which is directed toward the source of the malady.

In this connection it is interesting to note that self-knowledge and a knowledge of the psychological laws governing prejudice may be instrumental in eliminating prejudice. The dissemination of psychological knowledge of this kind is often much more effective than the dissemination of knowledge concerning the objects of prejudice.

V. DISCRIMINATION AND SCAPEGOATING

When prejudice exists toward a small minority which does not constitute a threat to the dominant majority, it may not result in any very serious injustice. When the minority becomes powerful or large enough to constitute a threat, however, persecution and discrimination may result. Selective housing covenants, restricted job opportunities, and many subtle persecutions and limitations of the personal liberties of the minority group may then follow. In times of great crisis and emotional perturbation, the minority group may be forced into the position of scapegoat, as, for example, was the case during the Nazi persecution of the Jews in Germany. *Scapegoating* has been defined as a "phenomenon wherein some of the aggressive energies of a person or group are focused upon another individual, group, or object; the amount of aggression and blame being either partly or wholly unwarranted." [9] Scapegoating is a serious social calamity and may result in complete annihilation of the people who are its victims.

VI. ANTISOCIAL BEHAVIOR

The antisocial behavior known as delinquency and crime is a special problem in the relation of the individual person to the society in which he lives. The study of delinquency and crime goes far beyond mere psychological analysis into the fields of sociology,

---

[9] *ABC's of Scapegoating*, with a Foreword by G. W. Allport (Central YMCA College, 19 South La Salle Street, Chicago).

THE PERSON IN SOCIETY 569

anthropology, economics, and ethics. In a sense, the basic psychological factors underlying delinquency and crime have already been explained, inasmuch as any experience which influences character and personality will also make for either social or antisocial patterns of behavior.

A. Juvenile Delinquency

The term *delinquency* has a more social than psychological connotation, since it generally refers to a situation in which a person has come into conflict with civic authority. This notion is reflected in the statement that "a child is to be regarded as technically a delinquent when his antisocial tendencies appear so grave that he becomes, or ought to become, the subject of official action." [10] Ordinarily, a child who commits misdemeanors, but is protected by his parents and by their neighbors because of his parents' status in the community, does not get classified as a delinquent. Yet his conduct may be just as undesirable as that of the delinquent in so far as moral behavior is concerned. Some children, too, become technically delinquent, not because their behavior is seriously antisocial, but because a peevish adult has been annoyed by their conduct. To think of delinquents as "bad," therefore, and of non-delinquents as "good," is to set up a false dichotomy.

In studying juvenile delinquents, we are dealing only with those who get caught or reported. It is probable that this is a highly selected group, differing from those who did not get caught or reported in such important characteristics as intelligence, social and economic status, ethnic group, and geographical location. It is also probable that the number of children who commit antisocial acts but who do not become the objects of official action is considerably larger than the number of those who come into conflict with the law.

The typical juvenile delinquent has an IQ below 100. It has been reported that 13 per cent of the delinquents studied had IQ's below 70, and could be classified as feebleminded.[11] These

[10] Cyril Burt, *The Young Delinquent* (New York, D. Appleton & Company, Inc., 1925), p. 15.
[11] W. Healy and A. F. Bronner, *Delinquents and Criminals: Their Making and Unmaking* (New York, The Macmillan Company, 1926); S. Glueck and E. T. Glueck, *One Thousand Juvenile Delinquents* (Cambridge, Harvard University Press, 1934).

findings have been corroborated by other independent studies both in the United States and in Great Britain. These results, however, should be interpreted with caution. In studying delinquents who are brought into court, we are likely to be dealing with a selected group, namely, those who got caught. Those who did not get caught, and were, consequently, not available for study, are likely to be much brighter. Porterfield's study, reviewed in Chapter XVIII, has already thrown light upon this problem.

B. Adult Criminals

The type of crime committed by adult criminals as well as by juvenile delinquents is related to general intelligence. Assault and battery, rape, and one-man hold-ups are committed, typically, by relatively dull persons. Complicated thefts or embezzlement, involving careful planning, are usually committed only by persons of very superior intelligence. In general, prisoners in federal penitentiaries are more intelligent than those in state or county prisons and jails. In a federal prison in Illinois, for example, the prisoners were found to have significantly higher scores on tests of intelligence than the wardens and other attendants who had charge of them. The average IQ of a group of women sex offenders in North Carolina was 83.3 as compared with an average for the entire group of 86.6. The average IQ of the women who had committed robbery was 99.[12]

It is as difficult to define "criminality" in psychological terms as it is to define "juvenile delinquency." Many kinds of immoral behavior which are basically antagonistic to the welfare of society cannot be punished because of legal technicalities or because the persons committing the crimes enjoy social prestige. Certain types of business manipulation are fundamentally unjust, yet they are tolerated by a society which would condemn much lesser violations of justice if they were committed by one man against another. Thus, serious crimes of injustice toward whole classes of the population may go unpunished because no legal machinery has been set up to handle them, and because people in general have taken the attitude that "business is business." Behavior of this kind is sometimes referred to as "white-collar" criminality.

[12] E. W. Ruggles, "An Analytic Study of Various Factors Relating to Juvenile Crime," *J. of Juvenile Research*, 16 (1932), 125–132.

VII. SOCIAL PSYCHOLOGY AND CHRISTIAN PRINCIPLES

Social psychology deals with the natural factors that influence a man's relation to his fellow men. Because he is by nature a social animal, the human being reaches the fullness of his development only in the community. The nature of the social groups in which he participates and the part he takes in them exert a decisive influence upon his personality.

In the Christian scheme of things, man is supernaturally united to his fellow Christians in the Mystical Body of Christ. This supernatural union in the Mystical Body of Christ does not destroy but perfects the natural solidarity of human society. Because he is destined for life in a supernatural society, the Christian achieves the fulfillment of his powers only when he fully realizes the social implications of his religion. The attainment of a mature personality, as we shall show in the following chapter, is, in fact, largely dependent upon the substitution of intelligent social behavior for selfish individualism.

SUGGESTED READING

BORING, E. G. (ed.), *Psychology for the Armed Services* (Washington, D.C., The Infantry Journal, 1945), Chapters 18–23.

PART VIII

Maturity and Old Age

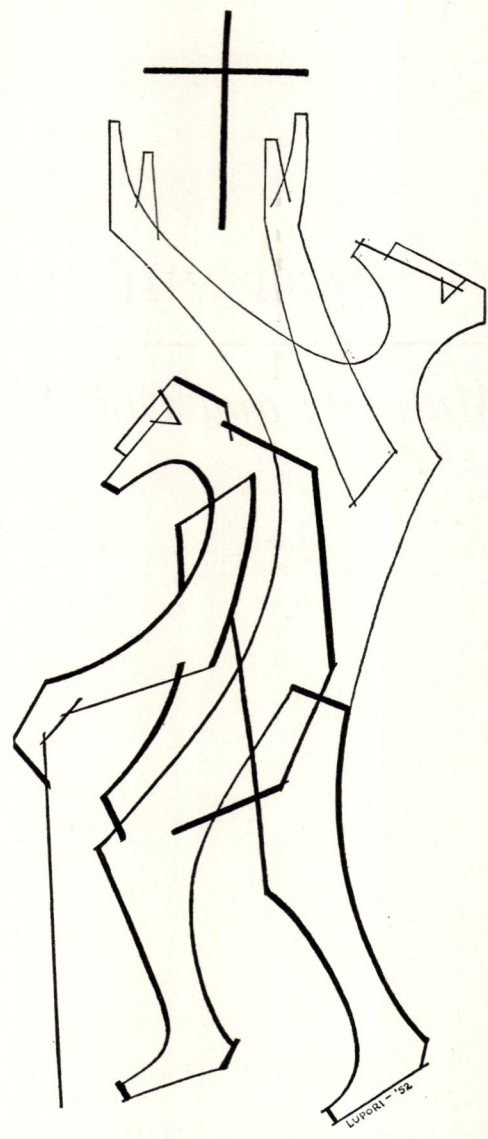

Maturity is the state of complete development. Maturity of body is not synonymous with maturity of soul. Christian man, coöperating with the grace of God, continues to grow spiritually even when the body goes into its decline.

XXI

Adulthood in Our Culture

> ... *the precise moment at which we become adult is ... that in which after some personal failure, struck by the feeling of our own helplessness, we at last exclaim: "Lord, deliver me from myself, I am only a poor, wretched man." It is only at that moment of honest humility that childhood comes to an end. Then man has grown up. It is then that the divine folly of Christianity can be manifested; in its presence we can no longer play at being clever, we are mature and can understand its higher wisdom.*—CHARLES MIEL, S.J.[1]

The climax of personality development is reached in adulthood. At this stage of life the basic attitudes, ideals, habits, and character traits have for the most part become crystallized. The inherited characteristics, the experiences and choices of a lifetime, have made the personality what it is. Chronological age alone, of course, does not make a man mature. Some people, in fact, never seem to grow up no matter how old they get. Yet adulthood presents to everyone new problems and opportunities which, if properly used, will insure the further development of personality. Adults are no longer subject to parents and guardians and are therefore responsible for the direction of their own lives. They are not, it is true, entirely free to make of themselves anything they would like to be, since their entire life history has to a considerable extent cast them into a characteristic mold. But each human person, within the limitations set up by his own peculiar experiences of life, is free to decide whether he will continue to grow or whether he will allow himself to be "fixated" at the relatively mediocre level of late adolescence.

[1] Fourth Sermon from Lenten Course at St. Joseph's, Marseille, 1927. Quoted in H. De Lubac, *Catholicism* (New York, Longmans, Green & Company, 1950), p. 265.

In this chapter and the next we are going to show you how adulthood is related to the rest of the life cycle, what the significant psychological aspects of this stage of life are, and what is meant by maturity.

I. EARLY MATURITY IN RELATION TO THE WHOLE LIFE SPAN

The span of human life known as early maturity (in contrast to later maturity or old age) falls, roughly, within the ages of twenty-five and fifty. Physically, it is characterized by stable growth in which regeneration takes place about as rapidly as degeneration. It is preceded by a period of progressive growth and followed by a period of regressive growth in which degeneration takes place faster than regeneration.

One of the more fruitful approaches to the understanding of adulthood in relation to the whole life span is biographical psychology, a field in which one of the leaders is Charlotte Bühler.[2] The methods she employed and some of the results and conclusions of her studies will be summarized here. In interpreting these studies, two cautions should be kept in mind. First, it should be remembered that the conclusions are summaries of general trends rather than binding principles illustrated by each and every individual life. Second, the studies were made by Bühler in Europe and have only limited validity in our American culture.

The basic materials used by Bühler were approximately 400 biographies of persons from different countries, social classes, and vocational groups. These biographies were supplemented by letters, diaries, and other documents whenever possible, and, in the case of living people, by clinical interviews. Among the vocations represented in the sample were physicians, engineers, business men, politicians, actors, priests, nuns, artists, scientists, lawyers, journalists, soldiers, pilots, mountain climbers, teachers, workers, waiters, servants, janitors, clerks, and farmers. The sample also included people who were not employed.

From the life histories of these four hundred people, three kinds of data were assembled and interpreted according to the principles of what we may call a longitudinal typology:

[2] C. Bühler, *Der menschliche Lebenslauf als psychologisches Problem* (Leipzig, Verlag von S. Hirzel, 1933). Also, "The Curve of Life as Studied in Biographies," *J. Appl. Psychol.*, 19 (1935), 405–409.

1. *External events of life.* Under this heading everything a person did was tabulated. The different fields of activity were classified as "dimensions" of behavior. The social dimension, for instance, was represented by such behavior as helping others, visiting friends, and enjoying one's family. The practical dimension included study, ways of earning a living, and the like. Ninety-seven dimensions were distinguished and an analysis was made of each dimension at different ages according to the prominence of each of the activities included under that dimension.

2. *Inner attitudes and reactions to events.* Under this heading all materials which revealed how the person thought about his own life were tabulated and analyzed in terms of age. Letters, diaries, and autobiographical notes were scrutinized.

3. *Accomplishments and productions.* An age analysis of both quality and quantity of work produced was made under this heading.

As a result of these biographical studies, five periods or phases were differentiated in the human life span. These periods, if we allow ourselves to throw the individuals out of focus and concentrate on the typical picture, are characterized as follows:

Period I. From infancy to about sixteen years of age the child lives at home and has a narrow group of interests centered around his family and school.

Period II. Typically, this period is ushered in between the sixteenth and twentieth year, and is characterized by the selection of an independent activity or by the independent acquisition of new relations with people. From this age until approximately twenty-eight years of age there is a great *expansion* of interests and activities, all of which are of a more or less preparatory character.

Period III. This period, beginning between the twenty-sixth and thirtieth year, with an average of 28.6 years, is a period of *culmination.* In most cases it begins with a definite choice of vocation and with the establishment of a home. It lasts until about 50 years of age. It is the most fruitful period of creative and professional work, and represents a high point in social relations.

Period IV. The fourth period begins at the average age of 48.5 years,[3] and is usually ushered in by a psychological crisis, such as retirement from work, illness, loss of friends or relatives, or economic reverses. It is characterized by a decrease in the number

[3] This age is much too early for our culture.

of dimensions of activity and by an increase in negative dimensions, such as illness or discontent.

Period V. The fifth period begins, on the average, at 63.8 years. Typically, it is characterized by retirement from work, by a decrease in social activities, and by an increase in hobbies requiring very little physical energy. Activity becomes more and more restricted.

It is interesting to compare the subjective experiences of these different periods of life. Typically, during the first period, the person's concerns and his attitudes and feelings are primarily the result of his individual needs. During adolescence, however, the individual raises the question as to why he should live at all. From this age on he not only wishes to live but must have some reason for living. By the time he has reached the *culmination* period, his subjective life is governed not so much by his own needs as by his accomplishment of tasks which he considers important in terms of goals set for him by society or by his own ethical or religious values. Progressively, as he grows older, interest in self is superseded by more objective interests, and, instead of being preoccupied mainly with his own wishes, he becomes more concerned about duties toward others. He is not content merely to live but must *live for* something. The above generalizations hold only for normal adults. In neurotic people, personal wishes take precedence over duties even in the third and fourth periods of life. When the neurosis is of a compulsive character, however, the whole subjective life of the person may be involved with duties, but the nature of these duties is different from that of normal people. Activities which normal people look upon as pleasurable may be placed by these neurotic persons in the category of duties, as, for example, visiting with friends.

The lives of some individuals lose their significance and are psychologically extinguished at a relatively early age. Women whose only aim is that of physical attractiveness and romantic love bloom for a short period and then decline. This is true also for persons whose lives have been built up around the satisfaction of personal desires and the pursuit of pleasure. Without significant goals of a spiritual nature, life becomes more and more of a burden and existence becomes meaningless as physical strength declines.

II. SEX DIFFERENCES

Sex differences are found in nearly every psychological characteristic, with the possible exception of measured intelligence and certain educational achievements. Physical characteristics in which men and women differ significantly and which condition psychological differences are rate of maturation, muscular strength, height, weight, body build, vital capacity, and different roles in the reproductive function. The fact that men, on the average, surpass women in physical size and strength, tends to make them more dominant and aggressive than women. The range of individual differences in most of these characteristics within either sex, however, is greater than mean differences between the sexes. Many individual men, for instance, are below the average height of women.

The social role of women is considerably different from that of men, and an education which does not take this fact into consideration may lead to widespread maladjustment. Women may compete successfully with men in college courses, even in those of a professional nature. But, once they are in a professional field, they usually find that their salaries are lower and that there are more limitations to their advancement than is true for men. Even when these conditions do not exist, however, and the woman becomes highly successful in her "career," the experience is often accompanied by a feeling of "incompleteness" or a lack of personal fulfillment.

III. THE ADULT WOMAN IN OUR CULTURE

It is not an easy thing to appraise the role of women in the contemporary world because myriad influences cause it to vary from one culture to another. The social class, the ethnic group, and the total cultural pattern in which she lives—all play a significant part in defining woman's role. Economic conditions and worldwide social and political changes are dynamically changing the status and role of millions of women throughout the world, and what is true today may be radically altered within a decade or so. In contemporary America there is a prevalent feeling that women are "free" in the sense that men are free, that they have achieved most of the rights and privileges which an earlier generation of "feminists" sought to secure for them. Nevertheless, we do not have to look very far to discover that the millennium for women has not yet arrived. Students of comparative cultures and penetrating observers of our own American culture find a profound unhappiness in the contemporary middle-class American woman. Margaret Mead, for example, writes as follows: ". . . the most articulate, the best educated, the most mobile group of American women is disturbed. . . . The position of women in America at present is explosive and potentially harmful." [4] And it has been pointed out by other writers that in our culture more prestige may be attached to the position of a woman in one or other of the various professions than to her position as wife and mother. While this is probably not altogether true, it seems likely that such prestige factors are operative at times.

The rapid historical developments of the past few decades have brought about a radical change in the position and role of women, and particularly of those belonging to the middle-class urban population. The battle cry of the "feminists" of an earlier day was that they must secure equality with men in every avenue of life: equal opportunities for jobs, even those of the most masculine type; equal pay; equal legal status; and equality with men in securing divorce and remarriage without incurring community censure. By "equality" these militant women seemed to imply "sameness," a proposed goal or ideal for women that is psychologically unsound. The ends they sought have to a very considerable degree been realized today. Yet it is doubtful that women are really happier as a result. The basic biological differences in men and women preclude the possibility that sameness of opportunity, experience, and status will of itself insure equality. Since men do not bear children it is impossible to claim that there are, or need be, no essential differences in the life of the two sexes.

Let us examine for a moment the assumption under which the leaders of the so-called feminist movement were operating. They started out with the view that historically men and women have been rivals and that women have been enslaved by men and deprived of their rights as human beings. Let us try to see to what

[4] Margaret Mead, "What Women Want," *Fortune*, 173 (December, 1946), 224.

extent it holds for the English and American societies which these early feminists were trying to reform.

One of the most painstaking research studies dealing with this problem is reported by Mary R. Beard in a book entitled *Woman as a Force in History*. The evidence amassed by Mrs. Beard successfully blasts the theory upon which the feminists operated, namely, that throughout history women have been subordinated to men. On the contrary, she shows that women have been a primary force in the history of the world and that their contributions have not been limited to their role as wives and mothers. She traces the intellectual leadership of women in academies and salons and depicts the influence they have had upon social and political changes. For all of modern woman's freedom, this influence does not appear to be greater today than it has been in past epochs. And many writers apparently believe that woman has less prestige today than she has had at other periods of history, partly because she is often competing with men rather than complementing them in their social role. The evidence amassed by Mrs. Beard and others indicates that in western culture, the unfavorable position of women as compared to men came only after the so-called Protestant reformation. As psychologists, we do not feel competent to evaluate all of the historical research bearing on this problem, but we do feel that at least some mention of historical influences should be made because of their bearing upon the psychological problems of women today. The serious student who wants to penetrate the subject more deeply will have to consult the authentic historical documents.

Historically, it appears that the contemporary "woman problem" is the natural outgrowth of the spirit of individualism ushered in by the Renaissance and by the Protestant religious revolt, a view that is shared by both Catholic and non-Catholic historians.[5] It is doubtful that the religious reformers could foresee the far-reaching consequences of their revolt against authority, and they would undoubtedly be horrified to find the social evils of divorce, child abandonment, birth prevention, adultery, and abortion laid at their door. But intellectually they sowed the seeds of individualism from which the contemporary attitudes toward the above social problems have progressively developed. The key notion

[5] E. W. Burgess and L. S. Cottrell, Jr., *Predicting Success or Failure in Marriage* (New York, Prentice-Hall, Inc., 1939), p. 1.

underlying a philosophy of individualism is that the individual rather than the family is the social unit. This gives rise to the idea that each individual has a right to live his life as he sees fit without considering its effect upon his family. According to this view, a woman as well as a man has a right to divorce her spouse and abandon her children if she feels that her own personality development requires it. She is free to bear or not bear children as she sees fit. This is sometimes called "living one's own life." It is legitimate, if one accepts this view, to enter into a series of experimental marriages until one finds an appropriate mate. The "happiness" of the individual rather than that of the group is the first consideration. We put the word "happiness" in quotation marks because we seriously doubt that real happiness ever results from putting this philosophy into practice in one's daily life.

It is of interest, too, to analyze some of the motives which appear to have inspired the crusading efforts of the militant feminists in England and America. One of the earliest of these, Mary Wollstonecraft Godwin (1759–1797), published her *Vindication of the Rights of Women* in 1792. The thesis of this book is that woman is everywhere in chains because of the malice and egotism of men, and that women must rise up and fight for their rights. This book contains many sweeping generalizations, unsupported by facts but burning with a passionate spirit of indignation. It has the sound of a clarion call to women in the English-speaking world. All women, of course, could not be interested in the feminist battle; but among those who were there appears to have been a preponderance of those whose relations with the particular men in their lives had been overwhelmingly frustrating. Certainly this was true for Mary Wollstonecraft herself. In childhood she had been subjected to beatings by a drunken father, and was released from his cruelty only when he deserted his family. Later she became enamoured of an American army officer named Imlay and had two illegitimate children by him. When he grew tired of her and deserted her she reacted by trying to commit suicide. Later she appears to have begged William Godwin to marry her, which he did in 1797, although he as well as she did not believe in what they termed the "slavery of marriage."

There may, of course, be normal women in the vanguard of feminism, but the odds are against it. Mary Wollstonecraft Godwin's unconscious but irresistible thirst for revenge and her pathologically warped attitude toward men may or may not have provided the theme upon which other feminists' lives have played with variations. But the idea is plausible. The normal woman in a normal human culture pattern, that is, one that does not show signs of decay, accepts the natural consequences of biological differences in the sexes without a feeling of being cheated—Freud and Mary Godwin to the contrary! Difference does not imply inequality. This becomes obvious when we penetrate the depths of human solidarity as expressed in the doctrine of the Mystical Body of Christ. The vocation of woman—that of mother—is necessarily different from that of man by reason of natural differences in biological function. In the words of Gerald Vann:

. . . different members [of the Mystical Body] have by definition different functions to fulfill according to their different gifts; and if you hold that grace perfects nature and makes that the material of the supernaturalized life, then you must hold also that the differences of natural as well as supernatural gifts determine the function the Christian is to fulfill in the Church. That is indeed the basis of the Christian doctrine of vocation.[6]

Women today, as in any age in which their major social contribution, that of child-bearing and rearing, is not held in honor, will necessarily be maladjusted. In America today this is probably true of women living in some geographical areas and in certain sub-cultural groups. It is probably not true of farm women and less true of lower-class than of middle-class women. It seems to strike the college-educated woman in certain localities with the greatest force.

Women today are free to compete with men in most of the professions, although medical, law, and certain other professional schools admit students on a quota basis unfavorable to women, and in most of the professions—including psychology—women earn less than men do at exactly the same jobs. Women can and do, however, succeed in the professions and are often able to compete successfully with men. A few such women are exceptionally gifted and can successfully combine a career with marriage and the rearing of a family. But they are the exceptions to the rule. Most women find that if their family is not to suffer, their career must take a second place. The woman who makes a real

[6] Gerald Vann, O.P., *Eve and the Gryphon* (Oxford, Blackfriars Publications, 1946), p. 28.

contribution to her profession is usually unmarried, or at least childless. Yet often at the peak of her career she finds that something is missing in her life, and the professional success that beckoned to her so glamorously in youth she now discovers is not a very soul-satisfying experience.

The "mothering" role of women finds its expression even in the absence of biological motherhood in the choice of a career. The majority of career women choose and find satisfaction in professions in which they are serving the needs of other people. Terman and Miles found, as the result of an exhaustive study, that women were decidedly more interested than men in "administrative occupations for young, helpless, and distressed." [7]

IV. MARITAL AND FAMILIAL ADJUSTMENTS

The happiness of most adults in our culture is significantly related to their marital adjustments. Marital adjustments and family relations are today, to an unprecedented degree, a major social as well as personal problem. A number of scientific studies have been made to discover what factors in the premarital lives of middle-class urban husband and wife are favorable to adjustment in marriage. The following factors have been reported by two or more investigators as being favorable to adjustment in marriage: The parents of the couple were happily married, neither of the partners had conflicts with father or mother, each of the partners was emotionally attached to both father and mother, and they had received sex instruction in childhood. The partners had been acquainted with each other for a relatively longer time than most married couples, their engagement had been relatively longer but not too long, they had married at a later age than most couples, and they had many friends. They had attended church and had attended Sunday school after the age of 18, and had been married by a priest, minister, or rabbi. There had been an absence of petting or spooning, the wife had engaged in no such activity at any time, and her virginity had been preserved.

An analysis of these factors indicates that childhood relations to both parents are important for successful marriage, and that

[7] L. M. Terman and C. C. Miles, *Sex and Personality* (New York, McGraw-Hill Book Company, Inc., 1936).

biological or economic factors are less important than cultural and psychological influences. Finally, the general participation in social activities by both partners is positively related to success in marriage.[8]

These studies indicate that it is possible to predict to some extent the probable degree of success in marriage; and furthermore, that definite steps can be taken to assure greater success in marital adjustment.

V. WORK AND JOB SATISFACTION

A. Place of Work in Adult Life

Work is a necessary and valid expression of the adult personality. It is not an unmitigated punishment for the sin of Adam, and to look upon work as a necessary evil is psychologically unsound. For man in his fallen state, work is not only a necessity; it is also a blessing. But not all work is equally conducive to the expansion of human personality. Some kinds of work are more "human" than others; they contribute more to the development of a wholesome personality. Other kinds of work not only do not contribute but actually stunt the complete development of human personality. Yet no necessary work need be an obstacle to the person who understands why he is working. Attitudes toward work and one's concept of self are intimately related. And most of all, the whole scale of values will determine the meaning and the place of work in the life of an adult. For the convinced Christian who accepts the beatitude, "Blessed are the poor," the major goal of work will not be monetary gain. For the ambitious man to whom "money is power," work will be evaluated in terms of financial returns.

Work plays a major role in the lives of almost all adults in nearly every culture pattern throughout the world. We shall limit our discussion of work in this book, however, to present-day American conditions, and chiefly to those of the middle-class. To what extent our generalizations hold for the extremes of socio-economic status we are unwilling to surmise.

[8] Burgess and Cottrell, *op. cit.*, pp. 359–360. The authors also point out that the American wife makes a greater adjustment in marriage than does her husband.

B. Job Satisfaction

Out of the many studies of job satisfaction that have been made, it is now possible to draw a number of generalizations which appear to hold true in most cases. Contrary to the widely accepted opinion that wage incentives hold first place, nearly all studies show that wages are not the most important factor in job satisfaction and in employee morale. Employers are often unaware of the factors which operate to produce good or poor morale in their employees. In one study,[9] for example, three thousand employees and several hundred employers were asked to rank in order of importance eight factors which presumably make for job satisfaction. Table 8 shows the respective average rankings of each item

Table 8

EMPLOYER AND EMPLOYEE RANKING OF FACTORS IN MORALE

Morale Item	Employee Ranking	Employer Ranking
Credit for all work done	1	7
Interesting work	2	3
Fair pay	3	1
Understanding and appreciation	4	5
Counsel on personal problems	5	8
Promotion on merit	6	4
Good physical working conditions	7	6
Job security	8	2

Adapted from Fosdick, in *op. cit.*, p. 119.

by each of the two groups of raters. The coefficient of correlation between the two rankings is approximately zero. Notice that the employers list "fair pay" first and "credit for all work done" seventh, whereas employees list "fair pay" third and "credit for all work done" first. This finding has been substantiated by other studies in which the most important factors appear to be those that give the worker a sense of personal dignity and worth. Unless a worker feels that his contributions are valued and that he is considered worthy of respect, no amount of money will be able to satisfy him. It has been found that the absolute amount of pay is not nearly so important as the amount received relative to what other members of the same social group get. In other words, money is important as a symbol of status within one's group, and a per-

---

[9] See S. J. Fosdick, in *Industrial Conflict: a Psychological Interpretation*, First Yearbook of the Society for the Psychological Study of Social Issues (Cordon, 1939), p. 119.

ADULTHOOD IN OUR CULTURE

son must make enough money to be accepted on an equal footing with his friends if he is to be satisfied with his job. Some studies show that a worker who complains about his pay is usually discontented with other features of both his work and his life outside his job. Typically, he is dissatisfied with the lack of recognition and interest shown in his work. Moore reports three typical attitudes on the part of the discontented worker, namely: (1) "You can't get anywhere in this place," (2) "No one ever notices anything you do here," (3) "Who could be interested in the type of work I have to do?" [10] It is also to the point to note the finding that men with three or more dependents were more satisfied with their jobs than were men with smaller families.[11] Other studies show that "variety" is an important factor in making a job interesting.

C. Efficiency

Efficiency is commonly defined as the ratio between the expenditure of energy and the amount of work accomplished. "The ideal of human efficiency would be the production of the maximal output of the highest quality in the shortest time, with the least expenditure of energy and with the maximum of satisfaction." [12] Psychological studies of efficiency have centered about two major problems, namely: (1) the selection of people with the proper interests, abilities, and aptitudes to succeed in given types of work, and (2) the discovery of the most efficient conditions and methods of work. Obviously, if a person is working at a job for which he has little aptitude, he will be working inefficiently. The amount of energy he will have to expend will be all out of proportion to what he will accomplish. For his own success and happiness he should, if possible, be guided into an occupation for which he has the requisite personal qualifications.

Assuming that the worker has the requisite aptitudes and abilities for a given job, there are certain conditions of work and certain methods of doing the work which are more efficient than others. Among such conditions are the following:

[10] H. Moore, "Employee Attitude Surveys," *Personnel Journal*, 19 (1940), 360–363.
[11] R. J. Cole, "A Survey of Employee Attitudes," *Public Opinion Quarterly*, 4 (1940), 497–506.
[12] A. T. Poffenberger, *Principles of Applied Psychology* (New York, Appleton-Century-Crofts, Inc., 1942), p. 364.

1. Work habits

Efficiency in work as in everyday living depends to a considerable extent upon the establishment of a relatively unvarying routine wherever feasible. Once habits of doing things according to a definite routine have become firmly established, the mind is free to exercise itself upon things worthy of its attention. As William James puts it in a much quoted passage:

> The more of the details of our daily life we can hand over to the effortless custody of automatism, the more our higher powers of mind will be set free for their own proper work. There is no more miserable human being than one in whom nothing is habitual but indecision and for whom the lighting of every cigar, the drinking of every cup, the time of rising and going to bed every day, and the beginning of every bit of work, are the subjects of express volitional deliberation. Full half the time of such a man goes to the deciding, or regretting, of matters which ought to be so ingrained in him as practically not to exist for his consciousness at all. If there be such daily duties not yet ingrained in any of my readers, let him begin this very hour to set the matter right.[13]

Routine has an important part to play in every occupation, from the simplest type of manual labor to the higher professions and business occupations. The busy doctor, in spite of many emergencies, cannot fulfill his obligations without establishing some kind of routine in his hospital visits and in his office hours. The business executive who leaves his correspondence to the caprice of the moment will probably never catch up. But routine is even more important in most industrial jobs, because here it extends not only to the time and place of the performance but to the several aspects of the performance itself. In factory jobs and various types of construction work and manufacturing, the first rule of efficiency is to eliminate useless movements as much as possible from the first day of working on the job. It also involves planning each step of the work process in such a way that one movement ends in a position favorable for beginning the next. In general, there should be no sudden changes of direction or speed and, whenever possible, the sequence of movements should fall into an easy rhythm. The position at which the worker sits or stands should provide for maximal leverage when strength must be expended. Both hands should be used as much as possible. Tools

---

[13] William James, *Principles of Psychology* (New York, Henry Holt and Company, Inc., 1890), Vol. I, p. 122.

required should be placed in the same place each time and at points where they, as well as the materials to be used, can be reached with the minimum amount of effort.

2. Monotony and boredom

Repetitive activities in which there is little or no variety easily give rise to boredom. The bored worker is an inefficient worker since he lacks the zest necessary to sustain effort. Most intelligent people prefer jobs which allow them to show initiative and in which some mental effort is brought into play, although this is not invariably true. Intelligent persons who are emotionally disturbed or who have psychotic tendencies often prefer jobs which allow them freedom to daydream without interference. Intellectually gifted people do not tend of their own volition to seek jobs that are repetitive and monotonous; but when their morale is high they are as efficient at such jobs as less gifted people. During the war many persons, especially women, took factory jobs who would not ordinarily have done so. In general, the morale of these people was high. Under such conditions there was no correlation between intelligence and susceptibility to boredom.

3. Time of day

People vary in efficiency at different hours of the day, as measured by production records. The man who comes to work in the morning in a rested state takes a few hours to work up to his maximal efficiency. Then fatigue gradually sets in, and by lunch time he has slowed down. (The bored worker, however, is inefficient most of the time but often shows a spurt before lunch or just before quitting time in anticipation of release.) After the lunch period there is again a time of maximal efficiency. Fatigue gradually sets in again, and by late afternoon the period of lowest production is reached.

4. Time of week

Production records in industry tend to show a gradual warming up from Monday to Wednesday followed by a sharp drop on Thursday. There is then a leveling off of production on Friday and Saturday.

required should be placed in the same place each time and at points where they, as well as the materials to be used, can be reached with the minimum amount of effort.

2. Monotony and boredom

Repetitive activities in which there is little or no variety easily give rise to boredom. The bored worker is an inefficient worker since he lacks the zest necessary to sustain effort. Most intelligent people prefer jobs which allow them to show initiative and in which some mental effort is brought into play, although this is not invariably true. Intelligent persons who are emotionally disturbed or who have psychotic tendencies often prefer jobs which allow them freedom to daydream without interference. Intellectually gifted people do not tend of their own volition to seek jobs that are repetitive and monotonous; but when their morale is high they are as efficient at such jobs as less gifted people. During the war many persons, especially women, took factory jobs who would not ordinarily have done so. In general, the morale of these people was high. Under such conditions there was no correlation between intelligence and susceptibility to boredom.

3. Time of day

People vary in efficiency at different hours of the day, as measured by production records. The man who comes to work in the morning in a rested state takes a few hours to work up to his maximal efficiency. Then fatigue gradually sets in, and by lunch time he has slowed down. (The bored worker, however, is inefficient most of the time but often shows a spurt before lunch or just before quitting time in anticipation of release.) After the lunch period there is again a time of maximal efficiency. Fatigue gradually sets in again, and by late afternoon the period of lowest production is reached.

4. Time of week

Production records in industry tend to show a gradual warming up from Monday to Wednesday followed by a sharp drop on Thursday. There is then a leveling off of production on Friday and Saturday.

5. Fatigue and rest periods

The symptoms of physical and mental fatigue differ and so do the optimal means for recovery from fatigue. In physical fatigue the muscles ache, the body feels heavy and relaxed, perception is dulled, and it is difficult to think. The physically tired person is usually ready to relax, and the best way for him to recover is complete rest. Not so for the mentally fatigued person. Although he wants to relax and rest completely he is often unable to do so. Typically, he is restless, irritable, and easily annoyed by things which ordinarily do not bother him, such as slight noises. These fatigue symptoms are aggravated if he is under emotional stress or finds his work distasteful. In extreme cases he will also suffer from mental blocks; that is, he will be unable to make decisions, remember names, or recall everyday items of information which ordinarily he recalls without any difficulty. Recovery from mental fatigue is best effected by diverting recreational activities or by physical exercise.

Physical fatigue seldom proceeds to the point of absolute exhaustion. Even though a man feels that he is going to drop in his tracks, he can, if the need is great enough, find his "second wind" and keep going. Furthermore, feelings of fatigue do not indicate the efficiency with which work is proceeding. Often people report feelings of fatigue even when their work records show no decrement. People who are highly motivated to accomplish something with which they are vitally concerned will often work feverishly hour after hour, with very successful results, only to collapse from fatigue the moment the inspiration runs out.

Industrial engineers have found that rest periods, provided at regular intervals, prevent fatigue and result in increased output. The optimal time for a rest period is at the moment when efficiency first begins to decrease noticeably. The ideal intervals and lengths of rest periods will vary from one job to another, since all jobs do not make the same demands upon the attention and strength of the worker. Rest periods should be sufficiently short so that the worker, in returning to his job, will not have to go through another warming up period. Another reason for short rest periods is that recovery from fatigue is at first rapid and then more and more gradual. For example, in one experiment, in which workers were required to lift weights, a comparison was made of the amount of time required for recovery from fatigue (1) after lifting the weight fifteen times and (2) after lifting the weight thirty times. Recovery after lifting weights fifteen times took only one-fourth as long as recovery after lifting the weights thirty times.

Human beings differ greatly in the rapidity with which they recover from fatigue, and the same person shows different recovery rates at different times and for different jobs.

6. Length of working day and week

During World War II, because of the shortage of workers, the working day and week in many war industries was much increased. Lengthening the number of hours worked, however, did not always increase production. In fact, there was some evidence that people come to work with a certain "set" as to how much effort they will expend regardless of how it is distributed in time. If this is true in wartime, when the motivation is presumably higher than in peacetime, it is probably true also for industry in general. In one British munitions factory workers had been required to work 58 hours a week, and a record was kept of production records. Later, the working week was reduced to 50 hours and a comparison of production records with the longer working week was made. Strange as it may seem, the hourly output went up 39 per cent with the result that weekly production output went up 21 per cent. In other words, by shortening the working week, the production record went up to what was the equivalent of 12 hours more work per week at the rate prevailing during the 58 hour week! To what extent these findings could be duplicated in other situations, such as studying in college, is uncertain, but it is a matter worth looking into.

7. Temperature and ventilation

It is harder to work in hot weather than in temperate or cool weather, and as a result the production records of factories go down during the summer. This loss in efficiency can be partly, but not wholly, controlled by air conditioning and improved ventilation. Even in winter when many people work in a room in which the windows are closed and in which there is no artificial ventilation, discomfort results and work is done inefficiently. At one time this discomfort was thought to be the result of oxygen deprivation, but we now know that this is not true. The air contains much more oxygen than is ordinarily needed and no matter how uncomfortable and stuffy a room is, the oxygen supply is usually more than ample. The discomfort and inefficiency result from the heat and excessive humidity and stagnation of the air rather than from lack of oxygen. Even in the absence of fresh air, relief can be obtained by any means that will cool the air or cause the air to circulate by means of fans.

8. Sleep

Studies designed to show the effect of loss of sleep on efficiency have at times yielded somewhat amazing results. Sleep is necessary for the maintenance of normal metabolism, and people who have been deprived of sleep for any length of time report feelings of great discomfort when required to remain awake or when they are unable to relax. Experiments show that men who have been deprived of sleep for as long as 60 hours can respond normally to a variety of short psychological tests, such as canceling numbers, naming colors, and steadiness. They all report symptoms of malaise, however, such as burning eyes, headache, buzzing in the ears, feeling dazed, and being "half dead." After one night's loss of sleep, emotional reactions are usually normal for people who are basically sound. But with 60 hours' loss, or even somewhat less than that, silliness, irritability, and nervousness are common. Hallucinations may appear and even delusions of persecution. Although 60 hours' loss of sleep may result in no impairment of efficiency on the psychological tests listed above, the capacity for sustained attention is lost. Success on the individual tests appears to result from the application of greater energy than usual to overcome the effects of drowsiness. This expenditure of extra effort cannot be kept up, and that is why sustained attention and effort is impossible. Moreover, the person suffering from loss of sleep finds it difficult if not impossible to shift his attention from one task to another, or, in a lengthy test, from one item to another. Yet human efficiency in many tasks may not be impaired by lack of sleep for as many as 48 or even 60 hours. Animals deprived of sleep for any marked period of time invariably die, even though all other conditions conducive to health, such as adequate food, drink, and temperature, are provided. When the brains of these experimental animals are examined after death, degenerative changes in the brain tissue are found.

9. Illumination

Good illumination is a more important factor in jobs requiring precision adjustment and keen visual acuity than in jobs consisting mostly of gross muscular activity. Both the intensity and the distribution of light have an effect upon efficiency. In general, light should be distributed as evenly as possible. A spotlight focused upon the work area and surrounded by relative darkness makes for visual fatigue. Uneven lighting produces glare, and glare cuts down efficiency by causing images on the retina to be blurred. The light source should never be directly in the line of vision but should be shaded. The lighting should be of sufficient intensity but need not be as intense as some specialists have recommended.

Experiments in which lights of different colors have been compared indicate that a yellowish light is best not only for initial visual acuity, but also for clearest vision after several hours of reading.

In industrial plants the introduction of an improved system of lighting is usually accompanied by higher production records. It is not clear, however, whether the increased production results from the lighting improvement per se or from the increased morale of the workers. Almost any change which convinces employees that their employers are interested in their welfare is accompanied by an increase in work output, at least temporarily.

10. Rate of work

A few studies have been made of the relative effect of different rates of working upon efficiency. The results suggest that for most types of work there is an optimal speed, below which and above which efficiency is impaired. The exact rate varies with the individual. In one study, the amount of oxygen consumed during walking at different rates was compared. Oxygen consumption is an indirect measure of the amount of energy being expended. The results of this study showed that, in general, men were more efficient when they walked at the rate of four miles an hour than they were at either three or five miles an hour.

11. Effect of drugs

a. Alcohol. Alcohol, even in small amounts, impairs the efficiency of the organism in both physical and mental tests. It depresses the higher brain centers, and as a result it impairs learning, memory, discrimination, and judgment. It dulls the senses in such a way that hearing and vision are less acute, and the range of vision is diminished. In small amounts, alcohol may slightly increase a man's muscular strength, although greater amounts produce muscular weakness. Small amounts impair muscular coordination, slow down reaction time, reduce skill and dexterity in complex activities, and interfere with performance on intelligence tests. Alcohol decreases general alertness and decreases or abolishes a man's power of self-criticism, depending upon the amount imbibed. Contrary to popular opinion, alcohol is not a stimulant. Its first effect upon the organism is to produce relaxation. Then, because it suppresses the activity of the higher brain centers, it releases inhibitions. Under the influence of alcohol, the timid man loses his fears, and talks and laughs without restraint, and may even become for the time being the life of the party. Unhappy and frustrated people, as we have previously shown, sometimes find alcohol an easy way of temporarily escaping the harsh realities of life.

Not all people tolerate alcohol to the same extent. Intoxication from alcohol is related to the total weight of the body and not to the absolute amount taken. For this reason a small amount of alcohol usually has a much greater effect upon a woman than upon a man, since women, in general, weigh less than men. Other things being equal, a person who weighs 100 pounds will tolerate only about half as much as a person weighing 200 pounds.

The conditions under which the alcohol is taken either facilitate or retard intoxication. An empty stomach, an undiluted sip from the bottle, and warm, poorly ventilated rooms—all tend to facilitate intoxication. A full stomach, especially one filled with fats or oils, tends to retard intoxication. Fresh air, a standing position, the dilution of the drink, and slowness in drinking it—these factors decrease the likelihood of intoxication.

Because alcohol dilates the blood vessels in the skin and makes the heart beat faster, it produces a sensation of warmth for a time. It does not really warm the body, however, because it increases the loss of heat. Similarly, when alcohol is first taken it diminishes feelings of fatigue, since it temporarily replenishes the depleted sugar reserves in the blood. But the effect is more apparent than real. The increase of sugar provided by the alcohol causes the pancreas to secrete more insulin. If too much insulin is produced, nervous tension results, the hands and face tremble, sweat becomes excessive, and anxiety reactions follow.

b. Tobacco. Studies of the effect of smoking upon efficiency have often led to ambiguous results. Some studies, for example, show that smoking is accompanied by a need for more oxygen since it causes respiratory efficiency to diminish. Other studies, on the contrary, show no diminished respiratory efficiency even in heavy smokers. Theoretically, we would expect smoking to have bad effects, since burning tobacco produces a number of poisonous substances which enter the blood stream. Apparently, it is not the nicotine in the tobacco which causes the harm. Most of the nicotine decomposes in smoking and very little of it enters the body. We know, however, that smoking is accompanied by an increased pulse rate in both experienced and inexperienced smokers and that it produces unsteady hands. We also know that very heavy smoking sometimes results in spots of retinal blindness. Studies of members of the armed forces during World War II gave results that suggest that less heavy smoking causes a blurring of vision and reduces visual acuity. There was some evidence, too, that excessive smoking sometimes produces decreased sensitivity to color.

c. Beverages containing caffeine. Coffee, tea, and certain cola beverages contain a substantial amount of caffeine, and caffeine, in general, acts as a stimulant. In moderate amounts it speeds up reaction time and increases mental alertness. Excessive amounts, however, not only do not improve efficiency, but actually decrease it. Excessive coffee drinking, for example, slows down reaction time and decreases muscular coördination and steadiness. What constitutes an excessive amount, however, varies from person to person. It is partly dependent upon weight, partly on individual sensitivity, and partly upon the amount of coffee that one habitually drinks. People who customarily drink one cup of coffee may find, after a time, that two cups are required to produce the same amount of stimulation that was formerly derived from one. People who do not habitually drink coffee, on the other hand, usually find that one cup is very stimulating. These people, too, are likely to find that three cups cut down their efficiency, whereas the habitual coffee drinker may find that his efficiency is not markedly diminished until he takes a fourth cup.

The amount of caffeine in an ordinary cup of coffee taken after the evening meal is not sufficient to keep the average person from sleeping at night, although it may do so if the person expects it to have this effect or, of course, if he has a caffeine allergy. The person who does not habitually drink coffee may be prevented from sleeping by two cups of coffee taken at night, and the habitual drinker may be similarly affected by three cups.

Some people are "compulsive" coffee drinkers. Even though they know that excessive coffee drinking can do them no good, they apparently cannot stay away from it. In this respect, they resemble "chain smokers." Compulsive coffee drinkers as well as chain smokers are tense, nervous people with many symptoms of unresolved personality conflicts.

d. "Pep pills." There are several drugs, such as benzedrine sulfate, which are much more effective than caffeine beverages in fighting fatigue. Benzedrine sulfate dilates the blood vessels of the brain and enables a person to stay awake for considerable lengths of time without feeling fatigue. But it does not of itself produce greater efficiency. The long-run effects of using benzedrine sulfate are unknown. The drug acts differently on different parts of the nervous system and its effects are often paradoxical—sometimes a mild dose increases alertness, sometimes it has no noticeable results, and sometimes it decreases alertness. In general, the use of these drugs has no place in everyday life, but should be reserved for emergency situations or when recommended by a physician.

VI. OTHER FACTORS ASSOCIATED WITH ADULT ADJUSTMENT AND HAPPINESS

Most older people who have been asked at what period of their lives they were happiest specify that they were happiest during the period of maturity, or roughly, during ages 25 to 45 or 50. That is, they do so if they have been married. Bachelors and spinsters are more apt to state that they were happiest in childhood and youth. Morgan [14] and Landis,[15] making independent investiga-

[14] M. Morgan, "The Attitudes and Adjustments of Recipients of Old Age Assistance in Upstate and Metropolitan New York," *Arch. Psychol.*, 30 (1937), No. 214.

[15] J. T. Landis, "What Is the Happiest Period of Life?" *School and Society*, 55 (1942), 643–645.

tions, secured results that were in rather close agreement on this point. In Landis's study, two-thirds of the bachelors and spinsters but only one-third of the married people claimed that they were happiest in childhood and youth. The married people give as their chief reasons for happiness in early maturity the joys of marriage and parenthood. People who in retrospect view childhood and youth as the happiest periods of their lives list as reasons the companionship and fun they had at parties and dances. The later years seem to be relatively empty for the single, full for married people. All persons list enjoyment and success in work as important reasons for happiness during early maturity, and people who have made poor work adjustments tend to be unhappy. Clinical psychologists are amassing evidence that good work habits formed in youth are among the most important factors making for wholesome adjustment in maturity. In some instances people with serious mental disturbances have been able to function effectively, earn a living, and stay out of trouble or out of a mental hospital because of excellent work habits formed previous to their illness which persisted in spite of their symptoms of deep personality disturbance. Landis and Morgan both found that the better adjusted people not only had plenty of work to do, but that they liked work. These people were also in better health, had more hobbies, and engaged in more recreational activities. In studying a group of graduate students, it was found that failure in love was a frequent source of unhappiness. The factors associated with happiness were success in dealing with people, enjoyment and success in work, and an attitude of "serious, deliberate, earnest, hardworking living rather than impulsive, light, amusing, dilettanteism." [16]

There is some evidence that the social and economic conditions prevalent at the time an individual is maturing bear a significant relationship to his emotional stability in adulthood. An illustration of this point is found in a study by Gundlach, [17] in which an attempt was made to relate emotional stability and political opinion to age and income. Although Gundlach was not able to demonstrate any marked correlation between emotional stability and

---

[16] G. Watson, "Happiness Among Adult Students of Education," *J. Educ. Psychol.*, 21 (1930), 79–109.
[17] R. H. Gundlach, "Emotional Stability and Political Opinion as Related to Age and Income," *J. Soc. Psychol.*, 10 (1939), 577–590.

age as such, he was able to show interesting trends when the data were analyzed in terms of the social and economic conditions which existed when the subjects of a given age reached maturity. People who had been brought up in the habits and attitudes of the 1920's but who had spent almost all of their maturity during and for a few years after the great depression showed a much higher than normal percentage of emotional instability and neuroticism. Less emotional instability was found among people who had been able to get established as adults before the depression but who had been too young for military service in World War I.

VII. WHAT IS MATURITY?

The word *maturity* means fullness or completeness of development. As applied to persons it usually refers to the final stage of development in which all human powers are fully developed. Generally we think of physical maturity as that stage of development in which the organism is capable of reproducing itself. But strictly speaking we should think of this stage not as one of complete physical maturity but more specifically as one of "reproductive maturity," since other organs or systems of the body are still developing. Complete maturity of the skeletal system is often attained a decade or so after reproductive maturity. And muscular development in men usually continues until the early twenties.

Psychologically, a person is judged mature on the basis of his characteristic attitudes and behavior. The mature person has clearly defined goals toward which he persistently works. He is master of his emotions and feelings and does not let them interfere with the objectivity of his judgments or with the fulfillment of the duties of his state in life. He takes responsibility for his own acts and does not blame his failures on others. He appreciates the good qualities of other people and rejoices at the good they do even when they surpass his own achievements. He can accept suggestions and criticisms and turn them to his profit. He is not unduly elated by success nor too much cast down by adversity. In a word, he is master of himself and is the slave neither of his own turbulent desires and emotions nor of the world of people and things about him.

What is meant specifically by psychological maturity varies with the scale of values accepted by the culture since these values define the "ideal" personality or the goal of development toward which persons are expected to strive. In a sensual culture physical strength and attractiveness may be at a premium, and the age at which the maximum of these qualities is attained will be considered "complete development" or "maturity." A materialistic culture may define maturity as the age at which a person makes his greatest earnings. A humanistic culture places a greater value upon intellectual and spiritual development and will consequently tend to look upon maturity as the period in which the intellectual powers reach their climax. A Christian, however, will not consider himself fully mature until his completely developed natural powers are elevated to a supernatural plane by the greatest possible infusion of divine grace. Until the Christian has attained to sanctity, therefore, he is not mature in the most significant sense of the word. Growing toward complete spiritual maturity in the Christian sense is the work of a lifetime. It does not end with the attainment of the biological or intellectual peak of development.

For the Christian, maturity means that state in which the moral virtues have been developed to the utmost so that the theological virtues can come to fruition. Grace builds on nature; and although man cannot merit grace nor by any effort of his own increase it, he can remove the obstacles in his soul which keep grace from being fruitful. The natural moral virtues are acquired according to the psychological principles of habit formation. They can be acquired both by the "good pagan" and by the Christian. The Christian who neglects developing the moral virtues will never attain true maturity. In practicing these virtues the baptized Christian grows in natural goodness but he also gains supernatural grace because, in baptism, he received the supernaturally infused moral virtues. The latter enhance wondrously the effect of the morally good life because they lift it up to the supernatural plane. Normally, grace elevates the soul only when the natural soil is prepared in which it can grow. It would be a mistake, therefore, to neglect the moral virtues—to begrudge the effort necessary to acquire them on the pretext that God's grace is alone sufficient. God's grace plus man's coöperation are necessary for the complete development of a mature personality.

XXII

Later Maturity and Old Age

There came to her ... the consciousness of power, of victory almost, in the mere fact of having lived, which gives to old age, however humble, its own peculiar dignity. "My life!"—says every soul—"that sum of happenings which is mine and mine alone, that wonderful and dreadful pilgrimage that I have made with Time. Whatever the record, I have lived, finished the course, bound myself to Eternity by the tendrils of experience and growth."—C. HOLME [1]

1. THE CULTURE PATTERN IN RELATION TO AGING

The study of later maturity and old age must be made against a background of social and cultural influences as they affect the aging person. Characteristics of old people in our culture are not necessarily the accompaniments of aging, but are to a considerable degree the result of cultural, social and economic conditions which meet or frustrate the needs and aspirations of older people. Some cultures, such as our own, place a high value upon youth. This value may even increase as the birth rate declines and as the relative number of young people as compared to old people declines. A generation or two ago people died at an earlier age and the ratio of children to adults was considerably greater than it is today and than it will probably be in the future. Medical advances and improved sanitation have made it possible for more people to continue living until advanced old age. These medical advances, however, have not increased the length of the prime of life, but have extended the period of old age and senility. The increasing life span, therefore, does not in itself provide the aging person with a richer life, but only with a longer one. As a result,

---

[1] Constance Holme, *The Lonely Plough* (London, H. Milford, Oxford University Press, 1931), p. 185.

old age in our culture is for many people a time of such great frustration and bitterness that it presents a major social challenge, and, in particular, a challenge to the Christian conscience.

The role which older people play in their milieu varies considerably with the culture pattern. In some cultures, such as the traditional Chinese, old people command respect and reverence just because of their age, irrespective of their personal merits or demerits. In such a culture, for example, a woman may have no authority in the family until she is a grandmother. Then, by reason of being a grandmother, her status automatically goes up, and she is then expected to assume an authoritative role in the household, a role which other members of the household respect. This reverence may even extend beyond the grave in the form of ancestor worship.

In certain primitive cultures young people are necessarily insecure in the absence of their elders because they rely in many matters upon the knowledge that older people have for meeting the ordinary problems of adult life. A girl, for example, may receive no instruction about childbirth until she becomes pregnant. She is then taken aside by older women who instruct her and help her to get ready for the birth of her child. In such a culture, children are not instructed early in life in anticipation of their needs as adults as they are in ours; formal education in school does not replace the informal, on-the-spot education which they receive as adults. Young people in such a culture are not under the illusion that they know all the answers and must admit that they do not. It is easy to see that the status of adults in such a society will necessarily differ from that of a culture in which the great majority of adults are not apparently useful or necessary to the well-being of the young.

Very few scientific studies of old age and its problems in our culture have been made, but certain trends appear to be evident. The elderly person as such enjoys no prestige in present-day America. The cynosure of all eyes is youth. It has been said that the Western world picked up this evaluation from Greek civilization. Our films, our radio and television programs, our sports, our advertisements, all testify that youth or early adulthood is the most desirable age in our culture. Once we understand this cultural value, we have a clue to many behavior anomalies in middle-aged and elderly adults, and particularly to behavior peculiarities of women. The young marriageable woman is most often featured in advertisements—even in advertisements for false teeth and hearing aids! Middle-aged women often affect the dress and manners of teen-age girls. Their behavior, too, must imitate that of the young girl. Women are usually flattered when they are told that they look more like the older sisters than the mothers of their grown-up children. Even successful professional women frequently refuse to state their birthdates in the biographical data that appear in professional handbooks. Professional men, however, do not seem to be reluctant to reveal their ages. Perhaps this is because professional men, unlike women and workers of a lower socio-economic status, may gain rather than lose prestige with age. This is not true, however, of the great majority of men, and it is certainly not true for women. The great majority of American men find that age is a handicap to getting a job or to keeping a job at which they have been employed for years. Many industries have a policy of not employing any new workers over the age of 40 or 45. Yet the average life span of men today runs more than twenty years beyond that age, and such a policy undoubtedly has a profound influence upon the personality adjustments of aging people.

Our culture pattern, apart from the specifically Judeo-Christian elements in it, does not define the duties of children toward their parents. This fact alone presents a constant threat to the security —emotional as well as economic— of the aging person. An old person has the same basic needs as the young: the need for a sense of personal worth, the need to be respected as a unique individual, the need to give and receive affection, the need for food and shelter and for satisfying forms of recreation. But contemporary social conditions make it increasingly difficult for old people to secure the satisfaction of these needs. A few generations ago, when our culture was primarily agrarian, old people lived with their children and performed chores on the farm according to their strength and ability. Houses were large and food was plentiful, even though money might have been scarce. Under such living conditions, an elderly person was not an economic burden, even when he was ailing and needed physical care. Today the pattern of living has been radically altered. The old person, like the child, is an economic burden in a family which must buy its food rather than raise it. Small houses and apartments are not adapted to the needs of the aged. Often if the members of a family are to take on the burden of caring for an aged relative, they must secure a larger apartment and pay a correspondingly higher rent. In many families both husband and wife work away from home; and if an elderly person making his home with them becomes ill, there is no one at home to care for him nor are there neighbors to assume such a task. If a nurse is hired, the cost is often greater than the salary of one or both of the wage earners. Under such circumstances it is difficult even for a family that genuinely wants to meet its responsibilities for the aged to do so. Old people who understand the situation are threatened with insecurity. Those who do not understand because of the different conditions that existed in their youth often become embittered complainers.

In an industrial society such as ours the personal worth of an individual may be assessed on a very superficial basis. Ours is a success culture, and we unconsciously evaluate people in terms of their success or failure in attaining the goals which our society considers important. Economic efficiency and the ability to produce material wealth are important considerations in determining prestige. The old person may have acquired great wisdom in the course of living, wisdom which a young person could not possibly possess because of his lack of experience, but the wisdom of the old is not appreciated in a materialistic culture unless the old person can also produce evidence of his material success. Needless to say, most old people are handicapped by reason of their declining physical capacities in competing with young people for material goods. As a result, old people are looked down upon as economic burdens and are considered of little worth in any sphere of life. They lack the prestige necessary to make their opinions carry weight. The limited number of old men who find themselves in positions requiring the experience of a lifetime, such as certain political or professional appointments, are exceptions. Young people, too, often resent older people who stand in the way of their advancement professionally. Regardless of the older person's merits and experience, the younger person who covets his position is likely to belittle him and dismiss his opinions lightly as outmoded or unrealistic. Older people are usually aware of these attitudes and are forced to adopt compensatory behavior in order to retain their sense of personal worth. Such compensatory behavior often leads to further rejection on the part of the young.

Age differences in attitudes and behavior, as we observe them in our culture, are not just the result of the physiological and psychological changes that take place with time. They often result from differences in the cultural situations in which members of the different age groups grew up. Many of the attitudes which older people hold today they also held when they were young, because those were the prevailing attitudes of their time. But ours is a dynamically changing culture, and new patterns of life and new ways of looking at life are continually coming in. Older people do not adopt new patterns as readily as young people for several reasons. One reason is that their needs have been "canalized" in certain directions. In youth these needs could have been satisfied in any number of ways, but with the advancing years certain specific satisfiers are sought after and other possible satisfiers are rejected. That is one of the reasons why old people resist change. Another reason is that old people do not learn as rapidly as the young, and so retain the patterns of behavior and the attitudes toward life which were appropriate in their youth but which do not necessarily meet the situation today. In this way the "radical ideas" of one generation become the conservative ideas of the next.

II. CHANGES IN ABILITY WITH AGE

Most human abilities increase rapidly during infancy and childhood and reach their peak in early maturity. They decline slowly during the middle years of life and rapidly during later maturity as senility sets in. The abilities which show the earliest decline are those which are most intimately related to bodily performance, such as athletic skill. However, there is no one-to-one relation between aging of the body and loss of efficiency, since practice and experience often compensate for physiological deterioration. The ability to drive an automobile without accident, for example, seems to increase up to the age of 50, even though reaction time, vision, and some other component capacities for driving show a decline. Experience and the more cautious attitude of the older person apparently compensate for his waning physical abilities. After the age of 50, however, the accident rate increases.

Age losses in visual and auditory acuity take place gradually. After the age of 50, sensitivity to light stimulation is decreased, the visual field becomes narrower, dark adaptation is slowed down, and there is a gradual reduction of visual acuity. Before the age of 60, the lens of the eye has lost almost all of its elasticity. Hearing losses first occur for the higher pitched tones. By the age of 50, there is already a slight loss of sensitivity to tones in the higher middle ranges of pitch. Motor abilities show a similar decrement with age although marked individual differences occur. Older adults who have continued exercising their motor abilities perform significantly better on tests than do young people who have had no experience. In other words, although the younger person may have a greater basic capacity than the older person, he may perform less well.

Older persons cannot compete with young persons in physical tasks or work which requires sudden spurts of energy. Often, however, their ability to persist in work which does not require violent effort improves during maturity.

Significant studies of adult intelligence have been made independently by Miles and Miles,[2] and by Jones and Conrad.[3] The adults studied by Miles were largely from urban groups living near the west coast, whereas those of Jones and Conrad were recruited from New England villages. The results of the two studies are in very close agreement.

Miles and Miles administered the Otis intelligence test to their subjects and studied not only the changes which take place with age, but also the relation of these changes to educational level. The total sample was divided into three groups on the basis of educational level, and interesting differences were found from group to group. The group which had never attended high school showed a more rapid decline with age than did the better educated groups. The peak of mental ability, as measured by the

[2] C. C. Miles and W. R. Miles, "The Correlation of Intelligence Scores and Chronological Age from Early to Late Maturity," *Amer. J. Psych.*, 44 (1932), 44–78.

[3] H. E. Jones and H. S. Conrad, "The Growth and Decline of Intelligence; a Study of a Homogeneous Group between the Ages of Ten and Sixty Years," *Genet. Psych. Monogr.*, 13 (1933), 223–298.

Otis test, was reached at about 18 years of age. With increasing age, those tasks in which speed was a factor showed a greater decrement than other tasks. The learning of material which conflicted with well-established habits also showed a marked decrement with age. Individual differences were very great, and Miles stresses the point that many older people continue to perform better than the average young person.

The amount of mental decline is correlated with the intellectual level of the person. Those who possess a high level of intelligence before later maturity may, even in old age, still be superior to the average adult of a much younger age.

Jones and Conrad attempted to test all persons in certain New England villages between the ages of 10 and 60. They obtained subjects by presenting a free motion picture in the community hall and then asking the audience to take the Army Alpha test during the intermission. People who did not attend the movie were visited in their homes and, in as many cases as possible, took the test there. The total group tested consisted of 1,191 people. The results of this study were in essential agreement with those of Miles.

An analysis of the Army Alpha subtest results shows clearly that all abilities do not decline at an equal rate. General information and vocabulary show no decline after the general level of mental ability has reached its peak until senility has set in. Tasks calling for a reorganization of established habits show a rapid decline with age. The greatest loss was shown on the analogies and the directions tests. In everyday life we notice selective forgetting in old age. Old people tend to forget recent events whereas they often remember events that occurred in childhood.

Mental ability declines in old age for a variety of reasons, one of which is the change which takes place in the circulation of the brain. With advancing age there is an increase in diseases which affect the amount of fuel the brain will receive, such as arteriosclerosis and hypertension. Arteriosclerosis results in diminished intelligence, and it may also bring about marked changes in personality, such as delusions of persecution.

III. AGE AND PRODUCTIVITY

The relation of age to productivity of various kinds has been studied by several different methods, and the results of such studies have often been in conflict. In this area of research, as in all personality studies, there is a discrepancy between results based on studies of individuals and results based on the analysis of group averages. We may, for example, find that the average age of dentists at the time of earning their highest income is 45; yet it is quite possible that no individual dentist reached his earning peak at that age. Such studies are misleading if we really want to understand individuals. In studying the productivity of women it is just possible that a bimodal curve would be obtained, showing greatest productivity just before marriage and then again at the "empty nest" stage after their children are no longer dependent upon them. If these ages were added together and an arithmetical mean calculated, the mean would probably fall somewhere in the early thirties, even though no individual woman would be producing at that time. Obviously, we would be mistaken if we were to conclude that the peak of productivity in women is in the early thirties. Yet some of the widely quoted studies of age in relation to productivity have been based upon such inadequate experimental designs.

The criteria of productivity have also varied from study to study. The most common criteria are (1) age at which the maximum amount of productivity occurred, (2) age at which the masterpiece was produced, and (3) age of greatest earnings. When the first criterion is used, the number of books, articles, inventions, compositions, works of art, or operations performed within a given year is computed. The year in which the greatest quantity appears is considered the year of greatest productivity, irrespective of the quality of the work produced and its cultural or social significance. No doubt, sheer quantity of work produced is an interesting fact to know about a human being, although even objective criteria of quantity are sometimes difficult to derive. Are we, for example, in making our count, to list separately each different book title, each musical composition, or each painting regardless of size? In a study of the productivity of psychologists it was found that it made a great difference in the results which measure one used. Younger psychologists wrote more articles and shorter ones; older psychologists wrote fewer articles and longer ones.

When the second criterion is used, that is, the age at which the masterpiece was produced, the selection of the masterpiece is usually made by a group of competent judges. Here, too, difficulties arise because the date of publication or the date at which the invention was patented or put on the market may be considerably later than the date at which the great idea underlying the production was conceived. Kant's *Critique of Pure Reason*, for example, was published in his fifty-fourth year. But there is reason to believe that the basic ideas presented in this book were in Kant's mind many years before, even though he did not get around to publishing until much later.

Perhaps the most complete and detailed studies in English of the relation of age to productivity are those of Lehman and his collaborators. Lehman's studies [4] show that the age at which the masterpiece was produced or written varies with the particular field of productivity. In general, Lehman found that the age at which the greatest work was produced was close to the age at which the greatest quantity was produced. The peak of accomplishment in writing lyric poetry occurs at about 25 years of age. Mathematicians, inventors, chemists, and short story writers reach their peak somewhere around 35 years of age. Astronomers and writers of religious and philosophical literature reach their peak much later, usually between the ages of 45 and 55. In every field, however, the individual differences are great and extend from the early twenties to the seventh decade.

The age of greatest accomplishment in areas involving physical prowess is considerably earlier than that for most intellectual pursuits, and declines much more rapidly. In almost every kind of athletic performance the peak occurs around the age of 25. A baseball player, a boxer, and the pilot of a jet propelled plane is an elderly man in his field by the age of 30, although occasionally a record is set by an athlete in his early thirties. But such an accomplishment is out of the ordinary, and when it occurs it has always been preceded by continuous practice and "training."

Lehman has also made a comparison of the age of peak accom-

---

[4] H. C. Lehman, "Man's Most Creative Years: Then and Now," *Science*, 98 (1943), 393–399.

plishment in fifteen types of creative endeavor in our day with that of earlier historical periods. Interestingly enough, for twelve of the fifteen fields, the peak accomplishment is reached today at an earlier age than in generations past. Earlier achievement today is characteristic of physics, geology, mathematics, inventions, botany, pathology, classical descriptions of disease, medicine and hygiene, philosophy, literature, economics and political science. This earlier achievement is, however, accompanied by a more rapid descent of the age curves after the peaks have been reached. The three fields in which there were no significant differences in the two historical periods were chemistry, astronomy, and oil painting.

IV. WHAT IS OLD AGE?

It is impossible to establish a definite chronological age as the beginning of old age. Some people are old at 30; others are still young at 50. People live at different rates, and some investigators even affirm that all people go through a definite cycle of physiological and psychological changes, at the end of which, regardless of age, they are ready to die, since at that time they have completed the entire life cycle. Not only do people live at different rates, but the same person lives at different rates at different periods of his life. Du Nöuy,[5] as a result of his studies of the rate at which wounds heal, has given us the concept of "biological time." Du Nöuy found that with increasing age surface wounds heal progressively more slowly. This relationship of age to rate of tissue repair was so precise that it could be expressed in a mathematical formula. Nevertheless, two individuals of the same chronological age may be of widely different biological ages.

Because we lack sufficient significant research we are today facing a major social crisis involving the well-being of old people without much expert information to guide us. People who work professionally with the aged, like social workers, psychologists, or psychiatrists, are often appalled at the inadequacies in the thinking and planning of younger persons who are responsible for older relations.

[5] P. Lecomte Du Nöuy, *Biological Time* (New York, The Macmillan Company, 1937).

We have already described some of the physical changes of age as they affect capacities and abilities. The more obvious characteristics by which we recognize old age are changes in the hair and skin, such as grayness, baldness, wrinkles, and a thinning of the skin; a general slowing down of movement; a decrease in strength and endurance. Other changes taking place include a gradual slowing down of the basal metabolic rate, the progressive atrophy of body cells accompanied by fatty infiltration, a gradual decrease in the elasticity of tissues, and a progressive retardation in the capacity of the cells to divide, which makes it increasingly difficult for the body to heal in case of injury or illness. There is also a progressive degeneration of the nervous system, which is accompanied by impaired hearing and vision, a decreased ability to focus and sustain attention, and by the loss of memory—particularly memories of recent events. We are all familiar with an aged person whose question we answered only to have him repeat the same question almost immediately or a short time later. And all of us, no doubt, have observed aged people looking for spectacles that have slipped down on their noses!

The degenerative changes of age take place gradually and cannot be measured week by week or month by month. They do not take place at the same rate in all of the organs of the body, and in a given person all of the symptoms of age do not appear with the same severity. An old person, for example, may be very deaf and yet have keen eyesight. For this reason no one physiological measure can be used as an index of aging. There are great individual differences in the age at which specific organs begin to deteriorate.

V. LONGEVITY

Longevity appears to run in families and results from the interaction of both constitutional and environmental factors. Evidence derived from animal research suggests that diet may significantly lengthen or shorten life. Rats were maintained on different kinds of diets to determine the effect of different diets on length of life. It was found that animals raised from infancy on diets which were insufficient to permit full growth but which contained all of the essential elements lived, on the average, twice as long as their litter mates who had eaten as much as they wanted. Perhaps this finding may help to explain the exceptional longevity of many saints who practiced great fasting and other bodily mortifications. In the lives of the saints we often run across statements such as "after subsisting on a meager ration of herbs (or some other relatively unnourishing food), often taken only once every other day, he died in the odor of sanctity at the age of 107"!

VI. ADJUSTMENT PROBLEMS OF THE AGED

The fear of growing old is apparently related to the fear of death. Death is a penalty, and all normal people have a natural repugnance to the thought of death. Every man knows that he will someday die, but as a rule he strives to keep this knowledge out of his consciousness as much as possible. Yet his adjustment to old age and to the final crisis of death depends upon facing his mortal situation realistically. Education in youth must be directed to this end; if one waits until old age it is usually too late. Often the most profound shock of life, apart from death itself, comes when a person is forced for the first time to realize that there is something very much wrong with him physically, something that will not be healed, something that is causing him progressively to decay. The ability to accept aging and death as the inevitable end of life on this earth is related to the degree of one's readiness to die. And readiness to die is related in turn to a number of influences in the natural order as well as to the degree of supernatural grace in the soul. The full realization of the meaning of the preface for the dead in the burial Mass, "For unto Thy faithful, O Lord, life is changed not taken away: and the abode of this earthly sojourn being dissolved, an eternal dwelling is prepared in heaven," produces a holy joy rather than fear. But this is the effect of God's grace which illumines and strengthens the soul; it transcends the natural order. Apart from God's grace no man can look upon death with equanimity. The most he can ever achieve by himself is a stoic endurance. Joy is one of the fruits of the Holy Ghost. The death of religious men and women is often characterized not only by resignation but also by a deep joy. For the person who during life has coöperated with grace and has progressively become detached from material comforts and from doing his own will, "to live is Christ, and to die is gain." In some religious communities the death of a sister is an occasion of general rejoicing, and the surviving members celebrate the event as they would any feast day.

Communists, in their attack upon religion, call it the "opium of the people," a means of dulling one's sensibilities, a means of retreat from reality. Nothing could be further from the truth. The Catholic Church has something to say about all of the great realities of life, and often it is to people of our day a "hard saying." It insists on the indissolubility of marriage and forbids an unhappy husband or wife to seek forgetfulness in an illicit love affair or remarriage. It forbids the irresponsible use of marital rights in forbidding the use of contraceptives. It will not permit the aged and the suffering to "run away from life" by the practice of euthanasia, nor will it permit the young to evade the harsh realities of caring for the dependent by such unlawful means. Surely the Church, far from encouraging us to escape from reality, is one of the most powerful allies we have in facing it. And when it comes to the supreme reality—the reality of death—the Church, and the Church alone, never lets us forget it. From the "Memento, homo" of Ash Wednesday, through every requiem Mass, until the final burial service, the Church continually reminds us of our last end, and of the final reality—the last judgment. The liturgy of the Church does not mince words in reminding us of that "Day of wrath! Oh day of mourning." Nor does it hide the grim reality of death by using such euphemisms as "passing on" or "passing away"; on the contrary it uses strong and unmistakable language such as that of the "Stabat Mater" in which we find the lines: "While my body here decays, may my soul Thy goodness praise, safe in Paradise with Thee." Only a person ignorant of the Church, or viewing it only from the outside, or one deliberately misconstruing her doctrine could accuse her of providing a means of escaping the harsh realities of life. On the contrary, religion sometimes demands the deliberate choice of martyrdom. And for the one reality from which there is no escape—the reality of death—the Church offers not escape but strength to face it, not as a disintegrating mass of protoplasm but as a person endowed with human dignity. For the aged man or woman who has lived according to the law of God, death holds no terrors but is an entrance into the fullness of life. Those responsible for the welfare of old people can often help them by reminding them of this fact and by encouraging them to use the means for assuring themselves of a happy death.

Other problems fade into insignificance beside this major problem of preparing for death. Yet they, too, are important enough for our consideration. The declining physical strength of the aging forces them to relinquish activities in which they formerly took pleasure. Attendance at clubs, membership in social organizations, and visiting the homes of friends become more difficult as time goes on. The old person who is no longer financially independent must often drop out of clubs because he cannot afford the dues or the costs of transportation. The narrowing of his interests leads him to increased introspection and to an overconcentration upon himself and upon his needs. At this point he often enters upon a "second childhood," a stage which lacks the charm of childhood because it does not offer the promise of future growth. Adults who associate with the elderly person at this stage often find his behavior repellent and, if they do not understand and sympathize, may let him know how they feel. This is usually a mistake, since at this age most older people have lost the power of self-criticism to such a degree that they can no longer profit from discipline and criticism. They interpret criticism as a rejection of themselves and become depressed or discouraged, or compensate by an even greater pampering of themselves. Typical of this stage is an increased interest in bodily sensations and comfort. The major portion of the day may be devoted to securing a comfortable place to rest or to planning, preparing, and eating meals. Interference with these activities may lead the elderly person to look upon the one who interferes as an enemy. He may consequently look upon him with suspicion and work out sly little schemes for "getting around him." Often the insecurity of old people shows itself in hoarding.

Old people have a tendency to relive past events and their conversation often revolves around the past. With very little or no encouragement they become extremely garrulous. This overtalkativeness has several sources: (1) Often it is a desperate attempt to secure or to retain the attention of people whose interest is waning. Or, (2) it may be partly the result of thinking out loud. When elderly people are left to themselves much of the time they devise ways of entertaining themselves, and talking to themselves may be one of them. The preoccupation with self and the loss of normal inhibitions may lead the old person to relapse into talking to himself when he converses with others. (3) The old person often feels called upon to drag out all of the details of a story, whether relevant or not, simply to prove to himself or to his listener that his memory is as good as ever. In relating a story the old person may recall each event as it occurred without arranging his thoughts in a sequence, giving the same emphasis to both trivial and important items. This characteristic is known as *circumstantiality*, and it is, of course, a great source of boredom to the person who must listen to it.

The critical period of adjustment to age occurs earlier in women than it does in men. For many women it occurs at the menopause, even though the menopause is not accompanied by any serious physiological disturbance. The majority of women apparently have no serious physiological symptoms during this period, although about 10 per cent of them do. Most women, however, seem to have a greater tendency toward being emotional at this time than they have previously had. Sometimes this exaggerated emotional state can be alleviated by the administration of hormones which retard the degenerative changes taking place in the reproductive organs. When endocrine therapy relieves the emotional symptoms, we can conclude that the cause of the symptoms has been primarily physical. Many women, however, in spite of good physical health and appropriate treatment, undergo a marked personality crisis at the time of the climacteric. In such instances the "meaning" of the physiological changes rather than the changes themselves appears to be the precipitating factor. The cessation of the menstrual function forces a woman to realize that she is getting old. In a culture in which age brings increased status and in which the old are assured of respect and protection from the young, the realization that one is aging does not come as an unpleasant shock. On the contrary, it may be welcomed as a relief from childbearing and as an entrance to a less strenuous life. In present-day America, however, it may mean none of these things; it may present a major threat to what has been a satisfying way of life. Our society tolerates divorce and remarriage. As a rule, men do not reach a climacteric until at least ten years later than do women. And for the man the climacteric is almost never as dramatic a physiological event as it is for the woman. It is not infrequent in our culture for men whose wives are aging to become interested in younger women, divorce their wives, and marry again. When this happens it may mean double frustration of the basic needs of the wife—her need to give and receive affection, and her need for economic security. Often it occurs at the time that her children are leaving home to establish families of their own, and the woman is forced to realize that she is no longer needed or wanted. How she will react to this situation will depend on the alternative satisfactions available to her, the personality characteristics and traits that she has developed in meeting the other adjustment problems of her life, the extent to which religion is a reality in her life, and the aspirations and goals that she has set for herself.

Even when husband and wife remain united and loyal to each other, the "empty nest" stage of life presents a challenge to the woman. The rearing of children is a full time job for most middle-class women as long as it lasts, but the time comes when they must "graduate" from it. The woman who has not thought through what middle age will mean to her and who has made no plans for this period of increased leisure is likely to become a burden to herself and to society.

In men, the crisis of aging usually comes at the time of retirement from full-time employment or is precipitated by the awareness of some physical symptom which makes it necessary to curtail activity. For men, this enforced idleness is usually more complete than it is for women, especially if they have not been accustomed to taking any responsibility for the efficient running of their homes. The man who has allowed his job to consume all of his energy and to become his all-absorbing interest often suffers acutely when he is forced to retire. If, on the other hand, he has cultivated hobbies and interests, and particularly those that can be pursued at home, his problem of adjustment is greatly mitigated. The man who enjoys "puttering" in the garden, repairing fences, and cooking savory dishes for his family makes a better adjustment to old age than the man who has no such interests. As a rule, these interests have to be acquired before retirement. Otherwise they seem to be acquired only when special teaching is available. Men who look forward to retirement and accept it eagerly when it comes are usually those who have some very absorbing interest outside of their jobs and which, until retirement, they have been unable to satisfy for lack of time or energy. The same generalization holds true for women.

For both men and women the death of a spouse may initiate a radical change in habits of living which have brought satisfaction. When the loss of husband or wife coincides with the loss of a job or with the onset of ill health, the incentive to adjust to the situation is often removed. The ability to adjust to the changing circumstances of life depends at all ages upon the degree of motivation to change. Loss of a loved one may substantially lower the elderly person's "level of aspiration." The old person who has no one but himself to live for may feel that the struggle is not worth while. This loss of zest for living, together with diminishing physical strength and increasing difficulty in learning, constitutes a major source of maladjustment among the aged.

The downward social mobility that so often accompanies a reduction in income in old age is also a source of frustration. The majority of the aged in our culture are never completely free from anxiety over their financial status. Sometimes when the concept of himself as an independent, self-supporting, and responsible person meets defeat as it becomes necessary to accept old age assistance, an older person undergoes a traumatic change.

VII. MENTAL DISEASE IN LATER LIFE

In later maturity there is a great increase in mental disorders with an organic basis. Involutional states (depressions of later life), arteriosclerotic conditions, and senile psychoses all have organic bases. The peak incidence of involutional psychoses is from 50 to 54 years of age, and it is four times as common among women as among men. Arteriosclerotic and senile psychoses occasionally begin as early as the forties, and there is a steady rise in the number of cases each year until 70; thereafter the rate of increase is marked.

VIII. THE MENTAL HYGIENE OF OLD AGE

Preparation for old age begins in childhood, since "the child is father to the man." Anxiety neuroses are very common in old age and often appear in people who have not previously been vulnerable to anxiety. A healthy adjustment to life requires that we take into account all of the aspects of reality that concern our mortal situation. All of us tend to cling to what we value; we struggle to protect ourselves from losing our prized possessions. Often we do not know what it is that we prize until we are threatened with its loss. People who by reason of birth and family status have occupied positions of unquestioned privilege and status may go through life with the mistaken notion that somehow, because of their personal merits, they have a right to these. When in old age the situation changes, they may suddenly come face to face with themselves and their personal limitations for the first time. They may find that their sense of personal worth and significance and the entire edifice of their emotional security have been built upon the insecure foundation of social prestige. They may be confronted for the first time with a knowledge of their own inner emptiness and personal unworthiness, a knowledge that cannot be assimilated at this late day into their personality structure. The best education for old age is a lifelong education directed to the acceptance of objective values outside of oneself. For the Christian it means using the things of this world and enjoying them, but only as means rather than as ends. It means the gradual attainment of inner detachment from all goods which have only a temporal value. Wealth, social position, friends, prestige, physical strength and personal attractiveness—all have a purely temporal value. They are important only insofar as they enable the person enjoying them to reach the ultimate goal of his life, union with God for all eternity. If they distract him from his goal, if they become ends in themselves, the possession of such goods will be a handicap. Viewed in the light of Christian principles, the sufferings, frustrations, and deprivations of old age may be of incomparable value to the elderly person in preparing him for death. Suffering may force him, in spite of himself, to see life as it really is. With the help of God's grace he can use these sufferings as a means of purifying himself from all that will prevent his eternal union with God. The aged person must be helped to realize that this is his last chance, that the state of his happiness for all eternity depends upon using it well. The Little Sisters of the Poor, whose vocation is that of caring for the destitute aged, recognize this as the major objective of their apostolic work.

In earlier periods, when the life span was shorter, education in youth may have been sufficient to care for the needs of people throughout the entire life cycle. This is no longer true. For people who will live sixty, seventy, or eighty years, some kind of continuous adult education is necessary to help them use these remaining years in a fruitful and personally satisfying way. Of course, adult education must not be delayed until extreme old age because by that time the old person is no longer able to profit by education unless he has retained the habit of learning new things through some kind of part-time adult education during the years before retirement. Probably no community at the present time has adequate facilities of this kind for its adult population, but as the need becomes recognized and as its social importance is demonstrated, it is probable that more educational and recreational programs suitable for older people will be developed. This is a fruitful field of research for psychologists today and one offering a great challenge to the social planner.

IX. VIEWPOINTS IN PSYCHOLOGY

We have now completed our discussion of the factors influencing human personality throughout the entire life cycle. We have presented the basic scientific facts and principles that throw light upon this subject. From time to time we have shown, in specific instances, the role which theological and philosophical knowledge plays in enabling us to interpret the scientific data of psychology. It remains for us now to develop these ideas more completely at this time.

In the next two chapters of this book, we shall discuss the theoretical framework which underlies the scientific study of psychology. We are going to present and evaluate, first, important trends within scientific psychology and show their relation to a Christian view of life. We shall then present some basic philosophical and theological notions concerning the nature of truth. Without such a knowledge of philosophy and theology the findings of scientific psychology can easily be misconstrued or applied incorrectly.

PART IX

Theoretical Framework of Psychology

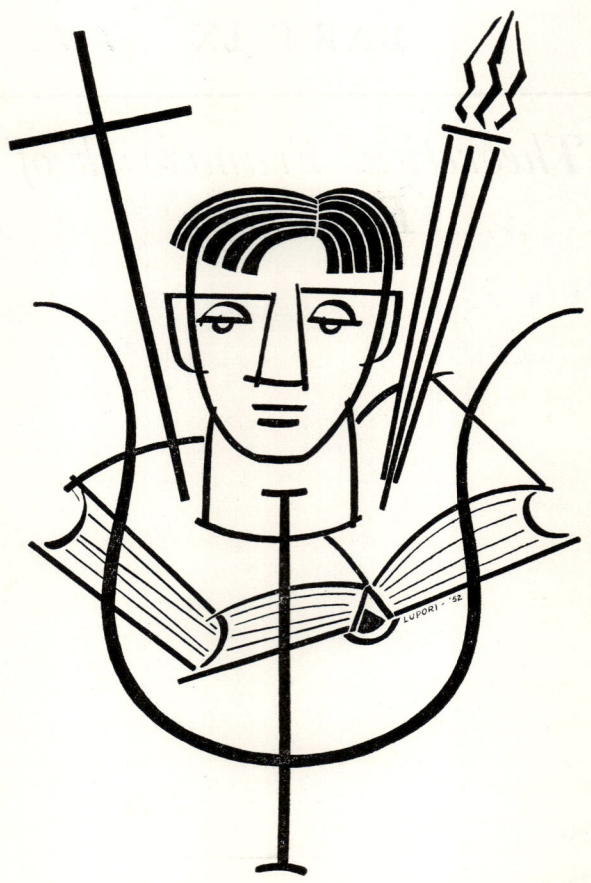

The data of scientific psychology must be interpreted in the light of philosophical and theological knowledge. In this picture, the Greek letter, psi, symbolizes scientific psychology. The torch symbolizes philosophy, and the cross theology.

XXIII

Trends and Viewpoints in Psychology Today

> *You who seek truth and are ready to recognize its countenance everywhere, do not set its servants up one against the other, even though they should be amongst those "incomplete angels," men of partial genius whom truth has visited without making its dwelling-place in them. . . . Let us regret their errors, but without violent condemnation; let us build bridges, not dig ditches between their doctrines. There is a great revelation in discovering the hidden links that exist between ideas and systems the most dissimilar.*—A. D. SERTILLANGES, O.P.[1]

I. PSYCHOLOGY AS A SCIENCE AND AS A PROFESSION

In the preceding chapters of this book we have outlined the nature, scope, and methods of psychology and have discussed the many factors which influence psychological development. We now turn to a consideration of psychology itself: (1) psychology as a systematized body of knowledge, and (2) psychology as a profession.

A. Psychology as a Systematized Body of Knowledge

Psychology today is a vigorous and rapidly growing science of almost unlimited possibilities. Its subject matter is expanding at an unprecedented rate. Its accumulated facts and principles are applied in all areas of human life, and the questions it has raised will challenge research workers for many decades to come.

Yet, in spite of its vast accomplishments, psychology as a science is still very young. Only recently has it divorced itself from

---

[1] A. D. Sertillanges, O.P., *The Intellectual Life*, trans. from the French by M. Ryan (Westminster, Maryland, The Newman Press, 1947), p. 120.

philosophy on the one hand and from physiology on the other. As compared to physics or astronomy, it is a relatively undeveloped science. A developed science is never just a collection of isolated facts and principles; it contains these facts and principles within a theoretical framework which gives meaning to the whole. Psychology is just beginning to construct for itself a satisfactory theoretical framework.

From time to time psychologists have, it is true, constructed a number of relatively distinct and often mutually exclusive theories of human and animal behavior. These several theories have given rise to different "schools" of psychology, schools which have played an important role in stimulating and guiding research. Curiously enough, the accumulation of facts in psychology has more often been the *result* of theory than the *prelude* to it. Yet most American pioneers in psychology thought that it was the other way around. They accepted the idea expressed in Francis Bacon's *Novum Organum* (1620) that a science progresses as it accumulates facts. William James, for instance, said that if enough facts are gathered they will eventually combine in some way or other. But historically the progress of scientific psychology has not been advanced in that way. The theories held by the early American "structuralists" and "functionalists" determined the direction of their research. Similarly, the characteristic viewpoints of the more recent schools of "Behaviorism," "Gestalt psychology," and "Psychoanalysis" have suggested hypotheses to be tested by later research. How these schools arose, what their basic tenets were, and what they have contributed to psychology as a whole will be the subject matter of later sections of this chapter.

B. Professional Psychology

Psychology today is not just a specialized branch of knowledge; it is also a profession. Among the recognized specialties in which professional psychologists are now certified are those of "clinical psychologist," "industrial psychologist," and "counseling and guidance psychologist." These are not, of course, the only fields in which psychologists are employed; they are, rather, the fields in which, to protect the public interest, certification procedures were first set up. A number of states today require that all psychologists be certified to practice their particular specialities. With increasing knowledge on the part of the public as to the kind of services psychologists render and of the great danger associated with charlatanism, it is probable that more legal certification will be required than is customary at present.

The contemporary status of psychology as a science and as a profession will be clearer if viewed against the background of its historical origins. In the next section we shall sketch in the main outlines of this background.

II. HISTORICAL ROOTS OF CONTEMPORARY PSYCHOLOGY

If we were asked to designate the time at which the modern period in psychology began, we might, depending on what we were emphasizing, specify the first half of the seventeenth century, 1860, or 1879. The first date refers to the advent of Cartesian philosophy, the second to the publication of Fechner's famous book, *Elements of Psychophysics,* and the third to the founding of Wilhelm Wundt's laboratory of psychology at the University of Leipzig. Each of these dates marks an historically significant step in the direction of "modern" psychology, as we shall try to show in the following paragraphs.

Descartes held that all material things, including the movements of the human body, could be explained according to mechanical principles. That is, the same principles that govern the operation of a machine govern the functioning of the human body. Descartes did not make of man a mere automaton; he held that man has a soul as well as a body. But in Descartes' view, soul did not influence body and body did not influence soul; therefore, the activities of the body could be studied without reference to the soul. Descartes, himself, was not a materialist. But, curiously enough, it was from his philosophy that the modern materialistic outlook in psychology received its impetus.

A later generation, rejecting the soul entirely, constructed a psychology which limited its study to bodily activities. It adopted the view that all psychology can be studied by observational methods alone. This notion limits the data of psychology to scientific knowledge and rules out philosophy. Thus, Descartes, while accepting the validity of philosophical knowledge himself, was indirectly responsible for its repudiation in psychology.

A second important landmark in the growth of scientific psychology was the publication of Gustav Fechner's *Elements of Psychophysics*, in 1860. In this book Fechner presented what he believed to be an exact mathematical formula for showing the relation of mind to body. Previous to Fechner's work, Ernst Weber had made extensive studies of the relation of actual differences in the magnitude of two stimuli to the perception of such differences. He had conducted numerous experiments to find out how much a given stimulus must be increased or decreased before a "just noticeable difference" can be perceived. As a result of these experiments he found, among other things, that a 30 gram weight was perceived as "just noticeably heavier" than a 29 gram weight and "just noticeably lighter" than a 31 gram weight. Similarly, a 15 gram weight could just barely be distinguished from a 14.5 or a 15.5 gram weight. In other words, differences between weights are perceived when the actual differences between them represent an increase or a decrease of $1/30$ of the "standard stimulus." The perception of differences in lengths of lines followed a similar pattern; it was relative to the length of the stimuli and was found to be a *constant fraction* of one of them. Thus, a line 101 mm. long was perceived as just noticeably longer than a line 100 mm. long, and a line 51 mm. long was perceived as just barely longer than a line 50.5 mm. long. In other words, relative rather than absolute differences in physical stimuli are perceived. Weber stated this principle in the form of the equation, $dR/R = C$, in which R stands for the "standard stimulus" (the one to which an increment is added to determine the just noticeable difference), $d =$ the amount added to R before a difference is barely perceived, and $C =$ a constant. In the lifted weight experiment, for instance, $C = 1/30$; in the experiment with lines, $C = 1/100$.

Fechner seized upon Weber's observations and devoted his life to the further development of *Weber's Law* (i.e., $dR/R = C$) because he saw in this law an exact mathematical expression of the relationship between the physical and the psychical world. Fechner believed that he had a clue to the unity of mind and body and that he was on the verge of a great philosophical discovery. It was this hope that kept him hard at work, performing experiment after experiment, and developing the new field of *psychophysics*. The result of his arduous labor was the formulation of his own law which stated that "When stimuli increase by a constant ratio, the sensations aroused by them increase by equal increments or steps." Or, stated differently, as the magnitude of the stimuli increase geometrically, the resulting sensations increase arithmetically. For instance, when the stimulus value is 10, the corresponding sensation is 1; when the stimulus is 100, the sensation is 2; and when the stimulus is 1,000, the sensation is 3, and so on. This relationship was expressed in the formula, $S = C \log R$, in which S represents the sensation, R the stimulus, $\log R$ the logarithm of the stimulus value, and C is a constant. This formula, known as *Fechner's Law*, means that the loudness, brightness, et cetera, of sensations are proportional to the logarithms of their exciting stimuli.

It is not our purpose in this book to develop the implications of either Weber's or Fechner's laws. We wish merely to show how the research of Weber and Fechner contributed to the growth of scientific psychology. Fechner's famous book showed that psychological data can be studied mathematically; it thus created a climate of opinion favorable to the establishment of a truly scientific psychology.

It remained for Wilhelm Wundt to give official recognition to the scientific status of psychology by founding a laboratory specifically for psychology in 1879. This laboratory soon attracted foreign students, many of whom were Americans, and thus the new scientific psychology took root in the United States.

You will have noted by now that this early experimental psychology was not concerned with personality as such. Nor was it interested in the individual person. Wundt's research was directed to discovering "constants" for human reactions just as physics has worked out constant values for different physical reactions. If you open a handbook in physics and chemistry you will find a table of Coefficients of Expansion for different metals. Suppose you want to determine how much a piece of pure iron will expand with a given rise in temperature. By consulting the appropriate table you can find exactly how much the iron will expand at various temperatures. All pieces of pure iron will respond to heat in the same way; there are no individual differences in this respect in pieces of pure iron. Wundt confidently expected that similar tables could be worked out for human reactions under different stimulating conditions. He found in his reaction time experiments that a motor attitude (attention centered on response to be made) led to a quicker response than a sensorial attitude (attention directed to stimulus). This was true of people in general. But, although there were certain characteristics common to all persons, great individual differences in speed of reaction were demonstrated under all conditions. Wundt expected these differences to disappear with practice; but since they did not, he had to abandon his plan to work out tables of "constant values" for human reactions under different stimulating conditions.

German experimental psychology was brought to America by Titchener, among others, who had been a student of Wundt. Titchener became the chief exponent of the first "school" of psychology in the United States, the school of *structuralism,* the basic tenets of which were Wundt's. In the following section we shall trace the development of theory in American psychology, starting with structuralism and continuing up to the present day.

III. SCHOOLS OF PSYCHOLOGY

A. Structuralism

Although Titchener claimed that the subject matter of psychology is "experience as dependent on an experiencing person," his psychology actually ruled out the study of personality. He held that the proper subject matter of psychology is "consciousness" and that the method of studying consciousness is "trained introspection." Consciousness is made up of three elements: sensation, affection, and image. These elements and their attributes are the stuff of which the mind is made; the problem of psychology is to analyze consciousness into its elements, to determine the way in which these elements are combined, and to study their attributes. In other words, the problem is that of determining the "contents" of the mind by a sort of "mental chemistry." Titchener, like Wundt, had resolved the mind-body problem by adopting the doctrine of psychophysical parallelism. His psychology has been variously labeled as "structuralism," "introspectionism," "existentialism," and "content" psychology.

It is evident, then, that structuralism was concerned with isolated mental contents rather than with the personality as a whole. Furthermore, it was interested in mind in general rather than the individual. In both of these respects it is poles removed from the contemporary scene in American psychology. In still another respect it is very different from our modern point of view: its emphasis upon psychology as a "pure science." For Titchener, the study of psychology was an end in itself. Psychological knowledge was not pursued because it might have practical applications; in particular, psychology did not exist to minister in any way to sick souls. Psychology was a pure science, uncontaminated by practical considerations. If this point of view had prevailed, psychology as a professional specialty would not exist today.

Almost from the beginning, however, the structuralist view was rejected and a more characteristic American school began to supersede it. This school, destined to exert a powerful influence on the direction of American psychology, is known as *functionalism*. It drew its inspiration from the psychology of William James.

B. Functionalism

William James, like Titchener, believed that experimentation should be used in psychology and that introspection was a valid method. He did not, however, stress introspection as the characteristic method of psychology. For James, as for Titchener, psychology was a natural science, but with James it was a biological rather than a physical science. James viewed mental processes as experiences of biological organisms; he did not study mental states in isolation from the living organism. This view was later made explicit in the *functional* psychology developed by James Angell, John Dewey, and others, and is the characteristic view of American psychologists. It sees mind in relation to its usefulness to the organism, a notion that leads naturally to applied psychology. Functionalism as a school disappeared when Behaviorism had reached its prime, but the spirit of functionalism still prevails in American psychology.

C. Behaviorism

The school of *behaviorism* grew out of functionalism and arose as a protest against structural psychology. The credo of this school was first voiced by John B. Watson in *Psychology from the Standpoint of a Behaviorist*, which he published in 1912. Watson repudiated "introspection" as a valid method of scientific study and rejected "consciousness" as the legitimate subject matter of psychology. Watson had received his Ph.D. degree in animal psychology and later extended the viewpoint and methods of animal psychology to the field of human psychology.

For Watson the only legitimate subject matter of psychology was the observation of behavior. At first glance, this notion would seem to place hampering restrictions upon the study of psychological processes. And, to a certain degree, this is true. It was not altogether true, however, because introspection was admitted through the back door by various tricks of language. "Introspection" became "verbal behavior," and "thinking" became "implicit" or "sub-vocal" speech. Moreover, the new emphasis on observation of behavior brought the world new knowledge of great value. It was a powerful stimulus to the development of child psychology and mental testing, for instance, and it greatly extended the horizons of psychological study. Behaviorism of the Watsonian kind is now extinct, but the basic notion of observing behavior is not. The naïve behaviorism of Watson, with its repudiation of philosophy, has been superseded by highly developed theoretical systems in which the philosophy of neobehaviorism has been made explicit.

Behaviorism was not the only school that arose in protest to structuralism. The German school of Gestalt psychology did so at about the same time as behaviorism. The Gestalt psychologists, however, were not protesting so much against introspection as a method as they were against the notion that experience can be analyzed into its separate components. We now turn to a consideration of the Gestalt school of psychology.

D. Gestalt Psychology

Gestalt psychology is radically different from both structuralism and behaviorism. Its basic tenet is that all mental experiences are organized wholes, patterns, or configurations. These patterns, it affirms, must be studied as wholes. Gestalt psychologists are opposed to the notion that complex experiences are built up through the combination of simple elements and that the complex experience can be analyzed by reducing it to its elements. They object to the analysis of mental experience on the grounds that such analysis destroys the very object of psychological study itself, just as the analysis of water into its components of hydrogen and oxygen destroys the water. The properties of water must be studied as water; the study of hydrogen and oxygen, except as they are combined in water, can tell us nothing about water as such. Similarly, mental processes must be studied as they are, as immediate given wholes, without analysis into elements.

Gestalt psychology got its start at the University of Berlin under the direction of Max Wertheimer, and became known to Americans through his students, Wolfgang Köhler and Kurt Koffka. Gestalt psychology is probably the best known of the "field" theories in psychology. Field theories, in general, deal with psychological data only in the total setting or "field" in which they occur.[2]

The next school to be considered, that of psychoanalysis, did not grow out of psychology at all; it was developed by an Austrian neurologist, Sigmund Freud. It was from this school, however, that modern clinical psychology received one of its chief inspirations, the other being the elaboration of psychometric methods applied to personality.

E. Freudian Psychoanalysis

Psychoanalysis began as a method of treatment, but rapidly developed into a complex body of psychological theory and a philosophy which has ramifications in all areas of human life. In this section, we shall treat of psychoanalysis under two different aspects: (1) Freudian psychology, and (2) Freudian method.

1. Freudian psychology

The basic ideas of Freudian psychology are as follows:

a. Libido. The libido, eros, or life instinct, is the vital energy of the person and is derived from the sexual instinct. It is a dynamic force, constantly moving, or flowing. Within the life history

---

[2] Perhaps the most important offshoot of Gestalt psychology is the *topological psychology* developed by Kurt Lewin. Topological psychology draws its theoretical constructs from topological mathematics. *Topology* is a branch of geometry which, like all geometry, deals with the properties of figures in space. Topology is a non-Euclidian and non-quantitative branch of mathematics. Topological space cannot be visualized as physical space within which it is possible to measure direction and distance. Topological space is concerned only with relations and not with quantities. Topological psychology is today being successfully applied to several areas of psychological research, but particularly to the fields of child psychology and to studies of group social processes and functions. In the eyes of some psychologists, Lewin's topological system is to contemporary psychology what Einstein's theory of relativity is to modern physics.

of the individual it is characteristically directed first toward self, then toward a member of the same sex, and eventually toward a member of the opposite sex. When conditions exist which disrupt this normal sequence of development, various personality aberrations result. An adult, for example, whose libido has been turned inward is said to be "narcissistic." Narcissism is self-love as contrasted to "object-love" or love directed to other individuals.

When the libido adheres to infantile love objects without progressing to a higher level, it is said to be *fixated* at an immature stage. If it has once progressed, however, and then flows back to a more infantile love-object, *regression* has taken place. *Repression* is the term used to signify what happens when the libido is dammed up; whereas *sublimation* occurs when the libido is directed into altruistic or socially approved channels.

b. The conscious, preconscious, and unconscious. Freud distinguishes three kinds of mental content: (1) conscious, (2) preconscious, and (3) unconscious. The mental content of which we are aware is *conscious*. That of which we are not immediately aware but which can easily be brought to mind is the *preconscious*. That of which we are not aware and of which we cannot become aware without specialized psychological help is the *unconscious*. The unconscious is the greatest part of mental life and is more powerful than conscious mental life in determining one's life pattern and actions. Unlike the conscious, the unconscious is not logically arranged nor verbalized. Its content comes from two sources: (1) that which was conscious but has been repressed, and (2) that which was never conscious, namely, the racial unconscious, inherited from primitive man. Freudian theory and method are centered almost exclusively upon the first of these sources.

c. Œdipus complex. Every child unconsciously desires to possess the parent of the opposite sex and supplant the parent of the same sex. The name "Œdipus complex" was taken from the play of Æschylus, *Œdipus Rex*, in which the son unknowingly kills his father and marries his mother. A basic notion of Freudian psychology is that adult personality patterns derive from the way in which the Œdipus complex is resolved during early childhood before the age of five.

d. Id, ego, and superego. These three terms did not appear in the early Freudian writings but are of later origin. The *id* is conceived of as a burning cauldron of instincts, the reservoir of the libido, and the unconscious source of all instinctive energy. Within the id, the pleasure principle rules supreme.

The *ego* is partly conscious and partly unconscious, and is at war with the id. The ego represents reason or sanity, and from the ego proceed repressions. This repression is brought about by means of a *censor*.

The *superego* is a partly unconscious conscience which is built up in the child as he learns "thou shalt" or "thou shalt not."

2. Freudian method

Freud, after practicing medicine in Vienna, went to Paris to study under Charcot, who was at that time becoming famous for his hypnotic treatment of hysteria and other functional nervous disorders. On returning to Vienna, Freud at first treated his patients as he had observed Charcot treating them, by means of hypnosis and electrotherapy. Gradually he discarded Charcot's methods, however, and came to rely more and more on a new method of his own, a method which is called *psychoanalysis*. This method is a kind of free association which aims to release the contents of the unconscious mind. The patient is encouraged to speak freely of anything that comes into his mind without any inhibitions. The psychoanalyst listens to his recital and notes symptoms of blocking, embarrassment, or significant sequences of ideas. These symptoms call attention to areas of conflict and it is the work of the psychoanalyst to assist the patient to become aware of the source of his conflicts. Theoretically, once the patient is aware of the unconscious roots of his condition, roots that extend back to very early childhood, he has the means to understand and so to control his psychological illness.

F. Offshoots of Freudian Psychoanalysis

Two of Freud's most distinguished students, Alfred Adler and Carl Jung, parted company with Freud and established schools of their own. Neither of these schools has attained anything like the acclaim which psychologists in America have showered upon Freud. But in Europe the situation is different and many psychologists as well as artists and writers look upon Jung's system as the most penetrating and complete formulation of human psychology that has yet been developed.[3] Since several eminent Catholic scholars have seen rich possibilities in synthesizing the psychology of Adler and of Jung with Thomistic philosophy, we feel justified in giving these systems a little more consideration in this volume than is customary in American textbooks.

After breaking with Freud, Adler became the leader of a school commonly referred to as *individual psychology*. This school attributes all human activity to an urge for mastery, just as Freudian psychology sees the source of all human striving in the sexual instinct. For Adler, even sex is explained as a means of satisfying the will to mastery. For Freud, on the other hand, the will to mastery is a particular manifestation of the sexual instinct. Jung differs from both Freud and Adler in that he does not attribute motivation in all persons to the same dominant urge. He recognizes individual differences in human motivation. The sexual instinct, for instance, may be the clue to one man's personality; the will to power may be the dominant driving force in another. In this respect, Jung's system bears a striking resemblance to the Christian notion of a "dominant passion." According to this principle, every human being has within himself the roots of the seven capital sins: pride, anger, lust, greed, envy, sloth, and gluttony. But each person is particularly attracted by one of these vices, and his tendency in this direction is known as his "dominant passion." Spiritual guidance is often directed toward helping a person discover his dominant passion as a means of gaining control over it. Catholic spiritual guides have always recognized the fact that some of these unworthy motives find expression in acts which at first sight may appear virtuous, and in doing so they have anticipated, in a sense, the Freudian doctrine of unconscious motivation. They have not, however, limited their conception of human motivation to one urge nor have they attributed sin to the perversion of only one of these urges, as, for example, to the root sin of lust or of pride. Catholic theologians, while consistently defending the dignity of man and his power to freely make himself into the kind of personality he wants to become, have, nevertheless, seen in man the possibility of just as much and probably more evil than even Freud could conjure up. In other words, they have seen

---

[3] W. P. Witcutt, *Catholic Thought and Modern Psychology* (London, Burns Oates & Washbourne, Ltd., 1944), p. 5.

not one motive but seven which might, if allowed to prevail over reason and the grace of God, effectively destroy a human personality

Rudolph Allers has probably made more use of Adler's theory of personality than any other Catholic psychologist. Allers was trained in both psychology and medicine and has a grasp of philosophy which other psychologists might well envy. In what is probably his most important book, *The Psychology of Character*,[4] Allers has effected a convincing synthesis between Adlerian psychology and Thomistic philosophy. For Allers, the Adlerian mastery urge is in a sense equated with the dominant human passion of pride. Allers has not been content merely to work out an academic system of psychology, but has carefully teased out of his theoretical formulations the educational and therapeutic implications.

Jung's conception of the unconscious differs radically from that of Freud. For Freud, all that is really important is the repressed life of the individual. For Jung, the individual repressed life is only an inconsequential part of the unconscious. What matters is the racial unconscious, an unconscious from which proceed mental impressions, impulses, and affections. It is a corollary to the sense world, and like the senses, it is a source of knowledge. This notion of Jung's is, of course, different from the Aristotelian-Thomistic principle that all knowledge comes through the senses. The average person finds it difficult to accept this facet of Jung's system; creative writers, however, have been very receptive to the idea since it appears to offer an explanation of what happens to them in those moments of creative frenzy when their pens fail to keep up with the ideas pouring out from an "inner source."

Several psychologists, in attempting a synthesis of Jung's ideas with those of the Aristotelian-Thomistic tradition, see in Jung's concept of the unconscious not so much a contradiction of the traditional view as an addition to it. These unconscious contents, they point out, present themselves to the conscious mind in the form of concrete symbols, either in dreams or in phantasy, and these symbols can be abstracted by the intellect in much the same way as concrete sense images are abstracted in the genesis of an idea.

[4] Rudolph Allers, *The Psychology of Character*, trans. by E. B. Strauss (New York, The Macmillan Company, 1931).

All psychologists interested in the unconscious have found it necessary to construct a theory of dreams. Freud, Adler, and Jung were no exceptions in this respect. For Adler, as for Freud, dreams are symbols of unconscious instinctive drives. In Adler's system they are symbols of the power drive; in Freud's system they are symbols of sexual desire. For Jung, dreams have a far deeper meaning than they have for either Freud or Adler. Jung noted that the same symbols appear over and over again in the history of the race, both in dreams and in myths or fairy-tales. He sees in fairy-tales the crystallized dreams of the race. These dream and myth symbols are not learned through individual experience; they spring from the racial unconscious. Through comparative studies of the folklore, mythology, language, and religion of different peoples, Jung claims to have found a restricted number of symbols with a relatively fixed meaning, even though the people using these symbols have had no communication with each other. These fixed symbols are called the *archetypes*.

Jung's recognition of the need man has for religion has perhaps more than anything else in his doctrine stimulated the interest of Christian psychologists in his system. Jung's view on this subject is epitomized in the following quotation:

> During the past thirty years, people from all the civilized countries of the earth have consulted me. I have treated many hundreds of patients, the larger number being Protestants, a small number Jews, and not more than five or six believing Catholics. Among all my patients in the second half of life—that is to say, over thirty-five—there has not been one whose problem in the last resort was not that of finding a religious outlook on life. It is safe to say that every one of them fell ill because he had lost that which the living religions of every age have given to their followers, and none of them has been really healed who did not regain his religious outlook.[5]

And again, Jung says, "Man is never helped in his suffering by what he thinks for himself, but only by revelations of a wisdom greater than his own. It is this that lifts him out of his distress." [6]

In the next section we shall try more explicitly to evaluate the contributions of these several schools.

[5] C. C. Jung, *Modern Man in Search of a Soul*, trans. by W. S. Dell and C. F. Baynes (London, Kegan Paul, Trench, Trubner and Company, Ltd., 1947), p. 264.
[6] *Ibid.*, p. 279.

IV. EVALUATION OF PSYCHOLOGICAL SCHOOLS

A. Contribution to Psychology as a Science

All schools have imparted something of positive value to psychology as a science. Some have made appreciable contributions to methodology; others have discovered important facts; still others have raised significant questions. Most schools, in fact, have pushed back the frontiers of psychology in all of these directions. In the early days of scientific psychology it was inevitable that different schools of thought should arise. The field was so vast and so little of it had been explored that no one person could possibly get a vision of the whole. Each psychologist formulated his own goals and mapped out the particular area of psychology which he was going to explore. In doing so he was often oblivious to the work of others in the field. Today, however, all psychologists are more or less cognizant of what their colleagues are doing. The boundaries that separate schools are gradually breaking down. Established facts and the methods that have stood the test of time are now a part of psychology as a whole. Schools of psychology have become relatively unimportant.

B. Contribution to Psychology as a Profession

Schools of psychology have also made their specific contributions to psychology as a profession. Even structuralism, which denied that psychology could or should become an applied science, invented methods and techniques that are used extensively in applied psychology today. Psychophysics, for instance, plays an important role in attitude measurement, instrument design, and in the selection of men for different specialized occupations. Functionalism, with its emphasis on the utility of mental processes, provided a "climate" of opinion in which professional psychology could develop. Behaviorism, too, with its emphasis on habit formation and upon objective observation, led naturally to the study of children. Its denial of instinct and of heredity resulted in a new interest in manipulating the environment so as to foster psychological growth. It was in this respect an important influence in the establishment of child guidance clinics. Most important, however, was the impetus it gave to mental testing, a field in which the great majority of professional psychologists are today employed. Lastly, the influence of psychoanalysis must not be overlooked. The Freudian viewpoint and method have opened up vast new clinical possibilities and have led to increased emphasis on psychotherapy and guidance. Since psychotherapy must be based upon a deep understanding of human motivation and adjustment, this view has been a powerful incentive to clinical research and practice.

It remains for us now to evaluate the several schools and current trends in psychology from the vantage point of Christian principles.

C. Trends in Psychology and Christian Principles

The growth of experimental and clinical psychology has been received with mixed feelings by many Christians. Even those who know little about modern psychology often view it with suspicion. Let us consider for a few moments what justification there may be for adopting such a negative attitude.

A careful scrutiny of all five of the schools of psychology just described (we are disregarding the offshoots of psychoanalysis) gives us a clue to their rejection by Christians. Underlying the scientific research of each of these schools is a philosophical notion of man that is incompatible with Christian principles. Basically, all of these schools have been materialistic in outlook, as we shall now illustrate briefly.

The structuralists' view that all mental processes can ultimately be reduced to images is basically a denial that thought is spiritual. The behaviorists' limitation of psychology to what can be observed by the senses is also implicitly a denial of spiritual reality. Gestalt psychology, too, while rejecting the notion that complex experiences can be analyzed in terms of their component sensations, is fundamentally a materialistic psychology. All mental life, according to the Gestalt view, is intrinsically dependent upon "brain fields." In rejecting sensations as the units of mental experience, Gestalt psychologists have substituted perceptions instead. Perceptual experiences, while undoubtedly more complex than sensations, are still bound up intrinsically with the material conditions that give rise to them. Perceptions differ essentially from intellectual ideas. Since the Gestalt doctrine explains *all* mental life in terms of perceptual patterns and ultimately of "dynamic

TRENDS AND VIEWPOINTS IN PSYCHOLOGY 639

brain fields," it rules out the possibility of an intellect not intrinsically dependent upon matter.

At the heart of the functionalist view of mental life is the Darwinian theory of evolution. Functionalists assume that man's mind has evolved from that of lower organisms and is not essentially different from that of other animal species. The Christian, of course, cannot accept such a position because it is a denial of man's spiritual nature.

Christians have, on the whole, been more critical of psychoanalysis than of other schools of psychology, probably because its moral implications are readily perceived. Freudian philosophy, unlike Freudian psychology and method, cannot by any stretch of the imagination be assimilated into a Christian scheme of life. It is frankly materialistic, deterministic, and anti-intellectual. Its "amoralistic" attitude toward human beings is a denial of an objective norm of good or bad, right or wrong; implicitly it is a rejection of the Ten Commandments.

It is important to note that it is not the scientific findings nor the clinical observations of psychoanalysts to which the Christian takes exception. It is the philosophical assumptions about the reality of God, the nature of man, and the nature of truth to which the Christian objects. For Freud, God is only a projection of man's mind: God does not create man; man creates God. In a sense, the Freudian and the Christian view of life take their starting points at opposite poles: the Freudian looks from the earth upward, and sees reflected in the heavens the image of earth. The Christian looks from heaven downward and sees heaven reflected upon the earth. To the Freudian, only the material world exists, and all of man's aspirations, be they social, artistic, scientific or religious, are projections or sublimations of his biological instincts. The basic reality is matter; the "spiritual" aspirations and activities of man are "caused" or, at least, proceed from his animal drives. The Christian, on the other hand, sees God as the primary reality —God, Who is a pure spirit. The created world, including minerals, plants, animals and men, is essentially "good" in every respect since it reflects or mirrors the attributes of God. Man's aspirations and cravings—his longing for goodness, for truth, and for beauty—are not sublimations of biological instincts. They are spiritual characteristics in which man mirrors the perfections of God, in Whose image he has been made. Man's literary and artistic creations, his scientific and practical achievements, even his procreation of other human beings, are all participations in the creative work of God. In the Christian scheme of things, the lower is interpreted and understood in terms of the higher. In the Freudian scheme, the higher is explained in terms of the lower. Both the Christian and the Freudian observe the same world of phenomena, but because of their divergent attitudes and values they may with reason be compared to the two men referred to in the lines:

> Two men looked out from prison bars
> The one saw mud; the other stars.

Catholic writers differ in their evaluation of Freud. Some, like Rudolph Allers,[7] contend that it is difficult if not impossible to use the method of Freud without at the same time being influenced by his philosophy. If by method one means the exact way in which Freud used free association and dream analysis, as a means for unearthing an Œdipus complex or a repressed incestuous desire, for example, then Allers' contention probably holds. Strictly speaking, Freud's method is focused upon a particular goal, and in using the method as Freud intended it to be used, one must of necessity accept the reality of the goal toward which it is directed; that is, one must accept the philosophical or theoretical assumptions underlying the technique. Most people, however, who use Freud's method are not using it in the pure sense. They are adapting it for purposes and goals of their own. Jung, for example, who broke away from Freud's school of thought, continued to use free association and dream analysis but with a radically different end in view from that of Freud.

This completes our evaluation of the several schools from a Christian point of view. We have seen that the Christian has with reason been suspicious of modern psychology. But we do not want to end with this negative criticism. Psychology is the most rapidly developing science of our day. Already it has made great contributions to modern thought and human welfare. In the next and final section we shall try to present a constructive Christian attitude toward psychology and its future progress.

[7] R. Allers, *The Successful Error* (New York, Sheed and Ward, Inc., 1940).

V. PSYCHOLOGY AND THE FUTURE

Psychology is making enormous strides both as a science and as a profession; we have reason to believe that it will continue to do so. As its factual basis is extended and as its methodology becomes firmly established, psychology is ridding itself of conflicting points of view. This trend, we confidently believe, will eventually eliminate "schools" of psychology. Psychology will then be an established factual science; its data will consist of demonstrated scientific facts rather than opinion. The need for negative criticism will be greatly diminished.

The above statements have important implications for the Christian student who finds himself attracted to psychology either as an academic specialty or as a profession. In the past, many students have avoided specializing in psychology because every major system of psychology had some objectionable features as viewed by a Christian. Catholic scholars have been prolific in their negative criticisms of psychology. Their research has been devoted chiefly to exposing errors in existing systems of thought. But we note a new trend in Catholic circles today.[8] The time has come, we believe, when Catholic scholars must more and more take the initiative in developing positive views. In psychology as in the arts, it is much easier to be a critic than a creator. Yet it is the creative thinker, the man of ideas, who attracts disciples to his cause and profoundly influences the spirit of his age. Psychology is here to stay, and negative criticism alone will not eliminate its undesirable features. Psychology today offers a tremendous challenge to the sincere Catholic student. He must not be content with static formulations of psychological data, in archaic language, and which have no apparent relevance to our own age. He must actively seek a new and meaningful synthesis

---

[8] In 1947, a group of over one hundred Catholic psychologists met to consider the advisability of forming an organization of Catholic psychologists. This organization, known as the American Catholic Psychological Association (ACPA), is now well established and has over 300 members. Psychologists who wish to become constituent members of this association must meet the eligibility requirements for associate members or fellows of the American Psychological Association. Since the American Psychological Association requires adequate scientific preparation for membership, this stipulation automatically eliminates people untrained in science from membership in the ACPA.

of scientific psychology with sound philosophical thought and with the revealed truths of religion.

Our discussion of scientific psychology in this book is now completed. But we are appending a chapter to serve as a bridge between scientific psychology and philosophy and theology. This chapter is necessarily incomplete; it is not offered as a substitute for books on philosophy and theology. We include it here because we want to impress you with the importance of interpreting your scientific knowledge in the light of relevant philosophical and theological truths.

SUGGESTED READING

ALLERS, R., "The Limitations of Medical Psychology," *Thought*, 17 (1942), 477–488.

BURNS, C., "Psychology and Catholics," *Blackfriars*, 31 (1950), 118–124.

DONCEEL, J., "Second Thoughts on Freud," *Thought*, 24 (1949), 465–484.

MARITAIN, J., *Scholasticism and Politics* (New York, The Macmillan Company, 1940), Chapter 6, "Freudianism and Psychoanalysis."

WITCUTT, W P., *Catholic Thought and Modern Psychology* (London, Burns, Oates & Washbourne Ltd., 1944).

WHITE, V., O. P., "Psychotherapy and Ethics," *Blackfriars*, 26 (1945), 287–300.

WOODWORTH, R. S., *Contemporary Schools of Psychology*, Revised Edition (New York, Ronald Press, 1948).

XXIV

Science, Philosophy, and Theology in the Study of Man

In the consciousness of the harmonious coördination and subordination of the truths of the natural and supernatural order, the thoughtful Catholic student finds the origin of that sense of spiritual steadiness and inner security which nothing in this world can replace, which constitutes his most precious heritage and is the privileged possession of those centers of learning whose breath of life is the Catholic faith.—POPE PIUS XII [1]

I. PSYCHOLOGY AND COMMON SENSE

When you began the study of psychology you were not entirely naïve about human nature and behavior. You had lived with people all your life, observed their reactions, and had probably developed your own set of generalizations as to how you could best get along with them. Your daily conduct in living with people is very likely based upon the common experience of everyday life rather than upon a set of scientific or philosophical principles. In fact, all knowledge begins with such common and unsystematized experience. Two questions arise in relation to common sense knowledge in understanding people: (1) to what extent is common sense knowledge valid and accurate? and, (2) how is common sense knowledge related to the scientific and philosophical study of man?

One of the discoveries that most of us make after studying

---

[1] From an address delivered by Pope Pius XII when, as Cardinal Pacelli, on October 22, 1936, he visited The Catholic University of America at Washington, D.C. Quoted in Jan Olav Smit, *Angelic Shepherd*, trans. by James H. Vanderveldt, O.F.M. (New York, Dodd, Mead & Company, Inc., 1950), p. 80. The address was published in *The Catholic University Bulletin*, V, 2 (February, 1937), 4–6 and also VII, 2 (February, 1939), 1–8.

psychology systematically for a while is that many ideas which we took for granted are either not true at all or are only partially so. The knowledge we acquire casually in the process of living is made up to a considerable extent of mere beliefs and opinions. Much of it does not stand up under rigid scientific and logical scrutiny. Yet there is, in our ordinary knowledge, a certain amount of truth. Common sense knowledge bears to scientific knowledge somewhat the relation that a rough map bears to a perfect map. In the rough sketch there may be disproportion, incorrectness in detail, even downright error in certain parts; yet some of the main features of the terrain stand out clearly, and this rough map serves especially as a guide and incentive for further more intensive work. The very imperfection in such a rough sketch demands improvement. The final perfect map will improve on the original but will not altogether change it.

Common sense knowledge includes (1) certain self-evident axioms or first principles of knowledge, such as every effect has a cause; a thing cannot be and not be at the same time; and the whole is greater than any of its parts. It also includes (2) sense perceptions, such as those which enable us to recognize that material objects are characterized by height, length, and breadth. And, lastly, (3) it includes the consequences which we immediately deduce from primary sense data and the first principles apprehended by the intellect.

Scientific and philosophical knowledge are of a higher order than that of common sense, although all three kinds of knowledge have their roots in the natural light of the intellect and are based upon the authority of evidence. Although common sense is less refined than scientific and philosophical knowledge, it can in many ways be a useful handmaid to the scholar. Thus, it may serve to point out erroneous conclusions even when it is not able to show why these conclusions are false. Descartes, it is said, was one day explaining his theory that motion is relative and that consequently it made no difference whether you said the object was moving toward the goal or the goal was moving toward the object. One of Descartes' hearers, however, claimed that if he were panting for breath in trying to reach a goal, he would be in no doubt as to which was moving—himself or the goal. Similarly, it is reported that Zeno was one day developing a logical argument which seemed to prove that motion was impossible. Diogenes, one of his listeners, said not a word, but demonstrated the falsity of the reasoning by simply getting up and walking away.

Specious reasoning in psychology must sometimes be refuted in exactly the same way. Some of the early theories of Watson on the training of children could easily have been refuted by common sense, without waiting for a generation of children to grow up and demonstrate the inadequacy of the theories. The arguments for absolute determinism, too, would be much more convincing if common sense did not demonstrate that human society would be impossible if we attempted to carry out the logical implications of such a doctrine.[2]

II. PSYCHOLOGY AND SCIENCE

A. The Meaning of Science

Throughout this book we have generally used the word *science* to mean the natural sciences. What we wish to emphasize in this chapter is that there are three valid sources of knowledge about man. Because of the naturalistic bias of many contemporary thinkers, there is a tendency at the present time to restrict "science" to the natural sciences alone. Strictly speaking, however, philosophy and theology are even more properly called "science" than are the natural sciences, for the natural sciences cannot penetrate to the *essences* of things. But "certain knowledge through causes" (the Scholastic definition of science) is achieved only by a discipline which can penetrate beyond accidents. The various special ("empiriological" as some scholastics call them) sciences can investigate only the accidents of things. Hence, while they come closer and closer to the ultimate truth of things, they never will attain it; their very method precludes this. All three kinds of knowledge help us to understand man.

First, some facts about man are known through a study of the

---

[2] Legal practice, like Catholic moral theology, places great stress upon the *intention* of the person. In law, punishments are meted out not according to the objective consequences of an act, but according to the intention the man had in performing it. A man may intentionally kill someone, for example, and the crime is labeled *murder*. If the killing was unintentional, however, it is labeled *manslaughter*. Society views these two crimes very differently and demands different punishment according to the amount of free will involved. Our basic notions of legal justice would collapse were we to assume that man is not free to formulate an intention of the will. If a society were to accept this view it would consequently destroy itself.

special sciences. For instance, you can learn a great deal about the process of digestion from a study of chemistry. Second, there are questions about man which cannot be answered by investigation through the special sciences alone. Such a question as "What is life?" demands more than science can contribute; it belongs to philosophy. Third, reason alone cannot attain to the fact of supernatural life. Theology—the study of what God has revealed to man—is the only discipline capable of treating of supernatural life. Both theology and philosophy are sciences in the strict sense of the term, as explained above. Theology, philosophy, and the natural sciences are needed by anyone who would see man as he really is.

B. Sources of Valid Knowledge

Much confusion in contemporary psychological writing results from the fact that the authors fail to clarify their theories of knowledge. You, as a Christian, are apt to be disturbed by the obviously pagan and anti-Christian attitude taken by many writers in the field of modern psychology. Unless you are equipped to evaluate such writing, you may fall victim to either one of two serious intellectual temptations, namely, (1) to accept an entire system of psychological thought, in spite of the fact that certain aspects of the system are untrue and violently opposed to Christian principles; *or* (2) to reject an entire system of psychological thought, even though most of it is true, because certain limited aspects of it are untrue.

In yielding to the first temptation, you run the risk of losing your faith, or at least your intellectual integrity. In yielding to the second, you cut your mind off from its appropriate object, the contemplation of truth. In either event, you prevent yourself from acquiring a deep understanding of human beings.

The following discussion of knowledge aims to help you avoid both these dangers and to evaluate contemporary psychological research and opinion.

As we said above, there are three valid sources of knowledge concerning human nature and behavior: revelation (faith), philosophy (reason), and special observation (science). Each occupies a distinct place in the hierarchy of knowledge. Since truth is one, there can never be any real conflict between the truths derived from any of these three sources; and failure to consider all three sources of valid knowledge may result in an inadequate or distorted view of human beings.

In the study of human beings, a synthesis of these three kinds of knowledge can be attained only if the three are clearly distinguished.

1. Faith

Accepting a truth on faith means accepting it on the authority of another. There are two kinds of faith, namely, human faith and divine faith.

a. Human faith. We exhibit human faith whenever we accept a statement on the authority of another human being without seeking to verify it. The small child, as well as the eminent scientist, frequently exhibits such faith. For example, most people accept facts concerning their parentage or their birthplace as told to them by parents or other relations. Such acceptance on faith is not an indication of stupidity or suggestibility. Human faith is not beneath the dignity of man, provided his reason tells him that the person whose word he is accepting knows what he is talking about, and is, moreover, an honorable person who can be relied upon to tell the truth. The scholar often reads biographical, historical, or scientific books and accepts their contents as true without laboriously investigating the sources or without himself repeating the experiments. The same scholar, however, will sometimes ridicule the Christian for accepting divine truths on the authority of God or His divinely founded Church.

b. Divine faith. Divine faith is the acceptance of truth on the authority of God, or of His Divine Son Who became man, or on the authority of the Church speaking as God's representative. Like human faith, it is preceded by an act of reason. It is because Catholics hold there are arguments convincing to reason (1) as to the fact that God has spoken to man and (2) as to the nature of His revelation, that Catholics look upon these revealed truths as sacred and deserving of their most profound respect. However, before such faith can be efficacious, it is necessary that God supply what is lacking to man's natural powers by granting supernatural grace.

Through divine faith, man is able to know many truths which he could not have learned through his reason alone. On the other hand, God has revealed truths which man could discover by his own reason, but if left to himself would discover too late, or mixed with error, or might never discover because unfitted for study by reason of temperament, inclination, lack of ability, or time. Faith serves reason in many ways, as Gilson points out in *The Spirit of Medieval Philosophy*. In the history of philosophy many problems for philosophical study have been suggested as a result of contemplating the truths of faith. Reason serves faith, too, by demonstrating the foundations of faith. Elsewhere Gilson points out that,

> . . . our faith in Revelation should not be a merely natural assent to some rational probability. When something is rationally probable, its contrary also is rationally probable. It is but an opinion. Religious faith is not an opinion. It is the unshakable certitude that God has spoken, and that what God has said is true, even though we do not understand it.[3]

Moreover,

> No man would ever admit that God has spoken unless he had solid proofs of the fact. Such proofs are to be found in history, where the miracles of God, and quite especially the greatest of all: the life and growth of His church, prove His presence, the truth of His doctrine, and the permanence of His inspiration.[4]

Revelation gives us an explanation of the fundamental conflict in men in the dogma of original sin. This problem of conflict is one of the most crucial in modern psychology. The Christian has, as a result of revelation, an understanding and a certainty in this regard that non-Christians lack.

2. Reason or philosophy

In a sense, philosophy stands midway between theology and the special sciences. For philosophical truth, like scientific, is attained by the use of *human reason* without appealing to divine revelation. Philosophy, however, differs from the special sciences in several important respects. Before discussing in detail the relations of philosophy and science it will be helpful to consider the nature of knowledge itself and the degrees of abstraction in human knowledge.

---

[3] E. Gilson, *Reason and Revelation in the Middle Ages* (New York, Charles Scribner's Sons, 1939), p. 77.
[4] *Ibid.*, pp. 81–82.

a. Differences between sense knowledge and intellectual knowledge. Aristotle compared sense knowledge to the impression left on wax by a signet ring. The impression left on the wax is an exact copy of the design on the ring, yet the ring itself does not remain in the wax. Similarly, sense knowledge is always a reproduction of the material stimulus which has impinged upon a sense organ. Yet the stimulus itself may be removed from the sense organ while the knowledge remains. Thus, even sense knowledge is to some extent "remote from matter." But because it is always knowledge of a particular, individual, and material object, it is not as remote from matter as is intellectual knowledge. Sense knowledge is common to both man and animal.

Intellectual knowledge is possible to man because of his spiritual soul. Because the soul is spiritual, it is not limited, as are all material things, by the laws of space and time. Its operations transcend the limitations of the material world. Originally, it is true, all knowledge comes to man through his sense organs. Sense knowledge is the material upon which the intellect works, and without sense experience the intellect cannot function. Yet because of the immaterial nature of his mind, man is not confined in his knowledge solely to the raw materials received from the senses. In sense knowledge he knows or possesses the thing known in this way: he grasps the object independently of its matter but not independently of the conditions of matter. In knowing the object intellectually, he begins with the data of the senses but he immediately disregards the particular, individuating and material qualities in order to arrive at the abstract essence of the object. This abstract essence is immaterial, and it can be predicated of every individual in its class, kind, or species; yet it does not belong exclusively to any one of them, not even to the concrete object from which it has just been abstracted. Thus it is rightly said to be potentially universal. This abstract, immaterial essence of the thing known is present in the intellect and is expressed by the intellect: it is the idea. It is not merely free from matter but it is free also from all the conditions of matter. Like the intellect itself, the idea is wholly immaterial. Thus intellectual knowledge can be acquired only by beings endowed with a spiritual or immaterial principle of nature. Animals have no such principle in their nature and consequently they cannot achieve anything higher than sense knowledge. Thus they are incapable of language,[5] of thought, and of passing on to their offspring a culture pattern or a set of values.

b. Degrees of abstraction or remotion from matter. It is possible to distinguish various degrees of intelligibility among the objects of human knowledge. These are called degrees of abstraction, and human science is generically divided in virtue of them. On the lowest level of abstraction, the object of human knowledge is natural bodies which are material and which by their nature are subject to constant change. For this reason they are called *mobile being*. This is the level of the physical sciences and also of the philosophy of nature. At the second degree of abstraction, being is considered as it is quantified or numbered. It treats of numbers, points, and geometrical figures which indeed refer to matter, since they deal with quantity, but they are not material and accordingly they are basically more knowable, since they do not change. They belong to the realm of mathematics. Finally, on the highest level, being is studied simply as being. That is, the objects considered have no necessary relationship to matter because they are either wholly immaterial realities, such as God, or realities that do not imply matter, as, for instance, being in general, substance, and the properties of being: unity, truth, goodness, and beauty. These objects are essentially unchangeable and hence they are the most knowable of all things. They constitute the proper object of the science of metaphysics and, in virtue of their dignity, they make it the highest of all purely human sciences.

c. Distinction of the special sciences from philosophy. Philosophy deals with knowledge which is grounded on *common* experience as distinguished from the *special* experience upon which scientific truth is based. By "common" experience we mean experience which all men can have even though they have not been trained in specialized techniques of observation. An example of such a common experience would be the observation that trees bud and send out leaves in the spring but lose their leaves in the autumn. No specialized training is required for a man to observe the cycle of growth and decay in nature. Such observation, therefore, is common experience. Special experience, on the other hand, presupposes technical training in modes of observa-

---

[5] That is, "conceptual" or "representative" language, as distinguished from expressive sounds, like cries of pain, or calls, such as that of a bird to its mate.

tion. Examples of such special experience, upon which scientific knowledge depends, are the use of the microscope, the telescope, and the x-ray machine, or the conduct of any controlled laboratory experiment. It is "common" experience that leaves change color with the seasons; it is "special" experience that leaves are composed of several layers of cells. The latter type of experience, requiring as it does the use of a microscope, is not experience which is open to all men. Before the invention of the microscope no man could have seen the different layers of cells in a leaf. Since the microscope has been invented, only men trained especially in its use can avail themselves of the experience it offers.

Philosophy is still more set off from science and gains in dignity in that philosophy seeks the *ultimate* causes of things while science seeks only *proximate* causes. The proximate cause of a human life is the parents; the ultimate cause is God. The proximate cause is studied by science; the ultimate cause by philosophy.

Philosophy, moreover, throws light upon the *essence* of man, that is, the human nature which underlies man's actions and habits. Science, dealing with man's actions and habits themselves, cannot of itself arrive at a knowledge of the essential nature of man.

3. Science

The natural sciences, in contrast to philosophy, deal with proximate causes and with specialized experience. They deal with limited aspects of bodies, and primarily with sense perceptible data. Scientific truth is arrived at by means of empirically or experimentally demonstrated facts. Its criterion of truth is always the evidence of the sense perceptible objects under consideration, although reason enters in to provide a framework for organizing and interpreting such data as are given by the senses. Unlike philosophy, it deals only with observable realities rather than with essential reality.

Since there are many aspects of human life which cannot be studied by scientific means, a knowledge of scientific psychology alone would give a very inadequate and limited understanding of human nature. On the other hand, psychology must take into account what science has contributed to our knowledge of learning, of growth, and of the development of attitudes, intelligence, and other psychological characteristics. Such scientific studies are necessary foundations upon which all modern applied psychology —whether in industry, social work, education, war, or medicine— is based.

III. APPARENT CONFLICT OF TRUTH

Truth is one. There can never be any conflict of truth derived from revelation, reason, or science.[6] It is not only unnecessary, but also undesirable for a Christian to shy away from the study of science lest it undermine his faith. The more truth we learn from any source, the more we know about the Author of truth. As Alfred Noyes has put it:

> What is all science then
> But Pure religion, seeking everywhere
> The eternal power that binds all worlds in one?
> It is man's age-long struggle to draw near
> His Maker, learn His thoughts, discern His law,
> A boundless task, in whose infinitude,
> As in the unfolding light and law of love,
> Abides our hope, and our eternal joy.[7]

At times, however, there may be an apparent discrepancy in the truth derived from these three sources. The discrepancy is really a spurious one. When such apparent conflicts occur the difficulty can usually be traced to one or more of the following factors:

---

[6] An excellent development of this idea is found in Christopher Dawson, *Progress and Religion*. In this book Dawson demonstrates that Christianity and science are not at all incompatible. The following excerpt illustrates his point of view:

It [Christianity] seeks not the destruction or the negation of nature, but its spiritualization and its incorporation into a higher order of reality. Consequently, the organization of the material world by science and law which has been the characteristic task of modern European culture is in no sense alien to the genius of Christianity. For the progressive intellectualization of the material world which is the work of European science, is analogous and complementary to the progressive spiritualization of human nature which is the function of the Christian religion. The future of humanity depends on the harmony and coördination of these two processes.—From *Progress and Religion*, by Christopher Dawson. Copyright, 1938, Sheed and Ward, Inc., New York.

[7] Alfred Noyes, *Watchers of the Sky* (New York, Frederick A. Stokes Company, 1922), pp. 228–229.

What is accepted as revelation may actually be a garbled or distorted version of truth. The following example illustrates the way in which truth may be distorted. Many people read Bibles and take the printed words literally. Some of these Bibles, however, have been translated inaccurately; others have been deliberately tampered with. Even when revelation is correctly given in a Bible, the person reading it may, because of his ignorance of biblical language, geography, and customs, misinterpret the passages. What this person accepts as revelation may not be revelation at all. It may be distorted in such a way as to give him a totally untrue impression.

What appears to be a sound philosophical inference may actually be a fallacy resulting from false reasoning. There are laws of logic which, if followed exactly, always yield valid truth, provided the basic premises are true. When these conditions hold, the human mind is capable of arriving at truth. Truth arrived at in this way is "perennial"; it is not altered by subsequent scientific findings. In this sense such truth is absolute.

In the history of philosophy we find many instances in which human reasoning has resulted in error. What has been accepted as truth, based on reason, may actually be a falsehood. The presence of such a falsehood does not indicate that man is incapable of arriving at truth by means of his reason. It merely indicates that the reasoner has either started with false premises or has erred in logic. The situation may be compared to that of a man who is trying to total his expenditures for a month. He takes up his receipts and puts in a column all of the figures given on the receipts. Obviously, if the amount written on one or more of the receipts is incorrect, the total figure will be incorrect. Or if, in adding the figures, a mistake in addition is made, the total figure will be wrong. The fact that such things happen should not blind us to the fact that, with correct receipts and with accurate addition, the right total could have been obtained. Similarly, the fact that men have arrived at false conclusions does not mean that with true premises and with correct reasoning they could not have arrived at true conclusions.

What appears to be a scientific truth may really be an error. Scientific findings are by their very nature tentative. Generalizations derived from them are never based upon the whole of reality but only upon that limited part of the material universe which has been subjected to investigation. Consequently, scientific "truth" is always relative and subject to change with further investigation.

When a scientific finding seems to be in conflict with a truth of revelation or of reason, one must carefully review the scientific generalization. The generalization may be correct in the light of evidence available at the time, but later investigation may show that it needs revision. In such cases it is necessary to suspend judgment until further data are available.

There are students who try to keep their knowledge of religion, of the humanities, and of science in separate mental compartments. In this way they hope to avoid mental conflict. Nothing could be more detrimental to their spiritual and intellectual development. The fully developed personality is the integrated personality. It sees life as "all of a piece." It apprehends all aspects of reality in their essential relationships and not as isolated bits of experience. The study of psychology, like every subject in the liberal arts curriculum, must be seen in its relation to the whole of life if it is to contribute toward the development of an integrated personality.

In the light of the above discussion it should be clear that the study of psychology involves the understanding of principles and the ability to apply these principles to new situations. It requires the mastery of certain tools of thought, such as logic and the scientific method. Above all, it presupposes an alertness to see the relation of psychology to everyday life and to other subjects in the college curriculum. Such study of necessity involves hard work; but the rewards accruing from such hard work so far outweigh the hardships involved that the burden becomes truly light.

IV. PSYCHOLOGY AND LIFE

In writing this book we have had in mind the words of Pope Pius XII, quoted at the beginning of this chapter. We have tried to present psychology in such a way as to make you conscious of "the harmonious coördination and subordination of the truths of the natural and supernatural order. . . ." If we have succeeded in attaining this objective, you will not now content yourself with an academic knowledge of psychology. You will ask yourself the questions: What can psychology contribute to my own life? What can I learn from psychology that will help me to understand my own personality and character? Will my life be richer as a result of such study? Will I have a deeper grasp of truth than I had before? Can I use psychology in everyday life—in my relations with other people and in my relations with God?

The answers you will give to the questions above will depend upon the depth of your understanding of psychology, and understanding is something deeper and more fundamental than mere knowledge. It is possible to know the facts and principles of psychology without necessarily being improved by such knowledge. A fact, to be significant, must be viewed not in isolation, but in relation to other facts. There are many facets to human life—scientific, philosophical, and theological. Some of these facets are on a natural plane; others are on a supernatural plane. For the Christian there is a supernatural life—a life illumined by the gifts of the Holy Ghost. There is a natural understanding to which man comes by his own unaided powers of intuition and reasoning. This understanding enables him to make practical judgments on a purely natural plane. If we lived only in a world of time and if everything ended with death, this natural understanding would be sufficient. But since man has a spiritual soul and is destined for eternal life, his understanding of this temporal world must go beyond what he can know by his own unaided reason. His understanding of natural phenomena and his right use of such knowledge will rest upon his ability to view this knowledge in the light of eternity. The ability to view all knowledge and all experience in the light of eternity reaches beyond his natural powers. It comes as a special gift from God; no one can acquire it for or by himself. "Understanding" and "Wisdom" are gifts of the Holy Ghost; they are pure gifts of God. We cannot merit them. But we can, unfortunately, place obstacles in the way of their reception.

Scientific and clinical psychology, in so far as their data are true, serve the practical function of all natural knowledge. Since the fall of Adam, man has had to acquire natural knowledge of many kinds in order to survive. Adam, in his original state of integrity, received from God the preternatural gift of a natural knowledge of the things that concerned his temporal life. That gift was taken away when Adam rebelled against God, and Adam and the countless generations of his descendants have waged a continuous war against ignorance in order to enjoy the good things of this earth and to provide the natural conditions of life upon which a supernatural life can be built. Supernatural grace of itself will not reap the wheat, grind the flour, or bake the bread. These things man has had to learn to do for himself. But "man does not live by bread alone"; his natural life must be elevated to a supernatural plane if he is to reach the fullness of life to which he is destined. All of man's natural knowledge, whether of agriculture, philosophy, or psychology, will contribute to his "fullness of life" only if it is viewed in the proper perspective—if it is interpreted in the light of eternal truths.

Science and philosophy study the natural man; they do not show us how man's nature is refined and elevated by supernatural grace. Yet when we are dealing with human beings, baptized in Christ, the natural man is a pure abstraction. The teacher, the clinical psychologist, the psychiatrist—all deal with the whole man, body and soul. But this whole man participates in the divine life of the Blessed Trinity. Supernatural grace, it is true, does not destroy nature; it refines and elevates it to a higher plane of being. All of man's life—his feelings, emotions, attitudes, thoughts, and actions—are thus raised to a new plane. The Christian, therefore, must not expect to understand human beings through science and philosophy alone. He must also know theology and understand the workings of grace in the human soul. The awareness of two facts, the freedom of the human will and the transcendent effect of supernatural grace, must permeate his scientific and clinical study of man. Only with this complete knowledge of man will his understanding be deep enough to meet the practical problems of everyday life in human society in such a way as to glorify God.

SUGGESTED READING

AGAR, W. M., *Catholicism and the Progress of Science* (New York, The Macmillan Company, 1940), Chapter I.
AGAR, W. M., *The Dilemma of Science* (New York, Sheed and Ward, Inc., 1941), Chapters I–III.
BRENNAN, R. E., *The Image of His Maker* (Milwaukee, Bruce Publishing Company, 1948).
DONCEEL, J. F., "What Kind of Science Is Psychology?" *New Scholasticism*, 19 (1945), 117–135.

GILL, H. V., S.J., *Fact and Fiction in Modern Science* (New York, Fordham University Press, 1944).
WELLMUTH, J., S.J., *The Nature and Origins of Scientism* (Milwaukee, Marquette University Press, 1944).

Index

Abnormalities, physical, 50-51
Abnormal psychology, 15
Abscissa, 274
Accident, effects on personality, 397-399; meaning of term, 6-7
Accommodation, 252
Achievement, intelligence and, 323-324
Achromatic experience, 136-138
Acquired characteristics, 74-75
ACTH, 156
Activity, meaning of term, 7
Adequate standardization, 321-322
Adequate stimulus, 127; for kinesthesis, 148; olfactory, 148; skin senses, 146
Adjustment, 213-214; atypical development and (see Atypical development); Christian goal, 215-216; compensation as, 209-210; disturbed person, 229; habit and, 231-233; identification as, 210-211; normative criterion, 215; pathological criterion, 214; patterns of behavior, 206-207; perception as a means toward (see Perception); projection as, 210; rationalization applied to, 207-208; at rational level, 220-224; regression as, 211; relationship of mind to body, 226-231; role of reasoning in, 230-231; sensitive level, 218-220; statistical criterion, 214-215; sublimation as, 212; supernatural level of, 224-226; thinking as (see Thinking); vegetative level, 216-218; withdrawal as a type of, 208-209
Adler, Alfred, 50-51, 633-636
Adolescence, 52, 469-471; adult relationships, 49, 51-52, 480-484; anatomical and physiological changes, 474; attitudes toward sex, 486; atypical rate of maturing, 478; basal metabolism and energy output, 475-477; body as the symbol of self, 479-480; boy-girl relationships, 484-488; circulatory system changes, 477-478; college students, 501-502; community role, 494-497; cultural effects on behavior, 386; educational opportunities, 500-501; occupational adjustment, 492-494; parental problems, 481-484; physical deviation, 478; physiological maturing, 473-475; prestige patterns, 488-490; religious outlook, 497-499; skeletal growth, 471-473; underprivileged, 499-500
Adrenal glands, 156-157
Adrenalin, 156, 157; emotions and, 188, 190-191
Adult biographies, 31-32
Adulthood, 575-576; adolescent relationships, 49, 51-52, 480-484; culture pattern and, 600-604; early maturity, 576-578; emotional stability and, 597-598; factors influencing characteristics, 59-65; happiest period in, 596-597; marital adjustments, 584-585; maturity, meaning, 598-599; place of work in, 585-596; sex differences, 579; woman's role, 579-584
Aerial perspective, 253
Æschylus, 632
Affective experiences, 183-184
Afferent neurons, 161
After-image, 139

INDEX

Age, behavior of women and, 601-602; changes in ability with, 604-606; culture pattern in relation to, 600-604; longevity, 610-611; mental disease and, 616; productivity and, 607-609
Agoraphobia, 373
Akenside, quoted, 159
Albanian babies study, 87-89
Alcohol, efficiency and, 593-595
Alcoholic psychoses, 362, 364
Alcoholics Anonymous, 379
Alcoholism, 378-380; conditioning cure, 278
Allergies, 227
Allers, Rudolph, 152n, 183, 635, 640
All-or-none law of nervous activity, 162
Allport and Vernon personality test, 545
Allport Ascendance-Submission Study, 520-521
American Catholic Psychological Association (ACPA), 641n
American Psychological Association, 641n
Amnesia, 300; hypnotic, 203
Analysis, 349
Andaman Islanders, 192
Androgens, 157
Anesthesia, 368; hypnotic, 203
Angell, James, 629
Animalism, 198
Animal research, 15, 197-199, 273, 276-280; application to human psychology, 291-294; insightful learning, 283-284, 285; latent learning, 289-290; maze learning, 281-283; negative adaptation, 284-285; trial-and-error, 280-283
Anthropology, 7
Anthropomorphism, 198
Anti-Semitism, 562
Antithesis, Darwin's theory of, 189
Anvil, 141
Anxiety states, 373-374
Apparent movement, 254
Applied psychology, 16
Apprehension, 243-244
Aptitude tests, 493-494
Aqueous humor, 131
Aquinas, St. Thomas, 5, 168n, 183, 218, 507; habits according to, 232-233; senses according to, 151-152 (see also Thomistic philosophy)
Archetypes, 636
Aristotle, 5, 151-152, 218, 347, 526, 541
Arithmetical mean, 335
Army Alpha test, 316, 325, 328; age ratings, 606
Army Beta test, 316
Army General Classification test, 316
Arteriosclerotic psychoses, 616
Arthritis, 227
Arthur Scale of Performance tests, 313-314, 317
Artistic ability, 465-466
Aspiration, level of, 512
Association, 346-347; primary laws of, 347, 526; secondary laws of, 526-527
Association areas, cortex, 172
Association fibers, 165
Associationists, British, 347, 526
Association neurons, 161
Asthenic body type, 542
Astigmatism, 139
Astronomy, 22
Athletic body type, 542
Atomistic approach to personality, 535
Attention, distraction and efficiency, 245-246; factors controlling, 247-248; fluctuation of, 246; process of, 241-242; stimuli arousing, 242-245; two-task, 245
Attitude, meaning of term, 522
Atypical development, 407-409; blindness, 393-394; feeblemindedness, 399-406; hearing defects, 394-396; illness and accident, 397-399; nature of a handicap, 411-412; orthopedic defects, 397; slow learner, 407; speech defects, 409-411
Audiometers, 396
Auditory area, cortex, 172
Auditory canal, 141
Auditory ossicles, 141
Auditory perception, 258-259
Auditory stimuli, 14
Autacoids, 154
Autobiographies, 31-32
Autonomic constitution, 85-86
Autonomic nervous system, 163, 176-178

INDEX

Autopsies, 169
Axons, 160-161, 162

Bacon, Francis, 624
Bacteriology, 22
Balzac, Honoré de, 267
Basal metabolism, 475-477
Basilar membrane, 141, 143-144
Baudelaire, Charles, 267
Beard, Mary R., 581
Beauchamp, Miss, 380
Beers, Clifford, 362
Behavior, abnormal, 378-380; analyzing, 308; antisocial, 568-570; basic drives in animals and humans, 195-199; cultural effects, 515; infant (*see* Infancy); nervous system and, 179; preschool child (*see* Preschool child); psychological measurement (*see* Intelligence tests)
Behaviorism, 40-42, 424-425, 624, 629-630, 637, 638
Benedict XIV, Pope, 370-371
Benzedrine sulfate, efficiency and, 596
Bernheim, on hypnosis, 200
Bernreuter Personality Inventory, 520
Bibliotherapy, 375-376
Binet, Alfred, 228, 310-311, 324; intelligence tests, 312-314
Binet-Simon Scale, 313
Binocular parallax, 250
Biographical studies, 31-32
Biological determinism, 91-92
Biological sciences, 8
Blackmore, quoted, 239
Bladder tension, conditioning, 278
Blame, 306, 512-514
Blindness, 393-394; obstacle-avoiding, 13-14
Blind spot of the eye, 133
Blood distribution, 188
Blood pressure, 188, 477-478
Blos, Peter, 479
Body build, 422-424
Bose, Sir Jagadis Chandra, 218-219
Boys, preadolescent, 466-468; prestige pattern, 490 (*see also* Adolescence *and* Children)
Braille, 393, 394
Brain, 164; brain stem, 173-174; cerebellum, 173; cerebral dominance, 172; cerebrum, 165-173; methods of studying, 167-171; operation on, 169, 178-179; size, 161; visual stimuli, 133-134
Brain stem, 173-174
"Brain waves," 170-171
Bray, volley theory, 143, 145
Breast feeding, 432, 444
Brigham, C. C., 328
Brightness, 136, 137
British associationist school, 347, 526
Broca, brain study, 169-170
Bronchial asthma, 227
Bronner, on child guidance, 499
Bühler Baby Tests, 296
Bühler, Charlotte, adulthood studies, 576-578; infant behavior studies, 425-426
Burks, Barbara, 383
Business, 11

Caffeine, efficiency and, 595-596
California Growth Study, 471, 475
California Guidance Study, 111
Canalization, 285-287
Cannon, emergency theory of emotions, 191; hunger experiments, 149; thirst experiments, 150
"Canon of parsimony," 198
Cardiac muscle, 153-154
Cartesian philosophy, 625
Case study method, 32-33
Catalepsy, hypnotic, 204
Catastrophe reaction, 427
Catatonic schizophrenia, 204, 364
Catholic Church, care in canonization, 370-371; future of psychology and, 641-642; reality and, 612-613; social class and, 57 (*see also* Christianity *and* Religion)
Cattell, J. M., 310
Central canal, 174
Central nervous system, 163, 164, 165-174
Central tendency, measure of, 36, 335
Cerebellum, 173
Cerebral cortex, 165-167
Cerebral hemispheres, 165
Cerebral palsy, 398
Cerebrospinal fluid, 174
Cerebrotonic person, 544

Cerebrum, 165
Character, influencing factors, 58, 59-65; meaning of term, 6; studies in development, 461-462
Character Education Inquiry, 461
Charcot, Jean Martin, 200, 633
Chesterton, G. K., 101
Child guidance clinics, 362
Childhood, Boyhood, Youth, Tolstoy, 479
Child psychology, 14-15
Children, adolescent (*see* Adolescence); adult personality and, 49-52; age pattern (*see* Age); atypical development (*see* Atypical development); canalized responses, 286-287; common behavior problems, 445; comparative studies, 82-86; discipline, 109-110; factors influencing characteristics, 59-65; family attitudes, 109; growth rhythms, 454-455; illegitimate, 113; institutional care, 112-113; intelligence tests and (*see* Intelligence tests); marginal conflicts, 100-101; maturation and learning, 87-90; mental disease, 381-382; middle childhood (*see* Middle childhood); notion of self, 511-513, 515; overprotection, 107-108; parental overambition, 109; parental rejection, 105-107; preadolescent, 466-468; prejudice in, 564-567; preschool period (*see* Preschool children); religious education, 446-447; rivalry for the affection, 108-109; sibling relationships, 111; social class differences, 444-445; social significance of, 52
Chimpanzee, visual sensation experiment, 257
Chinese culture, 601
Choroid coat, 131
Christianity, 115; adjustment goal, 216, 234-236; apparent conflict of truth, 652-654; attitude toward schools of psychology, 638-640; dominant passion principle, 634; faith, 647-648; insight into personality problems, 391; interior life interpreted, 224-226; man's relationship to man, 548-549; meaning of maturity, 599; preparation for death, 611-613; preparation for old age, 617-618; social class and, 57; social psychology and, 571 (*see also* Catholic Church *and* Religion)
Chromatic experience, 136-138
Chromosomes, 66
Chronological age (CA), 322-323
Chronoscope, 24-25
Ciliary muscles, 131
Circumstantiality, 614
Claustrophobia, 373
Clinical method, 32-33
Clinical psychology, 15-16
Closure, law of, 261
Clouding of consciousness, 241
Cochlea, 141
Co-conscious personality, 380
Coghill, G. E., 422
Cold, common, 227
College students, adjustment problems, 501-503; characteristics, 501; prejudice among, 562-564
Color blindness, 140
Coma, 241
Comics, personality influence, 122-123
Commissural fibers, 165
Common sense, 151; nature of, 643-645
Communication, group, 552
Communism, 57, 612
Community (*see* Environment)
Comparative psychology, 15
Completion tests, 296
Compensation, 209-210
Complex, emotional, 527-528
Concept formation, experiment on, 352-353; meaning of term, 351
Conception, 65
Concussion, 242
"Conditioned" fears, 28
Conditioned reflex, experiments, 276-280
Conditioning, 276-280
Cones, 130; color and, 134-135
Confession, children's first, 459-460
Conjunctiva, 131
Connecting neurons, 161
Conrad, H. S., 605-606
Conscious, Freudian, 632
Consciousness, nature of, 241; structuralism and, 628-629
Constancy, perceptual, 255-256
Constants, psychological, 311-312

INDEX

Constitutional psychopathic states, 376-378
Content psychology, 628
Contingent association, 347
Control, use in scientific experiment, 26
Controlled association, 346-347
Controlled experiment, 24
Convergence, 252
Conversions, crowd, 553
Cornea, 131
Corpus callosum, 165
Correlation coefficient, 37, 337-338; in family resemblance study, 80; of identical twins, 83
Correspondences, Baudelaire, 267-268
Cortex, localization of function in, 171-173
Cortin, 157
Cortisone, 156
Counseling and Psychotherapy, Rogers, 405
Cranium, 164
Creative thought, 356-360
Cretinism, 400-401
Crime, 568-570
Crippled children, 397
Critique of Pure Reason, Kant, 608
Cross-eye, 139-140
Cross-sectional methods, 53-54
Crowd behavior, 553-554
Crush, adolescent, 497
C.S.C. Religious Attitude Scale, 522-525
Cultural anthropology, 7-8
Culture, 57; adolescence and, 470-471; adult-adolescent relationships, 480-484; behavior dictated by, 515; child-training differences due to, 445-446; comics as influence, 122-123; emotional expression and, 191-192; family influence, 102-113; influence on personality development, 95-100, 549-551; learning and, 95-100; marginal aspects, 100-101; mental disorder and, 361-362, 385-390; movie influence, 120-122; "norm" concept, 387-388; participant observer studies, 556; patterns in relation to age, 600-604; radio and, 118-120; role of the school, 114-118; role of woman in, 579-584; stereotypes, 565; television and, 118-120; tested intelligence differences affected by, 327-330 (*see also* Environment)
Culture epoch theory, 420
Cytoplasm, 65-66

Daltonism, 140
Darwin, Charles, 29; evolution theory, 639; principles for interpreting emotional behavior, 188-189
Dawson, Christopher, 652n
Dax, 353
Daydreaming, 208-209
Deafness, 141, 144, 394-396
Dearborn, growth study, 340
Death, 611-613
Defense reactions, 206-207
Degeneracy studies, 79
Delayed reaction, 277
Delinquency, 568-570; adolescent, 495-497; identification with older delinquents, 498-499
Delirium tremens, 267, 380
De Lubac, Henri, 548
Demosthenes, 209-210
Dendrites, 160-161, 162
Dependent variable, in scientific experiments, 24-29
Depth, physiological cues, 250-252; psychological cues, 253-255
Depth psychology, personality, 536
Descartes, René, 625, 644
De Servorum Dei Beatificatione, Pope Benedict XIV, 370-371
Determinism, 91-93
Developmental psychology, 14, 45-53; applications of, 46-47; cross-sectional, 53-54; interaction of influences, 59-65; longitudinal, 53-54; professions and, 52-53; social class and, 54-57
Developmental quotient, 422
Dewey, John, 343, 629
Dictionary of Psychology, Warren, 192
Differential psychology, 15
Digestion, emotion and, 188
Diogenes, 644
Discipline, 109-110
Distance, physiological cues, 250-252; psychological cues, 253-255

Disturbed person (*see* Mental disorders)
Dostoevsky, Feodor, quoted, 377-378
Double images, 252
Draw-a-Man test, 328
Dream analysis, 528-530, 636, 640
Drives, 219, 273, 292; significance of studies, 195-199
Du Noüy, P. Lecomte, 609
Duration, of sensation, 129

Ear, 140-142
Ebbinghaus, memory study, 295-297
Ecstasy, 369, 370
Ectomorphy, 543
Education, adult, 618; differential opportunities, 500-501; handedness and, 408-409; readiness for school, 454-458; religious, 446-447; whole child concept, 448-450 (*see also* Schools *and* Teachers)
Effectors, 152-158
Efferent neurons, 161
Efficiency, effect of drugs and, 593-596; environmental conditions and, 591-593; fatigue and, 590-591; length of working period, 591; rate of work and, 593; repetitive activities, 589; sleep and, 592; time factor, 589; work habits, 588-589
Ego, child's concept of self, 462-464; Freudian, 632-633; notion of others, 513-515; notion of self, 511-513
Ego-involved situations, 513
Eidetic imagery, 268
Electrical stimulation studies, 170
Electrical theory of nerve impulse, 163
Electroencephalograph, 9, 170-171
Elements of Psychophysics, Fechner, 625, 626
Eliot, T. S., 415, 448
Embryo, environmental influences, 71-74
Eminent men studies, 77
Emotions, 183-184; adolescent, 479-480; Cannon's emergency theory, 191; Darwin's theory of, 188-189; expressive reactions, 191-192; infant development, 426-427, 428-430, 431-434; James-Lange theory, 190-191; mood cycles, 192-194; motivation and, 194-206; physiological accompaniments, 185-188; reading disability and disturbance of, 452-454; role of, 184-188, 298-301; stuttering and, 409-411
Encephalitis lethargica, 398
Endocrine glands, 154, 614
Endomorphy, 543
Environment, 58; adjustment to (*see* Adjustment); change in, as therapy, 374; child training differences due to, 445-446; community adjustment of adolescent and, 494-497; effects of abnormal embryonic, 71-74; influence on mental health, 383-385; institutional, 112-113; intelligence level and, 81; interaction with heredity and free choice, 59-65; learning and, 96-99, 272; methods of study, 75-86; perception influenced by, 257; personality development and, 95-100 (*see also* Culture)
Epilepsy, 362
Equilibrium, 140, 149
Eskimo language, 257
Essence, meaning of term, 7
Estimative sense, 151
Estrogens, 157
Ethics, motive and, 220; science and, 12-13 (*see also* Religion)
Ethnic groups, adolescent acceptance and, 492; child training differences, 445; mental disease and, 361-362; physical differences, 424; tested intelligence relationships, 327-330
Evans, pituitary grafts, 156
Exceptional child, 327
Excessive activity, Darwin's theory of, 189
Exhaustion, 371
Existentialism, 93*n*, 628
Experiment, scientific, 24-29
Experimental extinction, 276
Experimental psychology, 13-14
Expressive therapies, 375
External senses, 151-152
Exteroceptive senses, 151
Exteroceptors, 128

INDEX

Extirpation studies, 167-169
Extra-sensory perception, 269-271
Extroversion, 545
Eye, reading movements, 451; structure and function of, 129-133

Factor analysis, of intelligence tests, 331
Failure, 463
Fairy-tales, 636
Faith, 647-648
Family, adolescent acceptance and, 491; delinquency and, 496; emotional blocks stemming from, 452-453; personality development and, 95-100, 102-113; personality resemblances, 538-539 (*see also* Adolescence, Children, *and* Parents)
Family history studies, 76-79; differing degrees of biological relationships, 80-86
Farm children, 445-446, 496-497
Farsightedness, 139
Fatigue, 162, 589-591
Fear, 428-430
Fechner, Gustav, 311, 625, 626
Fechner's Law, 626-627
Feeblemindedness, 63, 327, 443; causes of, 406; clinical types, 400-402; delinquency and, 569-570; diagnosis of, 402-404; extent of, 399; legally recognized types, 399-400; meaning of term, 400; parental acceptance of, 405-406; treatment of, 404
Feeling, 183-184
Feré, hypnotism studies, 228
Fertilization, 68
Field-expectation theory of learning, Tolman's, 290-291
Field study, 29-30
Fissure, 165
Fleege, Urban, 484
Fluctuation, phenomenon of, 246-247
Forgetting, 297-301, 303, 509-510; Ebbinghaus' curve of, 297; role of the emotions in, 298-301
Formal discipline doctrine, 288
Form constancy, 256
Foster children studies, 81
Fovea, 131

Franz, brain studies, 167-168
Free association, 346-347, 526-528, 633, 640
Free association tests, 187
Free choice, 58, 90-93; habits and, 233; interaction with heredity and environment, 59-65; relation to personality problems, 390-391
Frequency theory, Rutherford's, 143, 144-145
Freud, Sigmund, 207, 229, 385, 526; Christian attitude toward, 639-640; dream analysis, 529-530; method of, 633; Œdipus complex theory, 426-427; psychology summarized, 631-633; unconscious motivation theory, 199
Frontal lobe, cortex, 165
Frustration-aggression hypothesis, 230-231
Functionalism, 624, 629, 637, 639
Functional psychoses, 364-366
Furry object fear, 28-29

Galileo, 9
Gall, Franz Joseph, 516
Galton, Sir Francis, 77, 312, 357
Galton whistle, 312
Galvanic skin response (GSR), 186-187
Ganglia, 176
Garrigou-Lagrange, R., 224-225, 370
Generalization theory of learning, 288
General psychology, 13
Genes, 67
Genetic psychology, 14
Genius, 357; meaning of term, 326-327
George Washington Social Intelligence Test, 521-522
Germ cells, maturation, 67-68; reproductive process, 65-71
Gerontology, 47
Gesell, Arnold, 73, 87, 422
Gestalt psychology, 332, 624, 630-631, 638; meaning of, 260-261
Gifted children, 78-79, 327, 443, 464
Gilson, E., 648
Girls, preadolescent, 466-468; prestige patterns, 489-490 (*see also* Adolescence *and* Children)
Gladstone, William E., 227

Glands, 154-158; abnormalities of human development and, 156; emotion and, 185, 188
Global approach to personality, 535
Glove anesthesia, 368
Gluecks, the, child guidance work, 499
Goals, learning directed toward, 99
Goddard, delinquency study, 79; intelligence tests, 313
Godwin, Mary Wollstonecraft, 582
Goldstein, Kurt, 354, 427
Gonadal hormones, 474
Gonadotropic hormone, 474
Gonads, 157
Good continuation, law of, 260-261
Graphology, 518-519, 530
Grasping reflex, 419
Gray matter, 161
Group, communication, 552; crowd behavior, 553-554; leaders, 556-558; psychology of the, 551-552; rumor mongering, 554-556
Group dynamics, 551-552
Group therapy, 375
Growth, adolescent skeletal, 471-473; patterns of, 340-341; pubertal spurt in, 469-470; studies of, 53-54
Growth hormone, 156
Guess-Who test, 488-490
Gundlach, R. H., 597
Gustatory area, cortex, 172
Gustatory sense, 146-147
Gyrus, 165

Habit, adjustment and, 231-233; establishing of, 290-291; meaning of term, 168n, 232-233; physical weaknesses and, 51 (see also Behavior)
Habit interference, 287
Habitual attention, 243
Habitus apoplectus, 541
Habitus phthisicus, 541
Half-vision, 140
Hall, G. Stanley, 34, 419-420
Hallucinations, 265, 267, 592
Halo effect, 524-525
Hammer, 141
Handedness, 407-409
Handwriting, personality expressed by, 530-531

Hartshorne and May studies, 526
Harvard growth study, 340
Harvard Psychological Clinic, 525
Hathaway, S. R., 538
Hanfmann-Kasanin test, 353-355
Hay fever, 227
Healy, child guidance work, 499
Hearing, 152; age and, 605; ear make-up, 140-142; infant, 416-417; stimulus for, 143; theories of, 143
Hebephrenic schizophrenia, 364
Heisenberg, principle of uncertainty, 222
Helmholtz, on ideas, 359; resonance theory, 143-144
Henning, odors classified, 148
Heredity, 58; acquired characteristics and, 74-75; alterations caused by abnormal environment, 71-74; biological processes of, 65-71; difficulties in human studies, 75-76; feeblemindedness and, 406; interaction with environment and free choice, 59-65; methods of study, 76-86; mental disease and, 383-385
High blood pressure, 227
Higher order conditioning, 279-280
Highlights, 253
Hippocrates, 541
Holistic approach to personality, 535
Homeostasis, 217-218
Hopi culture, 329
Hopi Indian children studies, 90
Hopkins, G. M., 361
Hormones, 154, 474
Hue, 136-137
Hull, C. L., hypnosis studies, 204-205
Hull's stimulus-response theory of learning, 290-291
Humanities, 8
Humoral theory of nerve impulse, 163
Hunger, 149-150
Hydrocephalic, the, 402
Hypermnesia, 300
Hyperopia, 139
Hypnoanalysis, 204
Hypnosis, 200-206; attitude of the Church toward, 206; body-soul unity evidenced by, 228; test medium, 190

INDEX

Hypochondriasis, 373-374
Hypothalamus, 173-174
Hypothesis, 23, 32
Hysteria, 367-371; meaning of term, 371
Hysterical anesthesia, 368

Id, Freudian, 632-633
Ideas, 347
Identical twins studies, 83-86
Identification, 210-211
Idiots, 400, 404
Illegitimacy, 113
Illness, effects on personality, 397-399
Illusions, 265-267
Imagination, 151
Imbeciles, 400, 404
Implicit speech, 630
Incentive, meaning of term, 220
Independent variable, 24-29
Indian girl, wolf cub, 73-74
Indians, intelligence testing study, 328-330; northwest coast, 386-387; stuttering nonexistent among, 410
Individualism, 581-584
Individual psychology, school of, 634
Industry, 11
Infancy, adult personality and, 49-52; emotional development, 426-427, 428-430; feeding, 432; intellectual development, 430; motor behavior, 421-422; physical development, 422-424; physiological and psychological needs, 431-434; reflex, 418-421; sensory reactions, 415-418; sex differences, 430-431; simple resistance, 427; social development, 424-428; toilet training, 431, 432-433, 444, 445 (see also Children)
Infant biographies, 31
Infections, 50
Injuries, 50
Inkblot personality tests, 333, 532-534, 563
Inner ear, 141
Innervation, 153
Insight, 349
Insightful learning, 283-284, 285
Inspiration, 356-360
Intellect, 308

Intelligence, 308-311; age and, 605-606; attributes of, 332-333; bi-factor theory, 330-331; brain size and, 161; crippled child, 397; disease and, 398; environment influence, 81; ethnic aspects, 327-330; general intelligence concept, 310-311; group differences, 54; infant development, 430; language development index, 443; mental set, 242; multi-factor theory, 330-331; personality and, 333-334; population distribution, 326; preschool development, 440-443; social significance, 309-310; tests for (see Intelligence quotient and Intelligence tests)
Intelligence quotient (IQ), 308-311, 323; achievement and, 323-324; delinquency and, 569-570; development of tests, 310-314; feeblemindedness and, 403-404; infancy tests, 422; interpretation of, 326; meaning of term, 308; musical sensitivity and, 464-465; occupational level and, 325; preschool children, 443; school progress and, 324-325; values of, 309-310 (see also Intelligence and Intelligence tests)
Intelligence tests, attributes of intelligence, 332-333; cultural influences, 320; development of individual, 311-314; factor analysis, 331; factors influencing, 328-330; diagnosing feeblemindedness, 402-404; Gestalt point of view, 332; group, 315; infant, 422; intelligence quotient and, 322-323; irregularities, 339-341; linguistic, 316; mental age and, 322; nature of, 314-315; objectivity, 321; performance, 316-317; person-to-person, 315-316; physically handicapped child and, 398-399; reading ability essential to, 451-452; reliability, 320-321; rural and urban differences, 330; statistical terms clarified, 334-339; validity criterion, 317-320 (see also Intelligence and Intelligence quotient)
Intensity, 129
Internal senses, 151-152

Interoceptive senses, 151
Interoceptors, 128
Interposition, 253
Interrupted learning, 298
Introduction to Comparative Psychology, Morgan, 198
Introspection, 40-42, 630
Introspectionism, 628
Introversion, 545
Inventories, 33
Involuntary attention, 243
Involutional melancholia, 363-364
Involutional psychoses, 616
Iris, 130
Isabelle, case history of, 89

Jaensch, on eidetic images, 268
James, William, 463-464, 624, 629
James-Lange theory of emotions, 190-191
Janet, hysteria studies, 367-368
Japanese, emotional expression, 192
Jews, 562
Johns Hopkins Hospital, 435
Johnson, Wendell, 409-411
Jones, H. E., 605-606
Journal of Parapsychology, 270
Judd, generalization theory, 288
Judgment, 344; central tendency of, 524, 525
Jung, Carl, 633-636, 640; personality types, 545-546
Juvenile delinquency, 495-499, 569-570

Kallikak, Martin, 79
Kallman, Franz J., 384-385
Kant, Immanuel, 608
Keeley cure, 379
Kelley, Father Gerald, 487-488
Kinesthetic sense, 148-149
Kinnebrook incident, 9
Kleptomania, 372
Knowledge, nature of, 648-651
Koffka, Kurt, 332, 631
Köhler, Wolfgang, 283, 631
Korsikoff's syndrome, 380
Kraepelin, mental disease studies, 385
Kretschmer, body types study, 542
Kuder-Richardson formula, 523

Kuhlman-Binet test, 399

Lamarck theory of characteristics, 74
Landis, J. T., 596-597
Language, child development in, 438-439, 443; deafness and, 394-396; influences on perception, 257
Language age (LA), 457
Lashley, brain studies by, 167-168
Latent learning, 99, 289-290
Laughter, significance of, 192
Law, 10, 24
Leadership, group, 556-558
Learning, canalization, 285-287; conditioning problems, 276-280; culture pattern and, 95-100; curve of, 273-276; distributed practice, 301; factors influencing, 95-96; forgetting and, 297-301; goal-directed, 99-100; informal, 118-123; insightful, 283-284; intention important, 301-302; interpolated, 303-304; knowledge of results, 304-307; latent, 99, 289-290; maze device, 281-283; meaningfulness of material, 297; memory, 294-307; nature of, 272-273; negative adaptation, 284-285; praise and blame in, 306; rational, 285; recitation in, 302-303; relationship between maturation and, 86-90; reward and punishment, 306; slow learners, 407; tools used in studying, 273; transfer of, 287-289; trial-and-error, 280-283; validity of animal-research generalizations, 291-294; whole, 302 (*see also* Education *and* School)
Learning curve, 273-276
Left-handedness, 407-409
Lehman, H. C., 608-609
Leipzig University, 40, 625
Lens, 130-131
Leonard, William Ellery, 48
Lewin, K., 116, 117, 631n
Libido, 631-632
Life history methods, 31-32
Light, theories of, 135
Liminal stimulus, 159
Linear perspective, 253
Linguistic tests, 316
Lippitt, R., 116

INDEX

Lip-reading, 395
Localization, 166
Logos, 5
Lombroso, criminologist, 516
Longevity, 610-611
Longitudinal methods, 53-54
Lourdes, cures at, 368
Love, 428-429, 485, 487
Lower class, 55

McKay, H. D., 495-496
Macrocephaly, 161, 402
Magic, 386
Maier, N. R. F., 345, 349-351
Malnutrition, 49
Man (*see* Society)
Manic-depressive psychosis, 194, 365-366
Manipulative development, 421-422
Manoptoscope, 408
Marginal man, 100-101
Marriage, criteria for successful, 486-488; culturally accepted attitudes, 102-105; factors favorable to, 584-585; old-age problems, 614-616 (*see also* Family *and* Parents)
Mathematics, 9
Maturation, 60-61; germ cells, 67-68; relationship between learning and, 86-90; studies of sequence, 87-90
Maturity, early, 576-578; meaning of, 598 (*see also* Adulthood)
Maugham, Somerset, 50
May studies, with Hartshorne, 526
Maze learning, 281-283
Mead, Margaret, 580
Measurement, psychological (*see* Intelligence)
Measurement of Intelligence, The, Terman, 333
Measures, methods of using, 36-40
Median, 335
Medicine, 10
Medulla oblongata, 173
Memory, 151, 294, 347, 509-510; distributed practice, 301; forgetting and, 297-301; intention important, 301-302; interpolated learning, 303-304; interrupted learning, 298; methods of studying, 295-297; recitation in, 302-303; reminiscence, 298; role of emotions in, 298-301; rhythm and, 298
Menarchy, 470
Mendel, Gregor, 29, 71
Mendel's law, 71
Menopause, 614
Menstruation, 227, 469-470
Mental age (MA), 312-313, 322-323, 457
Mental disorders, alcoholism, 378-380; childhood, 381-382; conflicting value patterns, 388; constitutional psychopathic states, 376-378; cultural influences, 385-390; exciting causes, 362; extent of problem, 361-362; functional psychoses, 364-366; inheritance of, 383-385; in later maturity, 616; mental hygiene, 362-363; migration and uprootedness threat, 389-390; multiple personality, 380-381; organic psychoses, 363-364; overstimulation threat, 388; predisposing causes, 362; psychoneuroses, 366-376; relation of free will to, 390-391; unrealistic goals threat, 388-389
Mental telepathy, 270
Merrill, Maud, 314
Mesmer, Franz Anton, 200
Mesmerism, 200
Mesomorphy, 543
Metabolism, 217
Method, scientific, 22-24
Microcephaly, 63, 402
Middle childhood, 448-450; acquisition of skills, 457-458; artistic talent, 465; basic developmental tasks, 450; capacity for self-criticism, 456-457; character development studies, 461-462; developing concept of self, 462-464; fortitude development, 458; musical talent, 464-465; number concept task, 454; physical growth and development, 449-450; reading task, 451-454, 457; right conscience development, 458; school readiness, 454-458; social interests, 458; spiritual values, 459-461; work maturity, 455-456; writing task, 454
Middle class, 55

670 INDEX

Middle ear, 141
Mid-parent, 80
Miles, C. C., 584, 605-606
Miles, W. R., 605-606
Military science, 11-12
Miraculous cures, 368-371
Mirror writing, 409
Modality, 129
Mode, 335
Mongolism, 401-402
Monotony, 589
Mood, 192-194
Moore, T. V., 376
Moral defectives, 400
Morgan, Lloyd, 198
Morgan, M., 596-597
Moro embracing reflex, 419
Moron, 400, 404
Moth environment experiment, 73
Motivation, 96, 292; basic human needs, 194-195; goals, 99-100; studies of basic drives, 195-199; unconscious, 199
Motive, 272; meaning of term, 219-220
Motor ability, 421-422, 605
Motor area, cortex, 171
Motor neurons, 161
Mouroux, Jean, 3, 393
Movies, personality influences, 120-122
Multiple personality, 380-381
Muscles, 152-154; attention set, 242; emotion and, 185
Musical abilities, 464-465
Myelin sheath, 161
Myopia, 139
Myrdal, G., 559
Mystical phenomena, 368-371
Myxedema, 401

Narcissism, 632
Nature, meaning of term, 7
Navajo culture, 329
Nazi government, morality trials, 555; persecutions, 230
Nearsightedness, 139
Necker cube, 246
Negative adaptation, 284-285
Negatively accelerated learning curve, 274-275
Negro, 559; child training, 445
Neonate (*see* Infancy)

Nerve cells, 160-161
Nerve impulses, 133-134
Nerves, 162; brain, 165; tracing nerve fibers, 170
Nervous breakdown, 502
Nervous system, 159-160; autonomic, 176-178; central somatic, 164-175; classifying, 163; nature of nerves, 162; nerve impulses, 162; peripheral somatic, 175-176; spinal cord, 174-175; synapse, 162-163; tissue, 160-161
Neurasthenia, 373
Neuroglia cells, 161
Neuron, 160-161, 162
Neuroses, alcoholic, 378-379; compulsive, 371-373; experimental, 277; obsessive, 371
Nodding, significance of, 191-192
Non-striated muscles, 153
Novum Organum, Bacon, 624
Noyes, Alfred, 127, 213, 652
Nucleus, 65-66
Nursing, 10-11
Nutrition, 49

Obesity, 480
Objective observation, 40-42
Object-love, 632
Observation, 20-21, 22-23, 40-42
Obstruction box test, Warden's, 195-197
Occipital lobe, cortex, 167
Occupational adjustment (*see* Adjustment *and* Work)
Occupational therapy, 375
Œdipus complex, 426-427, 632
Œdipus Rex, Æschylus, 632
Of Human Bondage, Maugham, 50
Old age, adjustment problems, 611-616; culture pattern, 602-604; nature of, 609-610; preparation for, 617-618 (*see also* Age)
Olfactory area, cortex, 172
Olfactory sense, 147-148
Ontogeny, 420
Ordinate, 274
Organic senses, 149-151
Organ inferiority, 50
Organismic age (OA), 457
Organ of Corti, 141
Otis intelligence test, 605, 606
Outer ear, 141

INDEX

Oval window, 141
Ovaries, 157
Overlearning, 297
Overprotection, 105, 107-108
Ovum, 61; in reproductive process, 65-71

Pain, in infancy, 418
Paired associates test, 295
Palmar reflex, 419
Palmistry, 518
Paralysis, 171
Paranoia, true, 365
Paranoid schizophrenia, 365, 386-387
Parents, 102-109; desire to absorb child's personality, 482-483; discipline attitudes, 483-484; overambitious, 481-482; overlax, 484; religious and moral responsibilities, 458-461 (*see also* Adulthood, Children, *and* Family)
Paresis, 364
Parietal lobe, cortex, 165
Park, R. E., 100
Partial correlation formula, 339
Participant observer, 556
Passion, 183-184
Pavlov, Ivan, conditioned reflex experiments, 276-280
Payne Fund studies, 120-122
Péguy, Charles, 59
Perception, 129, 508-509, 510, 626, 638; attention essential to, 241-248; characteristics of, 239-241; context influences, 264; eidetic imagery, 268; extra-sensory, 269-271; hallucinations, 265-267; illusions, 265-267; individual determinants, 263-264; past experience influences, 261-262; patterned, 260-261; prejudices and, 566; preschool child, 443-444; sound, 258-259; synesthesia, 267-268; time, 269; universal determinants, 262-263; visual, 248-257
Performance tests, 313, 316
Peripheral nervous system, 163, 175-176
Persecution delusions, 592
Person, meaning of term, 6, 507
Personality, 58, 95-96, 627; adjustment and (*see* Adjustment); atomistic approach, 535; childhood development (*see* Childhood); comics as influence, 122-123; conditioning influences, 279; cultural influence, 57, 549-551; developmental psychology, 57; developmental study of, 46; disorders of (*see* Mental disorders); ego and, 511-515; family influence, 51-52, 102-113; family resemblances, 538-539; four temperaments theory, 541-542; glands and, 537-538; holistic approach, 535; infant training and, 431-434; interaction of influencing factors, 59-65; Jung's system of types, 545-546; Kretschmer's body types, 542; learning and memory in relation to, 307; life cycle, 49-52; marginal aspects, 100-101; meaning of term, 6, 508; measurement of intelligence and, 333-334; methods of studying (*see* Personality study); moral standards and, 461-462; motivation in growth, 194-206; movie influence, 120-122; patterns of adjustment, 48, 206-212; psychological wholeness, 507-510; radio and, 118-120; role of the school, 114-118; Sheldon body types, 543-545; social class influence, 56; social development in infancy, 424-428; Spranger's theory, 545; television and, 118-120; type theories, 539-541
Personality study, 515-516; astrology, 519; dream analysis, 526, 528-530; expressive techniques, 530-531; free association, 526-528; graphology, 518-519; limits inherent in, 535-537; palmistry, 518; paper and pencil tests, 520-525; phrenology, 516; physiognomy, 516-518; projective techniques, 530-535; psychological methods, 519; rating scales, 524-525; situation tests, 525-526
Peterson, R. C., 120
Phenomenological self, 512
Philosophy, 645-646, 648-651; doctoral degree in, 325; human personality and, 17; reasoning errors in, 653; senses and, 151-152
Phobias, 373

Phrenology, 516
Phylogeny, 420
Physical determinism, 92-93
Physical sciences, 9
Physiognomica, Aristotle, 541
Physiognomy, 516-518
Physiological limit of learning, 276
Physiological psychology, 16
Physiological zero, 146
Physique and Character, Kretschmer, 542
Pineal gland, 157
Pintner-Paterson tests, 313-314
Pitch, 144
Pituitary gland, 154-156, 474-475
Pius XII, Pope, 643, 654
Plantar reflex, 418-419
Plateaus of learning, 275-276
Pneumograph, 185-186
Porterfield, A. L., 495
Porteus Maze Tests, 317
Possessed, The, Dostoevsky, 377-378
Post-hypnotic suggestion, 200, 203
Post-mortem studies, 169
Potlatch, 386
Pragnanz, law of, 260
Praise, 306, 512-514
Prayer, childhood value, 459-460
Preadolescence, 466-468
Preconscious, 632
Prefrontal lobotomy, 178-179
Prejudice, causes of, 561; college students and, 562-564; elimination of, 567; nature of, 558-559; origin in children, 564-567; tabloid thinking, 559-561; unresolved personality conflicts and, 561-562
Preschool children, common behavior problems, 437; language development, 438-439; mental development, 440-443; perception, 443-444; sex awareness, 435-437; social development, 434-435 (*see also* Children *and* Education)
Pre-natal influences, 61-63; abnormal environment, 71-74
Prescott, D. A., 496
Preventive therapy, 374
Prince, Morton, 380-381
Problem box, 280-281
Problem solving, 348-351
Productivity, age relationship, 602-609
Professions, IQ Averages, 325

Progress and Religion, Dawson, 652
Projection, 157, 210
Projection fibers, 165
Projective techniques, 530-535
Proprioceptive senses, 151
Proprioceptors, 128
Protestant reformation, results, 581-582
Proximity, law of, 260
Pseudo-sciences, 516-519
Psychasthenia, 371-373
Psyche, 5
Psychiatry, 8
Psychoanalysis, 624, 631-636, 638, 639
Psychogalvanometer, 9, 187
Psychological determinism, 92
Psychological measurement (*see* Intelligence)
Psychological zero, 146
Psychology, as a profession, 624-625; associated studies, 7-9; behaviorism, 629-630; Catholic criticism of, 641-642; contribution by schools of, 637-638; limitations, 536-537; ethical considerations, 12-13; field theories, 631; Freudian psychoanalysis, 631-636; functionalism, 629; Gestalt, school of, 630-631; historical development, 40-42, 625-628; meaning of term, 5-6; offshoots of Freudian, 633-636; practical applications of, 10-12; scientific approach, 20-21; scope of, 3-5; senses and, 151-152; sources of understanding, 16-19; structuralism, 624, 628-629, 637, 638; subdivisions, 13-16; theoretical framework, 623-624; value of study of, 654-656
Psychology of Character, Allers, 635
Psychology from the Standpoint of a Behaviorist, Watson, 629-630
Psychoneurosis, bibliotherapy, 375-376; conversion neurosis, 367-371; environmental therapy, 374; expressive therapies, 375; group therapy, 375; hypochondriasis, 373; hysteria, 367-371; nature of, 366; neurasthenia, 373; occupational therapy, 375; preventive therapy, 374; psychasthenia, 371-373; psychotherapy, 374-375; types of, 366-374

Psychopathic deviate, 376-378
Psychopathology of Everyday Life, Freud, 199
Psychophysical measurements, 311
Psychophysics, 508, 637
Psychoses, functional, 364-366; organic, 363-364
Psychosomatic disease, 226-231
Psychosurgery, 178-179
Psychotherapy, 374-375, 638
Puberty (*see* Adolescence)
Pubescent-adolescent growth cycle, 469
Pulse rate, 188, 477-478
Punishment, 110, 306
Pupillary reflex, 277-278
Purkinje phenomenon after dark adaptation, 416
Pyknic body type, 542
Pyramidal cells, 171
Pyromania, 372

Quantum theory of light, 135
Quartile deviation, 336-337
Questionnaire, 33-35

Rabbit, fear experiment, 28-29
Radio, personality influences, 118-120
Rage, 428-429
Random sample, 39
Range, 336
Rating scales, 33, 524-525
Rationalization, 207-208
Rational learning, 285
Rational level, adjustments at the, 220-224
Reactive depression, 373
Reading, 451-454, 457; disability, 451-454
Reading age (RA), 457
Reasoning, 344-345, 648
Recall tests, 295-296
Recapitulation theory, 419-420
Receptors, 128, 159; attention set, 242; auditory, 141; retina, 130; smell, 148; taste, 147
Recitation, 302-303
Recognition tests, 296
Reconditioning, 28-29
Redintegration, 256-257
Reflex arc, 174

Reflexes, in infancy, 418-421; smiling, 424-425
Regression, 211, 632; hypnotic, 203; movements, 451
Reinforcement, 276
Rejection, 105-107
Reliability coefficient, 320
Religion, C.S.C. Religious Attitude Scale, 522-525; education in, 446-447; indivisible nature of the soul, 381; Jung's view on, 636; marriage relationship and, 103; school training, 114-115 (*see also* Catholic Church, Christianity, *and* Philosophy)
Reminiscence, 298
Renaissance, 581
Repression, 632
Reproduction, biological processes of, 65-71; heredity and, 61-63
Reproductive maturity, 469
Research, 22
Resonance theory, Helmholtz, 143-144
Respiration, emotion and, 185-186
Responses, 159
Retarded child, 407
Retina, 130
Retinal disparity, 250
Retinal image, 248-250
Retinal rivalry, 252
Retroactive inhibition, 303
Retrospective falsification, 299-300
Revelation, human personality and, 17
Reward, in learning, 306
Rheumatic conditions, 227
Rh factor, 406
Rhine, J. B., 270-271
Rods, 130
Roe, Anne, 383
Roger, H. A., 348
Rogers, Carl, 405
Rolando, fissure of, 165-167, 171
Rorschach test, 333, 532-534, 563
Rote memorization, 297
Routine, 588
Rumor mongering, 554-556
Russell (A.E.), 358
Rutherford, frequency theory, 143, 144-145

Saccadic movements, 451
Ste. Anne de Beaupré, shrine of, 368

Saints, 369, 370
Sally (*see* Beauchamp)
Sampling technique, 39-40
Sarah Lawrence College, 550
Sartre, existentialism, 93*n*
Saturation, 136, 137
Savings method of learning, 296
Scale, meaning of term, 313*n*
Scapegoating, 568
Schizophrenia, 156, 355, 362, 364-365, 390; causes, 384; childhood, 381-382; daydreaming and, 208-209
Schools, curriculum influences, 117-118; personality development and, 95-100, 114-118; social organization of the classroom, 115-117 (*see also* Education *and* Learning)
Science, errors in, 653-654; meaning of term, 22, 645-647; natural sciences, 651-652; philosophy and, 648-651
Sclerotic coat, 131
Seashore Measures of Musical Talents, 465
Self (*see* Ego)
Self-ideal, 512
Semantic conditioning, 278
Senile degenerative psychosis, 363, 616
Sensation, 129
Sense appetites, 219
Sense organs, 127-128
Senses, localization of, 167
Sensory experience, equilibrium, 149; gustatory, 146-147; hearing, 140-146; human adjustment and, 218-220; infancy, 415-418; kinesthetic, 148-149; olfactory, 147-148; organic senses, 149-151; receptors, 127-129; sensation, 129; skin senses, 146; vision, 129-140
Sensory neurons, 161
Sequin Form Board, 317
Sertillanges, A. D., 20
Set, in attention, 242
Sex, 60; Adler theory, 634; child instruction in, 601; circulatory differences, 477-478; determination of, 69; differences at birth, 430-431; hysteria and, 371; libido theory, 631-633; maturity, 484-488; measurement of drive, 196-197; neuroses and, 373; preschool child's awareness, 435-437; sex-linked traits, 69-71; speech differences, 439
Sex-regulating hormone, 156
Shadows, 253
Shaw, C. R., 495-496
Sheldon's body-type theory, 543-545
Shell-shock, 371
Shock, N. W., 478
Shuttleworth, F. K., 340, 473
Siblings, family relationships, 111; studies of, 82-86
Sign language, 395
Similarity, law of, 260
Simon, Th., 310-311, 312-314
Situation tests, 525-526
Size constancy, 256
Skin, emotion and, 186-187
Skin senses, 146
Sleep, hypnosis and, 205
Slow learners, 452
Smell, 152, 417-418
Smiling, 424-425
Social class, adolescence and, 470-471, 474, 491-492, 499-500; adult-adolescent relationships, 480-484; child-rearing differences, 444-445; community adjustment, 494-497; learning and, 97-99; marriage relationships, 104; mental disease and, 361-362; physical development and, 422-424; significance in developmental psychology, 55-57; speech development differences, 439 (*see also* Environment)
Social psychology, 15
Social work, 11
Society, antisocial behavior, 568-570; areas of study about man, 7-8; Christian relationships, 548-549; group influences, 551-558; man's relationships within, 548-549; patterns in relation to age, 600-604; prejudice barriers, 558-568
Sociology, 8
Sociometry, 35
Somatotonic person, 544
Somatic nervous system, 163, 164
Somatotyping, 544
Somesthetic area, cortex, 172
Son of the Gods, film, 120
Sonneborn, T. M., 66*n*
Soul (*see* Philosophy)
Sound perception, 258-259

INDEX

Sound wave, 143
Sour grapes mechanism, 207-208
Soviet government, use of rumors, 555
Span of attention, 243
Span of visual apprehension, 243
Spearman, theory of intelligence, 330
Spearman-Brown formula, 321
Speech area, cortex, 172
Speech defects, 409-411, 439
Sperm, 61, 65-71
Sphygmomanometer, 9
Spinal cord, 164, 165, 174-175
Spinal reflex, 174
Spirit of Medieval Philosophy, The, Gilson, 648
Split-half technique, 321
Spontaneous recovery, 276
Spranger, values theory, 545
Squint, 139-140
Stammering, 409
Standard deviation, 336
Stanford-Binet tests, 296, 313, 322, 326, 399, 440-443
Startle reflex, 419
Static sense, 149
Statistical measures, 36-40
Statistics, 9; group *vs.* individual aspects, 339-341; in psychological measurement, 334-339
Stenquist Mechanical Aptitude Test, 407
Stereoscope, 250-252
Stern, on intelligence, 311, 323
Stigmata, 369
Stimulus, 127, 159; Fechner's Law, 626-627; Weber's Law, 626
Stimulus generalization, principle of, 291
Stimulus-response theory of learning, Hull, 290-291
Stirrup, 141
Stocking anesthesia, 368
Stoltz, growth studies, 471-473
Strabismus, 139-140
Stratified sample, 39
Stratton, lens experiment, 248-250
Striated muscles, 152-153
Structuralism, 624, 628-629, 637, 638
Study of Values, A, Allport and Vernon, 545
Stupor, 241
Stuttering, 409-411

Sub-cultures, 97-99
Subjective observation, 40-42
Sublimation, 212, 632
Subliminal stimulus, 159
Substance, meaning of term, 6-7
Sub-vocal speech, 630
Success, incentive value, 463
Suggestibility, hypnotic, 203, 204-205
Sulcus, 165 .
Superego, Freudian, 632-633
Supernatural grace, human personality and, 17
Suspensory ligament, 131
Sweet lemon mechanism, 207-208
Syllogistic reasoning, 355-356
Sylvius, fissure of, 167
Sympathetic behavior, 435
Sympathetic nervous system, 176
Synapse, 162-163
Synesthesia, 267-268
Syphilis, 63, 364

Tabes dorsalis, 148
Tabloid thinking, 559-561
Tadpoles, swimming movement experiments, 14
Talent, artistic, 465-466; musical, 465
Taste, 152; in infancy, 417-418
Taste buds, 146-147
Teachers, adolescent identification with, 498; child attitudes toward, 450; classroom influences, 114-118; psychology important to, 11; vocational guidance, 493 (*see also* Education *and* Schools)
Television, personality influences, 118-120
Temperament, 104, 192
Temperature, in infancy, 418
Temper tantrums, 427
Temporal lobe, cortex, 167
Terman, L. M., 323, 324, 333, 584; gifted children studies, 78-79, 443; intelligence test revisions, 313-314; interpretation of IQ, 326-327; married happiness studies, 103, 104; quoted on intelligence, 311
Testes, 157
Testosterones, 157
Thalamus, 174
Theelin, 157

Thematic Apperception Test (TAT), 532, 533-534, 563
Theology, 645-646
Theoretical psychology, 16
Theory, 24
Thinking, concept formation, 351-353; creative, 345, 356-360; direction in, 349-351; highest of all human activities, 360; inductive, 352; introspective approach, 346; meaning of, 343-345; problem solving, 348-351; rational learning, 347-348; role of, 342-344; scientific, 344; syllogistic reasoning, 355-356; tests of concrete and abstract, 353-355
Thirst, 150-151
Thomistic philosophy, 226, 344, 390, 634 (*see also* Aquinas, St. Thomas)
Thompson, H., 87
Thorndike, E. L., 280-281, 288, 330, 348
Threshold stimulus, 159
Thumb-sucking, 432, 444
Thurstone, L. L., 120, 331
Thyroid gland, 154, 400-401
Thyroxin, 154
Time, perception of, 269
Time-sampling, 29-30
Titchener, E. B., 628-629
Tobacco, efficiency and, 595
Tolman, E. C., 290-291, 293
Tolstoy, L. M., Count, 479
Tonal islands, 141, 144
Tongue, 147
Tonus, 153, 178; emotion and, 185
Topological psychology, 631*n*
Touch, 152
Trace reactions, 277
Traits, personality, 519
Transfer of learning theory, 287-288
Treatise on Memory and Recollection, Aristotle, 347
Treatise on the Soul, Aristotle, 5
Trial-and-error learning, 280-283
True-false tests, 296
True paranoia, 365
Truth, 652-654
Tryon, C. M., 488-490
Twins, 82-86, 439; maturation and learning, 87; mental illness and, 384-385

Tympanic canal, 141
Tympanic membrane, 141

Ulcer, peptic, 226
Uncertainty, Heisenberg principle, 222
Unconscious, Jung's conception of, 635, 636; Freudian, 632
Upper class, 55
Urban community, adolescent place in, 497
Utility, Darwin's theory of, 188-189

Vann, Gerald, 583
Variability, measures of, 36, 336-339
Variables, 24
Venereal diseases, 63
Verbal behavior, 630
Vertebrae, 165
Vestibular canal, 141
Vestigial acts, 188-189
Vindication of the Rights of Women, Mary Godwin, 582
Vineland Training School, 313
Viscerotonic person, 544
Vision, 152; achromatic experience, 136-138; abnormalities of, 139-140; after-images, 139; age and, 605; chromatic experience, 136-139; color, 134, 138, 140; in infancy, 416-417; projection of nerve fibers, 133; sensory experience, 129-140; stimulus, 135-136
Visual area, cortex, 172
Visual perception, 255-256; depth and distance, 250-255; environmental influences, 257; redintegration, 256-257; retinal image, 248-250
Vitreous humor, 131
Vocational guidance, adolescent, 492-494
Volley theory, Wever and Bray, 143, 145
Voluntary attention, 243

Wada, hunger experiments, 149
Walking, 60-61
Warden, C. J., 195-197
Warner, Lloyd, 56, 57, 97

INDEX

Warren, H. C., 192, 219
Washburn, hunger experiments, 149
Watson, John B., 28, 428-429, 629-630, 645 (*see also* Behaviorism)
Wave theory of light, 135
Weber, Ernst, 311, 626
Weber's Law, 626
Wechsler-Bellevue test, 320
Weir-Mitchell treatment, 373
Wernicke, brain study, 170
Wernicke's center, 170
Wertheimer, Max, 631; laws of perception, 260-261
Wever, volley theory, 143, 145
Whistle, Galton, 312
White, R., 116
White House Conference of 1931, 399
White matter, 161
Whitman, Walt, 95
Will, freedom of, 221-224
Wolff, Werner, 538-539
Woman as a Force in History, Mary R. Beard, 581
Women, age adjustments, 601-602, 614-615; hysteria among, 371; role of the adult, 579-584
Woodworth, R. S., 63, 355
Work, age and, 602, 604-606; criteria of productivity, 607-609; efficiency, 587-596; job satisfaction factor, 586; role in the lives of adults, 585
World War I, hysteria caused by, 371; intelligence tests in, 316, 325, 328; mental subnormality in, 399
World War II, hysteria caused by, 371; intelligence tests in, 316, 320; rumor study, 554-555; uprootedness ills, 389
Wordsworth, William, 342
Wundt, Wilhelm, 40, 625, 627-628

Zeno, 644
Zia culture, 329
Zillig, prejudice study, 566
Zuni Indians, 329, 386
Zygote, 61; in reproductive process, 65-71

THE CENTURY PSYCHOLOGY SERIES

Richard M. Elliot, *Editor*

Kenneth MacCorquodale, *Assistant Editor*

Social Psychology, by Charles Bird
Learning More by Effective Study, by Charles and Dorothy Bird
Psychological Counseling, by Edward S. Bordin
A History of Experimental Psychology, 2nd Ed., by Edwin G. Boring
Sensation and Perception in the History of Experimental Psychology, by Edwin G. Boring
Readings in Modern Methods of Counseling, edited by **Arthur H. Brayfield**
A Casebook of Counseling, by Robert Callis, Paul C. Polmantier, and Edward C. Roeber
Beauty and Human Nature, by Albert R. Chandler
Readings in the History of Psychology, edited by Wayne Dennis
Techniques of Attitude Scale Construction, by Allen L. Edwards
Modern Learning Theory, by William K. Estes, Sigmund Koch, Kenneth MacCorquodale, Paul E. Meehl, Conrad G. Mueller, Jr., William N. Schoenfeld, and William S. Verplanck
Schedules of Reinforcement, by C. B. Ferster and B. F. Skinner
Social Relations and Morale in Small Groups, by Eric F. Gardner and George G. Thompson
Great Experiments in Psychology, 3rd Ed., by Henry E. Garrett
Exceptional Children, by Florence L. Goodenough
Developmental Psychology, 3rd Ed., by Florence L. Goodenough and Leona E. Tyler
Physiological Psychology, by Starke R. Hathaway
Seven Psychologies, by Edna Heidbreder
Theories of Learning, 2nd Ed., by Ernest R. Hilgard
Conditioning and Learning, by Ernest R. Hilgard and Donald G. Marquis
Hypnosis and Suggestibility, by Clark L. Hull
Principles of Behavior, by Clark L. Hull
Development in Adolescence, by Harold E. Jones
The Definition of Psychology, by Fred S. Keller

THE CENTURY PSYCHOLOGY SERIES

Principles of Psychology, by Fred S. Keller and William N. Schoenfeld
Psychological Studies of Human Development, by Raymond G. Kuhlen and George G. Thompson
The Cultural Background of Personality, by Ralph Linton
Vocational Counseling with the Physically Handicapped, by Lloyd H. Lofquist
Studies in Motivation, edited by David C. McClelland
The Achievement Motive, by David C. McClelland, John W. Atkinson, Russell A. Clark, and Edgar L. Lowell
Current Studies in Psychology, by F. Joseph McGuigan and Allen D. Calvin
Principles of Applied Psychology, by A. T. Poffenberger
The Behavior of Organisms, by B. F. Skinner
Cumulative Record, by B. F. Skinner
Verbal Behavior, by B. F. Skinner
Diagnosing Personality and Conduct, by Percival M. Symonds
Dynamic Psychology, by Percival M. Symonds
The Dynamics of Human Adjustment, by Percival M. Symonds
The Ego and the Self, by Percival M. Symonds
The Psychology of Parent-Child Relationships, by Percival M. Symonds
Educational Psychology, by George G. Thompson, Eric F. Gardner, and Francis J. DiVesta. Also accompanying *Workbook* by the same authors.
Selected Writings from a Connectionist's Psychology, by Edward L. Thorndike
Introduction to Methods in Experimental Psychology, 3rd Ed., by Miles A. Tinker and Wallace A. Russell
The Psychology of Human Differences, 2nd Ed., by Leona E. Tyler
The Work of the Counselor, by Leona E. Tyler
Experimental Psychology, by Benton J. Underwood
Psychological Research, by Benton J. Underwood
Elementary Statistics, by Benton J. Underwood, Carl P. Duncan, Janet A. Taylor, and John W. Cotton. Also accompanying *Workbook* by the same authors.
Persons and Personality, by Sister Annette Walters and Sister Kevin O'Hara